THE
NATURAL HISTORY
OF MAKE-BELIEVE

THE
NATURAL HISTORY
OF MAKE-BELIEVE

*A Guide to the Principal Works
of Britain, Europe, and America*

John Goldthwaite

New York   Oxford
OXFORD UNIVERSITY PRESS
1996

Oxford University Press

Oxford   New York
Athens   Auckland   Bangkok   Bombay
Calcutta   Capetown   Dar es Salaam   Delhi
Florence   Hong Kong   Istanbul   Karachi
Kuala Lumpur   Madras   Madrid   Melbourne
Mexico City   Nairobi   Paris   Singapore
Taipei   Tokyo   Toronto

and associated companies in
Berlin   Ibadan

Copyright © 1996 by John Goldthwaite

Published by Oxford University Press, Inc.
198 Madison Avenue, New York, New York 10016

Library of Congress Cataloging-in-Publication Data

Goldthwaite, John.
The natural history of make-believe : a guide to the principal
works of Britain, Europe, and America / John Goldthwaite.
p.   cm. ISBN 0-19-503806-1
1.   Children's literature—History and criticism.   2. Fantastic
literature—History and criticism.   I. Title.
PN1009.A1G569   1996
809′.89282—dc20   95-31813

The author and publisher are grateful to the following for permission to reprint specified material:

Hans Christian Anderson: His Classic Fairy Tales by Erik Haugaard. Copyright © 1974 by Erik Christian
Haugaard. Used by permission of Doubleday, a division of Bantam Doubleday Dell Publishing Group, Inc.

2 4 6 8 9 7 5 3 1

Printed in the United States of America
on acid-free paper

To the memory
of my mother and father
with love
and appreciation

PREFACE

A literary history is a chronicle of how books have begotten books. It stands on the assumption that writers write by reading. To my knowledge, this guide is the first such history of the world's imaginative literature for children. It necessarily runs afoul of a popular supposition about children's books—that an *Alice*, a *Peter Rabbit*, or a *Charlotte's Web* is the inspired articulation of thoughts whispered through an author by that clever ventriloquist we now commonly refer to as the Inner Child. To all who are in thrall to such an origin myth for our favorite books, a literary history will, of course, provide only an interesting gloss on the subject rather than being an equally valid—or perhaps even the better—explanation for it. My designating the literature "make-believe" admittedly can hardly help to dispel such a superstition, but this has long been the label for it. As a way of naming a certain kind of magic in story that acknowledges its diverse expression while at the same time suggesting its true audience to be children, make-believe does seem a happier term than, say, fantasy or whimsy.

In detailing the history and nature of the literature, I have subscribed to no particular school of thought. The reader will find some social history in these pages and some of what I suppose must be called psychology. There is some pulling apart and putting back together of things. Little of what follows, however, should offend a commonsense understanding of the books. I will not apologize for giving this or that author more or less than a democratic share of the study. Certain works, I feel, have been underappreciated for their craft and historical importance and others celebrated for the wrong reasons, and I have allotted space accordingly. This is how it happened that a reading of the enigmatic *Alice in Wonderland* became a book-length study in its own right. In my hypothetical reconstruction of how it came to be written, I thought it best to risk the reader's impatience with an abundance of evidence. Imagining the thing as a short detective novel may lessen the pain.

"The Black Rabbit" and "Sis Beatrix" first appeared in *Signal: Approaches to Children's Books*. I am grateful to editor Nancy Chambers for her expert help and continuing enthusiasm and support over the years. Special thanks are due as well to a pair of early catalysts, Harlin Quist and James Raimes; to Brooke Goffstein and other friends for their abiding interest; to Edward and Annette Hochberg for a month's retreat to write "The Black Rabbit"; and to the staff of the Donnell Branch of the New York Public Library for their sporting assault on the stacks in my behalf.

To Leila, who cheerfully rode shotgun on this slow coach of a book for so many years as wife and librarian, go my best thanks, inadequate as they are; and to our daughter Jessica, for all the bumps along the way, my sadly inadequate apologies.

CONTENTS

THE
NATURAL HISTORY
OF MAKE-BELIEVE

The knowledge of the holy is understanding.

Proverbs 9:10

My people are destroyed for lack of knowledge.

Hosea 4:6

Therefore every scribe which is instructed unto the kingdom of heaven is like unto a man that is an householder, which bringeth forth out of his treasure things new and old.

Matthew 13:52

INTRODUCTION
A Shorter History of the Subject

This library of lies at the heart of children's literature, which to other ages has seemed the indulgence of fools or even a store of dangerous superstition, has become so ordinary a presence in our own lives as to pass without comment. The Man in the Moon has dropped down to earth for a visit. Over the hedge a rabbit in trousers is having a pipe with his evening paper. Somewhere else elephants are building a city, children discovering a gingerbread house in a wood, Jumblies sailing the world in a sieve. Early critics of such impostures would not have found them more foolish, perhaps, than our comic-book demigods, who in their divine tumescence and pajamas can leap tall buildings with a single bound, but they saw them as dangerous lies nonetheless. For the stock-in-trade of make-believe is simple and outrageous: this is a literature that deals in miracles. Every book we will open in this history is a miracle story. Some presumptuous scribbler, practicing the forbidden craft of smoke and mirrors, has suspended the laws of God and nature and conjured up a new creation from out of the breach. He may have worked his miracle offstage before the story began—a little man named Mole, interrupting his spring cleaning for a jaunt along the riverbank, is, in fact, a mole—or he may have dropped it into a routine narrative as a sudden wonder: Alice passes through the looking-glass; Jack raises a beanstalk to heaven; Dorothy whirls away to Oz. Traditionally, he will usher us into the tale with the wizard's open-sesame, "Once upon a time." Like cave explorers we find ourselves wandering through the dream of an impossible history, a wonderland in which every probability weighing against the lie has been cunningly annulled. What may be awakened in us

3

now is a state not of wanting to know what happens next, which is a rational response to a story's surprises, but of *wondering* to know, which is a surrender to the magic.

Enchantment can be a precarious mood for a young reader. Ideally it should occasion a shimmer of that innocence of mind in which might appear some new understanding of the world. Just as easily, however, it can foster a habit of credulity and a taste for mere sensation. Cautions against chasing after extravagant make-believes have been heard at the gates of every city in history. Finding the bookshops of 1800 clogged with vulgar entertainments, Wordsworth had declared the true wages of the Industrial Revolution to be a degrading thirst after outrageous stimulation and had bid London adieu. Today, in New York or Hollywood, even the popular novelist can be heard complaining of "an audience which can be reached only by phenomena, by superior pornographies or willfully meretricious accounts of the way we live now."[1] Johnny-come-latelies. Two and a half thousand years ago a scribe watching at the gates of Jerusalem had taken the same measure of his audience and, echoing Jehovah in the wilderness, announced the folly of putting "a parable in the mouth of fools."

This early sage was a coauthor, as it happens, of the world's oldest surviving children's book.[2] Proverbs is one of those venerable works everyone quotes from now and again without perhaps realizing his source. Here are all those dear old hoary truths about sparing the rod and spoiling the child, and the pride that goeth before a fall, and expressions, too, like "inherit the wind" and "the apple of my eye." The wisdom tradition of the ancient world that gave us a storyteller for adults like Aesop produced this contemporaneous Hebrew Aesop as well. Indeed, if you were to imagine an Aesop that was all morals and no stories, you would have a passable counterfeit of the biblical text. In their search for practical corollaries to the Ten Commandments, the priestly scribes did leave some of the make-believe in place, however:

> There be four things which are little upon the earth, but they are exceeding wise:
> The ants are a people not strong, yet they prepare their meat in the summer;
> The conies are but a feeble folk, yet make they their houses in the rocks;
> The locusts have no king, yet go they forth all of them by bands;
> The spider taketh hold with her hands, and is in kings' palaces.[3]

The notion that a body of story told solely for pleasure could be built up from some simple conceit that the ants are a people seems obvious enough, but it is not for these few fragments of old fables that modern make-believe is to be traced so far back in time. The passage that does recall us to this ancient union of the secular and the sacred, the rule book and make-believe, is one of the most numinous and troublesome accounts to be found anywhere in Scripture. What we are going to see happening in the nineteenth century is this singular text quite literally coming alive and stepping into the pages of some of our most famous children's books. To make good sense of the event, of course, we must first look through the literature of the past few centuries, and for this reason I am going to say only so much here about Proverbs and then break off, with the promise of returning to it when its time has come in the closing pages. For the moment, let the world's oldest children's book be the practical guide for teenage boys that we find announced in its signature wake-up call, "My son, hear the instruction of thy father, and forsake not the law of thy mother." A prosperous family may have boasted its own scroll of Proverbs — the opening address implies home use — but chiefly the book would have been found in the classroom. It is no leap to imagine Israel's young elite having to commit these sayings to memory and loathing every one of them. Today a librarian might catalog the wisdom of Solomon as a YA, or Young Adult book, but certainly with no expectation that it would ever circulate as such. This is a manual to be read to or at boys and by them only as homework. Here the eternal father stands, scandalized before the hormonal stupor of the eternal adolescent — "How long wilt thou sleep, O sluggard?" — and mocks the eternal moan from under the pillow, "Yet a little sleep, a little slumber." What the several authors of Proverbs wanted for Sluggo was that he throw off the mantle of the fool and live in righteousness before God by choosing the right habits, the right friends, the right wife. Still, there is not the note of emeritus complacency to these aphorisms that the reader might expect. "A whore is a deep ditch" is a matter-of-fact observation; take it or leave it. Experience writes proverbs, not prudery, and some sayings seem the work of pens dipped in regret. "It is better to dwell in a corner of the housetop, than with a brawling woman in a wide house" calls up an image of Dad as a be-sandaled W. C. Fields daily having to sneak his wince and bowler down some Jerusalem backstairs. "Go to the ant, thou sluggard; consider her ways, and be wise" was probably first said by a grasshopper. Indeed, the most universally popular make-believe ever told for children will be the story of just such a repentant idler, and will be written by one who knew too well whereof he spoke. For the next two and a half millennia, though, words to the wise, unadorned by make-believe, will be the stuff of which all formal writings for children are made. Each cultural flowering will refine its own coming-of-age codes, its catechisms and books of courtesy and caution. From Proverbs in the days of the First and Second Temples to the dawn of the Industrial Revolution, rote instruction will be the dreary business of children's books. For entertainment the young will have to look to the cottage kitchen, the workbench, tavern, or passing balladeer.

It would be easy to dismiss this early tutelage as a didactic burden the literature is well rid of; it would also be rather fatuous, I think, and this for three reasons. First, which I leave to the reader's own discernment, is the holy provenance and truth of these oldest of aphorisms. Second is the simple fact that even if we wished to do without them, we could not. Platitudes, truisms, all those copybook maxims Lewis Carroll relished lampooning in *Alice*, these are the house rules of literature. They represent the annoyingly stable world without which story can be only an ineffectual amusement. Today, when all is satisfyingly deconstructed by parody and burlesque, it may well seem otherwise; with no rules left to break, however, there can be no valid plots — and no new Peter Rabbits, Cats in hats, or Maxes storming off in search of Wild Things. Some cautionary proverb stands in the doorway as every true hero sets forth; its stated presence is especially wanted in children's books, to assure us that somewhere in the culture there remains a legal address to which the prodigal sons of story may return when the stomach growls, the chuckles dwindle, and night falls. If nothing in the world is proverbially held to be true absolutely, then neither will make-believe be understood to be true. Its heroes will drift away into the rarefied ethers of whimsy or surrender their virtue to the tender mercies of show business.

The third reason for not scorning this homiletic ancestry for story I cite only to acknowledge my own debt to history. The twentieth book of the Bible was such a staple of the Puritan diet that the United States could fairly be called The House that Proverbs Built; its teachings became the principles of that Puritan work ethic that would one day secure an idler the free hours to voice such nonutilitarian thoughts as these, and you the leisure to contemplate them in behalf of our children, who need no longer, in these intertestamental years, go to work at the apprentice ages of eight or ten or fourteen but can sit in their rooms dreaming of the world through the vast literature now available to them. Among the colonial schoolboys dozing over their copybooks there had been more than a few Yankees who took the old saws to heart. Substitute a shrewd opportunism for the piety of Proverbs and you would have something like the *Autobiography* of Benjamin Franklin, who with his early-to-bed, early-to-rise regimen did make himself healthy, wealthy, and wise — and enough of a diplomat to ensure for America a future so plummy that make-believe could in time become one of its chief exports to the world.

The fun began about the same time that Franklin did. The first true children's book preceded our aphorist into the world by nine years. This was a collection of tales retold by an academic, Charles Perrault, to amuse the children of the salons of the *ancien régime*. It appeared in 1697, some eight decades before Franklin would make his own ambassadorial debut in the salons of France. The world's second true children's book, an assortment of jingles, followed Franklin's birth by thirty-eight years and was the collation of a London printer, Mary Cooper. Fairy tales and nursery rhymes would have yet another century of singing in the shadow of the grownups' tutorials, but the way had been prepared for the unfettered amusements we today accept without question as the proper vehicle for easing our children into the world. The evolution of children's books in general over these three centuries has been the subject of much inquiry, particularly in the past twenty-five years or so. Critics, biographers, librarians, and enthusiasts have written exhaustively on individual authors or literary trends; historians, sociologists, psychologists, and now a new school of academics have dissected texts and authors from a variety of angles as a cultural phenomenon. What has eluded definition thus far is the make-believe at the heart of the literature. I would suggest here that the key to any such definition will lie first in our ability to distinguish the miracles from the lies, the true wonders from the tricks. A good beginning might be made by putting aside the biographical niceties and anthropological data for the moment and thinking instead of make-believe as a reality being disputed by two eternally discrepant sensibilities. The more popular of these was nicely expressed in 1895 when the children's magazine *St. Nicholas* summoned its readers to behold "a dear, delightful land" where good things were guaranteed always to happen:

> Ah, there the skies are always blue,
>   And hearts forget to grieve,
> For there's never a dream but must come true
>   In the Land of Make-Believe.

In this excerpt from the previous decade, a rather different tone is being struck:

> "Give ear to me, and go back."
> "On the contrary, I am determined to go on."
> "The hour is late!"
> "I am determined to go on."
> "The night is dark!"
> "I am determined to go on."
> "The road is dangerous!"
> "I am determined to go on."
> "Remember that boys who are bent on following their caprices, and will have their own way, sooner or later repent it."
> "Always the same stories. Good night, Cricket."
> "Good night, Pinocchio, and may Heaven preserve you from dangers and from assassins."

What we hear being voiced in these two passages are the contrary minds of the sentimentalist and the realist. The latter is a fantasist with his feet on the ground, who sends his readers forward into the world; the former, a fantasist with his head in the clouds, beckoning children to tarry a while on some privileged isle of play. Carlo Collodi, the author of *Pinocchio*, was a realist in his practice of make-believe; Beatrix Potter, whose Peter Rabbit would get into such trouble for not heeding his mother's advice, was another. Her contemporary James M. Barrie was a sentimentalist (albeit a shrewd one) whose thoughts were filled with fairies and flying over rooftops and daintily roguish little boys like Peter Pan. His Never Never Land is the apotheosis of that isle of play heralded by *St. Nicholas*'s "Land of Make-Believe." Most good children's books cannot be broken down this neatly, of course, and in any case it would be foolish to hobble a literary history with so simple a thesis. Still, some tacit contest between the two sensibilities does seem to obtain throughout the descent of make-believe, and it is worth keeping in mind as we explore who has been learning what from whom over the past three centuries, and in which of the two moods authors have been volunteering themselves as the tutors of other people's children.

The vehicles of this happy instruction are familiar to everyone; make-believe comes into our lives and sets the patterns of our minds clothed as the nursery rhyme, the fairy tale, or the beast fable. If the history of children's story is not terribly difficult to sort out, it is because these three forms have generally bred true to kind and in an orderly fashion. The opportunities for experimentation afforded by the picture book in the twentieth century have complicated the line of descent somewhat, but even here a standard taxonomy will apply. The picture book is a format, not a form, and I can think of no author who has actually created a new form by using a picture book to tell his story. All picture books will be found to be a second- or third-generation graphic expression of some ancient folk type or mingling of types. Margaret Wise Brown's *Goodnight Moon* is a lullaby in rhyming prose; Uri Shulevitz's *One Monday Morning*, a ballad; Russell Hoban's *How Tom Beat Captain Najork and His Hired Sportsmen*, a trickster tale. M. B. Goffstein's *Sleepy People* belongs to the same tradition of folk myth that produced "The Shoemaker and the Elves." Arnold Lobel's *Frog and Toad* books and H. A. Rey's *Curious George* are beast fables. Cross the beast fable with the fairy tale and you have Jean de Brunhoff's *Babar* or William Steig's *Sylvester and the Magic Pebble*. Virginia Lee Burton's *The Little House* is a Victorian melodrama retold as a silent-movie cliffhanger cleverly rephrased as a children's picture book, and all reflect that same ancient cautionary tale in which the country maiden falling prey to the wicked city is restored to rural bliss at the last moment, besmirched (here, literally, with soot) but uncorrupted.

Tracking the ins and outs of the three parent classes of make-believe has meant twice returning the reader from the present day to the beginning of the story, and I have everywhere tended to let ideas take precedence over any strict observance of the calendar. The result is bound to be some confusion, especially as the titles begin to accumulate. Here, then, is a short-list chronology of the major and a few minor works done once straight through for reference:

1697	*Histoires ou Contes du temps passé*, Charles Perrault
	Contes des fées, Madame d'Aulnoy.
ca. 1744	*Tommy Thumb's Pretty Song Book*, ed. Mary Cooper

ca. 1765	*Mother Goose's Melody*, ed. Oliver Goldsmith
1784	*Gammer Gurton's Garland*, ed. Joseph Ritson
1785–89	*Le Cabinet des Fées*
1804–18	*Tabart's Popular Stories for the Nursery*, ed. William Godwin[?]
1805	*Songs for the Nursery*, Tabart & Company
	Old Mother Hubbard, Sarah Catherine Martin
1807	*The Butterfly's Ball*, William Roscoe
1812–22	*Kinder- und Hausmärchen*, Jacob and Wilhelm Grimm
1835–72	*Eventyr, fortalte for Børn*, Hans Christian Andersen
1842	*The Nursery Rhymes of England*, ed. James O. Halliwell
1846, 1861	*A Book of Nonsense*, Edward Lear
1863	*The Water Babies*, Charles Kingsley
1865	*Alice's Adventures in Wonderland*, Lewis Carroll
1867	"The Golden Key," George MacDonald
1871	*Through the Looking-Glass*, Lewis Carroll
	Nonsense Songs, Edward Lear
	At the Back of the North Wind, George MacDonald
1872	*The Princess and the Goblin*, George MacDonald
1875	*The Little Lame Prince*, Dinah Mulock Craik
1876	*The Hunting of the Snark*, Lewis Carroll
1877	*Laughable Lyrics*, Edward Lear
1880–1918	*Uncle Remus*, Joel Chandler Harris
1883	*Le Avventure di Pinocchio*, Carlo Collodi
1885	*A Child's Garden of Verses*, Robert Louis Stevenson
1889	*The Nursery Alice*, Lewis Carroll
1889–93	*Sylvie and Bruno*, Lewis Carroll
1894–95	*The Jungle Books*, Rudyard Kipling
1897	*Lullaby Land*, Eugene Field
1899	*The Story of Little Black Sambo*, Helen Bannerman
1900–1920	*The Wonderful Wizard of Oz*, L. Frank Baum
1902	*The Tale of Peter Rabbit*, Beatrix Potter
	Just So Stories, Rudyard Kipling
1904	*Peter Pan*, James M. Barrie
1908	*The Wind in the Willows*, Kenneth Grahame
	The Roly-Poly Pudding, Beatrix Potter
	The Tale of Jemima Puddle-Duck, Beatrix Potter
1910–60	*Old Mother West Wind*, Thornton W. Burgess
1912	*The Tale of Mr. Tod*, Beatrix Potter
1912–40	*The Adventures of Uncle Wiggily*, Howard Garis
1920–52	*The Story of Doctor Dolittle*, Hugh Lofting
1922–23	*Rootabaga Stories*, Carl Sandburg
1926–28	*Winnie-the-Pooh*, A. A. Milne
1928	*Millions of Cats*, Wanda Gág
1931–40	*L'Histoire de Babar*, Jean de Brunhoff

1937	*The Hobbit*, J. R. R. Tolkien
	And to Think That I Saw It on Mulberry Street, Dr. Seuss
1946–71	*Kometjakten*, Tove Jansson
1950–56	*The Chronicles of Narnia*, C. S. Lewis
1951–73	*Pogo*, Walt Kelly
1952	*Charlotte's Web*, E. B. White
1954–55	*The Lord of the Rings*, J. R. R. Tolkien
1957	*The Cat in the Hat*, Dr. Seuss
1963	*Where the Wild Things Are*, Maurice Sendak

The last title here might easily have been written by the first author on the list, and vice versa. How important are the differences between the societies that greeted the two works I leave to the reader to decide. Perrault wrote for the scions of the court, the civil service, and the merchant class. His listeners were the same children of privilege who millennia earlier had pondered the book of Proverbs. Sendak's story belongs to a culture in which libraries and television have (at least theoretically) made all children equally privileged. A detail in *Where the Wild Things Are* that might have struck Perrault's readers as truly odd is something we take for granted today. The adventure itself would have seemed familiar enough to them: the traveler's tale has been a staple entertainment since Homer. Just who or what is crawling about the terra incognita is an enduring fascination; if no one cared, there would be no science fiction. More surprising to earlier readers would have been the author's remark that Max begins and ends his adventure in a place that is called "his very own room." There is no mention of such a place in fairy and folk tales about Red Riding Hoods and Hop o' My Thumbs. What could an ordinary little boy mean by having "his very own room" — and his very own bed, too, in which there is no room for his brothers?

Before the Industrial Revolution, the situation comedy of domestic life was quite different from what we know today. The comic-strip Calvins of yesteryear sat with the family, slept with the family, and hatched their nefarious infant plots in full view of the family. None but the rich had rooms in which to sulk and dream. Nor did the routine of the average household include Papa returning home from work with his evening paper and reading the kiddies to sleep with a children's book. Work was not a job you commuted to, the newspaper had yet to be invented, and had there been such a thing as a nursery, there were as yet no children, in the modern sense of an indulged class, to put in it. To picture such a scene, you must have first a middle class and then, to account for the sentimental or subversive forms that the literature will assume, a petit bourgeoisie. The Industrial Revolution provided both. With a new society in want of a literature to reflect its abiding concerns came a new perception of the child as a generic audience. The novel was born in the middle of the eighteenth century, and the first children's bookstore opened almost immediately thereafter. Most of the work fabricated for this burgeoning market encouraged children to piety or riches. Fairy tales and nursery rhymes were the stuff of cheap chapbooks and would remain a street trade of little account. The duty of a children's book was to lead its readers on a course of self-improvement. Since the fairy tale could lead only to folly and corruption, authors like Perrault and Sendak — comic realists with a complementary talent for the mysterious and the strange — were nowhere to be found at this time. For the next century the pleasures of story will be thought idle self-indulgence and the real business of children's books will be instruction in the arts of saying your prayers and getting ahead in the world.

Man's impulse to folly and corruption led him to that new species, the child, slowly and in three stages. Make-believe entered the nursery as a language that was spoken in the beginning, written in the middle, and shown at the end. The first age was a period not of original work but of gathering out of oral tradition whatever songs, tales, and fables might satisfy the market. Such activity has gone on throughout the ages and continues today, of course, but the important years for make-believe were the two centuries from the 1690s to the 1890s. For the first century and a half of this period of growth, children's story will be the work of antiquarian collectors and catchpenny publishers.

The second, or literary, age of make-believe, which ran roughly from the 1840s to the 1950s, was marked by the translation of these folk forms into a new narrative literature. The half century of experimentation from *Alice* to World War I is commonly regarded as the golden age of children's books, and with good reason. A single year might see major works by Lewis Carroll, Edward Lear, and George MacDonald, for example. In the half decade from 1881 to 1885 appeared *Uncle Remus*, *A Child's Garden of Verses*, the toy books of Randolph Caldecott, *Treasure Island*, *Pinocchio*, and, on the outskirts of children's books, *Huckleberry Finn*. No half or even full decade since 1885 has equaled this brief span for inventive surprise, save perhaps the years 1899 to 1904, which can boast *Little Black Sambo*, *Peter Rabbit*, *Just So Stories*, *Kim*, *Peter Pan*, and *The Wizard of Oz*. What we see happening in this literary age is the flowering of make-believe's three main parent classes. Out of the nursery rhyme will come nonsense (see Chapter 1); out of fairy tales, the narrative romance or muse fantasy (Chapters 2–5); and out of the beast fable, the animal story or place fantasy (Chapters 6–8). At this time, too, we see appearing an almost epicurean taste for sentimentalism and a rush to children's books as an ideal place to indulge it.

In the present age of make-believe, the spoken word of the storyteller is to be heard mainly on television and the written word has been replaced by the icon. Visual images had been used to edify and delight readers from the earliest days, but not until the 1880s did the illustrated children's book come into its own, and not until the rise of the modern picture book in the 1920s did the image begin to supplant the word as the primary vehicle for conveying a story. With the advent of the comic book, the motion picture, and television, the growth of make-believe as a literature of ideas came to a standstill. A literary audience became a mass market, make-believe became entertainment, and encountering the miracles of story became the passive activity of an audience trained to consume images and in ever greater need of Wordsworth's outrageous stimulation. What has been temporarily lost to the literature, I fear, is the sense of discovery and calling that animated its childhood and middle age. A literature should not be merchandized as an amusement park when it is predicated on the quiet surmise that a materialistic reading of the world is insufficient to account for who we are. Among the old generations of tutors given to dull instruction and the new ones given only to games, there have always been some authors who have understood that the true role of make-believe is to baptize the imagination, however, and for this reason the central concern for the critic of make-believe becomes, finally, a theological one. The abiding question to be asked of the literature is this: If rites are indeed under way in these little miracle stories, then with what waters are the children being baptized?

The realists and the sentimentalists will be filling their basins from different taps in the pages ahead. It will be from those major works that are expressly Christian in origin, however, that we are going to feel the splash of real surprise.

1

THE WORLD
THREE INCHES TALL
The Descent of the Nursery Rhyme

In the beginning, when thought was first being given to what books might best introduce the world to the children of the new middle classes of England and America, the most promising idea managed to escape notice. That a miscellany of jingles could be the makings of a book would remain for more than a century the intuition of a few printers and antiquarians who for pleasure more than profit would turn a modest trade from curiosities found in old books, plays, and broadsides and from ditties copied down from the street corner, nursery, tavern, and county fair. By the time of Edward Lear and Lewis Carroll, enough rhymes had been assembled that the best illustrators could be commissioned and the thing displayed at last as a proper book properly embellished, but we should perhaps keep in mind as we read through the literature that the splendid editions to come will be gracing a world of make-believe that was not born to win prizes. Its first authors were scavengers of cultural scraps. The earliest known edition of nursery rhymes measured just three by one and a quarter inches and sold for a few pennies.

Mother Goose (1744–)

There is an accidental charm to stuff extracted from the world. Put enough of it between the covers of even a small book and something felicitous happens. Out of apparent chaos the world reappears. There is nothing to Mother Goose but random snatches of silliness, and yet it is all here: cast, history, scenery, weather, the piecemeal world somehow arguing itself

13

whole again in song. No one author could have done it on purpose, and for comic amplitude only the rarest have ever equaled it. Iona and Peter Opie cite some 550 episodes in the singsong life of the world in their *Oxford Dictionary of Nursery Rhymes*—William and Ceil Baring-Gould boost the number to 884 in *The Annotated Mother Goose*—but Mother Goose is numberless, a steady-state universe with no big bang, no closure, no definitive edition. New songs are piping into existence in odd corners of the planet every day. Songs about beggars and kings, slatterns and ladies, butchers, bakers, scholars and thieves, mothers, children, simpletons, lovers, heroes and crybabies, the short and the tall and the fat and the lean. Anyone can be a face of record in Mother Goose. This is our family album. These are the gathered citizens whose names and follies we have passed along over the years like items of backyard gossip. They have been carrying on in cottages, castles, and tenements, in haystacks, pockets, coal scuttles, alleys, and pint pots, and pumpkins. They have been breaking their noses, oversleeping, making merry, stepping in puddles, dropping dead. As a grace to listeners who can hardly yet tie their shoes, no act is thought too small to be newsworthy. Boy jumps over candlestick; mouse runs up clock: true stories.

What young children need to know, Mother Goose has at hand. There are alphabets to learn, and counting rhymes, botanical lore, a bestiary, and an old-farmer's almanac. Mnemonics teach the days of the week, the months of the year, the bells of London. Plum puddings, Christmas pies, and hot-cross buns memorialize the holidays and holy days. Of course, there are sad things to learn as well. Turn the page from "One, two, buckle my shoe" and you may have a neighbor to bury:

> Old Abram Brown is dead and gone,
> You'll never see him more;
> He used to wear a long brown coat
> That buttoned down before.

Mother Goose begins with lullabies for the newborn and ends in the town churchyard where lie Cock Robin, sad Bessy Bell and Mary Gray, and the luckless Frog who would a-wooing go. Grief is poignant but short-lived in this literature of games and knee rides, however: behind a tombstone the next generation is already snorting, "My father left me three acres of land, / Sing holly, go whistle and ivy!"

As a literature Mother Goose is an invention of the English, but nursery rhymes, needless to say, are universal. This is the only book in the world that everyone in the world, literate and illiterate alike, knows some of by heart. A verse like "Ladybird, ladybird, fly away home" can be heard recited almost everywhere in some local tongue or other. Save for a few famous songs like "Three blind mice," "Hey, diddle, diddle," and "Hickory, dickory, dock," the rhymes we know best, perhaps, are those that have given us names for ourselves. The same attraction obtains with fairy tales—

think of "Snow White," "Jack and the Beanstalk," "Little Red Riding Hood," or "Cinderella." In Mother Goose the names are Bo-peep, King Cole, Jack and Jill, Georgie Porgie, Jack Sprat, Bobby Shafto, Little Jack Horner, Tommy Tucker, Simple Simon, Little Miss Muffet, Peter, Peter, pumpkin eater, and Tom, Tom, the piper's son. These are folks who for all we know of these things at the age of three, four, or five might wish to meet us one day. Their songs are perfect mnemonic devices for ensuring their foolish little biographies an immortality in our minds from infancy.

It is not surprising that nursery rhymes should be our most common cultural currency after the Bible. It is Mother Goose who first introduces us to who we are in the world, and it is she who brings us our first make-believe. Our infant imaginations are jollied awake as she translates the toes on our feet into pigs going to market, sends a cow over the moon, and tucks the world's biggest family into bed in a shoe. We have given a name to all this fun. We call it nonsense. The tendency is to speak of most famous children's verses as nonsense. From "the dish ran away with the spoon" to Carroll and Lear and so on to Dr. Seuss, inspired silliness has been the mainstream of nursery poetics; for want of any precise way of describing such diversions we have declared there to be no sense in any of them. The term nonsense eludes real definition here, I think.[1] Cows, it is true, do not jump over the moon or frogs court mice, but there is nothing unsensible about "Jack and Jill" or "Old King Cole" or a mouse running up a clock. Nonsense is often a term of convenience that only obscures how such stuff actually works on our imaginations.

Sir Edward Strachey was the first critic, I believe, to suggest the obvious, that nonsense be regarded as "the proper contrary of Sense."[2] We do tend to think of sense and nonsense as natural counterparts. The question left unasked by the equation is whether sense can ever be this tidily negated. The mind is stubborn in its need for order. Upset its expectations with a spiel of gibberish and, like a turtle looking to right itself, it will seek the stability of meaning every time. Nonsense might be defined more accurately as a flirtation with disorder, a turning upside down of the world for the pleasure of seeing it come right side up again. Out of frustration, or simply to keep our wits in tone, we "talk nonsense" and "make nonsense." What we mean to upset is not sense itself but the good, proverbial sense of our neighbors when it has gone stale or overbearing or fatuous. In literature, nonsense enlivens the proceedings by scrambling the narrative codes by which we understand what we are reading. It does this, however, and not always wittingly, as a means to an end undreamed of by brother turtle in his efforts to return to normal. As Strachey put it when emending his original definition, nonsense is not "a commonplace negative of Sense, not a mere putting forward of incongruities and absurdities, but the bringing out a new and deeper harmony of life in and through its contradictions. Nonsense, in fact, in this use of the word, has shown itself to be a true work of the imagination."[3]

It is this harmony that I suggest is the true opposite of sense, with nonsense being our rhetorical access road to a new overlook on the world. The contrary of sense can only be that which transports our disparate, sensible understandings into something—a kind of light, perhaps—that precludes and justifies them all. This harmony, which I am going to call "allsense," is the bounty residing in everything that we know generically as make-believe. When we come to C. S. Lewis we are going to see a wonderful and curiously instructive case study of the allsense being revealed to a child through works of art, but at what moment or to what child it may appear there is no way of telling. It is not a thing that can be written into a story, nor is it something you can go looking for as a reader. Either it happens to you or it doesn't. The pure moment is fleeting and probably rare when, or when in memory of an earlier reading, you feel a sudden uplift in the solar plexus and a translation of your whole being into a longing for something unnameable. This history is a study of the many kinds of works, images, or turns of phrase that might be the occasion on which the invisible atmosphere of make-believe becomes an enlightening ether and touches a child with a quickening of gladness. In Mother Goose it could be the gift of a fanciful thought like "I had a little husband, / No bigger than my thumb" or of any one of a hundred psalms to simple things made make-believe by their storyland phrasing—"Mary, Mary, quite contrary, / How does your garden grow?" perhaps, or this cameo of someone poaching other men's fishes, and likely their wives as well:

> Little Tommy Tittlemouse
> Lived in a little house;
> He caught fishes
> In other men's ditches.

On a larger scale, the allsense might be summoned by the idea of the book itself, which is the idea of the world, and by the physical fact of the book, which is the heft of that idea in the hand. Nursery rhymes are not unlike the magic realism of Gabriel Garcia-Marquez or Italo Calvino, in whose tales the miraculous becomes real by association with the mundane and the mundane is transformed by its association with the miraculous. When you hold a volume of Mother Goose in your hand, you are holding a weight of proof that the world is real and a thing of make-believe both.

A paradigm of how a marriage of the real and the unreal gives birth to our own imaginings can be found, perhaps, in this variation of a verse collected in 1805:

> The man in the moon
> Came down too soon,
> And asked his way to Norwich;
> The man in the South
> He burnt his mouth,
> With eating cold plum-porridge.

The only nonsensical conceit in this nonsense poem is the notion of burning your mouth on cold food. The rest is the stuff of fantasy. What we have here is the story of the miraculous advent of the man in the moon. It is a puzzling narrative by reason of having, in true nursery rhyme style, all its explanations left out. For a moment — and the younger the child the longer the moment — the mind must ponder these possibilities:

- that there is a man in the moon;
- that he can come here;
- that there was a right time to come and he came at the wrong time;
- that he had some business in Norwich,
- whatever Norwich is;
- and that in the South, wherever that may be,
- there is a mysterious someone like him already living.

By giving us so much to make sense of and so little information to work with, the verse sets us to questioning how these things can be. It puts us in that state of wondering to know which is the state of ignorant innocence necessary before the allsense can take possession of us and the make-believe become a living experience. It does this by employing an actual mechanism, if you will, for behind the spell that every such tale casts upon us is an author balancing the counterweights of reality and miracle. What he thinks may or may not be possible in the observable world his story will reveal through one of four narrative choices he can make. The first of these is the way of "The man in the moon" or a verse like "Hey, diddle, diddle," or of Mother Goose as a whole. These are *open* fantasies, in which the allsense is accepted as a quality intrinsic to the world as we know it. Fairy tales are open fantasies, as are most animal tales. The narrative classic of the type is *Pinocchio*, in which men and miracles commingle freely, and without gratuitous explanation, as a natural function of how the world works.

The second and now more common type is the *circular* fantasy, or there-and-back-again tale, that we find in *Alice*, *The Wizard of Oz*, *The Chronicles of Narnia*, and *Peter Pan*. The circular fantasy is a fairy tale that has grown weary under the empirical probabilities weighing against it and has wandered out of the world to find its miracles elsewhere. Apart from its early prototype, the riddle, the circular fantasy is uncommon in Mother Goose:

> How many miles to Babylon?
> Three score miles and ten.
> Can I get there by candle-light?
> Yes, and back again.
> If your heels are nimble and light,
> You can get there by candle-light.

The third and rarest type is the *closed* fantasy, suggested in Mother Goose by a historical verse like "Old King Cole." This is a circular fantasy whose access to the wonderful has been sealed off, as it were, so that we cannot actually imagine ourselves traveling there by candlelight, rabbit hole, tornado, secret wardrobe, or any way at all. Historical closure became the fate of all of Mother Goose late in the Victorian era. The most ambitious work of the type is J. R. R. Tolkien's *The Lord of the Rings*.

The fourth type is a phenomenon we would today call postmodern. Precedent for the *broken* fantasy appears in Mother Goose in the suppositional verse "If all the world were paper, / And all the seas were ink." As with the similar riddle, the make-believe here is presented as a verbal game. Every broken fantasy will at some point announce itself to be an artifice. The characters of the old Warner Brothers cartoons, for example, are forever breaking frame to wisecrack about the nature of their cartoon reality. Authors of this type of story are interested not in miracles but in displaying their wit at making semblances. In Tomi Ungerer's *The Beast of Monsieur Racine* the beast is revealed to be two children in a cloth suit. We think a king and queen are coming to visit a lonely child in Uri Shulevitz's *One Monday Morning*, but it is only the boy's rainy-day fantasy as he contemplates a deck of cards. Alice's dream and the theatrical rigging of *Peter Pan* mark them as fantasies of this type as well as of the circular variety. The artifice of their ancient prototype, "If all the world were paper," worked to a different purpose altogether. Originating in the Talmud, the Koran, and the closing line of John's Gospel, the conceit would one day become a piety to parody and therefore a broken fantasy at long last; but in the beginning, it served to express the infinite permutations of the Word of God. Its artifice was a kind of mimetic homage. In the modern broken fantasy there is no implied someone to pay homage to, nor is one wanted. Occasionally the popping of the bubble of belief is characterized by an underlying sadness, as in the Shulevitz book, but most commonly the mood is one of satiric insolence. The broken fantasy is a feigned make-believe, a changeling, a comical golem with its tongue stuck out. It wants us to know that we must be content with the magic trick of the transformation, for there is nothing to believe in beyond the skill of the magician. Amused, and possibly relieved, we do not stop to ask whether a semblance of make-believe can be valid with nothing greater to justify it. J. M. Barrie's giddy appeal to the audience in *Peter Pan*, "Clap if you believe in fairies," has for many proven to be justification enough.

It would be misleading to identify these narrative stratagems with particular periods in history—they are all available at anyone's discretion at any time—but, with some allowance for overlapping, they did succeed one another in a more or less orderly fashion. The first type to prevail was the open fantasy and the last the broken, with circular journeys in search of wonder coming in the middle. Not surprisingly, this descent reflects the progress of society in general over the past three centuries. The increasing difficulty in suspending one's disbelief has been a problem for literature and faith alike. The accommodations we see in the succession of narrative types mirror the rise of the various isms and ologies that were tar-babied together in the nineteenth century to replace a God grown ever more incredible to the educated mind. Man is predisposed to wonder, however, and fond as we are of our postmodern ironies and knowing burlesques, we have been loath to retire the older lores to the archives of history. A make-believe like the fairy tale remains for many a place to go on retreat, as it were, and a way of saying one's prayers. They may be pagan prayers, but at least the fairy tale is still recognized as a sanctuary and not a novelty shop. In Mother Goose, evidence of the miraculous continues to impinge on infant minds through verses like "The man in the moon" or Mother Goose's two major ballads, "Cock Robin" and "A Frog He Would a-Wooing Go," both of which are full-fledged fantasies of the anthropomorphic variety. These are the obvious make-believes, but they are not the only repository of the allsense in the world of nursery rhymes, or even the most important. What makes open fantasies as well of all those little character sketches and domestic notations like "Polly, put the kettle on" is their membership in a collective vision of the world that is itself open. In a child's imagination man and miracle are not yet discrete, and so it is in Mother Goose. The world of make-believe and the world as we know it are here the same world in the telling.

How Mother Goose actually came to speak for the muchness of the world is an uncomplicated story, the tale of a few collectors and of editions that in the beginning were of no more account, some of them, than cereal-box premiums. It begins with the charm of happenstance and the surprise of found money, like a childhood dream in which a dime appears shining in the halftone twilight of a roadway, and then another and another, and we stoop along happily filling our pockets. No author would think to invent such small literary change, but to find it lying all about unclaimed, there was the pleasure of the enterprise. It was the welcome pleasure, too, of a saving glimmer in the dark, for children's literature in the seventeenth and eighteenth centuries was largely a Puritan monopoly, and the dream in which the first sixpence of a nursery rhyme appeared shining in the road was the darkness of Calvinist exhortation at the crossroads of heaven and hell.

This no-nonsense reading matter for Puritan children had begun with the leavening of the 1646 catechism *Spiritual Milk for Boston Babes. In either England: Drawn out of the breasts of both Testaments for their Souls nourishment.* Its author was John Cotton, the grandfather of Cotton Mather, and when the Reverend John addressed his little readers with the words "[T]he Righteous shall go into life eternal, and the wicked shall be cast into everlasting fire with the Devil," he meant business. This was an age when the infant grave held even odds with survival and the most pressing business at hand was heading small souls in the right direction. If the parson had to frighten the wits out of them to face them about, so be it. The Puritans, like the ancient authors of their beloved guide, the book of Proverbs, understood the choices available to fallen man to be but two, and children were not exempted to wander where they would, for judgment was not negotiable. In Michael Wigglesworth's epical *Day of Doom*, for example, the God of 1662 is given this to say to all the babes who have died at birth: "I do save none but mine own Elect. . . . But unto you I shall allow the easiest room in Hell." The most infamous expression of this mind-set was the widely read *A Token for Children* by James Janeway, which appeared in England in 1671 and in an expanded version in America in 1700. A kind of latter-day book of saints and martyrs published "for the Encouragement of Piety," it detailed *An Exact Account of the Conversion, Holy and Exemplary Lives and Joyous Deaths of Several Young Children*. No doubt a cold comfort to those who did die young, it must certainly have helped to stun the survivors into that solemn countenance we traditionally associate with the Puritans. It should at least be said of such early work, however, that in response to a high infant mortality the Puritans retreated neither to the weepy deathbed scenes later so beloved by the Victorians nor to the modern complacency that a free ticket to heaven is everyone's birthright. What seems so grim to us today was lifeboat work for them, and they spared no efforts in their children's behalf.

One of the more liberal spirits to write for the nursery at the time was the Congregational minister Isaac Watts (1674–1748). His fellow Congregationalist John Bunyan (1628–88) had anticipated him in 1686 with *A Book for Boys and Girls: or, Country Rhimes for Children*, but this early experiment was not of the quality of Bunyan's masterpiece, *The Pilgrim's Progress* (1678–84). Children would be better served by Watts's *Divine and Moral Songs for Children* (1715). As evidenced by his hymns "Joy to the World" and "Our God, our Help in ages past," Watts thought less on man's sins and likely destruction than on giving thanks for a good world and trying to live in it the kind of sane and balanced life he saw prescribed in Proverbs. His psalms, fables, and lullabies were well enough crafted to remain in general circulation through the Victorian age; Lewis Carroll was to have some sport lampooning Watts's proverbial variations, "How doth the busy little bee" and "the voice of the Sluggard," but in their day such rhymes were more balm than bane. How moderating an influence they had on Calvinist thought can be seen in a memorable verse first published in Thomas Fleet's *New England Primer* of 1737 and later adopted into Mother Goose by the Victorians. This is the famous children's bedtime prayer,

> Now I lay me down to sleep,
> I pray the Lord my soul to keep;
> And if I die before I wake,
> I pray the Lord my soul to take.

Insensible as we are to the possible loss of paradise for our own selves, I suppose we would today regard this as a sentimental nicety. For a very long time it was thought the proper end to the day's business.

The full break with all these prayers at the gates of hell came around 1744, shortly after the appearance of Fleet's *Primer*. It came in the shape of a worldly toy of a book, measuring just three inches tall and titled *Tommy Thumb's Pretty Song Book*. This is, to the best of anyone's knowledge, the earliest collection of nursery rhymes, and so to its publisher, the London printer Mary Cooper, must go the credit for being the first to recognize that such charming drek could ever be the makings of a book. She left no record of her thoughts on the matter, but the 1740s being the decade of *Pamela* and *Joseph Andrews*, when the emergent middle class was becoming known to itself through the reading of novels, it seems likely that the *Song Book*, which sold for sixpence, was improvised to piggyback the grownups' stories home as a premium for the kiddies. Cooper's ear for a good jingle was unerring. Among the thirty-eight verses collected in her little pocket piece were "Girls and boys, come out to play," "Lady bird, lady bird," "Little Tommy Tucker," "London Bridge is falling down," "Hickory, dickory, dock," "Mary, Mary, quite contrary," "Baa, baa, blacksheep," "Who killed Cock Robin," and, the probable inspiration for the book's price, "Sing a song of sixpence." Each verse was accompanied by an amusing woodcut, and in keeping with the humor of the day the songbook even contained a few mildly scatalogical jokes:

> Little Robin red breast,
> Sitting on a pole.
> Niddle, Noddle,
> Went his head,
> And Poop went his Hole.

One of the most inspired guesses any editor has ever made was this simple idea of gathering a motley of rhymes under one title. With it Mary Cooper set into motion an age of collecting scraps of popular folklore that today shows no sign of abating. Noting, too, that *Tommy Thumb* was only the second volume of an indeterminate set that has not survived, we might assign credit to Cooper as well for being the first to understand a simple point ignored by modern picture-book publishers: while any book containing nursery rhymes is a Mother Goose book, the more rhymes it contains, the more of a Mother Goose book it becomes.

The name Mother Goose became attached to the rhymes through the offices of the publisher of note in Cooper's day, John Newbery. A parent of London's swelling middle class, having at home one of those newly defined and educable creatures, a Child, would sooner or later have come visiting at Newbery's shop, the Bible and Sun. Here were the needed spelling books and geographies, *The Pilgrim's Progress* and Aesop, and a growing shelf displaying an upstart genre written specifically for children, the exemplary history of such a paradigm of self-improvement as Goody Two-Shoes or Tommy Trip. The progress of these new pilgrims was to the Celestial City of social and mercantile savvy soon to be codified in Ben Franklin's

Autobiography. Inspirational hackwork for the scions of the new bourgeoisie, these melodramas mimicked the novels the parents were reading and promulgated a naive pragmatism with the Manichaean earnestness of a Sunday School tract. Tommy Trip is buffeted about the world, forearm to forehead, until the glad day he can cry aloud, "Free Trade and plumcake, hurrah!" as virtue and a stout heart win him his just and worldly reward. The infantile plots and bombastic rhetoric of these sagas of upward mobility made for clumsy, compelling reading. Their boosterish spirit lived on in thousands of Victorian potboilers, of which the Horatio Alger stories are the most famous. The few score such items that Newbery published between 1744 and his death in 1767 would establish him as the world's first and, for half a century, its only serious entrepreneur in children's literature.

He seems to have been an agreeable soul. Contemporary reports have him bustling about his shop arranging tops and games one moment and going out of pocket the next to rescue Dr. Samuel Johnson from penury. "Simple, jolly, resourceful, journeying up and down England in a great flurry of business," writes one historian.[4] In *The Vicar of Wakefield*, his friend and sometime employee Oliver Goldsmith characterized him for all time as that "philanthropic bookseller in St. Paul's Churchyard, who has written so many little books for children: he called himself their friend, but he was the friend of all mankind." Clearly a man with a mission, "[h]e was no sooner alighted but he was in haste to be gone, for he was ever on business of utmost importance."[5] The phrasing calls up the image of Clement Moore's right jolly old elf in *A Visit from St. Nicholas*, sneezing up and down chimneys with his sack of toys. Notwithstanding the man used his children's books to hawk a nostrum in which he held the majority interest, Newbery hovers over the world of children's literature like some Ghost of Christmas Past, smiling down on the prizes annually awarded in his name.

In none of his titles, however, do we find that free play of the imagination we now associate with children's books. With Newbery didacticism had merely found a new agenda. A devotee of John Locke's precepts on education and a true son of the Enlightenment, he meant his imprint to bespeak the sensible, the upright, and the practical, and every book hammered home its moral. Against the lure of make-believe he would argue that "People stuff Children's Heads with Stories of Ghosts, Fairies, Witches, and such Nonsense when they are young, and so they continue Fools all their Days."[6] The warnings in Proverbs against sluggards in their folly were proving quite as suitable to the pragmatic morals of the new Age of Reason as they had to the pious instruction of the Puritans. But it would be quixotic to scorn Newbery's injunction against make-believe. It was only in the preceding generation that an end had finally been put to the hanging and incineration of men and women for witchcraft. The superstition deplored by the Enlightenment was not merely the Nonsense of Fools but an evil reality.

The nursery rhyme bespoke the familiar world, however, and Newbery was ever a man to smile on a jolly sixpence. Sometime around 1765 he put into circulation an anthology of fifty-two of "the most celebrated Songs and Lullabies of the good old Nurses" under the title, soon to be legend, *Mother Goose's Melody*. Many of these jingles he had undoubtedly culled from booklets then in shop, but twenty-five were new. Since the history of the "old woman toss'd in a blanket, / Seventeen times as high as the moon" is known to have been a favorite of Goldsmith's and his touch being elsewhere apparent in the book, it is likely that Newbery's *Mother Goose* was actually the work of this younger colleague who simultaneously had been collaborating with his employer on the instructive history of *Little Goody Two-Shoes*. Here, collected together possibly for the first time (they may, in fact, have been taken from the lost first volume of *Tommy Thumb's Pretty Song Book*), were "Jack and Jill," "Pease Porridge hot," "Jack Sprat," "Little Jack Horner," "Hush-a-bye baby," and such non-Newberian examples of utter Nonsense as "Hey, diddle, diddle, / The Cat and the Fiddle." It was probably Goldsmith, too, who assigned to the rhymes the putative authorship that remains with them to this day. The good dame is a borrowing from Charles Perrault's famous collection of fairy tales, *Contes du temps passé*. The frontispiece to that work depicts a woman spinning tales to a trio of youngsters before a fire where sits the grinning ancestor of Lewis Carroll's Cheshire Cat. Mounted on the cottage door is a display plaque that reads CONTES DE MA MERE LOYE. This was Englished in 1729 as MOTHER GOOSE'S TALES, and it was undoubtedly from this earliest translation of Perrault that the sentimental Goldsmith, who would elsewhere transfigure his boss as the friend of all mankind, adopted Mother Goose as the new and universal friend of the nursery.

No jolly elf, surely, but in the long run no less a friend than Newbery was the antiquarian Joseph Ritson. Born in 1752, midway between the appearances of *Tommy Thumb* and *Mother Goose's Melody*, he would become a notorious pedant, Jacobin radical, and all-purpose crank. But he did have an eye for honest value in the world of letters, and to his understanding this meant antiquities, or what we today call folklore. His searches would yield the monumental *Collection of English Songs* in 1783 and in 1795 his most famous work, the two-volume life and ballads of *Robin Hood*. His folkloric labors had begun with a reading of Newbery's *Melody* in 1781. Ritson was the first collector actually to strike out in search of rhymes, and he can lay fair claim to being the nursery's first scholar. His person and habits recall a song of 1680 that will later materialize in Mother Goose like some phantom from a child's dream:

> One misty, moisty morning,
> When cloudy was the weather,
> There I met an old man
> Clothed all in leather;

Clothed all in leather,
With cap under his chin.
How do you do, and how do you do,
And how do you do again?

An ambiguous figure, and not one to be trifled with, perhaps. On the other hand, what can you say ill of a man who takes pleasure in stumping the byways for the small change of a jingle or two? Ritson will spot the gleam of seventy-nine new pieces along the roads of England and exhibit them in 1784 in his *Gammer Gurton's Garland: or, The Nursery Parnassus*. Here, assembled for the first time, are "There was an old woman who lived in a shoe," "Parsley, sage, rosemary, and thyme," "A diller, a dollar, / A ten o'clock scholar," "Goose-a-goose-a gander, / Where shall I wander?," "The man in the moon" discussed earlier, and a variant of "A Frog he would a-wooing go" with the lovely refrain, "Cock me cary, Kitty alone, / Kitty alone and I." Of pedagogic intent, a burden that is increasingly to weigh on children's books, he had none. Ritson was a pedant with no agenda save "the amusement of all little good children who can neither read nor run."

In the century from the 1740s to the 1840s, while these and lesser editions of Mother Goose flitted in and out of print, children's literature remained overwhelmingly moralistic and didactic. But a reputation was building for make-believe, along with a more liberal view of what truly profits a child in his reading. The opening of the nineteenth century would see a slight thaw in favor of imagination and humor in children's books. In 1805 the London firm of Tabart & Company brought out the first collection of rhymes with colored illustrations, *Songs for the Nursery*. This popular compilation would be well thumbed by future anthologists. It is here that "One misty, moisty morning" entered the corpus, along with "How many miles to Babylon," "Pussycat, pussycat, where have you been?," "Bobby Shafto," "Nose, nose, jolly red nose," "One, two, buckle my shoe," and "Little Miss Muffet." The previous year had seen the composition of the first modern verse to enter Mother Goose over the signature of a known scribe. Sarah Catherine Martin was a pretty chatterbox who, annoying her future brother-in-law one day, was admonished to "run away and write one of your stupid little rhymes." The thirty-six-year-old nuisance, an early love of William IV, returned with a set of lines more than equal to the insult. Published in 1805, *The Comic Adventures of Old Mother Hubbard and Her Dog* was doted on by a public with Napoleon too much on its mind and eager for a bit of silly fun. The little toy book inspired many imitations and has enjoyed a place of honor in Mother Goose ever since. Equally popular, though not so clean of line as to win inclusion in Mother Goose, was William Roscoe's *The Butterfly's Ball*, a bit of whimsy that would be imitated no fewer than eighteen times within two years of its appearance in 1807 and could still be heard echoing six decades later in Edward Lear's "Calico Pie."

The Regency marks the first of several junctures at which we can see make-believe being claimed by authors of very different sensibilities. In the years ahead some will be writing in the extroverted spirit of Ms. Martin, but increasing numbers are going to turn to more subjective and inspirational modes. The first way will lead to Edward Lear and Dr. Seuss, the second to Robert Louis Stevenson, Eugene Field, and A. A. Milne. Some good early work might be assigned to either camp: Sara Josepha Hale's "Mary Had a Little Lamb" (1830), Mary Howitt's "'Will you walk into my parlor?' said the spider to the fly," and Clement Moore's effortlessly brilliant *A Visit from St. Nicholas* (1823).

The beginnings of an affective children's literature can be traced largely to three popular books by the Taylor sisters, Ann (1782–1866) and Jane (1783–1824). *Original Poems for Infant Minds* (1804), *Rhymes for the Nursery* (1806), and *Hymns for Infant Minds* (1808), which collectively could be subtitled The Sentimentalizing of Isaac Watts, virtually invented the kind of writing that in degraded form can be found in greeting cards. The Taylors dispensed generic emotions with generic gestures and considerable craft. In the stuffy parlors of the nineteenth century their genteel brand of pathos would prove as contagious as a head cold, and keep readers dabbing and blowing for more than a century. "My Mother" may be the most beloved bad poem of all time. The equally famous opening to "Twinkle, twinkle, little star" quickly entered oral tradition and is consequently now an official member of the Mother Goose family.

The art of the stock response would find a permanent sponsor in the next generation with the rise of the ladies' home magazine and gain universal distribution with the advent of the railroad. This colonizing of the nursery by the emotive arts was obviously a welcome opportunity, as attested to by the thousands of lines soon to be heard echoing the Taylors' "Thank you, pretty cow, that made / Pleasant milk to soak my bread." It is this sensibility that will finally promote Mother Goose out of the chapbooks and make her over into the classic, quaint old bird in a bonnet that we all know, surrounded by milkmaids and dimpled tots in a generically lovely, preindustrial land of make-believe.

The man who drew up the papers retiring Mother Goose to the nursing home of history may or may not have had such an end in mind. James O. Halliwell (1820–89), later to become a noted Shakespearean scholar, was a precocious twenty-two-year-old when he published his first edition of *The Nursery Rhymes of England* in 1842. A collation of previous anthologies, the book teemed as well with original discoveries — "Old King Cole," "There was a crooked man," "Little Tommy Tittlemouse," "Old Abram Brown," "The Queen of Hearts / She made some tarts," "Polly, put the kettle on," "Three blind mice," "Jumping Joan," "I saw a ship a-sailing," "Georgie Porgy," and others — and to these Halliwell attached his numerous theories on their origins. In effect, he did for Mother Goose what Ritson had done for Robin Hood. *The Nursery Rhymes of England* would remain the

Mother Goose of record until Iona and Peter Opie published their *Oxford Dictionary* in 1951. Unfortunately, as "the first work to draw attention to the antiquity of the rhymes with any conviction,"[7] it provided a rationale for every anachronism to come for the next one hundred years. Antiquity cannot be denied Mother Goose, certainly. As the Opies discovered, as many as a quarter of all nursery rhymes could have been known to Shakespeare, and perhaps as few as thirteen percent postdate the close of the eighteenth century. But it is an error to draw from this information an image of Mother Goose as costume drama. Nursery rhymes are living stuff extracted from a living culture. You could if you liked—and some have liked—take the rhyme "Jerry Hall, / He was so small, / A rat could eat him / Hat and all" and dress up the hero as a medieval Tom Thumb. You could likewise portray the snoring old man of "It's raining, it's pouring" as a character out of *The Pickwick Papers*. But in fact "Jerry Hall" turned up in the middle of the Roaring Twenties and the old man who bumped his head when he went to bed is not known prior to Hitler's invasion of Poland. With very few nursery rhymes is cultural nostalgia ever the point. We do not sing lullabies to children or give them knee rides to instill in them a taste for times past. The purpose of a nursery rhyme is to make children happily alert to the present. "Three blind mice" was nearly two and a half centuries old when Halliwell spotted it, but it shows no sign of age and we do not recite it out of a longing for the good old days of the seventeenth century. Yet, after Halliwell this is precisely the use to which the rhymes were put. Collecting was displaced by visual interpretation as the driving force behind Mother Goose; the rhymes were decorously retired to a land of make-believe, and Mother Goose became, in effect, their history book.

The late Victorians took this lovelier, merrier England completely to heart. The players from that Golden Age were all there waiting in Halliwell: King Arthur, Old King Cole, Robin Hood in the mickle wood, Good Queen Bess, all the milkmaids and Simple Simons. Childhood and the childhood of the realm thus became intimately linked in the popular imagination in the second half of Victoria's reign. Out of this association would emerge the first real definition of the phrase "make-believe." Around the 1880s, for the first time, nursery literature would be understood by cultural consensus to have a single quality, a single mood, that one might go shopping for in a children's book and find.

The artists commissioned to portray this mood were a trio commonly regarded as the seminal book illustrators of their day: Walter Crane (1845–1915), Kate Greenaway (1846–1901), and Randolph Caldecott (1846–86). Crane's often droll antiquities were published as *The Baby's Opera* (1877) and *The Baby's Bouquet* (1879). Caldecott, a natural storyteller, brought great liveliness to a regressive idea in the series *Sing a Song for Sixpence* (1880), *The Three Jovial Huntsmen* (1880), *Hey Diddle Diddle* (1882), and *A Frog he would a Wooing Go* (1883). Greenaway's *Mother Goose* appeared in 1881. Her decorative friezes of Little pensive Men and Little pensive Women from the world of Jane Austen in this and others of her books bore an elegance and faux naiveté that enchanted even the tetchy art critic John Ruskin. The famous "Greenaway look" of generically pretty girls in frocks and bonnets can be seen in shop windows even today.

The era following these three constituted the first mannerist phase in children's literature, an adventure in the decorative book arts that lasted some fifty years. Its high-water mark was the Edwardian period, when advances in color printing caused a flood of illustrated children's books to be produced. A few score editions were devoted to Mother Goose alone at this time. Among the better-known titles from the period are *The Nursery Rhyme Book* (1898) and others by L. Leslie Brooke; Arthur Rackham's *Mother Goose* of 1913; and Jessie Willcox Smith's *The Little Mother Goose* in the following year. Blanche Fisher Wright's *The Real Mother Goose* (1916) is a complete misnomer, a commercial vulgarization of Greenaway and Crane that is sentimental, a little loud, and still in print. The school's romantic yearnings found their true home in the enchanted bedtime land portrayed in Anne Anderson's *The Old Mother Goose Nursery Rhyme Book*.[8] Her old woman who lived in shoe inhabits a forest neighborhood so desirable in its unreality that it could stand forever as witness to all the cozy pleasures we should know better than to want from make-believe but often do in spite of ourselves.

The artist who woke the literature up finally was the Russian émigré Feodor Rojankovsky (1891–1970). At bringing animals to life on the page Rojankovsky has had few equals. Children sprang as naturally from the menagerie stored in his pen, and so too did trees, skylines, rain showers, and bicycles. His *Tall Book of Mother Goose* (1942) is an abbreviated edition but comes very close to being the definitive modern collection nonetheless. It is the first in a century to assume that its audience and its subjects are the same boys and girls come out to play. The kids here have a roughed-up rosiness and wear real clothes and real emotions. Yet in Rojankovsky's signature naturalism there is as well an almost tactile intimation of make-believe. *The Tall Mother Goose* has been cited for lacking the extravagance of his fantastical *Frog Went a-Courtin'* (1955), but this charge misses the point of his work, and indeed of Mother Goose herself. You need not indulge in literal fantasy when the make-believe is already alive in your line.

The best anthologies following Rojankovsky will exhibit a preference for brusque comedy—a more than generous helping can be found in Raymond Briggs's *Mother Goose Treasury* of 1966—but even now it cannot be said that we are free of that first definition of make-believe visualized a century ago. The image of Mother Goose as a quaint old bird has remained fixed in the popular imagination and seems unlikely ever to die. In the 1980s children's-book illustrators began a general exodus back to the styles and pretensions of the fin de siècle, some in a sentimental or utopian spirit, some for purposes of burlesque, and some to travesty the very real children of Mother Goose as animals or cartoons, but in almost every case taking it as a given that Mother Goose and make-believe belong not to ourselves but to some idyllic age long past. This same rivalry between our tropism for the real world and our need for more pleasant lands can be seen in the other half of Mother Goose's story waiting to be told, the literary half, which began in the middle of the nineteenth century when Mother Goose extended her reach out of folk rhyme and into the world of narrative verse. Nursery poets looking to derive new forms from her quick rhythms and sketches are now looking to the emotive style of the Taylor sisters, some of them, and some few are looking to Sarah Martin and "Old Mother Hubbard." In Robert Louis Stevenson and Edward Lear, make-believe will find a master in each camp.

A Child's Garden of Verses (1885)

"It's awful fun," said Stevenson of his writing; "You just indulge the pleasure of your heart, that's all; no trouble, no strain . . . just drive along as the words come."[9] Certainly among the most versatile genre writers of all time, he was very possibly also the best. No kind of utterance seemed alien to him: travelogue, verse, play, farce, adventure story, a tale of psychological horror like *Dr. Jekyll and Mr. Hyde* or the kind of historical romance pioneered by his countryman Sir Walter Scott—no matter: with unerring panache he shaped them all into things of beauty for the patrician and middle classes. His readers revered him in his lifetime (1850–94), and upon his romantic death in the South Seas at the age of forty-four they competed to canonize him with one edition of collected works after another. The reader today will be familiar with his masterpiece, *Treasure Island* (1883), through the illustrations of N. C. Wyeth (1911) or the yet more definitive edition by Mervyn Peake (1949). Stevenson's one work for children survives only as a relic of another age, when little boys wore dresses and nursery books were kisses at bedtime. He enshrined this age for his readers by detailing his own childhood as an habitual daydreamer creeping about behind the furniture, climbing a cherry tree, studying the passing scene through the window of a railway car. The lilting verses are all as beautifully laid out as the toy soldiers parading across his sickbed covers in "The pleasant land of counterpane." What Stevenson saw of the world when peering over the horizon of childhood was the world of his storybooks, where "the dusty roads go up and down" and where, for our entertainment, live the "Little Indian, Sioux or Crow, / Little Frosty Eskimo." A book about childhood can never really be a children's book, nor a book about making believe ever really be make-believe, but the pretty pretense of *A Child's Garden* made it the children's book of the hour. Where Greenaway was giving innocence a look, Stevenson was giving it a voice and things to do and think and hum to oneself while being childlike. No one had ever lied up a stereotype so sweetly or at this artistic level before, and a genteel reading public doted on Stevenson's image of itself "[s]itting safe in nursery nooks, / Reading picture story-books." Not even the trauma of World War I could break the spell. When history gave the covers a shake and spilled the boys of Counterpane into the trenches of the western front, Stevenson's sensibility passed safely through the fire to reappear in two other books that families would lovingly commit to memory, A. A. Milne's *When We Were Very Young* (1924) and *Now We Are Six* (1927).

What had provoked him into portraying childhood as itself a pleasant land of make-believe was presumably a collection of verses in the Taylor mode by a Mrs. Sale Barker. The immensely popular *Birthday Book* (1880) was lavishly illustrated by Kate Greenaway with 370 drawings and twelve color pages. Casting about for further ideas, Stevenson appears to have gone next to the Taylors themselves. Here is Ann Taylor's pretty cow and, beside it, Stevenson's "The Cow":

Thank you, pretty cow, that made	The friendly cow all red and white,
Pleasant milk to soak my bread	I love with all my heart:
Every day, and every night,	She gives me cream with all her might,
Warm and fresh and sweet and white.	To eat with apple tart.

His axiomatic "The world is so full of a number of things, / I'm sure we should all be as happy as kings" might be traced to William Brighty Rand's *Lilliput Levee* (1863) and its oft-quoted lines, "Great, wide, beautiful, wonderful world / With the wonderful water round you curled." And in the verses of a fellow Scot once known as the Laureate of the Nursery can be seen, perhaps, the child Stevenson would cast himself as being:

Wee Willie Winkie rins through the town,
Up stairs and doon stairs in his nicht-gown,
Tirling at the window, crying at the lock,
Are the weans in their bed, for it's now ten o'clock?

Published in 1841, William Miller's comic poem ran to twenty lines; this first stanza was included in a Mother Goose anthology within a year of its publication and there it has remained ever since. It is one likely inspiration for the Victorian fad of dressing little boys in girls' smocks. It was as Wee Willie in his nightgown that Charles Robinson would portray the young Stevenson in 1896, and Jessie Willcox Smith in 1905, in the two most famous editions of *A Child's Garden*; and it is how A. A. Milne and E. H. Shepard would see Christopher Robin in the 1920s. In reality, Stevenson had been a rather unpleasant child, as he later confessed, but it was as a sweet Wee Willie that he cast himself, and a Wee Willie was how the world wanted him. Neither he nor Greenaway invented that Victorian phenomenon, the Cult of the Beautiful Child, but they did give it a face and a voice, and, thanks in large part to their work, Wordsworth's familiar gospel that "Heaven lies about us in our infancy" had by the turn of the century been transmogrified into an affectation of pretty clothes, baby talk, self-pitying chatter about lost innocence, and clapping if you believe in fairies.

The smugness that cloys in so many books of this next generation can be clearly heard in Stevenson's lyrical garden. Here he is in "System," turning make-believe into a snug activity of the how-glad-I-am-to-be-me variety:

> The child that is not clean and neat,
> With lots of toys and things to eat,
> He is a naughty child, I'm sure —
> Or else his dear papa is poor.

· This egocentricity is alien to Mother Goose, and it is ironic that Stevenson thought he was composing in her spirit. Some of the imagined inheritance came from a firsthand acquaintance with nursery rhymes, some from second: Ann Taylor's pretty cow, for example, was itself probably a travesty of the folk rhyme "Cushy cow, bonny, let down thy milk," which had first appeared in Tabart's *Songs for the Nursery* in 1805. For firsthand knowledge Stevenson may have looked to Greenaway's *Mother Goose* following his acquaintance with *The Birthday Book*, or, like Lewis Carroll and Edward Lear, he may have made a study of Halliwell's definitive volume. That he conceived of *A Child's Garden* as a new kind of Mother Goose and wrote with one or another volume in hand is not in doubt: his lines "over the hills and far away" and "How many miles to Babylon?" are direct quotes. Even the overall scheme of the book is anticipated by Mother Goose. Stevenson is working two subject areas contrapuntally in his hymn to childhood — the pleasures of playing at home and the anticipation of playing at large in the world as a grownup. His intimate asides and domestic narratives can readily be found in the lullabies of Mother Goose, and the knee rides, and potentially sentimental cameos like "I love little pussy, / Her coat is so warm." His tin-drum marching songs parade by to the beat of barroom ditties like "Nose, nose, / Jolly red nose." His wonderings on the width and abundance of the world are that ancient conceit "If all the seas were one sea," and when he dreams of growing up and setting forth he might just as well be announcing from the pages of Mother Goose, "I, Willie Wastle, / Stand on my castle." His resemblance to tradition is often so close that it would be hard to say, without ascription, to whom lines like these belonged:

> If I had a donkey that wouldn't go,
> Would I beat him? Oh no, no.
> I'd put him in the barn and give him some corn,
> The best little donkey that ever was born.

What signals this as a verse from Mother Goose is the absence of that self-consciousness we can hear in Stevenson's variation on a nursery rhyme in "Looking Forward":

When I was a little boy	When I am grown to man's estate
My mammy kept me in,	I shall be very proud and great,
But now I am a great boy	And tell the other girls and boys
I'm fit to serve the king.	Not to meddle with my toys.

In folk rhyme the eye is always on the donkey or on being old enough to serve the king. Mother Goose documents the life of the world with little news fillers, and neither she nor the reader cares who wrote them. In Stevenson everything documents the life of the reporter; and because he cares, so must we.

To what extent his personal stamp might have expressed an actual commonality of play, daydreams, and domestic routine among the upper middle class I leave to the reader to judge. The effect of the domestic verses, I think, was unfortunate, leading as they did to hundreds of inferior volumes that preempt a child's original response to the world by attempting to do his thinking for him. All such work presents us with a scrapbook entitled "This Is Your Life." This is how you play, say the rhymes; this is how you go to bed; this is what you dream. It isn't, really, and the child is put in the position of being a third party to someone else's play; but the seduction is sweet, and generations of parents took Stevenson's book to heart as the gospel truth of who they thought they had been and wanted to see in their own children.

The world verses, because they are about something else, are rather better on the whole. Although for the reader they must be make-believe at second hand, the atmosphere of make-believe is there. Stevenson's shores may be too green, his seas too blue, and the way too serene, but the world is promised, which is the great purpose of children's story, and he makes you want to come along. If true sentiment is everywhere confused with false in *A Child's Garden*, and nostalgia with accurate recall, Stevenson's desire to be afoot is real enough, and, in their storybook way, so too the dusty roads that go up and down and the painted stations whistling by. When he writes of his longing to travel through "forests, hot as fire, / Wide as England," no false note is being struck. This is just how a child would make up the world from maps found in the drawing room. However much Stevenson veered from a child's true perception from verse to verse, at the center of the book is a vision of the world, and his voice as he tells us about this world he sees is the voice of a man who couldn't wait to be joined with it, and went.

Several writers have elected as the most magical words in children's literature the phrase that Stevenson adopted from Mother Goose, "over the hills and far away." For me they would have to include his evocation of that big thing in the sky once worshipped by the old Egyptian boys whose lost toys he dreamed of discovering on his travels: "Great is the sun, and wide he goes / Through empty heaven without repose." In these two lines Stevenson captures what it is to be three feet tall and looking into the sky for the first time. This is how it feels to have a vision of the immensity of space and time and to know it to be benign.

If little else in *A Child's Garden* is the true stuff of make-believe, that surely is.

Lullaby Land (1897)

The Cult of the Beautiful Child found its American home in the immensely popular make-believe of the Chicago newspaper columnist Eugene Field (1850–95). Memorable flights of fancy like "The Sugar-Plum Tree," "Wynken, Blynken, and Nod," "Little Boy Blue," "The Shut-Eye Train," "The Duel" ("The gingham dog and the calico cat"), "Seein' Things" ("I ain't afeard uv snakes or toads"), and "The Rock-a-By Lady from Hushaby Street" first appeared in two volumes ostensibly addressed to children, *With Trumpet and Drum* (1892) and *Love Songs of Childhood* (1894). Field had the instincts of a good lyricist—these are vivid and inventive pieces—but, unfortunately, he could not resist clotting the works with rhetorical sweeteners. There are enough lisped verbs ("bringeth," "turneth," "findeth"), lollipop seas, fairies, dimpledown cheeks, and winkyblink eyes in these pages to curdle even the Taylor sisters' glass of milk at bedtime. The death of Little Boy Blue, which we witness through the dumb testimony of "the little toy friends" he leaves behind, is a classic of contrived pathos:

> And they wonder, as waiting the long years through
> In the dust of that little chair,
> What has become of our Little Boy Blue,
> Since he kissed them and put them there.

This prelude to *The Velveteen Rabbit* is the sentimentalist's answer to the infant deaths in Janeway's *A Token for Children*. The sentimental ancestry of all these verses is clear: from Stevenson's Nursery, Boy, and Land of Counterpane came Field's "make-believe soldiers in Good-Children Street"; from Hans Christian Andersen, the live toys and the pathos. Where Stevenson is restrained in his effects, however, Field is as self-indulgent as Andersen; where Andersen is bracingly sardonic, Field is merely maudlin. "Little Boy Blue" is a kitsch dessert designed to put a lump in the reader's throat. Why anyone would think to put a lump of sorrow in a child's throat, and use a lullaby to do it, I cannot say. The public ate up these Stevensonian cupcakes; they appeared in limited editions and educators even designed readers for the primary grades around them. Kenneth Grahame, in the 1890s himself a practicing mannerist, edited a Field anthology, *Lullaby Land*, that would be decorated, not unexpectedly, by the illustrator of *A Child's Garden of Verses*, Charles Robinson.

Like Stevenson, Field knew his Mother Goose and aspired to family membership. In the work of another contemporary poet he saw how the thing could be done, and in one verse he tried to do it:

Wynken, Blynken, and Nod one night
  Sailed off in a wooden shoe—
Sailed on a river of crystal light,
  Into a sea of dew.
"Where are you going, and what do you wish?"
  The old moon asked the three.
"We have come to fish for the herring fish
  That live in this beautiful sea;
  Nets of silver and gold have we!"
      Said Wynken,
      Blynken,
      And Nod.

It might have been Mother Goose, but it isn't; it might have been another "The Jumblies," which I think it wanted to be, but it isn't. Something has gone wrong here. There is nothing off-key in the heroes' names, nothing wrong with their sailing in a wooden shoe, nothing mishandled in the moon's question, and nothing terribly off-putting about their reply. All these are good enough to warrant the poem's inclusion in Mother Goose. After three more stanzas Field is going to throw it all away irrevocably by announcing that Wynken and Blynken "are two little eyes / And Nod is a little head" and the wooden shoe "a wee one's trundle-bed," but at this point it hardly mattered; he had already disqualified the allegory from Mother Goose with the barely suppressed epic pathos of the poem's tidal rhythm and the artifice of "a river of crystal light" and "a sea of dew." Chandelier effects have no business in Mother Goose. The nursery is no place to strive for grandeur of vision. Field had the instinct to emulate Edward Lear but not the sensibility for it. "The Jumblies" belongs to the comic tradition of Mother Goose and Sarah Martin's "Old Mother Hubbard;" "Wynken, Blynken, and Nod" belongs to the world of the affective arts and the generic gestures of the Taylor sisters. Field wrote not to awaken his readers' imaginations but to impress their emotions.

There may be such a thing as being too comfortable in one's culture to write honestly. A columnist with a national following, Field played to the needs of the Gilded Age. Lear, on the other hand, spent much of his life (1812–88) wandering about in relative anonymity and self-imposed exile. When he wasn't wandering physically, he wandered emotionally. "His nose is remarkably big," he sang of his most prominent feature, and, like the boll weevil, he spent his days tramping it cross-country, looking for a home.

A Book of Nonsense (1846, 1861), *Nonsense Songs* (1871), *More Nonsense* (1872), *Laughable Lyrics* (1877)

The historian Harvey Darton thought him "not a clear product of evolution."[10] Lear, who saw himself as a sport of nature, a Dong with a luminous nose, would have taken the remark as a joke on his person and agreed. But he was foretold. The language meant to have him. Nonsense was in the air when Lear was born; Darton himself cites a minor work of the period with the Learish title *Aldiborontophoskyphorniostinos*, and to this we could add a few other possible precedents like Samuel Foote's prose poem *The Great Panjandrum*. None of these minor instances are necessary to account for Lear's cast of mind, however; a Queerie Learie, as he called himself, became inevitable on the family tree of make-believe the moment Mother Goose embraced the two nursery rhymes "Hickory, dickory, dock" and "Hey, diddle, diddle, / The Cat and the Fiddle." From the one, a verse in which subject and meter convey the idea of counting, would come Lear the limericist, taking the count of everyone else on the family tree of man; from the other, a song in which a dish runs away with a spoon, would come a Lear singing of Owls eloping with Pussycats and Ducks, Nutcrackers, and Flies running away with Kangaroos, Sugar-tongs, and Daddy Long-legs. We needn't speculate about this; a favorite recreation of Lear's, long before he put anything to paper, was amusing children at the piano with nursery rhymes set to music. One would later recall how "with intense pathos of expression and gravity of face" he would play "'Hey Diddle Diddle, the Cat and the Fiddle,' or some other nonsensical words to the same air."[11]

A *Book of Nonsense* appeared when he was thirty-four. A modest collection of limericks, it nevertheless became famous enough to encourage him to augment it at the age of forty-nine and at sixty to publish a second collection, *More Nonsense*. With these 212 examples, each accompanied by a happily spastic cartoon, Lear became the first writer to master what, despite later accretions of sophistication, is essentially a nursery rhyme.

Who first penned a limerick no one knows. Its prototypes are not uncommon in folk rhyme. "Hector Protector," "Baby and I / Were baked in a pie," and "Hickory, dickory, dock" are all limerick in form. In 1796 the didactic children's author Maria Edgeworth had written or copied down a similarly phrased piece, "Hannah Bantry, in the pantry." Mother Goose and Lear would both adopt these lines, Lear reworking them into "There was a young person of Bantry, / Who frequently slept in the pantry." Even earlier than Edgeworth, in the 1760s, a group of Irish poets in County Limerick had played with the form as a local amusement. The word itself does not appear in circulation until 1898, but it would seem likely to refer to an Irish origin.

The first book of limericks was published in 1821. *The History of Sixteen Wonderful Old Women* was an anonymous set of comic homilies annotating the fortunes of some generally ill-starred ladies; in a way it could be read as the nursery rhyme's answer to the book of Proverbs. It is not all that funny to the modern ear, but it was catchy enough to inspire a host of imitations. One from the following year, *Anecdotes and Adventures of Fifteen Gentlemen*, contained a verse that caught Lear's eye:

> There was a sick man of Tobago,
> Who liv'd long on rice-gruel and sago;

> But at last, to his bliss,
> The physician said this —
> "To a roast leg of mutton you may go."

Whoever first coined the limerick as a form, its pedigree lies in folk rhyme, and for an origin myth I think we can credibly arrange a marriage between one nursery rhyme collected by Mary Cooper and one by Joseph Ritson:

> Hickory Dickory Dock,
> The Mouse ran up the clock;
> The clock struck one,
> And down he run,
> Hickory Dickory Dock.

> There was an old woman who lived in a shoe,
> She had so many children she didn't know what to do.
> She gave them some broth without any bread;
> She whipped them all soundly and put them to bed.

Try saying both rhymes at once and you might produce a sound like this, from *Sixteen Old Women*:

> There was an old woman of Surrey,
> Who was morn, noon, and night in a hurry;
> Called her husband a fool,
> Drove her children to school,
> That worrying old woman of Surrey.

It was some brawling old woman of Surrey, no doubt, that we saw in Proverbs, driving her husband upstairs to live on the rooftop.

That the limerick belongs to the Mother Goose family of verses Lear saw plainly enough. He may even have understood it to be the offspring of those same two rhymes collected by Cooper and Ritson. His fifth line, for example, always follows in the style of "Hickory, dickory, dock" and *Sixteen Old Women*, repeating or varying the first:

> There was an Old Person of Rhodes,
> Who strongly objected to toads;
> He paid several cousins, to catch them by dozens,
> That futile Old Person of Rhodes.

When you are writing a great many verses that are all of a kind, you are quickly going to run up against the problem of repetition. If your subjects must be either young or old and male or female, there are only so many ways you can say There was a Somebody of Someplace before you become tedious. Lear gives the matter only a cursory attention, really, but when he does his formula is a curious one. Two hundred and twelve times he tosses up his old and his young, his men and his women, and so entertainingly does he juggle these counters that you never notice how two Persons are missing who ought not to be in a feat this elaborate. In compiling two books over the course of some thirty-odd years, Lear will detail the peculiarities and pratfalls of eighty-nine old men, twenty-seven young and five old ladies, one young girl, and ninety "Persons" of either age category. Not once will he do the obvious and begin a limerick "There was an old woman" or "There was a young man." The absence of the first is especially odd. "There was an old woman" is a standard Mother Goose formula; limericks aside, more than a dozen nursery rhymes begin this way, and, given the precedent of *Sixteen Old Women*, we should expect to see Lear naturally falling back on a phrase that lends itself so readily to the meter. Its absence is conspicuous enough to call attention to itself. Indeed, whenever we might expect him to break the monotony by switching from Old Man to Old Woman, he shows us a cartoon of another man and uses the surrogate Old Person. Of the twenty-nine Old Persons in the first collection and the fifty-one in the second, twenty-eight and forty-two, respectively, are men. If we knew nothing at all of Lear's life, something might be deduced from so studied an avoidance of old women, and with it, too, I think, some of the reason why Lear, unlike Stevenson, chose not to intrude himself upon his verses for the nursery but learned to disguise himself instead as a Dong or a Yonghy-Bonghy-Bò, or as various Old Men of Dunrose, Cassel, Brigg, and West Dumpet.

With Lear, the child was truly the father of the man. Of all those who have elected to write for the nursery following some childhood dislocation or unhappiness, and done so with an almost paradoxically comic generosity, he endured the unhappiest childhood of all. That he was a homely boy with bad eyes and the family nose was the least of it. He was also the affectionate runt of an enormous litter: last in a line of twenty-one children. He might have been lost in the shuffle altogether had he not at five or six been stricken with epilepsy. The seizures were severe and came as many as twenty a month, a trial that would dictate the evasive course of his wandering life and cast over it the pall of melancholy that he would allegorize privately as his "Morbids."

The event that would tell him who he was and was to be in the world, however, preceded even this doleful knowledge of himself. Many authors of children's books have grown up without a mother or father; Lear, like Rudyard Kipling, had the singular experience of having both but being sent into exile by them. In each case there was good reason, but to a child, of course, all reasons are academic. When he was only four, his mother, distracted and exhausted, sent him to live elsewhere. Division of labor is the necessary norm in any large family and easily explained away, but the act did tell him who he was, and was to be, in the scheme of things. He was the odd man out.

What good held fast and grew in him was the work of his sister Ann, who undertook to raise this unhappy four-year-old when she was twenty-six. She brought him up rather strictly, but she was loving and had a sense of humor. From her came his knowledge of nursery rhymes, and as he grew she read to him from the Bible and books of mythology and a good deal in the modern poets. She taught him to draw and to paint and thus gave him the career that would sustain him over nearly five decades. His little exile was an event he could not lay to rest, even so. He had been shunted aside by his mother and largely ignored by both parents thereafter, and the damage had been done. How even a good parent could see to the needs of twenty-one children is inconceivable to the rational mind, but then children do not have rational minds. Some three decades later old men will appear in Lear's limericks as figures of fun and old women will exist not at all. That Lear would never once break the monotony with the standard formula "There was an old woman" was surely no accident. What he was deliberately avoiding, I am reasonably certain, was the pain of association, and what he was associating with the limerick form was the nursery rhyme that had helped give rise to it, "There was an old woman who lived in a shoe." That famous old woman who "had so many children she didn't know what to do" was his own mother. And what she had done, after putting her other twenty children to bed, was to set this last, demanding child on the doorstep, outside her affections, and leave him there.

His being Edward Lear, odd man out, may account too for the absence of any limerick beginning "There was a young man." An extraneous thumbling at home, what could he be to general society but a larger pratfall? Epilepsy made him a risky vessel to take public. In later years he could sing, "Our Sieve ain't big, / But we don't care a button! we don't care a fig!," but never in this early work does he suggest there is a young Jumbly on board, and not once does he portray a Young Person as male.

The frequent seizures may have made him overly sensitive to his other shortcomings. He does look homely in contemporary portraits but not disagreeably so, and no one seems to have cared, really. Throughout his life he would find a welcome and loyal friends wherever he went. He preferred the company of "colourful, uninhibited people . . . free from the fears of wrathful gods and the worries of convention."[12] With them he could share a laugh over his most public liability, that gaudy advance man for his person, the Lear family nose. There are ten verses about disproportionate beaks among these limericks where no young men can be found. Dealing with the nose may have been what prompted him to write limericks in the first place. In the world of the nursery rhyme he could give his beak a home in a universe of extravagant noses. This is what the first books are all about, I think, creating a society of oddfellows in which a queerie learie would not seem all that peculiar a species. Like Mother Goose, Lear came at a moment in history to take the census. Just how many sports of nature and victims of chance are there in the world? To the beat of "Hickory, dickory, dock," he counts them off: one, "There was an Old Man of the West"; two, "There was a young lady in blue"; three,

> There was an old person of Crowle,
> Who lived in the nest of an owl;

When they screamed in the nest, he screamed out with the rest,
That depressing old person of Crowle.

A Book of Nonsense and *More Nonsense* are the tally books of an habitual, watchful archivist. The habit of counting heads may have begun early. How many times as a child must Lear have listened to his parents counting off that long inventory of siblings before hearing the name Edward spoken? Now it was his turn to make the count, and not only could he count himself in this time, he also had the discretion of counting himself out on his own terms, wondering aloud, as he excused himself from the world of wrathful gods, who was the more odd, was it he or they:

> There was an Old Person of Basing,
> Whose presence of mind was amazing;
> He purchased a steed, which he rode at full speed,
> And escaped from the people of Basing.

Painting took him abroad. His talent had emerged early, under his sister's tutelage, and at fifteen, out of financial need, he had put it to work. A gift for rendering wildlife in the manner of Audubon won him several well-placed sponsors and commissions sufficient to keep him going. He was, for a few months in 1846, drawing master to Queen Victoria. But it was the topical landscape that would pay his way, and in search of picturesque street scenes, vistas, and ruins he wandered the Mediterranean basin, and once India, for years at a time. Trips home to England were infrequent. He seems to have felt more comfortable away, where he could nurse his seizures and his Morbids in relative privacy. Perhaps, too, the absurdity of being an afterthought set better with him at a distance. Exile became a permanent condition. He settled at last on the Italian Riviera, and there, for eighteen years until his death at seventy-six, he wrote his new nonsense songs and kept company with his eccentric cat, Foss. When the cat died, Lear followed as dutifully as an abandoned spouse.

The announced ambition of his life, "to achieve a mood of balance, harmony, and happiness,"[13] became the business of his art. It was the credo of a man unable to keep from falling down. He knew he was not a great landscape painter like his admiration, J. M. W. Turner. His letters document the pain of an artist forever having to confront what he cannot do. "I have found a new world," he laments of the Levant, "but my art is helpless to recall it to others."[14] His pictures were the kind of accomplished but unmemorable set pieces that migrate from the display easel to the guest rooms and back hallways of notable homes. Beginning in 1841 with *Views in Rome* and ending in 1870 with *Journal of a Landscape Painter in Corsica*, he augmented his income with portfolios for the armchair traveler. It is classically serene work and all the study of an epileptic seeking to balance himself along strong axes and find rest from the impending vertigo among stately trees and architecture. In those letters to friends that detail such matters, he longed for this same mood of happiness outside the picture frame. His last decades were comfortable enough, sparer in his mind than in his rooms —

> Two old chairs, and half a candle, —
> One old jug without a handle, —
> These were all his worldly goods . . .

— but periodically, to the end, he longed for a woman's company and the small, fatuous pleasures enjoyed by his Table and Chair:

> "What a lovely walk we've taken!
> "Let us dine on Beans and Bacon!"

The lines of his most accomplished song, "The Courtship of the Yonghy-Bonghy-Bò," he had been rehearsing most of his adult life:

> "I am tired of living singly, —
> "On this coast so wild and shingly, —
> "I'm a-weary of my life:
> "If you'll come and be my wife,
> "Quite serene would be my life!" —
> Said the Yonghy-Bonghy-Bò.

His unattainable ideal was Emily Tennyson, the laureate's wife, a friend with whom he shared intimacies and after whom he named his house Villa Emily. He almost did marry once, but, fretting over his liabilities, he shied away in the end from his Lady Jingly Jones, and

> Down the slippery slopes of Myrtle,
> Where the early pumpkins blow,
> To the calm and silent sea
> Fled the Yonghy-Bonghy-Bò.

This final retreat into exile he portrayed as the flight of a foolish Hoddy Doddy perched ridiculously atop a turtle that bore him away

> With a sad primaeval motion
> Towards the sunset isles of Boshen.

"The Courtship of the Yonghy-Bonghy-Bò" cannot be called children's literature exactly, nor could "The Dong with a Luminous Nose" or several others of his verses. I would not, on the other hand, want to be the one to argue against them as such. The songs were published in two collections when Lear was fifty-nine and sixty-five. The earlier of the two, *Nonsense Songs*, is more truly the children's book, with its nursery rhymes like "The Owl and the Pussycat" and "Calico Pie" and its narrative verse fantasies like "The Duck and the Kangaroo." *Laughable Lyrics* has children's fare in it, certainly — "The Quangle Wangle's Hat," "The Pelican Chorus," and "The Pobble Who Has No Toes" — but this is the book of Lear's exile and as much a lament as a celebration. The children's verses were the earlier written. In them Lear was following the example of his own favorite nursery rhyme, "Hey, diddle, diddle, / The Cat and the Fiddle." Most of his work is predicated, really, on just one line: "And the Dish ran away with the Spoon." Going into exile was once for him an impulsive, exhilarating act of liberation. As the Duck says to the Kangaroo, "My life is a bore in this nasty pond, / And I long to go out in the world beyond!" And so they all go — the Jumblies to sea in their sieve, crying, "We don't care a button! we don't care a fig!," and the Owl and the Pussycat eloping in their pea-green boat, and the Nutcrackers and the Sugar-tongs, who

> rode through the street, and they rode by the station,
> They galloped away to the beautiful shore;
> In silence they rode, and 'made no observation,'
> Save this: 'We will never go back any more!'

Out there in the Torrible Zone or down by the Zemmery Fidd where the Oblong Oysters grow was the promise of a second chance among the Jumbly Girls and Nupiter Piffkins. "And there they play for evermore / At battlecock and shuttledoor" — or hand in hand by the edge of the sand, dance by the light of the moon, like the Owl and the Pussycat. Illusion or reality, this is growing up into liberated adulthood as children do often see it and therefore can be read as the work of a storyteller properly honoring his contract to deliver the future to his readers and his readers into their future.

Lear was not a deluded soul, however, and never a mere illusionist. The defiant ending to "The Nutcrackers and the Sugar-tongs" — "And they never came back!" — became the plaintive refrain of the verse that follows it, "Calico Pie":

> And they never came back to me!
> They never came back!
> They never came back!
> They never came back to me!

Here, it is the escape artist himself who has been left behind. Paradoxically, while his purest nursery rhyme, written in direct imitation of Mother Goose, this is a verse that has probably baffled children as much as amused them. It is a suite of four nursery rhymes, really — "Calico Pie," "Calico Jam," "Calico Ban," and "Calico Drum." The last,

> Calico Drum,
> The Grasshoppers come,
> The Butterfly, Beetle, and Bee

looks to have been the first written. There is an intimation in these lines that Lear conceived his four-part poem by marrying the thumpety-thump form of the nursery rhyme, "Aiken Drum" to the subject of a nonsense song in vogue when he was a boy, William Roscoe's "The Butterfly's Ball." Or he may have drawn from an imitation of Roscoe's little hit, "The Peacock at Home":

> The Butterfly's Ball, and the Grasshopper's Feasts,
> Excited the spleen of the Birds and the Beasts:
> For their mirth and good cheer — of the Bee was the theme,
> And the Gnat blew his horn as he danced in the beam.
> 'Twas hummed by the Beetle, 'twas buzz'd by the Fly . . .

"Calico Pie" is a lament, albeit a dancing, comical one, and with it Lear gave the defiant exuberance of his first volume of songs what he must have judged to be its proper balance. He later did the same service for the sadder *Laughable Lyrics* by reversing "Calico Pie" to make "The Quangle Wangle's Hat," wherein all the creatures that never came back do return, to make their home with the lonesome Quangle Wangle:

> And all of them said, — We humbly beg,
> 'We may build our homes on your lovely Hat,
> 'Mr. Quangle Wangle, grant us that!
>   'Mr. Quangle Wangle Quee!'
>
> And the Quangle Wangle said
> To himself on the Crumpetty Tree, —
> 'When all these creatures move
> 'What a wonderful noise there'll be!'
> And at night by the light of the Mulberry moon
> They danced to the Flute of the Blue Baboon,
> On the broad green leaves of the Crumpetty Tree,
> And all were as happy as happy could be,
> With the Quangle Wangle Quee.

Something like this was necessary to the health of the second volume, much of whose mood came not from Mother Goose but from the morbids of Alfred, Lord Tennyson. Lear had for years been entertaining friends with piano arrangements of Tennyson's poems, and although he would often lurch off into parody, he venerated the poet. In the Nutcracker's complaint, "Must we drag on this stupid existence for ever, / So idle and weary, so full of remorse," can be heard perhaps an echo of "Tears, idle tears." Detecting Tennyson's languorous rhythms, too, in "Far and few, far and few, / Are the lands where the Jumblies live," we might suppose Lear's poem began as a piano improvisation on "The Lotus-Eaters." To Tennyson's

> Then some one said, 'We will return no more,'
> And all at once they sang, 'Our island home
> Is far beyond the wave; we will no longer roam. . . . '

we could easily append Lear's

> They whistled and warbled a moony song
> To the echoing sound of a coppery gong,
> In the shade of the mountains brown.

If Tennyson's melancholy music moved Lear's later lyrics, it did not survive his humors to the end. When the time came for Queerie Learie to inter himself in that great Mother Goose graveyard wherein lie Cock Robin and Old Abram Brown, he composed two obituaries for himself that are among his brightest inventions. "How pleasant to know Mr. Lear!" and "Incidents in the Life of My Uncle Arly" were a last leap of the language before he went heels up to join his cat. In the end, the Quangle Wangle's Hat was Lear himself, in whom some of the happiest possibilities of the English language came home to roost. He died alone but certain that posterity would remember him in words of his own choosing: "How pleasant to know Mr. Lear! / Who has written such volumes of stuff!"

Dr. Seuss (1904–91)

W. H. Auden wrote generously of Lear that "children swarmed to him like settlers. He became a land." The metaphor can be applied even more aptly to Theodore Geisel, whose comic invention was for fifty years extravagant and inexhaustible. I have not headlined this episode in the history of story "Dr. Seuss" rather than with a list of titles merely to be whimsical. "Seuss" is the primary make-believe here; the books are chapters in the history of a land called by that name. I will assume that the reader knows it well. Part picture book, part comic book, part movie, a Seuss title carries the child happily along like a ball bouncing through some demented Rube Goldberg contraption. Geisel's architectures aspire to the impossible, like rubbery Towers of Babel, and his characters leap about like boneless acrobats. The land of Seuss is like nothing else in children's literature, and to call it a land is almost a literal truth: in every library there are two shelves of it, and at the bookstore a wall.

Sorting out the make-believe from the commercial primers and more didactic fables, these emerge as the principal editions:

And to Think That I Saw It on Mulberry Street (1937)
Horton Hatches the Egg (1940)
McElligot's Pool (1947)
Horton Hears a Who (1954)
The Cat in the Hat (1957)

The first and third of these are actually books about making believe as an activity rather than being themselves make-believe. The boys doing the daydreaming here are all-American versions of the Robert Louis Stevenson who imagined where the dusty roads would one day take him, but Geisel's flamboyance gives a better sense, I think, of the myriad pleasures of making believe and, by extension, of the very real possibilities inherent in the world. He has been compared most often with Lear. This is accurate in one sense and not in another. Lear wrote nursery rhymes and comic laments, Geisel social fables in verse. It is easy to fault Geisel at times for having a heavy hand, especially in the later books, but in the titles just cited his morals are so natural an outcome of the story and so breezily delivered that the reader is hardly put out at finding them there. "An elephant's faithful one hundred per cent" is simply an announcement of the hero's character. *Horton* was not contrived to broadcast some social agenda, as would be the case with, say, *The Lorax* (1971).

In their use of language to create a place in the imagination, however, Geisel and Lear were pipers of the same clan. The legendary Dr. Seuss might have hatched out of some nest in the Quangle Wangle's hat. Geisel's coinages — Sneetches, Grinches, Ooblecks, the ludicrous place names — are family with Lear's Nupiter Piffkins and Lands of Tute. The eponymous locale of his first book, *Mulberry Street*, while in fact the boulevard of his upbringing in Springfield, Massachusetts, is also a place where wonders can be imagined coming home to roost just as they do in Lear, where all assemble to "dance by the light of the Mulberry moon."

Hints of Geisel's signature look as an illustrator were everywhere in evidence in the first decades of the century. The Funny Thing of Wanda Gág's *The Funny Thing* would look at home in any Seuss book, as would Lang Campbell's Skeezicks from the *Uncle Wiggily* stories. In the comic strips were Rube Goldberg and the dreamscapes of *Little Nemo*, *Krazy Kat*, and *Felix*. The land of Seuss bears a striking resemblance to the creations of his now forgotten older contemporary, the cartoonist and children's-book illustrator, George Carlson. Both Carlson and Geisel may derive in equal measure from Gustave Verbeck, whose newspaper strip, *The Terrors of the Tiny Tads* (1905–16), appeared throughout Geisel's childhood. These were nonsense fantasies in verse, with creatures sporting the bizarre morphologies that would become a Seuss trademark. Verbeck's Terrors suggest as well an early source for Geisel's exploration of one of the great subjects of children's story, anxiety. As Selma Lanes was early to observe, the land of Seuss is anything but escapist or merry; the stories usually hinge on some crisis guaranteed to kindle an uncommon amount of anxiety in hero and reader alike. In *The Cat in the Hat* Geisel brought home to roost a tradition stretching from "Little Red Riding Hood" to Hilaire Belloc's *Cautionary Tales* of 1908. The inaugural volume in a series of reading primers like *Green Eggs and Ham* (1960) and *Fox in Sox* (1965), *The Cat* stands apart from its pedagogic function as a genuine work of make-believe. Exploring with uninhibited glee every kid's desire to turn the house upside down once the parents are gone, the tale is conducted in such a way that the child listening to it "can sit back and experience genuine pleasure, knowing that the anxiety building up in him is vicarious and that no punishment will follow Seuss's forbidden pleasures."[15] *The Cat* is a chapter taken from another masterpiece of forbidden games, *Pinocchio*. The bad puppet's conscience, a Talking Cricket, turns up in Seussland — by way of the Disney movie, it would appear — as an admonishing, hysterical goldfish. Geisel reverses the more traditional anxiety about growing up, however. In "Little

Red Riding Hood," in *Alice* and *Pinocchio* and *Peter Rabbit*, it is a given that in order to be bullied or conned one must leave home and set off down the road to wherever it is that bullies and con artists hang out. The modern anxiety — exacerbated by the invasion of the home by radio and television — echoes the story "The Three Little Pigs," in which suspicious characters are in the neighborhood and coming to ring your bell. The Cat who appears at the door promising "lots of good fun that is funny" is the fishy character in this tale. While he and his cohorts, Thing One and Thing Two, run amok in the house, the children can only stand by as stunned witnesses to the hideous fulfillment of their own secret desires. *The Cat in the Hat* is one of the very few children's books where the parent reading aloud can emote to his heart's content without doing damage to the text and the child listening can relish the ride. Again from Lanes, a remark that applies equally to *The Cat* or *Pinocchio*, *Peter Rabbit* or any of the great stories: "Seuss has a perfect understanding of grownups' love of order and the rule of their laws — and of the enormous anxiety burden this places on small children everywhere."[16] To invoke this tension and release it satisfactorily is one of the great tricks in writing for children. Geisel was as much its master as he was of that other favorite theme, the wonders that are waiting to be dreamed on Mulberry Street or fetched up by fishhook from the far reaches of the world into McElligot's Pool.

The nursery rhyme has attracted many hands in the twentieth century; talking nonsense to children has been a favorite activity of writers like Spike Milligan in England and Jack Prelutsky in America, for example. But with these two poets of the absurd, Seuss and Lear, the story of Mother Goose's descent into narrative verse is pretty much told. We now return three centuries, to France, for the birth of the second great class of children's make-believe, the fairy tale.

2

A FACULTY FOR THE MUSES (I)
Fairy Tales and Tutors

When we have read enough fairy tales that we actually become insensible to the fate of their heroes (assuming it always to be a happy one), we may still read them for their artistry and odd surprises, or we may come to them as J. R. R. Tolkien did, looking for the source of enchantment, the awakening of some strange desire. What we can no longer do is take such stories personally. To a child, on the other hand, these are true hero tales. They hold the secrets to how he is to fare in the world and what manner of world it is that means to test him. When he asks, "Is that true?" he often means, "Can that happen to me?" The perils in these tales are many and fearfully stated: abandonment, hunger, failure, ridicule, death. A child hearing a fairy tale for the first time is at risk with the hero. He is this Aladdin, this Jack or Hop o' My Thumb; she is this Snow White or Cinderella. Hero and reader are that same pilgrim laboring under the spell of ill fortune, ignorance, fear, and ineptitude known as childhood. What they are about to learn, the adult no longer need discover—how, through patience, goodness, pluck, or planting the right seeds, they may one day break the spell to claim their inheritance of the world.

On this all fairy tales are agreed: that while we are called upon to make the journey alone and may come to fancy ourselves able to make it alone, we cannot in fact make it alone. A bit of help along the way from some croaking toad or crone will be required, or the less ambiguous intercession of a good fairy. Our own hands must see to the work—

As the Old One poked her horrid old head into the oven, Gretel gave her a push and a shove, closed the oven door, bolted it swiftly and ran away. The

Old One called and cried, and frizzled and fried, but no one heard. That was the end of her, and who cares?[1]

—but coming into our inheritance will sooner or later mean being able to tell the true friend from the false and the true teacher from the rogue or the fool. Even resourceful Gretel needed the advice of a helpful bird to break the spell over her childhood. What we all require, the tales tell us, is a child's faith in the goodness of passersby and the humility to follow directions.

The story of how the fairy tale itself grew up to assume its inheritance in literature is the story of a search for this true friend of our need. From Charles Perrault in the 1690s to C. S. Lewis in the 1950s, what we are going to see in the growth of narrative fantasy is a literature in want of some teacher to stand muse over it, like a Mother Goose, and to serve within it as a guide to our vicarious wanderings. It has not wanted for candidates. Perhaps the most popular recourse, not only in make-believe but in all the arts, has been to those muses invoked by Milton and the Romantics. What could be more suited to the literature than the vocabulary of ancient Greece, whose storyland gods are so like ourselves and therefore so comprehensible to children? And if the vocabulary of Parnassus, home of the Sacred Nine, is suited to this world of tales, why not, then, to a study of tales? My calling upon the Daughters of Memory to guide these pages would be a gesture acceptable to everyone from Dante to Tolkien, who theorized at length on the matter and created his own distant Olympus. Neither J. M. Barrie nor Kenneth Grahame, who introduced the god Pan into their tales, would have thought it odd, nor C. S. Lewis, whose Narnia teems with fauns and centaurs. To Erato, the muse of poetry, might go our opening pages, then, and to sister Thalia, muse of pastoral and comedy, the three concluding chapters of the book. The long middle would fall under the aegis of Polyhymnia, the muse of sacred literature; and Polyhymnia and history's muse, Clio, would share dual sponsorship of the book as a whole. If it seems a whimsical thing to propose, this is a literature with a weakness for passing fancies and ceremonial rhetoric:

"Rat!" he found breath to whisper, shaking.

"Are you afraid?"

"Afraid?" murmured the Rat, his eyes shining with unutterable love. "Afraid! Of *Him*? O, never, never! And yet—and yet—O, Mole, I am afraid!"

Then the two animals, crouching to the earth, bowed their heads and did worship.

Grahame's peep through the shrubbery at two English gentlemen on their knees, worshiping a goat, is hardly unique in the Land of Make-Believe. There is definitely something about whimsy that encourages authors to blurt out fancies they might be loath to expose elsewhere. From the Romantics to the mannerists of the fin de siècle, and so on through our own era, the search to name the literature's natural muse has sprung the lid on a Pandora's box of phantoms, fairies, and peculiar household gods. There did come one defining moment, however, in the nineteenth century, when three scribes surrendered their prose to a muse who walked on no cloven foot and asked no sentimental favors of authors on country strolls. They were Charles Kingsley, the author of *The Water Babies*, the fantasist George MacDonald, and Carlo Collodi, the father of *Pinocchio*. What they wrote, each independently of the others yet each alike, had been first intimated at the close of the seventeenth century in a little book of stories by the French civil servant and academic Charles Perrault (1628-1703), whose other muse, Mother Goose, was to cross the Channel to England to preside over the world of the nursery rhyme.

Histoires ou Contes du temps passé; Avec des Moralitez (1697)

Where Perrault found the tales of Cinderella, Sleeping Beauty, Hop o' My Thumb, Puss-in-Boots, Bluebeard, and Little Red Riding Hood—whether he heard them from a family nursemaid or cook or came across them in some old book—is not known; nor is it clear how much his own hand shaped these classic stories. He referred to them only as "tales from days gone by." The more or less inapt term that has since attached to them originated in Perrault's day, but upstairs rather than down, in the chambers of Versailles, where since the 1670s it had been the fashion among ladies at court to pass the time spinning elaborate fairy romances. These were baroque improvisations on motifs taken from classical texts and popular anthologies like the Neapolitan shocker *Lo Cunto de li Cunti* (*Il Pentamarone*, 1634-36) by Giambattista Basile. The *conte des fées*, or fairy tale, would become as lush an expression of French society at play as an oil by Watteau or Boucher. At its commonplace worst it catered to the dreams of those painted girls on garden swings that someday their princes would come. At its best it delved convincingly into more enchanted realms. The queen of the French romance was Marie Catherine, Comtesse d'Aulnoy, a woman of quick wit, comely looks, and a taste for narrative action and gothic fancy. If unkempt as art, her *Contes Nouveaux ou Les Fées à la Mode* (1697-98) brought invention and magic to what was fast becoming an overripe form of entertainment. Inspired by wonder tales as good as d'Aulnoy's "The White Cat" and "The Yellow Dwarf," the genre prevailed for nearly a century until at last it was gathered to rest in the monumental retrospective *Le Cabinet des Fées*, published in forty-one volumes between 1785 and 1789. With the French Revolution the fairy romance and the aristocracy vanished together. Not until the appearance of *L'Histoire de Babar* in 1931 would Gallic fancy return to storytelling—although of course throughout the nineteenth century it surfaced in other guises: the fairy romance in the thumping of ballet slippers, satirical fantasy in the drawings of J. J. Grandville, and a sense of wonder in the engineered romances of Jules Verne. Of the myriad tales contained in the century of labors known as *Le Cabinet* hardly a trace remains. Only one is still in print, Madame

Leprince de Beaumont's retelling of "Beauty and the Beast" (1756). The *Cabinet's* forty-one volumes of baroque excess have turned to dust in basement stacks; this one tale survives, like those of Perrault, and for the same reason: she wrote it down not so much to titillate society as to amuse children.

History's first real children's book was a conscious refinement of this fashion for lush enchantments. Perrault served two audiences. Some of the tales he addressed to the dreams and fears of those garden girls on swings, and some, like "Little Red Riding Hood" and "Hop o' My Thumb," to their younger brothers and sisters. At the time, even among the aristocracy, to be a girl of thirteen or fourteen meant giving thought to your trousseau. For the enjoyment of this pubescent crowd Perrault dished up the midnight courtship of Cinderella, the swoon of Sleeping Beauty, and a sketch of social climbing in the ancien régime with "Puss-in-Boots." As in most traditional tales, there are warnings aplenty. To the "Sleeping Beauty" we think we know he attached, as it were, a "Sleeping Beauty, Part Two," a little satire on the folly of marrying your prince before you have taken a long, hard look at your future mother-in-law. And then too, of course, a maid in want of a husband could always end up a collectible in some Bluebeard's bloody closet.

To each of these tales Perrault appended a Moralité in verse not unlike the morals of Aesop or the book of Proverbs. On the evidence of these warnings and morals it has been argued that he had fallen under the influence of John Locke's *Thoughts on Education* (1693) and was experimenting with the fairy tale as a new kind of teaching device. Children and what to do about them was a new topic on everyone's minds, certainly, but this is hardly a collection of adages disguised as make-believe. It is compatible with Locke's precept of putting into children's hands "some easy pleasant book . . . wherein the entertainment that he finds might draw him on," but only so far as that, for these fairy tales are education on the frontier of pure imagination where Locke had warned lay "useless trumpery" and "the principles of vice and folly." Perrault likely wrote them as a recreation while recounting the lives of La Fontaine, Corneille, Molière, Racine, Pascal, and Descartes for his *Hommes Illustres* (1696–1700). At any rate, it is difficult to see how anyone could read this book as anything but an entertainment. His morals call up a picture not of the schoolmaster but of Ben Franklin's ambassadorial flirtations in French salons a century later. "Young blood must when young blood will"—Perrault's advice to his "maids a-sighing"—is not moral counsel but the consenting wink of a wayward uncle. And like the later courtier, he enjoyed shocking the young ladies. Franklin's thrillers were tales of the American frontier; Perrault's came from the underground of story, the folk tale. We forget today what a heady treasury of sighs, squeals, chills, and dreams this little book must have been. Here are the last moments in the life of Little Red Riding Hood, and the chase of Hop o' My Thumb over hill and dale by the ogre in the

Seven-League Boots, and that ultimate cliffhanger, "Bluebeard," with its heroine at the window, knife to throat, crying, "Anne, Sister Anne, do you see no one coming?"

The nineteenth and twentieth centuries may have proven Locke in some measure a prophet and Perrault the first unwitting instrument of trumpery, vice and folly, but make-believe in 1697 had yet a long way to go before accumulating enough sins to warrant such a denunciation, and it is hard to accuse the godfather of the fairy tale of not getting children's literature off to a clean, indeed a brilliant start. He had the best eye of his day for a good story and one of the best ears ever for how a cottage tale should sound on the page. His little histories are eloquent, yet always as straightforward as the evening news. Here is one such item from the papers, reporting on a royal birth:

> A grand christening was held, and all the fairies that could be found in the realm (they numbered seven in all) were invited to be god-mothers to the little princess. . . . When the christening ceremony was over, all the company returned to the king's palace, where a great banquet was held in honor of the fairies.[2]

There was a christening, and the fairies were invited. It is always better to treat news from once-upon-a-time simply as news. Perrault neither dilates the prose to make room for his own presence nor indulges in the kind of ceremonial rhetoric we saw Kenneth Grahame resorting to earlier. By merely referring back to the public what the public had been telling itself throughout history, his tales set the pattern for all written children's stories. Accepting a simple byline has proved difficult for many reporters, as we shall see in the pages ahead, but Perrault's ideal is not easily achieved, whatever the intent. The clear presence of a voice but anonymity for the scribe is an elusive quarry. One narrative ploy that has worked rather well has been the use of an implied or actual persona, a storyteller within the story, to whom the author can entrust his or her own untrustworthy voice. Perrault declined to sign his work, ascribing it instead to his teenage son and referring the reader to a frontispiece portrait of the folk muse Mother Goose, spinning yarns for the amusement of three young people. This simple picture in fact has been the most enduring image in the descent of children's books. We find an adult telling a child a story at the opening of *Winnie-the-Pooh* and all the tales of the *Uncle Remus* collections. It is the scene implied by the first words of Andersen's fairy tales, *Pinocchio*, *Just So Stories*, many of the tales of Beatrix Potter and Wanda Gág, and, most recently, *In the Night Kitchen*, which Sendak launches with the back-fence gossip "Did you hear about Mickey?" In the legend of how *Alice in Wonderland* came to be written, with Lewis Carroll narrating to Alice Liddell as they rowed along the Thames "all in the golden afternoon," the image rose to the level of popular myth. What began with Perrault — when thousands of years of storytelling by the fireside suddenly became fixed in a book and a literature was begun—has often been debated as a point of aesthetics (I confess to doing so once myself) and has frequently been ignored by authors, for it implies that this is indeed a literature told for children, but no book written in ignorance of it has ever survived.

The second precedent Perrault set for children's books was a rather odd one to find this early in the game, for it involved playing a joke on the expectations of his listeners.

"Little Red Riding Hood" is the first story ever published that is recognizably a children's story in the modern sense. The thing is as straightforward as a game of pattycake or a knee ride with a big bump at the end. The inclination to think of it as a veiled parable about sexual seduction can be put aside. This is a story about stories about innocence. It is Perrault's ironic aside on the new literature he knew he was creating. Here is how he ends the tale by tickling his little listener's sense of their own vulnerability:

> Little Red Riding Hood took off her clothes, but when she climbed up on the bed she was astonished to see how her grandmother looked in her nightgown.
> "Grandmother, dear!" she exclaimed, "what big arms you have!"
> "The better to embrace you, my child!"
> "Grandmother, dear, what big legs you have!"
> "The better to run with, my child!"
> "Grandmother, dear, what big ears you have!"
> "The better to hear with, my child!"
> "Grandmother, dear, what big eyes you have!"
> "The better to see with, my child!"
> "Grandmother, dear, what big teeth you have!"
> "The better to eat you with!"
> With these words the wicked Wolf leaped upon Little Red Riding Hood and gobbled her up.

Generally speaking, all true children's stories make promises to their readers. Here are you, they say, unhandy and short, and there is the big world that one day will be yours. Listen to how it happened for Cinderella once upon a time, and Jack with his beanstalk, and Aladdin with his lamp. Nearly all the classical tales make this covenant. To make it is the reason we have a children's literature, and hardly a book has survived that has not honored the contract. The fairy stories in Perrault are all, except this one, parables to the same purpose. With the consumption of little Red, however, Perrault has fulfilled the destiny of this particular tale. "Little Red Riding Hood" is not properly a part of the fairy-tale tradition of growing up to take one's inheritance of the world; only later was it straitjacketed into the role. Rather, it is a fable—a cross between the beast fable and the cautionary tale, actually—and the point of this genre is that the story must end badly for the sake of some perhaps earnest, perhaps comical moral. It is not a form that sits well with some readers. Subsequent tellings have called into service any number of awkward ploys to save Red Riding Hood and her grandmother. The most popular has been the solution collected by the brothers Grimm more than a century after Perrault, with a bold huntsman halloing to the rescue. The wolf is slit open, the ingested pair released, and the wolf, sewn up again full of stones, drops dead from a coronary. Efforts to make the tale come out right have often yielded a denouement more grisly than the original. A general disinclination to leave well enough alone reached its absurd climax in 1976 when a puzzled Bruno Bettleheim accused the tale of being an unsatisfactory example of what it never meant to be in the first place. In *The Uses of Enchantment* the psychologist dismissed Perrault's version as trivial because it did not conform to a perceived fairy-tale pattern of escape, recovery, and consolation. This is the sort of confusion that comes of holding overly sentimental preconceptions about children's books. Bettleheim wanted stories to be *good*. But before a story can be good, it must be true to what it is. Bettleheim could not understand why Andrew Lang, himself not enamored of Perrault's version, printed it anyway in his *Blue Fairy Book* (1889). Lang, of course, recognized the better story, as had Dinah Mulock Craik in *The Fairy Book* (1863). The children's historian Cornelia Meigs sensibly summed up the tale in 1953 as "a game, with a great pounce at the end and, probably, a squeak of delighted horror from the small listener."[3]

How Perrault meant us to respond to "Little Red Riding Hood" is perhaps best shown by a book that was in part modeled after it, Hilaire Belloc's hideously funny *Cautionary Tales*, wherein sundry masters and misses are burned up, gobbled up, or stampeded flat for minor lapses in manners and sense. "Jim, Who Ran Away from His Nurse, and Was Eaten by a Lion" is "Little Red Riding Hood" retold, one French master bowing to the wit of another. With a change of gender the Morals of the two tales are interchangeable:

> Little girls, this seems to say,
> Never stop upon your way,
> And always keep ahold of Nurse
> For fear of finding something worse.

Read as a joke on a literature only at that moment being invented, the appearance of "Little Red Riding Hood" in 1697 suggests an interesting answer to the axiom that before the eighteenth century children did not really exist in any modern sense. In many ways, it is true, they did not, but before Locke speculated on their education, and before Perrault could write the first children's book, there had to have been already in place a very public perception of children as distinct entities in need of specialized training and entertainment. The existence of "Little Red Riding Hood" almost demands that this be so, for otherwise the story would be a joke without an audience. If such tales were not already understood to be a literature about growing up, who would enjoy the surprise when the heroine gets eaten up instead? A joke can work only when expectations to the contrary are waiting to be fulfilled.

This was the precedent set by "Little Red Riding Hood," then, the idea that, while it is predominantly an encouragement to growing up in the imagination and in the world, make-believe is also a literature of games, parody, and burlesque and can renew itself by eating its own pieties, as the wolf had eaten little Red. The consequences of this invitation to make sport have been both happy and sobering. To the good, it has kept the nursery open for nonsense and Cats in hats. To the bad, as can be seen in the mass of popular children's entertainment today, it has led to a practice so all-pervasive that many spoofs are now nothing but variations on spoofs. One must wonder what children can really know of a tradition that has become, through television and cartoons, such a parody of itself.

With Perrault's third and most important precedent, we come to the real subject of this episode in the descent of make-believe—the question of who is to stand muse over children's story and serve within it as guide to our wanderings. The personage bringing us our earliest intimation of who the true friend of our need will be is the wonderful visitor to these tales, the fairy godmother. In Perrault she makes her first appearance in any literature, and in retrospect she does seem inevitable and right for this kind of story. If we had to particularize the allsense with a form and voice, we might arrive at just such a person.

But what exactly is a fairy godmother? We are so accustomed to the phrase today that we hardly give her a thought, unless to make her a figure of fun or, in a better spirit, retell her as one of Mother Goose's quaint old cousins:

> [A] little old woman in a high-pointed hat and buckled shoes appeared in the kitchen, and where she came from no one could have told. Her eyes shone and twinkled like two stars, and she carried a wand in her hand.[4]

These are not Perrault's words but a later, sentimental gloss on the tale of Cinderella. The godmother made her literary debut as a figure of more consequence than this excerpt conveys. She did not enter twinkling. The seven fairies summoned at the opening of Perrault's first tale, "Sleeping Beauty," are authorities in the kingdom to whom even the king must defer. They come to sponsor the princess's baptism, and it is their power to bless or to damn her that drives the plot.

The reader may be getting ahead of me here in guessing that, with the advent of the fairy godmother, we have crossed the threshold of the church. The question that may be unanswerable of this historical moment is, Just which side of the threshold are we standing on? Are we coming in or lurking in the street? The seven fairies, like Clement Moore's St. Nicholas, seem a composite of Christian and pagan elements. The gifts they bestow on the princess, for example—beauty, sweetness, grace, the arts of dance and song, and the playing of every instrument—are gifts traditionally dispensed by the three Graces of Greek mythology and the muses Euterpe and Terpsichore. In "Briar Rose," the version collected by the Grimms a century later, and "undoubtedly derived from Perrault's text" in the Opies' estimation,[5] we can see the tale reverting to such a pagan ancestry. The fairy godmothers have vanished, and in their place appear thirteen "Wise Women." Yet one does not invite pagan deities to preside over a Christian sacrament; a godparent, after all, is someone entrusted with a child's continuing spiritual upbringing as a disciple of Christ. On balance, we should probably say that whatever the permutations of her biography, at her point of entry into children's literature the godmother is clearly perceived to be a Christian personage. And "Sleeping Beauty," even granting pagan influences, may only mark a return to a more ancient Christian source. The Gospels include what certainly looks to be an early type of her story. Here it is as it appears in Luke 8:52–55:

> And all wept, and bewailed her: but he said, Weep not; she is not dead, but sleepeth.
> And they laughed him to scorn, knowing that she was dead.
> And he put them all out, and took her by the hand, and called, saying, Maid, arise.
> And her spirit came again, and she arose straightaway. . . .

Both maids have reached puberty: in Luke she is twelve years of age; in Perrault, fifteen. Popular versions of "Sleeping Beauty" require the princess to be awakened by a kiss, of course, and that does not happen here. But neither does it happen in Perrault: the princess simply awakens when the prince kneels by her bed. Really, there is no reason to think the Gospel story could not have lasted through history, eventually to become a "Sleeping Beauty." Consider how Matthew concludes the event: "And the fame hereof went abroad into all that land." What Perrault found could easily have been the corruption of a popular miracle story disseminated across Europe by Christians over the intervening years. The Gospels make that same, saving allowance for worldly appetites that pagan and children's lores require. In Perrault the guests awakening in the disenchanted castle "presently began to feel mortally hungry" and are shortly bidding the lovers come down to the feast. In Luke, Jesus "commanded to give her meat."

Seven godmothers open Perrault's little book, but in the later "Cinderella" we find them resolved into one. This most universal of all fairy tales is very old and found almost everywhere in the world. It is a fairy in a fig tree who comes to Cinderella's aid in the Neapolitan *Pentamarone* of 1634, but not yet a fairy godmother. Featured as the helper in the British "Rashin Coatie" is a red calf, a gift from the girl's dead mother. The oldest known version, from China and dating back to 850 A.D. tells of a man who descends from the sky. In the Grimms' quite poetic "Aschenputtel" a white bird appears in a tree growing from the mother's grave. Grimm is our best-known repository of pagan helpers, with its Wise Women, its magical ravens, foxes, fish, bees, ants, and horses, and, of course, the elves who help the shoemaker on Christmas and the famous Rumpelstiltskin. "Aschenputtel" and "Rashin Coatie" are typical of the tale worldwide in conceiving of the helper as a creaturely agent of Cinderella's dead mother. Of the more than seven hundred known versions of the story, only in Perrault is the helper that creature called a fairy godmother. How he came by her no one knows. She may be a portmanteau fashioned by joining Madame d'Aulnoy's fairies to society's real godmothers, or she may have announced herself full-blown in some cottage or kitchen, with Perrault merely writing down what he heard. In any case, she is a figure peculiar to the Catholic south of Europe and, like the sponsors of Sleeping Beauty, clearly meant to be understood in a Christian context.

The stepsisters have just left for the ball when Perrault introduces her:

> Away they went, Cinderella watching them as long as she could keep them in sight. When she could no longer see them she began to cry. Her godmother found her in tears, and asked what was troubling her.
> "I should like—I should like—"
> She was crying so bitterly that she could not finish the sentence.
> Said her godmother, who was a fairy:
> "You would like to go to the ball, would you not?"
> "Ah, yes," said Cinderella, sighing.
> "Well, well," said her godmother, "promise to be a good girl and I will arrange for you to go."

Her entrance is rather curious when you think about it. She is not actually introduced; nor is she explained. She simply appears. In his Moral to the tale Perrault seems to be suggesting that we view this miracle as an instance of grace taking a shape in order to bestow grace:

> Beauty is a treasure rare.
> Who complains of being fair?
> Yet there's still a something more
> That good fairies have in store.
> 'Tis that little gift called grace . . .

What was always within Cinderella is now, by grace, made visible to others. She does not have to promise her godmother to be good; she is so already. Her story does not end with a grand wedding and the cheers of an adoring citizenry; it ends with her forgiving her stepsisters, accepting her own reward without remark, and seeing to their well-being before her own. Her wedding to the prince is barely mentioned. The universal fairy tale has become in Perrault's hands something of a Christian parable. It really is in a way the teaching story that some have found these tales to be. What it is teaching is something other than what has been argued, however. That the meek do inherit the earth is the happily-ever-after being suggested here, and forgiveness, the true moral.

To many, of course, "Cinderella" remains only a simple wish-fulfillment fantasy. Perrault knew that this was the root appeal of the tale. He knew too that he was dealing with a situation in which praying for help would be the natural thing to do. Given the period and the Catholic context, we might expect to find a girl in such a predicament down on her knees asking St. Catherine for that pretty dress and the eye of the prince. It is Perrault's nice distinction that Cinderella does not pray for relief from her unhappiness. Although bereft, she is not envious of her stepsisters and never thinks to ask for favors. This is what makes the tale a true parable and not merely a popular romance. But its author knew better than to play the priest with it. What keeps the parable as real as the meat that Jesus ordered up is Perrault's friendly concession to our own implicit prayer in this situation, the prayer that Cinderella does not think to make. The wayward uncle of those girls a-sighing in the garden never forgot what earthly needs motivate a good fairy tale. Of all the great authors the seventeenth century can boast, Perrault is the only one we still read for pleasure pure and simple, and this is so because in tale after tale he knew to keep pushing the swings.

This is how the children's story began, then, with a little book of worldly tales having a touch of the miracle about them. For our earthly and spiritual needs Perrault gave us the two muses who in one guise or another are with us today. The first, spinning yarns before the fire, was Mother Goose. The second, that friend of our need who comes and goes within the tales, he called a fairy godmother. It is with her that we see the first appearance in modern children's books of a personage who will be materializing in one narrative make-believe after another in the years ahead. Who this wonderful visitor to the world of story might actually be no one has dared say, not even those who have known her best. To some of the authors we will be reading she is going to be a familiar presence; to others her name will prove as elusive as Rumpelstiltskin's. I alluded earlier to St. Catherine, but it would be insufficient to read the universal muse as some intercessionary saint like Clement Moore's St. Nicholas. I am going to leave her as vaguely defined for the moment as she in fact would remain for the next hundred and fifty years, when a few scribes reading Perrault realized that a parable need be no solemn tract, nor even evident as a parable, but instead could be told with a lighter and more mysterious touch, as a fairy tale.

For those intervening years the muse bided her time. In France, the fairy tale became that painted caricature of itself, the fairy romance. Abroad, it was anathematized as a temptation simply too dangerous to be loosed on children. A literature of miracles, even small ones, is not always a welcome thing. The fairy tale had, and continues to have, for example, great appeal to the would-be shaman with intimations of the divine whimsy dancing in his head. It was partly a fear of this that branded the form with the scarlet letter two and three hundred years ago. The fact that it commonly came dressed to play the outcast did nothing to discourage such an estimation. A popular tale like "Jack the Giant-Killer" was not to be found in the pretty picture books we know today but — truer to its nature, perhaps — selling on street corners in ill-written, luridly illustrated chapbooks. The fairy tale, in short, was the pulp literature, the comic book, of its times. The pious of the seventeenth and eighteenth centuries saw it, not unjustly, as a flirtation with paganism (or with Roman excess if the pious were Puritan), and the impious as a dalliance with stupidity. To John Locke such stuff could only lead the growing mind to vice and folly. To the philosopher Jean-Jacques Rousseau it was of little moment in itself, since all books for children were to be discouraged as unnatural distractions. In the name of reason and common sense, the Enlightenment rejected fancy out of hand as "the Chit-Chat of an old Nurse, or the Maggots in a Madman's Brain,"[6] and an emerging children's-book industry agreed with John Newbery's estimation that this cheap trade would turn children into "Fools all their days." For the century thereafter — the Age of Admonition, as Cornelia Meigs has dubbed it — a tireless succession of Englishwomen and clergymen undertook, in tome after didactic tome, to convert children into paragons of piety and civic virtue and looked upon the fantastical with as leery an eye as any of their predecessors. In America that redoubtable father of the social studies text, "Peter Parley," could be heard insisting as late as the 1850s that fairy tales would "erase from the young heart tender and gentle feelings and substitute for them fierce and bloody thoughts and sentiments."[7] Even James O. Halliwell's *The Nursery Rhymes of England* he deemed a waste of children's time.

Narrative make-believe would enter the modern age finally through the back door of scholarship, its credentials tucked in the pockets of those antiquarians who, following the example of collectors like Joseph Ritson, would assemble the first scientific anthologies of national and ethnic folk-lores. It is equally to be noted, however, that the first major collection after Perrault was a general omnibus edition of tales chosen solely on their own merits. Children care little about national literatures unless taught to think in such terms, and make-believe and folkloric studies have frequently become confused over the years, with arguable advantage to the former. The omnibus edition is always the more natural vehicle for conveying the world of make-believe to the nursery. This first example was compiled for the same London firm responsible for *Songs for the Nursery* (1805). *Tabart's Popular Stories for the Nursery* appeared in three volumes between 1804 and 1818. Its editor was William Godwin, the husband of the feminist Mary Wollstonecraft and the father of Mary Shelley, the author of *Frankenstein*. Godwin was an early champion of children's books that put pleasure before instruction, and here he assembled the best tales then known from Europe and England, which included all of Perrault, "Beauty and the Beast," "Aladdin," and thrillers like "Jack the Giant-Killer." In 1807, under separate cover, he published for the first time anywhere one of make-believe's finest wonder tales, "Jack and the Beanstalk." A copy of *Tabart* was owned by the two antiquarians who are generally credited with making folk and fairy lores acceptable and of interest to the world at large.

Kinder- und Hausmärchen (1812–)

Jacob (1785–1863) and Wilhelm (1786–1859) Grimm published the first series of their children's and household tales in 1812, 1815, and 1822. The English translation, *German Popular Stories*, illustrated by George Cruikshank, appeared from 1823 to 1826. Grimm is a rich compendium of story, with two hundred specimens of fairy tale, beast fable, romance, hero tale, and episodes of domestic slapstick, jokes about stupid ogres and lucky simpletons, and tales that defy classification, like the moving barnyard elegy "The Death of the Little Hen." In addition to these, the Grimms categorized ten more as "Children's Legends," although a dozen or so more like them from the two hundred could be so listed. Here God, the Christ child, the devil, and Saints Mary, Joseph, and Peter play themselves in little parables that may have begun as ancient Sunday School stories for the German tribes then becoming Christianized. A millennium ago, for example, a monk invented the pretzel as a treat to entice children to church, designing it to represent their crossed arms as they prayed. Similarly, an origin myth like "The Twelve Apostles" could be read as a story pretzel invented by some priest or nun to help explain the faith to superstitious peasants wandering into the church for the first time. Who were these twelve apostles? Only poor country men like yourselves who when starving to death were laid to sleep in a cavern by angels. "They slept three hundred years, until the night when the Savior of the world was born. Then they awoke, and were with him on earth, and were called the twelve apostles."[8]

Some of the tales were of recent origin, being retellings of Perrault or, like "The Twelve Dancing Princesses," perhaps derived from *Le Cabinet des Fées*. Studies suggest that a few, such as "The Juniper Tree," date from the Period of Migrations that marked the fall of the Roman Empire. Some, like "The Straw, the Coal, and the Bean" and "The Valiant Little Tailor," were entertainments handed down from tenth-century minstrels. "The Water Sprite" suggests an Oriental origin. But the roots of those tales of forest magic that lie at the heart of Grimm reach back to the Middle Ages and the period of the chivalric romances. These are the tales we think of when we think of Grimm: "The Frog Prince," "Brother and Sister," "Rapunzel," "The Fisherman and his Wife," "Rumpelstiltskin," "Hansel and Gretel," and "Snow White and the Seven Dwarfs." There is an almost archeological fascination in conjecturing about the origins of folk tales. That familiar image of the suitor calling to his love, "Rapunzel, Rapunzel, let down your golden hair," for example—where did such a moment begin? Someone had to have thought it up, at some time, for some reason. In the period to which the tale has been dated, another legend of a maid in a tower was popular, the story of St. Barbara fortifying herself against her father's wish that she marry. Could "Rapunzel" not have been born in the complaint of some Romeo against the convent system that had cloistered his Juliet? Convents were the girls' boarding schools of the Middle Ages and the Renaissance. The aristocracy and the merchant class paid the convent's bills, the convent kept their daughters chaste, and a few girls would likely stay on to take holy vows. From the virginal St. Barbara, then, the frustrated swain took the image of the tower, and the abbess, or the church itself, he cast as the "enchantress, who had great power and was dreaded by all the world." A parable extolling Christian chastity thus became a worldly allegory of the spiritual life and desire at odds, with the lovers excommunicated and wandering the earth apart (she with their two children, no less) until at last they are reunited to live happily ever after. A tale that took shape outside a convent wall one day became the stuff of a troubadour's romance and later, perhaps overheard by servants, it entered oral tradition. Over the centuries it was purged of inessential sentiment and further altered and refined, until the day it reemerged in one of those middle-class homes where the Grimms collected more of their folk tales than was originally supposed. All of this may have happened, or none of it. Whatever the scenario, the "Rapunzel" gathered at the opening of the nineteenth century was a tale with a long and complex history. The Grimms, unfortunately, wished it to be a German tale, peculiar to the German people, and thus worthy of an age that had recently brought the world a Goethe and a Mozart. It should in no way detract from the virtue of these stories, or from their Germanic flavor, that they are not the remnants of Teutonic myths that the Grimms believed them to be. Many of the best of them the brothers had collected from their own middle-class, educated family and friends, and the claim that they all derived immaculately from the untutored *volk* was either wishful thinking on their part or a patriotic deception. To the eyes of the world, however, *German Popular Tales* provided living proof of an idea once common among the ancients and lately revived by the Romantics—that each people, each state, is inspired by its own unique genius and that the purest expression of this genius is to be found in the tribe's myths and folk tales.

The notion of an ethnically discrete and ancient heritage in need of no muse but the bloodstream and the state would prove an alternative theology congenial to all in an age of rapid secularization and militant nationalism. *German Popular Tales* provoked an outpouring of ethnic lores that has lasted more than one hundred and seventy five years and shows no sign of abating. With it has come a droll, and for authors indispensable, demonology of wizards and witches, goblins and giants and elves. For two centuries we have been delighting in these imps as the fairy tales of all nations have paraded by, flying their ethnic banners like entrants in some Olympiad of the imagination. This is the true legacy of the Grimms, I think—that we have nationalized the idea of genius again, for the first time since Rome.

Clan solipsism must conclude, of course, in some kind of shamanistic secularism wherein we come to worship each other, or paganism, wherein we come to worship our own make-believe. The pursuit of fame and folly can always be found hand in hand with that other great solipsism, which holds that there is a guiding genius within and native only to one's self. This twin to the myth of the tribe was recovered from the ancients in the Renaissance and reclaimed by the Romantics, who built an aesthetics on the thought that the natural and sovereign geniuses of the race are the poet and the child. In 1819, as the Grimms were at work on the third volume of their series, these two sublime entities arrived in Copenhagen in the person of a shoemaker's son anxious to write his signature across the consciousness of the world, Hans Christian Andersen (1805–75).

Eventyr, fortalte for Børn (1835–)

Andersen's "tales told for children" appeared serially in booklets, three or four stories each, over a period of thirty-seven years. In all, there are 156 of them, a considerable body of work for someone who thought himself first a novelist and playwright. The first booklet contained "The Tinder Box," "The Princess on the Pea," "Little Ida's Flowers," and "Little Claus and Big Claus." The second, published a year later, included "Inchelina" ("Thumbelina"); the third, in 1837, "The Little Mermaid" and "The Emperor's New Clothes." A dozen or so more of a like quality made Andersen famous throughout Europe and America: "The Steadfast Tin Soldier," "The Nightingale," "The Ugly Duckling," "The Fir Tree," "The Snow Queen," "The Red Shoes," "The Little Match Girl," and "The Shadow." These early examples, in which he mostly cleaves to known folk motifs, are the Andersen we know and belong to his best period, which saw two bursts of creativity, from 1835 to 1838 and again in 1844–45. After "The Snow Queen" he went on to write 125 more, retitling the corpus *Eventyr og Historier*, or fairy tales and stories, which latter category allowed him room for a miscellany of anecdotes, incompleted fables, conceits, bits of journalism, and one novella. Very few of these could be said to be for children, and when they are the invention has grown whimsical and lazy: "The days of the week wanted to have some time off so they could hold a party" ("The Days of the Week," 1871).[9] His talent for satirical animism still worked to good effect on occasion: "There once were five peas in a pod; they were green and the pod was green, and so they believed that the whole world was green, and that was quite right" ("Five Peas from the Same Pod," 1855); more often, however, it deferred to mere prettiness: "The butterfly wanted a sweetheart, and naturally it had to be a flower" ("The Butterfly," 1861). By his sixties he had run out of things to say, but he went on anyway, like a man talking into his beer: "You should have known my mother's sister! she was a lovely person . . . " ("Auntie," 1866). This is the Andersen who penned the immortal chestnut "'I can walk!' he sobbed. . . . 'Oh, my God! I can walk!'" ("The Cripple," 1872).

It is worth taking note of this creative collapse in the later stories because it suggests why so few of his earlier tales have survived. The claims made for Andersen's contributions to literature seem valid enough in general: he extended the world of the imaginary to include inkwells, darning needles, Christmas trees, toys, and teapots, and he quickened this world to life with his impulsive voice. He could transform the commonest setting into a privileged moment and reveal the unusual in terms that seem borrowed from some eternal primer on storytelling:

> Far, far from land, where the waters are as blue as the petals of the corn-flower and as clear as glass, there, where no anchor can reach the bottom, live the mer-people. So deep is this part of the sea that you would have to pile many church towers on top of each other before one of them emerged above the surface.
> Now you must not think that at the bottom of the sea there is only white sand. . . .
>
> Here the witch had built her house out of the bones of drowned sailors, and there she sat letting a big ugly toad eat out of her mouth, as human beings sometimes let a canary eat sugar candy out of theirs. The ugly eels she called her little chickens, and held them close to her spongy chest.
>
> "The Little Mermaid"

Much of Andersen is told with a glancing humor his early translators were ill equipped, and sometimes disinclined, to convey, and it has become a commonplace that they left him with a reputation for sentimentality that is undeserved. But neither is the disclaimer true, really, and Andersen's peculiar humor only confirms this. It was nothing like the humor of his English contemporary Edward Lear, with whom he shared the misfortunes of an unhappy childhood and a large nose, or the bumpkin slapstick of the Grimms' lighter tales. There is little here of Perrault's good-natured wink, or indeed of any kind of humor we would associate with the nursery. The short tale "A Drop of Water" is Andersen in a swallow:

> Surely you know what a magnifying glass is. It looks like one of the round glasses in a pair of spectacles; but it is much stronger, and can make things appear a hundred times larger than they are. If you look at a drop of water from a pond through it, a thousand tiny animals appear that you cannot see with the naked eye; but they are there and they are real. They look like a plate of live shrimps jumping and crowding each other. They are all so ferocious that they tear each other's arms and legs off, without seeming to care. I suppose that is their way of life, and they are happy and content with it.
> Now there once was an old man whom everybody called Wiggle-waggle, because that happened to be his name. He always made the best of things; and when he couldn't, he used magic.
> One day when he looked through his magnifying glass at a drop of ditch water he was shocked at what he saw. How those creatures wiggled and wag-

gled: hopping, humping, pulling, pushing, and eating each other up—yes, they were cannibals.

"It is a revolting sight!" exclaimed old Wiggle-waggle. "Can't one do anything to make them live in peace, and each mind his own business?" He thought and thought, and when he couldn't find an answer, he decided to use magic.

"I'll give them a bit of color; then they will be easier to study," he decided. He let a drop of something that looked like red wine fall into the ditch water—but it wasn't red wine, it was witch's blood of the very finest type, the one that costs two shillings a drop. All the little creatures immediately turned pink. Now they looked like a whole town of naked savages.

"What have you got there?" asked an old troll who had come visiting. He had no name, which among trolls is distinguished.

"If you can guess what it is," replied Wiggle-waggle, "then I will make you a present of it. But it isn't easy, unless you know it."

The troll who had no name looked through the magnifying glass. What he saw looked like a city with all the inhabitants running around naked. It was a disgusting sight, but even more disgusting to see was the way the people behaved. They kicked and cuffed each other; they beat and bit and shoved; those who were on the bottom strove to get to the top, and those on the top struggled to be on the bottom.

"Look, his leg is longer than mine! I will bite it off! Away with you!"

"Look, he has a lump behind his ear. It is small but it embarrasses him and gives him pain. We will really make him suffer!" And they pushed and pulled him; and finally they ate him up, all because he had a little lump behind his ear.

One little creature sat still, all by herself in a corner, like a modest, sensitive little maiden. She wanted peace and quiet. But she was dragged out of her corner, mistreated, and finally she was eaten up.

"It is most instructive and amusing," said the troll.

"But what do you think it is?" asked Wiggle-waggle. "Have you figured it out?"

"That is easy," answered the troll. "It's Copenhagen or some other big city, they are all alike."

"It's ditch water," said Wiggle-waggle.

The world is a muddle, the innocent are fated to a life of hurt, and one can only cast a mordant eye on the whole sad affair. Andersen's wit very ably directs this trim little tale, but it is all done in the name of tortured maidens and creatures with lumps, which is shading the world a bit black for a children's story. His identification with victims seems to have been compulsive. Elsewhere he would portray himself as a fir tree thrown out after Christmas, a steadfast tin soldier consumed by flames, a match girl frozen in the snow. The humor, when it can be found, is the bitter irony of a man who saw in himself the living proof that life is not fair. Every one of his tales is colored by the witch's blood of self-pity.

As a boy, Andersen was embarrassed to be poor. As a man, he was embarrassed to be alone. He lived the life of the extraneous bachelor, knocking on the doors of Europe's rich and famous, looking to become the world's best-loved adopted son. His demands on life were unreasonable, and he was stung whenever the world did not deliver. When the Snow Queen promises Kay "the whole world and a new pair of skates," she is speaking Andersen's mind. He wanted it all. In his search for it, he tried the patience of everyone he met, and he made sure that he met everyone worth knowing. The ordeal of making his acquaintance can be guessed from a minute's reading in any of his diaries or letters: "If it weren't too profane to say so I would maintain that I have understood the biblical quotation: 'The entire Writ is inspired by God.' . . . The few individuals around me must recognize me as a true *Digter*."[10] Andersen was the first—indeed, he may be the only—author in this study to be motivated purely by that modern malaise, the desire to be famous. To be a digter means more than being a creative writer; it means becoming a national oracle, a shaman. Andersen believed himself the true prophet of the modern sensibility. His stories he promoted shamelessly as "my gift to the world." The poor boy come to town had learned early, and yet had never learned, that, while provoking such dreams of glory, the world is a fickle mistress and remains indifferent to the happiness of the dreamer.

Women held this final power over his imagination. He wrote his fairy tales to them, for them, and sometimes about them. The ballerinas and actresses he courted smiled on the homely, fretful prince but left him imprisoned in the frog. He was the king's son at the foot of the tower, and no Rapunzel would let down her golden hair. Unrequited love gave him words while souring his heart: "The Ice maiden kissed him, and the eternal coldness penetrated his backbone and touched his forehead. He cried out in pain."

The habit of personification is a bad sign in a children's author paradoxically, and never more ill-advised than when driven by an animus against a whole class of creation. Anderson personified indiscriminately. Each year, for example, hoping for a windfall, he would renew his ticket in the Danish state lottery. Trusting his fate to the numbers made him as superstitious and vindictive a Christian as a Brazilian spiritist casting bones after Mass. His consistent bad luck brought only one image to his mind: "If Mrs. Lottery, who has now for years been a bag of lies, were to present me with a suitable sum this time I could make plans for going abroad; but I have no faith in that woman."[11]

The voice of the martyr is heard everywhere in the tales. The Fir Tree, the Little Match Girl, and the Tin Soldier are martyrs, and so also are Inchelina, the Little Mermaid, the scholar of "The Shadow," and even the Ugly Duckling in a way. Their histories are the old Lives of the Saints romanticized. All of them suffer; most die. They expire to heaven as nobler beings than the rest of us, for some higher cause than our base instincts could ever comprehend—love, art, innocence, goodness. The idea of being too good for the world has great appeal. A type of quasi-children's book has grown up from these tales of Andersen's. *The Velveteen Rabbit, The Little Prince, The Mouse and his Child,* Eugene Field's "Little Boy Blue"—

all these owe a debt to the man who, following after the Taylor sisters, turned storytelling into one of the emotive arts and tinted make-believe with the hues of pathos. The atmosphere pervading each of these little saints' tales to come is an atmosphere of gloom and sorrow.

He turned to God. If Mrs. Lottery and the ballerinas would not have him, God would, and God would one day bring him home to glory "on a sunbeam," like Karen in "The Red Shoes." All his life Andersen hectored heaven for signs of such favor. As a child, he had called on God to save him from bullies and the shame of poverty; as an adult, he filled his diaries with prayers for recognition and rewards. What celebrity he did win, and it was considerable, he took in good Calvinist faith as a sign of divine justification. The scoundrels who from the start had dismissed him for wearing his heart on his sleeve, these he cursed publicly for failing to see in him the true *digter*, the chosen one. His destiny rode his shoulder like a banana-republic epaulette. It made him boastful, anxious, vain, demanding, sulky, weepy, and accusatory. To his credit, he knew it and could satirize himself along with the rest. And he did have a better side. He was a parvenu and a snob, but he was also an advocate for the poor. He was maudlin, yet funny; a visitation of petty tyrannies on his hosts, yet charming company. Families were happy to welcome him into their homes. They were equally pleased a week, a month later, to help him down to the street with his bags.

None of these unpleasant data would be worth the incivility of an airing had he not made himself the business and the tone of his tales. This first writer to introduce the subjective element into storytelling is still the most subjective of all children's authors. A well-wrought tale for Andersen was only a vehicle for putting his case before the public as he played Cyrano to the world's Roxanne. He lacked that essential ingredient in a storyteller — the humility to absent himself from the tale in order to do it full justice. What made his work noticeable and of some importance historically also made it ephemeral in a way that folklore resists. The tales have not survived the twentieth century, save one as a Hollywood extravaganza, because Andersen's sensibility, so right at the time, eventually choked the life out of them.

Whether they were ever best understood as children's stories is arguable. Andersen was not a children's author, I think, but someone pretending to be a gifted child in order to impress the grownups with his skills. He did produce a few genuine fairy tales — "The Tinder Box," "The Wild Swans" — but more of his tales are fairy romances and allegories. "The Little Mermaid" really belongs to the world of classical ballet and to a sophisticated audience looking for ways of being creatively distraught. Andersen is to the folklore of the Grimms what *Le Cabinet des Fées* was to the simplicity of Perrault. What the centuries had purged from a tale like "Rapunzel" he put back in. His temperament was histrionic, and his motives theatrical: he wanted to stab the reader in his romantic heart. This is not what fairy tales do, nor children's story, nor make-believe.

A clue to how he fell out with tradition may be found in his autobiography, where we find him euphemizing his fretful life as "a beautiful fairy tale, rich and happy."

> If, when I was a small boy, poor and lonely going out into the world, I had met a powerful fairy godmother and she had said, "Choose your own course through life and your own destination, then I shall protect you and lead you according to the development of your mind and the way things must reasonably work out in this world," then my fate could not have been a happier one, nor more cleverly and well guided than it has been. The wonderful story of my life will say to the world what it says to me: that there is a loving God who directs all things for the best. [12]

Clearly, Andersen knew his Perrault. But none of what he handed his public here is what he really felt. He never told the kind of light and grateful tale these words imply he had. For every child who inherits the world in Andersen, five are subtracted from it. The one true word in this little fantasy is the word "if." "If," he begins his story; *if* he had had a powerful fairy godmother. The reader familiar with Perrault's "Sleeping Beauty" will recall that there is an eighth fairy in the tale, who takes it amiss that she has been invited to the christening only as an afterthought. It is she who sets the plot in motion when she declares out of spite that the princess will prick her hand with a spindle and die. This eighth fairy, I think, is the muse Andersen took from his reading of Perrault. His childhood had likewise been cursed by her. But unlike Sleeping Beauty, he had not been graced with a good fairy to be the friend of his need. And so, in spite, he carried his grievances to a tradition that did not want them and painted Perrault's gracious godmothers as an Ice Maiden, a cheating Dame Fortune, and the Antichrist, whom he called the Snow Queen. It is ironic that he should be the first children's author to think of himself explicitly in sacerdotal terms, as a mediator between God and man. He was not alone in this opinion of himself: within his lifetime others would be speaking of "the soft glow which surrounds him like a halo." [13] Alas, instead of letting the little miracles of his make-believe swim into view, he broadcast a sentimental religiosity across the surface of his work, creating a perturbation that almost always overwhelmed them. The result is not fairy tale, quite, nor children's story, nor make-believe; neither is it Christian or pagan, for he mixed his religious metaphors into a syncretic brew according to whim. It is something in between these things, a dysfunction, a falling out of the tradition. This is what comes of viewing the world through a magnifying glass and staining it with witch's blood. His "gift to the world" was not ever a gift *of* the world, really. In the end, his gift of fairy tales must be read as a cautionary fable on how not to write them.

What effect Andersen had on the next generation of writers in England is rather hard to define. The books that show the most influence history has sorted out and left behind. Throughout the Victorian age, from Thackeray's *The Rose and the Ring* (1855) to Andrew Lang's *Prince Ricardo* (1893), his example helped sustain a collateral fashion for fairy romances and burlesques that the fantasist George MacDonald would brand "of all forms of literature the least worthy."[14] In flights of fancy like Mark Lemon's *Tinykin's Transformations* (1869), Tom Hood's *Petsetilla's Posy* (1870), and Mary De Morgan's *The Necklace of Princess Fiorimonde* (1880), Perrault's godmother occupies a seat considerably lower than before, wearing the guise of garden fairy or decorative guest at court farces. If the Victorians had produced only works such as these, their contribution to the descent of story could be dismissed as a late echo of *Le Cabinet des Fées*. But the muse had a more earthly occupation in mind, and mannered fluff of this sort was not the future she intended for her literature.

The agent of change in translating the tale into narrative fantasy was Victoria's chaplain, Charles Kingsley (1819–75), who with one book created the first novelized make-believe for children, the first English prose nonsense, and the most ambitious Christian parable since *The Pilgrim's Progress*.

The Water Babies (1863)

This epic story about a ten-year-old chimney sweep in the north of England whose mother is dead and father a convict in Botany Bay runs to 265 pages, making it a parable nearly ten times the length of Andersen's "The Snow Queen." Ordinarily, fairy tales are not asked to support such a burden of material, so it is no surprise to find the book beginning to collapse at the center under its own weight. That it holds up as well as it does can be attributed perhaps to the author's confidence in his calling. Andersen had to plead his priestly role between the lines of every tale; Kingsley had no need to convince anyone of his role, least of all himself. He had merely to discharge the task at hand of writing a Christian fable for children that would have little of the Sunday School lesson about it and all the pleasure of a fairy tale. Being a man of many parts—cleric, teacher, novelist, naturalist, historian—he set out on three courses at once, announcing simultaneously that here was a new make-believe ("Once upon a time there was a little chimney sweep, and his name was Tom"), an evangelical parable ("He had never been taught to say his prayers"), and a novel of social reform ("He cried when he had to climb the dark flues . . . "), which last, as it happened, would almost immediately precipitate a change in England's child labor laws. What I want to present at this point is a brief trot to the story, offered on the assumption that the likelihood is virtually nil that the reader can (1) locate an unabridged edition of this book and (2) if so fortunate, persevere to the end of it. There will be more about *The Water Babies*, particularly its nonsense, in the next chapter, which deals with *Alice in Wonderland* and in which we are going to find the Reverend Charles

Dodgson reading Kingsley's brainchild with stupefaction and dismay and learning from it immeasurably.

Notwithstanding its fairy-tale opening, the story is set in contemporary England and proceeds in a realistic vein for nearly two chapters before Kingsley submerges it literally in the stream of make-believe and launches that voyage through the world by river and ocean that comprises the body of the book. Going aquatic for the fantasy might be expected from a naturalist fascinated by marine life; it was a necessary choice for the parablist. Water is baptismal, washing away sins, and the chaplain meant to give his chimney sweep one very thorough dunking. His tongue was only partly in his cheek when he closed the book with a moral, asking, "What should we learn from this parable?" and concluding that his little reader should forsake his "nasty, dirty, lazy, stupid life, and . . . learn your lessons, and thank God that you have plenty of cold water to wash in, and wash in it too, like a true Englishman." At this point in the tale, presumably, we have become accustomed to the ironies in his voice. He did not risk his odd humors on the reader at the outset:

> As for chimney-sweeping, and being hungry, and being beaten, he took all that for the way of the world, like the rain and snow and thunder, and stood manfully with his back to it . . . and thought of the fine times coming, when he would be a man, and a master sweep, and sit in the public-house with a quart of beer and a long pipe, and play cards for silver money. . . . And he would have apprentices, one, two, three, if he could. How he would bully them, and knock them about, just as his master did to him; and make them carry home the soot sacks, while he rode before them on his donkey, with a pipe in his mouth and a flower in his buttonhole, like a king at the head of his army. Yes, there were good times coming; and, when his master let him have a pull at the leavings of his beer, Tom was the jolliest boy in the whole town.

This prophetic sketch of how we are trapped into repeating the sins of the fathers is a very reasonable explanation of original sin for a children's book. The peril of growing up unbaptized Kingsley underscored with an image that owed a debt to Darwin's new *Origin of Species* (1859). It comes as a revelation in a mirror, a backward glimpse into ages past. Tom has been going about his chores, cleaning out the complicated chimney system of a manor house, when suddenly he tumbles into "a room the like of which he had never seen before . . . all dressed in white, — white window-curtains, white bed-curtains, white furniture." On the wall hangs a picture "of a man nailed to a cross, which surprised Tom much," and near it "a washing-stand, with ewers and basins, and soap and brushes, and towels, and a large bath full of clean water." In the bed, "under the snow-white coverlet, upon the snow-white pillow, lay the most beautiful little girl that Tom had ever seen . . . an angel out of heaven." He is puzzling over in his mind how such a perfect creature could need all this array merely for washing, when, looking round, he suddenly saw, standing close to him, a little ugly, black, ragged figure, with bleared eyes and grinning white teeth. He turned on it angrily. What did such a little black ape want in that sweet young lady's room? And behold, it was himself, reflected in a great mirror. . . . And Tom, for the first time in his life, found out that he was dirty; and burst into tears with shame and anger.

Kingsley does not tarry over his symbols. Everyone comes running at this point and, taking the chimney sweep for a thief, they put him to flight. "Tom paddled up the park with his little bare feet, like a small black gorilla fleeing to the forest." He scales a mountain and, in the valley below, collapses on the doorstep of a secluded cottage.

When he peeps inside, he sees what could be the frontispiece to Perrault's fairy tales come to life. Before the fireplace is "the nicest old woman that ever was seen. . . . At her feet sat the grandfather of all the cats; and opposite her sat, on two benches, twelve or fourteen neat, rosy, chubby little children." Mother Goose has become the local schoolmistress. She brings the exhausted boy into her little schoolhouse home and puts him to bed. Tom is by now delirious. He hears the girl from the white room calling to him to "[g]o and be washed." Wandering obediently outside, he stumbles into a nearby stream, lies down in the cool water, and, falling asleep, drowns. His pursuers "found a black thing in the water, and said it was Tom's body," but they are unaware that the adventure is only now beginning, for "his whole husk and shell had been washed quite off him, and the pretty little real Tom was washed out of the inside of it, and swam away . . . as lively as a grig, and as clean as a fresh-run salmon."

There is a theological point to this, beyond the naturalist's desire to see his hero one with the newts and minnows. Kingsley is heeding the scriptural injunction "Except ye be converted, and become as little children, ye shall not enter into the kingdom of heaven." To make Tom again a little child, Kingsley must return him to what he was before he came to accept "the way of the world" and his fate as a lackey whose only hope of happiness is to make a lackey of others. The chaplain gave it good measure: he shrank his sweep and his sweep's manly ambitions to just under four inches long. Tom becomes a "water baby."

We follow him now on a pilgrimage that will take him to a schoolroom equally benign but with a very different curriculum. Like a reader turning from Perrault's frontis to the make-believe within the tales, Tom has left Mother Goose's house in the real world for the realm of the fairy godmothers. His destination, downriver and far over the sea, is St. Brandan's isle, home of the water babies. Assembled in this pleasant primary school sometimes called Purgatory are all those children who were "untaught and brought up heathens" or who "came to grief by ill-usage or ignorance or neglect." Here they are schooled out of their benighted state by the fairy spirit of the Old Testament, Mrs. Bedonebyasyoudid, "who reads the news very carefully every morning, and especially the police cases," and by the fairy spirit of the New Testament, Mrs. Doasyouwouldbedoneby, "who is the loveliest fairy in the world." When our newcomer proves a hard case and his soul turns "all prickly with naughty tempers," Mrs. Bedonebyasyoudid declares, "I shall fetch you a schoolmistress, who will teach you how to get rid of your prickles." Tom does not find this welcome news, but his fears are ill founded. The substitute teacher is none other than the girl from the white room, whose name is Ellie. Since their first meeting she, too, has died (in an accident too coincidental, I'm afraid, to be credible even in a fairy tale), and now, six days a week for seven years (the details of which we are spared), she comes to teach him how to say his prayers and be good. On Sundays she goes home to heaven. At the end of the seven years, when Tom expresses a wish to join her there, the fairies declare that he may, on condition he first, like a true champion, go somewhere he does not like, do something he does not like, and help someone he does not like. The somewhere will be the Other-end-of-Nowhere. The someone he must help will be his abusive former master, who upon his own death was sent to this Other-end-of-Nowhere—which is to say, straight to Hell. Tom's mission, furthermore, is to find his way there himself—"to go on this journey, and see the world, like an Englishman." Only one person can advise him, the mysterious Mother Carey, who sits enthroned on an iceberg behind Shining Wall, where the good whales go to die. There she spends her days "making old beasts into new all the year round." She offers Tom a succinct definition of just how, in Kingsley's Anglican view, Purgatory works:

> "I heard, ma'am, that you were always making new beasts out of old."
> "So people fancy. But I am not going to trouble myself to make things, my little dear. I sit here and make them make themselves."

The journey to Mother Carey and from Mother Carey to Hell takes up fully a quarter of the book. It should be, as she said, about Tom's final efforts to remake himself. What we find instead is Kingsley converting his *Pilgrim's Progress* into a pocket *Gulliver's Travels*—for while John Bunyan is "as wise a man as you will meet in a month of Sundays," there were a few worldly bugbears clinging yet to the edges of the parable, and Kingsley itched to play Swift. And so, for some seventy-odd amusing if largely extraneous pages, we go with Tom to the nonsense lands of Hearsay and Leaveheavenalone, and to the island of the Tomtoddies, which is Swift's Laputa, first discovered by "the great traveler Captain Gulliver," and from there to the land of Oldwivesfabledom that St. Paul warned of in his letters to Timothy, and to several more besides, including Waste-paper-land, that courtyard to Hell

> where all the stupid books lie in heaps, up hill and down dale, like leaves in a winter wood; and there he saw people digging and grubbing among them, to make worse books out of bad ones, and thrashing chaff to save the dust of it; and a very good trade they drove thereby, especially among children.

Kingsley of course was making a new parable out of old ones in just such a way as this, although from better stock and to a better end.

The earliest parable to inform *The Water Babies* may have been a little story-poem from William Blake's *Songs of Innocence* (1789). A sweep named Tom, a heavenly intercessor, immersion in a stream, and a coming forth from this baptism to do one's duty can all be found in "The Chimney Sweeper":

> When my mother died I was very young,
> And my father sold me while yet my tongue
> Could scarcely cry "'weep! 'weep! 'weep! 'weep!"
> So your chimneys I sweep, & in soot I sleep.
>
> There's little Tom Dacre, who cried when his head,
> That curl'd like a lamb's back, was shav'd: so I said
> "Hush, Tom! never mind it, for when your head's bare
> You know that the soot cannot spoil your white hair."
>
> And so he was quiet, & that very night,
> As Tom was a-sleeping, he had such a sight!
> That thousands of sweepers, Dick, Joe, Ned, & Jack,
> Were all of them lock'd up in coffins of black.
>
> And by came an Angel who had a bright key,
> And he open'd the coffins & set them all free;
> Then down a green plain leaping, laughing, they run,
> And wash in a river, and shine in the Sun.
>
> Then naked & white, all their bags left behind,
> They rise upon clouds and sport in the wind;
> And the Angel told Tom, if he'd be a good boy,
> He'd have God for his father, & never want joy.
>
> And so Tom awoke, and we rose in the dark,
> And got with our bags & our brushes to work.
> Tho' the morning was cold, Tom was happy & warm;
> So if all do their duty they need not fear harm.

As for the good matrons at the heart of this new parable, a precedent in Perrault is clear enough; the question, rather, is, By what route might the fairy godmother have become a schoolmistress in Purgatory? Kingsley took reference, I think, to two books—I should say, to one book and a class of books. It would be premature to explore the first of these now, when there are other stories indebted to the same source and all best accounted for together. The second was a kind of book Kingsley detested, yet would find useful. His spirits of the two Testaments can be read, then, as a translation into make-believe of what had been the prevailing fashion in children's books for the entirety of the preceding century, that period dubbed the Age of Admonition. Being unwelcome at the front door of children's literature for so long, the muse could now, thanks to this fashion, simply go around to the side and come in through the back. And so we find her doing. She came in as a governess or tutor, and she got in through the unlikely offices of the philosopher Jean-Jacques Rousseau.

In *Emile* (1762) Rousseau had described the ideal learning situation as one in which the pupil is removed from the corruptions of society and learns not from books but from nature, with the aid of an unobtrusive and patient tutor to answer whatever questions might arise and now and then to offer guidance. This tutor would do, in effect, what Mother Carey does: make the pupil make himself. As for moral instruction, this was to be withheld until the fifteenth year, by which time, presumably, the pupil would be so naturally good and unbiased that such instruction would hardly be needed.

Kingsley had a sounder grasp of sin than Rousseau, though not so tightly Calvinistic a grasp as the cadre of educators, clerics, and novelists in England who, recognizing that Rousseau's benign neglect avails nothing, seized upon the tutorial idea and marched moral instruction back into the nursery where they felt it belonged. They added a new personage to the fictions of the day: the Wise Adult who, whether as parent, uncle, or governess, comes into the nursery to counsel the children in matters of comportment, piety, good deeds, and right thinking. Rousseau's unobtrusive teacher thus became a garrulous, moralizing, sometimes frightening pest. What no one had foreseen was that one day the pest would suddenly turn up in a form of children's literature that had been despised by all alike—the fairy tale.

Kingsley hated them all, these didacts, but their purpose was his purpose: to teach. He was familiar with Plato's advice "Let your children's lessons take the form of play" and knew that without humor and fantasy a book like his must always fail, but he was bound nonetheless to the general agenda. He understood something it is very easy for us to forget today— that with all children's story a tutorial relationship inescapably obtains, for every adult narrating or reading to a child is faced, implicitly or explicitly, with answering the eternal questions, Why? and Is that true? Kingsley's great mistake in *The Water Babies* was to allow himself one Wise Adult too many.

With his tutelary muses his instinct was sure. He knew to introduce the muse as a mystery and not as a schoolmarm tapping the blackboard with her pointer. And so it is that we find "a poor Irishwoman, trudging along with a bundle at her back" as Tom and his master are making their way to the manor house where Tom will discover himself to be a sooty ape in a mirror. "She had neither shoes nor stockings, and limped along as if she were tired and footsore; but she was a very tall handsome woman." Taking a shine to Tom, she "asked him where he lived, and what he knew, and all about himself, till Tom thought he had never met such a pleasant-spoken woman. And she asked him, at last, whether he said his prayers! and seemed sad when he told her that he knew no prayers to say."

To this juncture we have been reading as realistic a tale as *Oliver Twist*. With the Irish Woman comes something strange into the story. When the master and Tom have a falling-out, for example, and Tom is taking a cuffing, she calls the master's name, which she could not know, and threatens to expose the secret crimes of his past if he persists in beating the boy. The master is stunned. She leaves them with the admonition "I have one more word for you both; for you will both see me again before all is over. Those that wish to be clean, clean they will be; and those that wish to be foul, foul they will be. Remember." And with that, she passes into a meadow and vanishes.

Tom will see no more of her until his journey's end, but she will never be very far away. She is there at the stream in which he drowns, preparing his passage as the book takes its plunge from realism into make-believe:

> [J]ust before he came to the river side, she had stepped down into the cool clear water; and her shawl and her petticoat floated off her, and the green water-weeds floated round her sides, and the white water-lilies floated round her head, and the fairies of the stream came up from the bottom and bore her away and down upon their arms; for she was the Queen of them all; and perhaps of more besides.

At the end, when Tom has saved his old master from Hell and he and Ellie are reunited, the mysteries of the book all gather into one, and we learn who the Irish Woman is, and Mother Carey, and the twin spirits of the two Testaments. And yet they are not explained, either, for Kingsley closes the book with the heart of the mystery left intact:

> At last they heard the fairy say: "Attention, children. Are you never going to look at me again?"
> "We have been looking at you all this while," they said. And so they thought they had been.
> "Then look at me once more," said she.
> They looked—and both of them cried out at once, "Oh, who are you after all?"
> "You are our dear Mrs. Doasyouwouldbedoneby."
> "No, you are good Mrs. Bedonebyasyoudid; but you are grown quite beautiful now!"
> "To you," said the fairy. "But look again."
> "You are Mother Carey," said Tom, in a very low, solemn voice; for he had found out something which made him very happy, and yet frightened him more than all that he had ever seen.
> "But you are grown quite young again."
> "To you," said the fairy. "Look again."
> "You are the Irish Woman who met me the day I went to Harthover!"
> And when they looked she was neither of them, and yet all of them at once.
> "My name is written in my eyes, if you have eyes to see it there."
> And they looked into her great, deep, soft eyes, and they changed again and again into every hue, as the light changes in a diamond.
> "Now read my name," said she, at last.
> And her eyes flashed, for one moment, clear, white, blazing light: but the

children could not read her name; for they were dazzled, and hid their faces in their hands.

"Not yet, young things, not yet," said she, smiling.

It might seem a paradox to some, though the Victorians did not think it odd, that the man who would sit portrait for the "Muscular Christians" of his time should say, seven years after *The Water Babies* in a letter to John Stuart Mill on the subject of woman suffrage, that he has meant "to set forth in every book I write (as I have done for twenty-five years) woman as the teacher, the natural and therefore divine, guide, purifier, inspirer of the man."[15] *The Water Babies* is the first modern children's book to bear this thought. If only Kingsley had let his natural teachers teach and stepped back and been himself still, the book would have been an unqualified masterpiece. But the confident stance that enabled him to sustain the tale, where Andersen had run afoul of his priestly garb, became a careless overconfidence in other matters, and it is this flaw in Kingsley that finally causes the book to collapse under the weight of unwanted oration and opinion. Much of this weight was added, ironically, in a proper mood of celebration. In Tom's river and sea journeys, which I have hardly touched here, Kingsley was serving both his love of nature and his pastoral role as celebrant of the Twenty-sixth Psalm, "That I may publish with the voice of thanksgiving, and tell of all thy wondrous works." He had the spirit of the encyclopedist and the enthusiasm of the fascinated amateur. He was early, and unusual among clerics, in seeing that the daunting backward reach of Darwin's evolution, and the myriad creations it exposed to view, did nothing to faith but further glorify the Creation. *The Water Babies* is oceanic work, a sea-lane to salvation crammed with information to open Tom's eyes to the wonders of the world. Unhappily, Kingsley had yet a third agenda to satisfy in these pages, and that was the airing of his many grievances against the other half of creation, the social animal. So vast is the man's xenophobia, and so great a game does he make of his antipathies, so full of self-ironies and nonsense, that his slights against Americans, Papists, Jews, Negroes, and a host of others quickly gather themselves into such a company that it becomes almost pointless to take offense.

The historian Harvey Darton wrote of children's authors during Victoria's reign that "they were more nearly of the ruling classes. They had a modest feeling of prerogative audience."[16] Too cozy a sense of audience in a children's author can be a dangerous thing, sanctioning much mischief. It has been the chief failing in an otherwise brilliant tradition in British children's books. It would lead to the intimate tone and rich textures of the Edwardians but also make some books sound smug abroad. Kingsley was certain whom he was addressing. It was that "brave English lad, whose business is to go out and see all the world." His assumption that no one else would be listening in allowed him unkindnesses quite out of keeping with his calling. His preoccupation with skewering heathens outside the tribe even led him into being careless with the whereabouts and well-being of his story. To play coy in a fairy tale by repeatedly discussing whether one's story is "true" or not is simply inept. Kingsley was having such sport playing the comic monologist that he sometimes forgot what he was about altogether. When Tom is ready to go on at the end, presumably to heaven, Kingsley speaks of his becoming "a great man of science," as if he were reentering the world of the living instead. The reader closes the book, thinking, But the boy did die, did he not?

The Water Babies is a story divided against itself. It succeeds in being the parable it wanted to be because of Kingsley the priest; it fails because of Kingsley the preacher. Having installed a magical tutor within the story, whose teachings were acceptable and pleasurable because make-believe, he continued to tutor from outside the tale, thus placing his voice in conflict with the voice of his muse. It was a performance that Lewis Carroll, the Reverend Charles Dodgson, would view with disgust and annoyance. But in the end it may be vain to ask why Kingsley willfully burdened his parable with so much that impeded its progress. Gladness and exasperation drove the book through its paces equally. On the one hand, we have Kingsley singing of the natural world; on the other, throwing out civility, public reputations, and even a few obstructing orthodoxies like so much used furniture. As a result of his exasperation, the book is compromised; without it, there may have been no book at all.

We might take a more Platonic view to end here, and, shrugging off the Romantic's fancy that works of art are sui generis the children of genius, think, rather, of authors as characters in the evolving story of Story. The role played in the plot by Kingsley's intemperate housecleaning, then, was to prepare rooms for the universal muse and the name, as he called it, that-is-not-yet. This he did.

3

A TUTOR RECANTS

The Unwriting of Alice in Wonderland

It was Harvey Darton, I believe, who first declared *Alice in Wonderland* the recess bell that officially freed children from the classroom to the playground in their reading. The Reverend Charles Kingsley's policy that "the general tone shall be such as never to make the reader forget the main purpose of the book"[1] is sound advice, of course, if you have subordinated yourself to the real object of your story. Kingsley had not. A man with much on his mind, the author of *The Water Babies* had made a pulpit of his parable and with missionary zeal unburdened himself of a thousand complaints extraneous to the matter at hand. This would not be the way of the Reverend Charles Dodgson (1832–98), who even worked up a pun on the intrusion of purpose into children's tales:

> "Will you walk a little faster?" said a whiting to a snail,
> "There's a porpoise close behind us, and he's treading on my tail. . . . "

The reader may recall Alice's pert endorsement, "I'd have said to the porpoise, 'Keep back, please! We don't want *you* with us!'" The inspiriting role played by her little book in the descent of make-believe has achieved an almost credal status since Darton:

> broke new ground . . . handled childhood freshly . . .

> set free the imagination . . . revolutionized writing for the young . . .

> the true beginning of fantasy . . . had the sole aim of giving pleasure.

> revolutionary . . . the real beginning of modern literature for children . . . written purely to give pleasure without a trace of a lesson or a moral.

broke radically with the tradition of what children's books were supposed to be and set a new standard. Unlike earlier children's books and those of contemporaries, the "Alice" books teach no moral. . . . Carroll was the first to banish seriousness from children's books.

Carroll's humor . . . is sheer, unadulterated fun, free from both topical allusion and from wit. . . . The fetters of reality are broken and liberation is found in fantasy or laughter.[2]

I am not going to deny a certain validity to these professions of faith. As a narrator Dodgson made at least a pretense of taking the child's part, and in contrast to most earlier tutorials *Alice* does seem blissfully free to be itself. The belief that he wrote the book solely to give pleasure is far from true, however. The seriousness, the lessons, the morals are here; they are simply of a different order and more cunningly presented. The received wisdom about *Alice*, that by teaching nothing it freed children from literary bondage, has made the book something of a red herring in the annals of make-believe, actually—a pilot fish schooling us away from the main currents and feeding grounds of the literature. Are we not, for example, under the corporate impression today that carefree pleasure is the only true desideratum in children's stories? Would we not agree that fantasy and nonsense are a priori all innocent fun and a blessing on every child holding a book or a ticket to the movies?

In a way, this chapter will be a test of the second of these propositions. As for the first, let me suggest that not only is "sheer unadulterated fun" a false ideal for make-believe; it is one that is quite impossible to achieve. Twenty and thirty-five years down the line from *Alice*, two ingenuous books will appear that do seem to achieve it; if any stories are to be cited for making a clean break with didacticism, surely it should be this happy pair, *Treasure Island* and *Little Black Sambo*. Yet even with Robert Louis Stevenson and Helen Bannerman we are not free from instruction, only from the more obvious sorts, for every children's book teaches. It teaches the world it portrays and imprints us with a sense of how we are to respond to that world. In this regard alone, no one has taught children more doggedly than the author of *Alice in Wonderland*. Alexander Woollcott's 1939 portrait of the book as a "gay tapestry" and of Dodgson as a "shy, retreating man who left so much bubbling laughter in his legacy to the world"[3] is still pretty much the popular perception (witness the number of filmmakers who have come to grief pursuing it), but one rather at odds with the intellectual intensity of the Reverend's magic kingdom. How many extracurricular smiles can there be for a child, after all, in a tale whose heroine must reason and argue as hard and as fast as she can for her very survival? Alice laughs but three times. On each occasion her fancy has been caught by some minor absurdity—the antics of a footman, the flamingo she must use at croquet, and the news that the Duchess has boxed the Queen's ears. Against these weigh her unending puzzlement and the frequency with which, like a startled eye, this puzzlement dilates into apprehension, dismay, even terror. Add to these moments the four occasions she is provoked to actual tears and the seventeen to defensive fits of temper. A common epithet in the book is the word "poor"—"Poor Alice!," "Poor little thing!" If *Wonderland* is the recess bell in the history of children's literature, to what strange playground have we been excused?

"Curiouser and curiouser!" is the book's only reply. Scene by scene, riddle by riddle, Wonderland seems everywhere haunted by the sense that a key to its secret does exist, like that tiny golden key to the Queen's garden; yet so artfully does the author withhold it from us that no two critics have ever explicated the story in quite the same way. Alice's question to herself between tears, "Who in the world am I? Ah, *that's* the great puzzle!," is not only her own signature soliloquy; it is clearly a "to be or not to be" and "whether 'tis better" for the book itself. In tutoring his pinafored Hamlet through a world gone mad, this is precisely how Dodgson has phrased the fiction: as a cunning, great puzzle. What I write here I add to a very large critical literature in which pleasure and bewilderment (usually cleverly disguised) have been expressed in about equal measure. I do not hope to understand the adventure more clearly than others. I do propose to offer some relief from the burden of meaning by reading the book less as a message to be decoded than as an occasion of storytelling. The key may lie as much as anywhere in how Dodgson thought his way into and through these chapters. In making what must be a highly speculative inquiry, I am going to take Mother Carey's advice to Tom as he departed for the outskirts of Hell and, in good Looking-glass fashion, "go the whole way backward." Dodgson had taken this same retrospective look at his life and works: in 1889, as he neared the end of his literary journey, we find him putting into print a pair of books that in effect constitute a kind of epilogue or coda to the earlier tale and which I feel may supply those missing pieces necessary to complete the puzzle. What becomes especially manifest when reading *The Nursery Alice* and *Sylvie and Bruno* is the degree to which *Wonderland* was the work of the *Reverend* Charles Dodgson, deacon of the Church of England, a man who as the son of a minister was raised for the clergy and educated for the clergy and whose diaries are full of the fear of God. As the invention of an apprentice cleric, the question "Who in the world am I?" becomes particularly suggestive. The existential anxiety articulated by Alice is, not, after all, native to this branch of story but, following Shakespeare, to the modern novel and to philosophy and theology. Realigned to read "Who am I in the world?," the question implies a work of social satire, which describes *Wonderland* rather well; in its original phrasing, however, it speaks to the human condition and the nature of reality. Having what is popularly known as an identity crisis is precocious stuff for a fantasy about a child of seven. It calls attention to itself. One of the critics cited at the head of this chapter, Morton N. Cohen, has spoken of Dodgson as "a deeply religious man [who] practiced what he preached."[4] The interesting thing about the deacon's masterpiece is that he appears to have used it to do something else entirely.

Cheshire Puss

In 1888, as Charles Dodgson turned fifty-six, he did a curious thing. His little tour de force, *Alice in Wonderland*, was now fast becoming the most famous children's story ever told. As a consequence, it was now also threatening to become the defining fact of its author's life. He decided to rewrite it from start to finish.

This would be his third attempt at working the material, actually. It was a project he had entertained since resigning from his lectureship in mathematics at Christ Church, Oxford, in 1881. The first attempt had been a private affair to amuse the ten-year-old daughter of the Dean of Christ Church, Dr. H. G. Liddell. In it the young deacon had told of a girl rather like herself and filled the tale with jokes and allusions for her eyes only. In November 1864 he presented Miss Alice Liddell with the story in a gift edition of eighteen thousand hand-lettered words, the illustrations to which he had done, and done ably, himself. This presentation copy he called *Alice's Adventures Under Ground*. He had worked on it in his spare hours for some two and a half years.

The second, more public version he undertook, it is said, at the encouragement of friends. Between 1863 and 1865, adding new characters and episodes, he doubled the book's length to thirty-five thousand words. This is the *Alice in Wonderland* that we read today. It was published in November 1865 under the pen name Lewis Carroll and illustrated by the *Punch* cartoonist John Tenniel (1820–1914). Popular memory seals the history of the book here, in 1865, as an act complete.

Twenty-five years later, however, Dodgson returned to Wonderland, and this third time he meant to subtract from it. Out came the lampoons in verse. Out came Alice's soliloquies, which had given the story such immediacy. Out came the comic conversations (the Mad Tea Party being passed over as "a long talk," for example) and with them the book's wit. All the strangeness, all the ridicule of writers with a fishy purpose, all the acclaimed humor is gone. In the end Dodgson would sanction a mere sixty-five hundred words, hardly a fifth of the original. And what he did keep he retold so that a passage like this:

> "Here, Bill! The master says you've got to go down the chimney!"
> "Oh! So Bill's got to come down the chimney, has he?" said Alice to herself. "Why, they seem to put everything upon Bill! I wouldn't be in Bill's place for a good deal; this fireplace is narrow, to be sure; but I *think* I can kick a little!"
> She drew her foot as far down the chimney as she could, and waited till she heard a little animal (she couldn't guess of what sort it was) scratching and scrambling about in the chimney close above her: then, saying to herself, "This is Bill," she gave one sharp kick, and waited to see what would happen next.
> The first thing she heard was a general chorus of "There goes Bill!"

came out sounding like this:

> He sent Bill, the Lizard, up to the roof of the house, and told him to get down the chimney. But Alice happened to have one of her feet in the fire-place;

so, when she heard Bill coming down the chimney, she just gave a little tiny kick, and away went Bill, flying up into the sky!

Poor little Bill! Don't you pity him very much? How frightened he must have been!

The surprising purpose of this new work, *The Nursery Alice*, the author explained in a preface "Addressed to Any Mother":

[M]y ambition *now* is (is it a vain one?) to be read by Children aged from Nought to Five. To be read? Nay, not so! Say rather to be thumbed, to be cooed over, to be dogs'-eared, to be rumpled, to be kissed, by the illiterate, ungrammatical, dimpled Darlings that fill your Nursery with merry uproar. . . .

Rumpling a dog's ears had been his most glaring aesthetic mistake in the official *Alice*. In *The Nursery Alice* he has exacerbated the intrusion of a real, not a Wonderland, puppy into the story by giving the misplaced terrier a chapter all its own. It is worth quoting a part of "The Dear Little Puppy" to appreciate just how remarkable an achievement *Alice* is, coming from a man who could nestle so cozily among the rugs and pillows of the Victorian sensibility:

Have you got a little pet puppy at *your* home? If you have, I hope you're always kind to it, and give it nice things to eat.

Once upon a time, I knew some little children, about as big as you; and they had a little pet dog of their own; and it was called *Dash*. And this is what they told me about its birthday-treat.

"Do you know, one day we remembered it was Dash's birthday that day. So we said 'Let's give Dash a nice birthday-treat, like what we have on *our* birthdays!' So we thought and we thought 'Now, what is it *we* like best of all, on *our* birthdays?' And we thought and we thought. And at last we all called out together 'Why, it's *oatmeal-porridge*, of course!' So of course we thought Dash would be *quite* sure to like it very much, too.

"So we went to the cook, and we got her to make a saucerful of nice oatmeal-porridge. And then we called Dash into the house, and we said 'Now, Dash, you're going to have your birthday-treat!' We expected Dash would jump for joy: but it didn't, one bit!

"So we put the saucer down before it, and we said 'Now, Dash, don't be greedy! Eat it nicely, like a good dog!'

"So Dash just tasted it with the tip of its tongue: and then it made, oh, such a horrid face! And then, do you know, it did *hate* it so, it wouldn't eat a bit more of it! So we had to put it all down its throat with a spoon!"

I wonder if Alice will give *this* little Puppy some porridge? I don't think she *can*, because she hasn't got any with her. I can't see any saucer in the picture.

Even setting aside the thought that dimpled Darlings nought to five should have an *Alice* to call their own, there is nothing about *The Nursery Alice* to recommend it as a work of art. Out of allegiance to its author, a few aficionados have spoken for it, but porridge is porridge, and this kind of filler was a staple of every children's magazine of the nineteenth century. It is the rhetoric of the literary babysitter, the beleaguered editor or hired hack tending to a generic flock of sentimentalized, and here rather patrician, children. The conceit of "The Dear Little Puppy" is actually an elaborate one for *The Nursery Alice*. As suggested by Dodgson's allusion to a missing saucer, the book is otherwise little more than a series of captions to Tenniel's pictures. Shifting responsibility onto his illustrator as the prime teller, Dodgson has recast his delivery in the form of a magic-lantern show, or what we would think of today as a slide presentation:

> Doesn't Alice look pretty, as she swims across the picture? You can just see her blue stockings, far away under the water.
>
> *click*
>
> Mr. Tenniel says the screaming bird is a *Storkling* (of course you know what *that* is?) and the little white head is a *Mouseling*. Isn't it a little *darling*?
>
> *click*
>
> Oh dear, Oh dear! What *is* it all about? And what's happening to Alice?
>
> *click click click*

What is it all about, indeed? Later I hope to show that in fact this fondling stuff was, at some level of intent, an act of contrition and the necessary prelude to *Sylvie and Bruno*; for the moment, it should be noted that mawkish sentimentality, so unexpected from the acerbic Lewis Carroll, was a constant in Dodgson's career and not merely a late fancy as he slid into his dotage. Witness the cloying tale "Bruno's Revenge," which he wrote between *Wonderland* and *Through the Looking-Glass*, and even the two *Alices* themselves. Listen to the soporific closing to *Wonderland* and the equally pretty opening to its sequel:

> [S]he pictured to herself how this same little sister of hers would, in the aftertime, be herself a grown woman; and how she would keep, through all her riper years, the simple and loving heart of her childhood; and how she would gather about her other little children, and make *their* eyes bright and eager with many a strange tale, perhaps even with the dream of Wonderland of long ago; and how she would feel with all their simple sorrows, and find a pleasure in all their simple joys, remembering her own child-life, and the happy summer days.
>
> Do you hear the snow against the windowpanes, Kitty? How nice and soft it sounds! Just as if someone was kissing the windows all over outside. I wonder if the snow *loves* the trees and fields, that it kisses them so gently? And then it covers them up snug, you know, with a white quilt; and perhaps it says "go to sleep, darlings, till the summer comes again."

Kindly words from a man who has just confronted the loving heart of childhood with "Off with her head!" and "Really you are very dull!" and "Speak roughly to your little boy, / and beat him when he sneezes." There are two ways of putting the obvious question here: How could a man who normally sounded like the narrator of *The Nursery Alice* ever have written

Alice in Wonderland, and why would the author of *Alice in Wonderland* ever have perpetrated *The Nursery Alice*?

It is generally agreed, I think, that Dodgson did not suffer in any degree from a split personality. Nor is one required to frame our portrait of him. We are all of us harboring too many contrary moods ourselves to think his that unusual. The bite of Lewis Carroll and the unctuousness of the deacon are speaking likenesses of the same man. He was a man the admiring Alexander Woollcott had to admit was "puttering, fussy, fastidious, didactic."[5] Call him an eccentric, then, this "gentle, shrinking celibate."[6] Grant him his surprises.

Woollcott did the deacon an injustice, as it happens. He did not putter; he puttered prodigiously. He once found the time, for example, to catalogue his correspondence in the form of an index with ninety-eight thousand cross-references. At playing the scold he was not only fastidious, he was fearless, ambushing acquaintances with pained and stately notes of reprimand for minor discourtesies or impieties. His own piety made him a public nuisance. His illustrators were forbidden to illustrate on Sundays. Upon discovering that a stage production of *The Water Babies* contained a burlesque of a Salvation Army hymn, he campaigned to have the theater's license revoked. The infamous Bowdler edition of Shakespeare was a scandal to the prudish don, who wanted the plays purged of anything that might bring a blush to a maiden's cheek. This last is the mark also of a true sentimentalist. Dodgson's choices of entertainment ran to blatant kitsch. He doted on maudlin songs, the pathetic in drama, and paintings with titles like "First Communion," "The Naughty Boy," and "The Morning Kiss." Unembarrassed by his own bad taste, he was a snob and a lion hunter, chasing after celebrities with his camera and, like Hans Christian Andersen, courting the good opinion of princesses and actresses with unsolicited, inscribed copies of his books. When he first thought how *Alice* should be pictured for the world, his preference was not for the satirist John Tenniel but for the grandiosely decorative salon painter Sir Noel Paton. The poet laureate would be another feather in the deacon's cap. Dodgson made a habit of turning up uninvited on Tennyson's doorstep, camera at the ready. Friendly at first, the laureate had at last to declare himself permanently not at home. Unsurprisingly for someone who sensed at least a footnote for himself in the history of his time and prepared the way by cross-referencing his letters, such embarrassments as the Tennyson snub went unrecorded in Dodgson's diaries. Fame has ferreted them out, however, and presented us with the puzzle of finding in the man a plausible author for the *Alice* books, as well as a plausible answer to the question "Who in the world am I?" that his life so confounds.

No solutions are going to recommend themselves here, I think, unless we first set aside the legend of *Wonderland's* genesis as being any kind of explanation in itself. Undeniably, it is a pretty story, the young don being called upon for a fairy tale as he and a colleague rowed the three Liddell girls along the Thames one summer day, looking for a picnic site. It is one of the reigning myths of children's literature that *Alice* was plucked on that day, like a lily from the waters of the imagination. "Thus grew the tale of Wonderland," sang its bard to introduce the geste, and so have popular fancy and several films preserved it. For love of the little boat and its winsome crew, we have been quite willing to overlook the presence of some rather fretful porpoises swimming in its wake.

The most tenacious shadow looming below was spiritual. The problem of whether to follow his father into the ministry had been vexing Dodgson for years. The family's expectation had always more or less been that he would take holy orders in the Anglican Church, do parochial work at Oxford or elsewhere, and possibly in time become a priest. Young Charles, his piety notwithstanding, had balked. He did finally agree to try the partial solution of taking interim orders at Oxford "as a sort of experiment."[7] The position, or Studentship, which could be resigned without prejudice, would guarantee him a living for as long as he remained celibate. He accepted these terms officially on December 27, 1861, six months before the famous picnic that launched *Wonderland*. What happened next can only be guessed — a winter spent brooding over the compromise, perhaps, availing little. Six months later the question "Who in the world am I?" has found its way into the thoughts of an alarmed novitiate who has just obeyed a command to "DRINK ME" and "EAT ME." If there is a correspondence between the two events, the young deacon will not be testifying to it. His diaries for this period, never read by anyone outside the family, have disappeared.

A measure of notoriety has already been gained by one essayist bent on tracking the scent of theology in *Wonderland*. By Shane Leslie's inventive reckoning — whether wonderfully sly or woefully misguided is moot — the *Alice* books are in reality a sustained allegory satirizing the religious debates then embroiling the English, and in particular what is known as the Oxford Movement. The Mouse Alice meets in the Pool of Tears, who is said to hate cats and dogs, is thus a "Church mouse" with no great love for Presbyterians (our "dear little puppy") or Catholics (Alice's cat, Dinah). The Cheshire Cat is revealed to be one Cardinal Wiseman; the Duchess, a Bishop Wilberforce. The March Hare and the Hatter represent the Low and the High Anglican Churches, with the snoozing Dormouse standing for the general doziness of all England's congregations. In *Through the Looking-Glass* the Low and the High Churches become Tweedledum and Tweedledee. Bishop Wilberforce is transformed into the Red Knight, while the White Knight speaks for the world of science. The scenario reaches its bizarre climax with the coronation of Queen Alice. We are meant to understand by this event that our heroine, like Cardinal Newman (the White Queen), has decamped from the Church of England to embrace the Church of Rome. In his introduction to *The Annotated Alice* Martin Gardner understandably calls the whole thing "hilarious."

Dodgson certainly did not premediate *Alice* in order to articulate his spiritual quandary or to editorialize on religious issues. He had fallen into this new chapter in the art of storytelling, after all, partly by the accident of a command performance. Finding himself in a boat with three girls eager for a tale, he had sent the namesake of his favorite down a rabbit hole "in a desperate attempt," as he later wrote, "to strike out some new line of fairy-lore."[9] At its inception the story probably meant little more than its mechanics: how you begin such a tale and how you keep your audience attentive with comical turns and cleverly planted signs of its relation to you and yours to it. Like that later entertainment, *Winnie-the-Pooh*, the story of Wonderland began as something of a roman à clef. Here is your colleague on the picnic, the Reverend Duckworth, for example, climbing out of the Pool of Tears as the Duck; and here is yourself, a sure giveaway as the Dodo ("Do-Do-Dodgson," as you habitually stammer your name); and here as the Lory and the Eaglet come Alice's sisters, Lorina and Edith, who will later appear with Alice at the bottom of the Dormouse's treacle well. Clearly, these are associative games for the understanding of children, not scholars of church history.

As we come to Dodgson's two painstaking years working on the more evolved public version of *Wonderland*, certain problems do begin to arise, however. And it is here that we find critics withdrawing into opposing camps. At one extreme are those cranks convinced that there remains some secret to be unlocked to this conundrum of a book; at the other are the guardians of the legend, who dismiss such a thought as folly and for whom the only key to *Alice* is an appreciation of nonsense and how Dodgson employed it. Properly understood, they assert, the book has no meaning beyond the sport it makes of those who would go looking for meaning. Such associations as may obtain — a Duck, a Dodo — are innocuous counters in the game. Happy, unpremeditated child, *Alice* is the product of a genius freely inventing at the top of his form. Symbol hunters not only miss the point; they betray the spirit of the book.

As propositions go, this is lovely stuff, but it is hardly as self-evident as the enthusiasts would have it. The idea that there is nothing to *Alice* but nonsense and laughter is no more credible, really, than Shane Leslie's allegorical scheme. He erred in thinking the intellectual intensity of Wonderland could be chased into a single corner. They err in supposing that a few symbolic assignments made in a boat can safely preclude our suspecting Dodgson of later layering the book with hidden ones; he has made much too cunning a game of the search for meaning to be thought quite so innocent.

Between the either and the or, I suspect, lies a simple sequence of events, with the serpent of a private agenda slipping into the garden of delights at precisely the moment Dodgson began improvising associative games for the tale. True, he had denied himself a presence in Wonderland by declining to use the tutorial voice of a Kingsley, but his celebrated absence there is really misapprehended. No sooner was he out than he cleverly reinstated himself by coming around the back dressed as a Dodo and rejoining the adventure as a player. And once inside the tale, I would suggest, he began underwriting Alice's story with his own. "Who in the world am I?" is not the question of a seven-year-old child. It is the question of a thirty-one-year-old apprentice priest.

Here I want to jump ahead of the evidence with a rather bald assertion. There is a great deal of matter to come, and it might stay in focus better if I preface it now with my belief that *Wonderland* is not merely something of a roman à clef, as suggested earlier, but all of it a roman à clef. It is a baggy specimen, and much of the how and why of it must be conceded lost; nonetheless, I think it can be demonstrated that virtually the whole of the book makes reference to real events in the lives of Alice Liddell and her next-door neighbor and friend, the Reverend Charles Dodgson. The evidence is abundant that many minor characters and at least six of the principals represent people known to them both and that at least two major story sequences in addition to the Pool of Tears refer to events in which they played leading roles. Once these assignments are made, moreover, a plot will begin to emerge from the confusion with reasonable consistency. It will be Dodgson's own private plot, and it will speak not only of his spiritual quandary but, more immediately, of his social and artistic troubles. Some of the nonsense may now seem to have been contrived less for the fun of it than as a means of disguising the names behind the caricatures. If this makes the book sound more like a detective novel than a children's story, so be it. In *Alice* a crime is committed, remember, and there is a trial, with Alice called as a witness. So let me begin this search for the people behind the masks by collaring the most obvious suspect, the author himself. He has opened *Wonderland* with a personal appearance as the Dodo. Six years later he will close *Through the Looking-Glass* with a personal appearance as the White Knight. Might he not have put something of himself in the middle of the saga?

I think it is safe to say there is nothing of him in the White Rabbit, the Caterpillar, or the Duchess, or in the March Hare, the Hatter, or the King or Queen of Hearts. We might be hearing a memory of his student days in the complaint of the Mock Turtle; but otherwise these major players are clearly the targets or vehicles of Dodgson's burlesques and satire. That leaves two principals who are presented in a distinctly different light — so different, in fact, as to suggest that what he is telling us about Alice — "this curious child was very fond of pretending to be two people" — might as easily be describing the mental habits of her creator.

The earlier and more famous of the pair turns up, like the Dodo, at an opportune moment:

> The Cat only grinned when it saw Alice. It looked good-natured, she thought: still it had *very* long claws and a great many teeth, so she felt that it ought to be treated with respect.

In the two *Alice* books the only figures ever said to be intimates of the heroine are cats. In *Wonderland* it is Dinah, the pet she left behind, and in

Through the Looking-Glass, Dinah's two kittens. This new cat in her pilgrimage she will introduce to the King of Hearts, interestingly, as "a friend of mine." It is a sentiment expressed about no other personage in the book. The Cheshire Cat appears, furthermore, as the fulfillment of a wish: "Dinah, my dear!" sighs Alice during her tumble into Wonderland, "I wish you were down here with me!" A bit later we find her dreaming "that she was walking hand in hand with Dinah." And after five chapters a cat does appear:

> "Cheshire Puss," she began, rather timidly, as she did not at all know whether it would like the name: however, it only grinned a little wider.

Dodgson had been born in the county of Cheshire and raised there to the age of ten. This was also Alice Liddell's age when he began telling her the tale. Given the nature of their private games together, might he not have brought this to her attention and a pet name come of it? Or perhaps he was here indulging in a reverie of his little friend doing him that favor. Into *The Nursery Alice* he inserted a note of special pleading: "'Cheshire Puss!' said Alice. (*Wasn't* that a pretty name for a Cat?)" The many illustrators who have portrayed the Cheshire Cat as a sinister presence have skidded off the mark, I think. The creature is unsettling, as any adult can be to a child, but it is "good-natured" withal. Dodgson must have intuited these future misreadings, for he continued to chip away at the Cat's ambiguity:

> [Y]ou may be sure she was very glad indeed, when she saw the Cheshire-Cat, perched up in a tree, over her head.
> The Cat has a very nice smile, no doubt: but just look what a lot of teeth it's got! Isn't Alice just a *little* shy of it?
> Well, yes, a *little*. But then, it couldn't help having teeth, you know: and it *could* have helped smiling, supposing it had been cross. So, on the whole, she was *glad*.

And again from *The Nursery Alice*:

> I'm nearly sure you've *never* seen a nicer Cat! Now *have* you? And *wouldn't* you like to have a Cat of your own, just like that one, with lovely green eyes, and smiling so sweetly?

Find an author giving preferential treatment to one character while all about it others are being skewered, and you may well have found a semblance of the author himself. Not incidentally, I think, the Cat appears at a crossroad in Alice's journey. Everyone knows the experience of being at once both the protagonist of a dream and a disembodied viewer aware of things that one could not know as a mere player. This is how a child makes believe with dolls or toy soldiers, acting out the parts like a ventriloquist. It is also a fair likeness of a storyteller bent over his desk. The Cat looking down on Alice from its tree, all head and no body, is just how a character in the story, if she could look up from the manuscript page, would see the person who is writing the tale: a great head floating there, perhaps grinning over his act of creation but disinterested, too, in minding that events unfold in proper sequence, with not too much being given away all at once. Think of the following, doctored passage as a conversation between this character and the omniscient author who has brought her to this crossroad:

"Would you tell me, please, which way I ought to go from here?"

"That depends a good deal on where you want to get to," said the Author.

"I don't much care where — " said the Heroine.

"Then it doesn't much matter which way you go," said the Author.

" — so long as I get *somewhere*," the Heroine added as an explanation.

"Oh, you're sure to do that," said the Author, "if you only walk long enough."

The famous grin of the Cheshire Cat is the grin of one who knows what the character cannot know — where she will be going next and what is to happen to her there. Read in light of the later plea that we have "never seen a nicer Cat," it reminds me that Dodgson was not, at first, a professional author addressing a generic audience but a young mathematics instructor with the assignment of entertaining the dean's daughter. It had been his habit for years to amuse little friends like Alice Liddell with riddles, magic tricks, nonsense, and linguistic and logical conundrums that had piqued his own interest. Not infrequently, these games were played, by formal invitation and with parental approval, in his rooms. Remember how in the book's opening scene Alice falls through what appears to be a gentleman's study, a Wind-in-the-Willowsy place of cupboards, maps, and marmalade. Could her fall not be read as a passage through the rooms of the bachelor don who is creating this fantasy? At their far end she weeps herself a sea of tears, and out of it who should step but Uncle Charles[10] himself as the kindly Dodo. It is not hard to imagine the many times he must have sat her down at his desk with a puzzle to solve, discretely disappearing into another room and then, a moment later, popping back to see how she was faring with his wonderland of games on paper. Popping back to look in on a guest describes the situation exactly as the Cat makes its promised reappearance at the Queen of Hearts's croquet match. Alice has been set the conundrum of threading the wickets with a wayward hedgehog for a ball and a flaccid flamingo for a mallet. Displeasing the Queen with her play could mean the loss of her head. This is the most discomforting and, after the Pool of Tears, the most dream-like episode in the book. And it is just now, as Alice "was looking about for some way of escape," that she "noticed a curious appearance in the air. . . .

"It's the Cheshire Cat: now I shall have somebody to talk to."

"How are you getting on?" said the Cat. . . . "

Cracking conundrums was a pastime Alice Liddell and Cheshire Puss likely shared often as guest and host, pupil and tutor. The welcome reprieve of "How are you getting on?" — accompanied in real life perhaps by the arrival of tea—would have cued her that, here in Wonderland, the Cat checking on her namesake's progress was really her dear friend, Uncle Charles. Even a game can seem like an examination to a child when it is a game set up by an adult, and Dodgson well knew that there is nothing to ease a moment of panic like the sight of a familiar face.

A disembodied cat is an odd choice for conducting the business of a friendship, even so. Dodgson created the character on his second tour through the story, along with the Duchess, the Mad Tea Party, several of the satirical verses, and the trial of the Knave of Hearts. With the Cat, a newly astringent quality has been introduced into Wonderland. The solicitous voice of Uncle Charles can be heard, but speaking now from an ironic perch above the action, there to be recognized as a reassuring presence, no doubt, but one exempted from having to deliver the consolations of an older friend. *Wonderland*'s most famous speech, "We're all mad here," is delivered by the Cat with unnerving composure. In *The Nursery Alice*, Dodgson will eliminate it entirely; the Cat will direct Alice to the March Hare and the Hatter with the simple remark "They're both mad," as if this were something funny to look forward to. Missing is the dark insinuation that is also nowhere to be found in the private version of the tale:

> "But I don't want to go among mad people," Alice remarked.
> "Oh, you can't help that," said the Cat: "We're all mad here. I'm mad. You're mad."
> "How do you know I'm mad?" said Alice.
> "You must be," said the Cat, "or you wouldn't have come here."

She hasn't come, of course: Cheshire Puss has brought her. *Wonderland*, the public version, is mad both as a place of anger and as a place of madness, the one following inexorably behind the other. As Alice reflects in "Pig and Pepper," "It's really dreadful . . . the way all the creatures argue. It's enough to drive one crazy!" This, and not the "bubbling laughter" promised us by Woollcott and others, is the true temper of the book. It is a hot summer's day. Everyone is feeling anxious, flustered, cranky, violent. The White Rabbit hurries by, fretting, "Oh! the Duchess, the Duchess! Oh! *Won't* she be savage if I've kept her waiting!" The Mouse in the Pool of Tears is jumpy and bilious. Its companions are said to be cross, the Lory sulky, and a little crab sasses her mother. Alice is provoked into wishing Dinah were there to put an end to the pettish Mouse. In the White Rabbit's house she kicks Bill the lizard up the chimney. With the rude Caterpillar she is first a little irritated, then angry. A pigeon, mistaking her for a serpent, attacks her hysterically, then turns contemptuous and sulky, like Alice's sister the Lory. Saucepans and dishes fly in the house of the Duchess, and finally a baby is airborne as well. Alice reacts to the derision of the Hatter and the March Hare with growing indignation, then stalks off in disgust. In this combative mood she is ready to challenge the rages of the Red Queen. The book ends with the final revolt against this mad/mad crowd by a child who is said to be, or once to have been, timid, polite, humble, patient, and soothing.

Little of this appears in *Alice's Adventures Under Ground* and none of it in *The Nursery Alice*. The world in the middle that the Cat surveys is a madhouse indeed. To account for it, we must, I think, imagine Dodgson in a peculiarly choleric humor. As the Cat he is Alice's friend, but a friend who has brought her among mad people. He sympathizes with her tears and means to show her the way home in the end, but there is no getting around his having done her a large unkindness. By dropping her down a hole he has enlisted her into that same darkness where (I am supposing) he had found himself when a future in holy orders prompted the question "Who in the world am I?" The heady mixture of hostility and comedy in *Wonderland* bespeaks a mood that must have been both mordant and giddy; I assume that what turned the shy don giddy enough to work the trick was the realization that his little fairy tale supplied the perfect vehicle for sorting out his answers. He would say who he was by declaring who he was not. It would be a satire, and into it would go everyone who stood in the way of a happy ending for the Reverend Charles Dodgson.

He seems to have known himself quite well as a social animal, and where his talents lay. Measure his good work against the bad: everything he wrote testifies that as an artist his best self was adversarial. He was a master of make-believe only when at odds with some person or idea and on the attack with parody and burlesque. Aggravation was the yeast that raised his imagination to the level found in *Wonderland*. Deprived of an opponent, he simply collapsed into occasional verse and baby talk. The *Alice* in the middle is no make-believe for the nursery but a debator's rebuttal, the midnight thoughts of a running argument.

As to who his chosen adversaries might have been, there are any number of ready candidates. Two events of the day recommend themselves immediately. The first was the publication of Kingsley's *The Water Babies* at the very moment Dodgson sat down to write *Alice*. The second, more or less coincidental with it, was the auto-da-fé conducted by Mrs. Liddell with all of his letters to her daughter. These two affronts, I believe, not only permeate *Wonderland*, but also informed his decision to pull the book to pieces two and half decades later and to rephrase it completely as *The Nursery Alice*. The reason for this penultimate act of his career, it has been suggested, was the convenience of having in pocket a story toy for amusing tiny children met on trains. Or could it be that his stated purpose, "to be read by Children aged from Nought to Five," was a pretext for something he felt bound to do for other reasons? Revision this drastic suggests a more personal motive. *The Nursery Alice* is so radical a departure from its parent story, in fact, that it is hard not to think that Dodgson's intent was to have on record an *Alice* other than the *Alice* for which he was being celebrated. How else but as a repudiation of the earlier work can we explain his reverting to the rhetoric of the didacts and the sentimentality of the inspirational writers he had once so adroitly savaged? How else to account for the narrative pretense that *Alice* is more Tenniel's book than his own and that, like the projectionist at a magic-lantern show, his only role is very sweetly to explain the pictures?

In reality, *The Nursery Alice* is only the final sugarcoating in a process of revision that can be traced all the way back to the lyrical preface to *Wonderland*, "All in the golden afternoon." Here he characterized the adventure as the happy tale of a child

> . . . moving through a land
> Of wonders wild and new,
> In friendly chat with bird or beast —

I suppose we might read this reverie as the deacon's rethinking of what Lewis Carroll has wrought. And what he thinks — or, rather, what he feels — about his fantasy is itself a fantasy. "In friendly chat" is a description of some wholly other book than the one he has written.

In 1876 the sugarcoating came on a salver. Dodgson ordered his publisher to insert into copies of his nihilistic comedy *The Hunting of the Snark* a curious pamphlet that he hoped would establish the new work as being, against all instinct, a children's book. This pamphlet, which would be included with subsequent editions of all Dodgson's books for children, is "An Easter Greeting to Every Child Who Loves 'Alice.'" Beginning "My Dear Child," it rhapsodizes about God and about being awakened from ugly dreams by "a Mother's sweet voice." In the middle of the epistle there appears an apologia for *Alice* that seems at first merely a flourish of false modesty:

> And if I have written anything to add to those stores of innocent and healthy amusement that are laid up in books for the children I love so well, it is surely something I may hope to look back upon without shame and sorrow (as how much of life must then be recalled!) when *my* turn comes to walk through the valley of shadows.

Calling *Wonderland* an innocent and healthy amusement continues the pretense of "friendly chat" from a decade earlier. The intriguing thing here is how the idea of shame and sorrow has crept into the picture.

Alice betrays, in its ironies and ambiguities, the habits of a secretive mind, but I have no shabby theories to air regarding Dodgson's love of little girls. He did like to photograph them in the nude, and the models in a few of the pictures to survive are displaying their as yet nonexistent virtues in attitudes more common to the erotic arts, but these photos can probably be attributed to Dodgson's bad taste rather than to any bad habit. In arranging the girls this provocatively, I suspect he was only borrowing stock poses from that world of kitsch portraiture he so doted on. He portrayed himself truly, I think, when he cast himself as a White Knight in *Through the Looking-Glass*. A chivalrous tutor, he seems to have been quite incapable of making an improper gesture toward a child. He and his girls were each other's muses, and the terms of the exchange were children's games and perhaps a sentimentalized spirituality.

Still, the allusion to shame and sorrow in "An Easter Greeting" cannot have been a mere accident of his valedictory rhetoric. And to find him consummating in *The Nursery Alice* this old delusion of his about the true nature of the story only reinforces my suspicion that in rewriting everything about the book, he meant, at some level of awareness, to correct a perception about himself that he felt was being conveyed by *Wonderland*. We can see a glimpse of this in his special pleading for the Cheshire Cat, for example. And now here in 1876 and again in 1888, when "An Easter Greeting" was appended to *The Nursery Alice*, we find Dodgson thinking aloud in public about his mortality and his reputation. What else could the author of the most famous children's book in Christendom be amending with all these deletions and sentimental glosses but the animus of *Wonderland* and his responsibility for it? Those occasions of ill will that could not easily be elided he couched in painful apologies and explanations — carefully distancing the Duchess, for example, as "a very cross old lady." And all that business about chopping off heads? "Oh, that was only a joke."

It was a joke he was at some pains to deny ever having made, however. Vanishing behind a smokescreen of revisionism, the author, like his Caterpillar, metamorphosed into a prettier creature altogether. He vanished in order to forget that the jokes in this roman à clef had served to sustain a bout of rancor directed against the two people who were nettling him the most at the time, Charles Kingsley and Mrs. Liddell. Jousting with this pair had been his way of answering the question "Who in the world am I?" He was not who they were, say the parodies and burlesques of *Wonderland*. He was not a citizen at home in the assurances such people represented, not religiously, not socially, not artistically, not temperamentally. He was the Cheshire Cat — detached, aloof, free to come and go, to look and say, to name the mad. He was so, at least, until the day when, to renounce the shame of an ugly dream, the stubborn part of himself backed down from its lofty perch and tried to become one with them after all.

The Blessing

It would be an exaggeration to say that if there had been no *Water Babies* there would be no *Alice*, but I do think that without Kingsley's book to knock about, *Wonderland* might well have remained arrested in its earlier form as *Alice's Adventures Under Ground* and be known to us only as a Victorian curiosity now and then resurrected in small-press editions. I am not the first writer to note Kingsley's shadow on *Alice* — the literature is sprinkled with asides that *The Water Babies* "may have been" an influence or that the resemblances "are by no means superficial" — but I am unaware of anyone ever making much of it. Yet the similarities between the two books are unmistakable. Here, with the telltale names removed, are some roughly comparable passages from the two Reverends Charles; only a reader very well versed in one author or the other, I think, would be able to identify which passage belongs to whom:

"Nonsense; your elephant is contrary to nature."

All this time the Guard was looking at ———, first through a telescope, then through a microscope, and then through an opera-glass. At last he said "You're traveling the wrong way," and shut up the window, and went away.

"Can you tell me the name of a place that nobody ever heard of, where nothing ever happened, in a country which has not been discovered yet?"

Nothing is to be depended upon but the great hippopotamus test.

Any gentleman who has been confined during Her Majesty's pleasure may be unconfined during his own pleasure, and take a walk in the neighboring park to improve his spirits, after an hour's light and wholesome labor with his dinner-fork. . . .

"Now, *here*, you see, it takes all the running *you* can do, to keep in the same place. If you want to get somewhere else, you must run at least twice as fast as that."

always at lessons, working, working, working. . . .

"I think I'll go down the other way," said ——— after a pause; "and perhaps I may visit the elephant later on."

"You musn't go west, I tell you; it is destruction to go west."

"But I am not going west, as you may see," said ———.

And another, "The east lies here, my dear; I assure you this is the east."

"But I don't want to go east," said ———.

"Well, then, at all events, whichever way you are going, you are going wrong," cried they all with one voice.

"I see nobody on the road," said ———.

"I only wish *I* had such eyes," the ——— remarked in a fretful tone. "To be able to see Nobody! And at that distance too!"

"He said he *would* come in," ——— went on, "because he was looking for a hippopotamus. Now, as it happened, there wasn't such a thing in the house, that morning."

"That's what you call a History of England, that is. Now, take a good look at me! I'm one that has spoken to a King, I am: mayhap you'll never see such another: and, to show you I'm not proud, you may shake hands with me!"

"How long would it take a school-inspector of average activity to tumble head over heels from London to York?"

"That's enough about lessons," ——— interrupted in a very decided tone.

The passages from *The Water Babies* will be found shoelacing down the page from the upper left and ending with "working, working, working."

Analogous excerpts from *Wonderland* proving too recognizable for the purpose of this little exercise (save for the last, which is spoken by the Gryphon), I have substituted passages from *Through the Looking-Glass*, where I feel a strong echo from Kingsley can still be heard. The proper match to Kingsley's gentleman confined during Her Majesty's pleasure, of course, would be the Knave of Hearts, awaiting trial for stealing the Queen's tarts; and against Kingsley's "whichever way you are going, you are going wrong," the reader might check the Cheshire Cat's advice to Alice on *her* next move, "Then it doesn't much matter which way you go." A comparison of *The Water Babies* with *Looking-Glass* is recommended as well by the passage following Mother Carey's advice to Tom to "go the whole way backward," which I cited earlier as the way I intended to go myself through this maze:

> "Backward!" cried Tom. "Then I shall not be able to see my way."
> "On the contrary, if you look forward, you will not see a step before you, and be certain to go wrong; but, if you look behind you, and watch carefully whatever you have passed . . . then you will know what is coming next, as plainly as if you saw it in a looking-glass."
> Tom was very much astonished: but he obeyed her. . . .

In the chapter, "Wool and Water" in Dodgson's own *Looking-Glass*, we find the White Queen explaining to Alice how "living backwards . . . always makes one a little giddy at first." The news draws this response: "'Living backwards!' Alice repeated in great astonishment. 'I never heard of such a thing!'"

Other traces of Kingsley can be found in *Looking-Glass* (of these more later), but it is with *Wonderland* that the likenesses chiefly obtain, and I submit that major portions of that book are what they are and sound as they do because they arose in Dodgson's mind as the answers in a debate between this new children's book he was reading and the question of how he was to go about composing his own. Scene after scene in *Wonderland* imply that he built up his tale by consulting Kingsley's story and that he fell into his own way of saying a scene by muttering to himself as he read along, "Not that way, you old bore, *this* way!" Or, as he would have Alice put it, "Keep back, please! We don't want you with us!"

A claim that *Alice* reads the way it does largely because Dodgson was goaded in that direction by someone else's book is not going to sit well, I realize, with those who are committed to the myth of the story's origin, and they do have various remarks by Dodgson to support them. I repeat, however, that his recollection of what happened on that "golden afternoon" in July 1862 (on which day it rained, the record shows) can be credited only against the first telling of the tale and does little to account for the second, more rancorous version, for which another, and rather different, explanation is wanted. The accounting Dodgson did finally give for his later efforts has been taken without a misgiving as evidence in support of the reigning myth:

Alice and the *Looking-Glass* are made up almost wholly of bits and scraps, single ideas which came of themselves. In writing it [*Alice's Adventures Under Ground*] out, I added many fresh ideas, which seemed to grow of themselves upon the original stock; and many more were added when, years afterwards, I wrote it all over again for publication; but (this may interest some readers of *Alice* to know) every such idea and nearly every word of the dialogue *came of itself*. Sometimes an idea comes at night, when I have had to get up and strike a light to note it down — sometimes when out on a lonely winter walk, when I have had to stop, and with half-frozen fingers jot down a few words which should keep the new-born idea from perishing — but whenever or however it comes, *it comes of itself.* [11]

Other readers have noted the insistent tone of this romantic self-portrait. As Roger Sale has observed, "The point was apparently so important for Lewis Carroll that he had to say it four times in one paragraph and italicize twice as well." [12] On a first reading, I might take Dodgson's claim at face value; on a second, not. Sale does so because he is committed to the argument that Dodgson's improvisational narration led to the book's failure to cohere structurally. This is true, and the passage supports it; Dodgson's insistence that everything "came of itself" has a nervous edge to it, however, and it strikes me as the edginess of the man who proverbially protests too much. His testament here really seems to be answering, or anticipating, a charge that in adding to his "original stock" he may have borrowed from someone else's work. In fact, one such charge was made in his lifetime, in behalf of a fantasy entitled *From Nowhere to the North Pole*. It was an easily dismissed charge, since Tom Hood's book had been published nine years after *Wonderland* (and if anything owed debts to Kingsley and the fantasist George MacDonald), but the fact that it had been made at all may have put Dodgson on his guard that other charges could be forthcoming. His apparent attempt to head off these phantom accusers appeared in "Alice on the Stage," a piece written for *The Theatre* in April 1887, and again in *The Lewis Carroll Picture Book* in 1899, the year following his death. It has since become a cornerstone in support of the legend of the little boat and what came after. Dodgson biographer Derek Hudson, for example, in allowing that *The Water Babies* "may have influenced *Alice*," [13] thinks nothing need be made of it because Dodgson is on record that his ideas all "came of themselves." Martin Gardner used the passage to introduce *The Annotated Alice* in 1960, and in the same year Roger Lancelyn Green made much of it in his *Lewis Carroll*. Green's acceptance of it is much the most interesting, for he uses the testament to make a stunning claim for Dodgson: "It must not be thought that either of the *Alice* books is derivative; they are both original with the absolute originality of sheer genius." [14]

Green sounds even more certain of having found God in the person of a children's author in his biography of C. S. Lewis, for whose *Chronicles of Narnia* he paradoxically avers himself to have been an inspiration, but his brief for Dodgson is no less fervent:

> Those who have told impromptu stories to children know how easy and natural it is to weave such fantasies as Dodgson wove . . . only our stories are but clay models, and into his the genius of "Lewis Carroll" breathed the breath of life. . . . We, like all subsequent writers, are under his influence. [15]

The Reverend Charles Dodgson had need to believe in his own absolute genius, clearly, but I think the blasphemy implicit in Green's metaphor might have appalled him nonetheless. Creativity to a Christian, at least to a Christian as pious as Dodgson, is ordinarily understood to be a gift the recipient of which is in no way entitled to strut about as a solipsistic wonder (as Hans Christian Andersen did with "my gift to the world"). To Green's understanding, our own poor tales are a child's toys imitating God's work, but the deacon's epic is the Platonic Ideal itself. Through his genius, "Lewis Carroll," Dodgson has sniffed out the route back into Eden and taken a bite from the Tree of Life, that "ye shall be as gods." He is as Jehovah Himself, breathing the breath of life into the inert clay. (Andersen only wished to be High Priest.)

To what extent Green might believe this I cannot presume to say. In a culture that has become a sitz bath of fatuous rhetoric it might be only that. Nor do I mean to slight the ideas of individuality and originality here. Nearly every book in this study displays a heightened and potent idiosyncrasy of voice and invention, and of course there is, as in any endeavor, a great range in degree of talent and vision. But "the absolute originality of sheer genius" is leftovers from the table of the Romantics. "Absolute" necessarily means creating from nothing, and this has yet to happen in human history and never will. The Poetic Genius is the myth of those who have done with God and wish to raise up Man in His place.

"The revolutionary nature of 'Lewis Carroll's' achievement cannot be exaggerated," Green continues. Alice "danced joyously into Wonderland," made good sport of "joking with the Duchess," and "came home to her Victorian nursery without a spot on her character — or a suspicion of having learned anything more serious than the rules of a Caucus Race or the way to cut Looking-Glass cake." As a case of special pleading this is incomparable. And in refusing to read the book in hand, preferring to see in it only Woollcott's "gay tapestry," Green of course has no reason to regard *The Water Babies* as anything but a clammy ground fog to be burned off by Dodgson's "dawn of levity." He writes, "To see how utterly different this was from all that had gone before one has but to read *The Water Babies*, an absolute orgy of self-conscious didacticism. . . . "

He goes on to cite the redoubtable Harvey Darton that *Alice* marked the advent of "liberty of thought in children's books" and that henceforth "there was to be in hours of pleasure no more dread about the moral value . . . of the pleasure itself." Darton, so right about most books, has missed the mark here, I think, for *Alice* is a children's book in which dread and pleasure are more often than not synonyms for the same experience. "*The Water Babies* is a very find period piece, almost, indeed, a museum piece,"

Darton continues, but "the *Alices* will never be put in a museum, because they will neither die nor grow out of fashion."[17] Darton published this prophecy in 1932. Four years earlier Herbert Read had offered the more prescient opinion that "*Alice* has a suppressed background of culture which a true fairy tale never has. *Alice* will always delight our particular civilization; it will hardly become a part of our traditional folk-lore, like 'The Three Bears.'"[18] Read's "particular civilization" pretty much went up with the smoke of World War II, and with it went, very possibly to our detriment, a more innocent way of reading tales. However, for those still willing to take Dodgson's "it came of itself" at face value, it should be noted that in 1889, two years after staking out his claim to absolute originality, he prefaced his last work, *Sylvie and Bruno*, with a rather different version of Alice's beginnings:

> I do not know if 'Alice in Wonderland' was an *original* story—I was, at least, no *conscious* imitator in writing it. . . . [19]

Imitation is not the charge here, let me say. Custodians of the myth, beginning with Dodgson himself, have confused imitation with influence, provocation, material. To those who believe in absolute genius, the hint of plagiarism that goes by the name of imitation is the final, unforgivable sin. Rather than ask how one creates, from what materials, they prefer to imagine their heroes emerging *ex nihilo*, bearing great gifts.

Dodgson's *ex nihilo* was simply this:

> . . . random flashes of thought . . . suggested by the book one was reading. . . . [20]

It seems an easy enough thing to admit. For authors, assimilating, arguing, and inventing as they read is a standard operating procedure. It hardly warrants comment—unless, that is, one has some abiding interest in denying it.

Why the deacon chose to make his veiled confession at this particular moment, in what he hoped would be his greatest work, is something I want to look at shortly; in the meantime, the reader might think of it as a passing fancy, for he soon reneged on the confession and returned to insisting that his half-frozen fingers had plucked *Alice* from the air on lonely winter walks. His need to distance himself from his older brother in Christ, the Reverend Kingsley, far outweighed, I think, his instinct to tell the whole story. Kingsley was the key to an ill humor in *Wonderland* that Dodgson had been at pains to deny ever since his decision to indoctrinate newly arriving readers with the pretty pretense of "All in the golden afternoon."

When he finally did acknowledge those "random flashes of thought suggested by the book one was reading," he had been considering Kingsley, the man and his works, for some thirty-five years. In keeping with his other eccentricities, the oddly isochronal first entries on Kingsley that appear in Dodgson's diary for 1856 and 1857 suggest something beyond coincidence:

that here was a young man already so compulsively mindful of his reading habits that he would, from one year to the next, arrange a symmetry to his days for reading and reporting on certain authors.

On the third of January 1856, he noted of Kingsley's first novel, "Went on with *Alton Locke*, a powerful and grandly written book."

On the seventh of January: "Finished *Alton Locke*. . . . I wish he would propose some more definite remedy . . . it might stir up many fellow-workers in the same good field of social improvement. Oh that God, in His good providence, may make me hereafter such a worker! But, alas, what are the means? Each has his own nostrum to propound, and in the Babel of voices nothing is done."

On the third of January 1857: "Began reading Kingsley's *Hypatia*."

And on the seventh: "Finished *Hypatia*: it is powerful, like all that Kingsley writes — outrageous to taste in some parts."[21]

Some five and a half years before *Alice*, Kingsley appears in the diaries as a figure to be reckoned with. They are never to meet, and Kingsley will remain an unwitting player in the scenario, but these two clergymen, each the stammering son of a clergyman, are about to cross paths. Their point of intersection will be the world of children's books. Almost simultaneously both men will decide to write something never written before: a fantasy for children in which a central narrative tool will be the trope of nonsense.

Kingsley's route to the crossroads was the less likely of the two, as little in his life immediately suggests that this sort of tale was in the making. His childhood predicts the writer, but the Muscular Christian known to Victorian England surprised many when he brought forth a fairy tale. Growing up a solitary, self-conscious dreamer, he was yet full of precocious bravado, closing a letter at the age of seven, "I have more letters of consequence to write and here I must pause," and another, "Adieu! my dear Mrs. Knowles!"[22] Clearly, there would be no holding the boy back. England awaited. When he concluded *The Water Babies* with the thought "Thank God that you have plenty of cold water to wash in; and wash in it too, like a true Englishman," he meant to be funny, but he also meant you to do it, for God and Queen. His own life was an act of the will. He had been touched by death early, losing a sister at five and a brother at fifteen, and had come to terms with it at the age of twelve when within his view the racing fires of the Bristol riots overtook a mob lapping spirits from the gutter and turned it instantly into a row of blackened corpses. "It is good for a man," he wrote of the experience, "to be brought once at least in his life, face to face with fact, ultimate fact, however horrible it may be; and have to confess to himself, shuddering, what things are possible upon God's earth, when man has forgotten that his only welfare is in living after the likeness of God."[23]

As a youth he had scorned religious orthodoxy but saw nothing more worth the use of a life than to be a shepherd of the church. Pessimistic and prone to nervous collapse, he exercised his thoughts with the vigor of a reformer. A stammerer, he became an orator. His prejudices he tempered with ironic humor; his feverishly erotic imagination, with Christian chivalry and cold water. Through an act of the will, he wed his contradictions. A talent for addressing the human condition made him one of the celebrated speakers and authors of the day. When he died in 1875, he left a collected works of nineteen volumes — novels, natural histories, verse, children's books, lectures, sermons. It is all robust stuff, of the sort from which Classics Comics once were made: *Westward Ho!* (1855), *The Heroes* (1856), *Hereward the Wake* (1866). Though hanging by a thread spiritually and emotionally himself from time to time, he unfalteringly advised men to obey God, to be strong, to know nature, to esteem the wisdom of women, and to abjure vanity. As a man who turned sickliness into the big stick of a charismatic personality, he reminds me, not too improbably, of Teddy Roosevelt. The next Kingsley in Victorian England will be an agnostic, Rudyard Kipling.

During the years that Dodgson was putting students to sleep with his lectures at Oxford, Kingsley was drawing applause at Cambridge as Regius Professor of Modern History. Lean, square-jawed, chaplain to Queen Victoria, and five times a father, Kingsley was the very model of the Muscular Christian so desired in those days of dwindling congregations, and arguably the preeminent Protestant cleric of Victorian Britain. Dodgson by contrast was reclusive, eccentric, diffident about his calling, a stuffy Tory. In public achievements he was barely a dilettante. In other ways, though, he almost seems a Kingsley before Kingsley became Kingsley. I have wondered in the course of studying these two men if Dodgson might ever have seen a likeness of his famous counterpart — a photograph or frontis portrait, perhaps. Both men were handsome, but in diametrically opposite ways. Kingsley had the craggy look of an eagle; Dodgson's face, in all the photographs that have survived, of whatever age, is contemplative, sadly becalmed, with an unweathered, prepubescent softness. Put their portraits side by side and you might suppose them each the author of the other's book — Dodgson the dreamer of water babies and fairy faculty, Kingsley the brooding philosopher with the sharp tongue.

What becalmed the man and drove his wit inward behind the mask, there to busily translate discontents into humor? His career at the Rugby School has been suggested, and, his childhood having been untroubled as far as we know, this seems plausible enough. A stammerer and a muff at sports, Dodgson cannot have enjoyed these three years much. He later wrote, "I cannot say that I look back upon my life at a Public School with any sensations of pleasure, or that any earthly considerations would induce me to go through my three years again."[24] Whatever, or whenever, the exact cause (he lost his mother soon after matriculating at Oxford, but this event is unfortunately lacking in documentation), he seems to have suffered a rude awakening as an adolescent and begun shutting himself up, as Alice would later do, like a telescope, to become the punctilious, guarded adult of the photographs. Behind him lay a home life that must have seemed a paradise in comparison to what followed. The oldest boy in a brood of eleven, he had been the family wit and the leader of the games. His seven sisters adored him. The impact of these early years of being encouraged and cosseted by seven appreciative girls, I think, cannot be underestimated. If the key to his decades-long search for little playmates lies anywhere, it must lie in his effort somehow to replicate the happiness he gained from entertaining his sisters. Heaven for this Christian virgin would be a room full of entranced maidens.

Even in middle age, he could be found playing the wallflower, thinking his thoughts. Following an introduction at a gathering in 1879, Mark Twain remarked that next to Joel Chandler Harris, Dodgson was "the stillest and shyest full-grown man" he had ever met.[25] Derek Hudson's assessment that "Dodgson will never be a leader in that crusade of Kingsley's" is an understatement. The treed Tory, the stammering Rugby boy who climbed down too early from heaven, Dodgson had learned not to display his Cheshire grin for just anybody.

Before 1862 the imposing Kingsley had aroused only a disinterested admiration in Dodgson. In the years following, when the two men inadvertently became competitors for the favors of children and queens, all that changed. It changed because at the very moment Dodgson set out to claim a small territory in storytelling as his own — and set out in some desperation, as he noted — he found that a man he had been reading for years, a man "powerful" and "outrageous to taste" had just beaten him to it. Although with just the one book Dodgson will declare himself the better artist, he can hardly have seen himself as such when writing *Wonderland*. Kingsley is the literary lion, and he the novice. Pious to a fault, he has been diffident about taking holy orders; the irreverent Kingsley has, with seemingly effortless bravado, become a famous cleric. Dodgson teaches in a subject he loves but can hardly keep his students awake; Kingsley is a popular professor in a field he does not even know. Dodgson at thirty is "Nobody on the road" — seen by children, invisible to kings. Kingsley, now forty-three, has laid his own roads and arrived safely wherever he would go. Once in a world of his own making, he will appear confident, even insouciant as the Cheshire Cat; but now, in the real world, Kingsley's world, he must have felt more of a fretful White Rabbit. I do not see how he could have viewed Kingsley in 1862 and 1863 without envy and the sudden appearance of *The Water Babies* without dismay.

I realize there are some readers who will be disinclined to allow such an understanding of *Alice*. They will naturally invoke Dodgson's diaries as proof that there is nothing to it, for the diaries make no mention of *The Water Babies*. The absence of this of all books from the private records of a man who has made a habit of reading Kingsley is, of course, quite as conspicuous as any presence could be. Then, too, the diaries are a notoriously unreliable index to Dodgson's life. Annual volumes have vanished, pages have been torn from others, and events are nowhere reported that are known to have happened but would reflect badly on their hero. Kingsley is missing, but so is Edward Lear; and this is odd because, in addition to their all being contemporary writers of nonsense for children, Lear and Dodgson shared, for a time, the acquaintance of the laureate Alfred, Lord Tennyson. Missing information has caused much minor mischief in the literature on *Alice*. One historian felt encouraged to assert, for example, that Alice Liddell's father and Dodgson's superior at Oxford, Dean Liddell, was actually Dodgson's close friend. In fact, their relations were formal, they hardly ever conversed, and in their fallings-out over college matters they probably felt like choking each other to death.

In conjecturing how Dodgson might have felt about the author of *The Water Babies*, we should remember, too, that the deacon was a snob and not without a snob's ambitions. The unmentioned Lear had been Victoria's drawing master; Kingsley was now the queen's chaplain. When Dodgson finally wrote his near-confession about the book he had been reading when he composed *Alice*, the man thirteen years his senior had been dead the same span, his public reputation fading at last from that high standing we see reflected in the entry for January 23, 1875, that the queen made in her own journal:

> Poor Canon Kingsley, who has been alarmingly ill for the last three or four weeks, died to-day, and is a sad loss! His wife was very ill at the same time, and neither could go to the other, which was dreadfully sad, and terrible for the two daughters. He was full of genius and energy, noble and warm-hearted, devoted, loyal and chivalrous, much attached to me and mine, full of enthusiasm, and most kind and good to the poor.[27]

Dodgson made much of queens. There are the Queen of Hearts in *Wonderland* and the Red and White Queens in *Looking-Glass*, and that book's final coronation of Alice herself. He had hoped for Victoria's good opinion of *Alice*, awaited the summons to court, which never came, and kept up a pretense with his girl friends that he and the queen were corresponding. And when in 1864 he had the manuscript of *Alice* in hand, to whom did he take it but the queen's chaplain's publisher, and whom did he want for his illustrator? Not Tenniel but the same artist, Sir Noel Paton, who had provided the elegant frontispiece to the queen's chaplain's book.

Now, of course, little of this would make sense — indeed, it would all be a rank impertinence — if it did not follow from a reading of these two contemporary books by the Reverends Charles. I have pursued this line of speculation confident that the evidence is there that much of *Alice* is a running argument with Kingsley over how one goes about telling a children's story. In concentrating on Kingsley I do not mean to ignore sources that have been identified by other writers. These are matters of record and need little reiterating here. Most are singular borrowings. The very funny verse "You are old, father William," for example, is a parody of Robert

Southey's aphoristic bore, *The Old Man's Comforts and How He Gained Them.* "How doth the little crocodile" spoofs Isaac Watts's "How doth the little busy bee," and for "Twinkle, twinkle, little bat!" Dodgson helped himself to Jane Taylor's inspirational "Twinkle, twinkle, little star," mentioned in Chapter 1 of this study. These are the more obvious sources, the models Dodgson used for his skits and burlesques. Kingsley's influence is beaten into the whole, as it were. Before trying to find him, however, I want to mention one other writer who has not been cited much in the literature.

The reader will have noticed that the two *Alices* contain a number of scenes that are neither satire nor nonsense but something indefinably other, something never meant to be funny. When Alice has done reading the poem "Jabberwocky" in the looking-glass book she has found, this is how she goes downstairs and out of the looking-glass house:

> She just kept the tips of her fingers on the hand-rail, and floated gently down without even touching the stairs with her feet: then she floated on through the hall, and would have gone straight out at the door in the same way, if she hadn't caught hold of the door-post.

There is the mystifying episode in the railcar when the Guard tells Alice she is traveling the wrong way, and the even longer enigma "Wool and Water," in which the White Queen turns into a sheep clerking in a shop, the shop dissolves into a stream, Alice and the sheep row away in a boat, the boat and stream revert to being the shop, a chair sprouts branches, and the egg Alice has bought turns into Humpty Dumpty. Ostensibly, Dodgson has organized *Looking-Glass* according to the symmetries of the mirror and the chessboard. Nothing in this chapter is beholden to either scheme: "[T]he 'thing' went through the ceiling as quietly as possible, as if it were quite used to it."

The second chapter of *Wonderland* presents a more focused dreamscape of the same order when Alice, swimming in a sea of her own tears, is suddenly joined by the cast from Aesop's fables, four of whom are her own two sisters and the Reverends Dodgson and Duckworth. Whatever is going on here, it is not strictly nonsense. Nor do I believe that these scenes are hiding any philosophical secrets. If they must have a name, call them phantasmagorical transformations. They have been rendered rather faithfully, I think, after the unique manner of Dodgson's fellow clergyman, the writer George MacDonald. In 1858 MacDonald had published a fantasy for adults called *Phantastes* in which he created a fairyland to explore just such dream transformations as we find in *Alice.* In the following year the two men found that they were both given to the same "ridicule of smug formalism and copy-book maxims"[28] and struck up a friendship. MacDonald's daughters soon numbered among Dodgson's correspondents. (The kitten Snowdrop in *Looking-Glass* is named after one of Mary MacDonald's pets.) In 1863, when the deacon had his own fairy tale in hand, it was to MacDonald that he sent *Alice's Adventures Under Ground* for a first opinion, and in all probability it was MacDonald's encouragement that set him to thinking of a larger tale.

Despite their shared fondness for puncturing stale pieties, however, the two men were on very different journeys. In his imagination MacDonald was not of this world, whereas Dodgson seems unworldly only in photographs. The fantasy he devised is very much of this world, MacDonald's influence notwithstanding. In *Wonderland* we hear no echo of an ally's spiritual dreams, only an outcry provoked by an adversary's earthly oratory.

One small impediment needs to be removed before we look at those passages in *The Water Babies* with a corresponding echo in *Wonderland*. This is the claim that Kingsley's story was not available to Dodgson until he had already done the important work on his own tale. Thus we have Derek Hudson's unexamined assurance "[H]e can only have read the book when his own was far advanced"[29] and the obscuring fairy dust of Roger Lancelyn Green's assertion "It is unsafe to attempt to get nearer to Dodgson's sources of inspiration. There seems to be no doubt that he made up the stories on the spur of the moment. . . . "[30]

The least confusing way of refuting these claims is with a simple calendar of events. Unless otherwise noted, the following quotations are from Dodgson's diaries:

July 4, 1862	"in a desperate attempt to strike out some new line of fairy-lore" and "without the least idea of what was to happen next" Dodgson tells a story. Content unknown. Date disputable. Only on February 10 of the following year did he identify this as having been the day.
August 6	"had to go on with my interminable fairy-tale."[31]
August	*Macmillan's Magazine* begins serialization of *The Water Babies*.
November 13	"MS copy begun." This and the note following were jotted together in the margin of the diary, as if recalled together at a later date.
February 1863	"Text finished before Feb. 10, 1863." Again, contents unknown. Martin Gardner: "This first manuscript . . . was probably destroyed by Carroll in 1864 when he prepared a more elaborate hand-printed copy. . . . [I]t seems likely that this second manuscript differed in many respects from the first."[32]
March	Concluding episode of *The Water Babies* in *Macmillan's Magazine*.
May	*The Water Babies* published.
May 9	MacDonald encourages Dodgson to publish *Under Ground* and advises on changes. Presumably this is the

	earliest date on which Dodgson could have begun the expanded version.
April 1864	Tenniel agrees to illustrate the book after reading the text — "or parts of it," Hudson states, "though one must assume it was virtually complete by now."[33]
November 26	Dodgson sends the gift copy of *Under Ground* to Alice Liddell. This is the earliest text of her story to have survived, and the only autograph copy of any version known to exist. The printer's copy of *Wonderland* has never been discovered.
May 1865	Dodgson receives the finished book *Alice's Adventures in Wonderland* from Macmillan.

Hudson's conclusion that "he can only have read the book when his own was far advanced" is an evasion worthy of Humpty Dumpty, for Dodgson could easily have followed the story as it appeared in serialization. Moreover, "his own" book, presumably so far advanced, can only mean the first telling of the story, and we cannot even say what was in *Alice's Adventures Under Ground* for those two years before he delivered it to Alice Liddell. This we *can* say: that much of *The Water Babies* was in print and available to Dodgson before he set pen to paper on November 13, 1862, and all of *The Water Babies* was in print before he began the expanded version in the spring of 1863.

A few of the resemblances between the two books may be coincidental; some may be generic to fairy tales. Most, I think, are not accidents. Which are which I will leave to the reader to decide.

In *The Water Babies* a ten-year-old boy descends from the real world into a world of make-believe by falling, first, down a chimney into a strange room and, second, into a stream where he drowns. In *Wonderland* a girl who in real life is ten years old descends from the real world into a world of make-believe by falling down a rabbit hole into a strange hallway where she nearly drowns in her own tears. Each has been preceded into the land of make-believe by a visitor from that world to this — the Irish Woman and the White Rabbit. Tom, now a water baby, is said to be "3.87902 inches long." Alice complains about her own shrinkage: "[T]hree inches is such a wretched height to be." She has addressed this to the Caterpillar, himself three inches long and about to be transformed into a butterfly. When Tom is identified as a thumbling, he has been speaking to a dragonfly larva also about to undergo a metamorphosis. Dodgson's Caterpillar is "in a very unpleasant state of mind" ("Who are *you*?"), and so for the moment in Kingsley's dragonfly ("Don't speak to me."). Dodgson will pick up the insect motif again in *Looking-Glass*, and again there will be a precedent in *The Water Babies*. The mayfly whom Tom meets next speaks "in the tiniest, shrillest, squeakiest little voice you ever heard." Dodgson avoids repeating Kingsley's modifiers by reproducing his Gnat's speech in tiny letters:

"'I know you are a friend,' the little voice went on: 'a dear friend, and an old friend. And you won't hurt me, though I *am* an insect.'"

The Gnat engages Alice in a civil exchange about looking-glass insects. Kingsley's mayfly is equally civil but also, in the way of all Dodgson's characters, "as bold as nine tailors." In a passage that could be transplanted into *Alice* without causing a ripple, the mayfly perches on Tom's finger, and Tom responds just as Alice reacts to everyone she meets in her two adventures, especially to the aforementioned Caterpillar:

"Much obliged to you, indeed; but I don't want it yet."

"What what?" said Tom, quite taken aback by his impudence.

"Your leg, which you are kind enough to hold out for me to sit on. I must just go and see after my wife for a few minutes. Dear me! what a troublesome business a family is!" (though the idle little rogue did nothing at all, but left his poor wife to lay all the eggs by herself). "When I come back, I shall be glad of it, if you'll be so good as to keep it sticking out just so;" and off he flew.

Tom thought him a very cool sort of personage; and still more so, when, in five minutes he came back, and said — "Ah, you were tired waiting? Well, your other leg will do as well."

And he popped himself down on Tom's knee, and began chatting away in his squeaking voice.

The Gnat and the mayfly are quite alike in their now-you-see-me, now-you-don't exits, though Kingsley's ephemerid does return for a tragicomic encore:

. . . and began flirting and flipping up and down, and singing —

"*My wife shall dance, and I shall sing,*
So merrily pass the day;
For I hold it quite the wisest thing,
To drive dull care away."

And he danced up and down for three days and three nights, till he grew so tired, that he tumbled into the water, and floated down. But what became of him Tom never knew, and he himself never minded; for Tom heard him singing to the last, as he floated down —

"To drive dull care away-ay-ay!"

The mock pathos of this protracted fade-out compares well, I think, with Dodgson's closing for his tenth chapter in *Wonderland*, "The Lobster Quadrille":

. . . while more and more faintly came, carried on the breeze that followed them, the melancholy words: —

"Soo-oop of the e-e-evening,
Beautiful, beautiful Soup!"

Being desperate, as he said, to strike out some new lines of fairy lore and having not the least idea what was to happen next, is it not possible that Dodgson, in his running debate with Kingsley over how not to tell a story, might naturally have fallen into Kingsley's way of saying a scene nonetheless? Realizing this could explain why he later wrote that he was "no *conscious* imitator." The two books are altogether different experiences, but in expression and incident the one does often seem a Tweedledum to the other's Tweedledee. After their encounters with the Caterpillar and mayfly, respectively, for example, Alice and Tom next confront a Pigeon and an otter and are caught up in the same exasperating dispute with each:

"Serpent!" screamed the Pigeon.

"I'm *not* a serpent!" said Alice indignantly. "Let me alone!"

"Serpent, I say again!" repeated the Pigeon. . . .

. . . "but I'm *not* a serpent, I tell you!" said Alice. "I'm a ——— I'm a ———"

"Well! *What* are you?" said the Pigeon. "I can see you're trying to invent something!"

"I—I'm a little girl," said Alice, rather doubtfully, as she remembered the number of changes she had gone through, that day.

"A likely story indeed!" said the Pigeon in a tone of the deepest contempt. "I've seen a good many little girls in my time, but never *one* with such a neck as that!"

"Come away, children," said the otter in disgust, "it is not worth eating, after all. It is only a nasty eft, which nothing eats, not even those vulgar pike in the pond."

"I am not an eft!" said Tom; "efts have tails."

"You are an eft," said the otter, very positively; "I see your two hands quite plain; and I know you have a tail."

"I tell you I have not," said Tom. "Look here!" and he turned his pretty little self quite round; and, sure enough, he had no more tail than you.

The otter might have got out of it by saying that Tom was a frog: but, like a great many other people, when she had once said a thing, she stood to it, right or wrong; so she answered:

"I say you are an eft, and therefore you are, and not fit food for gentlefolk like me and my children."

These are some of the more general likenesses between the two stories (the reader might recall the shoelacing comparisons earlier in this section). If we now close the door on the past at February 10, 1863—taking the 1864 manuscript of *Under Ground* as a more or less true copy of what Dodgson had completed by that date—the most obvious question to ask is this: What is missing from *Under Ground* that surfaces in the expanded version and might have been "suggested by the book one was reading"?

The first new character to turn up may have been Dodgson himself, in the guise I suggested for him earlier. Here is the conclusion to Kingsley's otter episode, which it very much seems he used (dates notwithstanding) as his model for the exchange between Alice and the Pigeon: "And the otter grew so proud that she turned head over heels twice, and then stood upright half out of the water, grinning like a Cheshire Cat."

In order of appearance, the major additions for the expanded version are "A Caucus Race"; "Pig and Pepper," which introduces the Duchess and the Cheshire Cat; "A Mad Tea Party"; the introduction of the Duchess and Cat into "The Queen's Croquet-Ground" and "The Mock Turtle's Story"; the enlargement of "The Mock Turtle's Story" and "The Lobster Quadrille"; and the expansion of the trial of the Knave of Hearts from one page to the book's two concluding chapters, "Who Stole the Tarts?" and "Alice's Evidence." Some precedent for each of these can be found in *The Water Babies* save the trial of the Knave, the inspiration for which I will treat in a later section. What we find in Kingsley varies from a mere suggestion, like that for the Cat, to whole scenarios.

Dodgson's first new character may actually have been Alice—that is, a more universal, more beset and combative Alice. In this regard I want to discuss the sometimes cited, and always dismissed, Quaker crow episode in *The Water Babies*, but this too is a thing to be saved for later. The correspondence to be noted at the moment is the sequencing of events in the two books. Generally, Dodgson's new characters follow one another in the same order of appearance as their counterparts in Kingsley. Thus, as Tom goes from dragonfly to otter and Cheshire Cat, so Alice goes from Caterpillar to Pigeon to Cheshire Cat. As it is the Cat who directs her to the March Hare's house, we might now expect to find in *The Water Babies* some hint of this new character turning up in sequence. And we do find it, two chapters down the line, being mentioned in conjunction with the trope common to both writers and the one word besides "Alice" that Dodgson uses on nearly every page:

> If you think I am talking nonsense, I can only say that it is true; and that an old gentleman named Fourier used to say that we ought to do the same by chimney-sweeps and dustmen, and honor them instead of despising them; and he was a very clever old gentleman: but, unfortunately for him and the world, as mad as a March hare.

It may not be too farfetched to imagine Dodgson jotting down those "flashes of thought" as he read along in *The Water Babies* (whether month by month in serialization or all at one sitting in May 1863) and then working several of them up in the same order as his notes. *Alice* is episodic, recall; there is no plot to it that might inhibit such a progression.

The Cheshire Cat and the March hare turn up merely as names in Kingsley, of course, and may or may not have awakened Dodgson's interest. Two major episodes following the tea party at the March Hare's house, on the other hand, do appear to be studied variations on correspondingly developed scenes in *The Water Babies*. The one, I suggest, is a satire on *The Water Babies* itself; the other, a lampoon of Kingsley.

> "When we were little," the Mock Turtle went on at last, more calmly, though still sobbing a little now and then, "we went to school in the sea. The master was an old Turtle—we used to call him Tortoise—"
> "Why did you call him Tortoise, if he wasn't one?" Alice asked.
> "We called him Tortoise because he taught us," said the Mock Turtle angrily. "Really you are very dull!"

Going to school in the sea is what all the children are doing in Kingsley, of course. Some go to a good school, and some to a bad. The phrase "mad as a March hare" appears in the midst of his description of the earlier of the two, that purgatorial nursery school run by the spirits of the Old and New Testaments for children who have died of sickness or starved in alleys or been murdered or brought up heathens. Everyone there is contented but must learn to be more than that, for "[b]eing quite comfortable is a very good thing; but it does not make people good. Indeed, it sometimes makes them naughty, as it has made the people in America."

The bad school Tom discovers on his travels to the outskirts of Hell. This is the Island of Laputa from *Gulliver's Travels*, renamed the Isle of Tomtoddies by Mrs. Bedonebyasyoudid. Here, in the tradition of Swift's pedants and quacks, children cram learning until they turn into turnips — all head and no body: "their foolish fathers and mothers, instead of letting them pick flowers, and make dirt pies . . . kept them always at lessons, working, working, working" — working to solve such pressing problems as the length of time it would take "a school-inspector of average activity to tumble head over heels from London to York." And what happens to these turnips when they cram too much? They explode — "by dozens . . . like Aldershot on a field-day."

It is hard to determine whether Dodgson was parodying this episode in making his own school in the sea or simply borrowing the idea. How do you satirize something that, deriving from Swift, is already itself twice a satire? Dodgson and Kingsley are here of one mind pedogogically, as Dodgson and MacDonald had been of one mind over copybook maxims. If only Kingsley had practiced what he preached and not so often played his own Examiner-of-all-Examiners and "looked so big and burly and dictatorial, and shouted so loud to Tom to come and be examined that Tom ran for his life."

Whichever the case may be, a borrowing or a parody, Dodgson did take reference to the scene, for when Alice asks the Mock Turtle to detail the "regular course" at his school in the sea, his response includes a virtual quote from Tom as he makes his escape:

As he went down to the shore he passed the poor turnip's new tomb. But Mrs. Bedonebyasyoudid had taken away the epitaph about talents and precocity and development, and put up one of her own instead, which Tom thought much more sensible: —

> *"Instruction sore long time I bore,*
> *And cramming was in vain;*
> *Till heaven did please my woes to ease,*
> *With water on the brain."*

So Tom jumped into the sea and swam on his way, singing: —

> *"Farewell, Tomtoddies all; I thank my stars*
> *That nought I know save those three royal r's:*

Reading and riting sure, with rithmetick,
Will help a lad of sense through thin and thick."

In "The Mock Turtle's Story," the "three royal r's" become "Reeling and Writhing, of course, to begin with . . . and then the different branches of Arithmetic—Ambition, Distraction, Uglification and Derision."

The "lad of sense" here, of course, is now Alice, Uncle Charles's sensible little Gulliver navigating a world of rogues, crackpots, Yahoos, pedants—and didacts like Kingsley, perhaps, whom Dodgson may or may not have had in mind as both or either the Tortoise who taught them and/or the Gryphon's Classical master:

"He was an old crab, *he* was."
"I never went to him," the Mock Turtle said with a sigh. "He taught Laughing and Grief, they used to say."

Like Reeling and Writhing for reading and writing, and Ambition and Derision for addition and division, Laughing and Grief are Latin and Greek. But they translate rather well, too, as the terms of Kingsley's way with a story: the laughter of his nonsense compromised by the grief of having to sit through his interminable lectures.

There is another, and perfectly plausible, explanation for this parody of school days that has nothing whatever to do with Kingsley. According to Derek Hudson, it was all a bit of fun at the expense of the tutors who came to the Deanery to give private lessons to the three Liddell girls. Thus, the art critic John Ruskin, who came weekly, provided the model for the master who teaches Drawling, Stretching, and Fainting in Coils (drawing, sketching, and painting in oils). Still, I wonder, if "The Mock Turtle's Story" and "The Lobster Quadrille" are entirely the expression of a private joke to amuse Alice Liddell, why did Dodgson wait until the expanded, public version to make such a business of it? Also, this picture of stuffy tutors coming and going accounts only for the two "extras" of drawing and dance and leaves undocumented the identities of the Classical master and the Tortoise who ran the school. Presumably, it was the Tortoise who taught the Mock Turtle "Mystery, ancient and modern, with Seography" as a part of the "regular course." We might recall here that, as Dodgson sits reading *The Water Babies*, Kingsley is Regius Professor of Modern History at Cambridge, the author of a book on marine life (*Glaucus*, 1855), and a man treating his Oxford audience to a seographer's grand tour of the Atlantic Ocean.

A further hint that all of this, while likely incorporating events known to the Liddell girls, is overreachingly a joke private to Dodgson himself can be found in the Mock Turtle's song and in the earlier ditty that it displaced from the manuscript of *Alice's Adventures Under Ground*. "'Will you walk a little faster?' said a whiting to a snail" has an intricate history. Though probably not written until late in 1863, a place for it in the book was established as early as July 3, 1862. At the Deanery that day—the day before the famous picnic—the Liddell sisters had treated Dodgson to a rendering of the minstrel tune "Sally come up! Sally go down!" At some point over the next two years Uncle Charles reciprocated by rewording the song to read:

> Beneath the waters of the sea
> Are lobsters thick as thick can be—
> They love to dance with you and me.
> My own, my gentle Salmon!
> CHORUS
> Salmon, come up! Salmon, go down!
> Salmon, come twist your tail around!
> Of all the fishes of the sea
> There's none so good as Salmon!

and then installing the new lyric in the manuscript, *Alice's Adventures Under Ground*, that he delivered to Alice Liddell in November 1864.

This seems so straightforward as a moment of improvisational play that it might also seem a bit obtuse and finicky to be wondering here why Sally is under the sea turning into a salmon and from whence come these happy lobsters who will soon be dancing over to the public version of *Alice* for the Lobster Quadrille. But as it happens, lobster and salmon are there in Kingsley, and, as with the other characters, they appear in the right sequence to have been retrieved by Dodgson from his notes at exactly this point in the story. Beginning with the otter/Cheshire Cat episode and running for fifteen pages is Kingsley's ode to that worthy gentleman of the sea, and how there is no fish so good as the salmon. He tells us how otters prize and hunt them and how men pursue them; he describes the various streams in Britain in which they can be caught (*The Water Babies* is a *very* long and discursive book), and, finally, having exhausted the permutations of salmon lore, he introduces Tom to "the king of all the fish."

Immediately following the salmon hiatus comes the lobster:

> Tom had never seen a lobster before; and he was mightily taken with this one; for he thought him the most curious, odd, ridiculous creature he had ever seen.

Or, as the Mock Turtle will put it,

> "You may not have lived much under the sea—" ("I haven't," said Alice)— "and perhaps you were never even introduced to a lobster—"

For the real Alice the introduction came twice. The moment of exchange, from "lobsters thick as thick can be" to the Lobster Quadrille at that point in the story, was encoded by Dodgson into the Gryphon's instructions on how to perform the dance: "change lobsters and retire in same order." "Salmon, come up" was hand-clapping, good-natured fun for the Liddell girls; the point of the song that replaced it is how the gaiety of the dance might be spoiled by an encroaching "porpoise":

"Will you walk a little faster?" said a whiting
    to a snail,
"There's a porpoise close behind us, and he's
    treading on my tail.
See how eagerly the lobsters and the turtles
    all advance!
They are waiting on the shingle—will you
    come and join the dance?"

The tail of the whiting being trod upon, of course, is the tale that wants to dance. I am going to suppose that Dodgson is now four chapters into *The Water Babies*, falling out of patience with the didactic Kingsley, and eager to find some way of saying, "We don't want *you* with us!" The emerging purpose of the author in hand is Christian salvation. On page after page the hero is called upon to seek it like "a brave, determined, little English bulldog." Dodgson being in a state of snaillike diffidence about his own direction, he may have been less than thrilled by the poetic recitation of the diffident fishes with which Kingsley introduces the useful lobster episode. In this allegorical passage all the sea creatures are drifting along squandering their souls in a state of self-absorption. Basking sharks have grown dull from overeating; the lazy sunfish has lost its way; a fleet of "happy stupid" sea snails (n.b.) wanders by, singing, "Whence we come we know not; and whither we are going, who can tell? We float out our life in mid-ocean . . . and that is enough for us." A sea-ribbon, swept away on the gulf stream, informs Tom how it has been helped by other water babies like himself, "or I should have been eaten by a great black porpoise [n.b.]." And then, finally, comes the lobster, who will be a dancer in each of Dodgson's two verses.

Where better for a diffident deacon to execute a cake walk or quadrille than on such virtuous reproof of his own lack of resolve?

The further off from England the nearer is to France—
Then turn not pale, beloved snail, but come and join the dance.

In the conversation that follows, Dodgson added a note of special pleading in behalf of all little readers and how they are, and are not, to be wise:

"If I'd been the whiting," said Alice, whose thoughts were still running on the song, "I'd have said to the porpoise, 'Keep back, please! We don't want *you* with us!'"

"They were obliged to have him with them," the Mock Turtle said. "No wise fish would go anywhere without a porpoise."

"Wouldn't it, really?" said Alice, in a tone of great surprise.

"Of course not," said the Mock Turtle. "Why, if a fish came to *me*, and told me he was going on a journey, I should say, 'With what porpoise?'"

"Don't you mean 'purpose'?" said Alice.

The fish going on a journey here refers to Tom's pilgrimage but also to any child opening a book. Alice's surprise is Dodgson's defense of stories innocent of didactic purposes and of not burdening readers, heroes, heroines, and tutors with missions of salvation. His choice of meter for the Lobster Quadrille also smells of a rap at Kingsley, I think. He styled the poem after Mary Howitt's "The Spider and the Fly":

> "Will you walk into my parlor?"
>   said the spider to the fly —
> "'Tis the prettiest little parlor
>   that ever you did spy.
> The way into my parlor is up a
>   winding stair;
> And I have many curious things
>   to show you when you're there."

Here is the perfect parable for Kingsley's way with his child readers, a cautionary fable after Aesop or La Fontaine that ends, like *The Water Babies*, with the requisite dreary Moral:

> And now, dear little children, who may
>   this story read,
> To idle, silly, flattering words, I pray
>   you ne'er give heed;
> Unto an evil counselor close heart,
>   and ear and eye,
> And take a lesson from this tale
>   of the Spider and the Fly.

The diction of the poem would lead one to suppose, chauvinistically, that the spider, like the author, is female, when in fact the victim is female and the spider male — like Kingsley and a reader named Alice, perhaps. The "prettiest little parlor," then, would be Kingsley's book, and the "curious things to show" his encyclopedic enthusiasms, his "seaography." He welcomes in his readers only to wrap them up in stupefying verbiage and suck the joy out of them with lectures and morals. His purpose and craft and the spider's purpose and craft are one and the same.

Dodgson's animus toward Kingsley the orator may have carried over, by way of this nursery rhyme, into *Through the Looking-Glass*. There the flatterer, the "evil counselor," would be the Walrus, beguiling and consuming readers like so many little oysters. The "many curious things" of the spider and the factual and nonsensical curiosities detailed in *The Water Babies* are the very things the Walrus promises to reveal to *his* little pupils:

> "The time has come," the walrus said,
>   "To talk of many things:
> Of shoes — and ships — and sealing-
>   wax —

> Of cabbages — and kings —
> And why the sea is boiling hot —
> And whether pigs have wings."

There are no flying pigs in *The Water Babies*, or sealing-wax, either, alas, but the sea on three occasions *is* said to be boiling or boiling hot.

The Walrus, the spider, and the porpoise are all comical portraits of predators, to be sure, but rather ugly ones, too. They represent what I suppose Dodgson perceived to be the ugliness of luring children into a book only to bore them to death. It is this idea of ugliness that led him to create his one consummate caricature of Kingsley in *Wonderland*. He turned the trick by modeling the burlesque on one of Kingsley's own characters, Mrs. Bedonebyasyoudid.

In his school in the sea, remember, the Tortoise (a minor likeness, if you will) taught Kingsley's own subjects of history, ancient and modern, and Seaography, and the "three royal r's" that Tom sang about, which Dodgson expressed as "Reeling and Writhing" and "the different branches of Arithmetic — Ambition, Distraction, Uglification and Derision." Uglification is the most strained of these four transliterations. Not coincidentally, I think, it is how we find Kingsley's undersea teacher describing herself:

> "I am very ugly. I am the ugliest fairy in the world; and I shall be, till people behave themselves as they ought to do. And then I shall grow as handsome as my sister, who is the loveliest fairy in the world; and her name is Mrs. Doasyouwouldbedoneby."

Dodgson seems to be recalling this promised transformation in a passage elaborating on the Tortoise's curriculum:

> "I never heard of 'Uglification,'" Alice ventured to say. "What is it?"
> The Gryphon lifted up both its paws in surprise. "Never heard of uglifying!" it exclaimed. "You know what to beautify is, I suppose?"
> "Yes," said Alice doubtfully: "it means — to — make — anything — prettier."
> "Well, then," the Gryphon went on, "if you don't know what to uglify is, you *are* a simpleton."

If he thought Kingsley's Sunday School on St. Brandan's Isle a tedious place, what must he have thought of the ugly work afoot at the bottom of Kingsley's sea? Here, for four deliciously detailed pages, Mrs. Bedonebyasyoudid works out the salvation of malefactors in ways that will have children either laughing (as they laugh, say, at the punishments meted out to the grownups in Kipling's "The Elephant's Child") or frightened out of their wits. Doctors, careless nursemaids, foolish ladies, and cruel schoolmasters are all gathered down there having their ears boxed and their teeth pulled out every Friday for having, when alive, ill used the children in their care. The schoolmasters catch the devil's end of it. In a little origin myth you won't find in the abridged versions and which Kingsley might have titled

"Why the Sea Has Bubbles," an anti-Catholic bias is displayed that is so disproportionate as to be almost funny:

And after luncheon she set to work again, and called up all the cruel school-masters—whole regiments and brigades of them; and when she saw them, she frowned most terribly, and set to work in earnest, as if the best part of the day's work was to come. More than half of them were nasty, dirty, frowzy, grubby, smelly old monks, who, because they dare not hit a man of their own size, amused themselves with beating little children instead. . . .

And she boxed their ears, and thumped them over the head with rulers, and pandied their hands with canes, and told them that they told stories, and were this and that bad sort of people; and the more they were very indignant, and stood upon their honor, and declared they told the truth, the more she declared they were not, and that they were only telling lies; and at last she birched them all round soundly with her great birch-rod and set them each an imposition of three hundred thousand lines of Hebrew to learn by heart before she came back next Friday. And at that they all cried and howled so, that their breaths came all up through the sea like bubbles out of soda-water; and that is one reason of the bubbles in the sea.

Even if the Bible does promise divine justice, Tom "could not help thinking her a little spiteful." Her "spite" only elicits sympathy from the Reverend Kingsley, however: "no wonder if she was, poor old soul; for if she has to wait to grow handsome till people do as they would be done by, she will have to wait a very long time."

To be fair, the verbal abuse Alice takes from each new acquaintance is no prettier than Mrs. Bedonebyasyoudid's birchings. More hostility is conveyed in a few pages of *Wonderland* than in all of *The Water Babies*. Still, Dodgson seems to have seen uglification everywhere in his rival's work, both in its incident and its rhetoric; and he gathered up the punitive fairy and the author who punishes with his moralizing into one grotesque caricature in his own fairy tale:

"Tut, tut, child!" said the Duchess. "Everything's got a moral, if only you can find it." And she squeezed herself up closer to Alice's side as she spoke.

Alice did not much like her keeping so close to her: first, because the Duchess was *very* ugly: and secondly, because she was exactly the right height to rest her chin on Alice's shoulder, and it was an uncomfortably sharp chin.

"*Very* ugly" equates nicely with "the ugliest fairy in the world," and the digging chin likewise evokes the narrator who simply will not take his nagging presence elsewhere. There may be a veiled notation here as well that, being the same height as the Duchess, his heroine is the equal of all of them. She bears the squeezings of an unwanted adult as best she can for the moment, muttering only, "How fond she is of finding morals in things!," but in just a few pages we find her announcing, "Keep back, please! We don't want *you* with us!"

The Duchess makes her debut in the chapter "Pig and Pepper" in company with the Cheshire Cat. This seems fitting somehow, but an oddity is introduced: if I am correct that the Cat is really Dodgson and the Duchess Kingsley by way of Mrs. Bedonebyasyoudid, then why is the Cat said to be the Duchess's cat?

It may not signify, of course. Although a roman à clef, *Wonderland* is no point-by-point allegory. What matters is the general character and mood of the place, with its little troupe of players acting out similarly absurd roles. A few writers have surmised that something of Dodgson might be found in half the characters in the book, and we could easily find—and have found—Kingsley in several as well. I do think that with the Cat and the Duchess, Dodgson meant to be specific about who was who, but even here we should not imagine him inhibited by a memo pinned to his sleeve, *Kingsley = Duchess, I'm the Cat.*

Or it could be that the Cat is nobody's cat. When Alice asks the Duchess about "your cat" and later tells the King and Queen of Hearts, "It belongs to the Duchess," she is only assuming that it does. Neither Dodgson nor the Duchess has confirmed this. When the Duchess is about to make her entrance at the Queen's croquet match, the Cat, who got there first to ask Alice "How are you getting on?," dissociates itself from its supposed mistress altogether and disappears.

Or perhaps the reverse of Alice's assumption is the truth of it. Perhaps the Cat is "grinning from ear to ear" by the Duchess's hearth with the knowledge that what obtains in this curious world is the fact that if anyone belongs to anyone, the Duchess belongs to the Cat. Behind the grin is the subliminal footnote *She* is here because I have *brought* her here.

In this last regard it is worth noting that, just as Alice is about to be escorted off to hear the Mock Turtle's story, "the Duchess's voice died away, even in the middle of her favorite word 'moral.'" The now-redundant Duchess exits the tale at the very moment Dodgson wants to begin his parody of Mrs. Bedonebyasyoudid's school in the sea. Looking to make his point about Kingsley in another way, he has no more need of the Duchess's sharp chin.

The most telling evidence that he meant to spoof Kingsley with this portrait of the Duchess appears early in the second chapter of *The Water Babies*, which appeared in *Macmillan's Magazine* in September 1862, two months after the famous picnic and two months before Dodgson actually set pen to paper. It comes at the most critical juncture of the story, as Tom is drowning in the brook and being transformed into a water baby. To this point Dodgson has been reading what he has come to expect from Kingsley, the adventures of a naturalistic hero in the harsh Dickensian world of the Victorian reformers. Now, suddenly, the tale dives straight into the make-believe territory Dodgson is himself about to explore. Typically, however, the exasperating Kingsley has arrested himself in mid-dive for a chat. He begins the aside with his own dig at the literary theories of America's information specialist, "Peter Parley" (here called Cousin Cramchild). Better than any other passage I have quoted, this gives the full flavor of what it is like to read *The Water Babies* unabridged. Imagine that in a book of 275 pages, a good 200 of them sound like this:

> Some people think that there are no fairies. Cousin Cramchild tells little folks so in his Conversations. Well, perhaps there are none—in Boston, U.S., where he was raised. There are only a clumsy lot of spirits there, who can't make people hear without thumping on the table: but they get their living thereby, and I suppose that is all they want. And Aunt Agitate, in her Arguments on political economy, says there are none—in her political economy. But it is a wide world, my little man—and thank Heaven for it, for else, between crinolines and theories, some of us would get squashed—and plenty of room in it for fairies, without people seeing them; unless, of course, they look in the right place. The most wonderful and the strangest things in the world, you know, are just the things which no one can see. There is life in you; and it is the life in you which makes you grow, and move, and think: and yet you can't see it. And there is steam in a steam-engine; and that is what makes it move; and yet you can't see it; and so there may be fairies in the world, and they may be just what makes the world go round to the old tune of
>
> "*C'est l'amour, l'amour, l'amour*
> *Qui fait la monde à la ronde:*"
>
> and yet no one may be able to see them except those whose hearts are going round to that same tune. At all events, we will make believe that there are fairies in the world. It will not be the last time by many a one that we shall have to make believe. And yet, after all, there is no need for that. There must be fairies; for this is a fairy tale: and how can one have a fairy tale if there are no fairies?

This is not badly told, for a polemical essay. It is hardly going to suspend anyone's disbelief in fairies (a goal of questionable worth, even if there *were* fairies in *The Water Babies*, which there are not, although as a convenience Kingsley calls two of his personages by that name). I have often wondered, in writing about these two authors, if the Liddell sisters had followed the serialization of *The Water Babies* or read it the following year, and if Alice had run to tell Uncle Charles about it, and what she had to say (feeling distanced, no doubt, from a story that continually addresses the reader as "my little man"), and how he might have felt if she had. At any rate, here he was, trying to tell her a story of his own, and what should appear but the passage just quoted. Of all the aesthetic mistakes in Kingsley's book, this first blunder, appearing out of nowhere, I think must have provoked Dodgson the most.

The proof that at this moment he marked Kingsley down for a reckoning and began the train of thought that would transmogrify him into a Duchess can be found in the centered and italicized lines just quoted. For it is with the song "C'est l'amour, l'amour" that we actually find the Duchess quoting a line, not only from *The Water Babies*, but from one of Kingsley's own editorials. For the occasion she has planted her chin in Alice's shoulder. Alice has been remarking of the Queen's croquet match. "The game's going on rather better now." And the Duchess replies, "Tis so . . . and the moral of that is — 'Oh, 'tis love, 'tis love, that makes the world go round!'"

Kingsley and the Duchess are singing the same song. It is the Queen Mother of all those copybook maxims Dodgson loves to mock. The deacon is wincing but resolving too, I would suppose, that the game of storytelling *will* be "going on rather better now" if he has anything to say about it.

The supreme irony of the moment, of course, is that one day Dodgson is going to rewrite his story, and it is going to sound like this:

> And then she had a very long fall indeed. . . . If anybody *really* had such a fall as that, it would kill them, most likely: but you know it doesn't hurt a bit to fall in a *dream*, because, all the time you *think* you're falling, you really *are* lying somewhere, safe and sound, and fast asleep!
>
> And if she finds any *white* roses on the tree, do you know what will happen? It will be "Off with their heads!" Oh, work away, my little men! Hurry, hurry!
>
> But the Dodo — who was a very wise bird — told them the right way was to have a Caucus-Race. And what do you think *that* was?
> *You don't know*? Well, you *are* an ignorant child! Now, be very attentive, and I'll soon cure you of your ignorance!

Twenty-five years later, Dodgson has himself become the Duchess.

To do the right thing at the right season is a great art, as Aesop would have it — or Mrs. Bedonebyasyoudid. In *Wonderland* we see Dodgson at the edge of his antagonistic powers. He and Kingsley are equals in invention, but he has the instinct for delivery that Kingsley lacks: the ear for conversational speech, the eye for a shapely scene, the comic's perfect timing. The precipitous Kingsley wants everywhere for tact: "And I am very glad to say, that Tom learnt such a lesson that day, that he did not torment creatures for a long time after."

This is just how Dodgson will sound when he becomes the Duchess, but in *Wonderland* we have the child's understanding of things: "'How the creatures order one about, and make one repeat lessons!' thought Alice, 'I might just as well be at school at once.'"

Kingsley is the blustery priest, sending his lads off to see the world like proper English bulldogs. With the best will in the world he cannot help but cause the children in the pews to break out in flop sweat. Dodgson, partly by his nature and partly out of his antipathy toward Kingsley, saw himself as a coconspirator with the children. For this reason, *Alice* is a tutorial against tutorials. And Dodgson, it must be said, *is* funny. This is a side to *Alice* that I have neglected thus far. I do think his humor appeals more to adults than to children, in whom it is more likely to cause puzzlement or a shiver of dread than a laugh, but there is no denying him a talent for it or the range he displays in the two books. There is stuff here in the playful spirit of nursery rhymes, and, as with Humpty Dumpty, nonsense as a kind of philosophical inquiry, and also the sad kind of nonsense we find with the White Knight:

> "But you've got a bee-hive — or something like one — fastened to the saddle," said Alice.
>
> "Yes, it's a very good bee-hive," the Knight said in a discontented tone, "one of the best kind. But not a single bee has come near it yet. And the other thing is a mouse-trap. I suppose the mice keep the bees out — or the bees keep the mice out, I don't know which."
>
> "I was wondering what the mouse-trap was for," said Alice. "It isn't very likely there would be any mice on the horse's back."
>
> "Not very likely, perhaps," said the Knight; "but, if they *do* come, I don't choose to have them running all about."

Dodgson had that peculiar talent of the English for portraying their own bored disdain:

> "It wasn't very civil of you to sit down without being invited," said the March Hare.
>
> "I didn't know it was *your* table," said Alice: "it's laid for a great many more than three."
>
> "Your hair wants cutting," said the Hatter. He had been looking at Alice for some time with great curiosity, and this was his first speech.

Some of what he wrote prefigured surrealism:

> "Here I am!" cried a voice from the soup-tureen, and Alice turned again, just in time to see the Queen's broad good-natured face grinning at her for a moment over the edge of the tureen, before she disappeared into the soup.

And for the children there are perfectly rendered moments of outright slapstick: the White Knight's inability to sit a horse, father William somersaulting in at the door, Bill the Lizard going up the chimney and coming down to cries of "Tell us all about it!" Dodgson had an instinct for the humor that is a potential in all fairy tales. Here, Alice finds herself in the classic predicament of a Red Riding Hood or Snow White in the forest:

> "I was thinking," Alice said very politely, "which is the best way out of this wood: it's getting so dark. Would you tell me, please?"
>
> But the fat little men only looked at each other and grinned.
>
> They looked so exactly like a couple of great schoolboys that Alice couldn't help pointing her finger at Tweedledum, and saying, "First Boy!"
>
> "Nohow!" Tweedledum cried out briskly, and shut his mouth up again with a snap.
>
> "Next Boy!" said Alice, passing on to Tweedledee, though she felt quite certain he would only shout out "Contrariwise!" and so he did.

What Kingsley was chasing with his stumbling attempts at humor, Dodgson caught to perfection. Why the author of such accomplished stuff would not just blow his adversary off with a joke or pass him by altogether is a puzzle, perhaps, but I think we have already seen the answer: Dodgson was a master of comic make-believe only when going on the attack. The best products of his mind did not "come of themselves"; he always needed someone to perform for — his sisters, his girls, a kindred spirit like MacDonald — and someone or some piece of writing to perform against. Alice Liddell commissioned him to bring her into Wonderland, but once she was there he had little idea where to send her next. Unlike Kingsley, he had no real story to tell. The only way to sustain the fiction was to sustain the attack. And so he made his way through the twelve chapters by picking targets to burlesque, and when he had gathered enough routines together and settled a few scores, he sent his heroine home. Dodgson is best understood not as a writer at all but as a gifted specimen of the Victorian parlor performer — not unlike Lear at the piano, running cheerily maudlin variations on the poems of Tennyson. Too shy for such theatrics himself but with an abiding love of amateur and professional theater (he would later pay court to the famous actress Ellen Terry), he instead scripted little show pieces in prose, decorous versions for mixed company of the sort of comic sketch we see today on, say, *Monty Python's Flying Circus*. The burlesques and songs and dialogues in the two *Alices* are at heart performances.

Enter Kingsley, then, at the very moment Dodgson is commissioned to translate his knack for parlor amusements into an actual work of sustained prose. The younger performer is about to test himself on his first real stage, and suddenly, without warning, he must follow the act of a man who has the ear of the queen, renown in the pulpit, fame in the press, and the same kind of story to tell. Although the finished *Alice* is the work of someone grown bold with the discovery of his own voice, how could there not have been a moment of trepidation at the outset, a need to go on the attack, not merely for its own rush but first to shake off the flop sweat?

The anxiety of second billing is a commonplace with any performer, of course. Behind Dodgson's animus toward Kingsley, I think, lay something still more personal.

In his biography *Lewis Carroll*, Derek Hudson reports a fascinating discovery made in 1950 at the Croft Rectory in Yorkshire, where Dodgson had lived from the age of eleven, after the family's move from Cheshire. Beneath a floorboard in the nursery lay a cache of children's playthings that seems indisputably to have been hidden there by Dodgson and his sisters more than a century earlier. Among the ephemera were a white glove, a thimble, and a left-hand shoe — surely suggestive of the White Rabbit's dropped glove, the Dodo's gift to Alice of her own thimble, and the lines from the White Knight's song "Or madly squeeze a right-hand foot / Into a left-hand shoe." The most interesting discovery, however, was a small piece of wood on which were penciled the words

And we'll wander through
the wide world
and chase the buffalo.

A variation of these words also appears in the White Knight's song. Hudson writes, "[T]here seems to be little doubt that this is in Lewis Carroll's hand"—he thinks it may have been written when Dodgson was about fifteen—and speculates that the memento marks "a *cri de coeur*, evidence, perhaps, of an early longing to escape into some sort of Wonderland."[34] On this I would disagree. The time capsule under the floor could as easily be a promise to the future. The words on the piece of wood speak not of escape but of adventures to come. If a guess can be made, I would guess that, with his adoring sisters as witnesses to the shamanistic event, Dodgson deposited the message beneath the floor in 1846 when at fourteen he left for his three-year ordeal at the Rugby School. What great things are to be expected, it seems to say, of our dear brother Charles as he sets out into the wide world.

Rugby was going to teach him, however, that a stammering muff at sports, a White Knight who could not sit a horse, was not going to be one of England's buffalo hunters in the farthest reaches of the empire. That boyish dream was going to stay buried under the floorboard. What otherwise became of his hope for the future can be found, I think, in a strange verse he wrote many years later, in which the quarry is no longer the buffalo but that fabulous creature whiffling through the tulgey wood, the Jabberwock.

The opening stanza of the poem, "'Twas brillig, and the slithy toves," has become one of the best-known passages in English poetry. He had written these four lines in 1855, at the age of twenty-three, as an exercise in nonsense to amuse his family. The rest, in which the hero, "my son . . . my beamish boy," delights his father by slaying the dreaded Jabberwock, he composed at some later, unknown date. Because of its peculiar mood and its proximity in *Looking-Glass* to the White Knight, I am going to assume he did so between the two *Alices*, after playing out his hand as the Cheshire Cat. "Jabberwocky" is a fragment he retrieved from the past and enlarged into the future, a thought from his youth that he found useful in middle age. It is a puzzle to understand because he designed it to be so, both in 1855 and later. The story it tells is expressed as a ballad, but he has taken it a step further and phrased the ballad as a riddle. Where Dodgson seems to be inventing forms, he is always reinventing old ones. "The Walrus and the Carpenter," for example, is built up from nursery rhymes and fables from Aesop and La Fontaine.[35] With "Jabberwocky," as with any riddle, the outward form is a deception. The thing's true nature has been hidden behind a camouflage of verbal misdirection. The poem is actually twice disguised: it is printed in reverse, so that Alice must hold it before a mirror to read it, and its meaning is screened by coinages like "brillig" and "frumious." This is nonsense practiced as an intellectual game. The point of the game, as it had been for his family in 1855, is to appreciate the conjurer's cunning and then to test how good a detective you are at decoding the riddle and announcing its meaning.

Whatever we do take it to mean, and critics have read it various ways, we can see that it has at least somehow to do with heroism. My own feeling is that behind the spoofing ("in uffish thought he stood," for example, or "O frabjous day!"), Dodgson is laying the traditional heroic mode to rest and redesigning it to suit his own needs. "Jabberwocky" is both the fossil evidence of a boy's dream of hunting the buffalo and that dream's rebirth as something else. Dodgson has reconciled himself to living a life outside the age's heroic arenas of soldiering for the empire or soldiering for Christ as one of the new Muscular Christians. In neither sphere can he play one of Kingsley's brave English bulldogs. Instead, he will conduct his tutorials in private—a White Knight to little girls.

The Knight is, I think, the key to the riddle of "Jabberwocky." The suggestion Dodgson planted in the opening chapter of *Looking-Glass* seems deliberate enough and was meant to lead us to this solution: the boy who slew the Jabberwock grew up to become the White Knight: Uncle Charles is the beamish boy who slew the Jabberwock. Indeed, it is the association of the poem and the Knight, and not the advertized schemes of mirror and chessboard, that gives *Looking-Glass* its true symmetry. The pair appear in tandem at the outset (Alice has no sooner observed, "*The White Knight is sliding down the poker. He balances very badly,*" then her eye falls on the book containing the poem), the center of the tale is occupied by Humpty Dumpty's analysis of the poem, and at the close the Knight, once a chess piece, appears in the flesh (along with the buffalo and the left-hand shoe from under the floorboard) to defeat the Red Knight and escort Alice to the end of her journey. This is the real story of *Looking-Glass*, the progress of two heroes: little Alice and the chivalrous, kindhearted friend galloping to her aid. He has come bearing a rather untraditional resource for helping her make the leap into adulthood. But, then, Dodgson is an untraditional kind of hero. Like his Knight head down in a ditch, he can say, "What does it matter where my body happens to be? . . . My mind goes on working all the same. In fact, the more head downwards I am, the more I keep inventing new things." The Knight's new things—the bee-hive and mouse-trap of which he is so proud, for example—are Dodgson's new, great resource, his inventions in the realm of Nonsense.

As a way of saying, unsaying, resaying a thing, nonsense was perfected in one generation in Victorian England. The principal sayers were the contemporaries Kingsley, Dodgson, and Edward Lear. For Dodgson, at least, the matter of who had the first and best claim to the new realm seems to have been a point of honor, to be contested the way boys might argue whether Batman could take Superman in a fight. Or, as the Red Queen puts it to Alice, "You may call it 'nonsense' if you like . . . but *I've* heard nonsense, compared with which that would be as sensible as a dictionary!"

At the heart of nearly every debate and duel in the two *Alices* lies this question of what words mean and who is the true master of them. In *Wonderland* there is real rancor to the argument; in *Looking-Glass* Dodgson's temper has cooled, as evidenced by his tongue-in-cheek depiction of the heroic joust between the Red and White Knights for possession of Alice on the chessboard:

> "She's my prisoner, you know!" the Red Knight said at last.
>
> "Yes, but then *I* came and rescued her!" the White Knight replied.
>
> "Well, we must fight for her, then," said the Red Knight, as he took up his helmet. . . .
>
> "You will observe the Rules of Battle, of course?" the White Knight remarked, putting on his helmet too.
>
> "I always do," said the Red Knight, and they began banging away at each other with such fury that Alice got behind a tree to be out of the way of the blows.

Lest a child reading this be tempted to take any of it seriously, Dodgson describes the pair going at one another "as if they were Punch and Judy" and ends the fracas by dropping the two of them on their heads.

> When they got up again, they shook hands, and then the Red Knight mounted and galloped off.
>
> "It was a glorious victory, wasn't it?" said the White Knight, as he came up panting.

Unlike the sarcastic and acrimonious tussles in *Wonderland*, this combat has been conducted purely in the interests of slapstick. It is as if Dodgson had freed himself somehow to deal with the specter of Kingsley in a lighter spirit. Indeed, I would suggest this to be the case and that it was the act of writing "Jabberwocky" that enabled him to do it. The knight's combat and the duel in the poem can even be read as the same event rephrased, as if the boy who beheaded the Jabberwock had grown up to be a hero who can shake hands with an opponent once he has unseated him. One interesting difference between the two contests may further explain Dodgson's possessiveness over the vorpal blade of nonsense and how as the White Knight he found a more grown-up way of wielding it. In "Jabberwocky" it is the hero's father who celebrates the triumph:

> "Come to my arms, my beamish boy!
> O frabjous day! Callooh! Callay!"
> He chortled in his joy.

but later in the book the father has disappeared, and it is the Knight himself who sings of the "glorious victory." It may be significant, then, that in 1868, three years before publication of *Through the Looking-Glass*, Dodgson's own father had died — an event he would describe as "the greatest blow that has ever fallen on my life."[36]

In his biography of Dodgson, Derek Hudson reproduces a letter written by the Reverend Charles Dodgson to his eight-year-old son that convinces me that Dodgson must have inherited the habit of nonsense from his father. Promising to honor a request for gifts while on a trip to Leeds, Charles senior swears to roust everyone in the town until the wanted items are secured,

> & if they are not brought directly, in forty seconds I will leave nothing but one small cat alive in the whole town of Leeds, & I shall only leave that, because I am afraid I shall not have time to kill it.
>
> Then what a bawling & a tearing of hair there will be! Pigs & babies, camels & butterflies, rolling in the gutter together — old women rushing up the chimneys & cows after them — ducks hiding themselves in coffee cups, & fat geese trying to squeeze themselves into pencil cases. . . .

Clearly, there was a kinship between the two beyond mere blood. What it might have sounded like across the dinner table is anyone's guess. The relative absence of information about these years leaves the door open for imagining a scenario in which son and father are eventually pitted against each other. Charles senior is thought to have been puritanical and strict; he disapproved of the theater, his son's great love. Charles junior can easily be seen as a boy growing unhappy under the weight of family expectations, secreting under the floors things that would later resurface in needling jokes and parodies. Dutifully, he followed his father through Christ Church. In his choice of career he echoed his father's interest in mathematics. He thought like his father, in nonsense and pieties, and like his father he would write books. What could be less of a surprise than to find him rebelling against it all by refusing to take holy orders and taking instead the nom de plume Lewis Carroll and asserting, at last, a separate identity? It could be argued from this that in the older Kingsley Dodgson saw an image of his father and that behind his animus toward Kingsley (here the reader may recall his campaign to shut down a stage production of *The Water Babies*) lay a resentment of his father and all that damned soldiering one was expected to do for Crown and Christ.

Real evidence is lacking, however, that Dodgson was ever insecure or unhappy as his father's son. There is better evidence to the contrary, not least his testimony that his father's death was the greatest blow ever to befall him. His decision not to take holy orders need not reflect on his father at all, really. It is probably best to say that his father was his father, Kingsley was Kingsley, and Dodgson did not resent the one or confuse him with the other when he asked, "Who in the world am I?" His relationship with his father should be read as a straightforward one. It strikes me as being quite biblical, actually, in the sense of a son looking to please a father and wanting the father's blessing in return. What could be a more fitting way to look at the inheritance passing from Canon Charles Dodgson to Deacon Charles Dodgson than as a blessing in this oldest sense of the word? This is what lies at the heart of his animus toward Kingsley, I think: the feeling that in beating him into print with a nonsense story for children —

the first nonsense story in English letters—Kingsley had usurped Dodgson's right to the blessing, and not only usurped it but misused it as well. The blessing of the cloth and the collar Kingsley could have. Dodgson would compromise on this by being the deacon who could still frequent theaters. But Dodgson would not tolerate Kingsley's laying claim to the blessing of nonsense. This was his, a family tradition, a birthright not to be stolen away.

This is the state of mind I have imagined Dodgson in as he read *The Water Babies*; and I have wondered whether Alice Liddell had been reading it too as Dodgson, "in a desperate attempt to strike out some new line of fairy-lore," tried to satisfy her request for a story of his own. Had she exacerbated his annoyance by coming to him excited about this new tale by the very man who had stolen the blessing? Was Uncle Charles's story to be anything like this one?

Insult was added to injury yet further: Dodgson, whose best talents were adversarial, was going to need *The Water Babies*—its ideas, its scenes and characters, its mistakes—in order to find out where to go with *Alice in Wonderland*. "Without the least idea of what was to happen next," he would have to stalk this poacher, recovering anything and everything that smacked of what had been, after all, native to his own mind since childhood. Being the better hand, he would show Kingsley, and an audience newly alerted to the pleasures of nonsense, how to do the thing properly.

I suppose it is a bit much, finding the face of Kingsley behind so many personages here—the Tortoise and the Classical master, the cunning spider, the Duchess, the Jabberwock, the Walrus, the Red Knight. Should we accuse Dodgson of a monomania or congratulate him on his inventiveness with a single premise? It might be safer to see Kingsley as the original focus of the animus, fully realized in the Duchess, and these others as generic Kingsleys, permutations Dodgson created while keeping his imagination at its highest pitch. The Jabberwock does intrigue me, however, as Kingsley in a new guise. The beast and the priest both being creatures that jabber, the assignment seems almost too easy, but Dodgson did suggest the obvious reading of "Jabberwock" when he suggested to some children that they take the first syllable "in its ordinary acceptation of 'excited and voluble discussion.'"[37] "The jaws that bite, the claws that catch" recall, perhaps, the spider of "The Spider and the Fly," which Dodgson had associated with Kingsley in composing the Mock Turtle's song. The fourth stanza of "Jabberwocky" would stand as a coded abstract for the critical year of 1862:

> And, as in uffish thought he stood,
>   The Jabberwock, with eyes of flame,
> Came whiffling through the tulgey wood,
>   And burbled as it came!

In another letter Dodgson explained "uffish" as suggesting "the temper huffish,"[38] which nicely describes his quandary in that year as he faced the uncertain futures of both his life and his "interminable fairy-tale." And what should occur in the very month he made this moan? The Jabberwock comes whiffling through the tulgey wood of make-believe, burbling the words of *The Water Babies*. Following which affront,

> One, two! One, two! And through and through
> The vorpal blade went snicker-snack!
> He left it dead, and with its head
> He went galumphing back.

Dodgson has left *The Water Babies* dead by obviating it with a better book, as he had feared Kingsley was obviating his own in its infancy. The head he takes as a trophy is his lampoon of Kingsley as the Duchess, which he bears jubilantly to the father of his talents, who now can sing "O frabjous day! Callooh! Callay!" that his son has reclaimed the blessing. The blessing brought home is the gift of nonsense, and the weapon used to recapture it is nonsense as well—the vorpal blade being the proverbial swift sword of satire. Interestingly, to achieve this end, Dodgson had reached back into a time before Kingsley, retrieving from his earlier writings the stanza "'Twas brillig, and the slithy toves." With Kingsley slain, he reasserts this family entertainment as the true reality: the poem subsides quietly with a repetition of the familiar opening lines, as if to mark a return to the normalcy of the days before Kingsley came to annoy the peace, when Dodgson's nonsense was his and his alone.

By slaying Kingsley straightaway in Chapter 1, furthermore, Dodgson was able to clear the air to pursue a sequel to *Wonderland* that would be more truly, as he says through the Knight, a thing "of my own invention." It is not, actually: *Looking-Glass* is built up from appropriated parts quite as much as *Wonderland*; the thing has the rickety charm of a Rube Goldberg contraption glued together from kitchen and garage junk, with Alice the little ball riding the loops, leaps, escalators, ferris wheels, and change-ups, looking for a bucket to plop into. But the tenor has improved; when Kingsley, or the echo of Kingsley, twice more turns up, it is as a Walrus properly expressed as a character from fable and as a Red Knight met as an equal on the jousting ground of comedy. Dodgson is freer to be his own invention now as the White Knight. In this, the penultimate climax toward which the book has been driving—his sad goodbye to the real Alice—he can more justifiably say at last what he has always wanted to say of all of it: "it came of itself."

Knave of Hearts

The farcical grand finale of *Alice in Wonderland* Dodgson extrapolated from a simple nursery rhyme:

> The Queen of Hearts, she made some tarts,
> All on a summer day:
> The Knave of Hearts, he stole those tarts
> And took them quite away!

In *Alice's Adventures Under Ground* he had disposed of the Knave's trial in a few paragraphs. For the public version he expanded the ordeal into two chapters and some twenty pages. Martin Gardner, sensing something afoot, has surmised an echo here of Mr. Pickwick's trial in *The Pickwick Papers*. The extended fun Dodgson makes of the Knave's predicament certainly demonstrates Dickens's dictum that the law is an ass, but whether we have Dickens to thank for this scene seems doubtful. Three things should be noted from the outset about the climax to *Wonderland*. First, it marks a return to the action of "The Queen's Croquet-Ground," which had been interrupted two chapters earlier; the venue has now been moved indoors to a court of justice that is apparently also the King and Queen's throne room. Second, Dodgson has made the trial the occasion for a cast encore. Alice arrives with the Gryphon to find the King of Hearts seated as judge, with the Queen beside him. A crowd of "all sorts of little birds and beasts" like the mob at the Caucus Race has gathered, along with the entire deck of playing-card characters. The White Rabbit has assumed the role of herald, reading out the accusation against the Knave and standing by to correct the King's mistakes in interpreting the evidence. Twelve jurors are seated, one of whom is Bill, the lizard who went up the chimney. The witnesses waiting to be called are the Duchess's cook, the Hatter, the March Hare and the Dormouse, and Alice herself. Two major players are conspicuously absent, however, whom we might have expected to turn up, just as they had turned up at the Queen's croquet match. This is the third thing to note about the opening of the trial: the Duchess and the Cheshire Cat, who entered the tale together in the Duchess's kitchen, have now vanished together.

The Duchess does not rejoin the cast, I would suggest, because she is irrelevant to what is about to happen; the Cheshire Cat, because its presence would be redundant. What had broken the earlier sequence of events, remember, was the Mock Turtle and Lobster Quadrille interlude in which Dodgson had lampooned *The Water Babies*. That business is now done. Kingsley is not on the agenda for the final two chapters, and so the Duchess need not appear. The absence of the Cat is more curious. If I am right that the Cat is Dodgson, then normal expectation would have it arriving now as it had at the croquet-ground, to ask Alice, "How are you getting on?" Its failure to do so is doubly curious because the story line has more or less led us to expect it. When we left the croquet match to see Kingsley given a thumping, it was the Cat who was under sentence of death and not the Knave. A meek and minor player in the scene, the Knave had quickly been superceded by the appearance of Cheshire Puss, and nothing at all had been intimated about locking him up. The chapter's center of attention is the impudent Cat:

> "Who *are* you talking to?" said the King, coming up to Alice, and looking at the Cat's head with great curiosity.
> "It's a friend of mine—a Cheshire Cat," said Alice: "allow me to introduce it."

"I don't like the look of it at all," said the King: "however, it may kiss my hand, if it likes."

"I'd rather not," the Cat remarked.

"Don't be impertinent," said the King, "and don't look at me like that!" He got behind Alice as he spoke.

"A cat may look at a king," said Alice. "I've read that in some book, but I don't remember where."

"Well, it must be removed," said the King very decidedly; and he called to the Queen, who was passing at the moment, "My dear! I wish you would have this cat removed!"

The Queen had only one way of settling all difficulties, great or small. "Off with his head!" she said without even looking round.

"I'll fetch the executioner myself," said the King eagerly, and he hurried off.

This confrontation on the croquet-ground ends with King and executioner running wildly about, looking for the Cat's head, to separate it from a body that is likewise nowhere to be found. Yet now, as we return to the scene two chapters later, the Cat has failed to reappear, and it is the Knave who is at risk of losing his head. The obvious reading of this would have the Cat and the Knave representing one and the same person. I had said earlier that I felt there were two figures in the book besides the Dodo in whom Dodgson had invested something of himself. The Knave is the second. The Cheshire Cat cannot appear at the trial to ask, "How are you getting on?" because Dodgson is already there, exploring a reversal of his and Alice's earlier relation as author and character. Now it is he, the Knave, who is the friend in need and Alice who must serve as the fairy-tale helper by testifying in his defense.

The next question is obvious enough: if Dodgson is on trial behind the mask of the Knave, what is the charge against him? The Knave is accused of stealing the Queen's tarts. Could this have had any specific reference to Dodgson's private affairs? I am going to jump ahead of myself a bit here and say, yes, it did, and that the charge against him was basically one of overall boorishness. The concluding chapters of *Wonderland* are an argument in defense of a man who is standing upon his dignity.

To understand how he might have played the boor, and with whom, I think we must first look away from Dodgson for a moment, however, and consider Alice herself. What is it that *she* has been doing all through the book? What has been the point of this incessant bickering for her? These are *Alice's* adventures in Wonderland, after all, and it is *her* question, "Who in the world am I?," that wants an answer. What did Dodgson think he was teaching her here? What was his point in dropping her into a land where everyone is twice mad and dragging her, often in tears, from one rude encounter to another?

Humphrey Carpenter has made the canny suggestion that Alice's wanderings in Wonderland recall Dante's tour of Hell in the *Divine Comedy*:

Certainly it is to a Dantean underworld that Alice comes, where many of the inhabitants are condemned to a punitive repetition of their tasks—the Duchess perpetually enduring the pepper and flying pots and pans of the Cook, the Mock Turtle and Gryphon for ever sighing by the sea, the Mad Hatter and March Hare endlessly moving round the tea table while time stands still. Alice has had a glimpse of Paradise, a vision of "the loveliest garden you ever saw." But when she finally reaches the rose garden it is not Paradise, not an Enchanted Place, but a cruel parody of Heaven where divine justice takes the form of the Queen of Hearts forever screaming "Off with her head!"[40]

Carpenter is properly speculative in proposing such an interpretation, but the notion does have appeal. It appeals to me particularly because there is room in it for a Kingsley. The resemblances among the three books are numerous. Dante, leaving Hell, finds Purgatory to be on an island—an image Kingsley surely had in mind when setting his own purgatorial school on St. Brandan's Isle. There is this suggestion in *Alice* as well when she comes ashore out of a sea of her own tears. In all three books Everyman passes from venue to venue like a visitor going from booth to booth at a circus sideshow, viewing the freaks of nature and engaging the damned in conversation. What distinguishes our Everyman Alice from Tom or Dante is her exasperation and anger. Wanting to best Kingsley at his own game but knowing he could not merely copy his purgatorial scheme, could Dodgson have thought to go him one better? To do so would necessitate sending Alice either to Paradise or to Perdition. The former being unthinkable for Dodgson—his diaries testify to a dread of making any such trespass in a fiction—Perdition it must be. And what better for his frustration and rancor as he began *Wonderland* in Kingsley's shadow than to resurrect Dante's nine circles of Hell? Down she goes, then, poor Alice, to join Cheshire Puss in that "under ground," as he first titled the place, to listen to the ravings of the proud and the angry and the slothful and the envious and to experience at first hand the fate of the damned as the endless round of a mad tea party. Dante fainted at the prospect; Alice cries. But then, Dante had a Beatrice to lead him to Paradise. Alice, whose guide is the solicitous but unhelpful Cat, can only wake up to the world-as-usual.

To read *Wonderland* as a peek into Hell has charm, but a first-generation paternity in Dante seems unlikely. Dodgson's conscious fear of committing sacrilege would have prohibited him from dipping into sacred tradition to make sport, I think. *Wonderland* is a very worldly book. If it does harken back to Dante, it is perhaps by way of Dean Swift's profane comedy, *Gulliver's Travels*. As Kingsley would adopt his island Purgatory from Dante, so earlier, apparently, had Swift. His Gulliver goes on an island-hopping tour of humanity read as a freak show of manikins and giants, mad intellectuals and carnal Yahoos. *Wonderland*, like *The Water Babies*, proceeds in a comparable manner and for similar satiric purposes. As Gulliver travels from island kingdom to island kingdom, so does Alice wander from house to house in a playing-card kingdom, visiting the peoples native to each: a White Rabbit, a Duchess, a March Hare, and so on. Her book could easily have been subtitled, after Swift, *Alice's Travels into Several Remote Regions of Oxford*. She shrinks to become one with the local Lilliputians, grows to join the Brobdignagians, and tries to hold her own in debate with various Oxford Laputans. The differences between the two books—and they are critical ones—are differences of temperament and texture. Swift's satire, like Dante's, is passionate but disinterested; his allegory, classical in its decodable clarity. It is, as they say, timeless. Dodgson's agenda is more allusive and more obscure. The prose is no less lucid, moment by moment, but in the aggregate *Alice* is destined to become quaint to the future. Working out his new line in fairy-lore, Dodgson gathered enough sheer strangeness together that the book became a genre yet unknown in literature. If we were to cross the intellectual comedy of Italo Calvino with the mysterious *ficciones* of that other Cheshire Cat of modern literature, Jorge Luis Borges, and were to phrase the thing as a children's story, we might come up with something like *Wonderland*, or certainly the more philosophical *Looking-Glass*. *Gulliver's Travels* is free of such enigmas and perplexities. *Wonderland* is Swift at twilight, Swift growing dim among the period furniture. A dream possessed of odd, Victorian humors, *Alice* has (not least because of Tenniel's pictures) that "suppressed background of culture" that Herbert Read spoke of, which distinguishes it from the true fairy tale and the allegory and fixes it forever in the historical moment.

On the other hand, it is this sense of the moment—Dodgson's moment in time, Alice Liddell's moment in time—that provides the key to what all this must mean to Alice as she asks, "Who in the world am I?" Dodgson denied that there was any plot to the proceedings, but there is at least an episodic story line, and because of it we need seek nothing more complicated in the book here than what it is that Alice is doing in Wonderland. And what she is doing is asking her way from house to house and trying to remain civil in a neighborhood full of fatuous and self-absorbed grownups. In other words, she is doing what Alice Liddell had to do: she is making the social rounds. This is the defining Victorian moment; the proper response to the question "Who in the world am I?" is to selflessly turn it around to read "Who am I in the world?" And who you are in this situation is the self you present to society, and no other. You are a young lady expected to call on neighbors, peers, retainers, and shopkeepers and to show due respect to your elders, whether about the campus or receiving guests at the Deanery. You are *Miss* Alice Liddell.

Running all through *Wonderland* is an implicit, and perhaps here and there specific, critique of a class of book well known to Miss Liddell—the book of etiquette. In Dodgson's day, guides for the clumsy and the perplexed had been a staple of children's publishing for nearly four centuries, ever since 1477, when William Caxton brought out the *Booke of Curtesye* to instruct boys employed in the houses of the rich, and 1487, when for the common folk he published *The Book of Good Manners*. The advice we now find in newspaper and magazine columns the humorist Gelett Burgess sent up finally in 1900 with *Goops and How To Be Them, A Manual of*

Manners for Polite Infants; but for the Victorians an early education in deportment was indispensable to the maintenance of civilization, and the rules required to hold things up were Byzantine in their complexity. Dodgson viewed these with a jaundiced eye even as he insisted upon their proper observance in his own presence. In *Wonderland* he took the child's side and showed the grownups to be an uncivil lot, making and breaking rules to suit themselves while holding Alice to a standard of courtesy and grace. This is basically what the story is all about from her perspective. The Queen's croquet match may be a cruel parody of Heaven, as Carpenter would have it, but it is more exactly a portrait of a child at sixes and sevens in the Deanery garden. The Mad Tea Party may be the absurdist philosophical treatise some writers have found it, but it is more exactly just what it purports to be: a lampoon of having to endure tea with the grownups. Perhaps Carpenter is right, though, about the spirit of the exercise. What else could the moral of *Wonderland* be, really, but that Hell is having neighbors such as these?

There *is* a darker side, I feel, to all this spoofing of the social round. A ghost script can just be detected here that shadows Alice's progress through five chapters, from "The Rabbit Sends in a Little Bill" to "The Queen's Croquet-Ground." What these episodes constitute is Dodgson's premonition of Alice's (and Alice Liddell's) likely future as an adult. Viewed retrospectively, as a whole, the sequence of events from the White Rabbit to the Caterpillar and the Pigeon and then to the Duchess, the Cheshire Cat, and the Mad Tea Party coalesces quite readily into an image of Alice grown up a woman unfulfilled.

The first whisper of warning is sounded as she approaches the White Rabbit's house to begin her round of social calls. Consider how things are being said here:

> Very soon the Rabbit noticed Alice . . . and called out to her, in an angry tone, "Why, Mary Ann, what *are* you doing out here? Run home this moment, and fetch me a pair of gloves and a fan! Quick now!" And Alice was so much frightened that she ran off at once in the direction it pointed to, without trying to explain the mistake that it had made.
>
> "He took me for his housemaid," she said to herself as she ran. "How surprised he'll be when he finds out who I am!"

Upstairs in the Rabbit's house, she happens on a strange bottle and, drinking from it, balloons to such a great size that "there seemed to be no sort of chance of her ever getting out of the room again." A prisoner in a man's bedroom, she falls to thinking how

> "it's rather curious, you know, this sort of life! I do wonder what *can* have happened to me! When I used to read fairy tales, I fancied that kind of thing never happened, and now here I am in the middle of one! There ought to be a book written about me, that there ought! And when I grow up, I'll write one—

but I'm grown up now," she added in a sorrowful tone: "at least there's no room to grow up any more *here*."

Could this not be the prophetic portrait of a wife rueing her childish illusions about marriage? How many women have had cause to complain of their husbands, "He took me for his housemaid?" and to wonder, "What *can* have happened to me!" as they contemplate the empty promises of the fairy tales they used to read. When Alice thinks, "How surprised he'll be when he finds out who I am!," she is echoing the Cinderella story, and when in light of the cramped truth she protests, "There ought to be a book written about me," she is echoing all those women who have ever wished the true story told. (In fact, a story will be written about their plight shortly, by the Norwegian playwright Henrik Ibsen. *A Doll's House* appeared in 1879, when Alice Liddell was twenty-seven.)

That this farce with the White Rabbit is an omen of Alice stifled by a bad marriage is confirmed by the events that follow. She calls next on the Caterpillar, who asks, "Who are *You*?" and Dodgson subliminally answers for her with an image of babies and the trials of motherhood. The Pigeon following the Caterpillar, and the Duchess the Pigeon, doubly invoke the idea. The Pigeon is a portrait of the good mother, protecting her brood against serpents, and the Duchess a portrait of the bad mother, "tossing the baby violently up and down" and finally flinging it at Alice with the remark, "Here! You may nurse it a bit, if you like!" (We could also take this to mean, "See how roughly that old Mrs. Bedonebyasyoudid, Charles Kingsley, treats the readers in his care.") Having become both wife and mother, Alice will in time, as a matron like the Duchess, fill her hours with the endless tea parties and soirées with the aristocracy that we see portrayed in the two chapters to follow.

Numerous writers have pointed out the dire implications of some of Dodgson's scenes, but I do not recall anyone's having cited Alice's experiment here with motherhood as such a moment. It is truly a dark reading of the cards. Dodgson's estimation of his pupil as a babysitter or future mother clearly places her in company not with the good mother Pigeon guarding her nest but with the Duchess who abandons her child to go to the Queen's croquet match. His mood throughout this scene is rather hard to read. As his biographers and his letters attest, he categorically loathed little boys, so I think we can assume he is enjoying himself when he has the Duchess sing,

> "Speak roughly to your little boy,
>   And beat him when he sneezes:
> He only does it to annoy,
>   Because he knows it teases."

and I am not at all sure that he doesn't see this baby's fate as a fit subject for slapstick comedy. But the scene otherwise is for Alice Liddell's benefit, not his own, and as a caution to her it is anything but complimentary. She begins her stint at babysitting well enough: "If I don't take this child away with me," thought Alice, "they're sure to kill it in a day or two. Wouldn't it be murder to leave it behind?" But when the baby will not leave off its grunting she allows herself a change of heart: "If you're going to turn into a pig, my dear," said Alice seriously, "I'll have nothing more to do with you. Mind now!" And a moment later, when the baby has turned completely swinish,

> she set the little creature down, and felt quite relieved to see it trot away quietly into the wood. "If it had grown up," she said to herself, "it would have made a dreadfully ugly child: but it makes a rather handsome pig, I think."

What Alice has done here is fulfill her own prophecy, "Wouldn't it be murder to leave it behind?" Not coincidentally, I think, it is at this moment that Dodgson chooses to appear in the guise of the Cheshire Cat. The tutor looking in to see how his pupil is making out with the new problem, he finds that she has not done well with it. In the famous passage that follows, Alice asks which way she ought to go next, and the Cat, replying that it doesn't matter, declares the world to be mad:

> "[W]e're all mad here. I'm mad. You're mad."
> "How do you know I'm mad?" said Alice.
> "You must be," said the Cat, "or you wouldn't have come here."

The "here" she has been mad enough to come to can now be read as adulthood, marriage, motherhood. And here Dodgson predicts she will fail the test. The whole point of the Cat's appearance has been to ask about the baby in her care. Distracted by her questions, it has overlooked this and then vanished. A moment later, however, as Alice is going on her way,

> "By-the-bye, what became of the baby?" said the Cat. "I'd nearly forgotten to ask."
> "It turned into a pig," Alice answered very quietly, just as if the Cat had come back in a natural way.
> "I thought it would," said the Cat, and vanished again.

There is something almost vindictively sly about Dodgson's manipulation of this sequence. It has been suggested that he wanted to marry Alice Liddell himself. This seems unlikely. He could be extremely jealous of his girl friends, though. Over his lifetime he would collect a large family of these little sisters, and he did not like losing them, either to puberty, when his amusements began to pale, or to marriage, in which event he was known on occasion to react with bursts of temper. His acid portrayal of Alice as wife and mother in these scenes seems more the anticipated frustration of a tutor whose beloved pupil he knows will forsake him and all that he has taught her to go off and marry some ass from the landed gentry. The Cat's "I thought it would" might be read as Dodgson's "I told you so"—: "I told you that if you followed the beaten path you would marry a fool. I told you that your child would be some wretched boy and that he would behave like a perfect little pig. I told you that wanting nothing to do with him you would give him over, like the Duchess, to a wetnurse and nannies to raise. And you *felt quite relieved* to do so, as I knew you would, and ashamed of yourself for feeling so relieved. That is why you answered me *very quietly* just now."

Alice Liddell did do it, too, or some of it. She married into country society, bore three sons to her sportsman husband, and lived, it appears, happily ever after. An aggrieved Dodgson disdained to note the wedding in his diary—or the failure of his tutorials to divert her from the expected path. The tutor she did heed in the end was instead that notorious snob and husband hunter of Christ Church, her mother.

Millions of words have been written on *Alice*, but the person who best understood the book was perhaps the woman no one would, or ever did, think to query on the matter. In pursuing this thought, let me again make the caution that much is plausible with Dodgson and everything arguable. I have presumed the existence of a ghost script lurking in these five middle chapters, for example, that constitutes a cautionary fable against growing down while growing up and smaller in spirit while larger in body. I might make equal sense of its corollary, that Dodgson did not want Alice Liddell to grow up at all and tried in his weird way, with this unhappy look into his crystal ball, to talk her out of it. Similarly, although Mrs. Liddell falls comfortably into place in our roman à clef as the matriarch of Wonderland, the Queen of Hearts, this is not to say that the Queen must be Mrs. Liddell and Mrs. Liddell alone every moment she is on stage. *Alice* was assembled for a variety of reasons and in a variety of moods. Taking note that the Queen and her court are an animated deck of cards, we might easily find five, or thirteen, or fifty-two well-shuffled things going on at once in Wonderland, with some characters acting as wild cards and the exact nature of the game never certain. Logically, it must be the game of hearts, I suppose, with the Queen being passed around like an unwanted guest at the tea party; but if it is, it is hearts the Hatter's way, always "two days wrong." This indeterminancy about the book is what has made it such rich pickings for critics, whereas most children's books, in their transparent simplicity, must go begging for attention. From Dodgson's deck, any hand you deal is playable at least once around.

The sure thing about the man—and what I believe Mrs. Liddell understood about him all too clearly—was that he liked to poke fun at people. I doubt we will ever know who all of his targets may have been or if a character is the same target in one place in the tale as in another. The Duchess is Kingsley, but exclusively Kingsley probably only on the Queen's croquet-ground. Characters like the Hatter or Humpty Dumpty from *Looking-Glass* are likely composites based on innocuous persons or on no one in particular. And it is only of secondary importance, really, if none but a few of these personages were modeled on people known to Alice Liddell. What matters more is the spirit of the venture and how in *Wonder-*

land every single conversation is governed by the humor of a man who practiced ridicule as a form of recreation. This is one thing we might wonder about Dodgson and Alice on their picnics or strolling about Christ Church or off by themselves in a corner of the Deanery: were they sometimes whispering asides to one another of a sort that would later turn up in the book? The impulse to annotate humanity with unkind footnotes is hardly unusual. Everyone at some time or another has sat on the park bench insulting the passers-by under his or her breath: "What a White Rabbit that one is"; "He's as mad as a March hare"; "Look at the chin on *that* Duchess." The difference is that Dodgson whispered his brickbats to children.

That this was in fact a habit of his when entertaining his girl friends finds some corroboration in a letter he wrote in 1864 to a daughter of George MacDonald's. I quote Hudson's summary of it here because it contains an intuition about Dodgson and listening parents that will presently throw some light on his troubles with the Liddells. Following a marvelous conceit about ink that has evaporated out of his inkwell and then fallen down on him as black snow, "[h]e went on to explain that the hot weather had made him so sad and sulky that he had thrown a book at the head of a visitor, the Bishop of Oxford, 'which I am afraid hurt him a good deal.' And then, thinking perhaps that he had gone too far, and that Mary MacDonald might report this act of violence to her father, he added: 'Mem: this isn't quite true — so you needn't believe it. . . . '"[41]

What we see behind Dodgson's placid facade at this diffident time in his life is the aging schoolboy reluctant to surrender his peashooter, a malcontent ever in need of little Jabberwocks to slay and ever ready to take shots at people behind their backs. How a game of lampoons was then translated into a catalogue of anger, insult, stifled wives, beheadings, and abandoned babies is the question.

The original cause may lie with his father. Recall the letter in which Charles senior promised to "leave nothing but one small cat alive in the whole town of Leeds, & I shall only leave that, because I am afraid I shall not have time to kill it." The blessing of nonsense had come with barbs already in place.

The more immediate cause, I am reasonably sure, was Kingsley. The usurper of the blessing had put Dodgson in the mood for rough play in *Wonderland*. Interestingly, Kingsley may also have provided him with both precedent and warrant for it. A speaking likeness of Alice appears in *The Water Babies*, a likeness of Alice as a maiden meek and polite who must bear much abuse and whose pleadings fall on deaf ears. Earlier I had alluded to a Quaker crow episode in Kingsley. Lacking only his postscript that Mrs. Bedonebyasyoudid will turn the Quakeress into a bird of paradise, here it is in its entirety:

[O]n the shore there gathered hundreds and hundreds of hoodie-crows, such as you see in Cambridgeshire. And they made such a noise that Tom came on shore and went up to see what was the matter.

And there he found them holding their great caucus, which they hold every year in the North; and all their stump-orators were speechifying; and for a tribune, the speaker stood on an old sheep's skull.

And they cawed and cawed, and boasted of all the clever things they had done; how many lambs' eyes they had picked out, and how many dead bullocks they had eaten, and how many young grouse they had swallowed whole, and how many grouse-eggs they had flown away with, stuck on the point of their bills, which is the hoodie-crow's particularly clever feat, of which he is as proud as a gipsy is of doing the hokanybaro; and what that is, I won't tell you.

And at last they brought out the prettiest, neatest young lady-crow that ever was seen, and set her in the middle, and all began abusing and vilifying, and rating, and bullyragging at her, because she had stolen no grouse-eggs, and had actually dared to say that she would not steal any. So she was to be tried publicly by their laws (for the hoodies always try some offenders in their great yearly parliament). And there she stood in the middle, in her black gown and gray hood, looking as meek and as neat as a Quakeress, and they all bawled at her at once —

And it was in vain that she pleaded —

That she did not like grouse-eggs;
That she could get her living very well without them;
That she was afraid to eat them, for fear of the gamekeepers;
That she had not the heart to eat them, because the grouse
were such pretty, kind, jolly birds;
And a dozen reasons more.

For all the other scaul-crows set upon her, and pecked her to death there and then, before Tom could come to help her; and then flew away, very proud of what they had done.

Now, was not this a scandalous transaction?

This excerpt from the seventh chapter of *The Water Babies* appeared in *Macmillan's Magazine* in February 1863. Dodgson was just then finishing the first draft of *Under Ground*. In *The Annotated Alice* Martin Gardner footnotes the as yet unwritten Caucus-race episode with this remark:

It has been suggested [42] that he was influenced by the caucus of crows in Chapter 7 of *Water Babies*, a scene that Charles Kingsley obviously intended as barbed political satire, but the two scenes have little in common.

But in fact they do. Alice and Tom have both come ashore from a swim in the sea. In Dodgson's scene birds predominate, with the Duck, Dodo, Lory, and Eaglet gathering around Alice much as the crows crowd the Quakeress in *The Water Babies*. Kingsley's caucus has been preceded by a speech in which the last of the Gairfowl relates the sad tale of how her species came to its end (the Gairfowl, or great auk, became extinct when Dodgson was in his twenties). In *Wonderland*, of course, we have the extinct Dodo. And Alice. What these two scenes have most in common is Alice.

Kingsley, as it happens, may have found his little martyr in yet another man's work, which would make Alice a third-generation appearance of the image. In his short tale "A Drop of Water," remember, Hans Christian Andersen had described her this way:

> One little creature sat still, all by herself in a corner, like a modest, sensitive little maiden. She wanted peace and quiet. But she was dragged out of her corner, mistreated, and finally she was eaten up.
> "It is most instructive and amusing," said the troll.

The story was published in 1848 in a collection of five tales titled *A Christmas Greeting to My English Friends*. I am making what I think is a reasonable presumption that Andersen's "modest, sensitive little maiden" who is mistreated and eaten up became Kingsley's "prettiest, neatest young lady-crow" who is abused and vilified and pecked to death. Dodgson may have known the earlier work as well—note the likeness of his *Easter Greeting to Every Child Who Loves Alice* to Andersen's *A Christmas Greeting*— but it is more probable, given their several resemblances, that Kingsley's Quakeress marks the passing over of *Alice* from private games into social satire. The transitional word here is caucus, for it is with the Caucus-race episode that Dodgson opens Alice's social round with neighbors intent on verbally tearing her to pieces. It may also be Kingsley's crows that we are seeing at the very end of *Wonderland* when Dodgson imagines his playing cards to be a flock of hostile birds: "[T]he whole pack rose up into the air, and came flying down upon her; she gave a little scream, half of fright and half of anger, and tried to beat them off. . . . "

According to taste, it will be either "a scandalous transaction" or "most instructive and amusing" that *Wonderland* follows so faithfully after Kingsley's hard parable and so sardonically mirrors the world in Andersen's drop of water. Dodgson must have felt it was a proper education in the ways of the world. Alice's mother, it appears, felt otherwise.

Several writers have speculated on what caused the break between the Liddells and the man who came calling on their daughter. It was never destined to be a cordial relationship—the senior Liddells had scant interest in Dodgson and he in them—but from his first acquaintance with the family in 1856, when Alice was four, it dithered along satisfactorily for some six years before the real trouble began. Dodgson had always been conscious of a certain coolness from Mrs. Liddell. Frustrated in his attempts to photograph the three sisters, he had noted in his diary on November 14, 1856, that her guarded hospitality "may be meant as a hint that I have intruded on the premises long enough." Even so, he persisted, and by 1862 he and Alice had become quite close. A year and a half later we find him in open warfare with her father over college affairs. These little academic firefights will continue until a final, ugly campaign against the dean in the 1870s. By then, however, it hardly mattered. The alliance with Alice was coming to an end even as Dodgson began the first draft of his tale in the fall of 1862;

Mrs. Liddell, who at some unknown date would destroy all his letters to her daughter, was putting a stop to it herself.

As a climax to the romance, this falling-out wants some precipitating cause, and the novelist lurking in several critics has tried to supply one. A favorite scenario has Dodgson in love with Alice and at some point in the chronology scandalizing her parents by proposing marriage. This may be farfetched even for a man as eccentric as the deacon. If an idea of marriage had ever been transmitted to Mrs. Liddell, it would most likely have been a childish fancy initiated by Alice herself. "Promise me you'll wait until I grow up" is not an uncommon fantasy with children favored by some adored adult, and Dodgson was sentimental enough to have abetted the make-believe by gallantly swearing to honor her request. If such were the case, it is not difficult to imagine Alice boasting excitedly to her mother how Uncle Charles had promised to wait for her, and Mrs. Liddell — famous locally for seeking to marry her girls as high in society as possible — responding, like the Queen of Hearts, "Leave off that! You make me giddy."

Humphrey Carpenter has suggested that if any one event implicates a proposal of marriage from Dodgson it is to be found where, intriguingly, it cannot be found — in a page missing from the deacon's diary for the summer of 1863. On June 25 — roughly a month after George MacDonald had recommended expanding *Alice* for publication and Dodgson began casting himself as the Cheshire Cat — he recorded accompanying the Liddell family on a river picnic and being allowed to bring the three girls home by train, unchaperoned. It is the page following this entry that has been ripped from the diary, suggesting, perhaps, that recorded on it was some detail or opinion that, upon reflection, Dodgson (or later a family member or executor) wished suppressed. I think it unlikely that with her sisters present he would have raised, or responded to, the subject of marriage, even jokingly, if Alice were the point of it. But some untoward remark about something or someone may have been made during the train ride and later repeated to Mrs. Liddell by the girls, and, her censure being conveyed to him by Alice, he may have thought it prudent to strike his thoughts from the record altogether.

I am indulging in storytelling here, but something very like this seems to have happened in the preceding year, as Dodgson was beginning his famous tale. On October 28 he reported of Mrs. Liddell, "I have been out of her good graces ever since Lord Newry's business." What Lord Newry's business might have been no one seems to know for sure. Hudson and Gardner call it a mystery. Roger Lancelyn Green has offered an explanation of Mrs. Liddell's cold shoulder that I have not seen elsewhere but which seems plausible:

One of her protégés was a titled undergraduate, Lord Newry; she wished the rules to be stretched a point to allow him to give a dance, but Dodgson the scrupulous would not allow a golden tassel to sway his fairness of judgment, and he vetoed this when it was brought up at the college meeting.

Could we not expand on this to envision Mrs. Liddell wanting her eldest daughter, Lorina, and likely all three girls, to understand that in the sociable and titled Lord Newry they should recognize a good catch? A dance sponsored by her protégé would not only add to her own luster but would be an occasion for the girls to refine their social skills. Dodgson's "fairness of judgment" at council, then, may have been something else. If he indeed brought up marriage on the train the following year, he would not have been thinking of Alice at all, perhaps, but making a joke at the expense of Lord Newry or some other popinjay or about marriage in the abstract. The joke would have been intended for all of them, but especially for Lorina, now thirteen and first to come under their mother's tutelage as marriage counselor. Recalling his letter to Mary MacDonald, I can see Dodgson on either occasion playing that same, wayward, and now jealous uncle that Perrault had played with his girls. Perrault had warned them about bad marriages with the tale of Bluebeard; Dodgson, perhaps, was now cautioning them through the plight of Alice in the house of the White Rabbit. In place of the heroine at the window, crying, "Anne, Sister Anne, do you see nothing coming?," we have Alice, a prisoner upstairs, considering the folly of fairy tales and muttering, "There ought to be a book written about me, that there ought!" Mrs. Liddell, catching wind of such talk, particularly if it centered on Lord Newry, would certainly have put Uncle Charles "out of her good graces."

While a marriage scenario of one sort or another is certainly a possible explanation for the breach, *Wonderland* itself suggests that it would have been only a part of something larger. The real question being debated in Dodgson's tale is the question that has been asked all through the descent of the fairy tale: Who is to teach the children? Here, the question of whether it is to be Kingsley or Dodgson has been reworded to read, Is it to be Dodgson or Mrs. Liddell? This is the crux of *Wonderland* for Alice. If she is to come into her best inheritance, she must distinguish the true teacher from the false. And so: Will it be the woman to whom nature has assigned the role, or the man with the strange and funny birthright?

One makes a great presumption when tutoring other people's children uninvited. Dodgson had run up against the truth learned by all tutors and artists: that whatever seems obvious and right to them need not to everyone else. To Mrs. Liddell's understanding, he was quite literally, as we say, filling Alice's head with nonsense. And, worse, of the various moods that can be expressed by the nonsense trope, most are harmless fun, but Dodgson's brand of nonsense was disrespectful. All through *Wonderland* he is whispering to Alice, Who *are* these people all around you, and why are they so intent on your meaning what they mean? Like Rousseau, who would allow Emile only the one book, *Robinson Crusoe*, Dodgson will allow Alice only this one book of himself. All others he detonates with charges of "Stuff and nonsense!" Mrs. Liddell, equally possessive, was determined to have her back.

For one's daughters one always makes a presumption against inquisitive men, of course, and for this no explanation is required. And when the daughter is ten and the caller thirty, and he will not cease writing and coming to the door, then it has gone too far and something must be done. Over how many dinners did the Liddells listen to Alice repeating, in her innocence and pride, all the clever things that Dodgson had said before exchanging glances that now was the time to close the door forever on dear Uncle Charles?

Bumping into the family at a school function late in 1863, Dodgson noted in his diary, "Mrs. Liddell and the children were there—but I held aloof from them as I have done all this term."[44] This is the tone of one who, having been removed from a situation, nonetheless thinks himself still in charge of it. In this same mood he has only recently reinvented himself as the aloof Cheshire Cat and begun composing those scenes in *Wonderland* that will say to the world which teacher had the best curriculum after all.

Certain peculiarities of the Knave's trial recommend taking such liberties with the evidence as I have done here. In retrospect, the proceedings have a queer resemblance to those overwrought monologues we all rehearse when we think we have been unjustly treated. The natural defense to any misunderstanding of our behavior is to hone our rebuttals until we have arrived at a satisfactory fiction of the whole affair. Such a fiction, I think, is what we are reading in these pages. The few perfunctory paragraphs given the trial in the manuscript version of the story may reflect a day when Mrs. Liddell's charges were little to mutter about. By 1863, however, Dodgson will need a full two chapters to speak his mind. The argument—now dispatched with the cool humor of the offstage Cat—seems the work of a man in the habit of overstepping his bounds, who, when called out on it, stands upon his honor that he has been falsely accused. Here he is, years later in *The Nursery Alice*, still using the trial as a moment of special pleading:

> I'll tell you all about it, as well I can. The way the trial ended was this. The King wanted the Jury to settle whether the Knave of Hearts was *guilty* or *not guilty*—that means that they were to settle whether *he* had stolen the Tarts, or if somebody else had taken them. But the wicked Queen wanted to have his *punishment* settled, first of all. That wasn't at all fair, *was* it? Because, you know, supposing he never *took* the Tarts, then of course he oughtn't to be punished. Would *you* like to be punished for something you hadn't done?

Dodgson was not the Liddell's cross to bear alone in these years. The Tennysons also had become acquainted with the man's unwanted calls and injured dignity. His question "Would *you* like to be punished for something you hadn't done?" is the note sounded at the close of this relationship of some thirteen years as well. Dodgson seems to have been gripped in his mid-twenties by certain enthusiasms or ambitions that sent him chasing after happy families, as Andersen had done, and after famous Victorians whose notice might enhance his sense of a place in the world. He began ingratiating himself with the Liddells in 1856. The following summer he appeared at the doorstep of the laureate, asking to take some photographs. In 1859 he again took Tennyson by surprise, turning up one morning while the bard was mowing his lawn. Later he would protest that he was not one of those vulgar sightseers who made a habit of tracking the great man to his summer lair, but it seems he had done exactly that. The Tennysons were politely receptive. Photos were taken. Over the next several years Dodgson would volunteer to do the dog's work of preparing an index for "In Memorium," pay homage to Tennyson in print, and drop in on the family from time to time. In 1865 he sent them a copy of *Alice*. Neither Tennyson encouraged the friendship—Dodgson was not to become an intimate of Emily Tennyson's, like Edward Lear—but things might have drifted along satisfactorily were it not for Dodgson's sporadically odd behavior. The year before beginning *Alice*, for example, he sold one of his photos of the laureate to a commercial publisher. Its appearance in 1861 as a carte de visite from the company of Joseph Cundall likely took Tennyson as much by surprise as Dodgson's popping up while the poet was at his yard work. It may be because of this incident that we find Dodgson taking the otherwise peculiar step of writing Tennyson for permission to read poems that had not been published but were circulating privately. His letter of March 3, 1870, which brought the acquaintance to an ugly climax, displays an adherence to the proprieties that is quite absurd. "It is so long since I have had any communication with your family," Dodgson begins, "that you will have almost forgotten my name by this time, I fear. I write on a matter very similar to what I have written about to you on two previous occasions."[45] The matter was again a manuscript copy of a poem that had been passed along to Dodgson by a friend. "I have not even read it yet," he continues, "& shall do so with much greater pleasure when I know that you do not object to my possessing it. What I plead for is, first that you will make me comfortable in possessing this copy by giving your consent to my preserving it—secondly, the further permission to *show* it to my friends. I can hardly go so far as ask for leave to give away copies of it to friends, tho' I should esteem such a permission as a great favour."

As the letter suggests, Dodgson has been in the habit of annoying people with trifling impositions. He goes on to remind Tennyson of another poem and a similar request and how, in compliance with Tennyson's wishes, he had destroyed that earlier copy; "but," he argues, "*this* seems to me a different case." And so on. Years hence he will understand what it is to be a reluctant celebrity deluged with petitions and not enough hours to write the meticulous replies they require (he, too, will refuse to be drawn into it when his time comes). Tennyson was fed up. Clearly, Dodgson's over-nice concern was an excuse to reclaim the acquaintance and reengage the poet in a correspondence. The man, by Victorian standards, was a boor. The reply, from Emily Tennyson, was short and to the point: "Dear Sir, It is useless troubling Mr. Tennyson with a request which will only revive the annoyance he has already had on the subject. . . . a gentleman should understand that when an author does not give his works to the public he has his own reasons for it."

Stung by the imputation that he was no gentleman, Dodgson fired off a long retort upholding his dignity. "I may fairly ask you to point out what I have failed to do," he concluded, "that the most chivalrous sense of honour could require." Tennyson's no doubt exasperated reply has not survived, but it was insufficient, for at month's end Dodgson returned a furious summation of the episode that was intended to give him the last word in a duel he now knew was ended. It is worth repeating for the light it casts on the likelihood that standing on his honor with the Liddells was what motivated him to expand a few paragraphs into the final two chapters of *Wonderland*. The formal letter to Tennyson appears on the reverse of a sheet of paper; in it he accuses the laureate of having done the first injury but sourly accepts that he must settle for "a retraction . . . of all dishonourable charges against me" that is "without a shadow of apology or expression of regret." On the front of the sheet he has presented Tennyson with a ludicrous but telling dramatization:

"Sir, you are no gentleman."

"Sir, you do me grievous wrong by such words. Prove them or retract them!"

"I reiterate them. Your conduct has been dishonourable."

"It is not so. I offer a full history of my conduct. I charge you with groundless libel: what say you to the charge?"

"I once believed even worse of you, but begin to think you may be a gentleman after all."

"These new imputations are as unfounded as the former. Once more, what say you to the charge of groundless libel?"

"*I absolve you.* Say no more."

Tennyson's "I once believed even worse of you" may refer to the sale of his photograph, which I think we can assume was unauthorized. In the heat of all this denial from Dodgson, could there not be a blush of recognition that he has indeed played the hypocrite to his own high standards, that, the Cheshire Cat having worked some mischief, the Deacon must now hotly deny that there is anything of a Cat in him? Note here how Dodgson turns a grievance over in his mind until he has arrived at a fiction that satisfies his needs. This argument with Tennyson he has imagined as an excerpt from a play or novel; could not the same habit of mind have earlier converted his unpleasantness with the Liddells into the trial of the Knave? His way of dealing with an injury is to objectify it, first as drama and then as comedy. The sting of a rebuff will never quite go away—we can hear it in *The*

Nursery Alice ("Would *you* like to be punished for something you hadn't done?")—but at least he has the means of detaching himself, like the Cat, in order to label such things mad. In calmer moments, which I assume made up the greater part of his days, he could work them up as parodies and burlesques and even acknowledge how silly he'd been: around the time he is thrashing away at Tennyson he is also writing the mock battle between the Red and the White Knights and the funny scene in which Alice must arbitrate between "a couple of great schoolboys," Tweedledum and Tweedledee. In the trial of the Knave we see manifested this same talent for psychic survival that we find sketched in the letter to Tennyson and fully drawn in *Through the Looking-Glass.* Alice is rudely received everywhere in Wonderland perhaps in part because Dodgson had to bear the same treatment from the Tennysons and Liddells of the world; as the Cat, however, he has the satisfaction of scratching some sly humor from his predicament. Emily Tennyson may not have been the first woman sent out to dispose of him or Tennyson the first dithering husband to be fictionalized by Dodgson:

> "A cat may look at a king," said Alice. "I've read that in some book, but I don't remember where."
> "Well, it must be removed," said the King very decidedly; and he called to the Queen, who was passing at the moment, "My dear! I wish you would have this cat removed!"

The trial of the Knave really begins with this roman-à-clef moment on the croquet-ground. Dodgson likely composed it rather late in 1863, when he was recording in his diary, "I held aloof from them as I have done all this term." The royal procession and the croquet match were brought forward from the manuscript version, and the Cat and Duchess added. The resulting mix of early and late ideas makes it rather hard to read between the lines of the scene, but, still, there are unmistakable hints that "The Queen's Croquet-Ground" and its continuation in "The Mock Turtle's Story" were addressed, in both versions, to Alice Liddell's understanding that an actual day in the Deanery garden was being burlesqued here. The episode might be read as a masquerade, then, with Alice's parents appearing as the King and Queen of Hearts, the phantom Lord Newry as the White Rabbit, perhaps, and Uncle Charles coming and going as Cat and Knave. Kingsley will turn up later as the Duchess to lead Alice into the next chapter and there introduce her to Dodgson's lampoon of *The Water Babies.*

One little signal alerting the real Alice to pay special attention (for Dodgson did not intend to remain aloof forever) is the connection made in the book between playing croquet and boxing someone's ears. In the midst of her tears in the opening chapter, Alice had cheered herself by recalling how she had once tried "to box her own ears for having cheated herself in a game of croquet she was playing against herself." When we next hear of ears being boxed, it is here at the Queen's croquet match. The Duchesss, we are informed by the White Rabbit, has done it to the Queen, which news prompts from Alice "a little scream of laughter." I assume that these two occasions, although separated by six chapters, derived from the same thought in Dodgson's mind and that he felt they would strike a responding chord in Alice Liddell's.

The well-known "painting the roses red" incident that introduces the croquet match, I think, would have cued Miss Liddell even more strongly that the game of recognitions was again afoot. The Queen has stormed on stage with her entourage to find the playing-card gardeners dutifully prone, trembling for their lives:

> "And who are *these*?" said the Queen, pointing to the three gardeners who were lying round the rose-tree; for, you see, as they were lying on their faces, and the pattern on their backs was the same as the rest of the pack, she could not tell whether they were gardeners, or soldiers, or courtiers, or three of her own children.

The gardeners may simply be gardeners, of course; the scene may echo a moment in real life when Mrs. Liddell upbraided three employees for a job badly done. On the other hand, improbable as it may seem, the gardeners may be the Liddell sisters. There are three of them, note, not two or four, and the Queen does wonder if they might be three of her own children. Dodgson loved to play games of hide-and-seek with the identities of his girl friends, concealing their names in acrostic poems, for example, or anagrams. To this point in *Wonderland* he has played this game three times. In the dedicatory poem he allegorized the sisters as his classical muses, the "cruel Three" who "beg a tale":

> Imperious Prima flashes forth
> Her edict "to begin it":
> In gentler tones Secunda hopes
> "There will be nonsense in it."
> While Tertia interrupts the tale
> Not *more* than once a minute.

At the Pool of Tears, Prima, who is Lorina, the eldest, appears as the Lory, and Edith, the youngest, as the Eaglet. In the Dormouse's little tale of the treacle well in "A Mad Tea-Party," Lorina becomes Elsie, a homonym for "L.C.," from Lorina Charlotte; Edith is Tillie, from her nickname, Matilda; and Alice appears under the anagram Lacie. It would not be terribly surprising if, having worked these tricks in the first half of the book, Dodgson continued to do so in the second.

There are obvious problems with reading the three gardeners to be the girls. "Three of her own children" sounds deliberate enough, but the gardeners are spades when, if members of the royal family, they should be hearts, and they are the wrong sex. The first problem we can easily resolve, however, simply by imagining the girls to have been originally either in costume or in work clothes playing at being Mother's helpers. As for being spades rather than hearts, there may be a pun implicit here that they are twice in the wrong suit.

A third difficulty presents itself when we realize that if one of the gardeners is really Alice Liddell, then our heroine is twice present in the story at the same moment. Something very like this did happen with the treacle well, of course, which called up a no less complicated picture of Alice Liddell listening to a story about herself listening to a story about herself as someone named Lacie. We might recall, too, that Dodgson introduced Alice in Chapter 1 as a child who "was very fond of pretending to be two people" — which remark, as it happens, provides the tail of the sentence telling how Alice boxed her own ears at croquet.

And finally, after all, this *is* make-believe. In *The Nursery Alice*, Dodgson as much as admitted that no one in this scene is what he or she appears to be: "What funny little men they are! But *are* they men, do you think? I think they must be live cards, with just a head, and arms, and legs, so as to *look* like little men."

The numerical differences between these live cards replicates the differences in the ages of the Liddell sisters, who are thirteen, ten, and eight to the gardeners Two, Five, and Seven. The difference between Lorina and Alice is three years, as with Two and Five; the difference between Alice and Edith is two years, as with Five and Seven. The Two of Spades, then, would be Lorina, the Five Alice, and the Seven Edith. Five and Seven look to Two as their spokesperson, as younger sisters would. When no one is listening, the three carry on in a very childlike manner:

> "Look out now, Five! Don't go splashing paint over me like that!"
> "I couldn't help it," said Five, in a sulky tone, "Seven jogged my elbow."
> On which Seven looked up and said, "That's right, Five! Always lay the blame on others!"
> "*You'd* better not talk!" said Five. "I heard the Queen say only yesterday you deserved to be beheaded."
> "What for?" said the one who had spoken first.
> "That's none of *your* business, Two!" said Seven.
> "Yes, it *is* his business!" said Five. "And I'll tell him — it was for bringing the cook tulip-roots instead of onions."

Change a "his" to "her" and substitute the girls' names for the cards' numbers, and you hear this passage for what it is — the transcript of a "did — did not — did so" quarrel among children when Mother is coming and a scolding or spanking (beheading) is in the offing and blame is being passed down from the eldest to the youngest. The allusion to an earlier, childish mistake made by Seven, little Edith, in bringing the cook tulip-roots is furthermore so oddly specific and nonfunctional an afterthought as to almost insist that the scene is a redaction containing the vestigial trace of some actual event.

Whether Mrs. Liddell ever recognized herself, the dean, or the children in any of this there is nothing in the record to indicate. Unless Dodgson was deluding himself that the book would be taken as being all in good fun—as he deluded himself in the dedicatory poem that Alice's verbal brawls were friendly chats—he would hardly have made the Queen both recognizable and this outrageous. On the other hand, Mrs. Liddell did destroy his letters, which seems an act in want of more provocation than a mere dislike of the man. Perhaps Dodgson felt that making the caricature this grotesque simply obviated any chance of recognition. If so, he may have misjudged either his art or the suspicious eye of his reader at the Deanery.

Alice's behavior before the Queen makes sense, really, only if we see it as the reaction of a daughter at odds with her mother. Would a little girl being introduced to the actual queen of the realm ever behave this way? Note how out of proportion to the occasion Alice's response is when the Queen asks her if the little men lying prostrate before her are gardeners or three of the royal children. Only a moment earlier she was addressing the Queen "very politely." Her unexpected outburst now has the ring of a guilty party caught off guard:

> "How should *I* know?" said Alice, surprised at her own courage. "It's no business of *mine*."
> The Queen turned crimson with fury, and, after glaring at her for a moment like a wild beast, began screaming, "Off with her head! Off with—"
> "Nonsense!" said Alice, very loudly and decidedly, and the Queen was silent.
> The King laid his hand upon her arm and timidly said: "Consider, my dear: she is only a child!"

As the quarrel among the gardeners mimicked a spat among siblings, so this exchange seems the portrait of a family having a scene. It is, I think, Dodgson's camouflaged exposé of the Liddell family dynamics, with himself and half of Christ Church standing by uncomfortably as witnesses. The dean does not come off too badly, actually; Dodgson was yet a decade away from attacking him out in the open with satirical pamphlets like *The New Belfry* (1872) and *The Vision of the Three Ts* (1873). In 1863 he knew that his superior had no use for him and wanted Cheshire Puss shooed from the Deanery, but he did not here indict the dean as a parent. That pleasure he saved for Mrs. Liddell, mercilessly working the irony that the person insisting everyone lose their heads is the only personage in the tale to actually lose it. What we see in the passage just quoted is papa pacifying his wife for the child's sake. How accurate a picture of life at home with the Liddells this might be is anyone's guess. In the final chapter of the book, however, we have Dodgson's assurance that the wife was constitutionally prone to fits of anger and the husband to flurries of appeasement. While considering the evidence brought against the Knave, the King must weigh a bit of written testimony containing the words "before she had this fit."

> "[Y]ou never had fits, my dear, I think?" he said to the Queen.
> "Never!" said the Queen, furiously. . . .

"Then the words don't *fit* you," said the King, looking round the court with a smile.

If it was in Mrs. Liddell's nature to have fits, Dodgson's nudging Alice to stand up to the Queen may reveal a likely cause for it. To the rhubarb on the croquet-ground, add the exchange with which he chose to end *Wonderland*:

> "Hold your tongue!" said the Queen, turning purple.
>
> "I won't!" said Alice.
>
> "Off with her head!" the Queen shouted at the top of her voice. . . .
>
> "Who cares for *you*?" said Alice. . . .

It certainly sounds like a contest of wills between mother and daughter. What we may be seeing here is the fallout from Mrs. Liddell's exploding perception that what her Alice has gained from Uncle Charles's tutelage is really a taste for talking back. Consider how different is sister Lorina: on the croquet-ground the Two of Spades addresses the queen mother "in a very humble tone, going down on one knee." In a kind of visual double entendre Alice appears as a Jekyll and Hyde. As the Five of Spades she is the obedient daughter, prostrate before her mother's will; as Dodgson's creation she is the disobedient daughter quite literally standing up to her mother and, with Uncle Charles's favorite word, "nonsense," giving her a bit of lip. Even a single occasion of such behavior would account for Dodgson's diary entry that he had fallen out of Mrs. Liddell's good graces.

It should be possible to draw up a best-case scenario of this afternoon soap opera on the croquet-ground and its aftermath. Domestic comedy is how Dodgson saw it: in the trial scene we see him replaying it as a washtub weeper in the curious poem "They told me you had been to her, / And mentioned me to him." A plausible outline of the events might tell how one day in 1862 at a lawn party Mrs. Liddell threw a fit over something the children had or had not done. Dodgson may have been present or been told about it later. Putting his two cents in, he remarked to Alice sympathetically that her mother had had a fit over nothing. This innocuous opinion made its way back to Mrs. Liddell, either through Alice or through Mrs. Liddell's protégé, the White Rabbit, Lord Newry, who may have overheard it at the Deanery or been taken into Alice's confidence as she tried to defend herself to this young friend of her mother's. The queen of the household demanding to know what business any of this was of the Reverend Dodgson's, a defiant Alice sassed back, and Mrs. Liddell, already annoyed by Dodgson's nonsensical tutelage, withdrew her good graces from Uncle Charles for once and for all. The dean, who to keep the peace at home lived in a state of perpetual denial, pretended the whole thing had never happened. He was relieved to be rid of young Dodgson, anyway, whom he had always suspected of being capable of taking a remark like "You never had fits, my dear, I think?" and submitting it, like one of the Tennyson photographs, for a public viewing.

So it was, or might have been, that the Liddell family closed ranks in

1862 and 1863, leaving Alice to grow up to be her mother after all and Uncle Charles to retreat to his room to mount his injured defense.

He is being very good to himself with his self-portrait as the Knave. The demure fellow standing witness to the family squabble on the croquet-ground is displaying a nicety of feeling found in no other character in the tale, save perhaps the Dodo. Patiently he holds the King's crown; obsequiously he bows and smiles to the Queen; and with what good grace he accepts her verdict of "Idiot!" His delicacy with the gardeners cowering on the ground is telling:

> The King laid his hand upon her arm and timidly said, "Consider, my dear: she is only a child!"
> The Queen turned angrily away from him, and said to the Knave, "Turn them over!"
> The Knave did so, very carefully, with one foot.

The Knave executes the command "very carefully" because of what Dodgson knows here, that the cards are really Alice, Lorina, and Edith, and also because he is a *nice person*. Indeed, not only is the Knave the nicest person in the book; he is the *only* nice person in the book. Not even Alice is this tenderly portrayed. I am inclined to think that when Dodgson borrowed Kingsley's meek and martyred Quaker maid, who must stand trial precisely for *not* stealing, as the Knave is accused of doing, he had himself in mind as much as his heroine.

In playing first the guileless Knave on the croquet-ground, and then the knowing Cat, and then the Knave again, Dodgson worked his most artful sleight of hand. The ruse he is working here is like that stock comedy routine in which a dupe, sensing a nearby tongue protruding his way, turns to find the perpetrator staring innocuously into space, perhaps quietly whistling a tune. The dupe returns to his business only to feel the discomforting presence yet again, and again the perpetrator is caught looking innocent of the deed. Finally, when the dupe is thoroughly bolluxed, a fatuous grin comes out from hiding on the perpetrator's face. The dupe here is the King of Hearts, who wants Dodgson removed from the premises for refusing to kiss his hand. The fatuous grin belongs to the Cheshire Cat, who has been reintroduced to dare to "look at a king." When the insolent Cat is whisked away, Dodgson stands before the Liddell's judgment seat as the Knave, blinking in protest at the outrage being perpetrated against *him*. Technically, he can do this with a straight face because, yes, as the Knave, Uncle Charles is innocent of what Dodgson the Cat has done. Just how innocent was he of stealing away the hearts and minds of little girls and of playing the boor? For an insomniac bachelor who sat up nights devising cunning puzzles and redressing wrongs, we would have to conclude, not very. But clearly he felt he was innocent enough to be deserving of that same "retraction of all dishonourable charges" against him that he would later demand of Tennyson.

The hearts he has stolen as the Knave are of course the Queen's royal children and the tarts of the nursery rhyme by which the Knave stands accused. This will be the fifth appearance of Alice, Lorina, and Edith in disguise:

> The Queen of Hearts, she made some tarts,
>> All on a summer day:
> The Knave of Hearts, he stole those tarts
>> And took them quite away!

This time Dodgson provides clear proof that the make-believe is a code for the Liddell girls. He does so with a bit of evidence taken at the trial from the Duchess's cook. It is information that the King is reluctant to admit and the Queen frantic to suppress:

> The King looked anxiously at the White Rabbit, who said, in a low voice, "Your majesty must cross-examine *this* witness."
> "Well, if I must, I must," the King said with a melancholy air, and, after folding his arms and frowning at the cook till his eyes were nearly out of sight, he said, in a deep voice, "What are tarts made of?"
> "Pepper, mostly," said the cook.
> "Treacle," said a sleepy voice behind her.
> "Collar that Dormouse!" the Queen shrieked out. "Behead that Dormouse! Turn that Dormouse out of court!"

"What are tarts made of?" is a vestige of the nursery rhyme "What are little boys made of?" with its second verse, "What are little girls made of? . . . Sugar and spice / And all that is nice." These lines were first published in James O. Halliwell's *The Nursery Rhymes of England*, which we have seen before and from which Dodgson is known to have taken "The Queen of Hearts" and most of the verses used in *Through the Looking-Glass*. When he selected "The Queen of Hearts" for *Wonderland* he brought out this other rhyme as well. We can see another remnant of it in Alice's musings on the croquet-ground after she has met the Duchess:

> "Maybe it's always pepper that makes people hot-tempered . . . and vinegar that makes them sour — and camomile that makes them bitter — and — and barley-sugar and such things that make children sweet-tempered."

In the vestige of the poem that we see being used at the trial, nasty little boy tarts are made of pepper, as the cook can attest from her knowledge of the Duchess's baby, who "can thoroughly enjoy / The pepper when he pleases." Sweet little girl tarts are made of treacle, as the Dormouse knows from his acquaintance with things made of sugar and spice, namely, treacle, tarts, and little girls. The Dormouse's correction of the cook completes the identification of the Queen's tarts with little girl tarts to be identified with the girls in the treacle well, namely, Alice, Lorina, and Edith. The summer day on which the rhyme places the theft of the tarts may have reminded

Dodgson of the famous picnic of July 4 or of all those outings on which he stole their hearts away.

Present at the trial now as both an impartial observer and the implicit victim of the crime, Alice can serve Dodgson's needs in that same dual capacity she filled on the croquet-ground, where she appeared as both her own disobedient self, sassing her mother, and the compliant Five of Spades. The purloined tart being the only true witness to the alleged deed, she must, through her proxy, Alice, be called to testify on the Knave's guilt or innocence; but what Dodgson shows us here instead is a sleight of hand. When her name is read out as the next witness, Alice, the impartial observer, steps forward claiming to know nothing whatsoever of the matter and expressing surprise at being called at all. Behind her in actual fact is the culpable Cat, with its tongue stuck out, but by her testimony we see only the guileless Knave, as startled at being accused as Alice was at being called. What Dodgson wanted to convey by this, I suppose—to the Liddells, to the world, perhaps even to himself—was the thought that although Alice had indeed been "stolen," no crime had actually been committed. That is, by his lights, nothing untoward had ever happened or been said while she was in his company.

In the end, of course, the details of his culpability were of secondary importance to the Liddells, who simply wanted him out of their hair and gone from the minds of their children. In Dodgson's mind the imagined trial at the Deanery must have seemed an exasperating farce; to the Liddells it may have been simply good sense to decide, like the Queen, "Sentence first—verdict afterwards." Their being all of them polite folk, however, and colleagues, the defenestration of Uncle Charles would drag on for more than a year, from the lawn party in 1862 and "Lord Newry's business," through the train ride and missing diary page the following summer, to December 1863, when he wrote that he had held aloof from them all that term. Whatever did happen at the Deanery that finally decided the affair, it was long over as he composed these concluding chapters late in 1863 or early 1864. What he wanted from the exercise was what he would later want from Tennyson—the restoration of his pride and honor—and the satisfaction of having everyone see that the Liddells' judgment had been unwarranted and their behavior unworthy of the love he had shown their daughter. He was also looking to settle a score with a fifth columnist, a court snitch, who I think must have been the shadowy Lord Newry.

The evidence upon which the accusation against Dodgson finally rests in *Wonderland*—"the most important piece of evidence we've heard yet," as the King puts it—is a conundrum that to my knowledge no one has ever tried to solve, on the sensible assumption that it is exactly the gibberish it appears to be:

> There was dead silence in the court, whilst the White Rabbit read out
>   these verses:—

"They told me you had been to her,
 And mentioned me to him:
She gave me a good character,
 But said I could not swim.

He sent them word I had not gone
 (We know it to be true):
If she should push the matter on,
 What would become of you?

I gave her one, they gave him two,
 You gave us three or more;
They all returned from him to you,
 Though they were mine before.

If I or she should chance to be
 Involved in this affair,
He trusts to you to set them free,
 Exactly as we were.

My notion was that you had been
 (Before she had this fit)
An obstacle that came between
 Him, and ourselves, and it.

Don't let him know she liked them best,
 For this must ever be
A secret, kept from all the rest,
 Between yourself and me."

The usual supposition, that this is pure nonsense, devoid of any meaning, may be only half right. Nothing in *Wonderland* of this length and complexity is there without some attending association for Dodgson. The poem is such a tangle that those associations may now be irretrievably lost, but I want to look at it a moment anyway, on the assumption that it is nonsense only on its surface and is otherwise one of those coded puzzles Dodgson loved to invent. As he did with "Jabberwocky," he had dug through his files to find some old effort that might be adapted for the occasion. These six stanzas closely follow his eight-stanza poem, "She's all my fancy painted him," of 1855. As the title line suggests, this also was an exercise in scrambled pronouns. Unlike its successor, however, it was a spin on the parallel bars of nonsense purely for sport. By dropping two stanzas, rearranging and rephrasing the others, and installing the poem in the trial scene as "the most important piece of evidence," Dodgson in the end imputed a meaning to it. If most of that meaning must be conceded lost, we can at least see that there is a plot, or a parody of a plot, lurking in the lines. I suspect that more than one event may be implicated, with the confounding result that the pronouns may not even designate the same persons from one stanza to the next. Here is the perplexed King, then, "muttering over the verses to himself: '*We know it to be true—*' that's the jury, of course—'*If she should push the matter on*'—that must be the Queen. . . .'" In *Looking-*

Glass Humpty Dumpty's interpretations of "Jabberwocky" are most of them Dodgson's own, so I think the King must be right here in finding the "she" of the poem to be the Queen. The line "Before she had this fit" is what led him to remark, "You never had fits, my dear, I think," and pointed us toward Mrs. Liddell. The first stanza, then, taken as a message from Dodgson to Alice, might be paraphrased to read, "They told me, Alice, that you had been to your mother, and mentioned me to the Dean; she gave me a good character, but said I could not swim in the social stream."

What we might have here is a picture of Alice Liddell pleading Dodgson's case before her parents. The bafflement of pronouns prohibits our retrieving the particulars, but I think we can hold to a few observations about the poem. First, Dodgson meant it to demonstrate about the whole trial what anyone can plainly see, that the charges against the Knave (and so against himself) are unfounded. When the King continues, "'*I gave her one, they gave him two—*' why, that must be what he did with the tarts, you know—," Alice points out the obvious and, Dodgson must have hoped, telling fact "But it goes on '*they all returned from him to you.*'" One and two make three, note: three girls in the treacle well, three gardeners, three Liddells gone picnicking with Uncle Charles, and all returned safely home again. Consistent with his portrait of the Knave as impeccably *un*boorish, here in Alice's protest is Dodgson's summation of his character: that he is no bounder, no knave to steal and subvert the Queen's tarts, but a gentleman who always returns them spotless to their rightful place: "'Why, there they are!' said the King triumphantly, pointing to the tarts on the table. 'Nothing can be clearer than *that.*'"

Unfortunately, there *are* some details about the trial that could be clearer than that. The second thing to note about the poem is the fact that it exists at all. Here is a message conveyed in a private code and calling for utter secrecy between two conspirators:

> For this must ever be
> A secret, kept from all the rest,
> Between yourself and me.

The Knave denies having written it, and in so doing introduces a puzzle I am not sure can be solved.

"Are they in the prisoner's handwriting?" asked one of the jurymen.

"No, they're not," said the White Rabbit, "and that's the queerest thing about it." (The jury all looked puzzled.)

"He must have imitated somebody else's hand," said the King. (The jury all brightened up again.)

"Please, your Majesty," said the Knave, "I didn't write it, and they can't prove that I did: there's no name signed at the end."

"If you didn't sign it," said the King, "that only makes the matter worse. You *must* have meant some mischief, or else you'd have signed your name like an honest man."

The King's reasoning is Kafkaesque but correct, for the Knave has just given himself away as a liar. He has been standing "before them in chains, with a soldier on each side to guard him." The White Rabbit is beside the King, facing the Knave. The letter containing the incriminating verses has presumably been folded until now, and no one but the White Rabbit has seen its contents. The Knave must be the author of the verse and a liar because only the author could have known that it was unsigned.

It is not clear here whether Dodgson was merely being careless about who was standing where in the courtroom, within peeking distance of the letter, or whether he meant something by this slip. I assume that he would not be subverting his attempt to exonerate himself by suddenly admitting the Knave to be a sneak. I suppose the Knave could be understood as being innocent in his own mind, and a liar only to spare himself having to explain to dullards that, yes, he is guilty of the indiscretion of passing notes but innocent of any crime, for the notes are only harmless fun to amuse children. If this is Dodgson's brief, on the other hand, then he too is lying here—perhaps to himself, as when characterizing the book as a "friendly chat"—for all the deacon's notes are full of mischief. He stands guilty of meaning mischief exactly as accused by the King. Mischief—secret mischief, mischief directed against people for the amusement of a child—is the whole point of *Wonderland*.

I think Dodgson may not have been attending closely enough to detail to realize that he had named *someone* a liar with this exchange. His eye has been fixed elsewhere. He has been too preoccupied with exposing the dimness of the King to notice how he has implicated himself. He has also been rather intent on settling a score with the cunning fellow who introduced this "most important piece of evidence" into the trial in the first place:

"There's more evidence to come yet, please your Majesty," said the White Rabbit, jumping up in a great hurry: "this paper has just been picked up."

"What's in it?" said the Queen.

"I haven't opened it yet," said the White Rabbit; "but it seems to be a letter, written by the prisoner to—to somebody."

"It must have been that," said the King, "unless it was written to nobody, which isn't usual, you know."

"Who is it directed to?" said one of the jurymen.

"It isn't directed at all," said the White Rabbit: "in fact, there's nothing written on the *outside*." He unfolded the paper as he spoke, and added, "It isn't a letter, after all: it's a set of verses."

The Rabbit's excitement here is more than a little suspicious. The evasively intransitive "has just been picked up" suggests to the contrary that the letter has just emerged from the Rabbit's own pocket. It appears, too, that the Rabbit had earlier opened and read the paper and has only been waiting for the right moment to use it to seal the Knave's fate—a moment almost lost, as implied by its "jumping up in a great hurry." So the question becomes this: if the White Rabbit wished to incriminate the Knave with this missive, who besides the Liddells might have wanted to incriminate Dodgson with a similarly intercepted message addressed to Alice?

We needn't look far for the culprit. It was the student protégé of "Lord Newry's business," remember, who had recently put Dodgson out of Mrs. Liddell's good graces. Why the Rabbit should be assigned the role of herald at book's end may tell us something as well. Since a herald does not ordinarily serve as an officer of the law courts, which is the Rabbit's function here, other possibilities recommend themselves. The master of anagrams may have recognized, for example, in the depths of another sleepless night, that HERALD was an anagram for HER LAD, which aptly describes Newry's position at the Deanery. Then, too, a herald is one who delivers messages of state, and the Rabbit's business at the outset of the tale, when Alice spots him checking his watch and follows him down the hole, may have been just that. To Dodgson the lad was a gossip and a snitch. His being a herald would explain what the Rabbit was doing above ground in the first place; his playing Lord Newry suggests what else about him might have aroused Alice's curiosity. What did he know, and why was he rushing to the Deanery with it?

There is another meaning of the word "herald" that Dodgson may have had in mind. A herald is an official whose specialty is heraldry, the tracing of family pedigrees. Mrs. Liddell had married into the lower aristocracy when she wed the dean, and she would become notorious in college for sniffing out even better opportunities for her daughters. What a cozy love nest we would have, then: two snobs, each playing to the other's vanity—he eager to please his dean's wife; she eager to be pleased by a lord. Small wonder that the third snob in the comedy, seeing the shadow of his own aspirations in these two, perhaps, might wish to see them shown up.

Reading Lord Newry as the White Rabbit and the Rabbit as a snob and tale-bearer throws an interesting light on earlier scenes in the book—Alice's quasi-marriage to the Rabbit, for example, or this curious interlude between the Queen's invitation to croquet and the actual start of the game:

> "It's—it's a very fine day!" said a timid voice at her side. She was walking by the White Rabbit, who was peeping anxiously into her face.
>
> "Very," said Alice. "Where's the Duchess?"
>
> "Hush! Hush!" said the Rabbit in a low, hurried tone. He looked anxiously over his shoulder as he spoke, and then raised himself upon tiptoe, put his mouth close to her ear, and whispered, "She's under sentence of execution."
>
> "What for?" said Alice.
>
> "Did you say 'What a pity!'?" the Rabbit asked.
>
> "No, I didn't," said Alice. "I don't think it's at all a pity. I said 'What for?'"
>
> "She boxed the Queen's ears—" the Rabbit began. Alice gave a little scream of laughter. "Oh, hush!" the Rabbit whispered in a frightened tone. "The Queen will hear you!"

Happily, we know nothing of Lord Newry—a great convenience for the novelizing critic—and so, with apologies to the man's possible descendants, I offer the speculation that the young sycophant curried favor with all the Liddells, children included. Dodgson's treatment of the rabbity lord, an undercurrent running all through the book like his animus toward Kingsley, smacks of court intrigue. What we see on the croquet-ground and at the trial is a battle of innuendo between the White Rabbit and the Knave for the favor of the King and Queen on the one hand and Alice on the other. The Rabbit has won over the royal parents, finally, by maligning the Knave with dishonorable motives impugned to his courtship of the royal daughters. In *The Nursery Alice* Dodgson revealed that the Rabbit did indeed bear a personal enmity toward the Knave: "The White Rabbit is standing near the King, reading out the Song, to tell everybody what a bad Knave he is." What Dodgson would like to do to the Rabbit in return he establishes at the very beginning of the book with a parenthetical hope that all his little readers will do it for him:

[T]he Duchess was a very cross old lady: and the Rabbit *knew* she'd be very angry indeed if he kept her waiting. So the poor thing was as frightened as frightened could be (Don't you see how he's trembling? Just shake the book a little, from side to side, and you'll soon see him tremble). . . .

What we are seeing in this exchange between Alice and the Rabbit on the croquet-ground, I think, is Dodgson taking satisfaction on Newry in a more subtle way. He has something on the lad that he is expressing, almost gleefully, through the high anxiety of the Rabbit. What it is, the passage implies, is that Newry is currently himself in disfavor with Mrs. Liddell. The precipitous fellow has inadvertently put the Queen of Hearts in the ring with the Duchess, as it were, to have her ears boxed. To follow this metaphor, consider the equation being made by it: if the Duchess is boxing the Queen's ears, then Charles Kingsley is boxing Mrs. Liddell's ears. What this suggests to me, since Kingsley and Mrs. Liddell never met, is that to ingratiate himself with his patroness, the young lord has been bringing her children gifts. One of these, delivered in good faith, no doubt, was a copy of that new sensation for the nursery, *The Water Babies*.

The unlucky herald never guessed there might be something in the book to box their mother's ears, turning them red with recognition and anger. It appears in a most telling place, the little fable I quoted earlier, "Why the Sea Has Bubbles." Mrs. Bedonebyasyoudid is down at the sea floor, recall, administering justice to sinners not wicked enough for Hell but nonetheless needing "a taste of their own rods." The climactic paragraph of this episode begins, conspicuously, "And she boxed their ears. . . . " I say conspicuously because it must have been so to Mrs. Liddell, for the persons being smartened up at this point in the comedy are the cruel schoolmasters.

Dean Liddell had not always presided at Christ Church. He had moved up to the position from the headmastership of the Westminster School, where, I assume, corporal punishment was still the order of the day. It would have been as well for Lord Newry had he brought the children *The Communist Manifesto*. In that same fifth chapter where Dodgson would discover the phrase "as mad as a March hare" and Mrs. Bedonebyasyoudid's useful ugliness, Mrs. Liddell discovered, while reading to the girls, perhaps, that God was waiting for their beloved father to chastize him for officiating while other children were mistreated, and that the more he stood upon his honor the more his cries and howls were going to come "up through the sea like bubbles out of soda-water." She discovered next the even uglier news that for sins of her own she would be keeping him company. The schoolmasters got their comeuppance in the afternoons. Before luncheon Mrs. B. settled accounts with "a whole troop of foolish ladies" who had cramped their children's growth by making them conform to the current fashions. For them, too, there awaited an afterlife of being done by as they did. For Mrs. Liddell this would be a sore time of tottering about in wasp waists and "the most dreadfully tight boots" while nearby her husband was waiting to have his ears boxed and his head thumped with rulers.

It must have amused Dodgson to contemplate her reaction to this discovery. The Rabbit's whispered aside about the Duchess, "She's under sentence of execution," would indicate that Mrs. Liddell had had quite enough of this new thing called Nonsense and that Lord Newry's gift was headed where Dodgson's letters to Alice were soon to go. When the Rabbit sidles up to Alice, "peeping anxiously into her face" to discover, perhaps, the extent of the Queen's displeasure, Dodgson rubs his nose in his tutorial gaffe by having Alice reply dryly, "Where's the Duchess?"

Where she is, I think—and everyone else, too, for all one can tell from the pronouns—is in the rhyming soap opera that provides the trial's centerpiece. The "secret, kept from all the rest, / Between yourself and me" I would guess included at least one crack to Alice on what a muff Lord Newry was to have brought *The Water Babies* into the Deanery without first reading it himself. The cunning student, of course, had quickly hopped back into Mrs. Liddell's good graces by agreeing to spy on Uncle Charles. The evidence suggests he had been doing so for a year or more, gratis; but in her need to be rid of Dodgson she might have coached her protégé to new heights of infamy. The actual trial at the Deanery occurred sometime between Dodgson's train ride with the girls on June 25 and his holding aloof from them during the fall term. "In a great hurry" like the White Rabbit and announcing, "This paper has just been picked up," Newry delivered some purloined secret message and made his exit. Later, alone with her parents in the library, Alice found herself confronted with the incriminating note or poem, and possibly with all of Dodgson's letters.

"What do you know about this business?" the King said to Alice.

"Nothing," said Alice.

"Nothing *whatever*?" persisted the King.

"Nothing whatever," said Alice.
"That's very important," the King said. . . .

Alice knows nothing, runs Dodgson's bluff, because there is nothing to know. The Knave is innocent. The King is willing to take his daughter's word on it: the letters are harmless fun; Dodgson, though a pest and better gone, may not be such a malicious fellow after all.

Mrs. Liddell knows better. She may have chosen this moment to destroy the letters. Alice's friendly chats with Uncle Charles are now quite over.

"Stuff and nonsense!" said Alice loudly.
"Hold your tongue!" said the Queen, turning purple.
"I won't!" said Alice.
"Off with her head!" the Queen shouted at the top of her voice.

And so it ended, save for the version that Dodgson would construe for the world; and so it might have remained had he not also been playing the boor with someone whose displeasure would, by his own reckoning, make this little circus with the Liddells seem as consequential as finger shadows dancing on a wall.

The Vanishing

Which *Alice* do you prefer, then? In Wonderland the spirit of the Cheshire Cat presides, with its enigmatical grin and sly humor. Over and around *Wonderland*, the book and its reputation, hovers the artless smile of the Knave of Hearts, courteous servant, lover of children. For more than a century their story has been kept alive, not by any reciprocal love from those children, but by adult readers predisposed to one or the other contradictory pleasures of the tale — intellectuals to the camp of the Cat, sentimentalists to the camp of the Knave. *Alice* has enabled the former to wax sentimental without guilt and the latter to justify their sympathies by exercising the intellect. Their collusion has rewarded the future with a book whose place in the descent of make-believe is misconstrued and an author canonized in a faith he did not himself claim to practice.

Is *Wonderland* at all the children's story the sentimentalists suppose it to be? Yes, partly. It was first told to a child; it is about a child; it is convincingly told through a child's eyes. But that said, no. Dodgson has hidden agendas here that have nothing whatever to do with children's story or make-believe. He called his *Alice*s "the love-gift of a fairy-tale" and, yes, Alice does wander through a kind of fairy-tale landscape, but there is little of the traditional tale for a child to recognize in Dodgson's "Snow White" — no plot, no arousal and satisfaction of expectation — only endless confusion and anxiety. Of relief from the jealous rages of the wicked queen there is none. The helpers are not helpful. Alice comes upon a fairy-tale house whose "chimneys were shaped like ears and the roof was thatched with fur," but the woodland dwarves there — the Hatter, the Hare, and the Dormouse—are self-absorbed, inhospitable, twice mad. This new Snow White come in from the world elicits only their contempt. Whatever Dodgson may have construed "fairy-tale" to mean, he did not write one.

The agendas with Kingsley and the Liddells shunted the deacon instead onto that other line of fairy-tale descent that had begun with Mme. d'Aulnoy and *Le Cabinet des Fées*. This is the fairy romance, a form that lends itself readily to satire and farce and addresses itself primarily to adults. In Dodgson's day the notable example was Thackeray's *The Rose and the Ring*. Alice's social calls and appearance at court quite plainly announce *Wonderland* as a court farce in this same tradition. It is here that we see Dodgson making his innovations, turning farce into riddle with nonsense and philosophy and romance into an experience as astringent as Andersen's "A Drop of Water." To find any true signs of the fairy tale in the *Alice*s we must look to *Through the Looking-Glass*. This too is a court romance, with kings, queens, and knights, political satire, and a garden of talking flowers, but the two books are nonetheless distinguishable. There are *Wonderland* moments in the sequel, but there are no *Looking-Glass* moments in *Wonderland*. In the late 1860s Dodgson had shaken off his animus briefly by slaying the Jabberwock and was freer, as the White Knight, to play the helper of fairy-tale tradition.

He had always been in thrall, really, to this image of himself as the chivalrous, funny knight guiding little girls into the world. It is this that accounts for his believing *Wonderland* to be a true fairy tale. The reverie overrode the contrary evidence on the pages before him, and in the end it led him to gloss the book with the most ambitious pretense he ever entertained. The remodeling of Alice in "All in the golden afternoon" from a disgruntled, sassing daughter into a "dream-child . . . in friendly chat with bird or beast" he concluded with these lines:

> Alice! A childish story take,
>   And with a gentle hand
> Lay it where Childhood's dreams are
>   twined
>   In Memory's mystic band,
> Like pilgrim's withered wreath of
>   flowers
>   Pluck'd in a far-off land.

I am reasonably sure that this is a conflation of two of the world's most famous poems about childhood, Wordsworth's "Intimations of Immortality" and the "Introduction" to William Blake's *Songs of Innocence*, "Piping down the valleys wild." The thought being conveyed here in hushed tones and the appeal to Memory identify Wordsworth; the conspicuously antique "pluck'd" recalls the words with which Blake takes up his pen to write, "And I pluck'd a hollow reed." Bringing *Wonderland* into their fold was important enough to Dodgson that seven years later he closed *Through the*

Looking-Glass with paraphrases of the same two poems, thus bracketing the *Alice*s fore and aft with the one invocation. Blake's "And I wrote my happy songs / Every child may joy to hear" became

> Children three that nestle near,
> Eager eye and willing ear,
> Pleased a simple tale to hear —

and in his concluding stanza,

> Ever drifting down the stream —
> Lingering in the golden gleam —
> Life, what is it but a dream?

Dodgson echoed lines taken variously from Wordsworth, from his opening stanza to "Whither is fled the visionary gleam? / Where is it now, the glory and the dream?" The deacon's sigh about Alice, "Still she haunts me, phantomwise," might allude as well to Wordsworth's poem "She was a Phantom of delight."

For the occasion of a children's story we might expect a citation from Wordsworth; in *Looking-Glass* Dodgson was bidding Alice good-bye, as the poet had to the joys of his childhood. Because of their implications, however, the Blake quotations come as something of a surprise. In "Piping down the valleys wild" the visionary is relating his commission by the Christ Child to compose these songs of innocence ("Piper, sit thee down and write / In a book, that all may read.") and calling upon biblical tradition to do so. I cannot believe, given Dodgson's fear of blasphemy, that when aligning himself with Blake he was unaware of imputing to *Wonderland* a divine inspiration. The book being profane, the thought is startling and absurd. And yet it is consistent: his sentimentalization of Blake and Wordsworth into the late, rotting lily of Victorian religiosity is one with his delusion that his tale is an innocent "friendly chat." This last stanza identifying *Wonderland* as a pilgrim's wreath pluck'd in the Holy Land in effect declares the Knave to be innocent as well. He is innocent because his book is right with God. As for this Lewis Carroll fellow, the Reverend never knew the man.

The reason for the hypocrisy was simple enough: a celibate bachelor with insomnia,[46] Dodgson had too much time to think and so wayward a talent for it that pretenses by light of day became essential. Head down in his pillows like his Knight in the ditch, the more he said his prayers "the more I keep inventing new things." What these new inventions were he suggested in the introduction to an 1893 volume of mathematical oddities, *Pillow Problems: Thought out During Sleepless Nights*:

> There are sceptical thoughts, which seem for the moment to uproot the firmest faith; there are blasphemous thoughts, which dart unbidden into the most reverent souls; there are unholy thoughts, which torture with their hateful presence, the fancy that would fain be pure.

The unholy thoughts that he hoped his math tricks would displace have commonly been supposed sexual, and while one would expect that some naturally might have been, the weight of this statement suggests, rather, a war of ideas. The obvious inference is that in keeping time with God the earnest deacon was always, like his Hatter, "two days wrong" and inclining toward heresy.

There are only three things you can do with heretical apparitions should they trouble you to this extent: you can make yourself still, which is prayer; you can wrestle with them until a winner emerges; or you can pull the blanket over your head and mumble "pillow problems" to keep them at bay. This last stratagem is a fool's prayers, ceding the match to heresy by default. Dodgson's skeptical and blasphemous notions simply floated into the next room and formed their own world at his desk. The pious deacon could not sit down at such a place; a Cheshire Cat or a Lewis Carroll could.

Alice communicates this spiritual debate several times on her journey through Wonderland. She does so when articulating Dodgson's question "Who in the world am I?," for example, and again in this retort to the Duchess:

> "Thinking again?" the Duchess asked, with another dig of her sharp little chin.
> "I've a right to think," said Alice sharply, for she was beginning to feel a little worried.
> "Just about as much right," said the Duchess, "as pigs have to fly. . . . "

An inevitable consequence of strict Calvinism was the claustrophobic belief that one was either utterly bound within the faith or utterly free of it. Over the past two centuries, understandably, millions have chosen to be free, defecting into secularism, Unitarianism, paganism, what have you. Something in Dodgson apparently longed to join the crowd going over the side. What is lamentable, I think, is that a man of such gifts would do so by arguing, and then teaching, that thinking and faith are mutually exclusive propositions. Everyone thinks. Everyone thinks waywardly; everyone entertains heresy. There is no one who is not like the Knight head down in the ditch, for everyone's mind "goes on working all the same," whether he wishes it or not. At issue is not our right to think, or even to think waywardly, but whether out of intellectual pride in our own inventions we think we have thought the best. If I show a child a pear and say "pear" and the child, knowing the drill but wanting to be witty, says "apple," he has begun a career perhaps as a nonsense writer or comedian. There is nothing amiss here; from a spirited contrariness the language gains by a heartbeat. But nonsense is a trope, a means of clearing the way for the truth. It is not the truth itself. Should the child persist in calling pears apples he may, in his quest for applause, work up such a habit of waywardness that as an adult he will find himself vaporizing on how the difference between a pear and an apple is merely in the eye of the beholder, and of little account. Then he

will have turned thought against its purpose and willfully refused understanding; he will have substituted nonsense for the truth and turned the
blessing into a curse.

Apples, pears; pears, apples: this is the first idea presented to us in
Wonderland:

> Alice began to get rather sleepy, and went on saying to herself, in a dreamy sort
> of way, "Do cats eat bats? Do cats eat bats?" and sometimes, "Do bats eat
> cats?" for, you see, as she couldn't answer either question, it didn't much matter
> which way she put it.

Relativism may have smelled bad to the Christian Knave over his breakfast, but it was catnip to Uncle Charles from Cheshire as he nightly floated
down into his skeptical thoughts. Nearly every conversation in the two
*Alice*s springs from the convenience of this philosophical shrug; indeed,
without some assumption that all knowledge and truth are subjective and
contingent on circumstance, there could be no conversations in them at all.
"'When *I* use a word,' Humpty Dumpty said, in a rather scornful tone, 'it
means just what I choose it to mean—neither more nor less.'" The talking
egg may be an object of fun; nonetheless, what Dodgson is announcing
here is the one and only means by which two such books could have gotten
themselves told in the first place. "Just what I choose it to mean"—like the
Cheshire Cat's "Then it doesn't matter which way you go"—is the deacon's
self-proclaimed warrant to choose and to go however he will—to call nonsense the arguments of Hatters and Hares; to declare stuff and nonsense
the "divine rights" of Queen and God; to tweedle the strictures of his faith
with "Contrariwise" and "Nohow." At stake, he believed, was his "right to
think." This was his real answer to the question "Who in the world am I?"
He was someone who could think for himself and ought to be left to it.

There is a fallacy, of course, in his argument with God over free will and
accountability. Here, in the exchange introducing Alice's assertion of her
own right to think, the Duchess is instructing her with the challenge to

> "[b]e what you would seem to be"—or, if you'd like it put more simply—
> "Never imagine yourself not to be otherwise than what it might appear to others
> that what you were or might have been was not otherwise than what you had
> been would have appeared to them to be otherwise."

Unscrambling this is work for a logician, but unnecessary. The message—what Dodgson imagined Kingsley, or Christian doctrine, or God to
be telling him—is simply, "Never imagine." How or when he had arrived at
such a wrong conclusion I cannot guess. Perhaps he could not grasp how
God could accommodate a mind as wayward as his own. Perhaps he was
just plain contentious by nature and looking for a bone to pick, as he had
with Kingsley. If his midnight defections did proceed from some catlike
stubbornness against the Spirit, all the more compelling his need to maintain the pretense that *Wonderland* was a friendly chat and to enlist Words-

worth and Blake in the cause. A man who has allowed himself to be ordained only to then assert that the right to declare what is true lies with himself alone will need, at some point, to convince himself that his truth and God's truth are one and the same.

This is the messy dialectic of his life, then — the never-ending ups and downs of sleepless nights and pious days, of sense and nonsense, of the Cat undermining the Knave and the Knave covering up for the Cat. The deacon was his own odd couple. In 1876, in his third major work of nonsense, *The Hunting of the Snark*, he cast himself as tragic hero.

Enigmatic as the Cat's grin, *The Hunting of the Snark* has been quite as successful in eluding explanation. Dodgson's remark that he hadn't meant anything by it but nonsense has of course been taken to mean that while composing it he had no particular meaning before him. There is some truth to this, for what the poem is largely about is nonsense itself — the nature, practice, and proprietorship of the thing. The making of *The Hunting of the Snark* looks in fact to be history repeating itself. At the birth of *Wonderland*, a usurper to the blessing had appeared to give it new impetus; so too, I suspect, the publication of Edward Lear's *Nonsense Songs* pricked Dodgson's jealousy into play in 1871, the year of *Through the Looking-Glass*. For the next five years it would provoke him into realizing a book of rhymes bigger, funnier, more nonsensical than anything Lear could dream of making — an epic of nonsense, an *Odyssey* of nonsense. He subtitled it, grandly, "An Agony, in Eight Fits." ("Fit," an old term for canto, may recall "You never had fits, my dear, I think?" while "agony" contains, and perhaps described for Dodgson, the Greek word *agon*, a literary contest.)

The hero of this gallant farce would be Dodgson himself, in the role of the Baker, whose "courage is perfect!" It is he who will discover the fabled Snark in the end, and damn the consequences. Sailing to glory with him — or to extinction — go a Bellman captain and a crew consisting of a Boots, a Bonnet-maker, a Barrister, a Broker, a Billiard-marker, a Banker, a Beaver, and a Butcher. Critics have offered some odd explanations for this alliterated company. They may be simply the latest fruit of Halliwell's *Nursery Rhymes of England*. Casting about for ideas for his sea cruise, Dodgson would have found in his favorite source book the Butcher and the Baker of "Rub-a-dub-dub, / Three men in a tub." The double alliteration may have pleased him into pondering a whole crew of Bs; changing the tub's Candlestick-maker to a Bonnet-maker, he may have simply run the list from there. The book being conceived on a grander scale than anything in Lear, he may have looked to something like *The Canterbury Tales* for a general structure ("The Baker's Tale," "The Beaver's Lesson," "The Barrister's Dream") and perhaps to Coleridge's "Rime of the Ancient Mariner." Otherwise, just as there were traces of Kingsley everywhere in *Wonderland*, so *The Snark* resounds with Lear. When we read, for example, how "The man they called 'Ho!' told his story of woe / In an antediluvian tone," it is

Queerie Learie we are listening to. *The Snark* is told in the meter of Lear's "The Broom, the Shovel, the Poker, and the Tongs," and its matter echoes the stories of "The Duck and the Kangaroo," "The Nutcrackers and the Sugar-Tongs," "The Daddy Long-Legs and the Fly," and "The Jumblies." Here are three from Dodgson and three from the usurper:

'Must we drag on this stupid
    existence for ever,
'So idle and weary, so
    full of remorse, — '

'My six long legs, all here and there,
Oppress my bosom with despair;'

And every one said, who saw them go,
'O won't they be soon upset, you
    know!
For the sky is dark, and the voyage is
    long
And happen what may, it's extremely
    wrong
    In a Sieve to sail so fast!"

"This amply repays all the wearisome
    days
We have spent on the billowy ocean!"

"It is this, it is this that oppresses my
    soul. . . . "

" . . . beware of the day,
    If your Snark be a Boojum! For then
You will softly and suddenly vanish
    away,
    And never be met with again!'

I would suggest that it is this last passage, from "The Jumblies," with its dire warnings and comical crew, that put Dodgson in mind to take a sea voyage of his own. There are hints that he knew Lear's limericks and prose tales as well. A bit of business in "Fit the Seventh: *The Banker's Fate*" appears taken from *More Nonsense* (1872), as has been noted by others. Overlooked by annotators is Dodgson's quotation from Lear's first limerick in *A Book of Nonsense* (1846): "There was an Old Man with a beard, / Who said, 'It is just as I feared'" becomes in *The Snark*, "And the Bellman remarked, 'It is just as I feared!' / And solemnly tolled on his bell."

In the 1871 adventures of Violet, Slingsby, Guy, and Lionel in "The Story of the Four Little Children Who Went Round the World," we find Lear relating yet another ocean journey, and in his "History of the Seven Families of the Lake Pipple-Popple" may be prefigured the deacon's dreaded Boojum. No sooner have the children of the Seven Families been sent out to see the world than all come, like Dodgson's Baker, to a "vicious and voluble end." A Clangle-Wangle is stalking the landscape — "a most dangerous and delusive beast, and by no means commonly to be met with" — and also the fatal Plum-pudding Flea: "Presently they perceived, a long way off, an object of the most interesting and obese appearance. . . . The Plum-pudding Flea began to hop and skip on his one leg with the most dreadful velocity. . . . [H]e opened his mouth, and . . . began to bark so loudly and furiously and terribly that . . . everyone one of them suddenly tumbled down quite dead."

In *The Annotated Snark* Martin Gardner cites the various guesses that have been made on the origin of the word "Boojum." The matter remains unresolved, but, noting that Dodgson talks in his preface about the trick of making portmanteau words, as he had done for "Jabberwocky," we might at least assume "Boojum" to be in that same class of play. Perhaps the anagrammatist meant to say, simply, BOO to JUMBlies. If so, I think we can infer that in his contest with Lear, Dodgson held no real animus for the man. The "agony" is a professional joust, rather, between two knights of nonsense for rights to the territory. Alas for Dodgson's ambitions, Lear is the clear winner. *The Snark*, contains some wonderful conceits and lines, but, like Lear's prose nonsense, it is too self-conscious and too cluttered. And much, much too long: the pretense that an oversophisticated, 564-line epic could be thought suitable reading for children is absurd. The deacon's need to be greater at the game than Lear led him to assemble an apparatus of ill-matched parts so bulky and opaque that the only audience remaining for it is the aficionado or the professor wanting to take note, for example, of Dodgson's conspicuous use of coinages lifted from his earlier poem "Jabberwocky."

It was not for any aesthetic reasons, I suspect, but purely for show that the Jubjub bird and the Bandersnatch appear in *The Snark*, and the Beaver outgrabes in despair, and things are said to be uffish, galumphing, frumious, mimsiest, or beamish. What Dodgson meant to advertise with these ill-fitting allusions and epithets was his originality. They are present to demonstrate that he was in no way beholden to Lear's *Nonsense Songs* for his ideas. Bringing parts of "Jabberwocky" forward from *Looking-Glass* would establish that the five-year gap between "The Jumblies" and *The Snark* did not signify. The spliced-in language, clumsy as it was, would show that his new poem belonged to the same act of imagining as the earlier and that *The Snark* was therefore the work of a man whose ideas always "came of themselves."

The animus motivating the work—for Dodgson never wrote at this level without it—came not, as I have said, from his contest with Lear but from another quarter. If there is any likeness to Lear in the poem, it might be— and it is a slim might—the Billiard-marker, "whose skill was immense." Take this phrase to be the salute of one knight to another and it seems an appropriately contemptuous gesture for the occasion, delivered with the deprecating irony that the Billiard-marker's skill was immense at very small tasks. But more probably Lear is not present in the work at all as a personage. The party being lampooned here instead is the laureate, Alfred, Lord Tennyson.

Who better for a Bellman captain than the author of "Ring Out, Wild Bells," recent nemesis of the Reverend Dodgson and husband to an intimate of Edward Lear's? When we left the deacon and the laureate in 1870, remember, Dodgson had been cast out from the charmed circle and was spluttering with indignation. *The Snark* could afford him that last volley in the duel that earlier had been denied him. "Contemporary readers fancied a resemblance to Tennyson in Holiday's pictures of the Bellman," Gardner notes,[47] and I suspect this is no coincidence but followed either from Dodgson's instructions to his illustrator, Henry Holiday, or from an offhand remark that he had had Tennyson in mind. For the purpose of matching two versifiers, man to man at their craft, what could be more logical than to appoint as referee, or captain, the great poet whose acquaintance they held in common? Here in "Fit the Second" is the deacon's tongue-in-cheeck tribute to Tennyson's renown:

> The Bellman himself they all praised to the skies —
> Such a carriage, such ease and such grace!
> Such solemnity too! One could see he was wise,
> The moment one looked in his face!

His captaincy is a joke, of course. In the waters of nonsense Tennyson is useless. His map is "A perfect and absolute blank" and he "Had only one notion for crossing the ocean, / And that was to tingle his bell." The more pressing reason to write the laureate into the drama, however, was again to rehearse their parting exchange. The central confrontation in *The Snark* is not the Baker's fatal encounter with the Boojum, which the reader can see is inevitable, but his falling out with the Bellman. The third and fourth fits replicate perfectly the back-of-the-letter colloquy Dodgson sent Tennyson in 1870. The Bellman has been growing more and more impatient with the Baker's "story of woe," as had Tennyson with his chance visitor, and when the Baker reveals, "'I engage with the Snark — every night after dark — / In a dreamy delirious fight,'"

> The Bellman looked uffish, and wrinkled his brow.
> "If only you'd spoken before!
> It's excessively awkward to mention it now,
> With the Snark, so to speak, at the door!
>
> "We should all of us grieve, as you well may believe,
> If you never were met with again —
> But surely, my man, when the voyage began,
> You might have suggested it then?

Dodgson follows the Baker's protest, "I informed you the day we embarked," with a restatement of his argument in the 1870 letter:

> "You may charge me with murder — or want of sense —
> (We are all of us weak at times):
> But the slightest approach to a false pretence
> Was never among my crimes!

The Snark at the door I think we can assume to be — well, poetry, perhaps, flights of fancy, the blessing of nonsense, or, collectively, inspiration. Recalling Alice's "I've a right to think," we might take it to be thought itself, that chancy venture in which a Boojum of skeptical or unholy ideas can always be expected to make an appearance. Alice's fall into the Wonderland of relativism, for example, is a line of argument that for all one knows might anywhere swerve into a cul-de-sac wherein is scrawled the graffiti "Therefore, there is no God." And then the dreamer, too, must "softly and suddenly vanish away."

But since all the voyagers are eager to have it, let us call the Snark inspiration after all—to each seeker the sublime of his own poetic genius. Dodgson once told a child that "Snark" was a portmanteau word combining SNail and shARK, but he nowhere else mentioned this and in fact gave us the clue to its meaning in the poem itself, when he wrote that the Baker "told his story of woe / In an antediluvian tone." The phrase calls up the story of Noah and the Flood, and there in the word "Snark" is the ark itself. At a guess I would say he arrived at the name merely by transposing the "s" and "n" of DodgsoN'S ARK and that he meant by it a poetic vehicle so superior to Lear's that he could not resist saying BOO to the sieve of the JUMblies. His Boojum, metaphorically, then, is the maelstrom or the Sargasso stagnation that awaits every sinking inspiration. If the winds are with you, the Snark will bear you safe to your Ararat and rainbow, but there are no guarantees you will ever arrive.

Tennyson knew this well and jealously guarded his creative time, either by the interceptions of his wife or simply by excusing himself from an interview. Some such guarded moment, I think, must underlie the unpleasantness between the Baker and the Bellman in fits three and four. A plausible scenario might show Dodgson, in one of his surprise calls on the laureate, soliciting the poet to reveal the secret of his inspiration for *Maud*, say, or "Ring Out, Wild Bells" and then, during a lull, modestly introducing the news that he too engaged with the Snark every night after dark. Tennyson, taken unawares by a dilettante, is not amused. Dodgson had not previously mentioned being a poetaster but had represented himself as an academic with an interest in photography. Seeing that he has been flimflammed, Tennyson turns "uffish." He checks his watch, the door, anticipating the manuscripts about to emerge from the novice's pocket for his approval. He won't have it. He apologizes to the deacon that he hasn't the time, inspiration is knocking ("It's excessively awkward to mention it now, / With the Snark, so to speak, at the door!"); he must be at his work. There is a hint that Dodgson is not expected to return ("If you never were met with again . . ."), embarrassing the deacon into protesting that he has made no "false pretence." A decade later, of course, he does return, to be met with again, arriving via the mails to provoke the exchange that now requires the inclusion of Tennyson in his poetic contest with Lear. As always, he comes with his vanity cloaked in the self-deprecating ironies of nonsense. His insistence that those with whom he has played the boor acquit him of all dishonorable charges he portrays as only the meek and reasonable plea of "that mildest of men," the Baker—himself as the Knave of Hearts in a new guise.

The Hunting of the Snark, then, was conceived, it seems, to serve three agendas—answering Lear's challenge, answering Tennyson's accusation, answering his own original question, "Who in the world am I?" In *The Snark* he is again the man who thinks for himself. It is a comic portrait, like his depiction of the White Knight, but the portrait of a tragic hero withal—the intellectual who dares risk "the notion I cannot endure," to fall at last, "their hero . . . Erect and sublime," into the jaws of the Boojum. To safeguard this confession of intellectual pride, he invented his best excuse of all. After filling three stanzas with evidence of the Baker's habitual forgetfulness, he added, "[B]ut the worse of it was, / He had wholly forgotten his name." There can be, in other words, no holding to account a man who has forgotten who in the world he is, for whenever you find him writing out of some animus, or in contradiction to his faith, clearly *he is not himself*.

This I suppose was his final rationalization before the God who fills his diaries. It cannot have satisfied him completely, however, for he also made *The Snark* the occasion for his *Easter Greeting to Every Child Who Loves "Alice."* The outpouring of pious rhetoric in this public letter served to camouflage a dark—much less an Easter—fable much as the poem "All in the golden afternoon" had sprinkled fairy dust over *Wonderland*. The fear that he has played the boor before God is palpable. One moment he is claiming to have aroused with his children's tales "innocent laughter . . . as sweet in His ears as the grandest anthem that ever rolled up from the 'dim religious light' of some solemn cathedral"; in the next breath he is hoping to look back on his work "without shame and sorrow (as how much of life must then be recalled!) when *my* turn comes to walk through the valley of shadows."

The deacon's cannier reading of his last walk—"He had softly and suddenly vanished away— / For the Snark *was* a Boojum, you see"—is such a good rendering into make-believe of the proverb of judgment "For the turning away of the simple shall slay them" (Prov. 1:32) that I am inclined to think he knew the teacher's manual of Hebrew Scripture very well—and no doubt thoroughly disliked it. He was not altogether shy about appropriating from the Bible. It was his habit, for example, to annotate his diary on particularly brilliant occasions (such as meeting Alice Liddell for the first time), "I mark this day with a white stone." Here is the likely source of the deacon's delight, in Revelation 2:17:

> He that hath an ear, let him hear what the Spirit saith unto the churches; To him that overcometh will I give to eat of the hidden manna, and will give him a white stone, and in the stone a new name written, which no man knoweth saving he that receiveth it.

And in the stone *was* his new name: Lewis Carroll. But from Lewis Carroll came back nothing of the Spirit to the Spirit. How could the deacon not have read Proverbs as a reproach to the workings of his mind and the works of his pen and turned his back on them, even while helping himself to Scripture elsewhere? What were they most like, after all, but those copy-book maxims he had ridiculed with George MacDonald or the books of etiquette he had lampooned for Alice? "Lean not unto thine own under-standing. . . . Be not wise in thine own eyes." The world's oldest surviving children's book was a veritable anthology of Kingsleys warning him against "witty inventions" and pleading, How long will "the scorners delight in their scorning?" Mrs. Liddell, too, stood as a reproach to his sins of commission: the deacon in Christ's church at Christ Church was an agent provocateur, subverting the old books and mores and the old assumptions about how we let ourselves be brought up and by whom. His sins of omission were worse: he withheld his gift of the blessing from Him who filled his diaries and whom he knew to be the giver. He used his piety to buy his right to think what he pleased. In all his years of play with acrostics and anagrams, the one nearest to hand was the one he dared not preserve on paper — how in his own name DODGSON was a SON of GOD who would DODGe GOD to sing the ODD SONG of his own thoughts. To spell it out like this would have endangered the deal he hoped to cut — that as long as he refrained from giving offense by taking holy orders and *then* playing the Cheshire Cat; as long as he kept a respectful distance from the Bible and *The Pilgrim's Progress* with his parodies, then surely the blessing was his to command and he at liberty to say his mind at will.

But — and this makes all the difference — he set his mind down in a book for children. And in that book, as he now realized while composing his *Easter Greeting*, he had, to his shame, committed an actual blasphemy against the central tenet of his faith.

From Jesus, then:

"A new commandment I give unto you, that ye love one another. . . . "

And from Paul:

Though I speak with the tongues of men and of angels, and have not charity, I am become as sounding brass, or a tinkling cymbal.

This is Christianity in a word: charity: agape: love.
And this is what the deacon did with it:

"The game's going on rather better now," she said, by way of keeping up the conversation a little.

"'Tis so," said the Duchess: "and the moral of that is — 'Oh, 'tis love, 'tis love, that makes the world go round!'"

"Somebody said," Alice whispered, "that it's done by everybody minding their own business!"

This, remember, is Dodgson thumbing his nose at Kingsley's

and so there may be fairies in the world, and they may be just what makes the world go round to the old tune of

> "*C'est l'amour, l'amour, l'amour*
> *Qui fait la monde à la ronde*"

After his question "Who in the world am I?" and his assertion, also directed at the Duchess, that he has a right to think, this slap of ridicule is Dodgson's third key utterance in the book, and it is, he now understands, the turning away that shall slay him. What he has mocked, his book is without: of agape there is not the least trace in *Wonderland*. He has used the blessing to label the neighbors he is asked to love as being worthy only of contempt, and he has addressed this jaundiced view of the world to an audience of children. The effect of the absence of agape on one child, Alice, could not be clearer. At the outset we see in her all the virtues of anyone who might expect to inherit the earth: she is polite, humble, patient, soothing, and so on. But by the end of the tale, thanks to Uncle Charles's invisible whisperings, she is locked in screaming combat with the Queen, her mother.

Redressing this wrong increasingly occupied Dodgson's thoughts throughout the 1870s and 1880s. In 1881, after resigning his lectureship at Christ Church, he wrote in his diary,

> I shall now have my whole time at my own disposal, and, if God gives me life and continued health and strength, may hope, before my powers fail, to do some worthy work in writing—partly in the cause of Mathematical education, partly in the cause of innocent recreation for children, and partly, I hope (though so utterly unworthy of being allowed to take up such work) in the cause of religious thought. May God bless the new form of life that lies before me, that I may use it according to His holy will![48]

Twenty-five years earlier, he had written, as prologue to this hope, "What talents I have, I desire to devote to His service, and may He purify me, and take away my pride and selfishness. Oh, that I might hear 'Well done, good and faithful servant'!" Then had come thinking, and Alice and *The Water Babies*, and going to the theater, and with the compromise of the deaconry this early resolve was shelved. There it would remain for some twenty years or so, until it came to him finally what he had actually done in *Wonderland*, which he must now undo by emulating Kingsley and writing a Christian parable of his own. For without such an offering of the blessing, his loving words in the *Easter Greeting*, that his readers "rise and forget, in the bright sunlight, the ugly dreams that frightened you so when all was dark," were phrases devoid of real meaning.

Sylvie and Bruno appeared in 1889, *Sylvie and Bruno Concluded* in 1893. Dodgson ended the opus with what can only be an attempt at an apology to God, "an angel's voice . . . whispering, 'IT IS LOVE.'" Within the book his eponymous heroes sing his apology to Kingsley's "C'est l'amour, l'amour":

> For I think it is Love,
> For I feel it is Love,
> For I'm sure it is nothing but Love!

He had been working, along the way, to discharge one other item of business as well. If the new parable were to be an acceptable offering, he was first going to have to do something about *Wonderland*. Somehow he was going to have to unwrite it. Only then could *Sylvie and Bruno* be born free of taint. And so he began by composing yet another dedicatory poem for *Alice*, "A Nursery Darling":

> See how in sleep she seems to sing
> A voiceless psalm — an offering
> Raised, to the glory of her King,
> In Love: for Love is Rest.

The silly premise of *The Nursery Alice* — that children aged nought to five would want their own edition of the book — can be explained, I think, as a little trick that Dodgson worked on himself this time. When he first told the story, it had been to three girls the oldest of whom were ten and thirteen — old enough and bright enough that he could air every sophistication and sarcasm in the telling. But if he were now to scale his ambition down below the level of wit and tell the story to a five-year-old, then there would be no chance of his misspeaking it. He may have grasped this only intuitively, but some such awareness does seem necessary to explain the utter collapse of the original into this mawkish a caricature of itself.

Out came everything that might frighten a child or be construed as an affront to the Lord's commandment. Dodgson effected the rehabilitation of *Alice* in the simplest way possible — he began the tale by denying it any semblance of reality whatever: "Once upon a time, there was a little girl called Alice: and she had a very curious dream. Would you like to hear what it was that she dreamed about?" This deflating news, that there is nothing here but someone else's dream, not only neutralized the story; it required the narrator to become positively histrionic to make up for the loss in interest. Those scenes in the original that were sound enough in themselves, with no real animus informing them, have been swamped by Dodgson's unctuous gush. When Bill goes up the chimney, it's "Poor little Bill! Don't you pity him very much?" The "C'est l'amour," slander, needless to say, is nowhere to be found. Dodgson has himself become the Duchess, and the old Duchess is a sweetheart:

> So Alice is just resting from the Game, for a minute, to have a chat with that dear old thing, the Duchess, and of course she keeps her mallet under her arm, so as not to lose it.
> "But I don't think she *was* a dear old thing one bit! To call her Baby a *Pig*, and to want to chop off Alice's head!"
> Oh, that was only a joke, about chopping off Alice's head: and as to the Baby — why, it *was* a Pig, you know! And just look at her *smile*! Why, it's wider than all Alice's head: and yet you can only see half of it!

Having traduced his faith, the born-again sinner is rolling out all the agape he can muster. The deacon in his zeal is brimming over with agape; his lips are wet with it. The excess is positively Dickensian:

All alone, all alone! Poor Alice! No Baby, not even a *Pig* to keep her company!

He has just got up to say to Alice, "Your hair wants cutting!" That was a rude thing to say, *wasn't* it? And do you think her hair *does* want cutting? *I* think it's a very pretty length—just the right length.

This is what Dodgson supposed agape to mean for a story. His error is so naive and so awful that it proves, I think, that he simply had no understanding of what constitutes a real fairy tale. True agape exists in make-believe as an intimation of light, a gladness playing invisibly through the prose, with the author lost in his story and nowhere to be seen. J. R. R. Tolkien caught something of this when he spoke of every true fairy tale's bearing the signature of a *Eucatastrophe*, "the Consolation of the Happy Ending." This

> sudden and miraculous grace . . . does not deny the existence of . . . sorrow and failure: the possibility of these is necessary to the joy of deliverance; it denies (in the face of much evidence, if you will) universal final defeat and in so far is *evangelium*, giving a fleeting glimpse of Joy, Joy beyond the walls of the world, poignant as grief. [50]

Tolkien is pertinent here: there is no *Eucatastrophe* in simply waking up from a nightmare, no joy in the wake of *Wonderland*, only relief to be out of it. Otherwise, however, Tolkien has put his emphasis, and his *Eucatastrophe*, in the wrong place. *Evangelium* is not for seeking "beyond the walls of the world"; it is to be felt *in* the world, and because of this grace the *Eucatastrophe* is to be located not at story's end but prefiguring the narrative in its opening "Once upon a time" and inhabiting the story throughout. The felt presence of this gladness is what I called, in Chapter 1, the allsense.

Dark things happen underground, of course, because the light does not go there. Events turn strange, tempers flare, children cry. In Dodgson's hideaway from God there is no promise of a *Eucatastrophe* because the author has occluded the light. This is what all his pretense about the essential goodness of *Wonderland* was meant to deny. That he could deny it to himself as well is borne out by the fact that when he finally came to write his great parable on agape, he had no more understanding of a true *Eucatastrophe* than he did before. *Sylvie and Bruno* is an eight-hundred-page Victorian double-decker twice the length of both the *Alices* combined. A court farce again, in the tradition of *The Rose and the Ring*, it is a turgid, sentimental, damp closet of a book stuffed with fairies, dreams, dual worlds, shifting realities, love affairs, palace intrigues, baby talk, strained nonsense, hymns to Love, and sermons on prayer, keeping the Sabbath, and Dodgson's liturgical preferences. The deacon out-Duchessed Kingsley by 535 pages in the end, and it must be reckoned some kind of ironic justice that when the pillager of another man's Christian parable came to write his own he produced this colossal a stinker. *Sylvie and Bruno* is not even arguably the most unreadable book of the nineteenth century. Apparently, God could afford the loss.

And enough. This is the history of the writing and unwriting of *Alice in Wonderland* as I have construed it. Was it such a precedent-setting book, then, after all? I think it was, but not in the ways that have been claimed for it. By occluding the light, Dodgson inverted the terms that must obtain in order to write a true tale for children, and in this sense the book has no legitimate place in the descent of make-believe. The central question of this literature has been from the beginning, Who shall teach the children, and in what spirit? Dodgson lent an aura of righteous innocence to one of the great sophistries of the age, that art is a pastime that makes nothing happen. The corollary to this in children's literature holds that, having been liberated from the oppression of the old didacts, our make-believe, whatever its content, is now all innocent play. I have argued that, to the contrary, every children's book teaches. *Wonderland* teaches the content of Charles Dodgson's mind—all of it, including the subtleties of his "sceptical thoughts . . . blasphemous thoughts . . . unholy thoughts." He brought every reader down the rabbit hold with Alice into a place where it doesn't much matter which way you put a question, or how you re-dream the world, or what you believe to be true because everything, after all, is relative. This will be described by some as innocent intellectual play, I suppose, but it is also teaching. Furthermore, it is religious teaching. Some will say it was his right to teach. I will not argue it. The question, rather, is whether a practicing Christian can declare himself hors de combat as a scribe for the faith and teach paganism to children without being an apostate and traitor. Suspecting that his fate was, indeed, to "softly and suddenly vanish away," the deacon called in his will for a small, unadorned stone to be set over him. His heirs, having, as I suspect, destroyed the diaries testifying to his spiritual doubts, raised up instead a Victorian triple-decker variously inscribed "His Servants Shall Serve Him," "Where I am, There Shall also my Servant be," and "Thy Will be Done." His nephew wrote his biography. It must be counted an irony that his survivors should have suppressed the evidence of his doubts only to build monuments in book and stone to his apostacy as Lewis Carroll. In this, of course, they were only the first of many. Recall Roger Lancelyn Green and others, fawning before the idol of a book that was "original with the absolute originality of sheer genius." Dodgson had broken the First Commandment more subtly, taking the ban against setting other gods before God quite literally and creating with Wonderland, so he thought, a world of No Other Gods. But there *was* a god of sorts there, whom the custodians have now enshrined—that demiurge of the modern Self, the Poetic Genius, grinning over his mad world as the Cheshire Cat. And the Cat, as Dodgson knew in his heart, was a sinner. It sinned by breaking with tradition in the name of genius while at the same time refusing to let God speak through the blessing. In so doing, it loosed children's literature from the Christian universe—of which it was too often an admittedly unlovely expression—and in effect wrote the handbook for a subliterature of wonderlands that would be variously secular, pagan, gnostic, or messy New Age confabulations of all three, substituting new terms incommensurate with the old and making new worlds to compete with God's. The free play of the imagination is in itself neither a bad nor a good thing (though the benefit of the doubt must be given to the good); the problem lies in our having made a fetish of it for its own sake. The lie that Dodgson invented for it was the notion that children's story, or any art, could be a privileged vehicle, exempt from examination or accountability, for any and every thought to percolate up from someone head down in a ditch. Never mentioned in this assertion that the imagination and all its product are sacrosanct is the reality that wherever the light of agape is occluded, Poetic Genius will be found floundering in the dark, spitting out scorn and nonsense.

4

A FACULTY FOR
THE MUSES (II)

The Name of the Muse

More than a century and a half separate Perrault's fairy godmother from Dodgson's apoplectic Queen of Hearts. The reader may recall my dating this the meantime during which the muse had come round by the back door. To the Puritans her little stories had seemed the catchpenny enticements of the great seducer. The Enlightenment and later didactic tutors dismissed them simply as a trashy subliterature or else as baroque excess, and, in either case, food for fools. Anticipating Dodgson, Hans Christian Andersen very nearly reclaimed the imagination for children through the tale but then chose for his muse a Snow Queen's kiss of death and occluded his pages by pleading for our tears instead. Not until Charles Kingsley realized his Irish Woman by wedding Perrault's visitation of grace with the teaching adults of Rousseau and the didacts did the fairy godmother at last emerge as the natural tutelary muse of children's story. Translating the tale into narrative fantasy called, too, for a certain competence at managing larger structures, and this Kingsley had at his command by virtue of his faith. As with Perrault in spirit, so with Bunyan in trust: the grand design implicated by Christian teaching, which the Reverend Dodgson would forfeit, gave Kingsley the whole world to give away to his readers and a fitting venue for the muse of fantasy again to call home.

Invited now to tell her tale was the first, and perhaps still the only, author in all this history to regard the images and miracles of make-believe as actual representations of reality and not merely a literary convenience. The Scottish cleric George MacDonald (1824–1905) dreamed dreams. His stories are the recorded stuff of those dreams, and a pilgrimage, invitation in hand, to discover the sense of them, and the source.

"The Golden Key" (1867), *At the Back of the North Wind* (1871), *The Princess and the Goblin* (1872)

Portraying the muse as tutor would have come naturally to MacDonald even if the literature had not recommended it. Between graduating King's College in Aberdeen and taking up the ministry, he had scratched out a living for himself and his new bride by giving lessons; a novel, *The Tutor's First Love*, would follow from this formative period, in addition to the muse fantasies for children. His first faerie literature appeared in 1858. *Phantastes*, a hallucinatory, almost impenetrable romance for adults, will have an inordinate effect on several authors to come, including C. S. Lewis. Its moderate success upon publication led MacDonald to London with his growing family, there to write tirelessly over the years, producing three or four books to every one of his eleven children. These have long since been forgotten, as their titles—*The Maiden's Bequest, The Minister's Restoration, The Curate's Awakening*—suggest they might. His first book for children, *Dealings with the Fairies*, contained a story that is still read today, however: "The Golden Key." *At the Back of the North Wind* and *The Princess and the Goblin* followed within a few years. These three tales would be the simple lights he lit along the darkening progress of his imagination toward its valediction in 1895 with *Lilith*, an even more troubled and impenetrable dreamscape for adults than his first.

MacDonald's was a life of teaching as a shepherd of the flock on the one hand and wandering new pastures looking to be taught on the other. His thousand or so pages of published sermons are orthodox enough, even if he did chafe under the doctrinal severities of Calvinism, but his strange dreams—what were they? For guidance he looked to an earlier Congregational minister who, like himself, had had to preach in rented halls and through the pages of books. Bunyan's *Pilgrim's Progress* was a bulwark of orthodoxy, yet one of the seventeenth century's great wonder tales. Perhaps this lifelong favorite of MacDonald's held the key to synthesizing the doctrine and the dream and bringing his faith to completion. At any rate, he had no doubt whom he must play in Bunyan's grand scheme: when his family mounted its own dramatization of the allegory for a paying public, it was he who spoke the lines "My name is Greatheart; I am the guide of these pilgrims, which are going to the Celestial Country." This was how he would phrase his parables for boys and girls—as the fairy tales of pilgrims setting out for the Celestial Country. It was the one beautiful dream he had to relate, whose tides might run against the "melancholy, long, withdrawing roar" of Matthew Arnold's Sea of Faith in "Dover Beach." From boyhood Greatheart had seen a presence hovering over this ebb tide of the age. He knew it to be the friend of his need; he knew it wanted the story told. What he did not yet understand about the face he saw, which Kingsley would call the Name-that-is-not-yet, was how to speak of it, and on what authority. By pronoun and implication it must be Catholic. Or else, perhaps—Mac-Donald being Protestant to the bone—some new knowledge of God.

He was no Kingsley, to announce outright what he had seen. At the right hand of the presence whole landscapes of imagery were assembling to haunt his understanding. Greatheart dreamed of encastled libraries, and librarians who know his name even as he was unsure of theirs, and a glory of books beside which the literary achievements of this world seemed only a child's earnest paraphrase. Images drawn from such a storehouse would need some new way of telling. *The Water Babies* had announced itself a make-believe, and its author had come along to explain each detail. Greatheart's make-believes would be transcriptions of things actually witnessed by the author but left a mystery. His story sessions would convene at dusk, in strange woods and forgotten hallways. The tutorials would be intimate, hushed, and would call for great patience. MacDonald was going to lead his readers into that terra incognita between heaven and earth where the silence of God is the undeconstructible text, every thought a prayer, and every prayer answered by visions.

When using a tale to help children say their prayers, of course, one must initiate the reader with familiar landmarks and recognizable voices— a forest and helpers in the forest:

> There was a boy who used to sit in the twilight and listen to his great-aunt's stories.
> She told him that if he could reach the place where the end of the rainbow stands he would find there a golden key.
> "And what is the key for?" the boy would ask. "What is it the key of? What will it open?"
> "That nobody knows," his aunt would reply. "He has to find that out."
> "I suppose, being gold," the boy once said, thoughtfully, "that I could get a good deal of money for it if I sold it."
> "Better never find it than sell it," returned his aunt.
> And then the boy went to bed and dreamed about the golden key.

In the original, by the brothers Grimm, "The Golden Key" is not a tale as much as a rhetorical device for opening or closing a session of storytelling. The boy goes into the forest, finds the key, and, digging about in the ground, uncovers an iron chest:

> "If the key does but fit it!" thought he; "no doubt there are precious things in that little box." He searched, but no keyhole was there. At last he discovered one, but so small that it was hardly visible. He tried it, and the key fitted it exactly. Then he turned it once round, and now we must wait until he has quite unlocked it and opened the lid, and then we shall learn what wonderful things were lying in that box. [1]

Here the tale ends, with the contents of the box left to the reader's imagination. In his own parable Greatheart has postponed the box altogether, making its discovery the journey of a lifetime. "'You must look for the keyhole,'" a woman advises the boy; "'That is your work.'" The key that is better never found than sold, of course, is the key to those spiritual treasures we are invited to lay up in heaven. The boy's pilgrimage begins one evening at his window, which looks out on a forest said to border on Fairyland:

> The forest lay to the east, and the sun, which was setting behind the cottage, looked straight into the dark wood with his level red eye. The trees were all old, and had few branches below, so that the sun could see a great way into the forest and the boy, being keen-sighted, could see almost as far as the sun. The trunks stood like rows of red columns in the shine of the red sun, and he could see down aisle after aisle in the vanishing distance. And as he gazed into the forest he began to feel as if the trees were all waiting for him, and had something they could not go on with till he came to them.

Here the difference between a fairy tale transmitted by oral tradition and a more literary tale like MacDonald's becomes manifest. In Grimm the boy finds the key in the forest while lighting a fire to warm himself. In Greatheart's version he is obeying a call to the imagination. Physical need has ceased to motivate events, while at the same time, paradoxically, the physical world has come alive, almost as a character in itself, a fairy-tale helper to facilitate the felt spirituality of the journey. "The object is to move by suggestion," MacDonald would argue in defense of his method; "where there is the faculty of talking with suitable vagueness, and choosing metaphor sufficiently loose, mind may approach mind."[2] For the purpose of a children's story this way with the narrative is something of a gamble, of course, leading, as likely as not, to mere mystification. On the other hand, the rewards can be substantial. As we draw near to things in MacDonald, those emblems of the physical world that we think we know from the old tales begin to unfold as revelations. Witness the rainbow falling in the darkened forest and how it only glows the brighter as the boy approaches:

> He stood gazing at it till he forgot himself with delight — even forgot the key which he had come to seek. And as he stood it grew more wonderful still. For in each of the colours, which was as large as the column of a church, he could faintly see beautiful forms slowly ascending as if by the steps of a winding stair. The forms appeared irregularly — now one, now many, now several, now none — men and women and children — all different, all beautiful.

The golden key to his transfiguration the pilgrim may already possess — imagination, vision, a simple heart, the faith to enter the kingdom as a little child. Like Tom with Ellie in *The Water Babies*, Mossy will make his journey in the company of a little girl, Tangle, whose story is here also told. The two innocents wander as soul mates through a terra incognita haunted by images salvaged (as I suppose) fresh from MacDonald's own sleep. Their implied marriage is a sojourn on a plain of shadows rippling about them like the waters of a lake. They mingle there with the shapes of trees and birds and forms half bird, half human; with shadowy children, men and women, lovers, brothers and sisters, and things "of unspeakable beauty or grandeur."

> As they walked they waded knee-deep in the lovely lake. For the shadows were not merely lying on the surface of the ground, but heaped up above it like substantial forms of darkness, as if they had been cast upon a thousand different planes of the air. Tangle and Mossy often lifted their heads and gazed upwards to descry whence the shadows came; but they could see nothing more than a bright mist spread above them. . . .
>
> "We *must* find the country from which the shadows come," said Mossy.
> "We must, dear Mossy," responded Tangle. "What if your golden key should be the key to *it*?"
> "Ah! that would be grand. . . . "
>
> How long they were in crossing this plain I cannot tell; but before night Mossy's hair was streaked with grey, and Tangle had got wrinkles on her forehead.

Phantoms ascending a rainbow, the world as a plain of shadows—little here will appeal to the literal understanding; rather, it is meant to place the reader in a state of wondering to know. "If you do not know what it means," wrote MacDonald of his work, "what is easier than to say so? . . . It is there not so much to convey a meaning as to wake a meaning."[3] This is Greatheart at play in the realm of the Platonic Forms, that cosmology wherein all things material, while real enough, are yet shadows or semblances of things perfect in the mind of God. By this understanding, the natural good for man is to rise, both in soul and works, to the source of his being. Kingsley had explored these same ideas in his historical novel *Hypatia* (1853). Wanting to exemplify his belief in woman as the teacher of man, he had looked to the life of the famous philosopher at the Neoplatonic School at Alexandria, murdered in 415 A.D. by a Christian mob on the apparently trumped-up charge that she had set the pagan authorities against them. Neoplatonism had been formulated originally as an alternative to orthodox Christianity, but no critical inconsistencies obtain between Platonic conjecture and the revealed truth if one refrains from extrapolating cultish mythologies from the Dialogues. Plato has been an influence on Christian thought from "the example and shadow of heavenly things" in the Epistle to the Hebrews to the fictions and apologetics of C. S. Lewis. Any Christian artist is a Platonist in some general sense, for, as MacDonald wrote, "It is God's things, his embodied thoughts, which alone a man has to use." The summons to receive a wakened rather than a conveyed meaning should not, let me note, be mistaken for an invitation to read what you will out of the work, claiming equal validity for it. MacDonald may have been a maverick, but he was no relativist obeying some tropism toward disorder, like Dodgson. Christian pilgrimage is the frame of reference here. Great-heart did not attribute his inventions to his own genius but wrote in the belief that "[a] man may well himself discover truth in what he wrote; for he was dealing all the time with things that came from thoughts beyond his own."[4]

How to translate these thoughts into stories had come to MacDonald partly from a reading of the German Romantic Friedrich von Hardenberg (1772–1801). "Novalis," as von Hardenberg signed his poems and tales, had been raised in the Moravian branch of Lutheranism, a sect not unlike the Congregationalism of Bunyan, Milton, Watts, and MacDonald, with its doctrinal openness to new intellectual and mystical understanding. In Platonism, for example, both writers found justification for a freer play of the imagination than Calvinism offered, and the latitude to indulge a rather un-Protestant taste for imagery and rhetoric. If there was a danger to the experiment for a Christian writer, it lay not with the general theory of Forms but with the cultural enthusiasms of the age. The reemerging themes of genius and nationalism that were soon to embrace the brothers Grimm in their pagan fold were mingling seductively with a misperception of the allsense that the German Romantics called the "dark sublime." Feyness and inexplicability were the femme fatales luring these Romantics away from the rationality of the Enlightenment. How much more meaningful nature seemed when read as a Gothic melodrama peopled with numinous virgins and uncanny children; how much truer the truths of the imagination and the heart when reserved to the doomed and the dead. With its poetic leap over worldly vulgarities and its supposed insight into the spirit world, the Romantic corner of the psyche has fascinated parties as various as Coleridge, Andersen, Poe, Wagner, and the pre-Raphaelites, and, following MacDonald, children's authors like J. R. R. Tolkien, C. S. Lewis, and Maurice Sendak. Mistaken for a property of the allsense, the dark sublime must lead, unfortunately, to melancholy, even morbid literary effects (witness Russell Hoban's 1967 *The Mouse and his Child* or any of the myriad "sword and sorcery" fantasies of the past half century) and is probably best invoked sparingly in children's literature, if at all. Its siren call to private revelation invites the artist to alienate himself from the real community and even, in time, should he not become a drunkard or a suicide, to align himself with the drumbeat of some abstracted vision of the state. The call to the reader is the call to the power of wizards.

For his children's tales, at least, MacDonald was able to borrow von Hardenberg's allusive way with a story without falling prey to such temptations. He remained Bunyan's Greatheart on such occasions, wandering pen in hand after the source of his dreams, looking to connect his readers with a true embodiment of the allsense. Novalis had imagined the spiritual journey as a quest for a mysterious blue flower. MacDonald first sought the country whence the shadows came, and then, in *At the Back of the North Wind,* he reversed the motion of the pilgrimage to accommodate a presence come out of the silence between heaven and earth to whisper at a knothole by a little boy's bed.

Diamond is the name given this coachman's son who sleeps above the horse stalls; some call him "God's baby;" one calls him a genius. To passersby he is "not right in the head, you know. A tile loose." Whichever is the case—and MacDonald typically leaves it quite vague—he is easily the most thoughtful and eloquent little boy in all of children's literature. And one of the most imaginative, for he fancies that the wind is a woman who visits him in the night. What is hard for the reader to buy into, ironically, is the everyday story unfolding here, of how Diamond's father, with his one horse and hansom, sets up in London as a cabby and how Diamond befriends the streetsweep, Nanny, and finds a patron in the scholarly Mr. Raymond. At bringing neighborhoods to life MacDonald was no Dickens. His true talent lay in welcoming the muse into the world and his readers into a state of wondering to know. Kinswoman to Kingsley's Name-that-is-not-yet, his North Wind has it in her power to concentrate her being into a furious blur the size of a bumblebee or to blow herself up as wide as a gulf of weather, with clouds of billowing hair. She appears to Diamond as a young girl, a wolf, a shooting star. Most often she comes to him as a woman, to be his teacher, confidante, and comforter. That presence MacDonald had seen hovering over his own boyhood has here become a tutor the likes of whom Rousseau could not have dared conceive. Because Diamond is going to die and does not know it, she will be fortifying him against his coming fears with a flight northward to Purgatory, that inevitable next place in his journey. There, like Tom behind the Shining Wall in *The Water Babies*, he "felt so still and quiet and patient and contented, that . . . it was something better than mere happiness. Nothing went wrong at the back of the north wind. Neither was anything quite right, he thought. Only everything was going to be right some day." There is a touch of the evangelical novel about all of this, but never the melodrama or the sentimentality. We are subjected to no Little Eva deathbed scene when Diamond dies. The book's last words are laconically serene: "I saw at once how it was. They thought he was dead. I knew that he had gone to the back of the north wind."

If truth be told, at nearly three hundred pages, and proceeding at a leisurely nineteenth-century pace, *North Wind* is too uneventful a book to hold a child's interest for long. There is no clear narrative line to the make-believe, and the realistic component is less than compelling. What the patient reader might find worthy of note are the conversations between the North Wind and Diamond, which constitute a satisfying Platonic dialogue on the existence and nature of God, and why the world is the way it is, and why innocents like Nanny must suffer while the wicked prosper. In these walk-along-with-me chats we see MacDonald playing his favorite role of Greatheart, escorting new pilgrims to the Celestial Country. The unhurried, thoughtful solicitude accords with what photographs we have of the man, with his full beard and burdened eyes. I am reminded of William Carlos Williams's portrait of Abraham Lincoln, and how "the least private would find a woman to caress him, a woman in an old shawl—with a great bearded face and a towering black hat above it, to give an unearthly reality."[5] What the private wants to know from Greatheart is the answer to every child's question, Is that true?—or, as here implied, Is there a God? MacDonald chose to explore the problem in *North Wind* in the form of a tutorial on his favorite subject, the nature of dreams. There are whole chapters here on dreams and their strangeness and possible meanings. Throughout the second half of the book an argument evolves that MacDonald was not embarrassed to drive home to a conclusion:

"And you've got your dreams, too, Nanny."

"Yes, but I know they're dreams."

"So do I. But I know besides they are something more as well."

"You ain't a dream, are you, dear North Wind?"

"I'm either not a dream, or there's something better that's not a dream, Diamond."

"I couldn't be able to dream anything half so beautiful all out of my own head; or if I did, I couldn't love a fancy of my own like that, could I?"

"I think not. . . . I don't think you could dream anything that hadn't something real like it somewhere."

"The people who think lies, and do lies, are very likely to dream lies. But the people who love what is true will surely now and then dream true things. But then something depends on whether the dreams are home-grown, or whether the seed of them is blown over somebody else's garden wall."

"Everything, dreaming and all, has got a soul in it, or else it's worth nothing, and we don't care a bit about it. Some of our own thoughts are worth nothing, because they've got no soul in them. The brain puts them into the mind, not the mind into the brain." "But how can you know about that, North Wind? You haven't got a body."

"If I hadn't, you wouldn't know anything about me. No creature can know another without the help of a body."

"*Could* it all be dreaming, do you think, sir?" he asked anxiously.

"I daren't say, Diamond," I answered. "But at least there is one thing you may be sure of, that there is a still better love than that of the wonderful being you call North Wind. Even if she be a dream, the dream of such a beautiful creature could not come to you by chance."

"Yes, I know," returned Diamond. "I know."

When the boy tells his friend Nanny, "I like dreams even better than fairy tales," he is speaking MacDonald's own mind. I think we can assume Greatheart's nightly visitations to have been more potent than most men's; he trusted them like an Old Testament prophet, read them like a Joseph in Egypt, and wrote fairy tales, for both children and adults, that may be more autobiographical than has been supposed. Dreams, and thus also make-believe, were not true for him merely in the abstract, as truths of the imagination; they were either literally true or semblances of the truth expressly phrased to his understanding. The presence he had seen hovering over Arnold's ebbing Sea of Faith, to whom he now played the faithful secretary, was no solipsistic phantom but the very embodiment of "thoughts beyond his own." This is the best reason for reading *At the Back of the North Wind* today, as one man's announcement of Platonic Christianity as the living reality on this plain of shadows.

A Christian muse parable more suited to the understanding of children followed within the year. *The Princess and the Goblin* has the narrative interest of a "Sleeping Beauty" or a "Snow White." The trials of eight-year-old Irene and her hero of twelve, the miner's son, Curdie, are played out against that simplest of Christian schemata, heaven up, hell down, the world in the middle. A great hall built into the side of a mountain provides the fable's worldly stage. Here the princess has come to be brought up by country people. Below the castle floors lie the tunnels where Curdie and his father work at their excavations, and deeper still, in the bowels of the mountain, lie the caverns of a fairy-tale hell peopled by the literary ancestors of H. G. Well's Morlocks, Tolkien's Gollum, and the gnomes in C. S. Lewis's *The Silver Chair*. These goblins are not some race apart, appropriated from pagan lore, but human beings who once upon a time, seeking a tax shelter, had literally gone to ground. Degraded over the generations into misshapen parodies of the original stock, these tax-exempt bogeys are reduced to skulking about their netherworld, nursing ancient grudges. What we see in this reversal of the upward metamorphoses of "The Golden Key" is MacDonald's solution to the doctrinal bind of Calvinist damnation: God does not consign men to hell; they choose it themselves, of their own free will (a point forcefully made by Dickens thirty years earlier in *A Christmas Carol* when the ghost of Marley wails to Scrooge, "Mankind *was* my business!"). The little devils hope to take their vengeance by tunneling into the castle and abducting Irene as a bride for their goblin prince. Hidden away upstairs in the castle, however, someone is hard at work undermining this plot to storm the gates. Irene discovers her in what has since become a classic moment in the fantasy pilgrimage, that peek up forgotten staircases and down curious passageways until all hope of finding the way back is lost. On the third floor of the castle—what ought to be the topmost floor— Irene wanders into a maze of dusty halls and shut doors. One staircase seems to promise a way out, but "alas! It went the wrong way: instead of going down, it went up." Up to heaven, as it were; and there, sitting at a spinning wheel in a little room where no room should be, she finds a very old, very beautiful lady dressed in black velvet, with long hair as white as snow.

"Do you know my name, child?"
"No, I don't know it," answered the princess.

"My name is Irene."

"That's *my* name!" cried the princess.

"I know that. I let you have mine. I haven't got your name. You've got mine."

To satisfy the child's grasp of "old," the muse tells Irene that she is her great-great-grandmother, but MacDonald's attic apparition is really the ancient of days.[6] "You will be able to understand this much now," she allows the princess. "I came here to take care of you."

On her spinning wheel this new fairy godmother is working a spool of spider's webbing for her Sleeping Beauty. When the time comes for their descent into the caverns beneath the mountain, Irene and Curdie will have that same advantage given Theseus by Ariadne for the labyrinth of the Minotaur. A second gift will be the ability to distinguish the light of her lamp from all others and so use it as a beacon to guide them home again. "It does not happen above five times in a hundred years that anyone does see it," she tells her little charge. "The greater part of those who do take it for a meteor, wink their eyes, and forget it again."

Once downstairs, Irene does wink in a way, like Diamond before her, by accepting, almost, what everyone says about the lady in the upper room, that she is only a dream. Whenever she does doubt the truth of the attic, the whereabouts of the staircase to her grandmother eludes her. When her faith is strong, it reappears. This comes as no surprise to her father when he hears of it. The "look which she could not understand" reveals not that he disbelieves her story but that he knows about the woman in the upper room what MacDonald knows about her:

> "You won't come up and see my huge, great beautiful grandmother, then, king-papa?" said the princess.
>
> "Not this time," said the king very gently. "She has not invited me, you know, and great old ladies like her do not choose to be visited without leave asked and given."

The Princess and the Goblin is really a higher form of Sunday School story, if you will, but at no point is the child alerted that he is reading a parable about the workings of grace. To awaken rather than impress the meaning, all has been subsumed within the language of the fairy tale. When the muse baptizes Irene, what the reader sees is not a rite but a wonder. In this most extraordinary baptismal scene in literature we have the Platonic realization of what Kingsley had suggested with Ellie's white room, when Tom discovered his original sin in the mirror. The font now awaiting Irene's immersion is a silver bath with "no bottom, but the stars shining miles away."

> "Do not be afraid, my child."
>
> "No, grandmother," answered the princess, with a little gasp; and the next instant she sank in the clear cool water.
>
> When she opened her eyes, she saw nothing but a strange lovely blue over

and beneath and all about her. The lady and the beautiful room had vanished from her sight, and she seemed utterly alone. But instead of being afraid, she felt more than happy—perfectly blissful. And from somewhere came the voice of the lady, singing a strange sweet song, of which she could distinguish every word; but of the sense she had only a feeling—no understanding. Nor could she remember a single line after it was gone. It vanished, like the poetry in a dream, as fast as it came. In after years, however, she would sometimes fancy that snatches of melody suddenly rising in her brain must be little phrases and fragments of the air of that song; and the very fancy would make her happier, and abler to do her duty.

The tale must unfold a while yet, as MacDonald discharges the promises of his goblin plot, but with this baptism of the imagination and its awakening of the allsense Greatheart has brought things to their innermost conclusion. He has sealed his testament to all that he understands "from thoughts beyond his own." The story of how these rise up in the mind like a remembered melody to guide the pilgrim home again is his best true story about the world, beside which all other make-believes are vain imaginings, devoid of soul and worthless.

The one thing yet remaining to be done in translating the fairy tale into narrative fantasy would proceed from thoughts very similar to these in the following decade. Back across the Catholic south of Europe MacDonald's North Wind and Novalis's mystical blue flower were coming together in a new likeness of the muse, *la bella Bambina dai capelli turchini*, the beautiful Little Girl with blue hair. What the literature so far lacked—a more open and communal fantasy, told in a wide-awake prose and set square in the middle of a wide-awake world—she would now provide, through the offices of a Florentine journeyman, Carlo Lorenzini.

Le Avventure di Pinocchio: Storia di un Burattino (1883)

There is surprisingly little reliable information available in English on the author of this most translated of all children's books. Born to a cook and a lady's maid, Carlo Lorenzini (1826–90) appears to have devoted his first three or four decades to living up to his puppet's ambition "to eat, drink, sleep, and amuse myself, and to lead a vagabond life from morning to night." His mother's employer, the Marchesa Ginori Lisci, got the truant off the streets for a time by enrolling him at a local seminary, but a good forty years would pass before this kindness bore fruit. By one account he finished his studies; by another, his own, he went over the wall at sixteen. In either event, he soon struck out for a life of journalism, soldiering, and gambling. At two of these endeavors he enjoyed some small success, founding a pair of journals over the years and winning a citation for valor in his second enlistment against the Hapsburg Empire. In the 1850s, to keep up with his gambling debts, he began churning out romance novels and light comedies, which he published under the name "Collodi," after the village of his mother's birth. An interest in educational reform led him in the following decades to produce a series of popular school texts, a translation of Perrault, and, finally, some stories of his own. He died relatively obscure and probably broke. Along the way he had edited a Tuscan dictionary, promoted the unification of the Italian states, and been made a Knight of the Star of Italy.

As to why he would undertake to discharge his debts in 1881 with a cautionary tale on the wages of playing the puppet to one's appetites and not with a more agreeable kind of book, some priority must be given to the man's patriotism. In this century of nationalistic fervor, which had seen a new Germany announced to the world through the *märchen* of the brothers Grimm, Collodi was mindful of the literary needs of Italy's own struggle for a national identity. The eyes of the world, he knew, were on the Risorgimento, and he knew too that the eyes of Italy's children, newly awakened to their freedom, might be looking to the future as some vast Funland. Certainly nothing in *Pinocchio* could be clearer than its author's intention to inspire children to stay in school and seek honest work rather than run off to live the sweet life, as he had done. The textbooks that he wrote just prior to *Pinocchio*, and continued to write during the eighteen months he devoted to his puppet, were tutorials entertainingly designed to capture and hold a child's attention. The new fable would serve the same end through pure storytelling and perhaps, if he were equal to the task, provide Italy with an entry worthy to march alongside Perrault, Andersen, and the Grimms in the century's Fairy-Tale Parade of All Nations.

Had *Pinocchio* turned out to be merely another disguised tract, of course, it would quickly have followed the rest of Collodi's work into obscurity. Since its serialization in the children's magazine *Giornale per i bambini* (July 1881–January 1883), it has instead gone on to become one of the world's favorite stories. The secret to its wide appeal can be read in the eyes of almost any child listening to it: Pinocchio (the name means pine nut) is the universal boy running loose through the universal world; he survives one hair-raising episode after another and in the end arrives safely home to receive the final accolade of "Bravo, Pinocchio!" The kid, in short, has screwed up at everything, as most children do, and still come out of it a hero. So timeless, so culturally uncluttered is his tale that children in the streets of ancient Rome could have listened to it with perfect understanding. It is their eternal story—a tale told, as it happens, by one of their own, one of the *ragazzo di strada*, the street kids, about the boy he used to be. He meant to be earnest about it, but he could be exuberant, too, in all the other things a story must be about. The result is an epic comedy of errors in celebration of life even while, like Aesop or Kingsley, it warns us to have a care. Collodi has swept up all of folklore in the telling: characters wander in from puppet theater, from the commedia dell'arte, from the beast fable, from fairy lore and saints' tales, from real life. Here men and their imaginings scrabble for their suppers on the same streets: carpenters and innkeepers commingle with talking cats and foxes; fishermen, grave-diggers, cops, and school kids, with crickets and owls and dogs and crows. It is into these free streets that Pinocchio dashes as soon as Geppetto has carved him feet; it is here he is distracted into bartering his new spelling book for a seat at the puppet show; and it is here that Collodi cannot help but tip his pedagogic hat to the serendipities of sin over the rewards of prudence:

> On the stage Harlequin and Punchinello were as usual quarreling with each other, and threatening every moment to come to blows.
>
> The audience, all attention, laughed till they were ill as they listened to the bickerings of these two puppets, who gesticulated and abused each other so naturally that they might have been two reasonable beings, and two persons of the world.
>
> All at once Harlequin stopped short, and turning to the public he pointed with his hand to someone far down in the pit, and exclaimed in a dramatic tone:
>
> "Gods of the firmament! Do I dream, or am I awake? But surely that is Pinocchio!"
>
> "It is indeed Pinocchio!" cried Punchinello.
>
> "It is indeed himself!" screamed Miss Rose, peeping from behind the scenes.
>
> "It is Pinocchio! It is Pinocchio!" shouted all the puppets in chorus, leaping from all sides on to the stage. "It is Pinocchio! It is our brother Pinocchio! Long live Pinocchio!"
>
> "Pinocchio, come up here to me," cried Harlequin, "and throw yourself into the arms of your wooden brothers!"[7]

In the artfully offhand way of good make-believe, a pair of miracles has just been performed here, without our being allowed so much as a moment to recognize them as such. First is the sudden fulfillment of the audience's rapt belief in the show as the marionettes spring to life and, independent of the puppet master, rush forward to command the stage. Second is the subliminal effect of this little event on the reader. In coming to life, the marionettes have inadvertently revealed the existence of some mysterious brotherhood of the wood by which they have knowledge of what they could not know in a merely real world—Pinocchio's name. By this narrative flick of the wrist, every small reader's fear of the world has been negated for the moment and his greatest wish come true: the world knows our name; we are welcome. This is the gladness inherent in what I have called open fantasy, the gladness of Mother Goose with her invitation, "Girls and Boys, come out to play; the Moon does shine as bright as day." Caught up in the spirit, Collodi will continue to deal generously with his subjects. The scene has threatened to end badly, with Pinocchio being collared by the puppet master as a handy log to fuel his supper fire. But look: the ogre is revealed to have a soft heart—and Pinocchio a noble one: when Fire-eater spares him only to elect Harlequin for the flames, the selfish puppet uncharacteristically volunteers to throw himself in for the sake of his new friend. The ogre is so moved by the gesture that he suffers a sentimental sneezing fit, pardons them both, and sends Pinocchio home with five gold pieces to buy Geppetto a coat. Collodi has chastened his usual reading of the streets, which sees opportunists and assassins everywhere and ready fools at every corner in between. *Pinocchio* is many things—folk epic, cautionary fable, parable on original sin—but the gladness everywhere pulling against the pessimism of the tale signals it as being something more, a parable about the workings of grace in the world. It is this sense that someone indeed does know our name that makes the work not simply a lesson about suppressing one's urges and shouldering responsibility but a redemptive comedy about the human condition.

One cannot sit down planning to write a Divine Comedy as a literary or pedagogic exercise and hope to come up with much, of course. Read one way, the précis of Collodi's life, with its respectable accumulation of minor achievements and awards and its middling prose, does not suggest he had a *Pinocchio* in him. Indeed, the book is such a unique event in his life, so far exceeding anything else he wrote (I am trusting several sources here), that one must wonder just where it did come from. It came, I think, from the Collodi who, in the reading of one critic, was "a school dropout, a knockabout journalist, hack playwright, odd-jobber on the fringes of literature, possibly the father of an illegitimate child but too scatterbrained apparently even to have been sure about this."[8] It is a story about *la dolce vita* and the wages of sin, told by no civic-minded do-gooder but by a man who had dealt away his own life in smoke-filled rooms. The only way a comedy of redemptive grace can be written is the way of Dante or Bunyan or the former slave trader who suddenly burst out with the hymn "Amazing Grace"—it must flow naturally as one unpremeditated psalm from the story of one's own life. *Pinocchio* is the autobiography of a gambler. It began, apparently, in the kitchen of the castle where his old mother worked as a seamstress; there at the age of fifty-five, broke and with debts to discharge, Collodi sat down with the modest ambition he ascribes to Geppetto, to "make a beautiful wooden puppet . . . that should know how to dance, to fence, and to leap like an acrobat. With this puppet I would travel about the world to earn a piece of bread and a glass of wine." At the moment, the wood-carver is Collodi himself. He is going to pay his way in the world by making a puppet for our amusement, and the puppet he will make dance for us is the travesty of his own life. Listen to the puppet: he thinks like a gambler; his repetitive adventures have the up-and-down regularity of the gambler's compulsive routine—the wild forays, the self-recriminations and vows to reform, followed by yet another plunge. The "sacred Field of Miracles," a confidence trick of the Fox and the Cat, could stand as the perfect moral to the Aesop fable of any gambling man's life, whether he is to be found anteing up at the poker table or at the stock exchange: plant your gold piece, have patience, watch the money tree bloom.

The wonder of the book as a subsumed autobiography is that there is nothing very personal about it. Like "Amazing Grace" or Lear's nonsense songs, it stands purged of all vanity. Collodi had retreated the proper distance from it and could tell his instructive fable with grand and generous hyperbole. Another gambler, Hans Christian Andersen, had vented his self-pity over that bitch, Dame Fortune, by fashioning a Snow Queen and an Ice Maiden. Collodi played his sorry affairs as a reciprocal comedy of self-justification and self-recrimination. Pinocchio's foolish mumblings are very likely excerpts from the running monologue of the life of his creator:

> "Really," said the puppet to himself as he resumed his journey, "how unfortunate we poor boys are. Everybody scolds us, everybody admonishes us, everybody gives us good advice. To let them talk, they would all take it into their heads to be our fathers and our masters—all: even the Talking Cricket. See now; because I don't choose to listen to that tiresome cricket, who knows, according to him, how many misfortunes are to happen to me! I am even to meet with assassins! That is, however, of little consequence, for I don't believe in assassins—I have never believed in them. For me, I think that assassins have been invented purposely by papas to frighten boys who want to go out at night. Besides, supposing I was to come across them here in the road, do you imagine they would frighten me? Not the least in the world. I should go to meet them and cry: 'Gentlemen assassins, what do you want with me? Remember that with me there is no joking. Therefore go about your business and be quiet!' At this speech, said in a determined tone, those poor assassins—I think I see them— would run away like the wind. If, however, they were so badly educated as not to run away, why, then, I would run away myself, and there would be an end of it."
>
> But Pinocchio had not time to finish his reasoning, for at that moment he thought that he heard a slight rustle of leaves behind him.
>
> He turned to look, and saw in the gloom two evil-looking black figures completely enveloped in charcoal sacks. They were running after him on tiptoe, and making great leaps like two phantoms.

As a puppet with his assassins, so the deadbeat in the alley with his creditors, perhaps. Collodi was not about to renounce the error of his ways, however, without at the same time celebrating the route he had taken. *Pinocchio* speaks with the sobriety of one whose last illusions have been stripped away and the giddiness of a man astounded to find himself still in one piece. In full voice, Collodi cannot be denied. *This is who we are* is his happy discovery—all of us, in all our motley array. His voice is not in search of anything; it knows. It knows Pinocchio's heart; it knows the world. The antithesis of MacDonald's associative vagueness, his voice and his world are wide awake. *Pinocchio* and *The North Wind* are rather alike as tales of boys who meet their true teacher, but Collodi took on faith what MacDonald would spend his story to explain, and his prose as a consequence is light and quick where MacDonald's is shadowy and wandering. While no less literary than his northern counterpart, he held to the ways of oral tradition and the ideal established by Perrault and centered always on the concrete rather than the implied event. *Pinocchio* is all talk, all action. Collodi improvised scenery as he went along, and never a twig or a raindrop more than was needed. Among children's authors he most closely approximates how a child makes believe. In the 250 or so pages of the book there are not two pages of descriptive matter. What is happening here is happening of itself, and plunging forward with a headlong grace:

> The shore was crowded with people who were looking out to sea, shouting and gesticulating.
>
> "What has happened?" asked Pinocchio of an old woman.
>
> "A poor father who has lost his son has gone away in a boat to search for him on the other side of the water, and today the sea is tempestuous and the little boat is in danger of sinking."
>
> "Where is the little boat?"
>
> "It is out there in a line with my finger," said the old woman, pointing to a little boat which, seen at that distance, looked like a nutshell with a very little man in it.
>
> Pinocchio fixed his eyes on it, and after looking attentively he gave a piercing scream, crying:
>
> "It is my papa! It is my papa!"
>
> The boat meanwhile, beaten by the fury of the waves, at one moment disappeared in the trough of the sea, and the next came again to the surface. Pinocchio, standing on the top of a high rock, kept calling to his father by name, and making every kind of signal to him with his hands, his handkerchief, and his cap.
>
> And although he was so far off, Geppetto appeared to recognize his son, for he also took off his cap and waved it, and tried by gestures to make him understand that he would have returned if it had been possible, but that the sea was so tempestuous that he could not use his oars or approach the shore.
>
> Suddenly a tremendous wave rose and the boat disappeared. They waited, hoping it would come again to the surface, but it was seen no more.
>
> "Poor man!" said the fishermen who were assembled on the shore, and murmuring a prayer they turned to go home.
>
> Just then they heard a desperate cry, and looking back they saw a little boy who exclaimed, as he jumped from a rock into the sea:
>
> "I will save my papa!"

Of all works of make-believe, *Pinocchio* is the most passionate. The hero's fears, temptations, and recriminations are every child's fears, temptations, and recriminations. True, the book is a comedy, and, yes, the reader does enjoy an intellectual advantage over the hapless puppet; but even so, a child can become quite caught up in the tale emotionally. Children are masters of disguise and victims of inarticulation; as the naif who must blurt out his every thought and emotion, Pinocchio becomes the little fellow deputized to speak their minds and run their races. His story is catharsis at the edge of your seat. When Walt Disney revamped it for the screen as a sentimental melodrama, this is the one thing even he could not fail to understand about the book.

As it was a unique event in its author's life, so does *Pinocchio* stand alone in the literature of its time, even among its own class. It very much belongs with the tutorial muse fantasies that preceded it to the north, but it belongs to every other tradition as well. At least five or six distinct strains of storytelling can be detected here, each with a long history this well-read dropout may have plumbed. *Pinocchio* is a puppet show and folk tale, a cautionary tale and a beast fable, a religious parable and a fairy tale. Most of all, of course, having a fairy, it is a fairy tale. It is introduced the fairy-tale way, "Once upon a time," and told the fairy-tale way, expeditiously, with trials, a naive perseverance, and an emphasis on the importance of recognizing which are the true teachers and which the false. Its hero is the stock fool of tradition, who must surmount obstacle after obstacle—usually himself in Pinocchio's case—in order to claim his inheritance of the world. The puppet's progress also somewhat resembles that of the holy fool, Parsifal, who was negligent of his mother's counsel to heed the advice of the women he would meet on his adventures. When he at last found the Holy Grail in this fairy tale for grownups, he forgot what he was supposed to say and lost it again. Harlequin, the secular fool, is Parsifal's fallen heir. Pinocchio, being another Harlequin, is another Parsifal, now struggling against the grain to rise to his former rank as holy knight. He has again fallen under the purview of a woman, here the Blue Fairy, whose counsel, if taken, will lead him to the grail of full boyhood. We watched as Tom traced a similar route in *The Water Babies*. I have no reason to suppose that Collodi knew Kingsley's book, but, interestingly, Pinocchio is living out the very life that Kingsley had foreseen for his hero if he were not to be scrubbed clean of his folly. In the end, Pinocchio, too, is baptized in water and reborn. As Tom was rid first of his soot and then of his prickles, so too is Pinocchio when the Blue Fairy sends fishes to nibble away his humiliating donkey skin. Furthermore, both tales avail themselves of the same jackass legend from antiquity—the Land of Cockaigne, of cakes and easy living, where Pinocchio is turned into a donkey, is one of Tom's stopovers on the way to Hell. Here, Kingsley has turned it into the place where the fools of the fabled town of Gotham go:

> [H]e saw the end of such fellows, when he came to the island of the Golden Asses, where nothing but thistles grow. For there they were all turned into mokes with ears a yard long, for meddling with matters which they did not understand, as Lucius did in the story. And like him, mokes they must remain, till, by the laws of development, the thistles develop into roses. Till then, they must comfort themselves with the thought, that the longer their ears are, the thicker their hides; and so a good beating don't hurt them.

Authors bent on redeeming boys full of bad ways will tell stories that are alike in general outline, no doubt, and draw from some of the same sources. As a literary parable, *Pinocchio* does, however, mark a decided advance over Kingsley's *Water Babies*. Because his hero was not merely some test subject for a homily, but the boy he used to be, Collodi could speak naturally through his puppet and not trouble himself to keep popping up in the narrative as tutor. The felicity of voice occasioned by this release into the reality of the thing allowed him to leave unspoken whatever allegorical suggestions might obtain. *Pinocchio* is the most perfect Christian parable since *The Pilgrim's Progress* because it isn't one. It is a tutorial on the facts of life, true enough, but what we are experiencing is a make-believe as transparent and as sprightly as one of Perrault's fairy tales.

This is one source that Kingsley, MacDonald, and Collodi all shared, and which, of the three, Collodi best turned to his advantage. The style of *Pinocchio* has been described as a continuation of the colorful Tuscan dialect he employed when translating Perrault into Italian in 1875.[9] Specific tales implicated by the carryover might include "Bluebeard" and "Hop o' my Thumb" as provocation for the suspense and harum-scarum of the puppet's encounters with ogres of his own. Collodi's habit of speeding columns of dialogue down the page may owe something to the "Grandmother, what big eyes you have" exchange that closes "Little Red Riding Hood." The one indisputable borrowing from Perrault is the gilded coach of Cinderella's fairy godmother, drawn by a team of mice and driven by an elegant coachman. When the Blue Fairy sends her own coach to retrieve Pinocchio from the hanging tree, it too is drawn by mice; the decor is baroque, and the coachman is a Poodle — that is to say, a Frenchman. Tracing *Pinocchio* back to the *Contes du temps passé* makes a nice completion in the descent of make-believe. Perrault found his tales of fairies and castles in cottages and kitchens, and there sits Collodi in a castle kitchen two centuries later, reinventing the fairy tale in the spirit of his forebear.

Let me add to this happy thought only the caution that Collodi's sense of tradition was likely running at too intuitive a level to be mistaken for anything like Dodgson's intricate splicings in the dead of night. The immediate source and inspiration for *Pinocchio*, I again suggest, was Collodi's own reprobate life. What tricks of the trade he might have acquired along the way would have been assimilated at once to the purpose at hand. Unlike Dodgson, or Andersen or Kingsley for that matter, the only literary figure he was in competition with was himself. *Pinocchio*'s subtitle, *The Story of a Puppet*, could truthfully be reworded *Confessions of Carlo Lorenzini, a Sinner Saved*. And the subtitle to that would read *For Those Who Love a Good Laugh*. Like Perrault, Collodi was a man of the world and a seasoned swing pusher. He was not about to despise the world for the sake of a moral. What Margery Fisher has noted of Pinocchio's final transformation could be said as well of his maker: "Although he does reform . . . readers will note with some relief that he does not change for the love of goodness but for the love of people — a distinction which not all moralists make when they write fantasy for children with a concealed lesson in it."[10]

The grace that enabled Collodi to play generously with his lesson may have come, paradoxically, from the very agent called upon to bear the weight of that morality. The Blue Fairy does not enter the story until the fifteenth of these thirty-six chapters, but so complete is her command of the book thereafter it is hard not to imagine her waiting in the wings all the while—perhaps as early as the Perrault translation, perhaps always. Her entrance as *la bella Bambina dai capelli turchini*, the beautiful Child with blue hair, is one of the strangest events in children's literature. Seeking refuge from his would-be assassins, Pinocchio has come to "a small house as white as snow." Again and again he knocks on the door, but to no avail.

> Seeing that knocking was useless he began in desperation to kick and pommel the door with all his might. The window then opened and a beautiful Child appeared at it. She had blue hair and a face as white as a waxen image; her eyes were closed and her hands were crossed on her breast. Without moving her lips in the least, she said in a voice that seemed to come from the other world:
>
> "In this house there is no one. They are all dead."
>
> "Then at least open the door for me yourself," shouted Pinocchio, crying and imploring.
>
> "I am dead also."
>
> "Dead? Then what are you doing there at the window?"
>
> "I am waiting for the bier to come to carry me away."
>
> Having said this she immediately disappeared, and the window was closed again without the slightest noise.
>
> "Oh, beautiful Child with blue hair," cried Pinocchio, "open the door for pity's sake! Have compassion on a poor boy pursued by assas . . . "

When the Child does return to the window, the assassins have concluded their grisly business. Thinking to dislodge the gold sovereigns clenched in Pinocchio's mouth, they have left the puppet hanging from a tree for the night. Stirred to life by the compassion he had a moment ago begged of her, she summons her Falcon to break the knot around his neck, and then away too flies her Cinderella coach to the rescue. "The Fairy, who was waiting at the door of the house, took the poor puppet in her arms, and carried him into a little room that was wainscoted with mother-of-pearl, and sent at once to summon the most famous doctors in the neighborhood."

Everyone knows the gist of what follows the rescue—how Pinocchio makes a fuss over taking his medicine and sprouts a broomstick nose while lying to the Fairy about his hidden gold—but even this comical passage bears the spectral imprint of things "that seemed to come from the other world."

> "In short," cried Pinocchio, bursting into tears, "I will not drink that bitter water—no, no, no!"
>
> "My boy, you will repent it."
>
> "I don't care."
>
> "Your illness is serious."
>
> "I don't care."
>
> "The fever in a few hours will carry you into the other world."
>
> "I don't care."

"Are you not afraid of death?"

"I am not in the least afraid! I would rather die than drink that bitter medicine."

At that moment the door of the room flew open, and four rabbits as black as ink entered carrying on their shoulders a little bier.

"What do you want with me?" cried Pinocchio, sitting up in bed in a great fright.

"We are come to take you," said the biggest rabbit.

Needless to say, "taking the tumbler in both hands he emptied it at a draught."

"We must have patience!" said the rabbits. "This time we have made our journey in vain." And taking the little bier again on their shoulders they left the room, grumbling and murmuring between their teeth.

A nightmarish flight to a ghostly maiden, a pearly room, and murmuring pallbearers—rather an odd business for a folkish comedy of the streets. It reads, if you will, as Perrault might, had he opted to whisk the fairy godmother of "Cinderella" into "Hop o' My Thumb" to stand in the way of the ogre leaping the hilltops in his seven-league boots. Now the lad making his escape is a boy of wood and the ogre halved into a Cat and a Fox in charcoal sacks, "running after him on tiptoe and making great leaps like two phantoms." Why the fairy had first to die and be resurrected as a child with blue hair is the abiding mystery of the scene.

As it happens, though, we have come across something like it before. The raising of a maid from her sleep is not unique to Collodi. In *The Water Babies* a girl is startled awake in a white room, who will later teach the hero how to lose the prickles of his lower nature; there is the awakening of Sleeping Beauty, with its recollection of Christ's "Maid, arise;" and in *The North Wind* we see the way of a boy with his muse and how "the instant Diamond touched her, her face began to change like that of one waking from sleep." In Collodi a boy has again awakened an agent of salvation, touching her to compassion, and the face he has called to life is to give him life in return not once but repeatedly.

Putting aside, for the moment, the at least tacit possibility that the puppet has taken sanctuary at a church or a convent, we might best understand why this is all so strange an occasion by referring it forward to the Fairy's final appearance in the book, when she bestows the gift of real boyhood on her charge. There, for the first and only time, she comes to Pinocchio not in the flesh but in a dream. That the climax to the adventure should be expressed in this way inclines me to think that Collodi may have dreamed the Fairy's advent as well. She speaks to the fleeing puppet without moving her lips, which is how understanding comes to us in dreams, and her window closes without a sound. Indeed, everything here, from the nightmarish flight to the murmuring pallbearers, has the feel of storied dream-stuff, with this one beautiful apparition arriving at the center of it like one of those rumored visitations of MacDonald's that comes blowing over somebody else's garden wall.

I will hazard a guess that these three chapters in some sense also express their author's own immediate quandary as he wrote them. Like Pinocchio running with his five gold pieces straight into a necktie party, Collodi had reached middle age with but a few sovereigns to his name and creditors in hot pursuit. He was, in short, at the end of his own rope by the age of fifty-five. His quandary was simple and pressing: if he was to write his way out of debt—the only real avenue open to him—how was he to go about it, exactly, with what manner of tale? The answer, of course, he had rehearsed only a few years earlier when translating French fairy tales into his native Tuscan dialect. This is one way of reading the lynching and resurrection of Pinocchio—as a transfer of title from one author to another. The Fairy's return and her summoning of Cinderella's coach to rescue a lad at the end of his rope are really the story of how an indifferent storyteller, Collodi, has been rescued by a master storyteller, Perrault. Given the preternatural character of the scene, this solution to his quandary very likely had come to him, or been confirmed at least, in his dreams. And with it had come something unexpected and mysterious—the image of a Child, whose hair was blue and face as waxen as an icon's, to guide this children's story. Not to tempt Providence by tampering with the vision, he set it down as he had dreamed it, a wonder not to be compromised by narrative whys and wherefores.

Some speculation along these lines does seem necessary, I think, if we are to account at all satisfactorily for the emotional intensity of Pinocchio's progress throughout the rest of the book. A bond of devotion obtains here that would be unusual in even the closest of tutorials. Having raised each other from the dead, as it were, and returned together into the world, the little rogue and his muse quickly proclaim their love for each other:

> "What a good Fairy you are," said the puppet, drying his eyes, "and how much I love you!"
>
> "I love you also," answered the Fairy, "and if you will remain with me, you shall be my little brother and I will be your good little sister."

The three excruciating trials Pinocchio must endure for his betrayals of this love, which have so distressed some critics of the book, can better be understood, perhaps, if we recall the rationale offered in *The Water Babies* for the rigors that come with the privilege of any divine tutelage. Like Mother Carey, the Blue Fairy is not putting in her hours simply to pass out cupcakes and hugs, as sentimentalists would prefer a children's muse to do; she also is in residence "to make things make themselves." Pinocchio's hard times, like Tom's before him, are the necessary apprenticeship to his mastery of "the thing he does not want to do," which if it is to mean anything must be done with a glad and not a grudging heart.

Our wooden Parsifal begins badly, as might be expected, turning his quest at once into a harlequinade by throwing away the first of the Fairy's gifts to him, the company of his father. Waiting to greet Geppetto on the road, he is again accosted by the Fox and the Cat, who, appealing this time to the low resolve of the gambler, trick him into burying his gold in the Field of Miracles. Misfortune follows misfortune, and it is nearly half a year before he can return to the Fairy's house. Alas, the penalty for trifling with the gifts of the muse is the despair of losing the muse herself. Where the house once stood Pinocchio finds only

> a marble stone, on which were engraved these sad words:
>
>
>
> HERE LIES
> THE CHILD WITH THE BLUE HAIR
> WHO DIED FROM SORROW
> BECAUSE SHE WAS ABANDONED BY HER
> LITTLE BROTHER PINOCCHIO
>
>
>
> I leave you to imagine the puppet's feelings when he had with difficulty spelled out this epitaph. He fell with his face on the ground and, covering the tombstone with a thousand kisses, burst into an agony of tears. He cried all night, and when morning came he was still crying although he had no tears left, and his sobs and lamentations were so acute and heartbreaking that they roused the echoes in the surrounding hills.
> And as he wept he said:
> "Oh, little Fairy, why did you die? Why did not I die instead of you, I who am so wicked, while you were so good? . . . And my papa? Where can he be? Oh, little Fairy, tell me where I can find him, for I want to remain with him always and never to leave him again, never again! . . . Oh, little Fairy, tell me that it is not true that you are dead! . . . If you really love me . . . if you really love your little brother, come to life again . . . come to life as you were before! . . . Does it not grieve you to see me alone and abandoned by everybody? . . .
> . . . And in his despair he tried to tear his hair; but his hair being made of wood, he could not even have the satisfaction of sticking his fingers into it.

Pinocchio's second trial with the Fairy sours this agony of tears into a rage of temper. His orphan wanderings have taken him to the Island of Industrious Bees, and there he has found the Fairy reborn as "a woman almost old enough to be your mama." Against the urgings of every splinter in his body, he now promises to stay in school, work diligently, and thus earn the gift of being a real boy and the consolation of his poor papa. But of course the vagabond again falls among bad company, and when he straggles home at last after many misadventures, what does he find but the door locked against him? The lady's maid peering from an upper window refuses to wake the Fairy, and, being a snail, takes forever herself in coming to the door. To be locked out in the rain and cold after all his misfortunes is more than Pinocchio can bear; in a tantrum over what he considers a terrible injustice, he puts his foot through the door, nailing himself in place for the night. The hard lesson of the muse at this juncture is what Diamond had to learn of the North Wind, how "she always came of herself and never when he was looking for her," and the princess Irene of her grandmother in the upper room, whose staircase vanished whenever the girl lost faith in it. Come morning, with the obligatory fairy-tale caution "woe to you if you behave badly a third time," the Fairy does renew her promise to make Pinocchio a real boy, however.

> And he kept his word for the remainder of the year. Indeed, at the examinations before the holidays, he had the honor of being the first in the school, and his behavior in general was so satisfactory and praiseworthy that the Fairy was very much pleased, and said to him:
> "Tomorrow your wish shall be gratified."
> "And that is?"
> "Tomorrow you shall cease to be a wooden puppet, and you shall become a boy."
> No one who had not witnessed it could ever imagine Pinocchio's joy at this long-sighed-for good fortune. All his school fellows were to be invited for the following day to a grand breakfast at the Fairy's house, that they might celebrate together the great event. The Fairy had prepared two hundred cups of coffee and milk, and four hundred rolls cut and buttered on each side. The day promised to be most happy and delightful. . . .

The third of Pinocchio's misdeeds is a heart-wrenching dance to the edge of the pit. With the great breakfast and boyhood at hand, he allows his shiftless friend, Candlewick, to entice him aboard the devil's coach to Funland. To his credit, he does balk for a full ten pages before betraying the Fairy, but in the end, rather than be left behind by the other boys, he capitulates to the temptation and rides away with them to the fabled Land of Cockaigne. There, where there's never a wish but must come true, it is nothing but games and merriment for months on end. Soon enough, however, the runaways wake up to find themselves turning into mokes, donkeys, beasts of burden. These new working-class stiffs are promptly sold off to haul market wagons, most of them, or, if they are truly unfortunate, harnessed to the devil's coach and driven to death enlisting the next allotment of dropouts for the workforce. Pinocchio is sold to a circus where he is swiftly taught obedience, not to the Fairy's forgiving rules, but to the crack of a whip. And one day, to his horror, he finds himself leaping and braying like a jackass before his beloved muse herself:

> "Courage, Pinocchio! Before you begin your feats make your bow to this distinguished audience—ladies, gentlemen, and children."
> Pinocchio obeyed, and bent both his knees till they touched the ground, and remained kneeling until the director, cracking his whip, shouted to him:
> "At a foot's pace!"
> Then the little donkey raised himself on his four legs and began to walk round the theater, keeping at a foot's pace.
> After a little the director cried:

"Trot!" and Pinocchio, obeying the order, changed to a trot.

"Gallop!" and Pinocchio broke into a gallop.

"Full gallop!" and Pinocchio went full gallop. But while he was going full speed like a race horse, the director, raising his arm in the air, fired off a pistol.

At the shot the little donkey, pretending to be wounded, fell his whole length in the circus, as if he were really dying.

As he got up from the ground amid an outburst of applause, shouts, and clapping of hands, he naturally raised his head and looked up . . . and he saw in one of the boxes a beautiful lady who wore round her neck a thick gold chain from which hung a medallion. On the medallion was painted the portrait of a puppet.

"That is my portrait! . . . That lady is the Fairy!" said Pinocchio to himself, recognizing her immediately; and overcome with delight he tried to cry:

"Oh, my little Fairy! Oh, my little Fairy!"

But instead of these words a bray came from his throat, so sonorous and so prolonged that all the spectators laughed, and more especially all the children who were in the theater.

Then the director, to teach him a lesson, and to make him understand that it is not good manners to bray before the public, gave him a blow on his nose with the handle of his whip.

The poor little donkey put his tongue out an inch, and licked his nose for at least five minutes, thinking perhaps that it would ease the pain he felt.

But what was his despair when, looking up a second time, he saw that the box was empty and that the Fairy had disappeared!

He thought he was going to die: his eyes filled with tears and he began to weep. Nobody, however, noticed it, and least of all the director who, cracking his whip, shouted:

"Courage, Pinocchio! Now let the audience see how gracefully you can jump through the hoops."

Con quanta grazia. The ironies here I assume were intentional. He who was saved by a coach has been delivered by a coach to a place of torment. He who must leap gracefully is without grace. He who pretends to be dying *is* dying. The soul's pilgrimage that in *The Water Babies* was always rather vague — saying your prayers, losing your prickles — is here being detailed in very human, very understandable, very painful terms. In the eyes of Collodi the realist, the most necessary step on the journey may have been that great leveler of pride and willfulness, a sense of shame. Some critics have accused him of a kind of overzealous cruelty in visiting such humiliations on his hero. I cannot recall a single complaint, however, in which the critic has not gone on to betray an aversion to parables in general and even a certain obtuseness over the many ways a parablist can go about his business. *Pinocchio* is as passionate as a children's tale can be, certainly, but it is simply moving along at too frenetic a pace to be mistaken for anything but a comedy. Nor does it let us for one moment forget that it belongs to a particular school of comedy. Pinocchio is a performer from the *commedia dell'arte*, a theatrical tradition in which every gesture, boast, pratfall, and misery is magnified to its utmost extent for absurd effect. The Fairy, while not herself a figure of fun, is nonetheless implicated in the performance, along with all her finger waggings, warnings, and punishments. Note in this passage how Collodi's lightness of touch allows her to be both the teacher of his moral and a player in a comic sketch:

"[W]hen boys have good hearts, even if they are scamps and have bad habits, there is always something to hope for: that is, there is always hope that they will turn to better ways. That is why I came to look for you here. I will be your mamma."

"Oh, how delightful!" shouted Pinocchio, jumping for joy.

"You must obey me and do everything that I bid you."

"Willingly, willingly, willingly!"

"Tomorrow," rejoined the Fairy, "you will begin to go to school."

Pinocchio became at once a little less joyful.

"Then you must choose an art, or a trade, according to your own wishes."

Pinocchio became very grave.

"What are you muttering between your teeth?" asked the Fairy in an angry voice.

"I was saying," moaned the puppet in a low voice, "that it seemed to me too late for me to go to school now. . . . "

"No, sir. Keep it in mind that it is never too late to learn and to instruct ourselves."

"But I do not wish to follow either an art or a trade."

"Why?"

"Because it tires me to work."

"My boy," said the Fairy. . . .

And so on. What she is spelling out here is a more than reasonable program for any kid in the habit of disappearing into the streets for five months at a stretch, I think, and, for a lecture, agreeably presented. The kind of moment Kingsley loved to belabor with editorial asides Collodi has kept dramatic and playful. The laying down of rules makes some people wince in any context, of course, and I realize that there may be readers impervious to the humor of a scene like this. Should the comic strip *Calvin and Hobbes*, say, or the first five seasons of *Cheers* strike you as funny, however, then I would think the situation here, of a muse having to play straightwoman to an imp, would also appeal, and for the same reasons.

It is the comical tenor of *Pinocchio*, along with the rapid narrative pace of each emotional transaction, that enables us to bear a shock like the puppet's humiliation before the Fairy; conversely, it is Pinocchio's recurrent suffering that keeps us alert to how much more there is to his story than simple buffoonery. Since Collodi wisely chose to leave the essence of the parable implicit, let me suggest it by saying that no harlequinade can be sustained at this inspired a level without being informed by a firm belief that the world is also sustained in its travels. Such a belief is the one just warrant for inflicting pain in a children's book in the first place, I should add, for only by its felt presence can the pain be borne. In *Pinocchio* the news that the world is indeed sustained is twice told — once by the sublime confidence of the author's voice, twice by the presence in the tale of the Blue Fairy. Like her sisters, the Irish Woman and the North Wind, she is on the premises to do more than merely fine-tune a boy's inclination to play hooky. A good report card and advancement to the next grade are only outward signs of her work. This is a comedy in which there is suffering, and it is suffering assigned to a purpose. You do not turn one of the *ragazzo di strada* into a pure knight simply by making believe he is one. This is not some quaint costume drama. If Pinocchio is to deny himself in the end to care for Geppetto in his old age, then shame and anguish are demons that must be engaged along the way. Whatever is required to live a life that is fully human is required as well of this order of story. Today we seem to be under the impression that children's books are better when born free of didactic intent, perhaps even of reality itself, and that this wonder has actually been achieved. I have said that this is naive. Not only is every muse fantasy necessarily a tutorial; so is every children's book. Because it presents the child with a portrait of a world he is, in real life, only just coming to know, every book teaches a new way of thinking about that world. If it is dense and troublesome, like *Alice*, it teaches the world as a place of perplexity. If it is as frivolous as, say, a Muppet version of "Cinderella," it teaches frivolity. To pretend that children's books are the playground of the imagination, with no intrinsic pedagogic content and no accountability to reality, is to deny the very nature of the reading experience in childhood, which is, all of it, a learning experience. The question, as Collodi well understood, is not whether a book teaches but what and how and whether its intent is to humanize a child or merely to socialize him. *Pinocchio* is a call to school, yes, but, more than that, it is a wastrel's comic parable of childhood, written in sympathy with those who know best what it is to mean well, to have a good heart and yet poor resolve in the face of temptation. In this crazed but, in the end, heroic manikin a child can see, writ large, all his own desires, excuses, fears, failures, and triumphs as he plays the puppet to his instincts and needs; the lecturing that irritates some adults he will accept unquestioningly as the natural landscape of his world, the very air that he breathes every day at home and at school. *Pinocchio* is really the most naturalistic of all children's books. Our modern, abstracted, and sentimental notions of childhood are nowhere in evidence in these pages. Nineteenth-century authors were not so queasy about announcing common-sense truths to children; they used books to do properly what television now does for us in the raw while children's authors dream of better worlds someplace else. George MacDonald, the second of our trio of parablists, also elected to speak of the Land of Cockaigne and how "all men, if they do not take care, go down the hill to the animals' country; that many men are actually, all their lives, going to be beasts."[11] Children used to be given *Gulliver's Travels* to read, for lack of anything else. Now we have better tales for them, or at least tales more suitable, but that does not mean Swift's Yahoos, or the ghost of the Yahoo residing in all of us, should be squirreled away out of children's sight and their stories be little more than telegraphed wishes that we were nicer folks than we actually are much of the time.

Pinocchio's honest naturalism about children and the world they must survive is precisely why the rules that so discomfort the adults in the audience must be laid down hard and frequently. No romanticizer, Collodi took in the streets with a dry eye. He noted the thieves, the dropouts and the drudges, the child molesters, the sure parting of a fool and his money. He warned against the illusory promises of the sweet life, not because he despised them as a moralist, but because he knew better than most how they could not fail to kill the soul and rot the state. In the midst of such eternal temptations, is it such a bad idea to invoke a muse to keep her eye cocked for the runaways or for an author to address children from a sure moral and spiritual base? "It is not the commands and prohibitions, as such, which adults impose that the child resents," Auden wrote of the arbitrariness and confusion of *Alice*, "but rather that he cannot perceive any law linking one command to another in a consistent pattern."[12] It is no accident that the rules are pressed hardest by the Fairy and Pinocchio's pain the greatest when he fails her expectations of him. She is the only law that can deliver him from his folly. The police and the courts can lock him up, but that is all they can do. She is the one legal address to which the prodigal hero can return, and only she can grant him the means of discovering his innate goodness and nobility. She alone can bear the true message of the book—that we are acknowledged for who we are and that forgiveness and grace are always within reach. Her pupil is like the children of Israel, forever suffering punishment for worshipping neighboring baals and forever again being favored by Yahweh's renewal of the covenant. The repetitive ups and downs in the puppet's fortunes—taken, as I have supposed, from the life of a man who had wasted his days playing a forgetful Parsifal at the gaming tables—clearly speak this same message: the covenant is not withheld. Our vagabond's adventures end with the most pleasing words a child could hope to hear, as the Fairy paraphrases the benediction in Matthew, "Well done, thou good and faithful servant: thou hast been faithful over a few things, I will make thee ruler over many"—

> "Well done, Pinocchio! To reward you for your good heart I will forgive you for all that is past. Boys who minister tenderly to their parents, and assist them in their misery and infirmities, are deserving of great praise and affection, even if they cannot be cited as examples of obedience and good behavior. Try and do better in the future and you will be happy."

The final miracle in this saga teeming with the miracles of make-believe is the long-awaited transfiguration of Pinocchio from block of wood to boy of flesh. Following, as it does, a benediction from Scripture, the event implies a most unusual sense of warrant in Collodi. The man who went over the seminary wall is known to have been a devout Catholic nonetheless, and theologically astute. That he would presume to invoke a miracle worker "from the other world" to serve as factotum in a profane comedy of the streets, and do so without some sure sense of warrant, seems highly unlikely. Putting the words of God in her mouth without such an indulgence seems an impossibility. Yet apparently Collodi did intend to draw a biblical parallel here. As Pinocchio is embarking on his near-fatal rendezvous with the Cat and the Fox, the Talking Cricket sends him off with the blessing, "Good night, Pinocchio, and may Heaven preserve you from dangers and from assassins." A moment later, where do we find the puppet but at the Fairy's front door, seeking sanctuary?

Who is she, then, this muse who watches over the universal boy as he runs through the universal world? As the child who dies to be reborn a woman, she bears a striking resemblance to her protean sisters in Kingsley and MacDonald, of course. As the Irish Woman was revealed to be Mother Carey and the Spirits of the two Testaments, so is the Blue Fairy all things to her own story, appearing as a little girl and a blue goat and in dreams, much as the North Wind had appeared as a little girl and a wolf and in dreams. Like her sisters she is omnipotent and omnipresent but always, when met along the way, unostentatious and unassuming. Cinderella's coach is at her command, yet she chooses to walk the road barefoot after Pinocchio like the Irish Woman or to wait patiently for him in an upper room, like the grandmother Irene in the attic or Mother Carey at the top of the world. She likes to keep abreast of things, like Mrs. Bedonebyasyoudid with her morning paper, and troubles herself to make the coffee and butter the rolls when she might be out ruling the storms and the seas like the North Wind or the Irish Woman. In asking who she is, then, this down-to-earth miracle worker, we are asking as well after the names of the muses in Kingsley and MacDonald and how it is, by the bye, that independently of one another three contemporary Christian authors derived from Perrault virtually the same tutorial personage to preside over their parables. These are not easy questions to answer. In good fairy tales, as Kingsley knew, the important things do not come prelabeled, as they do in allegories:

> "Now read my name," said she, at last. And her eyes flashed, for one moment, clear, white, blazing light: but the children could not read her name; for they were dazzled, and hid their faces in their hands.
> "Not yet, young things, not yet," said she, smiling.

The argument has been made by several writers, reasonably enough, that if the Blue Fairy is suggestive of anyone, it is of the Virgin Mary. Certainly, as a devout Catholic in Catholic Italy, Collodi would have been mindful of the association. He does introduce the Fairy as having "a face as white as a waxen image," as if the child laid out to rest were to be understood as an icon in a church or convent. Other than this, however, the implication of an intercessionary saint does not really match the evidence. There is the obvious discrepancy, for example, that Pinocchio's patroness appears not as the Mother of the Church but as a child and a "good little sister." Nor would the Virgin Mary be a muse sufficient to the needs of the tale. Indeed, in none of these fantasies could a saint answer for the miracles being performed. From the Irish Woman to the Blue Fairy, the muse's powers must be absolute. She must enter into the world bodily and in a variety of guises. She must baptize, confer grace, and grant remission from sins. In the cases of Tom and Pinocchio, she must translate the hero into a higher state of being. She cannot be a saint, in short, because she was never herself once human. As Mrs. Bedonebyasyoudid explains, "I never was made, my child; and I shall go for ever and ever; for I am as old as Eternity, and yet as young as Time."

To understand this wonderful being we must look higher, and to go higher in Christianity means looking to the Trinity.

The theological concept of Divine Immanence, the idea that God is neither remote nor unknowable but indeed present in the world, would have been a familiar one to all three of these writers. It is an idea that lends itself readily to children's literature but presents certain conceptual hazards when expressed in story terms. MacDonald saw the problem when he created his North Wind. He knew he was flirting with pantheism, which is where the suggestion of immanence must lead when flying loose; that is why he was careful to distinguish his muse from some deification of nature by taking reference to the necessary parallel doctrine of Divine Transcendence. The whole truth must remain within the mystery that has been revealed to us, in other words; or, as Mr. Raymond advises Diamond, "There is a still better love than that of the wonderful being you call North Wind." The more general hazard in visualizing God as he did seems to have troubled MacDonald not at all. Kingsley and Collodi likewise proceeded as if on a sure warrant. In none of their tales is there the least sign of doubt that they had told the truth when assigning to the Divine Immanence a woman's face and voice. Grace in orthodox teaching is ordinarily a silent tutor, a rather abstracted idea of inspiration to be associated with a masculine pronoun when personified at all. For Kingsley, MacDonald, and Collodi, as perhaps earlier for Perrault, the voice that whispered to them was the voice of a woman, and the face of grace made visible to them was the face of a woman, and they must all have understood the implication of it. Only one Person of the Trinity is theologically and historically free to bear such a voice and face, and that is the Holy Ghost. Hers is the name the children could not yet read in *The Water Babies*. The Irish Woman, the North Wind, the grandmother in the attic, the Blue Fairy—they are all of them Herself. More technically, we might call them fictional theophanies of the Holy Ghost—God's immanence made manifest in daily life through story. She is the universal muse and the friend of our need for whom the literature had been searching for the century and a half following Perrault. And to make Her presence felt, if you will, She commissioned three scribes to tell it at the same moment.

MacDonald's North Wind calls for a second footnote here. Unlike his grandmother Irene, she herself cannot be the Holy Ghost but only an agent or emissary. Though she carries Diamond to Purgatory, note, she may not enter herself, for "I am nobody there." Also, she several times alludes to receiving and obeying orders. The Holy Ghost, being consubstantial and coequal in the Trinity, does not take and execute orders. That understood, however, we can still read her as a representative of God's immanence in the world. As a theophany of the Holy Ghost once removed, she comforts Diamond and instructs him in the ways of heaven and earth; for the time being she is the allsense taken form and voice. That is what all these ladies are, from Cinderella's godmother to Pinocchio's Blue Fairy—grace taking human form in order to bestow grace. Extending this thought to make-believe in general, I would even propose that what we have here, addressed to the understanding of children, is all of it a literature of the Holy Ghost, whether She appears in person or, as with Mother Goose, is felt through our perception of the allsense and the gladness it argues for the world. In neither category, let me repeat, is She a muse to be tucked away in some quaint realm of once-upon-a-time and indulged for sentiment's sake. She is a muse of the country roads, the city streets, our kitchens, and perhaps, sometimes, the still small voice of our dreams. This is where Kingsley, MacDonald, and Collodi locate Her, in the open fantasy of the real world, where Her grace can enspirit the meek, the wondering, and—this is the hard, the Pinocchio part—all those willing to sacrifice their own self-interest to God's wish for the world.

Whether one feels that, being a literature about the Holy Ghost, this might also be a literature *by* the Holy Ghost will depend on the reader's predisposition to believe such a thing or not. Clearly, these three parablists felt so, like Dante and Bunyan before them. Their books stand as witness to it. In the penultimate scene in *Pinocchio* Collodi even closed the implied equation here—that a literature of and by the Holy Ghost is also a literature *for* the Holy Ghost—by dramatizing the necessity of returning to God, and so to the world, those gifts that one has received. The puppet has been hard at work for five months supporting his old father—a penance, perhaps, for his five months in Funland—when he is brought news of the Fairy's fate by her lady's maid, the exasperating Snail. What follows is a scene unique to these fantasies, and another sign, I think, that Collodi hoped to achieve more with *Pinocchio* than merely erase his gambling debts:

"My dear Pinocchio, the poor Fairy is lying in bed at the hospital!"
"At the hospital?"
"It is only too true. Overtaken by a thousand misfortunes, she has fallen seriously ill, and she has not even enough to buy herself a mouthful of bread."
"Is it really so? Oh, what sorrow you have given me! Oh, poor Fairy, poor Fairy, poor Fairy! . . . If I had a million I would run and carry it to her . . . but I have only forty pence. . . . Here they are: I was going to buy a new coat. Take them, Snail, and carry them at once to my good Fairy."
"And your new coat?"

"What matters my new coat? I would sell even these rags that I have got on to be able to help her. . . . "

List what calamities you will from modern history as the thousand misfortunes of the muse—the ebbing of Arnold's Sea of Faith and a concomitant rise in militant nationalism and shamanistic secularism; murder; degradation; the list is long. Listen to the muse airing her fears in MacDonald's *The Princess and the Goblin*:

"I do wish I were as old as you, grandmother. I don't think you are ever afraid of anything."

"Not for long, at least, my child. Perhaps by the time I am two thousand years of age, I shall, indeed, never be afraid of anything. But I confess I have sometimes been afraid about my children."

In children's books God may still worry about Her children, and out loud, for all to hear. *Pinocchio, The Water Babies, At the Back of the North Wind, The Princess and the Goblin* might be read, then, as a new wisdom literature to add to the old, a little library against the slippage of an age's faith and its drift into a new age of cultish whimsies. Along the way the muse has looked into some odd corners to find the scribes to do the job. In the beginning there was the worldly Perrault, pushing his swings; then Andersen, perhaps, who thought that he was the point of it all and turned on the muse instead. Then came the establishment cleric Kingsley, with his unorthodox leanings, and MacDonald, a disenfranchised minister haunted by dreams, and Dodgson, possibly, who could not make up his mind and fell from grace, and, finally and best of all, Collodi, whom the muse had followed over the seminary wall to his epiphany in a kitchen four decades later. Jesus had once instructed his own scribes in the writing of parables, telling them to bring forth from their treasures things new and old. He then gave the world the Holy Ghost, and the Holy Ghost, afraid for Her children, called upon six new scribes to do likewise. A happy enough ending to the tale: four of them got it right.

5

A FACULTY FOR
THE MUSES (III)

Over the Rainbow

Although women began taking a share in the descent of the fairy tale soon after the publication of *Alice in Wonderland*, it would be another four or five decades before any claims could be made to full suffrage of the imagination in narrative fantasy. The energies of most women writing for children at this time were directed, rather, at humanizing a tutorial literature that, while ostensibly naturalistic, had for a century been obsessively extolling the virtues of saying your prayers and minding your manners. Some of these new stories of boys and girls growing up are still read today: *Hans Brinker* (1865), by the founder of *St. Nicholas Magazine*, Mary Mapes Dodge; *Little Women* (1868), by Louisa May Alcott; *Heidi*, by the Swiss author Johanna Spyri, first translated into English in 1880; Frances Hodgson Burnett's *Little Lord Fauntleroy* (1886) and *The Secret Garden* (1911); Kate Douglas Wiggin's *Rebecca of Sunnybrook Farm* (1903); and Lucy Maud Montgomery's story of a Canadian upbringing, *Anne of Green Gables* (1908).

The first women to test the waters of narrative make-believe were not so gifted with survival skills, and only one would succeed at creating a muse fantasy as satisfying as, say, *The Princess and the Goblin*. In 1869 the poet Jean Ingelow (1820–97) had tried her hand with *Mopsa the Fairy*, a wonderfully lucid tale scene by scene but so brooding and intellectually detached overall as to be even more baffling than *Alice* in the end. Ingelow is a good example, perhaps, of an author too possessed by the dark sublimes to have a real audience among children. Whereas the story is merely opaque in *Mopsa*, however, it is missing altogether in each of the two

201

best-known books by Mrs. Molesworth (Mary Stewart, 1839–1921), *The Cuckoo Clock* (1877) and *The Tapestry Room* (1879). Her teasing insistence keeps us alert to what wonderful things are imminent in the gloamings of a Victorian drawing room, but never once in these diffuse and rambling impostures are we involved in anything more urgent than a sight-seeing tour through the make-believe scenery of some Butterfly- or Rainbow-land. Both these authors had accepted Dodgson's invitation to explore mysterious other realms, and, once arrived, they had no more idea than he of where to go next. Unlike Cheshire Puss, unfortunately, neither had they any comedy in them to keep us amused in the meantime.

The first woman to write a tale that was fully awake to its purpose was Dinah Mulock Craik (1826–87), whose single muse fantasy was the only one of these early works buoyant enough in the telling to spell survival.

The Little Lame Prince (1875)

Having published a superior omnibus edition of fairy tales in 1863, Mrs. Craik knew her way backwards and forwards in the genre, but not until the appearance of MacDonald's *North Wind* and *The Princess and the Goblin* did she see what next step she might take in telling such stories. *The Little Lame Prince* is obviously derivative of these two fantasies but is a felicitous example of the form nonetheless, cleanly told in a voice that could almost be the voice of Collodi's Blue Fairy. Listen to her as she plays the matter-of-fact muse with her crippled hero one moment, only to turn as defensively solicitous as an older sister the next:

> It could not be said that the Prince missed his mother — children of his age cannot do that; but somehow after she died everything seemed to go wrong with him. From a beautiful baby he became sickly and pale, seeming to have almost ceased growing, especially in his legs, which had been so fat and strong.
>
> But after the day of his christening they withered and shrank. He no longer kicked them out in either passion or play, and when, as he got to be nearly a year old, his nurse tried to make him stand upon them, he only tumbled down.
>
> This happened so many times that at last people began to talk about it. A prince, and not able to stand on his own legs! What a dreadful thing! What a misfortune for the country!
>
> Rather a misfortune to him also, poor little boy! but nobody seemed to think of that.

This parable of how a misfortune was overcome is everywhere informed by an understanding of how fairy tales work, and for whom, and through what miraculous agencies. It is not a little in debt as well to the stock plot of an heir to the throne being deprived of his birthright by a conniving uncle. Sent away like the princess Irene to be raised in exile, the unhappy boy is soon visited by a mysterious godmother much like Irene's grandmother in the upper room. This little old woman, who always addresses him with a tender solemnity, had earlier been present at Dolor's christening, recalling the gift-bearing fairies of "Sleeping Beauty." Like all the muses in this literature she will bind her patronage to the empirical laws the hero must himself live by, but the baptismal gift of her love is constant:

> "My child, I cannot alter your lot in any way, but I can help you to bear it."
> . . . She touched his poor little legs. "These are not like those of other little boys."
> "Indeed! — my nurse never told me that."
> "Very likely not. But it is time you were told; and I tell you, because I love you."
> "Tell me what, dear godmother?"
> "That you will never be able to walk or run or jump or play — that your life will be quite different from most people's lives; but it may be a very happy life for all that. Do not be afraid."

Against his growing melancholy at being cut off from the world she leaves him a curious piece of cloth, drab and shabby to the eye but in reality a magic traveling cloak. Riding on this gift of imagination and vision like a magic carpet, Dolor can now fill his lonely hours with wondrous journeys. Since Craik several times employs the biblical epithet "comforter" to describe her muse, I am quite certain she meant her to represent the Holy Ghost and the cloak to be a gift of the Spirit. Elsewhere, she suggests her meaning in terms made familiar by MacDonald and Kingsley: "I am your godmother, child. I have few godchildren. Those I have love me dearly, and find me the greatest blessing in all the world." The Holy Ghost would have fewer godchildren in an age of rapid secularization, of course. That this is not God's doing but the unhappy consequence of man's free will she reveals to Dolor much as the grandmother does to the princess Irene and the North Wind to Diamond: "I could not come to you until you had said you wanted me; but now you do want me, here I am."

Craik's lesson about suffering, that with faith, imagination, and patience any disability can be overcome, is tidily conveyed by the subsequent events of the story as she conducts her gentle tutorial in the make-believe way of saying things. Prince Dolor regains his crown, like a proper fairy-tale hero, and, having appointed a worthy successor, sets out on his last and greatest adventure. At book's end we hear an unmistakable echo of MacDonald's conclusion of four years earlier: "They thought he was dead. I knew he had gone to the back of the north wind."

> King Dolor was never again beheld or heard of in his own country. But the good he had done there lasted for years and years. He was long missed and deeply mourned — at least, so far as anybody could mourn one who was gone on such a happy journey.
> Whither he went, or who went with him, it is impossible to say. But I myself believe that his godmother took him on his traveling cloak to the Beautiful Mountains. What he did there, or where he is now, who can tell? I cannot. But one thing I am quite sure of, that, wherever he is, he is perfectly happy.

Six years after her disappearance into the Beautiful Mountains, the muse will reappear in Florence to shepherd a puppet on his way; and then, following *Pinocchio*, she will vanish as a personage altogether from her literature. But, after all, with the blessing of "Bravo, Pinocchio!" bestowed upon it, what more was there to be said? The point in future will not be one of imitation but of finding suitable new ways of saying, "Well done!" What the muse left behind of herself was the right narrative voice for the work at hand. This is what we are hearing, I think, in a little book by one of the first women to experiment with make-believe, Helen Watson Bannerman (1862–1946).

The Story of Little Black Sambo (1899)

The first writers of any consequence to tell tales explicitly for the nursery were Mrs. Bannerman and her English contemporary Beatrix Potter. Each would choose to work within the compass of books made to fit tiny hands and with stories modeled after the folk tale and the beast fable. Bannerman's pocket-sized comedy, some three by five inches in the original and likely the inspiration for Potter's small volumes, preceded *Peter Rabbit* into print by two years. It was the fourth title published in a popular library of nursery entertainments called The Dumpy Books. No word could better describe *Sambo*, certainly, with its plain boards and pawky illustrations. But then, there can be great aesthetic virtue in dumpiness—a conveyed sense of friendliness and intimacy and sometimes, as we see here, the air of a charmed amateur at work. As for the amateur's story, everyone knows how Sambo goes for a walk in his fine, new clothes, only to lose them to the ferocious tigers, and how the tigers, while fighting over who is the grandest tiger in the jungle, run themselves into the pool of butter that will be used to fry up the splendid pancake banquet at the end. If there is a more perfectly composed, more perfectly expressed literary tale in the English language, I do not know of it. How much of the story Bannerman might have taken from earlier tales and how much she made up from whole cloth is not certain. It never occurred to her to say, and it never occurred to anyone to ask. Helen Watson was the daughter of an army chaplain, who, after a childhood on the Portuguese island of Madeira and an education in Scotland, wed an army doctor and spent thirty years of her married life on station in India. How she came to write the book has been disputed, but apparently she began it in 1898 while returning to Madras by train after leaving her two young daughters in the charge of a nurse at a mountain resort. She mailed them the story to cheer them up and then later sent it to England for publication.

The book has come under fire in recent years for obvious enough reasons. Adopting a name for her hero that had been in popular usage at least since *Uncle Tom's Cabin* no doubt seemed natural at the time but has proven an unfortunate choice in the long run and a cause of discomfort to any reader of color. In retrospect, we might suppose her to have been politely racist in a patronizing, upper-class way; given the warmth of the piece, however, and the fact that her girls were then only two and five, this seems unlikely. *Sambo* was written as a nursery tale, and by nursery rules. Sambo is called Sambo in the same way the lads in English tales are called Jack or those in German tales, Fritz. The historical process that delivered up a sobriquet like Sambo is an ugly thing to contemplate, to say the least, but to Bannerman the boy was a hero, not a joke. It is clear, too, that she meant to call up the memory of an earlier, famous tale for children, the title of which at once reveals why her character is dubbed not just Sambo but Little Black Sambo. Little Black Sambo is *Little Black* Sambo because Perrault's Little Red Riding Hood was *Little Red* Riding Hood. The resemblances between the two tales are unmistakable. Each tells of a young child in danger from wild beasts, and in each the child is too young to do anything about it but hide or be eaten. Both characters are identified by their colorful clothes: Red Riding Hood's red hood, made by her grandmother, and Sambo's red coat and blue trousers, made by his mother, as well as the beautiful green umbrella and purple shoes bought by his father at the bazaar. It is this reference to "Little Red Riding Hood" that convinces me that while working with earlier tales in mind,[1] Bannerman essentially created this ingenious fiction herself. *Sambo*, I would suggest, is a deliberate reversal of Perrault's story, one kind of joke jousting with another. It is also the deftest solution yet to the problem of how we keep the child from the belly of the beast in these tales. In Grimm there is the awkward stagecraft of a nearby woodcutter crying "Hark!" and rushing in to open up the wolf with his ax. Bannerman had a better eye for the pleasures of the trickster tale; she rescues her hero the proper way, by letting the vain villains finish themselves off instead, chasing one another round a tree, faster and faster, until there is nothing left of them. And, as if that were not trick enough, she stands Perrault completely on his head by arranging it that not only are the villains kept from eating the hero; the hero gets to eat the villains in the end, fried in their own juices and stacked high on his plate as a hundred and sixty-nine pancakes "as yellow and brown as little Tigers." This is how make-believe for the nursery entered the twentieth century, then, as a delicious joke played on the literature's first true story for children, which was itself a joke played on a form yet waiting to be created.

Why Bannerman ever thought to amuse her daughters by turning "Little Red Riding Hood" upside down in the first place can be inferred, I think, from the gaiety of her voice, which is almost as innocent of art as her pictures. It is a voice that could say, for the first time in story, with no buts or if-onlys, "And then wasn't Little Black Sambo grand?" Her book is a celebration. It is a celebration of nothing more nor less than the happy fact of being a child. Although it happened not so very long ago, this was something utterly new in children's literature. Here was a storyteller with no agenda to discharge and no need herself to hide behind a tree from the presence of tigers in the world. What Perrault's tales had announced as the ideal for children's literature was the felt presence of a storyteller but the absence of the scribe. This was it, and this is why, although it is a folk and not a fairy tale, I have included *Sambo* here with the muse fantasies. Bannerman's voice is the voice of the muse come onto the scene to speak as a friend to hero and listener and world alike. Her benediction on Sambo is the Blue Fairy's "Bravo, Pinocchio!" brought into the nursery as a gift to be freely given. The lad is to be saved and praised not for any deeds that he has done, for he is too young to have done any, but merely because he is Sambo. "Wasn't Little Black Sambo grand?" is the grace note the literature had been waiting to hear.

Books being most of them self-conscious acts of premeditation, the number of literary works that are as easy about themselves as Mother Goose or the fairy tales have of course been very few — perhaps only the best of Lear and Seuss, and Perrault's retellings, and *Pinocchio*, of those we have looked at thus far. Collodi did come on the scene carrying an agenda in his pocket, but his was a unique feat at the time, achieved, as I have supposed, because of his particular allegiance to the muse. *Little Black Sambo's* playful rescue of Little Red Riding Hood for the sake of a happier tale was also an anomaly in its time. From the "Aesthetic Eighties" through World War I, most authors of narrative fantasy were about other business — as, indeed, they continue to be today — and were going about it in rather an affected fashion. Their business, as it must always be in this literature, was the business of miracles; their problem, in an age of rapid secularization, was how to redefine them so as to preserve them for the sake of the story. For what do you tell children when your instincts are for whimsy but you are either without a faith or no longer certain of the underlying warrant for dealing in miracles in the first place? Inherent in virtually any fantasy we might name from the past hundred years or more is this problem of belief; and in every narrative choice that was made can be heard an echo of that moment when the author balanced the counterweights of empirical reality and miracle and asked what wonders were yet possible to relate of a disenchanted world without straining credibility, or, conversely, what things might be found if, giving up on the world, we were to leave it to search for our miracles elsewhere.

In the latter years of Victoria's reign, those writers choosing the real world as the setting for their miracles increasingly began to favor secular mimics of the muse to preside over their fancies, or showy pagan surrogates borrowed from history and folklore. Animated by the national and ethnic mythologies then being assembled, children's authors were catching up at last with the literary paganism that had been a mainstay of adult letters for centuries. Thus the growing profusion of pantheistic deities, fin-de-siècle fairies, and colorful demonologies in children's books from the 1880s onward, and the appearance of everyday divines like the flying nanny of P. L.

Travers's *Mary Poppins* (1934). The best muse forgery contemporary with *Little Black Sambo* was a curiosity from the popular arts, Winsor McCay's *Little Nemo in Slumberland* (1905–11), a comic strip run riot with art nouveau splendors, fearsome gods and fetching goddesses, and the court capers of the fairy romance. It is from the world of entertainment, too, not surprisingly, that we hear the first raspberries being directed at the literature, and at the truth of it and the sham alike, as if there were no distinguishing between them. Crockett Johnson's genial spoof of the muse business, *Barnaby*, appeared in 1942. In the opinion of its middle-class, Charlie Brownish hero, "What this house needs is a couple of good Fairy Godmothers." What he gets, hurtling through his bedroom window and landing in a less-than-inspiring heap, is a sawed-off, semicompetent godfather named O'Malley, whose magic wand is a cigar.

The Story of Doctor Dolittle (1920)

One of the best of the secular mimics was the benign creation of Hugh Lofting (1886–1947). The eponymous veterinarian is not the kind of character to impose himself on a popular culture, but his adventures have stayed in print with a modest insistence for more than seven decades now. The series that began in 1920 ran for twelve volumes more, ending in 1952 with *Doctor Dolittle's Puddleby Adventures*. The stories are neither compelling nor memorable, but they are pleasant enough in their journeys about the world. If Lofting was only adequate as a writer, he was, however, something of a poet as an illustrator. After the first volume, his pictures increasingly assume the responsibility for conveying a strange reality that is only tenuously captured by the prose. It is the work of a quieter Lear, a less ornate Charles Robinson (of *A Child's Garden of Verses* fame), measuring out his lines with a thoughtful, pre-Thurberesque clumsiness. His pictures cast an odd spell. What they are really about is not character, or landscape, or incident — though of course that is what they show — but how light and hesitation create a palpable sense of being arrested in time. They are not frozen in time, like so many bad tableaux in children's books, as much as they are portraits of temporal moments arrested in space. Periodically in each book there will come a respite, a time of quiet when the expedition's chronicler, Mr. Lofting, can whisk out his sketch pad and capture the moment for posterity. The doctor and his animal friends may then exhale sheepishly and resume the important business of getting to the South Seas or Africa or the moon.

Like Mary Poppins, the self-effacing Dolittle is a surrogate muse whose powers, as even a child can recognize, are only a kind of wish fulfillment. The nanny and the veterinarian lack the authority that comes when author and reader unquestioningly share the same beliefs and the same assumptions as to what this order of story is about and how it is empowered. Still, Lofting's conceits, constituting as they do an open fantasy about a more-or-less real world, are engaging, and the pictures in any case redeem the enterprise with a pensive gladness that is altogether too rare in children's books.

In the fantasies most appealing to the twentieth century, the answer given to the problem of belief in miracles will be the second, which renounces the world and looks elsewhere for a seat of gladness. This new subgenre, born of Charles Dodgson's desire to peek into a universe of his own making, is what I labeled at the opening of this study the circular fantasy. Our there-and-back-again expeditions to these modern Wonder-, Fairy-, and Slumberlands will resemble Alice's journey into strangeness and perplexity only in their structure, however. Our destination is now going to be that place announced by Guy Wetmore Carryl in *St. Nicholas Magazine* in 1895, when he invoked "a dear, delightful land" in his verse "The Land of Make-Believe." No moment in the literature better captures our crossing over from faith to secular pretense than this little variation on a children's hymn by Isaac Watts from two centuries before. I have spliced together a stanza from each author to underscore the obvious debt. The opening lines belong to Watt's "A Prospect of Heaven makes Death easy."

> There is a land of pure delight
> Where saints immortal reign;
> Infinite day excludes the night,
> And pleasures banish pain.

> Ah, there the skies are always blue,
> And hearts forget to grieve,
> For there's never a dream but must come true
> In the Land of Make-Believe.

Muse fantasy is to become less and less a meaningful kind of literature in the twentieth century and these circular flights to the Land of Make-Believe more and more our babysitter of choice. I would be presumptuous in saying of any one of them to what extent it might be a secular whimsy manufactured for sport and to what extent an encoded wish for some place invested with grace when the real world seems devoid of it. The author may have only been playing with this new vocabulary of make-believe, or he may have been alert to its meaning but too doubting or too embarrassed to make a real pilgrimage of the journey. In either case, it does not really matter. In rejecting the world as the proper residence of grace, these tales are all of them escapist mechanisms and, as a literature of miracles, spurious. They outwardly resemble the parables of Kingsley, MacDonald, and Collodi but, like *Alice*, have become too unreal to be in need of a muse. They have shed the cause and the purpose of the literature and settled for the pleasantries. They are the stories MacDonald ascribed to the lesser faculty of Fancy. By his Platonic understanding they must be false dreams because they are based not on a perception of grace in the world but on sentimentality, which is the emotion that rushes in to fill the void whenever faith ceases to inform our daily lives.

The two most famous of these circular fantasies, *The Wonderful Wizard of Oz* and *Peter Pan*, followed Carryl's verse announcement by just a few years. Expressions of that mannerist phase then busily converting Mother Goose and the fairy tales into an arm of the decorative arts, they will take narrative make-believe in a very similar direction. As folklore was being excerpted from daily life and set in an imaginary Golden Age, so too will enchantment here be bleached from the world, to decamp over the rainbow for Munchkin- and Never Never Land.

Peter Pan (1904)

The famous tale of the boy who wouldn't or couldn't grow up is the only major children's story to have been written originally for the theater. It is a play, and that is literally what it is—not make-believe as a creation anyone would actually mistake for a version of reality, but a play about playing at make-believe. As the viewer sits witness to the lead actor jerking about on a wire and singing "I'm flying!," he must make of it what he will. The experience of reading *Peter and Wendy* (1911), the clumsily managed novelization of the drama, is not unlike watching the play itself: the spectator is everywhere mindful of the artifice.

Never Never Land, the enchanted isle to which Peter takes the Darling children, Wendy, John, and Michael, is Collodi's Funland sanctioned at last as a place in which to play children's games forever and ever. Pirates and Indians and fairies and mermaids have been thoughtfully provided. In Never Never Land, making believe means having lovely thoughts. This is the announced secret to flying—"You just think lovely wonderful thoughts," Peter explains, "and they lift you up in the air." Still, as sore a test of the reader's credulity as it is, *Peter Pan* is a bit smarter than its whimsy would suggest. Never Never Land is a boy's paradise, but it is also a kind of purgatory. Like the abused and abandoned children cared for by the muse in *The Water Babies*, the Lost Boys are babies who fell out of their prams and into the care of fairies. They don't know any stories and want a real mother who can tell them some. The author of this conceit, J. M. Barrie (1860–1937), was a prolific and popular novelist and playwright, and foremost among the Edwardian sentimentalists. His impish hero, named after the Greek god of the frolic, is the final enshrined icon in the Victorian Cult of the Beautiful Child. He may be a bitter echo, too, of Robert Louis Stevenson's "The Unseen Playmate"—"He loves to be little, he hates to be big." Barrie himself had stopped growing at five feet, a fact that tortured him all his life. He was rather like Hans Christian Andersen, a smart, damaged talent, living in rooms, attaching himself to happy families. *Peter Pan* is really about the author himself, who could never grow to a normal height or to the full sexuality of his god, Pan, and who was destined to stand tiptoe like his Peter, peering through other people's windows. In a sense, the play's purpose, like that of Andersen's fairy tales, was to arouse pity and admiration for its author in a mutual catharsis immodestly staged as a public spectacle. Though it could hardly be called a parable, it does aspire to the same end, a revelation of the truth, and echoes earlier fantasies with the pretense that the muse is a part one can audition for like any other part in a play:

> Then all went on their knees, and holding out their arms cried, "O Wendy lady, be our mother."
>
> "Ought I?" Wendy said, all shining. "Of course it's frightfully fascinating, but you see I am only a little girl. I have no real experience."
>
> "That doesn't matter," said Peter, as if he were the only person present who knew all about it, though he was really the one who knew least. "What we need is just a nice motherly person."
>
> "Oh dear!" Wendy said, "you see I feel that is exactly what I am."
>
> "It is, it is," they all cried; "we saw it at once."
>
> "Very well," she said, "I will do my best. Come inside at once, you naughty children. I am sure your feet are damp."

Every decade or so, someone mounts a major stage production of this coy business, or some film version is released, and parents dutifully bring their children into theaters to puzzle out a fable that confounds their every instinct about growing up and then cozens them into clapping for fairies. Barrie puts a lump in our throats and a cunning noose around our necks with his fairy patter. Every time a child is born, you see, its first laugh becomes a fairy; and every time a child says it doesn't believe in fairies a fairy falls down dead. Now Tinker Bell has drunk the poison Captain Hook meant for Peter. Are you going to save her by publically announcing your faith in fairies, children, or are you going to commit murder in your disbelieving little hearts? In cold print the scene lacks the immediacy of the theater experience, of course; it cannot intimidate from the reader the same emotional rush that an audience can when responding to the plea.

> Her voice was so low that at first he could not make out what she said. Then he made it out. She was saying that she thought she could get well again if children believed in fairies.
>
> Peter flung out his arms. There were no children there, and it was night time; but he addressed all who might be dreaming of the Never-land, and who were therefore nearer to him than you think: boys and girls in their nighties, and naked papooses in their baskets hung from trees.
>
> "Do you believe?" he cried.
>
> Tink sat up in bed almost briskly to listen to her fate.
>
> She fancied she heard answers in the affirmative, and then again she wasn't sure.
>
> "What do you think?" she asked Peter.
>
> "If you believe," he shouted to them, "clap your hands; don't let Tink die."

Many clapped.
Some didn't.
A few little beasts hissed.

If this blackmail were not so embarrassingly silly, it would amount to child abuse. It is false, too, in the way of all Edwardian euphemisms. "Do you believe in fairies?" is a blushing evasion, perhaps a rejection, of the question "Do you believe in God?" The existence or nonexistence of God, needless to say, is entirely independent of the persuasion of our applause, but never mind: what Barrie is here proposing, with revival-tent fervor, is that, in the supposed absence of God, make-believe be raised up as the absolute good. This, again, is the Romantic's appeal to Poetic Genius, and a very dubious theology. Clapping if you believe in fairies is making believe in kind with reading horoscopes and table-rapping for spirits and feeling good about ourselves when we think we have been left out in the cold as a race. In this it does suit the times, which have favored whatever is unreal and whimsical in story. It had a hand in making the times, too, of course. It is in no small measure due to Barrie that the spirituality inherent in make-believe has become confused with emotional uplift in the twentieth century. As I hope has been demonstrated in this study, make-believe means to stir the imagination, not the emotions. Spirituality is not emotional, it is spiritual: the two are not even remotely the same. *Peter Pan* can only be one of MacDonald's false dreams, a show-business origin myth for an age whose scenery is all improvised of cardboard. It has endured because it always sends us home warm and smiling, assured of the fun that can be had from making things up.

The Wonderful Wizard of Oz (1900)

Barrie's best conceit in *Peter Pan* was rather a good one. A crocodile is stalking Captain Hook. In the stomach of the implacable reptile a clock is ticking. This is Hook's only warning of the beast's approach, and he lives in mortal dread of what will become of him the day the clock stops ticking and his foe begins its silent running. The fourteen volumes of the *Oz* series by L. Frank Baum (1856–1919) are full of inventions like this, and better. Baum was the Edison of narrative fantasy, finding ways of lighting it up and making it talk that no one had ever thought of before. The product of his two decades of tinkering are an often ill-written but always pleasing jumble of effects. *The Marvelous Land of Oz* followed *The Wizard* in 1904, with *Ozma of Oz*, *Dorothy and the Wizard in Oz*, *The Road to Oz*, and *The Emerald City of Oz* appearing annually from 1907 to 1910. In this last fantasy Baum tried to turn a circular journey into a closed one by declaring Oz forevermore invisible and thus inaccessible to its chronicler, but popular demand led him to resume his annual production in 1913 with *The Patch-work Girl of Oz*. *Tik-Tok of Oz* followed, and then *The Scarecrow of Oz*, *Rinkitink in Oz*, *The Lost Princess of Oz*, *The Tin Woodman of Oz*, *The*

Magic of Oz, and *Glinda of Oz*. I cite them all to suggest how spendthrift were Baum's powers of imagination, and also how hastily he wrote, for even these fourteen novels are but a fraction of his output for children in this period. Oz is undoubtedly the most pleasant of these pleasant lands of make-believe, but it is a place I think you really must discover in childhood to love. To come to them fresh as an adult is to be let down by a pedestrian style and by stories with little sense of purpose beyond getting out the next entertainment. Contrary to the claim that *Oz* is the first truly American fantasy, written in plain American English, the books are fraught with European borrowings, fin-de-siècle affectations, and unplain wee folk like Munchkins and Winkies talking wee talk. Charles Perrault wrote better American English than Baum. A place already charmed by the fairy dust of escapism is in no need of a muse, but Baum supplied one anyway. His secular mimic, Glinda the Good, makes an attractive accessory to the adventure, like the court fairies of earlier romances or Eugene Fields's Rock-a-By Lady from Hushaby Street. Baum was essentially a pulp writer who drew at need from every passing fashion, sometimes to the benefit of the story, sometimes not. Much of the credit for those images of Oz that settle lastingly in the mind must go to his illustrators, W. W. Denslow in the inaugural volume and John R. Neill thereafter. Some credit should fall as well, perhaps, to the American writer Frank Stockton, whose fairy tale "The Castle of Bim" may have been Baum's inspiration for sending a little girl and a company of eccentric wayfarers in search of a miracle worker who turns out in the end to be a fraud.

Plots notwithstanding, this is what *Oz* is really all about — wayfaring in a new land. The pleasure of being there is the thing, and bumping into new and wonderful characters, like the person in Mother Goose who went out one misty, moisty morning and said How do you do? to the old man clothed all in leather. The world may not know our name, as it does in *Pinocchio*, but in Oz it is always interested enough to ask. A walker in this enchanted land will make the acquaintance of many fellow travelers and find them the friends of his need. That is what they are there for, of course. They are the helpers from the old fairy tales, now Americanized into Scarecrows, Tin Men, Tik-Toks, Highly Magnified Wogglebugs, and Johnny Do-its. Through them the books do create a genuine feeling of gladness. Because the charm of Oz grows in direct proportion to its distance from reality, however, it may be that we are being gladdened by a lesser kind of happiness and left feeling a little bereft that the real world should be the drab place of hunger and destruction here portrayed, while the real residence of gladness lies somewhere over the rainbow.

Rootabaga Stories (1922), Rootabaga Pigeons (1923)

Over the rainbow, "where the railroad tracks run off into the blue sky and then forty ways farther yet," can be found the very pleasant land imagined by the poet and folklorist Carl Sandburg (1878–1967). Of all American fantasies, this collection of forty-nine tales about the Rootabaga Country is the one most alive in its language. Regrettably, it is a gathering of fancies so arbitrary and whimsical that they tend to evaporate from memory like a dream once the book is closed. You may recall riding the zigzag railroad to a wonderful place where you heard about the Potato Face Blind Man and Blixie Bimber and Bimbo the Snip, and Spink and Skabootch, and Dippy the Wisp and Slip Me Liz; you may recall how "the two skyscrapers talked with each other the same as mountains talk," and How the Animals Lost Their Tails and Got Them Back Traveling from Philadelphia to Medicine Hat; and you may recall the Haystack Cricket and How Things Are Different Up in the Moon Towns, and a hundred things more; but their moorings to your own reality were as tenuous as spider strands and proved as ephemeral. The illustrations by Maud and Miska Petersham are likewise beguiling, but nothing being told of the Rootabaga Country is being fully realized as a story—that is, as a narrative engaging the reader at any level of personal risk—and nothing plants itself very deeply in the mind as a consequence. A few of the tales have been excerpted to advantage as picture books—Harriet Pincus's rendition of *The Wedding Procession of the Rag Doll and the Broom Handle and Who Was in It* (1967) is notable—but few will stand alone. What settles in the memory are the details. Sandburg had a way with bugs, for example:

> Then the zizzies came. The zizzy is a bug. He runs zigzag on zigzag legs, eats zigzag with zigzag teeth, and spits zigzag with a zigzag tongue.
>
> Millions of zizzies came hizzing with little hizzers on their heads and under their legs.
>
> There was a corner house with corners every way it looked. And up in the corners were bugs with little bug houses, bug doors to open, bug windows to look out of.
>
> In the summer time if the evening was cool or in the winter time if the evening was warm, they played games—bugs-up, bugs-down, run-bugs-run, beans-bugs-beans.
>
> They entered the Potato Bug Country. And they had luck first of all the first hour they were in the Potato Bug Country. They met a Potato Bug millionaire.
>
> "How are you a millionaire?" they asked him.
>
> "Because I got a million," he answered.
>
> "A million what?"
>
> "A million *fleems*."
>
> "Who wants fleems?;"
>
> "You want fleems if you're going to live here."
>
> "Why so?"
>
> "Because fleems is our money. In the Potato Bug Country, if you got no fleems you can't buy nothing nor anything. But if you got a million fleems you're a Potato Bug millionaire."

The lighter Sandburg goes with his lyrical effects, the better the results, generally. Here he celebrates the harvest of talent in the American hinterland by summoning forth a string of ball towns hiding in the tall grass. Passengers in the railroad trains look out of the windows and the tall grass stands up so they can't see the ball towns. But the ball towns are there and the tall grass is full of pitchers, catchers, basemen, fielders, short stops, sluggers, southpaws, and back stops. They play ball till dark and after dark they talk ball. The big fast ballplayers in the Rootabaga Country all come from these ball towns in the tall grass.

Implicit in the matter and the spirit of these stories is an announcement made by *Little Black Sambo*, that the new energy informing this branch of children's literature in the twentieth century will come no longer from the fairy tale but from the folk tale.

Millions of Cats (1928)

Folk and fairy tales kept congenial company in the early collections for children, but as they were translated into literary forms in the nineteenth and twentieth centuries these two related branches of story went their separate ways. The fairy tale evolved into the muse parable, which in turn became secularized into the circular fantasy. The analogous translation of the folk tale was not into narrative fiction but into the picture book. The greater portion of original work for the nursery can be traced to some folkish origin. Russell Hoban's turn on the trickster tale, *How Tom Beat Captain Najork and His Hired Sportsmen* (1974), is only one of the better examples, from among thousands, of how folk tradition has been put to new uses.

The translation into graphic formats began in Germany in the 1860s with a series of comic picture stories by Wilhelm Busch (1832–1908). The nubile line and firecracker animation used by Busch to detail the misadventures in *Max und Moritz* (1865) and *Plisch und Plum* (1882) have influenced a number of modern illustrators, including Fritz Kredel, Maurice Sendak, and William Steig. In the 1920s Busch's line and liveliness were adopted by the daughter of Bohemian emigrés to Minnesota, Wanda Gág (1893–1946), who applied them variously in journals like *New Masses* and in children's books. Gág gave Busch's pleasing contours an earthier substance and a kindlier direction. Her thick, rustic line shapes a homely presence for each person, chair, tree, cloud, cat, or house portrayed, with every figure intimately forested in its own shadows. The result is a world that is engagingly idiosyncratic and friendly. *Gone Is Gone: The Story of a Man Who Wanted to Do Housework* (1935) is a tale we have seen played out, with the same disastrous results, on a hundred television comedies. It is a small book physically, a sturdy little chapbook told in an amused voice, as if Gág were recalling this anecdote of her grandmother's while rolling out the pie dough.

Where *Gone is Gone* is a straightforward domestic folk comedy, *Millions of Cats*, the story of a lonely old man and woman who want a cat for company, is that and something else besides. As she runs her layouts inventively up and down the pages and sends her old man up and down them in search of the wanted cat, Gág runs us gracefully right into a realm of make-believe. What else can a tale be in which somewhere over the hills we find

Cats here, cats there,
Cats and kittens everywhere,
Hundreds of cats,
Thousands of cats,
Millions and billions and trillions of cats.

Millions of Cats has the best of two worlds—the cozy familiarity of folklore and the more expansive air of fantasy. Implicit in *Little Black Sambo* had been the announcement that because there is a kind of grace in everyday life—a new red coat, a plate of pancakes, stupid tigers—the folk tale and make-believe need not be thought separate or incompatible forms. We can actually feel that promise being given full play in Gág's little adventure; the gladness of her sense of discovery is palpable. What she is conveying to us here is more than a comical folk story; it is the understanding that make-believe can be found residing in every leaf and rolling hill and that any mundane event, like the getting of a cat, can be an occasion for celebrating the whole world.

An entirely contrary thought was about to take command of narrative fantasy for older children. A product perhaps of too much war and crime, too big a nuclear arsenal, too crass a popular culture, this new thought was the subversive idea that an imaginary realm might be so sealed off in space or buried so deep in time that it could not be reached even by a make-believe ride on a tornado or a tumble down a rabbit hole. The genre to come of this surmise followed *Millions of Cats* by a decade. An offshoot of the antiquing process we saw at work in Mother Goose and the fairy tales, it reached full flower in the 1950s and has been overrunning the garden ever since. If Mother Goose and *Pinocchio* can be called open fantasies and *Alice* and *Oz* circular fantasies, this last phase, in which the author has severed his ties with the world altogether, might well be called the closed fantasy. It is an escapist genre and marks, I think, a dead end in the descent of the tale. It has proven fruitful for fantasy writers over the past four decades, but it is so solipsistic that it can only go on replicating itself ad infinitum. And when you have read one sword & sorcery fantasy, I'm afraid, you have pretty much read them all.

The Hobbit (1937), *The Lord of the Rings* (1954–55)

The earlier of these two tales by the Oxford professor of languages and literature J. R. R. Tolkien (1892–1973) is properly a children's story; the second, as Edmund Wilson observed, is "a children's book which has somehow got out of hand."[2] *The Hobbit* recalls another famous fantasy of the

English shires in which villagers, squires, and yeomen have been translated into creatures of field and stream. Kenneth Grahame reclothed his shiremen as the local fauna, whereas Tolkien has here imagined a new species, but in general *The Hobbit* and *The Wind in the Willows* are rather alike. For the animal fellowship that liberated Toad Hall from usurping stoats Tolkien substitutes a hobbit and a band of dwarfs liberating a usurped treasure trove from a dragon. Peaceable, pursy Bilbo Baggins of The Shire, with his homely digger feet, is quite like the self-effacing Mole, who in the right company also discovers in himself a talent for derring-do. Gandalf the Wizard, who taps Bilbo for the mission, has the cosmopolitan assurance of Rat, while the dwarfs could easily be the gruff, underground cousins of Badger. Bilbo's trek through Mirkwood is a mirror image of Mole's misadventure in the perilous Wild Wood, and so on. Unfortunately, Tolkien had neither Grahame's quickening way with a story nor his love of nature working for him. His taste was for things old and generic, and he was quite content to deploy stock images and narrative gestures drawn from his reading. That conjuring another dragon in an age of science fiction might simply be dull seems not to have troubled him, nor how deadening an effect it would have to drag out over several chapters what in a true fairy tale would have been conveyed by a tremor of mystery and a flash of scales. But then, by design Tolkien did not write fairy tales. As his essay "On Fairy-Stories" suggests, he preferred a hybrid fiction blending Faerie romance and heroic saga. He understood what story means to do but would not allow himself all the means with which to do it. A tale, he said well, works to satisfy "certain primordial human desires. One of these desires is to survey the depths of space and time. Another is . . . to hold communion with other living things."[3] A survey of space and time implies a circular fantasy; but coming and going like Dorothy in *Oz* was an operative mode that Tolkien expressly banned from his ideal aesthetics. Stories worked for him only when locked away "in an abyss of time so deep as to work an enchantment upon them." The redeeming enlargements of the real world we have seen in earlier fairy tales and narratives were so alien to his understanding that he hardly recognized them as proper tales at all. Most good fairy-stories, as he called them, were "about the *aventures* of men in the Perilous Realm or upon its shadowy marches."[4] He felt he could bring this Dark Sublime of Faerie into view by creating a "Secondary World" to contain it; the result of course was the triple-decker *The Lord of the Rings*, whose nearly twelve hundred pages the perplexed and exasperated Wilson would characterize as "interminable adventures the poverty of invention displayed in which is, it seems to me, almost pathetic." The critic's exasperation may have followed, too, from a prescient recognition that literary Modernism, of which he was the century's foremost chronicler, was drawing to a close and that this burdensome apparatus of recherché effects was come to replace it.

Faerie, whether dark and perilous or light and glad, can never, let it be said, be contained. If not a gift outright, it might be sought and suggested, but in either case the enchantment will lie in the story's language and not in any accumulation of events and feigned mythologies, for no Secondary World, however well imagined, can in itself be more than an inferior substitute for the real one. The opening volume, *The Fellowship of the Ring*, does get the adventure off to a promising start as Tolkien sends his hobbits again eastward and the reader comes to know Bilbo's heir, Frodo, his batman Sam, and the rest of the company. This first stage of the journey, through The Shire and the Old Forest to Weathertop and Rivendell, is eerily pleasurable. As the saga unfolds, however, it becomes depressingly apparent that not only will true wonders be lacking in the nine hundred and seventy pages yet before us; the author is everywhere actually going to talk his "deep enchantment" up from its secret places and right off the page to land with an inane thud at the feet of our expectations. The one bright exception is the reappearance of what was the best in *The Hobbit*—his mewling, wormy creature of the underworld, the Gollum. A degenerate scion of the original hobbit stock, this lisping antihero may have descended as well from the goblins in MacDonald's *The Princess and the Goblin*, on whom it is something of an improvement.

Discovered in one's teens, Middle-earth can be an interesting enough world to roam about in, but, unless one is nostalgic by disposition and tolerant to a fault, the book will pall rather rapidly. A stock company of travelers plods over a corduroy road of prose and through an endless series of stagey and redundant forced marches and battles until the final banality is at hand and the fearsome Ring of Power is simply disposed of in a volcano. Perhaps the best way to read the epic is to do what Grahame's Rat liked to do with boats, and that is to mess about in the maps, of which there are several. Tolkien claimed that Middle-earth was born of his habit of inventing make-believe languages, but it seems to be as much about the pleasures of geography. Those furtive dashes from copse to copse and on from Weathertop to the safe-house at Rivendell echo all our childhood afternoons slipping through woods and backyards, from one hideout to the next, capguns or quarterstaffs at the ready, until Mother—here the faerie queen, Galadriel—calls that it is time to come in for supper. At this level, the level of *The Hobbit*, the story might have succeeded. It goes all to hell after the first volume, I suspect, because Tolkien tried to glorify a boyhood game as an ideal for adults. His real agenda was not enchantment at all in the end but the invocation of a high heroic age where great deeds had once been done. The costume drama that this reclusive don conjured from his armchair adventuring would have made even the drawing-room swashbuckler Howard Pyle blush. Tolkien had survived some of the ghastliest battles of World War I; his friends had not. Nor, apparently, had his memory of the war. There is none of the observed truth of, say, an *All Quiet on the Western Front* to these clashes, even granting them their terms as make-believe. He regressed, it seems, into a compensatory dream of how a war ought to be fought, not with bodies piling up stupidly in trenches — that was all wrong, you see — but in the grand manner, with stirring rides and deeds of valor. The evil that men do to one another he saw as the unreal thing; true reality would be an age when heroes could cry out like eleven-year-old boys, "By Elbereth and Luthien the Fair, you shall have neither the Ring nor me!" and not be thought ridiculous. The irony must have escaped him that the make-believe swagger he was here honoring was precisely the kind of toy-soldiering that had led to the horrors of World War I to begin with.

This taste for the fake exultations of the battlefield he acquired largely from listening to Wagner. *The Lord of the Rings* is heavily in debt to the Icelandic sagas and Prose Edda and to a variety of Celtic and Teutonic myths and legends, but as much as anything it is a rehistoried and repeopled diminution of Wagner's opera cycle *Der Ring des Nibelungen*. The premise of both works is the same: a magic ring that will spell the doom of whomever possesses it is forged to rule the world. The prehistory of *Das Rheingold* became Tolkien's elaborate apparatus of historical and genealogical appendices. The heroic posturings of *Siegfried* he generously distributed among various bands of heroes. *Die Walküre* became the furious rides and battles, and *Götterdämmerung* the final convulsion and the pathetic grandeur of the Fellowship's parting. Here he is, displaying the fruits of having listened one time too many to "The Ride of the Valkyries":

> . . . foremost on the field rode the swan-knights of Dol Amroth with their Prince and his blue banner at their head.
> "Amroth for Gondor!" they cried. "Amroth to Faramir!"
> Like thunder they broke upon the enemy. . . .

> Fey he seemed, or the battle-fury of his fathers ran like new fire in his veins, and he was borne upon Snowmane like a god of old, even as Oromë the Great in the battle of the Valar when the world was young. His golden shield was uncovered, and lo! it shone like an image of the Sun. . . .

> Thus came Aragorn son of Arathorn, Elessar, Isildur's heir, out of the Paths of the Dead, borne upon a wind from the Sea to the kingdom of Gondor; and the mirth of the Rohirrim was a torrent of laughter and a flashing of swords.

Very seldom does one encounter emotion this fraudulent and writing this bad in any genre. And there will be a hundred pages more of flashing and breaking like thunder before Tolkien brings the pother to its last, breathless gasp of cliches. The little adventure that began in *The Hobbit* and ran along well enough through Book One of the sequel founders in the end in a gathering sea of what Wilson summarized as "balderdash." It founders because Tolkien was good to his word: he meant to lose himself in an abyss of time, and so he did. Cut loose from fairy-tale tradition, he went as deaf to the sound of his voice as a man drowning and ended by writing Faerieland's answer to *Conan the Barbarian*. In real fairy tales or in a fantasy like *Pinocchio*, the drama is played out, and the world redeemed, along ordinary country lanes and city streets. Jack climbs a beanstalk to a kingdom in the sky, but only because he has made a deal in the road for some beans while on his way to market. To the deeply pessimistic Tolkien, such leaps from the mundane to the wonderful were not imaginable. An abyss of time through which to work a deep enchantment had become his idée fixe; if redemption were to be found, it would be found in the long ago, for the real world had none to offer. This devout Roman Catholic saw the world, paradoxically, as being devoid of grace. A man can write only what his imagination gives him to write, if he is to write at all, of course, and must be read on his own terms. On the other hand, if he practices one thing while professing another, it is of some interest, and in preferring his own imaginary, pre-Christian, antediluvian, pre-Edenic world to the one in which he lived Tolkien does seem to have been committing a classic act of bad faith. Creating a Secondary World, after all, is in effect a declaration that God's creation is deficient. Tolkien's end-run around the First and Second Commandments makes him the second Christian writer in this history to have lived by the fool's parable "Stolen waters are sweet, and bread eaten in secret is pleasant." To what extent he was aware of his apostasy is as arguable as it was with the Reverend Dodgson. His essay "On Fairy-Stories" reveals, somewhat disjointedly, that it did worry him from time to time, at least. He closed the piece insisting that, appearances notwithstanding, a secondary creation like his own was indeed "drawing on reality" and "by grace" was perfectly consistent with "the Christian Story."[5] Since the whole essay is essentially a defense of the "escapist aspect of fairy-stories" as a "more profound" response than any other to "the ugliness of our works, and of their evil,"[6] it would be instructive to find in it some explanation of why renouncing the world for places lost in an abyss of time should be thought anything but a rejection of God's plan for the world, but no such explanation is offered. Nor do we find any indication of why he supposed such a heretical notion could have come to him "by grace," or how it could fall that grace would set a Christian to daydreaming of nature spirits, wizards, rings of power, and "gods of old" when these things are so often condemned in the Bible that no scholar could ever claim to be ignorant of the prohibitions against them. It is a most curious definition of grace, too, that would suppose it God's wish that millions of children be initiated into the pleasures of this literary paganism. But then, "On Fairy-Stories" is not the disquisition on aesthetics it purports to be. It is, rather, an attempt to justify the bread Tolkien preferred to eat in secret and a pretense, like Dodgson's, that it squared with the bread he ate on Sundays.

After Tolkien's death, more appendices to *The Lord of the Rings* were discovered, and then more and still more yet — enough to support a cottage industry of Tolkieniana. The twelve hundred pages originally released to the public were only the man's introductory remarks; for his entire adult life, this Catholic scribe had been down in the dark pagan sublime of Middle-earth, scratching about and mumbling to himself like his creature, the Gollum. In light of this vast and compulsive output, it is hard not to suppose that he was searching all the while for his *Eucatastrophe*, the *evangelium* he so valued that with a "sudden joyous turn" would make his life's imaginings ring true. If so, he might have known better what to expect. Down there in the abyss, joy was going to elude him to the bitter end.

Tolkien's confidant at Oxford in matters of faith and literature was his younger friend and fellow don, the noted Christian apologist Clive Staples Lewis (1898–1963). What the two men shared most was a sense of alienation from society and a love of old legends. They read to each other from works in progress, and together they recited Wagner librettos and talked about the old gods in their twilight. As Tolkien was bringing *The Lord of the Rings* to completion, his friend was likewise at work, drafting a series of seven novels that, when completed, would constitute the first major tutorial muse fantasy and Christian parable since *Pinocchio*. Lewis's imagination was to take him on a more circular route than Tolkien's, however, to a parallel universe called Narnia, where parties of earth children could be tested in the rigors of adventure and tutored in the ways of God.

The Lion, the Witch and the Wardrobe (1950), Prince Caspian (1951), The Voyage of the Dawn Treader (1952), The Silver Chair (1953), The Horse and His Boy (1954), The Magician's Nephew (1955), The Last Battle (1956)

"Supposing," wrote Lewis when explaining how he meant to story matters of faith, "supposing that by casting all these things into an imaginary world, stripping them of their stained-glass and Sunday School associations, one could make them for the first time [sic] appear in their real potency?"[7] What he meant to do with his Christian parable had not, in fact, been done before. He meant to make Christ Himself the muse of the tale. It was the potency of Christ that he wanted to bring out, the presence of a Christ, as he wrote in *The Silver Chair*, "so bright and real and strong that everything else began at once to look pale and shadowy compared with him." His rationale for taking the reader to another world to achieve this end he reiterated at the close of *The Voyage of the Dawn Treader* when his Savior, the lion Aslan, tells the children about to embark for home, "there I have another name. You must learn to know me by that name. This was the very reason why you were brought to Narnia, that by knowing me here for a little, you may know me better there."

The journey to this understanding had begun a decade earlier, at the outbreak of World War II. Some schoolgirls evacuated from London were being billeted with the Lewis menage at Oxford; the occasion suggesting a tale, Lewis worked up a trial sketch for one:

> This book is about four children. . . . They all had to go away from London suddenly because of Air Raids, and because Father, who was in the Army, had gone off to the War and Mother was doing some kind of war work. They were sent to stay with a kind of relation of Mother's who was a very old Professor who lived all by himself in the country. [8]

The Chronicles of Narnia began in a good and basically harmless spirit, then, in the tradition of the school-holiday story. Lewis's chatty lingo and easy rhythms recall the English storyteller Edith Nesbit, a favorite of his childhood. To Nesbit can go some of the credit for the trial sketch being brought forward as the opening to *The Lion, the Witch and the Wardrobe* after lying idle for seven or eight years. The magic wardrobe leading to Lucy's rendezvous at a lamppost in the snows of Narnia is a borrowing from Nesbit's story "The Aunt and Amabel," published when Lewis was ten. It may be that the best writing in the series reflects this interim, Nesbit period when Lewis had yet to take a hard fix on his meanings. There are passages in *The Chronicles* that seem fresh from his first discoveries of how to get in and out of Narnia and of the kinds of magic that could be practiced in such a place. When he let Nesbit's voice speak for him in conjuring new and wonderful things, he spoke rather well. She herself lacked an instinct for fantasy, although taking her cue from Mrs. Molesworth and H. G. Wells, she wrote several of them anyway. In *Five Children and It* (1902), *The Phoenix and the Carpet* (1904), and *The Story of the Amulet* (1906), the prose is clear and comely but the invention thin. Nesbit could round the circle of her circular fantasies nicely but wanted for interesting places to send her children, and could find little for them to do once they arrived. She is best understood as a comic realist:

> "Oh, hats, how hot it is!" said Robert. "Dogs put their tongues out when they're hot; I wonder if it would cool us at all to put out ours?"
>
> "We might try," Jane said; and they all put their tongues out as far as ever they could go, so that it quite stretched their throats, but it only seemed to make them thirstier than ever, besides annoying everyone who went by.
>
> Five Children and It

If Lewis had been content to stay with his narrative model, the work might have achieved a greater unity than it did. But he was too instinctively mimetic to hold to a single voice; each new narrative need in this long series brought to mind the best examples of its kind from his vast reading, and he fell like an acolyte into that manner of saying the scene. Lucy's foray into Narnia is a page taken from that first, famous story of a little girl wandering a new world, and her encounter with the Faun at the lamppost is really Alice's encounter with the White Rabbit in Wonderland. Later in the same book, a book being told as a holiday adventure, we find Lewis calling up conjunctive resonances from the King James Bible as his leonine Christ is taken down from the cross and echoing Kenneth Grahame's "Then the two animals, crouching to the earth, bowed their heads and did worship."

Incompatible borrowings can be found all through the series; sometimes the mingling echoes work to advantage, and sometimes they seem only the comfortable murmurings of The Man Who Read Too Much. In imagining his world between worlds, he would draw heavily from MacDonald's adult work, *Phantastes*; but, sorry to say, Lewis was no Greatheart; despite the felicity of many passages in *The Chronicles* there will be no final giving away of himself to the task of guiding his pilgrims to the Celestial Country, only, in the end, a stop here, a stop there, and always the trilling whistle of the troop leader.

When these various influences do level out into a single, pervasive voice in the series, moreover, it is not Lewis's voice that we hear but the voice of the literary storybook. This is a sound never perfected by more than a few children's authors, and its limitations are manifest. Katharine Pyle's "Jack and the Beanstalk" and "Aladdin" are possibly the best "Jack and the Beanstalk" and "Aladdin" ever told,[9] but they are rather patrician tellings and their subjects are made middle class and wholesome in a way foreign to their own lives. Never, however, did Pyle speak in the affected manner of her more famous brother, and this is just what we so often hear Lewis doing. Like Howard Pyle or, later, Tolkien, he could not resist trying his hand at the high heroic style, and, like them, he sounds perfectly archaic and silly doing it:

> "Fair Consorts, let us now alight from our horses and follow this beast into the thicket; for in all my days I never hunted a nobler quarry."
> "Sir," said the others, "even so let us do."

Speaking out of several inherited traditions betrayed him into making some truly fatal blunders. His central problem in building the parable had always been the difficulty of portraying his Lion of Judah, Aslan, in such a way that the Christ figure would speak with the needed authority yet without intimidating the tale back into those stained-glass and Sunday School associations Lewis wished to avoid. The odds against him were long, and he did not really surmount them—or, rather, he surmounted them and toppled over onto the other side of good judgment. His provenance for an anthropomorphized godhead lay in two biblical apocalypses:

> And as for the lion whom you saw rousing up out of the forest and roaring and speaking to the eagle and reproving him for his unrighteousness, and as for all his words that you have heard, this is the Messiah whom the Most High has kept until the end of days. . . . in mercy he will set free the remnant of my people, those who have been saved throughout my borders, and he will make them joyful until the end comes, the day of judgment. . . .
>
> 2 Esdras

> Weep not: behold, the Lion of the tribe of Judah, the Root of David, hath prevailed. . . .
>
> Revelation

And this was his storybook solution to the dilemma:

> "Wow!" roared Aslan half rising from his throne. . . .

Even a child might question the "real potency" of a Christ given to yelling "Wow!" At this point in the tale the reader may be noticing how shaky the props truly are that support Narnia. The muse was never made to look foolish by misspeaking like this in *The Water Babies* or *Pinocchio*, or the stories of MacDonald or *The Little Lame Prince*. A suspicion begins to arise that *The Chronicles* may not be, after all, quite as inspired as one would hope of a parable written by the most famous Christian apologist of the day. It may be a good time to ask of Lewis what I asked of Dodgson and Tolkien: why an avowed Christian would choose to make his witness by setting up a creation in competition with God's. His reason had seemed clear enough—to portray Christ so vividly in make-believe terms that children would know him as "bright and real and strong"—and there are moments when he does approach this end. There are many more, however, when the Lion of Judah simply looks goofy. And there are even some scenes ugly enough to suggest the presence of a debilitating animus driving these seven books, just as one had driven *Alice in Wonderland*.

Spiritual estrangement is the most obvious reason for creating a world sequestered off to the side of reality, of course. Lewis's career as misanthrope, misogynist, xenophobe, and classroom bully has been well and depressingly documented. Like Tolkien, too, he lacked Kingsley's fascination with the natural world as a bright given of our existence. Here and there we see him paying lip service to the beauties of creation, but nature—that is, real, not make-believe, nature—is generally viewed as a crawly, fallen state to be avoided whenever possible. The spirit of Psalm 26, to "tell of all thy wondrous works," is little in evidence for a practiced Christian apologist. Unlike Kingsley, Lewis ignored, or never saw, what might have been useful to him in his daily disenchantment, how the psalmists could praise God and with the very same words raise a moan about the world without giving offense.

Subtract man and nature from the parable and what does the author have left? He has his storybook stereotypes, his pessimism, and here a Christ who must be an uncertain presence largely dependent on the parablist's own prejudices. In Narnia they will be the prejudices of a man who, as Lewis wrote in *Prince Caspian*, fills all his spare hours with "thinking and dreaming about the old days, and longing that they might come back." It was not idle talk when the biblical prophets and wisdom writers warned against the spiritual snare-net of nostalgia. In the haze of sweet regret, grace must seem a phantom thing, to be found only in the antiquities of books or the promise of the New Jerusalem. The alienated Christian is necessarily at odds with perhaps the most famous passage in the New Testament: "For God so loved the world that he gave his only begotten Son." Lewis so deplored the world that, once deprived of his usual method, that of arguing His Christ into being, and having now to evoke him in story language instead, he could do it only by making some other, some presumably better world for him to inhabit. This first and more obvious reason for creating the parallel universe of Narnia was the negative reason: it allowed Lewis to leave out everything about the world that he disliked or to summon up what he disliked in such a way that he could knock it about however he wished. Making the way straight for Jesus was his warrant.

The second reason followed from the first: a Narnia gave him a place to put in everything that did please him. This is where Tolkien fell out with his friend, finding in the way he peopled his Platonic "shadowland" an utter disregard for the laws of consistency that must be observed when writing any fantasy. The new world must seem all of a piece, naturally evolved to its own fullness. Narnia is all pieces of other fullnesses, hastily thrown together like stage props retrieved from a warehouse. The only law of consistency Lewis observed was the law of his own fancy. His characters— medieval lords and ladies, talking horses and beavers, Greek fauns, witches and magicians, Father Christmas, elves, werewolves, mermaids, an evil ape, a dragon, and Cyrano de Bergerac played by a mouse—mill about like actors from various costume dramas in a Hollywood back lot. Narnia is much like Barrie's Never Never Land, a theatrical set that will be knocked down when the curtain falls on the apocalypse of act seven and the assembled cast is dispersed either to heaven or to hell. Platonism has here become an excuse for artistic license, as if the author could throw into the mix anything that came to mind, on the specious reasoning that anything he thinks into existence must already exist—indeed, be favored—in the mind of God. Lewis's supposition that this was so led him into a theological morass. As eclectic as the books are in their stylistic borrowings, so are they equally syncretic in borrowing from the pantheons of the world's pagan faiths and demonologies. As a Protestant fundamentalist, Lewis liked to ridicule other faiths in his pages, attacking Islam in *The Horse and His Boy*, for example, and in *The Last Battle* belittling Roman Catholicism, but he held fire if he happened to fancy the faith's imagery. When the children first encounter Aslan in *The Lion, the Witch and the Wardrobe*, the king of heaven is found to be sporting in the forest not with his saints but with Dryads, Naiads, a unicorn, centaurs, and a bull bearing the head of a man. The Lord of this hellenized, New Age land of make-believe is really more the son of Zeus and Hera than any recognizably Christian Christ.

I would hazard a guess that Lewis was emboldened to become this precipitous in his misreading of Plato by William Blake's infamous dictum, "Everything possible to be believ'd is an image of truth."[10] I would guess, too, that he was encouraged into thinking the time ripe for a sorcerer's apprentice by Walt Disney's recent homage to pagan mythologies, *Fantasia* (1940). The Judeo-Christian idiom had by now pretty much become a thing of the past, having in the nineteenth century rapidly lost its authority as a common language for the arts as biblical literacy declined and the fairy tales and myths of all nations and creeds became universally popular. A Romantic like Keats, affecting Greek ways, could rephrase Blake's bill of goods into the comely lie that any beauty is truth and any truth beauty, and declare, "that is all/Ye know on earth, and all ye need to know." The

Moderns similarly reanimated themselves by looking to primitive art. As a pop travesty of this long search for a new metaphoric language in what everyone was eager to call the post-Christian era, *Fantasia* stands as perhaps Hollywood's greatest ode to eclectic kitsch. To the strains of Stravinsky and Moussoursky, cartoon fauns and centaurs gambol, Pegasus soars, wizards beckon the elements, dinosaurs thunder, and hippopotami pirouette in pink tutus. If Lewis needed encouragement to throw into his drama whatever he pleased, he would certainly have found it at the movies. The temptation to poke through neighboring mythologies has always been great, of course, for paganism affords the artist more cunning, new ways of feigning miracles than he could accommodate in three lifetimes. That men are ever "vain in their imaginations" is a warning sounded everywhere in Scripture, from Sinai through Proverbs and the prophets to Paul, who cautioned,

> Professing themselves to be wise, they became fools,
> And changed the glory of the uncorruptible God into an image made like to corruptible man, and to birds, and four-footed beasts, and creeping things.

Nesbit's magic wardrobe must have offered the professor of English an escape from doctrine too convenient to pass by. And what harm could there be, after all, in something that was only make-believe? Taking license with the Platonic Forms, he could use this secondary world to play his religion to the tune of his own fancy. Becoming a demiurge unto himself empowered him now, not merely to leave out what he did not like and to put in what he did, but to say all those extraneous things he wanted to say that he could not get away with in the world of real men and women or in his usual world of orthodox, fundamentalist thought. That this was yet a third reason motivating the creation of Narnia he as much as announced in his offhanded Platonic *summa*, "I wrote fairy tales because the Fairy Tale seemed the ideal Form for the stuff I had to say."[11] When he wrote that he had things to say, he meant it as a pedagogue of the old school. Beyond saying his story, beyond saying his parable, he made *The Chronicles* serve every petty prejudice and every theological revision that could be fitted into the general scheme. And it is here—and not, as he told it, with the White Witch of the North—that evil entered Narnia. It is Lewis's own original sin of pride that infects this new world and brings about its fall.

On Being Boys and Girls

Several parties of children are assembled for the various adventures in Narnia. In *The Lion, the Witch and the Wardrobe*, *Prince Caspian*, *The Voyage of the Dawn Treader*, and *The Last Battle* it is the Pevensie clan: Peter, Susan, Edmund, and Lucy. In *The Dawn Treader* Lewis added as the hapless foil of the piece a Pevensie cousin, the unlovely Eustace Scrubb, "a puny little person" whose parents "wore a special kind of underclothes."

In *The Silver Chair* the struggling foil and heroine, Jill Pole, is joined by a Eustace newly reconstituted as one with a certain potential for heroism after all. In *The Magician's Nephew* the children are Polly and Digory, and in *The Horse and His Boy* the Narnian children, Shasta and Aravis. The first adventure had begun in the spirit of a school holiday, but this was a deception: these children are about to be examined more rigorously than ever they were at school; one of them Lewis is literally going to damn to hell. Unlike a Pinocchio, moreover, they will not even enjoy the freedom and dignity of their own thoughts along the way. The oft-scolded Pinocchio was only being asked to look to his studies, after all; he was otherwise free to think and run loose as he chose. In Christian terms he had the full free will necessary to make his actions meaningful. Lewis's children are puppets in a way that Pinocchio was not. It is possible, of course, that they are lacking free will by default; for where Collodi could quote straight from a child's brain and heart, Lewis seems not to have had a clue. His children are stock characters from series books, and they think in the clichés of series books. Occasionally they sound at least as convincing as Nesbit's children, but usually not, for he lacked Nesbit's ear for child-talk. The Pevensies and their friends speak the rhetoric of adventure and school stories. As a consequence, Lewis could ignore them as real persons and deal with them punitively at his leisure. The voice of the hall proctor stalks these pages, monitoring the children's every move and thought. Lewis judges their already predestined decisions, counts the demerits of their tears, and sets them to monitoring one another for lapses in right behavior. He is the sort of teacher who entertains the class by belittling the one or two kids whom no one much likes anyway. As much as he hated his own school days, they were good enough for him, and they ought to be good enough for us. There will be no nonsense about coeducation and enough corporal punishment to teach the way of things. The subject under study, in short, is not Christianity, or Christian ethics, but the kind of quasi-military comportment honored in the boy's books of R. M. Ballantyne and Captain Marryat, favorites of Lewis's youth. Poor "puny little person" Eustace, with his beetle collection, his miserable excuses, and his parents who wear funny underwear (what *can* this mean, by the way?), will become a hero not through any real agency of his own but because Lewis, having made his point about the sort of boy he detests, now wants to explicate the rules by which a worm can become One of Us.

If the books had quite so regimental a feel to them as I am here making out, of course, they would not be as popular as they apparently are, especially with girls. Lewis is sly. The going seldom seems too rigorous as you read along; the voice editorializing in the background is solicitous enough in the right places to be encouraging. Instead, the lessons are being insinuated; the method is one of innuendo. Incredibly, Lewis will sometimes even cozy the reader into a conspiracy against one of the main characters. Again and again in *The Silver Chair*, Jill Pole is spotlighted as a person who, being a girl, is not up to the challenge. She forgets her instructions, causes accidents, and

> I hope you won't lose all interest in Jill for the rest of the book if I tell you that at this moment she began to cry. There was a good deal of excuse for her.

At first reading this sounds a kindly way of putting the matter, not unlike Dinah Mulock Craik tending to her little lame prince. But it is not kindly; it is patronizing, and, worse, it is a betrayal of Jill. The relationship between Lewis and his characters is here exposed: he is the false friend of their need, ever ready to throw a wink over their shoulders to the reader. No one need be reminded of the man's public testimony on the inherent inferiority of girls to notice how often in these pages he allows them only the little things, and without much conviction even then. Rarely do we find him saluting a girl without crossing his other fingers behind his back:

> Polly absolutely refused to do any exploring in new worlds until she had made sure about getting back to the old one. She was quite as brave as he about some dangers (wasps, for instance) but she was not so interested in finding out things nobody had ever heard of before; for Digory was the sort of person who wants to know everything, and when he grew up he became the famous Professor Kirke who comes into other books.

It is everywhere painfully clear in *The Chronicles* that if girls are to be of any use, either in this world or in the New Jerusalem, they must learn to conform to the code as set out in boy's adventure novels. If they must tag along, that is, they had better follow orders, show pluck, and not blubber over all those things they can usually be expected to blubber over. Most will be found wanting along the way, naturally, and the reasons will be tediously familiar: "She's not like Lucy, you know, who's as good as a man, or at any rate as good as a boy."

I do not pretend to understand why girls like these stories as much as they do. As far as I can tell, boys have not cared for them much. It may be that boys are quicker to sense when another boy is making a grab for the whistle and clipboard. Insofar as girls today can more readily take their intellect and talents as a given, I suppose it is natural that they should be attracted to the challenges being offered them in Narnia. Lewis does court them with the occasional bouquet. Lucy acquits herself well, and so in the end does Jill, and the warrior maiden Aravis, of *The Horse and His Boy*, "was proud . . . and true as steel." The seduction here for girls, I suspect, is their implicit induction into a private club previously reserved for boys only. As they read along, they may not care what an elitist clique for Top Boys and Girls it is, or how exclusion from it will be for everyone else the quite literal loss of heaven in the end. Harvey Darton had noted the Victorians' "modest feeling of prerogative audience." In Lewis's keeping, this feeling has turned immodest and smug, allowing him to post his own keep-out signs on the clubhouse door:

"Squints, and has freckles," said Caspian.

"Oh, poor girl," said Lucy.

Once you have granted yourself license to say the snide thing, you are only a smirk away from the wicked one. In *Prince Caspian* appears what may well be the vilest passage ever to poison a children's book. Aslan has been coursing through Narnia, winnowing the wheat from the chaff, the saved from the damned, when he arrives with his entourage at a schoolhouse where a class is in progress:

"If you don't attend, Gwendolen," said the mistress, "and stop looking out of the window, I shall have to give you an order-mark."

"But please, Miss Prizzle—" began Gwendolen.

"Did you hear what I said, Gwendolen?" asked Miss Prizzle.

"But please, Miss Prizzle," said Gwendolen, "there's a LION!"

"Take two order-marks for talking nonsense," said Miss Prizzle. "And now—

"A roar interrupted her. Ivy came curling in at the windows of the classroom. The walls became a mass of shimmering green, and leafy branches arched overhead where the ceiling had been. Miss Prizzle found she was standing on grass in a forest glade. She clutched at her desk to steady herself, and found that the desk was a rose-bush. Wild people such as she had never even imagined were crowding round her. Then she saw the lion, screamed and fled, and with her fled her class, who were mostly dumpy, prim little girls with fat legs. Gwendolen hesitated.

. . . "You'll stay with us, sweetheart?" said Aslan.

"Oh, *may* I? Thank you, thank you," said Gwendolen.

Lewis's hatreds were petty, his enemies weak. The role of tutor-as-bully was one he relished, both at Oxford and in his books. Apologists for his work have written that his sadism should not be exaggerated. His pupil and biographer Roger Lancelyn Green, who will also promote the Reverend Dodgson as demiurge, sniffily dismisses Lewis's detractors as "watchful dragons." Well, perhaps. These same apologists refer to the master as "Saint Jack" and have even submitted to Rome that he be considered for beatification. Nevertheless, somewhere among the world's vast population of dumpy people with fat legs, there is one crestfallen schoolgirl who understands all too well the message of saintly Jack in this passage. So let us not ourselves simply pass it off as make-believe. The happy entourage here cavorting through Narnia is not a gathering of Christ and his Elect; it is a party of the Smart Set frolicking down the avenue and laughing at the pokey people they pass. Sweethearts named Gwendolen are in; girls with fat legs or freckles are out. In the care of Saint Jack, the Last Judgment has become a beauty contest: no Prizzles allowed at that heavenly pub, The Lion and the Lamb, and no freckles and no dumpies, either. For the extraordinary assumption behind this passage must be that there are no girls with fat legs among Lewis's readership—or else, perhaps, that their feelings are too inconsequential to matter. It is an assumption that makes Lewis either the most obtuse children's author who ever lived or the most fatuous.

If the latter, the word evil springs to mind, and, if not evil, then certainly the word shame. These lines, and many others like them, were written in cold blood. Lewis had ample opportunity to edit them out or to rewrite them in a better spirit. He chose to let them stand. His editors and publishers, to their own shame, have let them stand as well. People commonly, and unnecessarily, I think, worry about the violence in some children's books. Here is the real violence. Mother Goose would have slapped this saint silly.

Charles Kingsley may inadvertently have opened the door to this kind of mean-spiritedness when he promulgated a whimsical and potentially dangerous doctrine to explain the prickles that appear all over Tom's body—a phenomenon that he assures the reader

> was quite natural; for you must know and believe that people's souls make their bodies just as a snail makes its shell. . . . And therefore, when Tom's soul grew all prickly with naughty tempers, his body could not help growing prickly too, so that nobody would cuddle him, or play with him, or even like to look at him.

In *The Water Babies* this is a phenomenon presumably restricted to Purgatory, where visible signs will help us to purge ourselves of sin. In Lewis it has become corrupted into a doctrine that speaks of the living. The implication is clear. This is the predestined damnation of Calvinism that MacDonald had wanted no part of: ugly people are ugly because they have ugly souls. If, like C. S. Lewis, you have been gifted with a true eye for God's favor, you can, simply by looking at them, save boys and girls the trouble of looking into their mirrors to see for themselves if they are saved or damned. Freckles and fat are unmistakable signs; tears and odd hobbies render you suspect as well. Indeed, whomever Mr. Lewis deems contemptible or risible, pray that you aren't one yourself—for Mr. Lewis, children, speaks for God.

It is a shabby performance, lacking even the Puritans' reservation that for children excluded from heaven there will at least be "the best room in hell." Lewis's critics have called his method and message fascistic; certainly, it is anything but Christian to teach children to judge their neighbors. Dumpy girls with fat legs are Lewis's Jews. This is wicked enough; to implicate Christ in such a travesty is to commit, by one's own canon laws, a great sin. I have argued that an author ought not to think of himself as a priest, as Andersen had done; nonetheless, when you are writing a Christian parable, your story does become in effect the body of Christ, and your readers communicants. A priest who would offer communion to four children and knowingly, out of personal malice, slap shut the mouth of a fifth would be guilty of an unpardonable offense. Just so with the scribe.

On Being Men and Women

Not unlike Kingsley, but in a poorer spirit, Lewis used his tale to vent whatever opinions he held on whatever subjects. In general, these ring with the bravado of the barroom, a place where he particularly liked to hold forth. Whatever achievement one might name from the Renaissance on, he was against it. He deplored democracy and denied any wisdom to the separation of church and state. He held science and social welfare in contempt, ridiculed modern education, and advocated the beating of students. In *The Dawn Treader* he dismissed any and all benefits of progress out of hand: "We call it *Going bad* in Narnia." Most of the opinions expressed in *The Chronicles* are merely petty, however. He took digs at vegetarians, teetotalers, nonsmokers. Some others are so personal as to be pointless, such as his announced distaste for people who sleep with their windows open. His views on men and women and how or whether the twain shall meet are likewise caricatures of real thought. There are no real men or women in these stories, just as there are no real children. His men are either storybook knights or weaklings defined by a craven subservience to women, whose sole pleasure and evil purpose it is to emasculate the sorry beggars. Lewis had no difficulty mating beavers happily, but whenever we find him placing a man in proximity to a woman, or in situations that might suggest a muse relationship, it is to expose the pairing as unnatural and wicked. The pattern is so consistent as to suggest an intrusive neurosis: "He's a great baby, really: tied to that woman's apron strings; he's a sap." Lewis feared women and disliked them categorically. Femininity he saw as an imperfection, the sin of Eve, unspiritual and sinister.[12] Like Tolkien, the only women he could admit to feeling comfortable with were "shapes that looked like women but were really the spirits of trees." Whenever he sees them in a more threatening role, he retreats, interestingly, into the sadomasochistic rhetoric of pulp literature:

> . . . Jadis the Queen of Queens and the Terror of Charn. Her teeth were bared, her eyes shone like fire, and her long hair streamed out behind her like a comet's tail. She was flogging the horse without mercy.

Otherwise, grownup women are simply unpleasant: "I know of nothing so disagreeable as being kissed by a giantess." All women were giantesses to Lewis. The evil witches and queens in *The Chronicles* are all of them "tall and great." What in Kingsley and MacDonald were signs of nobility only struck fear in the heart of C. S. Lewis. Any man drawn to quality in a woman he brands a fool or a baby or a sap. He recognized but two kinds of woman: seducers and dominatrixes. Not that he minded borrowing from them, as he had done with Edith Nesbit. Ironically, the very scene in *The Silver Chair* in which a sap's mistress weaves her malevolent spell over the children is a conceit lifted from the author Jean Ingelow. The Lady of the Green Kirtle's sophistic argument denying any reality beyond the light of her underworld sun is an argument presented in *Mopsa the Fairy* about the moons of Fairyland.

In his autobiography, *Surprised by Joy*, Lewis wrote, "in the hive and the anthill we see fully realized the two things that some of us most dread for our own species—the dominance of the female and the dominance of the collective." It would be interesting to know whom he was implicating as being down there alongside him in his psychic bunker, but no matter; a valid analogy between human and insect life cannot be drawn, nor can one equate the feminine with the collective. Aware that psychologists might pounce on this almost pathological simile, he naively tried to head them off at the pass by tracing his fear of insects back to a nursery book given him by his mother. In it a Tom Thumb is menaced by a stag beetle whose mandibles could be opened and shut "like pincers" by pulling on the "devilish contraption" of a cardboard tab. "How a woman ordinarily so wise as my mother could have allowed this abomination into the nursery is difficult to understand," he wrote, but of course it was only a mechanical toy book of a sort most little boys would pounce upon. Apparently, Lewis never forgave his mother for this innocent mistake: the only mention of her in the story of his life is this one citation for her insensitivity. The memory of it haunts *The Chronicles*; insects are frequently invoked, or otherwise implied, as in this image from *The Magician's Nephew*:

> "You!" said the Queen, laying her hand on his shoulder—a white, beautiful hand, but Digory could feel that it was strong as steel pincers.

I draw the equation reluctantly, but it is Lewis himself who has led us to it. Women, even those so ordinarily wise as his mother, come bearing pincers and knives. Let your guard down for a moment and the dreadful thing will surely happen.

Put the creatures in charge of educating children, as Kingsley had advised, and you need only await the breakdown of civilization:

> I shall say as little as possible about Jill's school, which is not a pleasant subject. It was "Co-educational," a school for both boys and girls, what used to be called a "mixed" school; some said it was not nearly so mixed as the minds of the people who ran it.

Who does run it is a little revelation that Lewis saves for the great battle in the playground that ends *The Silver Chair*:

> And then the Head (who was, by the way, a woman) came running out to see what was happening. And when she saw the lion and the broken wall and Caspian and Jill and Eustace (whom she quite failed to recognize) she had hysterics and went back to the house and began ringing up the police. . . .

I doubt that there exists anywhere in children's literature a more dishonest parenthetical remark than this, or a more supercilious use of the phrase "by the way." There is nothing "by the way" about anything in these stories, and certainly nothing "by the way" about this arch slur or about the fact that the Head will summarily be removed from office for incompetence. To assess how truly malicious an aside it is, substitute for "woman" the word "Jew" or "Negro." And then give a thought to the man's jacket photo and to how puckishly he beams out at us while lighting his pipe. We are the prerogative audience he is cozying up to with these remarks — we, and our children.

The impulse to reopen a tale that had lain fallow for eight years had risen from this same unquiet corner of his psyche. Some billeted refugees would prompt *The Chronicles*; Christ would give them a purpose and Nesbit open the door, but the actual provocation for executing these seven novels sprang from his need to put a woman in her place — or two women, perhaps, or all of them. He had reason to speak of the dominance of the female, and yet a second reason in the bargain, that had added insult to the injury. His mother having died when he was ten, Lewis at nineteen had attached himself to a demanding lady twenty-six years his senior; for the next thirty years of his life he would live with her secretly as lover and devoted errand-boy. A measure of self-loathing seems to have accumulated over the decades. The exasperation that poured out of him suddenly and into *The Chronicles* in 1949 was precipitated by his humiliating public defeat the year before at the hands of the second imperious woman in his history, the Oxford philosopher Elizabeth Anscombe. As Lewis biographer A. N. Wilson tells it, "The debate took place early in 1948 at the Socratic Club, and instantaneously became legend. Elizabeth Anscombe . . . shared his taste for fisticuffs. . . . She was quite equal to the bullying and the exploitation of the audience to which Lewis resorted when he was boxed into a corner. . . . That evening at the Socratic Club was the first in the Society's history that Lewis was thoroughly trounced in argument."[13]

Worst of all, the object of the debate had been one of his very own books, *Miracles*, and the inadequacy of his argument for the existence of God. What his fellow Christian had established, furthermore, was his own ignorance of himself as a dualistic gnostic. As his friends attested, he took it badly, and took it badly for a long time. I am sure Wilson is correct in concluding that *The Lion, the Witch and the Wardrobe* "grew out of Lewis's experience of being stung back into childhood by his defeat at the hands of Elizabeth Anscombe."[14] I would suggest, though, that it stung him back into the broodings of adolescence rather than the innocence of childhood, and into a state of wanting to do with the event what Charles Dodgson had done with his trial-in-absentia at the hands of the Liddells. Between the lines of *The Lion, the Witch and the Wardrobe* I suspect we are hearing those same midnight rehearsals that in *Alice* had also yielded up a knave of hearts pure and shining before a howling queen. To Lewis, Anscombe was a White Witch of the North, and so he portrayed her. For the story part he referred back to that other Queen of Reason and Christ-killer, Hans Christian Andersen's Snow Queen, whom he now brought forward, sleigh and all, to whisk Edmund away to her palace of ice, just as she had done with little Kay. The lurid crucifixion scene in the same book, ostensibly an allegory of Christ's passion, so little resembles it, in fact, that it can be read only as Lewis's final rehearsal of the debate at the Socratic Club, with Anscombe now made to look grotesque, her followers loathsome, and Lewis himself long-suffering and noble.

The great apologist enters the hall:

> A howl and a gibber of dismay went up from the creatures when they first saw the great Lion pacing towards them, and for a moment the Witch herself seemed to be struck with fear. Then she recovered herself and gave a wild, fierce laugh.
>
> "The fool!" she cried. "The fool has come. . . ."
>
> "Muzzle him!" said the Witch. . . . Everyone was at him now. Those who had been afraid to come near him even after he was bound began to find their courage, and for a few minutes the two girls could not even see him—so thickly was he surrounded by the whole crowd of creatures kicking him, hitting him, spitting on him, jeering at him.
>
> "The cowards! The cowards!" sobbed Susan. "Are they *still* afraid of him, even now?"
>
> The Witch bared her arms . . . whet her knife . . . drew near. . . . Her face was working and twitching with passion, but his looked up at the sky, still quiet, neither angry nor afraid, but a little sad. Then, just before she gave the blow, she stooped down and said in a quivering voice,
>
> "And now, who has won?"

The real intent behind Lewis's treatment of children in *The Chronicles* becomes clear. The codes of behavior and forced marches, the ridicule, the bouquets—or, as here, making two girls stand witness to his humiliation—they are all to one and the same purpose: to keep them from growing up into the kinds of men and women Lewis could not abide. Girls like Lucy and Jill who learn to accept orders will presumably not become the sort of loud and intrusive woman given to arguing with a man like C. S. Lewis. A Eustace Scrubb, if rescued from his craven ways, will not one day be one of the fawning rabble awarding points in the debating hall to the likes of an Elizabeth Anscombe. Improperly tutored, he must become like Uncle Andrew in *The Magician's Nephew*, an absurd pawn given to muttering, "A devilish temper she had. . . . But she was a dem fine woman, sir, a dem fine woman." The contempt Lewis heaps upon cartoon men attracted to cartoon shrews throughout the series may also have been an attempt to distance himself from any charge that he was a weakling himself. Having lived most of his adult life at the secret beck and call of a very much older woman, and fearing the psychologists, he well might have trumped up these caricatures in part to announce that, although implicated by the evidence of his life, he was not this kind of fellow, never had been, never would be. He was, he wanted it known, Belfast Jack Lewis, good for a brawl, any time, any where.

On Being Christians

Notwithstanding a five-year spread in publication dates, *The Chronicles* were apparently the work of little more than a year, with the seven novels following one another in a white heat and every old book Lewis had ever enjoyed — Christian, pagan, and secular alike — being thrown indiscriminantly into the pot to sweeten his animus. This new Kingdom of Narnia belonged, ostensibly, to Christ, "that by knowing me here for a little, you may know me better there"; but supporters of Lewis, seeing an entanglement of problems, have vacillated over whether he ever really intended the books to constitute a Christian story at all. Roger Lancelyn Green feels "it would spoil their effect to attempt to interpret them allegorically or symbolically — certainly for children. They are and must be read simply as stories."[15] The Custodial Fallacy used to be fairly common in nursery studies. Since children do not read literary criticism, however, and can hardly be disenchanted by it, they will not mind my asking a few questions more of the work.

What is a child to make, for example, of that passage in which Christ is seen sporting in the forest with an entourage of Naiads, Dryads, centaurs, and the like? Would he not conclude, if only unconsciously, that Christianity and Greek mythology are stories with equal claims to the truth, and perhaps even the same story in the end? Lewis did not think he was advocating an all-gods-are-one-god theology; in a thinly veiled dismissal of Mohammed as a false prophet in *The Last Battle* he presents the idea as the sophistical argument of a villain:

> "But you others, listen. Tash is only another name for Aslan. All that old idea of us being right and the Calormenes wrong is silly. We know better now. The Calormenes use different words but we all mean the same thing. Tash and Aslan are only two different names for you know Who."

But can a Christian scribe have it both ways with other faiths? Can he decide that one — Islam — is a dumpy person with fat legs and another — Greek mythology — a Gwendolen? And having picked a favorite, can he then pluck out the imagery and with impunity leave the theology behind? The synchretistic Lewis was not only promiscuous in his borrowing habits; he was arbitrary. If the make-believe of classical Greece made a congenial complement to his understanding of the Christian story, why not the whole of it? If centaurs and minotaurs are "good" and will be Jesus's playmates in the great by-and-by, why not every creature with a like provenance? So whimsically eclectic a world is Narnia that there may be no sorting it out: "a bull with the head of a man" is good in Lewis's reading of the world that

Daddy Zeus made, but "bull-headed men" are evil. The distinction escapes me. And it seems to have escaped Lewis that by associating Christianity with a dead make-believe he was implying to children that Christianity might itself be just a make-believe. If invoking Dante as his sanction for bringing the Greeks into a Christian parable, he must have forgotten that the centaurs of the *Divine Comedy* are not to be found frolicking with Jesus in Paradise but tormenting men in Hell. The make-believe you proselytize to others against God's law in this life, goes the parable, will be the company you keep in the next.

Whenever a professed Christian feels he must create some wholly other world to explore the meaning of his religion, he is flirting with bad faith. When he fills that world with the make-believes of other religions, he is playing at polytheism. When he further sets sorceresses to rule over it, and werewolves, incubuses, and wraiths, he is dabbling in Manichaean dualism, the idea that standing opposed to God's good creation is another, separate and equal, or nearly equal, creation given over to evil. Much popular entertainment in the twentieth century has been dualistic. Without its change-lings and poltergeists, its vampires, zombies, and other Halloween treats, Hollywood would be hard put to turn a profit. I do not mean to moralize here, having enjoyed such things often enough myself, from the D.C. Comics and ghost stories of my youth to *Nosferatu* and Jack Vance's gnostic classic, *The Eyes of the Overworld*. But in a culture now awash in such fancies, I must wonder if they might not inure many readers to the superstition that evil is a corporeal reality that rules in the world with a free hand. In the Bible, Satan is a minor presence, either an adversary-at-law in heaven's court, or, in his fallen state, a seducer obedient to any truly felt command to step to the rear. In no way does he have the power to create anyone or any thing or to destroy anyone save by abetting them with whispers. The darkness that is in the world we are quite adept at casting ourselves, by eclipsing God's will with our own; and for this, to save us from ourselves and from the excesses of our make-believes, we have the agency of the universal muse, the Holy Ghost. Muse fantasies like "Cinderella," *The Water Babies*, *The North Wind*, *Pinocchio*, and *The Little Lame Prince* reflect this; they are Christian in spirit. Circular fantasies like *Alice* or closed ones like Tolkien's, with its pursuit of a personal supernatural power, do not reflect it and are heretical. Narnia is an olio of thoughts somewhere between these realms. On the one hand are Lewis's syncretic flirtations with paganism; on the other, a number of theological gestures recognizably a part of Judeo-Christian tradition. *The Magician's Nephew* comprises a Narnian creation myth, with its own Adam and Eve; *The Lion, the Witch and the Wardrobe* exhibits a crucifiction of sorts; and *The Voyage of the Dawn Treader* takes us to the beauty of the lilies where Christ was born across the sea. *The Last Battle* is modeled on the biblical apocalypses that gave Lewis his Lion of Judah and on the "wars and rumours of wars," the false prophets and Second Coming promised in 24 Matthew. *The Chronicles of Narnia*, in short, are one man's version of the alpha and the omega of the faith, and a new scripture in seven books.

It could be questioned, of course, whether the Last Judgment can ever be a fit subject for a children's book, particularly when delivered by someone with Lewis's punitive instincts. His summary damnation of Susan has probably disturbed more readers than anything else in the series. Certainly her apostasy and loss of heaven is unconvincing; worse, it is done without the least suggestion of God's possible forgiveness. "Her interests" writes Green in defense of the master, "are narrowly confined to the Shadowlands (this world) and she is, of her own free will, 'no longer a friend of Narnia.'"[16] How casually Saint Jack condemns all normal teenagers to the taste of everlasting death. There is no "free will" in these books. Susan falls away because Lewis has predestined her to fall away. And for what? For the convenience of making a point and the satisfaction of yet again putting a female in her place. It is preposterous to think that anyone would turn apostate who had visited another world and there actually met Christ in the flesh, much less witnessed his crucifixion, wept over him ("The cowards! The cowards!"), and seen him rise from the dead. Lewis would have us believe of this Mary Magdalene that she sloughed it all off shortly thereafter for some lipstick and a pair of nylons.

The crucifixion in *The Lion, the Witch and the Wardrobe* is equally specious, a transmogrification of the Passion into a pagan sacrifice with sadomasochistic overtones. Critics have called it variously "fresh and powerful . . . most moving" and "unpleasant."[17] As a travesty of the true crucifixion it is twice-over blasphemous, being in the first instance as poorly written as the wretched Gwendolen episode and in the second a misappropriation to tell of Lewis's own discomfort under the eyes of the Judases at the Socratic Club while Elizabeth Anscombe, "working and twitching with passion," brought her argument to its climactic "despair and die."

For eight years his parable had lain in a drawer. Only following the Anscombe debacle did he understand where to go with it. And it was the wrong place, and he went for the wrong reason, to proclaim himself a true martyr for the faith, "neither angry nor afraid, but a little sad" at being a victim of Woman the Anti-Christ. It was easily done, of course. In the Manichaean adventure *The Magician's Nephew*, he could yet claim the last word in the debate by revamping the witch who had unmanned him as Jadis, "the Queen of the World," boasting of her destruction of "the city of the King of Kings" and how "[a]ll in one moment one woman blotted it out forever." The world was going to hear from the resurrected warrior just how wicked a thing it had been to offer this "dem fine woman" a Socratic forum in which to exercise a Reason that was not among her sex's natural or rightful faculties.

This is how the muse came to be portrayed in her own literature in the twentieth century, then, not as a renewal of the inspiration of Perrault,

Kingsley, MacDonald, Collodi, and Craik, but, in a stunning reversal of the whole tradition, as a throwback to Andersen's Snow Queen and the muse as Christ-killer. In setting man against woman in a Christian muse parable, Lewis in effect created an allegory in which Son and Holy Ghost are at odds with one another and the Holy Ghost basely traduced by an up-and-coming apostle. Only a contortionist at exegesis could extract a credible precedent from Scripture to support this nonsense. Christ—how can I put this strongly enough?—Christ was not crucified by a woman. Or, since make-believe can put up a very obscuring haze, by Woman. There is nothing—nothing—in Scripture to encourage such a bizarre extrapolation. To redress an imagined wrong against himself, Lewis turned mankind's crime against God into a little thing and a false thing and a hateful thing. He equated himself with the crucified Christ and flattered himself with the witness of credulous children. The crucifixion in *The Lion, the Witch and the Wardrobe* is a tutorial designed to pillory Elizabeth Anscombe and then to rub Lucy's and Susan's noses in the wickedness of their sex.

How Lewis came to portray himself as a Fallen Warrior wept over by girls can be found nicely spelled out in his autobiography, *Surprised by Joy* (1955). Like Tolkien, he was an ardent Wagnerian, a devotee of what they together called "Northernness." In boys' make-believes this term might translate as a kind of they'll-be-sorry-when-I'm-dead fantasy, the bang-bang-they-got-me Game of Falls aggrandized to tragic dimensions. This lifelong mind-set had begun very early, when Lewis first read the words,

> *I heard a voice that cried,*
> *Balder the beautiful*
> *Is dead, is dead—*

and "uplifted into huge regions of northern sky, I desired with almost sickening intensity something never to be described. . . . " Northernness claimed him again at puberty, this time through an edition of *Siegfried and the Twilight of the Gods*, illustrated by that poseur of the Dark Sublime, Arthur Rackham. Setting his emotional dial permanently on Wagner, the neophyte pagan surrendered himself to the secret pursuit of "ecstasy, astonishment, 'a conflict of sensations without a name.'"

Some of these sensations do have a name, actually. In the Christian story they are the sensations of Simon Magus, the aspiring wonder worker who tried to buy the gifts of the Holy Ghost from St. Peter, so as to have wings to soar with the gods. Dreams of glory of course are quite normal in youth; Lewis's were a classier version of our century's favorite gnostic fantasy, the comic-book superhero. Prolonged into maturity, however, the pride of the imagination can lead only to a spiritual and intellectual pratfall. *Surprised by Joy*, I should say, is a reasonably honest chronicle of the process. If the story of Lewis's spiritual development suffers at all, it suffers from a reflective intellectualization that is not always convincing. When he tells us, for example, that in his enslavement to Northernness he was meant "to acquire some capacity for worship against the day when the true God should recall me to Himself," I am not persuaded. This is precisely and wholly the purpose of make-believe, in fact, but we have no testimony other than Lewis's that God ever deals in raptures of this ilk, and when Lewis later converted to Christianity he did not, as one would expect, abandon Northernness as an example of man worshipping his own make-believe but brought it with him into his new faith in Christ and into his new Christian parable.

Blown in through the window reopened by the Anscombe affair, the idea of Northernness everywhere chills the air in Narnia. At a very obvious level, it can be seen in Lewis's oafish prejudice against all things Southern. Below are some remarks about the Calormen (callow colored men?) from *The Horse and His Boy* and *The Last Battle*:

> What you would chiefly have noticed if you had been there was the smells, which came from unwashed people, unwashed dogs, scent, garlic, onions, and the piles of refuse which lay everywhere.

> Then the dark men came round them in a thick crowd, smelling of garlic and onions, their white eyes flashing dreadfully in their brown faces.

> . . . all of them, both men and women, had nicer faces and voices than most Calormenes.

> "This boy is manifestly no son of yours, for your cheek is as dark as mine but the boy is fair and white like the accursed but beautiful barbarians who inhabit the remote north."

This last remark is no more plausible in context than if a Polish Jew were to pause before boarding the cattle car to admire the accursed but beautiful barbarians of the Waffen-SS. It is Lewis again spreading the gospel of Northernness. The armchair warrior's need to dominate the landscape, and not the humility simply to live in it, is what animates these chronicles of Christ in His Kingdom. In his critical writings Lewis liked to commend the child mind over the adolescent, but it is the voice of the teenager we hear in the land, and the clash of arms rather than the still, small voice of vision. Lewis was baptized by the banks of not one but two rivers, the Jordan and the Rhine, and, like Tolkien, he spent most of his imaginative life camped by the latter, enraptured by Wagner's fanfares to pagan glory. His tragedy was that it need not have been, as it was, too little agape too late to matter. He had known true glory from the age of five or six, when he experienced a profound visitation of what I have tried to suggest by the term "allsense." What he describes in *Surprised by Joy* is the kind of universal awakening of a meaning that obviates any and all understanding of the world as North and South or male and female. It came to him, as these things often will, in two stages. First came the object of his desire, when his brother

> brought into the nursery the lid of a biscuit tin which he had covered with moss and garnished with twigs and flowers so as to make it a toy garden or a toy forest. That was the first beauty I ever knew. . . . I do not think the

impression was very important at the moment, but it soon became important in memory. As long as I live my imagination of Paradise will retain something of my brother's toy garden.

The desire itself arrived on a summer day years later when, standing in a garden, Lewis was suddenly overwhelmed by a memory of the toy garden and bathed in a sensation he would compare to "Milton's 'enormous bliss' of Eden." This second stage he called a memory of a memory, meaning that he understood the first stage Platonically, as a memory in itself—of Paradise. Memory may in this first instance be an arguable term; knowledge is perhaps better. His first knowledge of Paradise was complemented at the time by another poignant acquaintance with heaven's shadows on earth, the green, distant hills that were visible from his nursery window. The sight of them "taught me longing . . . made me for good or ill, and before I was six years old, a votary of the Blue Flower."

Here again is Novalis's blue flower—a discovery, perhaps, from his reading of MacDonald. Like Novalis, Lewis would make a life's pilgrimage of pursuing "an unsatisfied desire which is itself more desireable than any other satisfaction. I call it Joy. . . . it might almost equally well be called a particular kind of unhappiness or grief." Or, as he later put it, an "inconsolable longing."

In an essay on Protestant mystics, W. H. Auden has nicely explained the risks inherent in all such experiences. They were risks that Lewis understandably could not see in childhood and which I think he imperfectly understood as an adult. Such Platonic visions

> are, in themselves, blessings and a good; there is nothing in any of them that is contrary to Christian doctrine. On the other hand, all of them are dangerous. So long as the subject recognizes them as totally unmerited blessings and feels obligated by gratitude to produce, insofar as it lies in his power, works which are good according to their kind, they can lead him towards the Light. But if he allows himself either to regard the experience as a sign of superior merit, natural or supernatural, or to idolize it as something he cannot live without, then it can only lead him into darkness and destruction. [18]

The votary of the blue flower who longed for the paradise of the little garden and for the hills beyond would come to locate the seat of what he could not live without in the idea of Northernness and in Wagner and the Eddas. The emptiness left by a vanished childhood bliss found an analog in the vast physical absences of the pagan North, and Lewis called the two things one. It may or may not seem odd, then, that when he converted— first to theism, then to Christ—it was through a long process of intellectualization in which Joy played no part whatever. I am not at all sure what to conclude from his failure to return from the back of the north wind with good news like MacDonald. Perhaps associating Joy with the Dark Sublime of things pagan and, in truth, brutal rendered him incapable of comprehending it in the end, so that finally he could only give up on it (or it on him) as sterile. The autobiography closes with the surprising and dispiriting conclusion "No slightest hint was vouchsafed me that there ever had been or ever would be any connection between God and Joy." I can only suppose from this that it was out of some stubbornness against the Spirit that Lewis failed, or refused, to distinguish between the Joy of the tiny garden and the pangs of his later discoveries. After his conversion, he should have known that God was never going to "vouchsafe" his pagan enthusiasms a second visitation. Why then, too, he would not have granted God authorship of the first vision dumbfounds me. As Auden stated, and as visionaries have attested, such a gift is a call to service. Its purpose is to deliver such a blow of bliss that the recipient, usually a child, will not fail to understand in due course of time what the imprinting of such a vision must suggest — that there is a God in heaven; that some kind of Platonic relationship between heaven and earth does obtain; that Creation is good and dualism therefore a fallacy; that there is a grace which is freely given; and that this grace being the cause of his gladness, the duty of the scribe, and his joy, is to awaken others to it through his art. This is Christ's charge to the instructed scribes in Matthew 13 and the pledge of Psalm 26, "to publish with the voice of thanksgiving." Again, Auden:

> The vision of the splendor of creation . . . lays a duty upon one who has been fortunate enough to receive it, a duty in his turn to create works which are as worthy of what he has seen as his feeble capacities will permit. And many have listened and obeyed . . . for it is the wonder which is, as Plato said, the beginning of every kind of philosophy. [19]

The ability to obey as an artist — to say something for children as simple, perhaps, as "Great is the sun, and wide he goes/Through empty heaven without repose" — calls for a large humility before God and the world. Lewis resisted his story's tropism to return to its original, Edenic state, and thus he failed to envision Narnia in the spirit of that first knowledge of creation. Over time the parable of the toy garden became refracted by Wagner and things Northern, and, seeing, Lewis saw not and, hearing, he heard not. Northernness, by now an habitual bias, lingered on after the fading of the glory to inform *The Chronicles* as an aesthetic and racial ideal and from habit followed the distortion of the Christian message the work presumably had been written to announce. The Christ of Narnia is not the Jesus of the Gospels but a new Messiah for a Lewis who continued to see through a glass darkly — a Christ given to rambles with fauns one moment and a leonine godhead for a storybook warrior cult the next. The first portrait is merely foolish; the second presents us with a more commonplace and more dangerous slippage from the truth. The moment of betrayal comes at the end of *The Silver Chair*, when Aslan permits Prince Caspian to accompany Jill and Eustace back to that mixed-up school whose head bully was, by the way, a woman. There, in order "to set things right" with these "cowards and children," the Lion of Judah commands the boys to take up their swords and Jill to cut herself a switch. Putting "the strength of Aslan in them" for the coming fight, he then turns his back to the scene — signaling that his own eternal rules are now suspended — and releases the children to charge into their schoolmates. "Jill plied her crop on the girls and Caspian and Eustace plied the flats of their swords on the boys so well that in two minutes all the bullies were running like mad. . . . "

Lewis titled this satisfying little episode "The Healing of Harms." But what Christ is it that heals with the sword? It can hardly obtain that the recipients of this schoolyard justice are themselves bullies or that no one actually gets gut-stuck in the melee. The matter here is that Christian teaching has reverted to the Dirty Harry theology of the *lex talionis*, an eye for an eye and a tooth for a tooth. Lewis has contrived a Christ willing to turn his back while his chosen children, in the name of vengeance, beat up another group of children. We have seen this puppet Christ often enough before, marching at the head of innumerable armies and mobs convinced that they and they alone have been sanctioned by God "to set things right" in the world. The scribe from Belfast has here succumbed to the universal temptation to reject a scene from Scripture that is found to be neither congenial nor even reasonable. The scene in question — the only scene in the Gospels that could possibly apply — is the aborted fight in the Garden of Gesthemane, where Peter takes up the sword to hack off the ear of the temple servant Malchus. If you will not hear the truth, the gesture seems to say, what need have you of an ear? Jesus's interdiction, "they that take the sword shall perish with the sword," so disarms the disciples that they can only do what most men would do when denied the release of a fight — they run. Knowing that he was denied the sword by faith, Lewis ran from the cross as well — but only to reemerge in Narnia, a make-believe land where he could announce with disgruntled Christians all through history that pacifism was too hard a commandment, even a contemptible one. Surely it could not apply to this circumstance or to him (for he was no coward); surely God meant it to apply to that one event alone. Look, here are some bullies: if we rough them up for Jesus's sake, all will be well.

Whatever a Christian's personal lapses, pacifism is an ideal that he is bound by faith to honor whether it suits him or not. To scorn it before children is corrupt. Lewis's asides on the subject are the cunning insinuations of Matthew's "false prophets, which come to you in sheep's clothing, but inwardly they are ravening wolves." Pacifism to Lewis was the kind of cowardly waffling you could expect from the likes of a "puny little person" such as Eustace Scrubb, who, when threatened, will squeal, "I'm a pacifist. I don't believe in fighting." Against Eustace's contemptible example in *The Dawn Treader* Belfast Jack set his ceremonious hall proctor, Reepicheep the Mouse, that tiny champion whose threats had caused Eustace to make his craven excuses. Reepicheep is Lewis's idealized Grail Knight. When he embarks for Aslan's country beyond the world's end, Lewis paints his departure in a romantic haze, complete with the Malorian gesture of returning the good sword to the baptism of the waters:

> . . . They helped him to lower his little coracle. Then he took off his sword ("I shall need it no more," he said) and flung it far away across the lilied sea. Where it fell it stood upright with the hilt above the surface. . . . hastily he got into his coracle and took his paddle, and the current caught it and away he went . . . and since that moment no one can truly claim to have seen Reepicheep the Mouse. But my belief is that he came safe to Aslan's country and is alive there to this day.

This last sentiment is an unmistakable paraphrase of the stoical closings to *The North Wind* and *The Little Lame Prince*. The sanctimonious Reepicheep, however, is really only a hypocrite with delusions of grandeur. The message he bears, unlike the good news of those earlier books, contradicts everything that Jesus taught. He is proud, vain, judgmental, and quick to anger, and he lives by the sword. His final surrender of the weapon is the empty gesture of his reactionary maker, who in real life liked to brag in barrooms that no nation could ever have enough nuclear warheads at the ready.

This is what you do when your God asks things of you that are unthinkable; you create another world where you can sneak in your complaints under the guise of make-believe. Your readers will not mind, for people, as you well know, come to make-believe with the smiles of trusting presupposition on their faces and, charmed, tend to approve whatever they find. What Lewis here wants his prerogative audience to sanction is the notion that violence, being intrinsic to man's nature, is permissible if conducted properly—under civilized rules, against mutually agreed upon enemies, preferably by knights—rather than being the sorriest of all specimens of original sin. What we see him doing at the end of *The Silver Chair* is really quite stunning. I cannot imagine a betrayal of one's faith more complete than this last picture of Christ at the playground, putting weapons into the hands of children.

However innocent its beginnings, the story of Narnia was animated by one compelling need following the Anscombe debacle. It was not a need to reveal Christ to children but to have a place where Lewis could pass judgment on people with impunity. *The Chronicles*, after all, are exactly that, the story of a world created and a world destroyed, with some saved and many damned. It was a poor enough choice of subject for a children's parable; the one figure that make-believe least needed revived in a scribe was John of Patmos; but, worse, it was a dangerous choice, for the fatal temptation in writing about final things will always be that itch to make the Last Judgment oneself. Any scribe foolhardy enough to attempt it must at least take care to recognize in himself and edit out any baser instincts that might compromise the work. The humility to do this is what is so lacking in the Apocalypse According to Saint Jack. Lewis was as empty of true sympathies as he was full of shabby opinions. Browsing on his pipe and winking out at his readers, he knowingly played the bully to the end, revising nothing, blithely grading people and assigning the best rooms in heaven and in hell. He fancied himself the blue-eyed boy chosen to cast the first stone, and he came to the work mindful of deserving targets and with his pockets laden with ammunition. The first stone and the last judgment are so much the agenda for Narnia that they seem the only real reason for its existence in the end. Here Lewis would have all to himself a land not to be peopled and celebrated, like, say, an Oz, but to be destroyed when he was done with it, in his own personal Day of Wrath.

Perhaps cloistered dons who spend their lives in a state of intellectual make-believe should be discouraged from recycling their reading into children's books. What Tolkien and Lewis contrived for themselves were new corners of that same land into which Dodgson had fallen in his diffidence, the land of "Oldwivesfabledom," as Kingsley said it from 2 Timothy, "where the folks were all heathens." The three dons sprang from the zeitgeist and they fed the zeitgeist, pleasing a vast audience of readers both secular and Christian alike. The day was theirs among fanciers of make-believe, for, as Paul saw must happen repeatedly throughout history,

> the time will come when they will not endure sound doctrine; but after their own lusts shall they heap to themselves teachers, having itching ears;
> And they shall turn away their ears from the truth, and shall be turned unto fables.

Dodgson had meant his fable as a more or less secular joke on his own little corner of the world, and his Wonderland theologically a place of No Other Gods save the demiurge of his own genius. Tolkien and Lewis were more knowing and deliberate in the ways they skirted the First and Second Commandments. Giving over their Secondary Worlds to pagan make-believes, and charming the ears of children and the gnostic disaffected with unsound doctrine, these two alienated reactionaries may, as a consequence, have done as much to diminish their faith as any two Christians who ever lived. That fundamentalists could work such a wonder is not a paradox, I think, for, while in some ways dissimilar, the fundamentalist and the gnostic have succumbed to the same spiritual temptation. Each is possessed of a discontent with God for the state of His world, and each has resolved to do something about it, with one choosing a public means and the other a private. The gnostic takes from Scripture what he needs and chases off after special revelation in the fancies of the moment, looking for ever more grandiloquent metaphors to express his own specious godhead; the fundamentalist, blinding himself to the possibility that God might indeed be at work somewhere in the fictions of the present, clings with literalistic zeal to the inerrancy of a particular text and to whatever polity he thinks it implies. The gnostic daydreams of being a Merlin or a Superman and writes theological science fiction; the fundamentalist would deny man a creative role in understanding and perpetuating sacred truths and frets, rather, how through corporate political action or personal violence, he might deny others the exercise of a free will he everywhere sees abused. In short, the one fortifies the walls, while the other flies over them to his own personal Oz. What they share is a dualistic pessimism about the world, an itch for power, and a mistrust of God.

In Tolkien and Lewis we can see both these tendencies at play. The apostate dreamer in Tolkien, hoping not to give offense, hid his pagan world away in as remote a pre-Christian past as he could imagine. Lewis, unlike Tolkien, or Dodgson for that matter, who both at least suspected the truth about their work, remained oblivious to himself as a shareholder in man's common stock of bad faith and announced his fancies as a superior wisdom. Out of a distaste for Irish Women and Blue Fairies, who made unreasonable demands, and out of a stubbornness that the source of his longing must lie among legends where not even a North Wind could stir him, he abandoned tradition and pitched his battle tent by a mythical and oh so sweetly musical Rhine. There he sulked like some Teutonic Achilles and forged a kingdom in his own image, without charity, where he might tutor children in the ways of the slur and the sword. His pursuit of a private Joy and a private Apocalypse led the century's most popular Christian apologist to close his mind to that standard Protestant handbook, the Epistle to the Romans. There it is written that understanding lies nowhere else but in "righteousness, and peace, and joy in the Holy Ghost." The reason the reader will not find any of Lewis's Joy in Narnia is rather simple, I would suggest, when understood in a Christian context. It is missing because nowhere in these facile pages is there the least evidence that the parablist was ever willing, like Pinocchio, to cough up his last forty pence for the muse.

Where the Wild Things Are (1963)

American children's books were a literature at ease in Zion at mid-century. Picture books were in the main wholesome, pleasant, civic-minded. Longer works like *Rabbit Hill, Johnny Tremain, Charlotte's Web*, and the novels of Laura Ingalls Wilder reflected a comfortable middlebrow populism and a modest sense of mission. The central figure in the little renascence to follow was Maurice Sendak (1928–) and the central book *Where the Wild Things Are*. Like Dr. Seuss's *The Cat in the Hat*, published four years earlier, Sendak's "wild rumpus" marked a break with the complacent work of the period and a revival of the more fractious spirit of Perrault and Mother Goose, Collodi, Lear, and the German cartoonist Wilhelm Busch.

The arc described by this circular fantasy is the simplest line that a story could ever take: a child leaves home, has a brush with the world, and returns home again. We have seen it in a host of fairy tales, in *Little Black Sambo*, and the reader will recognize it as well as being the plot of *Peter Rabbit*. Exactly which books did inform *The Wild Things* must remain conjecture at this point. Sendak is the most eclectic student the literature has yet known, and perhaps the most acute. Each of his books bears the track of a thoughtful search through the world of story for clues to his own signature as an artist and to the right mode for each experiment. The number and range of authors and artists he has drawn from is daunting, and it would be no surprise if this best known of his works, apparently so simple a thing in retrospect, turned out to have a rather complex history.[20] It was published in the Fall of 1963, but as late as April of that year the now famous illustrations had yet to be conceived and the story itself was a rambling and unfocused montage of fantasy images entitled *Where the Wild Horses Are*. The brief transit of six months from misdirected fancy to published book would seem to imply that the new tale had been in the offing for some time, gathering strength. *Wild Things* was the fifty-fourth book to bear Sendak's name as illustrator, and the sixth to be written by him as well. It brought to full voice the earlier discontent of Pierre in *The Nutshell Library* (1962), whose refrain of "I don't care" may be an echo of Pinocchio's "I don't care" speech when refusing to take his medicine. What we are likely seeing in the sudden abandonment of the wild horses notion is Sendak's final resolve to be done with his long, lyrical apprenticeship — see *The Moon Jumpers* (1959), for example, or *Mr. Rabbit and the Lovely Present* (1962) — and to sign himself in as a member of the bad-boy comic tradition in children's books. *Wild Things* had stubbornly refused to arrive anywhere from its inception in 1955 to the eve of its demise in April 1963. In a moment he was rid of it and looking, evidently, to every bad-boy story he knew. Whatever his exact ancestry — Busch's *Max und Moritz*, say, or William Steig's Small Fry cartoons in *The New Yorker* — Max is the eruptive darker brother of the polite, pensive hero of the *Little Bear* series (1957-68), now given leave to shout, sulk, scheme, and dream. Sendak's new egoists — Pierre, Max, Hector Protector, Mickey of *In the Night Kitchen* (1970) — will be good boys whose tempers, tousled hair, and pug noses betray an itch to be known as kids who could run with the Brooklyn branch of Collodi's *ragazzo di strada*. Indeed, Max's quarrel with his mother is a Pinocchio moment, a break with the nearest muse to hand. Protesting "I don't care" or "I'll eat you up," as he does when his mother calls him a wild thing, is pretty much a pro forma requirement in children's stories, of course. Defying the muse is itself never the point, but how one goes about it. Andersen and Lewis each nursed a grudge and turned the muse into a castrating femme fatale. Max does the normal, the healing thing with his fury here: he blows it off. The glare on his face as he is sent to his quarters marks as pure and as decisive a breach with the muse as the slam of a bedroom door. The resultant fantasy, in which he can accept himself as a hero on his own terms, is clean as a result, and because it is clean Sendak is free to be generous, as Lewis was not, and admit that his hero, even at the height of his glory, is yet in need of "someone who loves him best of all." And the muse is there at the end, diplomatically out of the room but with supper waiting.

The trajectory of Max's there-and-back-again adventure, and even the details themselves, are everywhere to be found in the literature, once you start looking. Margaret Wise Brown's *Little Fur Family* (1946, and published by Sendak's own editor, Ursula Nordstrom) shares the same Peter Rabbitish plot of a child poking about in a "wild wild wood" before coming home to his supper; in her *Child's Good Night Book* (1943) she had spoken too of "Sleepy Wild Things," anticipating the moment when Sendak's Wild Things take a nap after their wild rumpus. Brown is only one of many plausible sources for the book, however. I have already cited Potter's tale, and "Little Red Riding Hood" and *Little Black Sambo*, Steig's pugs, and Busch's Max, from whom Sendak's imp likely took his name. The Wild Things themselves are an eclectic crowd, anticipated not only by Brown but also by her own probable source, Kipling's "The Cat that Walked by Himself," in which story a Woman tames the "Wild Things out of the Wild Woods." There is some precedent for an island of Wild Things in the movie *King Kong*, a source acknowledged by Sendak, and the droll Wild Thing later used as a curtain decoration for the opera made from the book bears a striking resemblance to an Apocalypse manuscript in the Cloisters Collection of New York's Metropolitan Museum of Art. The splayed teeth of the devouring beast, the pleated hair and bulbous nose, the big, round, comically crazed expression — all these suggest it as the very model for the Wild Thing in question. [21]

A Kipling association naturally recalls *The Jungle Books*. Sendak's Wild Things acknowledge Max as their king because he "tamed them with the magic trick of staring into all their yellow eyes without blinking." This is Mowgli's trick over the wolf pack, which established him as master of the jungle. Mowgli the wolf-boy in turn suggests a source for the wolf suit that announces Max's membership in a fiercer family than could be found in the children's books of middle America at mid-century.

Any or all of these sources may have helped to precipitate the book out of its lyrical fog in April 1963. I should say here, too, that there needn't have been anything terribly studied about the transaction; often a tale will come into focus in a moment's recognition of what family of story wants to claim it. If, on the other hand, we were to settle on some one make-believe as the true forebear of *Where the Wild Things Are*, I suspect it would be none of the titles mentioned earlier but rather George MacDonald's *At the Back of the North Wind*, for in MacDonald we can see both the source for Sendak's lyrical approach and his later solution to it. Sendak himself has said of the Scot that he was "probably the greatest of the Victorian writers for children" and "someone I try to copy in many ways." [22] The phantasmagorical transformations in MacDonald — for example, those that informed several scenes in the two *Alices* — also prefigure the transformation of Max's

room into a forest and an ocean tumbling by with a private boat. In Mac-
Donald's illustrator, Arthur Hughes, we find as well an obvious paternity
for Sendak's way with the art of the line drawing. He has credited Hughes,
in fact, with being a seminal influence on his career. The suite of seventy-
four pictures for *At the Back of the North Wind* is the most likely course of
study I know for Sendak's famous black-and-white technique—the pen-
stroke that speaks so precisely of mystery and the eye for the myriad har-
monies that can be achieved within a tight compass. Here, surely, is the
inspiration for his editions of MacDonald's *The Golden Key* (1967) and
The Light Princess (1969) and for his collection of Grimm, *The Juniper
Tree* (1973), the stories of Isaac Bashevis Singer and Randall Jarrell, and
his own *Higglety Pigglety Pop!* (1967), whose heroine, Jennie the dog, goes
on a mystical pilgrimage very like Mossy's and Tangle's. Sendak is best
understood, I think, as an artist of the black-and-white moment, a nineteenth-century artist. *Where the Wild Things Are* is really a nineteenth-
century dream that has been streamlined and colorized for a television
audience. Readers familiar with Barbara Bader's *American Picturebooks*
(1976) may recall the three pages from the book there reproduced in black
and white and at one-seventh their actual size. Without the lyrical softening
of the pastels, the story becomes more intense and a bit more disturbing. It
would be interesting to see this dimension of the book brought out in a
collateral edition, printed just so, like the little books of Edward Gorey.
Whether this would make suitable reading for children I leave to everyone's
individual discretion. The story gave adults enough of a start the first time
around, raising some alarm, unfounded, of course, that children might be
frightened by it. Sendak, however, had only returned to the way story used
to be before it became wholesome and toothless—to a time when authors
unsoftened by sentimentality expected a children's tale to reach into most
all the places that any work of art must reach.

The likely prototype for *Wild Things* appears in the middle of *The North
Wind*. There, Sendak's hero, his wild beasts, and the victory over one's own
demons can all be found laid out, at rather baffling length, in a verse
narrative of five quatrains and seventy-one rhyming couplets entitled "Little
Boy Blue." This poem, which appears to have been inspired by William
Roscoe's *The Butterfly's Ball* (1807), reads exactly like a rough draft of the
picture book still decades away—rambling and inchoate like Sendak's
fantasy montage with the wild horses but full of the matter that will precipitate out to become *Where the Wild Things Are*. MacDonald's Diamond has
found the perplexing poem at the back of a book he is using to teach
himself to read. As he explains to his mother, its hero "was a rather cross
little boy . . . instead of running home to his mother, he ran away into the
wood and lost himself." Once in the forest, the runaway discovers that he
can make the creatures bow to his will:

> "You must follow me, follow me, follow, I say,
> Do as I tell you, and come this way. . . . "

> He called, and the creatures obeyed the call,
> Took their legs and their wings and followed him all.

Even so, being king of the forest is not any more fulfilling for him in the end than it will be for Max:

> Then Little Boy Blue began to ponder:
> "What's to be done with them all, I wonder?"
>
> Then Little Boy Blue, he said, quite low,
> 'What to do with you all I am sure I don't know.'
>
> But before he got far he thought of a thing;
> And up he stood, and spoke like a king.
>
> 'Why do you hustle and jostle and bother?
> Off with you all! Take me back to my mother.'

This is how Sendak ends his own wild rumpus:

> "Now stop!" Max said and sent the wild things off to bed without their supper. And Max the king of all wild things was lonely
> and wanted to be where someone loved him best of all.

Both scenes are being played by MacDonald's allusive rules, with unspoken meanings waiting to be awakened in each. In *The North Wind* Little Boy Blue must get by a snake that stands between himself and home:

> He rose; and up rose the snake on its tail,
> And hissed three times, half a hiss, half a wail
>
> Little Boy Blue he tried to go past him;
> But wherever he turned, sat the snake and faced him.
>
> 'If you don't get out of my way,' he said,
> 'I tell you snake I will break your head.'
>
> The snake he neither would go nor come;
> So he hit him hard with the stick of his drum.
>
> The snake fell down as if he were dead,
> And Little Boy Blue set his foot on his head.

You will not find this particular moment in *Where the Wild Things Are*; taming the beasts and putting them to sleep has sufficed for the occasion in that book. But the scene, or one very like it, does appear in Sendak's next picture book, *Hector Protector* (1965). There, the same indomitable hero can be found vanquishing a persistent serpent very much like MacDonald's. In sending their knights on quests away from home and mother, these two authors were not looking to awaken quite the same meaning, of course. Sendak was looking to the uses of the imagination in *Wild Things*, MacDonald to original sin and the fall out of Eden (Diamond: "I suppose it was a young one of the same serpent that tempted Adam and Eve. . . . That killing of the snake. . . . It's what I've got to do so often.") Having vanquished the evil within him, as Max will dispel his anger, Little Boy Blue is free to come home a hero:

> And all the creatures they marched before him,
> And marshalled him home with a high cockolorum.

It is this note of personal triumph, I suspect, that marched *Wild Things* out of the lyrical fog in the end. We may even be seeing MacDonald's closing phrase brought to life as the Wild Things marshal Max up and down on their shoulders in the six wordless pages of the "wild rumpus." Prominent in the grand parade is a giant, strutting, roosterish creature, a visual pun, perhaps, on the words "high cockolorum."

"Little Boy Blue" is an anomaly in *The North Wind*, a theatrical set-piece popping up in the middle of an otherwise quiet and contemplative story. It may have caught Sendak's eye for this reason, for, as evidenced by his later career as a set designer for operas and ballets, his work has always inclined toward theater. Many of his books, indeed, exist somewhere between literature and literature as a kind of performance art. *The Moon Jumpers*, *The Sign on Rosie's Door*, *In the Night Kitchen*, *Higglety Pigglety Pop!*, and others are about acting out roles; sometimes it happens literally on a stage, as in the Mother Goose Theater of the last title cited. What is being celebrated on the stage of *Where the Wild Things Are* is the raw and inventive ego of childhood. The tradition to which Sendak belongs as a performer, let me repeat, is the tradition of Perrault and Mother Goose, Wilhelm Busch, *Pinocchio*, *Little Black Sambo*, and Beatrix Potter. It is not the tradition of *Peter Pan* or Eugene Fields's "Little Boy Blue" or much of Sendak's own earlier work. Unlike Robert Louis Stevenson's Little Bear of a narrator in *A Child's Garden of Verses*, who only dreams of what he will do and noodles to the reader about how he makes believe, Max acts out the make-believe, with the result that *Wild Things* is both about a thing and the thing that it is about. It is Sendak's *Treasure Island*. As Stevenson's more extraverted tale became the classic boy's experience of piracy, so *Where the Wild Things Are* is now, for every child, where the wild things are. And because it is a celebration of childhood, purged of sentimental illusions, it can end with that expansive, simple gesture that concluded *Pinocchio* and opened *Little Black Sambo*. Home at last, Max pushes back the hood of his wolf suit; written across his face is the glow of completion, the sense of a thing well done and rewarded. Like Sambo, he is grand, and for no other reason than that he is Max. Like Pinocchio, he has won his "Bravo!"

With the publication of *Where the Wild Things Are* in 1963, this study comes to a close chronologically. I have crossed the line here and there to cite more recent titles of interest, but the past three decades are best left to the future to sort out, I think. For the rest of this history we are going to look back from Sendak's Wild Things to a literature that is all of it about wild things, and nothing but wild things. As the muse was making her definitive appearance in *Pinocchio* more than a century ago, a way was being prepared for a body of narrative fantasy that would do what the fairy tale was not going to do in the twentieth century—create new lands of make-believe set in the real world, where the seat of the allsense is properly to be found. The parent book of this third great class of make-believe would appear fortuitously a mere six months before Collodi introduced his universal wooden boy. This pivotal year, in which one kind of story reached its climax and another was born, was the year 1881.

6

THE BLACK RABBIT

A Fable Of, By, and For the People

1

Appropriating animals to tell the story of our lives is a stratagem as old as Aesop, but as a development in the history of telling stories to children it appears rather later than might be supposed. The ancient beast fable, by which we are advised of our folly, and the modern animal fantasy, which like the fairy tale gives us the benefit of the doubt for the sake of deeper satisfactions, are very different kinds of story, and the translation from one to the other began only a century ago in the 1880s when the animal fantasists to come were all growing up within range of the same events, the same books. Kenneth Grahame had reached his early twenties, Kipling and Potter were in their mid-teens, and in America Thornton Burgess and Howard Garis were a few years shy of puberty. What events they shared were the manifest destinies of empire, electricity, and later the automobile, and, perhaps most importantly, of urbanization. All came of age while emigration from farm to city was reaching its height and people's experience of the country was becoming more and more a matter of memory and of weekends, holidays, or retirement. As to what pertinent reading they might have shared, Lear's nonsense songs had recently expanded the nursery rhyme into a narrative verse form suitable to the adventures of an Owl and a Pussycat and a Duck and a Kangaroo, but until the year 1881 there is little in story that would be of imaginative use to this next generation of storytellers, no leap into such an advanced state of anthropomorphism as they themselves would practice.

That is not to say there were no characters waiting in the wings for new parts to be written for them. There are a number of creatures popular in the old lore who suddenly proliferate in books at the turn of the century. The mouse, for example, who with its vaguely human domesticity has been with us since Aesop, we find Potter turning into some of her subtlest characters: Tom Thumb and Hunca Munca, Mrs Tittlemouse, and the mice of her sad meditation on Aesop, *Johnny Town-Mouse*. Less ancient than the mouse but now no less a familiar of the nursery scene is that descendant of Southey's famous tale, the bear, who rumbled benignly into the playroom when news of Teddy Roosevelt's refusal to shoot a cub he'd rendered motherless on a hunting expedition helped popularize the bear as a stuffed toy, a fad newly arrived from Europe. It has been a parade of teddy bears and Little Bears, Ruperts and Paddingtons and Winnies-the-Pooh ever since.

Some animals, of course, are more easily seen to be us than others. Despite Kipling's truism that he always walks alone, the cat has proven to be more adaptable to human ways, and a more appealing stand-in, than any other creature in story. (The equally domestic dog seems too noble or conversely too slap-happy, and is in either case too lacking in a certain human suppleness of body and character, to lend itself to very many anthropomorphic situations.) And conveniently the cat begins where children's literature is said otherwise to begin, in the seventeenth century with Perrault. Since his Puss put on boots and fooled the king, we have had a Cheshire Cat, a Tom who chases Jerry, T. S. Eliot cats, the "millions and billions and trillions of cats" of Wanda Gág, and now a Garfield. The more humanized heirs of Perrault's Puss-in-Boots begin in modern times with J. G. Francis's *Cheerful Cats* in *St. Nicholas Magazine* and with Potter's Tom Kitten, whose mother kept house like any human mother. They in turn helped set the stage not only for myriad domestics of kitchen and barn but for a Krazy Kat, a Felix, a Cat in the Hat, and, more recently, Robert Crumb's randy hipster, Fritz.

As busy as children's story has been with the comings and goings of the mouse, the bear, and the cat, however, and as ancient as two of these are in the literature, modern make-believe does not begin with them. The homely explanation for what children read and watch today and where it comes from is rabbits. Arrange the major works of make-believe from the past century in chronological order and there emerges a clear line of descent going back as far as Potter's Peter, the first animal-child hero in a story, and then back a little farther still, to the 1880s, when the coming generation of fantasists was still impressionable and its members all within imagining range of the same ideas and images. What we find in that decade is what we should expect to find, given the otherwise inexplicable proliferation of animals in story over the next decade and a half. *The Jungle Books* and *Just-So Stories*, the *Hollow Tree Stories* of Albert Bigelow Paine, the tales of Beatrix Potter, *The Wind in the Willows*, and *Old Mother West Wind* and

Uncle Wiggily—the appearance of all these books within fifteen years of each other indicates that in the 1880s story must have taken a significant turn in their direction; and in fact what we do find happening in that period is the beast fable suddenly shedding its ancient moralizing intent and taking on the affective weight of modern prose fantasy. In 1881 one creature in particular is put forward in print who, becoming a favorite with the reading public, will open up new possibilities for storytelling—possibilities that will be apparent to everyone at much the same time.

Curiously, for all that it is obvious that one book is the common source for so much modern make-believe, it is a line no writer on children's literature has ever pursued. Critics have almost unanimously preferred to lay the great change in children's books from the nineteenth to the twentieth centuries not to rabbits, not even to anthropomorphism in general, but to such an event as the introduction of color printing and the efforts of printer Edmund Evans to enlist Walter Crane, Kate Greenaway, and Randolph Caldecott in the production of toy books in the 1860s, -70s, and -80s. Out of this alliance ostensibly evolved the representative form of our own time, the picture book. There is more convenience than truth in settling on such a moment, however; while lending a wanted, if irrelevant, respectability to critical talk about children's books, it has allowed us to overlook other possible precedents for today's books, and to ignore the humbling fact that the dominant form of entertainment for children in this century, prior to TV, has not been the picture book but that heir to the cheap literature Evans wanted his imprint to transcend, the comic book.

The real deficiency in our invoking Crane, Greenaway, and Caldecott as the founders of modern children's books, though, is that it tells us only what the books would look like—and that only in small part—and not what they would be about. For if as a test we were to gather together all the lasting examples of make-believe from the past century and go looking in them for what most have in common with the past, we would not come up with the great three, we would come up with something like *Uncle Wiggily*, a paternity so embarrassing to anyone promoting the genre as an art form that the old rabbit gentleman—syndicated hero of 15,000 stories and some seventy-five books—has got his rheumatism crutch inside the door of not one of the scores of studies written on the subject. Nonetheless, what we read to children today evolved from the telling of stories, not from the manufacturing of books of prestige, and is the result of one writer after another having discovered the various things you can do with rabbits in stories—and after rabbits with (more) cats, (more) mice, and with bears, elephants, monkeys, donkeys, pigs, ducks, frogs, and the like, until today nearly every species from Aesop's ancient menagerie, and many a new one besides, has become the hero of its own adventures in picture books, novels, comic books, newspapers, movies, and on TV. Winnie-the-Pooh, Babar, Rupert of the English comic strips, Curious George, Mickey Mouse and

Donald Duck, Pogo, the Cat in the Hat, Frog and Toad, Big Bird from *Sesame Street*, William Steig's Sylvester, Wilbur from *Charlotte's Web*: these are only the most famous of them; they speak for thousands.

In such an advanced state of anthropomorphism no characters even remotely like them existed in literature before the year 1881. They themselves, and not the books they come in, are the great change in children's story. The year 1881 marks their birthday and the coming into our nursery lore of a vast zoo parade led by Peter Rabbit and Uncle Wiggily and Thornton Burgess's Peter Cottontail. The grand marshal of the parade, however, and the granddaddy of every beast in mufti today, is that one prolific hare whose influence over story I believe Potter was acknowledging slyly in her rhyme that begins, "Now what is that tapping at Cottontail's door?" and concludes, "Why I really believe it's a little black rabbit!"

It is from this hare, the first animal personage in children's story, that modern make-believe springs; it is the force of his personality on the public imagination that caused a shift in the direction of story — his personality and that of the old man telling us about him; and it is with him, Brer Rabbit, and with his teller, Uncle Remus, that any look into the origins of our modern nursery lore rightly ought to begin.

2

Uncle Remus: His Songs and Sayings, the compilation of Atlanta journalist Joel Chandler Harris (1848–1909), was published in December 1880,[1] to become, overnight, one of the famous American books of the nineteenth century. "The new craze," Angus Wilson calls it, slightingly, in his biography of Kipling,[2] who adored the work. "Mr. Bright was very much taken with *Uncle Remus*," Beatrix Potter noted of a family friend in her journal; "when papa showed it to him he used to read it aloud till the tears ran down with laughing."[3] Harris's protest that "[t]here is nothing here but an old Negro man, a little boy, and a dull reporter," delivered in alarm at the number of children, folklorists, and other correspondents descending on him through the mails, is characteristic of the repertoire of disavowals the shy author suddenly had to adopt to get himself through the day. The "nothing" was of course something brand-new in story. Chaucer's pilgrims, Scheherazade, and the titular Mother Goose notwithstanding, never before had the image of the storyteller or the occasion of the telling been made so real to life or so appealing as with this old Negro and this complaint white child. And it was not just the conception of the book that was new, or even of the first importance, though it seemed so at the time to Mark Twain and others; it was the tales themselves: here, within an old man's memory of plantation life and transcending it onto an international stage, was a world still very much alive and kicking, a realm of make-believe unlike anything that had appeared in American letters or indeed anywhere, delivered with the air of a thing freshly discovered. Around and about its neighborhoods roamed characters unknown to fantasy, speaking in accents of English few had ever heard outside the South and which none had ever seen in print (the dialect of regional writers and minstrels was exposed as wholly bogus; the rhetoric of contemporary fiction, as florid and tiresome).

As they told of their hero, Brer Rabbit, these tales were, and sounded in every syllable, as big as life and twice as natural. So real were they and so real seemed their putative black narrator that southern children introduced to the real author by Twain, who had taken Harris in tow, disbelieved that this portly white man could possibly be their Uncle Remus. In New Orleans a crowd was overheard whispering, "Look, he's white." But that was the luck of these tales: whereas all but a few like "The Tar Baby" would surely have been lost[4] as the Civil War disrupted the flow of story from one generation to the next and Negroes born into the troubles of Reconstruction became less and less interested in what the old-timers had to tell, the tales instead passed safely through an honest scribe and into literature. Harris's genius had been to recognize virtue in men and story and to succumb to it. What he rescued of the oral tradition he reproduced faithfully; not one of the tales is whitewashed with whimsy or bathos or cheap effects (a fate that would catch up with them, however, in Walt Disney's *Song of the South*). Harris retold them according to the best tellings he had heard, from men he had troubled himself to know since boyhood.

Nights with Uncle Remus followed in 1883, *Daddy Jake the Runaway* in 1889, and in 1892 came *Uncle Remus and His Friends*, the first collection to be illustrated by A. B. Frost. (The famous Frost reissue of *Songs and Sayings* appeared in 1895.) The years 1905–1918 saw the publication of five more collections, with the tenth and last published from manuscript in 1948.[5] In 1948 too—serving as a corrective to the Disney film, much as Wanda Gág's *Snow White* had served as a corrective to Disney's *Snow White* of 1939—came the standard children's edition, *The Favorite Uncle Remus*. Richard Chase's *The Complete Uncle Remus* followed in 1955. Whereupon the book that had become all the rage on publication and which for seventy-five years had been an honored classic of American letters simply runs out of credibility and evaporates into the haze of history. Talking in dialect and the image of a slave as a man contented with his lot (more or less) did an injury, blacks knew, to their children, and whites, with the rise of the civil rights movement of the 1960s, quickly abandoned the work as an embarrassment. An Uncle Remus may have been the right, the necessary, choice of character for the telling of these tales, but he was, everyone agreed, the wrong one for the preserving of them. By 1976 a Bicentennial-inspired survey of children's-book professionals could yield, consequently, a list of the ten best American children's books of the previous two hundred years on which no place could be found for the one book that for its art and historical importance ought to have headed the list. The centennial of *Songs and Sayings* passed with hardly a whisper of recognition. No mention at all is made of the work in most modern histories of American children's books.

There is an undue irony it the absence of *Uncle Remus* from a tally of home-grown greats. Harris himself had declared, in an 1879 call for a native Southern fiction that would transcend the merely provincial, that there could come out of the South no contribution to our understanding of what was American that did not incorporate the black character and no advance out of the old rhetoric into a clear, colloquial prose that did not acknowledge the black contribution to spoken English. "I want you to illustrate the matter in your own way, which is preeminently the American way," Harris wrote A. B. Frost in 1892 as they prepared *Uncle Remus and His Friends* for publication. "We shall then have real American stuff [*sic*] illustrated in real American style."

Real American tales as real Americans told them, pictured by an American with an instinct for the real earth on which make-believe must stand. It is one of the few happy pairings in children's literature, this collaboration in black and white—equal to Tenniel's *Alice* and to Shepard's *Wind in the Willows*, a book that descends from it. Today, despite several efforts to recast the tales into standard English, *Uncle Remus* is an unbook. No one can rightly object to this eclipse on extraliterary grounds. We can regret that the best of all American books ever handed down to children is a book we cannot in good conscience read them. We can regret, too, that a body of folklore equal to Grimms' or the *1001 Nights* is a heritage black students are unlikely to know in its original form, as their great-grandparents spoke it. We can regret that to enjoy these tales at all we must take ourselves to some Preservation Hall of the imagination, but we cannot deny that justice was due.[6]

What does need correcting, however, is the regrettable fact that the only American children's book to exert a profound influence on storytellers at home and abroad has become a book without critical standing. In its own day so famous as to make the usual kinds of acknowledgement by the next generation of storytellers superfluous, it is, in the absence of overwhelming testimony, seen now as a work of no apparent importance whatsoever. Its influence on the major English fantasists from Kipling to Milne and on such popular Americans as Thornton Burgess and Howard Garis, from whom so much of our nursery reading derives, has gone unremarked, as far as I can discover, by any writer on children's literature. Yet before the publication of *Uncle Remus* in 1881 there was nothing like, and for fifty years after there was little else of note in make-believe but the *Uncle Remus* order of serial adventures in the countryside. However else we regard the book, it is irrefutably the central event in the making of modern children's story.

In this and following chapters I want to look at just what there was in *Uncle Remus* that was so new to story—how it suggested to Potter, Thorn-

ton Burgess, and others fresh possibilities for the telling of stories and how
what they made of these possibilities has yielded the stories we read to
children today. In doing so I have decided to let the tales talk for themselves. Thirty years ago it could be assumed that the reader would have
some familiarity with *Uncle Remus*, but this is no longer the case. And
anyway, a literature in which even a sneeze is heroic ("Bimeby he sneeze —
huckychow!") is a literature that wants quoting. As we listen, we should
remember that although Harris's dialect is a phonetic approximation it is
nevertheless the genuine article and not the mugging of an Al Jolson in
white gloves and black face. Harris, from having spent as much time on
Negro back porches as anywhere else in his boyhood, could by his own
account think in dialect — his fellow Southerners, remember, had at first
assumed that he *was* black. We have, as well, Mark Twain's word (in *Life
on the Mississippi*) that "in the matter of writing it he is the only master the
country has produced."[7]

Keeping this in mind as the historical basis for the telling, we should
perhaps however abandon the term dialect and in its place substitute the
word style or voice. Dialect is a linguistic not a literary tag; it suggests that
the language in question is a degraded English, rather than a form of
expression with its own legitimacy. Think of *Uncle Remus* as story, as
make-believe, and the dialect becomes the right and happy sound of the
world being created in the tales. Harris himself denied there was anything
degraded about it: "The difference between real dialect and lingo is that the
first is preservative, while the latter is destructive, of language. Judged by
this standard the negro dialect is as perfect as any the world ever saw." And
of its stylistic advantages: "It has a fluency all its own; it gives a new
coloring to statement, and allows of a swift shading in narrative that can be
reached in literary English only in the most painful and roundabout way."[8]
The stories he attempted to write for children in standard English in the
1890s, in fact, are so painful and roundabout in contrast to the *Uncle
Remus* tales it seems natural to conclude that through the black style of
speaking Harris found a release into storytelling that was not otherwise
available to him.

The dialect affords us a release into the tales as well: this perfectly rendered, it deflects us straightaway into something we see is make-believe and
catches us believing before we can think not to. It would not help us to
believe to say of a character in any other way that when he laughed "he laff
en laff twel he hatter hug a tree fer ter keep fum drappin' on de groun'."
But *Uncle Remus* is tall-tale stuff calling for tall words, and these are the
right words to inhibit our skepticism. A fear of language, a self-
consciousness in its use, so common to Harris's mannered times, is quite
foreign to these tales. In the line "Ole Miss Goose she wuz down at de
spring, washin', en b'ilin', en battlin' cloze" there is not the faintest echo of
an author caught in the act of thinking twice before speaking. The event
and its expression are perfectly married. Miss Goose exists, the clothes

exist, the eternal battle between them exists, and we ourselves are as natural to the scene as if we had happened upon it while out for a stroll. That "fluency all its own" allowed Harris—like Lewis Carroll a stutterer—to forget that he himself existed and to become one with the tale he was telling. Consequently, there is the purest delight in listening to *Uncle Remus* and to the variety of things its language can do. Harris's easy virtuosity with the dialect catches each tale in mid-leap, like Brer Rabbit himself. Rendered into standard English the stories can (as many editions attest) only sit there in the rhetorical mud like Brer Fox with "a spell er de dry grins."

This is a speaking voice at perfect pitch:

> Ole Brer Wolf, he wuz settin' out on de back piazzer smokin' en noddin'. He 'ud take en draw a long whiff, he would, en den he 'ud drap off ter noddin' en let de smoke oozle out thoo he nose.

> "Brother Rabbit and his Famous Foot,"
> *Nights*; "Brer Rabbit Loses his Luck"[9]

> . . . ole Cousin Wildcat drawed back en fotch Brer Fox a wipe 'crosst de stomach, en you mought a heerd 'im squall fum yer ter Harmony Grove. Little mo' en de creetur would er to' Brer Fox in two. W'en de creetur made a pass at 'im, Brer Rabbit knew w'at gwine ter happen, yit all de same he tuck'n holler:
> "Hit 'im agin, Brer Fox! Hit 'im agin! I'm a-backin' you, Brer Fox! Ef he dast ter run, I'll in about cripple 'im—dat I will. Hit 'im agin!"
> All dis time, w'iles Brer Rabbit gwine on dis a-way, Brer Fox, he wuz a squattin' down, hol'in he stomach wid bofe han's en des a moanin':
> "I'm ruint, Brer Rabbit! I'm ruint! Run fetch de doctor! I'm teetotally ruint!"

> "How Brother Fox was too Smart,"
> *Nights*; "The Creetur with No Claws"

In "The Laughing Place" the verb "to think," rendered into action three times in fifteen lines, takes on a versatility that would be a missed opportunity in Standard English:

> Dey sot 'bout en make marks in de san' des like you see folks do w'en deyer tryin' fer ter git der thinkin' machine ter wuk.
> Brer Rabbit, he put his han' ter his head, en shot his eyeballs en do like he studyin'.
> He tap hisse'f on de head, he did, en 'low dat dey wuz a heap mo' und' his hat dan w'at you could git out wid a fine-toof comb.

> "Brother Rabbit's Laughing-Place,"
> *Told by Uncle Remus*

Here the comic promise of the language turns two potentially prosaic howdy-dos on the road into the opening patter of a vaudeville act:

> "How you fine yo'se'f dese days, Sis Cow?" sez Brer Rabbit, sezee.
> "I'm sorter toler'ble, Brer Rabbit; how you come on?" sez Miss Cow, sez she.
> "Oh, I'm des toler'ble myse'f, Sis Cow; sorter linger'n twix' a balk en a break-down," sez Brer Rabbit, sezee.

> "Miss Cow Falls a Victim to Mr. Rabbit," *Songs and Sayings*;
> "Miss Cow and the Persimmon Tree"

"Heyo, Brer Tarrypin, whar you bin dis long-come-short?" sez Brer Fox, sezee.

"Loungin' roun', Brer Fox, loungin' roun'," sex Brer Tarrypin.

"You don't look sprucy like you did, Brer Tarrypin," sez Brer Fox, sezee.

"Loungin' roun' en suffer'n'," sez Brer Tarrypin, sezee.

"Mr. Fox Tackles Old Man Tarrypin," *Songs and Sayings*;
"Lounging 'round and Suffering"

Listen to this epic opening to a domestic squabble over some chickens:

. . . ole Miss Fox wuz so mad dat she can't say nothin' en do jestice ter 'erse'f, so she des stan' dar en make motions wid de broom w'at she had in 'er han'.

Brer Fox, he wipe de persweat off'n his face en eyes en say, "Hit seem like ter me dat I year you talkin' ter some un des now; w'at wuz you sayin', sugar-honey?"

Soon ez she kin ketch 'er breff she 'low, "I'll sugar you! I'll honey you! W'at make you fetch vittles home ef you gwine ter sen' um off agin? W'at you wanter put yo' se'f ter de trouble er totin' um ter dis house w'en you know you gwineter give um 'way des ez soon ez you tu'n yo' back on de place? En w'at business you got sen'in' ole Miss Rabbit de two fine fat pullets w'at you brung home, w'ich dey make me dribble at de mouf de fus' time I seed um? En I aint mo' dan seed um, 'for' yer come ole Brer Rabbit a-bowin' en a-scrapin', en a-simperin' en a-sniggerin', en he 'low dat you done sont 'im fer de pullets. Ef it had 'a ' des 'a ' bin his own lone sesso, he'd 'a ' never got dem pullets in de roun' worril — I'd 'a' gouged out his goozle fus' — but yer he come wid a letter w'at you writ! How come you given' pullets ter old Brer Rabbit en his family w'en yo' own chillun, 'twix' yo' laziness en de hard times, is gwine roun' so ga'nt dat dey can't make a shadder in de moonshine?"

"How Brother Rabbit Brought Family Trouble on Brother Fox,"
Uncle Remus Returns; "Trouble in the Fox Family"

I cannot think of another American children's book that does not sound lifeless and slack by comparison. Carl Sandburg's *Rootabaga Stories* comes to mind, but this tour de force is a miscellany of unrealities, the studied effort of a poet at heightening standard English to describe very unstandard goings-on in a land where "the railroad tracks change from straight to zigzag" and the folks are called Gimme the Ax, Bimbo the Snip, and the Potato Face Blind Man. What we hear is the virtuosity of Sandburg's voice at making things up. What we hear in *Uncle Remus* is the real world talking itself alive through the voices of the people living in one corner of it. They are talking animals, true, but they are living just next door. Their tales are fantasy, but what we hear in them is the noise of our neighbors.

3

What were these neighbors up to in their tales that so impressed the next generation of storytellers? What is happening in *Uncle Remus* that hadn't been told in story before: It will be difficult to demonstrate any kind of answer to this without first dispelling the notion that we any longer know what the folklore collected by Joel Chandler Harris comprises. Mention of *Uncle Remus* today, if it calls to mind anything more than the Disney movie, will still evoke for most readers only the images of a benign old black man, a tar-baby, and Brer Rabbit "down dar in de briar-patch' laffin' 'twel his sides hurted 'im." The impression left us is one of episodes nearly alike in relating how one pair of baggy pants bamboozled another pair of baggy pants on a Georgia cart road in the old plantation days. But the Negro trickster tales—183 in the Harris collections alone—are a more various lot than this. For two and a half centuries before Harris, black American storytellers had been shuttling back and forth across the larger body of Negro folklore, weaving into their comedies of the social arena threads of myth and legend, fairy tale, and ghost, witch, and devil tales. What Harris unfolded before the public in 1881 was a folk portrait of a people as textured and complete as any ever recorded.

It was, too, while complete in one sense, a body of story that was only the beginning of its kind. Mingled in among the folk motifs of the beast fable are clear signs of the narrative fantasy to come. To show these moments in relief against the spare lines of a more ancient tradition I have set out below a brief description of seven major types of story in the *Uncle Remus* corpus. They are not necessarily recognized folk types. I have been interested simply in identifying whatever might best set each apart in the reader's mind from other *Uncle Remus* stories. It is worth nothing at the outset that, contrary to a common misconception about them, few of the tales bear any but a superficial resemblance to the instructive fables of Aesop. Many, in fact, seem more the chapters of a family saga than fables at all.

Mammy-Bammy Big-Money

Oral tradition provides few way-markers along the course of a tale's evolution, so it is not surprising that the origins of the *Uncle Remus* stories are obscure. While thoroughly American in character, they are pretty much agreed to be of African derivation, but the point has eluded definition. In the story "Brother Rabbit Doesn't Go to See Aunt Nancy" (*Seven Tales*), published from manuscript in 1948 but set down possibly as early as 1889, I think we may nonetheless catch a glimpse of that otherwise indeterminable moment in history when the ancient trickster tale changes clothes from African to American homespun.

> All de creeturs hatter go once a year fer ter make ter peace wid ol' Aunt Nancy . . . she wuz de granny er Mammy-Bammy Big-Money . . . Her rule went furder dan whar she live at, an' when she went ter call de creeturs, all she hatter do wuz ter fling her head back an' kinder suck in her bref an' all de creeturs would have a little chill, an' know dat she wuz a-callin' un um.

Thomas English, in his introduction to this last *Uncle Remus* collection, identifies Aunt Nancy with Annancy, or Anansi, the spider hero of Jamaican folklore. "Half 'oman an' half spider," Aunt Nancy lived in a house of fog, Mother Nature as Witch of the West Indies. She is also, in her male incarnation, Anansi the trickster hero of African lore. If we claim the obvious, then, that Anansi-Annancy-Aunt Nancy followed the slave route to America, could she not in this tale be a dream of Africa calling the creatures back to their homelands? Or perhaps it is not a dream but a nightmare. There is a clammy air of fear and guilt about the passage quoted above, as if it were saying, in a fierce whisper, where you are is not where you come from and not where you belong: come to me. Perhaps a captive race, having created a new culture in a new world, is prone to being pained by thoughts of an origin it can no longer comprehend.

Up in middle Georgia, however, an unfazed Brer Rabbit declines to honor this old ancestor. She has no hold over him, he declares; and when she threatens to come to him instead, "he went on chawin' his cud like nothin' aint happen." His muse of choice will be Aunt Nancy's granddaughter, the home-grown, piney-woods witch-rabbit, Mammy-Bammy Big-Money. There may be a historical underpinning to this tale: throughout the nineteenth century the suggestion had been put forward that the solution to slavery in America was the resettling of Africa by American blacks. A few attempts were actually made; from them came the founding of Liberia. But on the whole the experiment gained little support. Blacks were no more given to it than whites. "What I gwine to do in Affiky?" asks Uncle Remus when the idea of an exodus back to the homelands is put to him; "I aint no Affikin nigger."[10] And this would appear to be as well the coded message of Brother Rabbit's refusal to go see his Aunt Nancy. Here we are, the story seems to say; this is home, these woodlots and truck patches and misery. And I hear the listeners responding, like the communicants in a church, like the housekeeper Aunt Tempy, exclaiming "in an ecstasy of admiration, 'le' 'im 'lone, now! Des le' 'im 'lone!'" It is here we will live by our wits and survive, say all the tales — like Brother Rabbit. And the listeners shout with Aunt Tempy, "Dar now!"

> De time is right now, en dish yer's de place —
> Let de sun er salvashun shine squar' in yo' face.
>
> "Revival Hymn," *Songs and Sayings*

So it is Mammy-Bammy Big-Money who comes to preside over the woods of the American South, and it is she who stands as Brer Rabbit's personal muse in times of extremity. Of the seven tales in which she is mentioned or makes an appearance, the most notable are "Taily-po" (*Uncle Remus Returns*), in which she raises a wildcat from the dead to discomfort Mr. Man, and a suite of three tales in *Nights with Uncle Remus*, "Brother Rabbit and His Famous Foot," "Brother Rabbit Submits to a Test," and "Brother Wolf Falls a Victim." The first of these, a tale in rhyming prose, describes the theft of Brer Rabbit's lucky rabbit's foot, a gift from his witch-aunt in the woods, and his journey to Big-Money for advice:

> She live way off in a deep, dark swamp, en ef you go dar you hatter ride some, slide some; jump some, hump some; hop some, flop some; walk some, balk some; creep some, sleep some; fly some, cry some; foller some, holler some; wade some, spade some; en ef you ain't monst'us keerful you ain't git dar den . . .
> "Mammy-Bammy Big-Money, I needs yo' he'p."
> "Son Riley Rabbit, why so? Son Riley Rabbit, why so?"
> "Mammy-Bammy Big-Money, I los' de foot you gim me."
> "O Riley Rabbit, why so? Son Riley Rabbit, why so?"
> "Mammy-Bammy Big-Money, my luck done gone. I put dat foot down 'pon de groun'. I lef' um dar I know not whar."
> "De Wolf done tuck en stole yo' luck, Son Riley Rabbit, Riley. Go fine de track, go git hit back, Son Riley Rabbit, Riley."[11]

In the second and best-known of the three tales (see, for example, Ennis Rees's modern rhyming version in *More of Brer Rabbit's Tricks*, illustrated by Edward Gorey), Son Riley, his lucky foot notwithstanding, "b'gun ter feel he weakness"—off he goes again to his witch-aunt in the woods, wanting to know how come "he ain't kin fool de yuther creeturs no mo', en dey push 'im so closte twel 't won't be long 'fo' dey'll git 'im." To restore his confidence, Big-Money sets him two tasks. The first is to fetch her a squirrel sitting in a tree. After a moment's thought, Riley hides himself inside a bag with two rocks.

> He wait little w'ile, en den he hit de rocks tergedder—*blip!*
> Squer'l he holler, "Hey!"
> Brer Rabbit wait little, en den he tuck'n slap de rocks tergedder—*blap!*
> Squer'l he run down de tree little bit en holler, "Heyo!"
> Brer Rabbit ain't sayin' nothin'. He des pop de rocks tergedder—*blop!*
> Squer'l, he come down little furder, he did, en holler, "Who dat?"
> "Biggidy Dicky Big-Bag!"
> "What you doin' in dar?"
> "Crackin' hick'y nuts."
> "Kin I crack some?"
> "Tooby sho', Miss Bunny Bushtail; come git in de bag."

Having caught his squirrel and having for his second task snared a rattlesnake, Brer Rabbit returns

> ter whar de ole Witch-Rabbit settin' at; but w'en he git dar, Mammy-Bammy Big-Money done make 'er disappearance, but he year sump'n way off yander, en seem lak it say:
> "Ef you git any mo' sense, Son Riley, you'll be de ruination ev de whole settlement, Son Riley Rabbit, Riley."

A curious, almost subliminal thing has been happening as this three-part sequence unfolds in its printed form. Like a horror movie in which a hand and then a staring head emerge from a coffin, and finally the thing itself leaps out to chase us all around the cellar, Mammy-Bammy Big-Money is slowly being revealed to us. In the first tale we see "black smoke comin' outer de hole in de groun' whar de ole Witch Rabbit stay," and we hear her voice, "hoarse and oracular." In the second tale we see through the smoke "'er great big eyeballs en 'er great big years." And in the third, like the corpse in the cellar, she rises. The occasion for this horribly funny third tale is the discontinuance of Brother Wolf. Between them Big-Money and Riley have cooked up a grisly trick to rid themselves of the old boy once and for all. Arriving at Brother Wolf's door, Riley plants the hook:

"Brer Wolf! O Brer Wolf! I des now come fum de river, en des ez sho' ez youer settin' in dat cheer, ole Big-Money layin' dar stone dead. Less we go eat 'er up.

"Sho'ly youer jokin'," protests Brer Wolf; but Brer Rabbit assures him it's "de fatal fack," and together they race to the river, gathering neighbors along the way, until "dey had a crowd dar des lak camp-meetin' times." And "sho nuff, dar lay ole Big-Money all stretch out on de river bank." Now Brer Wolf is in his glory. He struts about, "monst'us biggity," canvassing his neighbors how much each of them thinks a fair division of the spoils. The wary brothers "speck he better take de fus' choosement," and under examination each volunteers over to Brer Wolf a little more of his share, until at last Brer Rabbit offers they do him the honor of tying him on and letting him eat the witch-rabbit all up—"'en den we kin pick de bones,' sezee." Swollen with conceit, Brer Wolf allows himself to be lashed to the corpse, and with a big wink at the others he "retch down en bite Big-Money on de back er de neck. Co'se w'en he do dis, Big-Money bleedz ter flinch.

"Take me off! She ain't dead. O Lordy! I feel 'er move!"

Brer Rabbit tries to rally him: "She er sho'ly dead, Brer Wolf! Nail 'er, Brer Wolf! Bite 'er! gnyaw 'er!"

But Brer Wolf's fate is as secure as that of Melville's Ahab. Hollering "lak de woods done ketch a-fier: 'O Lordy! Ontie me, Brer Rabbit, ontie me!'" he goes to the river lashed to as irreversible a force of nature as Moby Dick. And "she git ter de bank er de river, en she fall in—*cumberjoom!*—en dat 'uz de las' er Brer Wolf."

This last tale is a fable warning us of our greed and conceit and a consolation prize congratulating us on our talent for surviving them in others, but it is something more than either. Because of the intimate texture given it in the telling, it has become, as well, a horror story in a modern vein. "Brother Wolf Falls a Victim" would have been right at home as a set piece in D.C. Comics' *Haunt of Fear* or *Tales from the Crypt* in the 1950s. Illustrated by Graham Ingalls or Jack Davis, Brer Wolf's terror would have appeared stark naked across the page, his penultimate speech balloon gone rigid with the cry "O Lordy! I feel 'er move!" Considering this, we might ask if the one, two, three, smoke, ears, and out-of-the-hole emergence of Mammy-Bammy Big-Money is coincidental, then, or contrived. Were in fact these three tales ever told serially, for the gathering chill? Only a narrator of unusual skills could have worked such a feat of extemporaneous storytelling, so I think it is more likely an incidental bit of dramaturgy contrived by Harris himself in the course of assembling this second collection. My eventual point being that everywhere in *Uncle Remus*—both in the frame stories concerning Uncle Remus and the little boy and within the tales themselves—we are moving in small, sometimes accidental steps away from the pure economy of the fable and toward the more sustained fantasy of the next generation of storytellers.

Uncle Remus points us toward a number of modern genres, and not all of them literary. It points us toward the wisecracking Warner Bros. cartoons of the 1940s and toward the more benign satire of newspaper strips like *Pogo*. It points us toward our modern love of parody in general and even, in a way, toward rock 'n' roll.[12] And, apposite to this story, *Uncle Remus* is taking us forward into modern children's story. Not all the tales in *Uncle Remus* take a fearsome turn; in fact, most do not. There are stories that, beyond exhibiting a human immediacy never before granted animals in story, have a great friendliness and gentle humor about them; and it is from these that the beast fable becomes redirected toward a new audience in the children's room. In the second of the three tales cited above, the conversation between Brer Rabbit and the squirrel, and the benign, childlike nature of the trick itself, provide a clear example of this redirection. If I had set out to explain today's stories for young children in a more allusive way and had titled this book *How Story Got Its Bushy Tail*, I would have built my origin myth around just such a passage—or around any of the dozens like it in *Uncle Remus*—and I would not be far off the mark. In the name "Miss Bunny Bushtail" alone—a name shortly to be used verbatim by the author of *Uncle Wiggily*—can be heard virtually all of popular and commercial twentieth-century anthropomorphism.

Myths

In her handbook to the *Uncle Remus* tales, *Joel Chandler Harris—Folklorist*, Stella Brookes catalogues as mythical those tales which conform to folklorist Stith Thompson's criterion that we see in them the world as it was before becoming the world we now know. Such stories explain the origins of the heavenly bodies, the tribes and their rituals, and how the animals came to differ from one another. There are twenty-four of these precursors of Kipling and Burgess in the *Uncle Remus* corpus, most of them straightforward fables like "Why Mr. Possum Has No Hair on His Tail" and "Why Mr. Cricket Has Elbows on His Legs." In "The Origin of the Ocean" (*Nights*) a delightful image anticipates the theory of continental drift: "One time way back yander, 'fo dey wuz any folks a-foolin' 'roun'," Mr. Lion enlists Brer Rabbit to join him on a hunt; catching nothing himself, he lays claim to Brer Rabbit's take, which puts Brer Rabbit in mind to rid himself forthwith of Mr. Lion. Having tricked his adversary into leaping to the opposite bank of a creek they've camped beside, Brer Rabbit then cuts "de string w'at hol' de banks togedder, en, lo en beholes, dar dey wuz! . . . De banks dey keep on fallin' back, en de creek keep on gittin' wider en wider, twel bimeby Brer Rabbit en Mr. Lion aint in sight er one er n'er, en fum dat day to dis de big waters bin rollin' 'twix' um." Such a tale could explain of course not only the origin of the ocean but also how Brer Rabbit comes to be in America and Mr. Lion over-seas in Africa; and as such it could be said to be both a survival from African lore and a more recent tale as well.[13]

Famine Stories

Three tales not listed by Brookes as myths, and one in particular, seem to me to have something of the myth about them nonetheless. They are not origin stories but straightforward trickster tales imbued, unless I misread them, with residual mythic elements. Like the Mammy-Bammy Big-Money trilogy discussed above, they appear sequentially in *Nights with Uncle Remus*. I would guess them to be, at heart if not in their attire of detail, very old, predating the Africans' removal to the Americas, for the reason that a story of famine would have less application here: slaves suffer every kind of deprivation; their own gardens may blister in the sun; but they are not often starved to death. Nor, being slaves, do they have the opportunity of selling one another at market, as happens in these tales and did happen historically on the west coast of Africa when blacks of one tribe would sometimes sell blacks of another tribe to the slave trade. Slaves only get sold; they don't do the selling. And even allowing for the tendency of fable toward the wilder sides of reality, it is difficult to imagine American slaves, who had to suffer the breaking up of their families, entertaining themselves with as unnatural an act as selling your mother to fill your belly unless they were merely repeating tales that had come down to them from the old times.

The one other explanation that enables us to see these tales as being ancient yet dating only from the decade before the Civil War is the Bible. It is possible that the troubles related here are an image of Africa (read Egypt) introduced to the slaves through Bible stories told by those early black preachers who brought Christianity into the Quarter. If so, it does not really affect our reading of the stories. When delivered by a preacher to ready believers, myth by literature is still myth.

In "Brother Rabbit Gets the Provisions," famine has struck the neighborhoods; in "Cutta Cord-La" it is the hardest of hard times; and in "Aunt Tempy's Story" the leaves on the trees "look like dey gwine ter tu'n ter powder, un de groun' look like it done bin cookt. All de truck w'at de creeturs plant wuz all parched up, un dey wa'n't no crops made nowhars. Dey dunner w'at ter do." What they decide to do in each of these tales is to sell members of their families for the price of some corn meal. In the first tale Brer Rabbit and Brer Wolf agree to sell their mammies; in the second they agree to murder and sell their gran'mammies; and in the third Brer Rabbit and now Brer Fox will sell their wives and children. That is, Brer Wolf and Brer Fox will commit these unnatural crimes; Brer Rabbit, having slipped his own kin to safety, will proceed to trick his coconspirators out of their ill-gotten gains.

In the first and third stories the trick is the famous horse-tails-in-the-mud swindle: having duped Brer Wolf into running a footless errand—and Brer Fox in the third story having gone off on one of his own—Brer Rabbit hides the wagon of provisions bought with the blood money, cuts off the horses' tails, and plants them in a mud hole in the road. Brer Wolf and Brer Fox find him there, hanging onto the tails, bawling for the others to help before horses, wagons, and provisions sink into the mire forever. Brer Wolf comes up with the two tails for his exertions and goes home chagrined, while Brer Rabbit "git all de vittles, en he aint hatter sell he old mammy n'er." Brer Fox goes berserk in the mud hole and drops dead trying to raise the phantom wagon. In the middle story, having helped Brer Wolf eat up the goods bought with his gran'mammy's carcass, Brer Rabbit hides his own gran'mammy in a coconut tree, where he feeds her by means of a basket that can be raised and lowered by the cord of the story's title. Brer Wolf, disguising his voice as Brer Rabbit's, calls to her to raise him up, but Gran'mammy is not fooled and the old boy must resort to having a blacksmith sear his throat with a red-hot poker to alter his tone. Luckily Brer Rabbit happens by just as Gran'mammy is hauling up the now successful wolf; he calls out to her, and with a cry of "Cutta cord-la!" she sends Brer Wolf plummeting to his death.

To locate whatever it is about these tales that might be a vestige of Africa, where famines are a reality, or of Africa by way of the Bible, we must go back to the tone that is set for them in the first, when Brer Wolf and Brer Rabbit agree to fill their bellies by selling their mothers. Two events in this story bear notice that are not elsewhere found in *Uncle Remus*; the one I would guess to be historically recent, the other older, perhaps originating in a tribal taboo. The first is a little confrontation on the road as Brer Wolf and Brer Rabbit are driving Brer Wolf's wagon to town with his mammy on board disguised as a sack of corn. They meet a man. The man, who has no name, does not reappear in the tale and plays no part in its resolution, inquires where they are going, and the two reply:

> *Gwine 'long down ter town,*
> *Wid a bag er co'n fer ter sell;*
> *We aint got time fer ter stop en talk,*
> *Yit we wish you mighty well!*

Now, ordinarily the brers do not cross paths with Mr. Man in these tales unless he is there specifically to be duped, and that very infrequently. But this fellow is present merely to be present and to hear their verse. He is not mentioned again. And this leaves us to wonder how such a meeting on the road comes to be in the tale at all. Was it something laid in late in the story's history or a vestige of a more developed and now forgotten sequence? Was it a fragment in Harris's notes that he could not really account for but felt obliged to include? (Its inclusion left him needing a bridge back into the tale, so we find interjected at this point an exchange between Uncle Remus and the little boy on the beasts' "constant a-gwine on dat a-way" in verse.) The odd thing is, if you sing the brers' reply—more or less to the tune of, say, "Camptown Races"—it sounds remarkably like a strut, a cakewalk. So I would make a cautious guess that this is a modern imposition, a bit of jittery burlesque popping up in a myth of prohibition, with Mr. Man as John Law[14] running a wagon-check on two suspicious plantation slaves. There may be an echo, too, though, of something more mysterious, and perhaps biblical. With heaven's retribution yet to come, the brers' "We wish you mighty well" suggests an attempt to deflect the judgement of a higher, and not necessarily human, being, as if—to raise everyone one step in the hierarchy of animate life—two Old Testament sinners about to commit an unnatural act were confounded by meeting an angel on the road and tried to hide behind its expectation of them by being comically obsequious.

Heaven is not fooled, however, and it is not amused. In the next scene its rage is conveyed to the sinners, and to Brer Wolf in particular, by a revolt of nature which as a piece of psychological landscaping is unique in *Uncle Remus*.

> Now, den, dey tuck'n kyar Brer Wolf mammy ter town en sell 'er, en dey start back wid a waggin-load er vittles. De day wuz a-wanin' en de sun wuz a-settin'. De win tuck'n blow up sorter stiff, en de sun look red when she settin'. Dey druv on, en druv on. De win' blow, en de sun shine red. Bimeby, Brer Wolf scrooch up en shiver, en low:
> "Brer Rabbit, I'm a-gittin' mighty cole."
> Brer Rabbit, he laugh en 'low:
> "I'm gittin' sorter creepy myself, Brer Wolf."
> Dey druv on en druv on. Win' blow keen, sun shine red. Brer Wolf scrooch up in little knot. Bimeby he sing out:
> "Brer Rabbit, I'm freezin'! I'm dat cole I dunner w'at ter do!"

It is this scene, so odd for folklore, that feels old to me,[15] while the actual myths, about matters older than history, feel brand-new. The only thing about the tale that is incongruent with the spell of animism blowing through it is that Brer Wolf, having been royally trumped by heaven's agent and King of the Creeturs, Brer Rabbit, escapes with his life. But of course he escapes only as far as the next tale, where gran'mammy rabbit is waiting for him up in that coconut tree.

Tales of the Supernatural

There are fifteen tales of the supernatural in *Uncle Remus*. Two are ghost stories, two involve encounters with the devil, and the rest are witch tales.

Many are told in the more difficult Gullah dialect of the Georgia Sea Islands. Only four — of which "Taily-po" has been mentioned earlier — are Brer Rabbit stories. "Uncle Remus's Wonder Story" (*Daddy Jake*), probably the best-known of the supernatural tales, is a beast fable of sorts but does not concern the brers; nor, regrettably, does it live up to its title. "The Little Boy and His Dogs" from the same collection is arguably the best of the fifteen. More dream than tale, with magic too strong for paraphrase, it tells how a little boy leads two fine ladies to the fork in the road, only to have them turn into panthers, and how is rescued by his dogs Minnyminny Morack and Follerlinsko.

Tales of the Grotesque

The little boy, troubled by the gruesome demise of Brer Wolf's grandmother in "Old Grinny Granny Wolf" (*Nights*), remarks to Uncle Remus, "I don't think Brother Rabbit would burn anybody to death in a pot of boiling water." The old man tries to put him off with a joke, but in the next tale he has to admit, "W'en ole Brer Rabbit git he dander up, he 'uz a monst'us bad man fer ter fool wid." He is indeed. To effect Brer Wolf's comeuppance in "Old Grinny Granny Wolf" he contrives the death of his adversary's crippled, blind, and half-deaf grandmother by talking her into a pot of boiling water as a cure for her ills; donning the old lady's clothes, he then plays dutiful granny to the returned Brer Wolf and tricks his enemy into eating his kin for dinner. This is a very different Brer Rabbit from the dapper fellow famous for tripping up the local bullies. In a handful of such tales Riley comes mighty close himself to being the Old Boy in disguise. Like Loki, the trickster god of the Norse myths, whose mischief when turned to bitter malice brings down the known world, he wreaks more harm than his own salvation warrants.

Clearly Harris was made uneasy by the ferocity of these tales. His solution to their withering effect was to stand Uncle Remus in harm's way. When Brer Rabbit plays a trick on Brer Fox in "Mr. Rabbit Nibbles Up the Butter" (*Songs and Sayings*) and it is the innocent third party, Brer Possum, who loses his life, Harris allows the boy to comment on the cruelty of this, and Uncle Remus to talk him down gently. The old man's bluff throughout the wilder stories is to josh the boy along that it's time to pull out your handkerchief, honey, here comes the sad part, and to conclude each tale with a line or two suggesting that, however ferocious the creatures are, it is according to their nature, and that in this they "got de 'vantage er folks," who ought to know better.

Indeed, while creatures are ferocious, it is only folks who deserve what they get, and a few of these tales do derive their cruelty from being satires of specific human foibles. In "How Old Craney-crow Lost His Head" (*Told By*; "Why Craney-crow Flies Fast") the foolish bird, noticing his brother birds asleep with their heads tucked out of sight and concluding they've taken them off for the night, decides he "don't wanter be out'n de fashion," and at Brer Rabbit's suggestion allows "Doc" Wolf to lop off his pitiful bean so as to keep up. In the sequel story, "Brother Fox Follows the Fashion" (*Told By*), the same fate awaits Brer Fox, who doesn't "like fer ter be laffed at on de count er plain ignunce." And Mrs. Fox, so worried what folks might otherwise have whispered "'bout de tacky Fox fambly," can conclude with more relief than regret as she studies the husband she's just blipped with an axe, "Ole honey look like he dead, but he better be dead dan outer de fashion."

Still, the black comedy of *Uncle Remus* is seldom grand guignol. Harsh, perhaps; unremitting, yes, in Feodor Rojankovsky's sense of telling the truth like a tale and a tale like the truth; but where in many of the tales the narrative might have taken a wholly gruesome turn, what we find instead is a suspenseful restraint and that same delicious tension that makes a tale like Perrault's "Little Red Riding Hood" so enjoyable.[16] The tales that actually threaten to stampede our darker fears are few. And where they do threaten, of course, Uncle Remus is close at hand, ready to inquire "with a great display of solicitude . . . .'Whar'bouts in de tale wuz you tooken sick at?'"

The Little Rabs

Very young children, or their animal surrogates, appear so frequently today in children's books and so much of children's literature is addressed so intimately to them that it is odd to think that barely a century has passed since they first entered story as figures central to their own make-believe. In stories predating *Uncle Remus* they turn up infrequently, and if we claim the fairy tales as exceptions we must in the same breath note that their heroes and heroines are really perceived as being mature enough to set out into the world, whatever their assumed ages. Few are as young as Hansel and Gretel, and in few tales is coming home to resume life with a parent seen as the proper end of the adventure. Cinderella is marriageable; Rapunzel bears an illegitimate child; innumerable Jacks become kings. Something like can be said of Alice or Tom of *The Water Babies* or Pinocchio; they are old enough to take their knocks. Only in a few beast fables do we find children competent to do little in the face of danger but hide from it, and offhand I can think of only "The Wolf and the Seven Little Kids" (in its *Uncle Remus* version in *Nights* this appears as "The Fire Test," and it is the little rabs who are eaten up) and "Little Red Riding Hood" (more beast fable than fairy tale, really) as examples.

It is with two *Uncle Remus* fables of 1880 and 1892 that we see attention beginning its shift to young children in children's story. The tales are "A Story About the Little Rabbits" (*Songs and Sayings*) and "Why Brother Wolf Didn't Eat the Little Rabbits" (*Friends*; "The Fresher the Better"). "De chilluns" are mentioned in four other tales in *Songs and Sayings*; in the opening story, "Uncle Remus Initiates the Little Boy," one of them tumbles in the door "hollerin', 'Oh, ma! Oh, ma! I seed Mr. Fox a comin!'" but it makes only this one walk-on appearance, as do the rabs in two of the other tales. In "The Awful Fate of Mr. Wolf," a fourth story from *Songs and Sayings*, they have edged in a bit from the periphery. "Mighty skittish" when they hear "Brer Wolf go gallopin' by" they are still there at the story's climax when, watching their daddy prepare the old boy's demise, "dey hatter put der han's on der moufs fer ter keep fum laffin'."

What we have in "A Story About the Little Rabbits"—and for the first time of note in make-believe—is just what the title promises us: the very young in their very own story. And it *is* their story, and not just any story, that we are listening to here. It is theirs, not because the tale is a significantly different folk type from "The Wolf and the Seven Little Kids," which it isn't, but because the language being used to describe them has itself taken an attentive and affectionate turn in their direction:

> . . . dey minded der daddy and mammy fum day's een' ter day's een'. W'en ole man Rabbit say "scoot," dey scooted, en w'en ole Miss Rabbit say "scat," dey scatted. Dey did dat. En dey kep' der cloze clean, en dey aint had no smut on der nose needer.

Such "good chilluns," says the story, "allers gits tuck keer on." And indeed a stricture laid down elsewhere by Harris does not quite hold true for this hybrid of beast fable and fairy tale. "De creeturs never had no godm'ers," Uncle Remus tells the little boy in "Brother Rabbit and the Chickens" (*Told By*); "dey des hatter scuffle an' scramble an' git 'long de bes' way dey kin." It's true, the creatures had no godmothers—not like Cinderella's, at least (a story the little boy has just related to Uncle Remus), but Brer Rabbit did have his Mammy-Bammy Big-Money, and in the present tale the little rabs discover they have a friend they did not know they had. Cornered at home by Brer Fox, the rabs have been set three tasks, failing which they will give him the excuse he wants to eat them up. Being too little to solve Brer Fox's conundrums, the rabs "sot down en 'gun ter cry," and it is then they hear "a little bird singin' on top er de house." The bird sings out the solutions and "up dey jump, de little Rabbits did," to confound Brer Fox until "der daddy, he come skippin' in, en de little bird, he flewed away."

The bird, of course, is the magical figure of the helper found in so many fairy tales. It is a first cousin to the little white bird that provides Cinderella with her ball gown in the Grimms' version of that story and to the pigeons and doves that earlier helped her sort out the lentils thrown into the ashes by her stepmother. The helper does not appear otherwise in trickster tales because the trickster must win by his own wits or the tale is pointless. It appears in this tale because the characters are very young children, who haven't the wits to guarantee survival—until of course they're shown that in fact they do.[17]

The second of the two major stories about the little rabbits is, to use the preferable title from *The Favorite Uncle Remus*, "The Fresher the Better."

Like "Brer Coon and the Frogs" it is one of the three or four funniest — and in the interplay of its parts perhaps the most artful — of all the *Uncle Remus* tales. To an adult reader it will really seem to belong more to the grown-ups than to the children; the fun here lies in listening to Brer Wolf and Brer Fox lick their chops and plot their strategy as the little rabs frisk and frolic:

> Brer Wolf look at um en 'low, "Aint dey slick en purty?"
> Brer Fox chuckle, en say, "Oh, I wish you'd hush!"
>
> "You better do de talkin', Brer Wolf, en lemme coax de little Rabs off. I got mo' winnin' ways wid chilluns dan what you is."
> Brer Wolf say, "You can't make gourd out'n punkin, Brer Fox. I ain't no talker. Yo' tongue lots slicker dan mine. I kin bite lots better'n I kin talk. Dem little Rabs don't want no coaxin'; dey wants ketchin' — dat what dey wants."

and in watching Brer Rabbit use a jug of molasses to dupe Brer Wolf into thinking he'd do better to make a meal of Brer Fox. ("What kinder truck dat? Hit sho is good." "Hit's Fox-blood." "How you know?" "I knows what I knows . . . en de fresher 'tis, de better.")

But if the eye of the tale is on the elder brers, we have only to recall the spare lines of Aesop or to consider the various prototypes of a tale like this, in which little rabbits or kids or pigs are featured, to see again how black affections and black English have made the children something more than merely the stock victims of folklore. In retrospect it seems quite natural that for his *Uncle Remus* debut A. B. Frost should have passed over the two likeliest rouges since Carroll's Walrus and Carpenter and chosen to illustrate instead that moment of relief at story's center when the little rabs gather around their daddy in the road. Historically the comic ferocity of the grown-ups is already become a thing of the past. The mood of the future is that fond observance Frost overheard in the tale and pictured for us.

What we have, then, in "The Fresher the Better" and "A Story About the Little Rabbits" is something quite new in make-believe, the first truly affecting portrait of young children in their literature. They run at their own pace, *blickety-blickety* behind the *bookity-bookity* gait of the grown-ups; they are granted the right to cry when things aren't going well, and the moment help is in sight, toting that jug of molasses, all peril is forgotten and it's "Lemme tas'e, daddy! Lemme tas'e, daddy!" Those urchin bodies gathered in the road in their jeans and homespun in Frost's picture of them are, though rabbits, real children, never before seen in make-believe at this tender age outside *Mother Goose* and a few toy books. They are a portrait of the very young that will enable the next generation of storytellers to reimagine children's literature along entirely new lines.

Miz Meadows en de Gals

One feature of animal fantasy distinguishing it from folklore is the presence in the former of a memorable place for the story to happen, while in folklore the place is perfunctory. You cannot map the settlement in which these tales occur, the way you can map Grahame's riverbank, or Milne's hundred-acre wood, or Jansson's Moomin Valley. There is no detail in the text by which to orient the brers' quarters one to the other or to chart the progress of their comeuppances; nor would there be, considering that such tales must serve as well in Virginia and Texas as in Georgia. Harris located Brer Rabbit and his neighbors in the truck patches and woodlots behind a plantation in middle Georgia, but nothing in the tales themselves so restricts them. They were local to every corner of the South; the absence of any interior geography follows from their nature as folklore. At least we can say this — theoretically it is true; but in actuality there is something mappable in the stories after all — a named place in the settlement that, providing a geographical center, localizes events to itself.

An actual map of "de neighborhoods" is impossible, but, by focusing on this one identifiable dot, we can almost make out, along the periphery of our vision, the details of some storybook American township emerging — a Yoknapatawpha County of the animal world. The place in question is not the plantation where Uncle Remus spins his tales — plantations go unmentioned in the tales as Harris retold them; it is not the town to which the brers sometimes bring their produce, and it is not the house of any of the brers, for we do not know where those houses are. But it is a house (the tales suggest it to be not more than a few miles from any one brer's quarters), and it is an odd sort of house indeed to be turning up in a collection of beast fables: in it live a number of congenial women given to entertaining the brers "same ez a town man." An amiable miscegenation of women and creeturs obtains in this lore as the most natural society in the world. In tale after tale one or another brer will take a notion to "drap in en see Miss Meadows . . . en shake han's wid de gals, en set dar, smokin' his seegyar" while the gals, "dey talk, en dey sing, en dey play on de pianner," and "laff en giggle same like gals does dese days."

The residence of Miss Meadows and the gals is the great gathering place, the social watering-hole, for the beasts of *Uncle Remus*. When there is a frolic in the settlement or molasses in the pot for a candy-pull, a brer will "fetch his flank one swipe wid 'is tongue en he'd be comb up" and down to Miss Meadows's he'd go. There may be trouble at home — no vittles for the little brers, a nagging wife — but down at Miss M's he can set out on the porch with the ladies and get "ter runnin' on talkin' mighty biggity." Miss Meadows and the gals are that audience dreamed of by every thirteen-year-old boy with a boast in his pocket. Their admiration gives every trick and strut its extra kick. When Brer Rabbit and Brer Tarrypin run their famous race, Miss Meadows and the gals are there to witness it. When Brer Rabbit tricks Brer Fox into becoming his riding horse, Miss Meadows and the gals are there to "praise up de pony." Their laughter is sporting and affectionate. "Yer we is a-gigglin en a-gwine on scan'lous," says Miss Meadows, "yit hit done come ter mighty funny pass, sez I, 'ef you can't run on en laff 'fo' home folks."

There are limits to the laughter, of course. When Brer Fox is reported to have called Brer Tarrypin "Stinkin' Jim" it's a wink and "Oh, my! You year dat, gals?" and the ladies "make great wonderment how Brer Fox kin talk dat a way 'bout nice man like Brer Tarrypin." But when the boys start cutting up each other on the premises and the furniture, too, the boss lady of *Uncle Remus* "done put 'er foot down, she did, en say dat w'en dey come ter 'er place dey hatter hang up a flag er truce at de front gate en 'bide by it." And the brers do abide by it. The one thing no brer wants is "losing' his stannin' at Miss Meadows'."

Who was this housemother who is said to be unique in folklore, and how did she ever get herself and her company of gals incorporated into a body of beast fables out of Africa? Harris's explanation never went much beyond Uncle Remus's "Don't ax me, honey. She wuz in de tale, Miss Meadows en de gals wuz, en de tale I give you like hit were gun ter me." Either he did not know, or, if he did (which I suspect is the case), he chose to keep it to himself. Writing his first illustrator, F. S. Church, that he "cannot pretend to know what is meant by Miss Meadows," he adds, as if to be rid of the subject, "She plays a minor part in the entire series"—and this Harris, the storyteller, must have known was a misrepresentation of the spirit of the work, and even of the actual count. Miss Meadows is mentioned or prominent in a third of the tales in *Songs and Sayings*, eleven in *Nights*, and can be found here and there in later volumes—not a great number out of the 183 finally collected, but as many as any of the groups described in the first part of this article comprise, and enough to establish her by numbers alone as one of the presiding figures of the work.[18] "One of the greatest and most wonderful things he ever did was to create [*sic*] the character of Miss Meadows and the gals," eulogized one of Harris's literary friends years after his death; "I think it is the subtlest, most whimsical creation ever accomplished out of the imagination. There is nothing like it anywhere else it the literature of the world." Other readers were no less taken with Miss Meadows—*Uncle Remus* having been in its day the kind of book to raise family feeling among strangers, much as *Winnie-the-Pooh* and *The Lord of the Rings* have done in ours. "One thing I want to know badly," Kipling wrote Harris in 1895, "but from what nature-myth or *what* come 'Miss Meadows and the girls?' Where did they begin—in whose mind? What do you think they are?"[19]

If she and her gals had to have sprung from a nature myth, very possibly the root truth of their existence, certainly saying so afforded Harris an agreeable way out of his quandary. And so to Church's suggestion that "perhaps they mean just *Nature*, in which case I should depict them as pretty girls in simple costumes," Harris cautiously replies, "your conception will give to the sketches a poetical color . . . which will add vastly to whatever interest they may have for people of taste. [N.B.] By all means let Miss Meadows figure as Nature in the shape of a beautiful girl in a simple but not unpicturesque costume. As it is your own conception, I know you will treat the young lady tenderly . . . "

Church portrays Miss Meadows again in *Nights with Uncle Remus*, once in the frontispiece, where she appears as a slim Georgia Venus embowered with her swain, Brer Rabbit, in a sort of valentine of boughs and flowers, and again in the thirteenth tale, where she appears, picnicking with Brer Rabbit, as King Deer's daughter. The implication, vis-à-vis the nature myth, that Miss Meadows descended from this "nice young lady of quality" is pure speculation, but an agreeable enough image that Harris adopted it for his other fictions. To Jincy, the half-witted child of nature in his first novel, *Sister Jane*, he gives the surname Meadows, as befitting a boy who can whistle the birds from the bushes; and in *Little Mr. Thimblefinger*, the first of his five books written expressly for children, we find Miss Meadows telling the children who are listening to her and Mr. Rabbit's stories, "wherever you find mountains, hills, and rivers, there you'll find the Meadows family." Wherever, that is, save anywhere else in folk story. The idea that Miss Meadows is Nature does not seem susceptible of proof in the end.

How *do* you get from a King Deer's daughter to a Miss Meadows and a house full of women living by the side of the road? Oral transmission tends to conserve, not invent, and here, on the one hand, we have a simple courtship story in which Brer Rabbit can once more display his skill at outfoxing Brer Fox, and on the other hand we clearly have something more complex—a *mise en scène* with a social history. We are left suspecting, too, that folklorists are predisposed to find mythical origins in any character they can't otherwise account for, much as archeologists will label as ritual object any artifact whose function they can't identify. The very element— Miss Meadows—put forward by Brookes as "the most convincing evidence . . . in proof of the folklore element throughout the series" appears as well to be the most literary element in the tales, the part most likely to have been embellished by Harris in contradistinction to his claim about the tales that "Not one of them is cooked, and not one nor any part of one is an invention of mine. They are all genuine folklore tales."

To account fully for Miss Meadows and her girls, we have to imagine, I think, either that Harris added something to their portrait or that during the antebellum years there had lived among the slaves of middle Georgia a black Dickens (an appealing idea which, while improbable, would account for characters who are more than stock figures from folklore yet less than fully realized literary personages). Suspecting Harris, we needn't impugn his honesty or his faithfulness to the tales in speculating about the origins of Miss Meadows. Retelling a story is a subtle business. The Grimms are known to have reworked the tales they collected, and Italo Calvino in the introduction to his *Italian Folk Tales* advertises the virtues, even the necessity, of doing so. Nor does an author always understand what he is doing as he does it, particularly an author who can think in dialect and has become one with the tales he is telling. When Harris claims the tales are genuine and not one of them cooked, it is not clear he meant anything more than that he set down the characters and events as they were given to him; as to detail and dialogue, we know he had to supply these to many tales, having had only the barest of outlines to work from. The tale, then, would be genuine, but its character would owe something to Harris's elaboration, however closely he had worked to the structure and flavor of the original. This becomes manifest in the later tales especially, which are three and four times as long as those in the earlier collections. As B. A. Botkin characterizes Harris's work in *A Treasury of American Folklore*, "his renditions . . . are perhaps more properly literature than folklore" — which would account possibly for the confusion, quoted above, as to who "created" Miss Meadows.

It suggests to me also that Harris may not only have put something into, he may have taken something out of, his portrait of Miss Meadows. in a footnote to "The Fate of Mr. Jack Sparrow" in *Songs and Sayings*, he writes, "It may be well to state that there are different versions of all the stories — the shared narrators of the mythology of the old plantation adapting themselves with ready tact to the years, tastes, and expectations of their juvenile audiences." Following tradition in this sense could explain his similar remark to F. S. Church that the book make an appeal to "people of taste."

What was there of Miss Meadows in the tales originally, then, that Harris or an apocryphal black Dickens had to work with and that Harris might have wanted to soft-pedal to a genteel public? The first reading that occurs to a modern student of *Uncle Remus* is, I think, substantially correct: Miss Meadows is the madame and the gals the merchandise of a sporting house. How else are we to account for a house full of women with no visible means of support in the years before Emancipation? Here are the piano and the frolics with brers who continue to come "courtin'," even when married and with chilluns at home. Here is the story "Mr. Terrapin Shows His Strength" (*Songs and Sayings*; "Take up the Slack"), in which Miss Meadows's bed-cord is loaned out for a tug-of-war, with its joke, which Harris allows to stand, "In dem days, Miss Meadows's bed-cord would a hilt a mule." Why else would a woman's bed need to be so resilient save as a place of business? The tales are occasionally frank about the brers' private lives: "Miss Brune wuz Brer B'ar's ole 'oman, en Miss Brindle wuz his gal. Dat w'at dey call um in dem days." ("The End of Mr. Bear," *Songs and Sayings*). And I think it is safe to assume that it is not into polite society that Brer Rabbit is sending Brer Fox when he asks him "fer ter take his place en go down ter Miss Meadows's en have a nice time wid de gals," and the tale tells us, "Brer Fox, he in fer dem kinder pranks" ("Mr. Fox Gets into Serious Business," *Songs and Sayings*.)[20]

These were trickster tales, after all, not bedtime stories; the brers are the neighborhood rascals, not stuffed toys. And it follows that Miss Meadows might as likely be the local bawd as Mother Nature, and her gals in better voice off the piano stool than on it. A suggestive distinction is made between the brers, who hang about cadging free meals, and "dese yer town chaps, w'at you see come out ter Harmony Grove meetin'-house." The town men we can easily suppose the paying customers who kept Miss Meadows in business, whereas the brers, though home folks, and lively company, were freeloaders and sometimes more trouble than they were worth:

> Dey wuz dat flirtatious dat Miss Meadows en de gals don't see no peace fum one week een' ter de udder. Chuseday wuz same as Sunday, en Friday wuz same as Chuseday, en hit come down ter pass w'en Miss Meadows 'ud have chicken-fixin's fer dinner, in 'ud drap Brer Fox en Brer Possum, en w'en she'd have fried greens in 'ud pop ole Brer Rabbit, twel 'las' Miss Meadows, she tuck'n tell de gals dat she be dad-blame ef she gwineter keep no tavvum. So dey fix it up 'mong deyse'f, Miss Meadows en de gals did, dat de nex' time de gents call, dey'd gin um a game. De Gents, dey wuz a-co'tin', but Miss Meadows, she don't wanter marry none un um, en needer does de gals, en likewise dey don't wanter have um pesterin' roun'. Las', one Chuseday, Miss Meadows, she tole um dat ef dey come down ter her house de nex' Sat'day evenin', de whole caboodle un um 'ud go down de road a piece, whar dar wuz a big flint rock, en de man w'at could take a sludge-hammer en knock de dus' out'n dat rock, he wuz de man w'at ud git de pick er de gals.

In his introduction to *Nights with Uncle Remus*, Harris tells how for two hours one night he swapped tales with a crowd of men in a railyard outside Atlanta; it is unlikely that such a group, telling the above tale, "How Mr. Rabbit Succeeded in Raising a Dust" (*Songs and Sayings*), would be telling each other quite the same story as the mammy up at the big house with the master's child in her lap. In the railyard the euphemism "marry" would not have been the word that brought on the laughs. And Harris is being just playful enough at the end of the tale to justify our thinking him not only party to the joke but tweaking his morally upright narrator — and himself — as well, for censoring it.

> Brer Rabbit got one er de gals, en dey had a weddin' en a big infa'r.
> Which of the girls did the Rabbit marry? asked the little boy, dubiously.
> I did year tell un 'er name, replied the old man, with a great affection of interest, but look like I done gone en fergit it off'n my mine. Ef I don't disremember, he continued, hit wuz Miss Molly Cottontail, en I speck we better let it go at dat.

Two other passages suggest that Harris knew which side of the tracks could claim Miss Meadows as its own. Both appear in *Nights*. In "Brother Rabbit's Love-Charm," told in the Gullah dialect of the Sea Islands, the narrator Daddy Jack is thrown off his pace by an interruption from Uncle Remus:

> "One tam, B'er Rabbit is bin lub one noung leddy."
> "Miss Meadows, I 'speck," suggested Uncle Remus, as the old African paused to rub his chin.
> "'E no lub Miss Meadows nuttin' 't all!" exclaimed Daddy Jack, emphatically.
> "'E bin lub turrer noung leddy fum dat. 'E is bin lub werry nice noung leddy."

This can be read, of course, simply as one storyteller demanding elbow room from another: you tell your stories, Uncle Remus, and I'll tell mine. But there is something else here, I think. Daddy Jack knows who Miss Meadows is, and in his indignation he appears to be making a distinction between young ladies who are nice and young ladies who are not nice, with Miss Meadows understood to be among the latter. This understanding is supported by a passage in the earlier tale "Brother Wolf Says Grace." Uncle Remus is telling the story here to Daddy Jack and the little boy. Aunt Tempy, the housekeeper, has decided to listen in:

> "Well, den," said Uncle Remus, "we ull des huddle up yer en see w'at 'come er Brer Rabbit w'en ole Brer Wolf kotch 'im. In dem days," he continued, looking at Daddy Jack and smiling broadly, "de creeturs wuz constant gwine a-courtin'. Ef 'twa'n't Miss Meadows en de gals dey wuz flyin' 'roun', hit uz Miss Motts.[21] Dey wuz constant a-courtin'. En 'twa'n't none er dish yer 'Howdy-do-ma'm-I-'speck-I-better-be-gwine,' n'er. Hit 'uz go atter brekkus en stay twel atter supper."

Uncle Remus's broad smile to Daddy Jack in Aunt Tempy's presence looks mighty like a knowing smile to me. "Howdy-do-ma'm-I-'speck-I-better-be-gwine" is too close to the vulgar "Wham, bam, thank-you, ma'am" not to be its first cousin,[22] and the breakfast to supper hours, mentioned in other tales as well, are an odd time of day to be paying calls, especially on a "Chuseday," unless you're courting a whore. These are the profession's off-hours, when the boyfriends come rascaling around, and a brer can "set dar, smokin' his seegyar same ez a town man."

Harris would have had compelling reason to play down such material, even as he tried to honor its integrity as folklore. He was himself reticent and modest and not, we gather from his biography, insensible of the sanctity of women, one of his day's more exalted proprieties. His first consideration in muting Miss Meadows, though, would have been the response of a child in the room—both the little boy in the frame story, whose curiosity caused Harris to stand Uncle Remus in harm's way, and the child reading or listening to the book itself, over whose impressions Harris would have no control once the book had left his hands. Thinking of these child readers, and perhaps too of the "people of taste" who bought them their books, Harris went so far in *Little Mr. Thimblefinger* as to change the Miss in Miss Meadows to Mrs., even though here she and Mr. Rabbit are much too ancient for a frolic and are cohabiting just "for company's sake." Along with the chivalrous manners of the day went an almost morbid insistence on the innocence of children, the sanctity of childhood. Harris's friend Eugene Field, who would lullaby his Wynken, Blynken, and Nod down a river of crystal light and into a sea of dew, could publish, for semiprivate consumption, a sentimental joke in verse (*Little Willie*, 1895) in which a boy with a loose bladder climbs into his father's bed and inundates the old man "in seas of brine . . . Yet there he lay, so peaceful like,—/ God bless his curly head!" Even urine could be holy water, if it was a child's pee. Nineteenth-century children's writers thought nothing of dispensing violence in their stories, and plenty of it, but sex, unsublimated and unsentimentalized, was out.

Whatever Harris may or may not have abridged of her character, certainly Miss Meadows will appear wholesome to children in the tales as we know them. There is no more evidence of hookery here than I have given, and what little there is is so arguable that it has never even been argued. In 1948 the editors of *The Favorite Uncle Remus* did not hesitate to greet their child readers with a sociable "Miss Meadows and the gals cordially invite you to meet Brer Rabbit, Brer Fox, Brer Tarrypin, and their other friends. . . . " That house by the side of the road suggests a place where the brers can gather peaceably under the tutelage of a good woman, and no more.

What we may be losing by not reading the obvious from Miss Meadows, however, is our full sense of what these few dozen inclusions might have meant to adult listeners on the porches and in the railyards of the antebellum South and, in the years immediately after the war. It is interesting, for example, that Harris could find "few Negroes who will acknowledge to a stranger that they know anything of these legends." It is interesting but not surprising. Prisoners don't ordinarily share their jokes with their jailers, and certainly not if the jokes are at the jailers' expense. These were tales told on the sly, a private literature for slaves and a few white children. They gave a free place to live together, at least in story, to a people who must otherwise live kenneled like dogs in other people's backyards. They are a literature of captivity, of irreverent reports passed from one prisoner to the next. Like other captives in history, the blacks created their lamentations and their satires. The lamentations we hear in spirituals and blues; the satire, in the trickster tales.

The tales are satirical, of course, in the sport they make of the strong in behalf of the weak but clever, or of the foolish, who lose their heads for wanting to be in the fashion. But the real satire in these tales lies in the language itself. It is the master's English, but inflected in such a way as to make it, like Brer Rabbit, as big as life and twice as natural. Black English is the sound of constricted souls insisting on life, their life, through every syllable. It becomes a way of knowing yourself by the way you speak another man's lingo, when his lingo has been forced on you. What is being satirized by the language of these tales, ultimately, is the stultification of a life lived in standard English.

Still, this is satire by indirection, when we might reasonably expect to find something more overt in the tales, a pointed finger mocking the master behind his back. There may have been such moments in black lore, of course, moments that have not survived. We know of his folklore only what the Negro, looking ahead to freedom and not back to slavery, elected to remember and to concede to the white collector. But even so, there should be a trace of resistance in the tales—the resistance of laughter—and such a vestige does survive, I think, in the Miss Meadows stories. She and the gals I read to be a parody of white gentility, not a slavish imitation of it, and thus itself the object of the mockery, but a laugh in its face. There is something clearly societal, not fabulous, understood in "Mr. Terrapin Appears upon the Scene" (*Songs and Sayings*; "Stinkin' Jim") when Brer Rabbit hustles a rambunctious Brer Fox out of Miss Meadows's, telling him "dat ef he didn't go 'long home en stop playin' his pranks on 'spectable folks . . . I'd take 'im out and th'ash 'im"— or in "How Brother Fox Failed to Get His Grapes" (*Nights*; "All The Grapes in the Neighborhood") when Miss Meadows announces to the girls, "I lay I done wid Brer Fox, kaze you can't put no pennunce in deze yer men-folks. . . . Yer de dinner bin done dis long time, en we bin a-waitin' lak de quality"—and how we read these allusions to polite society must depend on how a slave would have understood them, which to my understanding would have been as an inside joke. So that when we hear in the first of these two tales, "'Law, Brer Tarrypin,' sez Miss Meadows, sez she, 'you don't mean ter say he cussed?' sez she, en den de gals hilt der fans up 'fo 'der faces," we are not laughing at Miss Meadows for putting on airs but with her at the ever so delicate feelings of the white women who do. It is *her* joke, and she and her gals are themselves never every far in these moments of affection from the release shared by the listeners to the tale, when "dey holler and laff fit ter kill deyse'f."

The brers never laugh at Miss Meadows behind her back, as they do at each other; they hold her in awe, rather, and not, I think, merely for her services, but because unlike anyone else in slave society she is free, independent, and bringing home the bacon. It is true that light-skinned blacks were known to affect white dress and manners (see, for example, the several instances described in *Uncle Tom's Cabin*), and literature has always found useful the propensity of whores to ape society. But Miss Meadows is altogether too agreeable, too much at the heart of this conspiracy of story, to be the butt of even its most lighthearted jokes. She and the tellers of the tales are in league—they are "home folks"—and their humor is directed outward from the private circle, spoofing a common enemy. The point need never have been made outright that a black whore is a better woman than the master's lady; it would have been recognized by all who listened. But the joke and the satirical thrust of the tales is lost if we do not assume Miss Meadows to have been a whore.

Let me finish with the lady by attempting briefly to reconcile her putative role as a vehicle of satire with the idea that she is Nature. Earlier I said that we must imagine how oral transmission could get us from King Deer's daughter, a "nice young lady of quality," to Miss Meadows, the whore, and remarked that such an evolution did not seem susceptible of proof. As an exception to this I would suggest a possible, and purely speculative, transition through a variant telling of the famous race between Brer Rabbit and Brer Tarrypin. There are several variants in Negro lore—Harris reports one in the introduction to *Songs and Sayings*, a race between B'er Deer and B'er

Cooter for the hand of a lady, and another from the Creole in his introduction to *Nights*, in which to the victor goes the hand in marriage of one Mamzel Calinda. Of more interest, however, is the variant discussed in the article "Folklore of the Southern Negroes" by William Owens in *Lippincott's Magazine*, December, 1877.[23] It was this piece that set Harris to collecting the tales he had first heard as a boy. In the Owens variation "Buh Rabbit and Buh Frog are admirers of the beautiful Miss Dinah, and try their best to win her. The lady likes them both, but not being permitted to marry both, she resolves to make her choice depend upon the result of a foot-race . . . the goal for the winner is to be a place in her lap." The story then proceeds as it does in *Uncle Remus*, resolving itself about the same trick. Here, though, the frog sings out as he wins the race, "I beat you there, I beat you here:/I've beat you back to Miss Dinah's lap!" We could interpret this phrase as denoting a place name, of course, or the corruption of one: in the same way that we use the words lip, arm, shoulder, toe, and so on to describe geographical features, we might also use the word lap. What is of more significance here, however, is the appearance of a metaphor equating marriage with a lady's anatomy—as lyrical, and not as coy, a euphemism in this setting as that of the maid in *Mother Goose*, now expurgated, who required her suitor to "produce a little Ore,/'E'er I make a little Print in your Bed, Bed, Bed." Produce a little ore, win the race, bridle the fox, and that place in the lady's lap is yours.

What in the story of King Deer's daughter is as vague as the happily-ever-after of fairy tales is here made specific. We see what we see nowhere else in these stories: a sexual reference attaching itself to a tale of courtship. By this one phrase alone—assuming that tales evolve much the same way everywhere—it is possible to reconstruct the passage from King Deer's daughter to Miss Meadows and her house of gals by the side of the road. At the time these tales were being told, in Europe the godmother/helper figure of the fairy tales was becoming a literary personage by taking reference to a variety of pagan, literary, and biblical sources, out of which thought in the minds of two generations came Andersen's Snow Queen, Kingsley's Irish Woman, MacDonald's North Wind, and Collodi's Blue Fairy. Just so, though still at the level of oral transmission, Miss Meadows could quickly have evolved from King Deer's daughter—a generation or two would suffice with Miss Dinah as intermediary—by taking reference to a personage known to the tellers, the local whore. For once you have fixed the sexual image of the lap in the tale, it is only natural that some teller will associate it with the nearest lap of any renown; and once the whore is named, you have created a social milieu whose implications will begin to inform the story. Allow a Miss Meadows, or a Miss Dinah or Miss Motts, to fulfill her desire to "marry" *both* the contestants in the race, in other words, and you have created a place in the tales where all the brers will want to gather. This lap of luxury becomes the central *mise en scène* of the series, and the tales you are telling are no longer simple fables but social comedies.

Miss Meadows would not be the first whore subsumed within children's literature. There is Jumping Joan in *Mother Goose*, who when no one is with her is always alone, and Maid Marian of *Robin Hood*, who in a development perhaps analogous to that of Miss Meadows entered the ballads via the May Games of medieval England "a smyrking wenche indeed."[24] In children's story these Magdalenes are washed clean. There is little left of the sporting house in *Uncle Remus*; whatever happened to Miss Meadows, whether Harris bowdlerized her or she had become suppressed naturally, her house and the gals now connote — well, sociability. Mayhem is rarely a feature of any episode over which she presides. The brers display their skills and wit — a race, a tug-of-war, a competition to see who can win a gal by tricking the dust from a rock — and there are no tricks to the death. These congenial tales have the air of something that is happening not in a ferocious past but today, when the witness of women calls for better behavior and we hold ourselves accountable for our actions. With Miss Meadows and the gals looking on, the talking animal trades in his wilder inclinations for the pleasure of playing to the gallery. Civilized without yet being emasculated, he is ready to enter the nursery.

4

I do not want to overstate the case for *Uncle Remus* — my sole subject here being children's story — but I do think its impact on English-speaking culture between 1880 and the 1950s, both in and out of literature, is greater than would ordinarily be conceded to any book both accessible to children and hugely popular. Greater and also difficult to assess: the books appealed to so many readers from so many levels of society and for so many reasons, and spilled over into the culture so generally, that tracing their aftereffects would be as delicate a business as digging branch lightning out of a sand dune. It is easy enough to demonstrate their influence on popular forms of entertainment, quite another thing to unearth any solid influence on serious literature. Yet, given its presence in literate households, *Uncle Remus* must have helped set the imaginative terms of their knowing for several generations of readers (to borrow a phrase from Roger Sale), and so I think it must be reckoned a contributing, if unlikely, cause of modernism — helping to change, for example, the way that we speak in prose and the way that fiction came to be organized in the first decade of the century.

But clearly this shift of emphasis in how we read the world and retell it in turn is most easily seen where the main energy of *Uncle Remus* was discharged, in children's story. Tales of make-believe before 1881 were variations played out all on a human theme; their heroes were young adults or children sent into the world to be put at physical and spiritual risk and rewarded, usually, with the honorific "grown-up." With *Uncle Remus* a new cast was brought on stage, and all that changed. Our perception of story changed, and our perception of how time passes, and our appreciation of how much of our life is a life in the world and how much a passage through it. Before *Uncle Remus*, story was a curtain rising on our expectations and setting again when the tale was done with us. We fell with Alice down the rabbit hole and woke with her at dream's end, to say good-bye. However resonant her adventures in Wonderland, they were a singular experience in our minds. They were singular because we each perceive ourself to be a singularity in the world, one sensibility heeding its own progress towards the grave, and reflexively we look to art for news of our fellow travelers. But with *Uncle Remus*, or any open-ended saga, we can break free of this habit of imagining, to perceive ourselves members in good standing of the community that will survive us. If our own lives, our singular stories, are inexorably falling off into the future, here, in the serial, duration and death are an illusion: we are invited to live awhile where time is arrested and the world peopled, unchanged, forever.

How this shift in our response to story came about becomes clearer, perhaps, when we go beyond what story meant to the slave and look at what it could *not* mean to him. And what it could not mean to him was freedom — the freedom to go where he would like to go in his imagination and to be what he would like to be. Before the modernism of Kafka and Beckett this freedom, or the promise of it, was the given of almost all Western literature, however pessimistic this or that work may otherwise have been about man's free will and his pursuit of happiness.

The slave stories of *Uncle Remus* are precursors of modernism in this one sense, then: they were not, they could not be, anything like the European model of popular story, which from the fairy tale to the novels of Scott and Dickens had taken the form of the romance. This type of story, which begins in Western civilization with *The Odyssey* and continues on the cheap today, a slave simply hasn't the wherewithal to tell. There are no heroic exploits in his storypack to pull out for the amusement of his own or his master's children. The man can have no dreams of glory to relate when he knows that "sold South" will be the extent of his travels. There will be no embryo Robin Hoods gestating in his lore, no Sinbads cruising his seas, no Jacks setting out to slay giants and win a kingdom. A slave cannot send a corn-rowed Alice to argue some sense from the nonsense of the master's world or imagine a soul unfolding as that world works on the instincts of a Pinocchio. A black Pinocchio does not grow up to be a real boy; he grows up to be the master's "boy." The only kingdoms he can hope to gain are Canada or Kingdom Come; the only giants he can hope to slay are hunger, fear, and pain. Little in his inherited stock of images from Africa and nothing in his life as a captive would lead the slave to dream such dreams or tell such tales. A Robert Louis Stevenson is free to contemplate his possibilities, walk out of his life, and reappear aboard some westward-sailing ship, the man of his choice. But a slave can do no such thing, and his kind of story will be different. The hero he imagines for himself must stay put, like himself, and survive in place. Never mind the keys to any kingdom but the last; the rewards he will conjure up will be a decent supper and the victory of getting through the day.

In celebrating those who must beat the odds wherever fate has made them resident, however, the slave storyteller has one great advantage over the roving ego of the romantic looking to wrest a story from his contest with the world: the slave is immune to the pathos that underwrites all such dreams of glory. Romanticism is a solitary sport, and the slave's life is of necessity communal. The romantic hero is born an orphan and dies alone, having lived to rewrite the world in his image. The slave's hero is born to the community, its legitimate son, and, being one with the community, is immortal. Black storytellers fell into this immortality of communal laughter over solitary tears by simply, but with genius, making the best imaginative use of the terms of their bondage. Stepping back, so to speak, into the woods and swamps surrounding the plantation, they could imagine themselves in another, a more natural, "neighborhood" and let their minds wander — "studyin' en laffin'" and getting even — down the same paths and through the same silences as the fox and the rabbit.

When you have gained at least the stealthy freedom a fox or a rabbit enjoys, you can find in the dangers of slave life an object for play, and before long you will be building an imaginable life in the midst of an unimaginable one. Become a rabbit running free through the neighborhoods, and what began as a compensation for your hardships can take on a life of its own. And the more you talk about your dream self and share him with the neighbors, the field hands, the children, the more you will warm to the game and gain speed, until you have outrun the master's English into an exuberance of your own, a verbal release from having had to talk like a nigger all day. As he gains in velocity, your hare takes on the weight of reality, and you, too, when the master says you are dirt, will emerge from this course of story as big as life and twice as natural, your secret self having attained by imaginative acceleration the weight of a man who lived before the slave time and will live long after it.

This disclosure of *Uncle Remus*, that a people so confined could tell stories so exuberant, proved a happy discovery for certain readers at the turn of the century who were themselves looking for a release into some new order of available reality. What these readers shared, Kipling excepted, was what the slaves had shared and what freed blacks continued to share: an immunity to the glory of empire building and an unfamiliarity with that ghostly emotion that underwrites all tales of romance, the pathos of the dying fall. Colonialism, after all, becomes, however you play it, a glorious bore, and worse, a burden of guilt, having led only to more slaves. The idea of empire was going bankrupt even in Kipling's day. And the dying fall, whether one is dying for love or for country, what is it but another way of saying, they'll be sorry when I'm dead? Unless of course you happen to survive your adventures in the world, in which case you must either come home to puzzle out the remainder of your life or else end up some adulterous sot in the outback, awaiting your Somerset Maugham. So it is no wonder that a book like *Uncle Remus* would have had great appeal for certain readers at the close of the century, as the terms of romance literature became less and less plausible.

Inevitably, many of these readers would be women. A few writers like Jean Ingelow, in *Mopsa the Fairy*, or Dinah Mulock Craik, in *The Little Lame Prince*, had in earlier decades fallen gracefully into the rhythms of the muse romance, but I suspect that like any author, male or female, they often wrote such books because the epic fairy tale was the prevailing available mode for storytelling. Of necessity the heroes these women dreamed up to see the world in their stead were boys, not girls. For a woman to leave home unescorted at all still meant, even in fiction, putting on pants and slipping out the door in the dead of night, pretending it was all a dream. To make the hero of the fantasy a girl, as Mrs. Molesworth does in *The Cuckoo Clock* and *The Tapestry Room*, meant attempting nothing bumptious but casting a spell of poetic reverie over your travels into other realms. There is little written by women of the period that is not in keeping with the classic division of children's literature into girls' books and boys' books: domestic introversion for the one, worldly extroversion for the other; *The Secret Garden* for the girls, *Treasure Island* for the boys. By and large, women writers of the nineteenth century, like Louisa May Alcott and the early Frances Hodgson Burnett, accepted their condition as the given of their fiction even as they strained against it. Domestic realism became such an enforced habit of imagining that even a twentieth-century fantasist like E. Nesbit found herself in better voice spelling out the domestic groundwork for the fantasy than in imagining the fantasy itself. Her inventions are nowhere near as interesting as the little conversations she devises for getting her children from one scene to the next.

Needless to say, this is a simplistic portrait of some of the women who wrote for children around the time of *Uncle Remus*, but it should suffice to show how a reader like Beatrix Potter might have responded to the exuberant disclosure of the work, seeing a parallel between the plight of black American slaves and her own constrained existence as the daughter of a starchy upper-middle-class family for whom schooling and a profession were nothing she need worry her little head over. In the next, Beatrix Potter's, chapter of this book, I want to show how she found in *Uncle Remus* a way of releasing the fantasy latent in her uneventful life—how *Uncle Remus* revealed that stories fit for readers to read could be made of such modest stuff as she had at hand.

This message was welcome news as well to a number of men of the period who found themselves geographically and emotionally distanced from a popular culture that, when not fatuously reinventing fairies, was metaphorically forever heading West. For Kenneth Grahame, Thornton Burgess, Howard Garis and, later, A. A. Milne, the reality of make-believe lay—as it does with young children—less in the haunted past or some unconquered elsewhere than in the present and the local. These writers, when they dreamed, saw the world from the point of view of a six-year-old—often with sophisticated embellishments but nonetheless looking up at the world from below and out at the world from a recalled center of childlike perception. For them the contemporary taste for the sentimental lullabies of Eugene Field, as he looked back on childhood and lied for our tears, or the quasi-religious bathos of Oscar Wilde's fairy tales, were poor substitutes for the active pleasures of making believe; the calling-all-boys dreams of glory of a Howard Pyle or an N. C. Wyeth, with their nostalgic King Arthur and costume-party buccaneers, were romance too much degraded into the merely picturesque to suggest any possibilities for living that could be conveyed to children. The sum effect of such literature is to leave us feeling that it is more pleasant to retreat into daydreams than to reimagine the world from the realities at hand.

Make-believe, to feel right and promising, would now instead have to be found closer to home. The publication of *Uncle Remus* gave this need a place and a way to happen. By anthropomorphizing the fauna of the rural neighborhoods, *Uncle Remus* gave storytellers fresh material with which to reconstruct the world in terms that could be at once familiar and magical with suggestion. A new set of images; see what you can build. This is what we find in the best work of the next fifty years or so: worlds made on the *Uncle Remus* model that comprehend the myriad details, speaking voices, variables of time and space, and allusions necessary to evoke a world. The fields and briar patches of the rural South, the ponds and creeks, cart roads, kitchens, and front porches brought to life in *Uncle Remus*—together with the sense conveyed there of a world properly evolved to its fullness—these particulars and this sense we find Potter, Grahame, and Milne transposing and adapting to the English countryside; Kipling (the only traveler in this generation of stay-at-homes) to the more exotic jungles of India; Thornton Burgess to the fields of Massachusetts; and, in time, Jean de Brunhoff to an Africa that lay just around the corner from Paris, Walt Kelly to Georgia's Okefenokee Swamp, and Tove Jansson to the coast of Finland.

In the following chapters, while treating Potter, Kipling, and company as originals in their own right, I want to examine just how they went about making these new worlds of make-believe and in what spirit—how they were guided by *Uncle Remus* both as a great wonder tale and, more practically, as a virtual blueprint for how such a literature should be organized and spoken. For some, like Grahame, it would be a matter of only a moment's recognition; for others, like Potter, a matter of back-and-forth reference and experimentation over many years. However brief or prolonged the influence, the results would be strikingly similar from storyteller to storyteller as a host of previously unspoken desires, images, and affinities comes to life in story at the turn of the century, and without, for some time thereafter, many lies being spun about the world under the guise of writing for children. For a while after *Uncle Remus* the world as retold in story could be comical, savage, sentimental, rude, serene, and all the same world in the telling. With Mole and Rat, Peter Rabbit, Pooh, Old Mother West Wind's children, and Mowgli's brothers, a feeling for the eternal daily life of the world can now intercede to stall time and mortality indefinitely in our behalf. Nor is that sense of well-being we experience while reading these serial adventures a spurious one: the world has been fairly accounted for in each of them.

7

SIS BEATRIX

The Fable in the Nursery

1

When we first read of Peter Rabbit and his three sisters that they "lived with their Mother in a sand-bank, underneath the root of a very big fir-tree," we enter a fictional state of being that is, as Selma Lanes has put it, "now and forever."[1] It is a new state of being in story, akin to "once upon a time" but sweeter somehow and more resounding; and for this reason alone Beatrix Potter's humble sand-bank must stand out as one of the paramount addresses along the passage of story from folklore to modern children's tale. What Lear had made of the nursery rhyme and Collodi of folk and fairy tales, Potter would now realize from the implications of the one remaining form of folklore, the fable. The *terra incognita* mapped by Joel Chandler Harris in the *Uncle Remus* stories would not be settled by her alone — Kipling, Grahame, Milne, and the Americans Thornton Burgess and Howard Garis would all stake out a patch, each with its own distinctive look and voice — but Potter's sand-bank comes closest, I think, to being the ideal way of saying what *Uncle Remus* implied for make-believe. Hers is the key translation of the fable into the kind of intimate book that is at once a mature work of empathic art and unmistakably, and once and for all, a book for young children.

To give us this new sense of now and forever at the sand-bank Potter had first, of course, to get there herself somehow, and I find it curious, given the nature of her journey, how little has been made of her life in books when so much of it was spent in them listening to how other people lived their lives. A small catechism recited from time to time includes the Authorized Version of the Bible, which she went to, as she said, to chasten her style, and Randolph Caldecott and a few others, but no writer I know of has done more than cite a title or two by way of acknowledging on her behalf some slight debt to tradition. Potter's life has seemed one of those privileged moments in history, like Lewis Carroll's famous picnic on the Thames—a life of and about books but beyond books somehow, and so thoroughly English as to need almost no other explanation. The excruciating progress of this dutiful daughter crippled by shyness and self-doubt was anyway not toward a life in letters but toward what every child wants: sovereignty, independence, a life of her own in the world. The kingdom she gained from the sale of her books, finally at forty-seven, was by her own choice a farmyard in the north of England, a quiet husband, and sheep.

There is a finished quality to the Potter life and the Potter tales that feels inviolable, a reproach to all efforts at understanding. You see her twenty-three little titles standing shoulder to shoulder on the bookstore shelf in their regimental jackets and they look to be not the twenty-three separate and often fitful starts that they were but twenty-three chapters mustered from one serene act of imagining; the work of a veteran hand that drew down the years with a calm purpose, rebuffing effort, doubt, and failure like so many flies on the parchment. That the tales first appeared in a motley array of sizes, designs, formats, and colors is so much history. You look at the uniform set that marketing has made them today and everything falls sublimely into place: England, the hedgerows and cottages, and Miss Potter there in the lane, inquiring of a hedgehog or rabbit like Agatha Christie's Miss Marple sleuthing for clues. God is in His heaven, say these little books. All is right with the world.

This uniformity we see in the books we have inclined to see in the life, understandably enough; and the uniquely English character of the life we have assumed is all there is to know of the books. In his monograph on Potter, Marcus Crouch rolls the national pudding properly, with breadcrumbs: "Beatrix Potter was a product of English society and her books were prompted by and mirrored the English country scene."[2] Well, and why not? She is so distinctive and so distinctively English, what more could we need to account for the tales but a girl arrested in adolescence and desperate for expression, and an England to express her? To suggest that out of a dread, perhaps, of her own imagined incompetence Potter had developed as compulsive and eclectic an eye for the craft of story as she had for nature seems almost an impertinence.

The small body of writing that has grown up around her work, faithful to what can only be called a Potter mystique, has shied away from such speculation and has specialized, rather, in the iconographic remark. Graham Greene's summary praise of Potter as an "unromantic observer who never sacrifices truth for an effective gesture"[3] was a lead others have been happy to follow. In her estimable biography, *The Tale of Beatrix Potter*,

Margaret Lane several times asserts, for example, that this or that book "is completely free from any touch of sentimentality" and that Potter's animal portraits "seem always to add to one's knowledge of animal character rather than distorting it."[4] The judgment is later echoed by Eleanor Cameron's "There is neither prettiness, preciousness, nor sentimentality in her pages,"[5] and even the iconoclastic Humphrey Carpenter can maintain that "she completely avoided the trap of sentimentality in writing about animals."[6]

Here is the children's book historian John Rowe Townsend suffering an uncharacteristic lapse in his assessment of the tales to deliver six insupportable truths at one sitting:

> [T]here seems no point in drawing up an order of precedence. Preferences among the best twelve or fifteen of the books are apt to be personal. The firm ring of the words, the precise composition and characterization of the drawings, the dry humour and the decisive and satisfying conclusions are common to them all. They differ in their individual nature but they are alike in excellence and they are all parts of a body of work that has a country-grown flavour and firmness.[7]

When the idea of precedence, which presumes aesthetic criteria, becomes a matter of preference, which presumes taste, we are dealing at best in categoric, not close, truths about a subject. Potter's tales are not alike in excellence; the ring of the words is not always firm, nor the composition always precise. Far from being decisive, the endings of *The Tale of Samuel Whiskers*[8] and *Ginger & Pickles* have been designed deliberately to avoid closure. The turning of their last pages reveals a series of epilogues, each with the force of a new chapter in a novel.

On the more general claim that there is neither prettiness nor preciousness in her pages, there are, when you come to inquire, enough dear-littles and teeny-weenys to satisfy the most doting grandmother. Jeremy Fisher "had the dearest little red float." (What boy gone fishing ever thought of his gear in these terms?) In the *The Tailor of Gloucester* we find "little teeny weeny writing" and "the most beautifullest coat." Ginger and Pickles had "a little, small shop" and the kittens in *The Tale of Tom Kitten* came equipped with "dear little fur coats of their own." This last witticism is more insipid than we might expect from the Potter we think we know, but not from the Potter who gives us names like Timmy Tiptoes or Twinkleberry, or describes a catnap as "forty winky peepies." The prettiness in *Mrs. Tiggy-winkle*, when the heroine's "little black nose went snuffle, sniffle, snuffle, and her eyes went twinkle, twinkle, twinkle," is catching, but unlike that "nice singey smell" in the kitchen, it does little to shore up a book that opens with an echo of Victorian baby talk.

> One day little Lucie came into the farmyard crying — oh, she did cry so! "I've lost my pocker handkin. Three handkins and a pinny! Have *you* sen them, Tabby Kitten?"

By the time of *Mrs. Tiggy-winkle* in 1905 Potter was a practiced hand at such whimsy. Frustrated in her hope to be taken seriously as an adult with a mind and talent to use, and I suspect out of a fear that someone might take her seriously one day after all, she had, in the decade previous, rendered scores of pictures that can only be described as a typical *fin-de-siècle* retreat to the nursery: elves and fairies, mice pushing perambulators, guinea pigs snuggling in sewing baskets. She made for herself a fairyland, as she later wrote,[9] and this preciousness, which she did not disdain in herself, easily carried over into books like *The Tailor of Gloucester*, *The Pie and the Patty-Pan*, and the *Appley Dapply* and *Cecily Parsley* nursery-rhyme books. If it is negligible in her best work, it is still frequent enough to be annoying. In her worst it verges on the egregious. *The Fairy Caravan* begins "In the Land of Green Ginger there is a town called Marmalade, which is inhabited exclusively by guinea-pigs" and contains the impossible passage "Bless its little pittitoes! No, it must not kick its blanket off its beddie beddie!"

This quaintness, and not her ironic distance, seems to be the quality in her tales that many, perhaps most, readers respond to, given the strong market in Potterbilia; and they are responding to something that is in fact present in the work. We cannot say that her portraits never distort animal character; she was capable of skewing whole books toward the sentimental. As orders of imagining go, there is no difference in kind between a bad Potter tableau and a picture by Racey Helps or Molly Brett or the Margarets Tarrant and Tempest, whose work finds it widest circulation on whimsical postcards. She was simply better at it, warmer, more appealing and less trivial somehow. The need to falsify that critics exempt her from, the need to escape into whimsy, rises and falls in Potter like a fever — or perhaps more accurately like a blush as the obedient daughter trundles out her characters for the inspection of those maiden aunts she recognized were the real audience for a book like *The Tailor of Gloucester*. Only in her few best books is falsification for effect negligible or absent. *Mr. Tod* is devoid of it, *Peter Rabbit* and *Jemima Puddle-duck* nearly so. It is a minor distraction in *The Roly-Poly Pudding* and *Two Bad Mice*. The *Flopsy Bunnies* would have escaped it altogether were it not for that last winsome greeting-card portrait of the helpful Mrs. Tittlemouse in her new cloak and muff. (Curiously, in *The Tale of Mrs. Tittlemouse*, where we might have expected such mugging for smiles, there is none. It is one of Potter's best secondary works.)

Affection in Potter is not a fault that can be passed over unless one has already adopted a purely custodial stance toward the work. It is hard to overlook, for example, how coy gestures spoil a good secondary tale like *Benjamin Bunny*. This is one of those rare children's stories that catches the unheard quiet at the heart of childhood, the held breath at the edge of a larger world. The pace of the short, hesitant paragraphs as Peter and Benjamin step about McGregor's garden exactly spells out the feel of two boys poking around where they don't belong yet are bound to go. What a disappointment, then, to find her using this realized moment as an excuse to play dress-up, tucking the woebegone Peter decoratively into a red handkerchief, the nonchalant Benjamin into purple clogs and a floppy tam-o'-shanter ludicrously too big for him. The book's cover-plate, showing Benjamin overwhelmed by the tam, betrays the real point of the tale, that we are meant not to share the stealth in the garden but to coo over a foolish and huggable child. It's too bad, really. *Benjamin Bunny* is less a book addressed to children than a book about children, illegitimately addressed to adults with a taste for the sweet and the sentimental. That Potter was capable of betraying her best talents is something that critics have been at pains to overlook, but it is an inescapable part of her character.

The other Potter, the one who counts in the end, is that stoical naturalist who cuts against the popular grain: dry-eyed, earth-wise, a little uncanny, the Potter that critics want known when they turn to absolutes in their praise. This is the no-nonsense Potter of the laconic prose and clipped paragraphs, who can imagine how a cat shopkeeper with mice for customers "could not bear to see them going out at the door with their little packages." Here there is an ironic, almost savage edge to the word "little," as befitting the real, not a falsified, situation between cats and mice—and between us townsfolk as well. When this Potter is in control of events Mr. Drake Puddle-duck's more sinister inclinations will emerge as he sidles up to steal Tom Kitten's clothes, and the yard of Mr. Tod will be found with "many unpleasant things lying about that had much better have been buried." Jane Gardam has drawn on a childhood recollection of Potter for as good a sketch of this side of her character as I have seen. In the following passage Gardam's mother, having discovered *Squirrel Nutkin* in a shop, has taken her daughter in tow and

proceeded to Sawrey, which was not far from our farm. I remember a little, bent, sideways-glancing person looking at me over a gate, and a sense of toughness and purposefulness of a high order. I was being led along by a hand—my mother's—and high above me was my mother's face, pink with pleasure at seeing the bunny lady.

She was no bunny lady to me. That she put rabbits in trousers worried me not a bit. They were real rabbits, often ridiculous and vicious, and real trousers of the sort that ought to be spelled with a W—trousers with bumpy flies. There was ruthlessness in the text as well as the heavenly beauty of the pictures and the sense of immense trouble taken. Look, for instance, at the drawing of the cat trussed up with string in *The Tale of Samuel Whiskers*, ready to be rolled up in pastry. Nobody could draw a cat trussed up with string, like a breast of lamb with stuffing, without a model. I believe that Beatrix Potter trussed up that cat and drew it, and its anguished face[10] is a portrait, the portrait of a cat whose relationship with it owner was, to say the least, a little odd.[11]

Two Potters, then, each expressing the view from the same aging child's eye. There is the Potter who remains a player within the work, practicing a high, precise art, innocent of imposed meaning, and, on a sort of internal time-sharing plan, there is the Potter who could step back into that safe place where dressing up dolls and rabbits and fairies could seem an allowable proxy for real story. Gardam saw the one by the gate that day; her mother saw the other. They were as inseparable, no doubt, as any of us in our contradictions, but they do contend with one another in the tales, and the reader of her life is left to wonder at the real source of her achievement. If one or the other Potter could be credited with discovering that now and forever at the sand-bank, which Potter would it be? It is a matter about which she herself had little to say. Her remarks on her craft are too few and too obliging in the wrong ways to be of any real help to us in reconstructing how she became the innovative translator of folklore that she was; and at least for the moment I think we are better off looking to the life after all. In her journal, which she wrote between the ages of sixteen and thirty-one, and here and there in her letters, she left enough of a record for us to re-create some part of the journey to the sand-bank and to see in that short span of years in the 1890s some little of what was going on when the essential imagining was done and only the making of the books remained.

2

"I had no idea of what the world would be like," she wrote of her childhood from the vantage point of eighteen; "I wished to trust myself on the waters and sea. Everything was romantic in my imagination."[12] The better part of these hopeful early years she spent sequestered upstairs, but it does not seem to have been an unhappy time. Tutors came and went. She kept a menagerie and busied herself with the little things that plied their trades about the wainscoting and yard. Each summer there was a country vacation to revel in, and at all times she read and drew and dreamed. There is no reason to suppose that before adolescence she ever imagined her life would not proceed along normal, perhaps even exciting, lines. Sometime in puberty, however, a suspicion arose in Potter that the world might be denied her after all, and the upstairs solitudes she could bear as a child began to resemble more and more the silences of an unwanted exile.

There is the opinion that shyness is an inherited disease, like diabetes. She herself believed so, and if it did not run in the family genes it certainly ran in the family manner. The Potters lived that cramped, bourgeois life of inherited wealth depicted in Galsworthy's *The Forsyte Saga*. Decorum was all, and it was thought unsuitable for a girl of Beatrix's station to have run-about access to a world of tradesmen and worse. With this came an almost fatal lack of contact with other children and the world at large. The "brilliant colour,"[13] as she called it, which once had merely been childhood reticence, now seized her terribly, and it was never to let go. She may have been mindful, too, of the liability of having cousins too pretty to stand beside in a gathering. Photographs of the period, showing the girls posed together, are rather sad to contemplate. Potter was not unattractive at this age, but in company looks always pained or solemn, and it is not hard to imagine that, as the years went by and nothing happened that ought to have, she must have suffered the humiliation of knowing that somewhere in the family someone was saying, what *are* they going to do about poor Beatrix? For a girl who believed, as Potter did, that a woman's place was beside a man and that women's suffrage was a craze of the lunatic fringe, this would have been devastating.

Signs of distress appear in the journal quite early. She had begun this curious document in her mid-teens in 1882 and before she was done with it fifteen years later would amass more than two hundred thousand words of daily reportage, family sketches, opinions on art and politics, and confession. It is a curious piece of work not so much for being penned in code and in a script so minuscule as to doubly dissuade anyone from reading it but for the even, knowing spirit in which much of it is delivered. Her ease of expression is not surprising in itself for an adolescent of her time and class; what does surprise is the manner. "Radicals furious because old Gladstone is trying to make terms with the Tories. There is no doubt what has driven him to his senses, it is the Egyptian difficulty."[14] This is the voice not of a seventeen-year-old semirecluse who draws fairies but of someone intimate, or pretending to be intimate, with the very seats of power. Most probably it is her father's voice. It has the ring of dinner-table debate and calls up an image of papa Potter pausing in his cigar to repeat what he had had to say at the club that afternoon on the failings of the P.M.

A case can be made that in this affection of worldliness we can hear apprentice work for the more astringent wisdom of her books, but as journal writing it doesn't lead Potter to anything but more of the same. It helped to keep her going by giving her something to do and some way of pretending to be in the world and counting for something, but when there is pain to report, the pain puts the lie to it. Only two days after her "old Gladstone" entry she is found lamenting, in envy of "swarms of young ladies painting" at the National Gallery—and possibly, too, of her younger brother Bertram, who is away at school—"If I was a boy and had courage!"[15] Her summation of the following, her nineteenth, year puts a tremor to months of even-handed reportage: "Much bitterness and a few peaceful summer days . . . I am terribly afraid of the future."[16]

In 1897, at the age of thirty-one, she was to abandon the journal for her books, and in 1913, at forty-seven, she would complete the cycle by abandoning her books for the husband and farming that would fill her remaining thirty years. But for now there was no foreseeable future at all.

Her decision to become a painter was life on too short a lead. Her father, though himself an amateur photographer, habitué of galleries, and friend to the painter Millais, would never tender more than the grudging support of a few lessons at home and the infrequent trip to a museum or the Millais studio. Going out the door with him could be a trial in itself. "If only I had not been with papa," she writes of one expedition; "he does not often take me out, and I doubt he will do it again for a time."[17] This for the embarrassment of her hat having blown into a fountain. When she turned to scientific portraiture in the manner of Audubon and Edward Lear, for which she showed great promise, there was even trouble over her going to a neighborhood museum to draw specimens. Nowhere in the record is there any evidence that Beatrix and her parents so much as played a parlor game together; nonetheless, the Potters meant to keep their one daughter convenient for the duration of their own lives, and escape was a notion they wanted her disabused of from an early age.

Naturally, there were scenes. "My temper has been boiling like a kettle,"[18] she reports more than once, and no wonder: here she had found the one thing she knew could give her both pleasure and the possibility of a life in the world, and it was going to be denied her. For the next decade there is in the journal little sense of an accessible future, only the worldly pretense of a lived life mingling with a barely suppressed desperation. The days are "wearisome, disappointing,"[19] and she is afraid. Afraid of being always the plain cousin, always treated like a child, always upstairs alone in a house where, as her biographer notes, the ticking of the clock could be heard everywhere. This was the way it was going to be forever. Her parents and her own hateful shyness were going to see to it.

When you are a prisoner — and worse, a willing prisoner suffering from stagefright before the world, unable, from a want of nerve and money and a destination, simply to pack a bag and get out — there is only one safety exit left to you, and that is through the inner door of daydreams. Potter daydreamed. For ten years, twenty — it became such a habit with her no one can really say when it started or stopped as a primary activity — she dreamed and set her dreams to paper: small immaculate watercolors of courtly mice in frocks, a fairy in pink on a leaping mouse, five little guinea pigs tending a row of sprouts. She became remarkably adept at depicting things pleasant to dwell on.

All make-believe is based on a measure of the whimsical, of course. Without some benign sense of the unreal (or unreal sense of the benign) children's story would be a very different, and a colder, thing than it is. The craft lies in knowing when to express the whimsical and when to hold it in check. In *Peter Rabbit*, once having wed the images of boy and beast, Potter otherwise holds the impulse in check. She does not have Peter picking lollipops from trees or tucking a lost little good feeling into his pocket and forgoing McGregor's garden to gather berries with his sisters. There is nothing in the book that can be described as whimsical beyond the fact that Peter is a rabbit with a boy's name and a boy's instincts. This is the simplest degree of whimsy, basically the same kind found in folklore like *Uncle Remus*. It involves a translation of reality by one necessary lie—here, the lie of anthropomorphism. As a narrative ploy such a translation has the effect of neutralizing the inhibitions and anxieties aroused by realistic literature and so of liberating our larger sense of the world's possibilities. Potter's discovery was how natural and right a way it is for telling a story to young children.

Add a gratuitous lie to the first and you will have created a second order of whimsy guaranteed to compromise your story with the affections of prior intent. The crossing over from one realm to the other can be made by as simple a gesture as a change of name. When Potter follows *Peter Rabbit* with a sequel titled *Benjamin Bunny*, she has imbued the translating image with a special quality that will hold her story to its implications like a magnet. Putting pants on a bunny is not the same as putting them on a rabbit. A trousered rabbit is free to have his story told; the bunny, merely by being called a bunny, is now promised in advance to the audience as an emotional treat and must stand there from time to time, as Benjamin does, to look endearing. For the most part in her tales Potter avoids the bunny trail; indeed, she is one of the masters at the naming of characters: Hunca Munca,[20] Mr. Tod, Samuel Whiskers, Jemima Puddle-duck, Jeremy Fisher, Chippy Hackee, Tommy Brock—these appellations have the feel of absolute historical veracity. More importantly, the dignity of the characters so named, and their freedom to do as they will in their stories, is preserved where Benjamin's is compromised. Naming Peter's sisters Flopsy, Mopsy, and Cotton-tail was a whimsical gesture of this second degree, but in their case, which is to stand in comic contrast to their brother, it works to good effect: the sound is right, with just enough charm and no more.

There is a third degree of whimsy that follows inevitably from the implications of the second; it is not different, merely a compounding of the gratuitous lie to the point where charm becomes not just a valuable adjunct to the story but an end in itself. This is the land of *The Little Prince* and *Puff the Magic Dragon* and the communal narcotic of Disney World. Potter's depiction in *The Flopsy Bunnies* of Mrs. Tittlemouse snuggled prettily in her cloak and muff is a good example of how her early regression would linger on into the books, a bad habit she could avoid but never quite break. Another and more serious lapse into third-degree whimsy is *The Tailor of Gloucester*, that simple Grimm fairy tale held subservient to Potter's quiet pageantry of period charm. She knew full well, of course, that the picturesque is inimical to art, but these were the years when her earliest landfall in attempting a story (in 1893) would be the island in *Little Pig Robinson* where "sweets grew upon the trees, . . . and muffins ready baked." It was a time when what she knew to be true in life was enough of a reproach, perhaps, to what she needed to be false in art that the truth never effectively crossed her mind.

What did cross her mind briefly, beginning in 1890, was the practical notion of putting her daydreams to good use by selling them to card publishers. Whose idea this first was, actually, is not known with any certainty; it may have occurred to everyone at much the same time as a solution to the vexing problem of what they were going to do about poor Beatrix. When a friend of the family drops by in 1890 to recommend she apply some of her whimsical cameos to Christmas-card designs, it is almost too convenient, and suggests that he had been summoned to encourage Beatrix in a project her parents hoped would mollify her ambition without leading her out of the house. Canon Rawnsley will appear again in 1900 when Potter is seeking, unsuccessfully, a publisher for *Peter Rabbit*. A founding member of The National Trust with some influence, he will offer in place of her own text, which has been found wanting, a trivializing and silly set of rhyming quatrains—forty-two pages of them—that must have required considerable effort on his part. When Potter the following year did find herself negotiating with the Warne publishing house after all, and that they preferred her own version, she wrote to them to say, "I do not know if it is necessary to consult Canon Rawnsley; I should think *not*."[21] Her attitude toward the avuncular canon seems at best to have been one of wary ambivalence.

Examples of her designs that survive from this period are not particularly good. She seems less than fully at ease with her role as a decorative illustrator. Certainly, there is a patronizing air about the whole enterprise that might have put her off, and if her experience with a German publisher in 1892 was typical, no doubt in later years she wished that episode buried and forgotten. She had done them a set of frog drawings that would later turn up in a children's annual as "A Frog He Would a-Fishing Go," accompanied by doggerel more witless than Canon Rawnsley would supply for *Peter Rabbit*. Potter knew what good writing was. Even if her pictures were not her best, to see them set to foolish lines could only have embarrassed and disgusted her. Shortly after the book's appearance we find her squaring accounts by devising her own variation on the fishing frog; and in 1905, when considering *Jeremy Fisher* as her next book, she will buy back the old illustrations—not, I think, to use them as models, as has been suggested, but simply to get rid of them. Whatever she might have hoped for it, her foray into the card business cannot have been satisfying at any level—too little gratification for the artist, too little money for the prisoner, and too much rue for the patronized daughter. It did, however, get her negotiating with the outside world at a somewhat adult level, and it afforded her the important experience of seeing herself in print and of knowing that numbers of people were looking at her pictures and possibly deriving pleasure from them.

3

A word often associated with Potter is inspiration. In almost everything that has been written about her it is said that she found the inspiration for this or that tale in one of her pets or in the countryside — I suppose we are to assume while strolling along the hedgerows. It is all left very vague, as if it were a self-evident fact that if you have a pet, or a hedgerow to stroll beside, a story will naturally ensue. The pets and the country were important, but to leave it at that begs the question of how exactly during the next several years an illustrator of greeting cards could have used these things to develop into a master storyteller.

Part of the problem may lie in a general tendency to confuse the idea of inspiration with the process of invention, by which works of art actually get made. Inspiration, as being akin, let us say, to daydreaming, only faster, might be applied to a passage in Mozart or a canvas by Van Gogh, but it is a superfluous concept in thinking about an artist like Potter. Her work is a manifestation not of sudden burst of insight but of painstaking invention, that process of trial and error by which new things are always made. Roger Sale has described her life as "growing, finding itself with almost terrifying slowness."[22] The same might be said of her books. A page of Potter is the work of days, weeks, and the revisions of more days and weeks in some following year until the thing comes right. If she is inspired it is as a result of being constantly in the process of inventing the next thing, of pursuing a phrase or dab of color to its logical conclusion.

Inspiration in Potter is no sudden happening into print but an evolution of thousands of tiny decisions as one idea suggests its successors and her instinct tells her which succeeding line or phrase best serves the sequence. To say that her pets Peter and Benjamin were the inspirations for their books tells us too little about how she worked and how her fictional world gathered in her imagination. Really, it tells us nothing at all, and obscures a central fact of her career, that her books happened not when the word "inspiration" implies they happened but a decade earlier and as a direct result of her efforts at depicting fictional worlds that had gathered in other people's imaginations.

In 1893 Potter had decided to become a professional book illustrator. She knew now that if she were ever to get out from under she would have to put her talent and her self-doubt to a larger test and do this thing the hard way — the way the grown-ups did it, not with pretty vignettes and courtesy renumeration but with whole books and whole pounds in payment. Fortunately, it was not going to work for her in the way she thought — nothing in her life ever did; and between the years 1893 and 1900 she would give up in frustration more than once. But she had taken the right step and she had gone to the right books. By the time she finally realized that hers was too peculiar a talent to picture anyone's words but her own, the books she put back on the shelf had already stood her in good stead. They had shown her the way to the sand-bank.

This is a point likely to cause some confusion, so it might be well, before looking at the books she chose to illustrate, to make a distinction about the nature of Potter's originality. Some readers will find it too radical an assessment but, weighing the evidence, I think it is fair to say that Potter never told a wholly original tale in her life. Every plot she used was someone else's plot, and more scenes than would seem plausible were other people's scenes in paraphrase. It is simply the way she worked. To remark on it does not deny, it only serves to define, her originality. Like Lewis Carroll, or Maurice Sendak today, or even like Shakespeare and Coleridge, Potter was an eclectic reader of the world of story, a gatherer and a translator. What we find in her tales are fragments of those books she first thought merely to illustrate, and then reprocessed instead. Where the original collectors of the nursery rhymes she loved to quote were gatherers only; Potter, like Lear and Stevenson, reimagined what she found and made of it what we have come to think of as the now-and-forever Beatrix Potter tale.

Oddly, and rather sadly in retrospect, she misunderstood her own talent and to the end of her life was afraid of being caught out as a cheat. "Copying," she called it. "It is a risky thing to copy," she confided to her journal as early as 1883; "shall I catch it?"[23] Sixty years later we find her writing her publishers to complain of an article in *The Listener* that compares her favorably with Bewick and other major illustrators. "Great rubbish, absolute bosh!" she retorts, and turns on the hapless author with the information that she had read the piece with "stupefaction." It was not modesty that prompted this outburst. As her biographer notes, "she plainly thought she was being accused of copying these artists."[24] It is on her mind, too, throughout the 1890s when she has begun the serious work of converting vignettes and tableaux into real stories. When someone observes of a set of pictures she has done that they are very much in the style of Caldecott, her entry in the journal is a dry "comparisons are undesirable."[25] The fear of being thought a copyist is such a recurring theme in her life it can only mean that copying is exactly what she did.

In 1893, when her period of study in books began in earnest, she was acutely sensitive to her technical liabilities. She knew she could not draw the human figure. She could be brilliant at copying from nature, but often when humanizing an animal she would have difficulty finding a solution to the simplest problem—the shoulders on rabbits, for example: where are they? Little conundrums like these persist into the books a decade later. No sooner does she slip a jacket on Peter than she loses track of the shoulder and sometimes an elbow as well (pages 12 and 20 of *Peter Rabbit* especially). At least a small part of her success in drawing mice, I suspect, can be laid to their tiny joints being more easily overlooked than a rabbit's.

When you draw a mouse you can show a forearm poking from a bulge of fur and no one will really care where the shoulder went.

As a writer Potter had, and knew it, no instinct for constructing plots or engineering a complex set of narrative actions. When she needs Mr. Tod to play a trick on Tommy Brock, for instance, she devises a ruse so complicated and is so long in setting it up that after a few pages of it the reader is willing to take it on faith alone. She had a faulty ear as well for the unobtrusive flow of narrative fiction; other differences aside, one cannot imagine her writing a *Pinocchio* or *The Princess and the Goblin* or even a single fairy tale of, say, four thousand words that did not depend on the narrative breaks afforded by the turning of the page every fifty words or so. Her true style is epigrammatic; her typical paragraph, like a remnant scissored from some longer passage. Each of her tales is a progress of precise moments excerpted from something larger, smoother, and left behind. She will record the vital minutiae of one such moment, and instantly we are at the next, with cause and effect often left suspended in the elision between paragraphs:

> Sometimes a beetle lost its way in the passages.
> "Shuh! shuh! little dirty feet!" said Mrs. Tittlemouse, clattering her dust-pan.

Working at length, she succeeds best with *Mr. Tod*, but generally, the longer her books the more unstable the structure and the more noticeable a slackening of effect. It is in books like *Peter Rabbit*, *Mrs. Tittlemouse*, *Jemima Puddle-duck*, and *Two Bad Mice* that she settled on her ideal way of telling a story: twenty-six pictures, and twenty-six pages of text ranging from about ten words a page to sixty-five, with a variable rhythm set up between them so that each page presents in its very look a slightly different event from the one before. She will make of this — the sum of things she cannot do — an art form in itself.

That she had found the solutions to many problems in other people's books she regarded as the skeleton in her closet. She had found solutions, too, by playing against what she had found, as Carroll had played against *The Water Babies*, but this was a side to her method that she undervalued. Throughout her life she will vacillate between dismissing her work as undeserving of attention and outbursts of "absolute bosh!" whenever someone comes too close. She will freely talk up the inescapably obvious source, like Caldecott for *Jeremy Fisher* or Aesop for *Johnny Town-mouse*, but those she feared might show her up to be an inept amateur by comparison (or, worse, a thief), those she kept to herself — even to dissembling in the instance of *Jemima Puddle-duck* that its source was, or was in the main, *Little Red Riding Hood*. Her first success, *Peter Rabbit*, was in particular open to the charge of being a mere patchwork of ideas. Owning up that scenes in the book were paraphrases of scenes in other books would have been like confessing the need of a Rawnsley. It is interesting in this light that the canon is not mentioned once in her journal. It is not terribly surprising, however. You do not, even in a secret code, admit to an episode that has made you out a helpless child counseled by a fool. Lewis Carroll withheld embarrassments such as this from his own diary—there is no mention, for example, of the humiliation he once suffered at the hands of Alfred, Lord Tennyson; and Potter was no more likely to cite her deeper sources than to credit the help of the good canon. To do so, to admit that virtually *every*thing was a copy—or was done by a process she thought of as copying—would have been to announce her desperation and ineptitude to the world and to compromise its opinion of her real achievements, however small she thought them.

There is no record of what Potter's or her father's libraries contained in 1893. We know those influences, like Caldecott and the Bible that she had credited herself, and allusions in various letters point to her having read Jane Austen (a likely source of clarity in her style) and *Uncle Tom's Cabin*, and virtually complete editions of Mrs. Ewing and Mrs. Molesworth. All in all, the evidence suggests that the Potters' shelves boasted the notable books of the day. *Little Pig Robinson* implies not only Lear but Defoe, and a character like Mr. Jackson ("Tiddly, widdly, widdly! Your very good health, Mrs. Tittlemouse!") intimates a mimetic love of Dickens. Indeed, throughout Potter's work we find unmistakable clues that she did in fact at one time or another own a given book.

Take the narrative premise of *The Roly-Poly Pudding*, for example. Here you have an adventurous kitten downstairs and, upstairs behind the wallboards, a phlegmatic rat. How do you bring the two of them together? No one that I have read has noted the book's resemblance to that other classic of English children's literature, Kingsley's *The Water Babies*. Both are set in the North Country; both tell of a boy named Tom; in each book Tom climbs up the inside of a chimney and tumbles, covered with soot, into an upstairs chamber where he makes an unpleasant discovery—in Kingsley, the "little black ape" of his own reflection in a mirror; in Potter, that other of her Dickensian characters, Samuel Whiskers. In Kingsley a girl startled from her bed by the intrusion screams out and brings running "a stout old nurse from the next room," who "dashed at him . . . so fast that she caught him by the jacket." In Potter, Samuel Whiskers, wanting to know what Tom means "tumbling into my bed all covered with smuts," squeaks out "Anna Maria! Anna Maria!" and "an old woman rat . . . rushed upon Tom Kitten, and before he knew what was happening—His coat was pulled off. . . . " Surely Potter knew the book. This close a paraphrase cannot have been coincidental.

She may have been familiar as well with that once popular antique from 1783, Dorothy Kilner's *The Life and Perambulations of a Mouse*. This tale about four mice named Nimble, Longtail, Softdown, and Brighteyes had reappeared in print in 1870, when Potter was five, in the collection *A*

Storehouse of Stories, edited by the noted children's author Charlotte Yonge. Its premise so exactly states Potter's own condition it is hard not to think she knew it as a child and that at some moment in late adolescence had remembered and gone back to it. The narrator of *The Perambulations*, finding herself in the company of storytellers—like Beatrix among her books—apologizes to the reader that an "insipid" life has left her with no tales to tell. Whereupon, a bit of folkish magic: she is saved from all embarrassment by "a little squeaking voice" that bids her to "write mine, which may be more diverting." It is almost as if Potter's entire career were a response to this tiny call to arms, and the books in her lap (and the pets, if you like) the voices that saved her.

A text Potter did freely cite as an influence was the Bible, and one tale at least can be laid directly to her reading of it. *Two Bad Mice* was prompted initially by her association with her publisher's niece; it was written to celebrate a doll's house and to entertain a particular child. But now and again in Potter (as in *Squirrel Nutkin*) we glimpse an allegorical urge that is nothing if not playful. A doll's house and a child are the occasion for *Two Bad Mice*, but Genesis and the story of the Garden of Eden are the source of its style and incident. Read the two stories side by side (keeping in mind that none of this should be taken any more solemnly than Potter did herself). The doll's house is the garden (at eighteen she had eulogized her own childhood as a paradise lost); Hunca Munca and Tom Thumb, like Adam and Eve, are naked in the garden, and thereafter—a doll's clothes having been heisted—Hunca Munca at least is clothed. The policeman posted by the door following discovery of the trespass is the angel sent to guard the gates of Paradise; and the two bad mice atone for their sins in the end by sweeping up and paying a crooked sixpense as restitution for damages. It is very neatly done.

The comic effect Potter wanted to achieve is more easily heard, perhaps, if we merge her own and King James's English into a single passage:

> Such a lovely dinner was laid out upon the table! She took of the fruit thereof, and did eat, and gave also unto her husband with her; and he did eat.
>
> Then there was no end to the rage of Tom Thumb and Hunca Munca, for underneath the shining paint it was made of nothing but plaster!
>
> And the eyes of both of them were opened, and they knew that they *were* naked; and they broke up the pudding, the lobsters, the pears and the oranges; and they sewed fig leaves together, and made themselves aprons.

Knowledge gained for Potter is what we might today call getting wised up to reality. In the Bible she found and used to wry effect literature's first example of the coming-of-age novel.

Whenever we find her using a particular text as her model, we almost always find in that text some likeness to Potter herself. In Kingsley and throughout Dickens we have the stories of unloved children; in Lear, the bliss of running way. The Bible story that became *Two Bad Mice* may have called to mind her own lost childhood and provoked a desire to do to her fake existence what Tom Thumb did to fake doll's food: "bang, bang, smash, smash!" Whenever she recognizes herself in the literature, it seems, she wants to take some remembrance away with her. Perhaps, in the appropriating way of children, she was building her own world of story out of what belonged to her anyway because it *was* her. She is known to have had a set of Mrs. Ewing's works, for instance. The popular *Story of a Short Life* was published in 1885; Potter is nineteen and still abides in the nursery; she is currently in disgrace for allowing her hat to blow into a fountain. On page one of the novel she reads how the father of the little hero, having settled into his armchair, discovers that his son has presumed to lurk nearby:

> Put your hands down, Leonard! Put your tongue in, sir! What are you after? What do you want? What are you doing here? Be off to the nursery, and tell Jemima to keep you there. Your mother and I are busy.

This inadvertent parody of the Victorian patriarch at bay, hilarious to us, would have been a more sobering discovery for Potter, and, given her way with other books, there is a possibility that with the reflex of a hurt and angry child she snatched away the name Jemima and ran with it. If so, like Tom the piper's son who ran with the pig, she ran with it over the hills and two decades away, finally to bestow it on the barnyard fowl in Sawrey who is otherwise credited with being the inspiration of *Jemima Puddle-duck*.

There are other possible sources for the name Jemima; with them comes an ancillary sense of Potter's copying habits that harkens back to *The Perambulations* of Dorothy Kilner and the desire of an insipid girl to belong to a gathering of storytellers. What these, and other, sources suggest is that Potter was, in effect, making a claim to kinship with the books she copied; that she was gathering in the real family she never had and no doubt, in 1893, felt she never would have. Earlier I hazarded the speculation that her fear of being thought a copyist was largely a fear of being thought inept and derivative. I think so still, but this more personal undercurrent to her method of gathering and translating stories betrays something more. It implies that an "absolute bosh!" served to screen a fear of also being thought too bereft, too naked, too pathetic. Throughout her adult life Potter took conspicuous pride in her command of the stoicism she admired in her ancestors—a stoicism that would make her a comic rather than a tragic or merely pretentious artist; and if you are the hard case Potter wished to think herself, you do not want biographers and critics coming round in later years to tell the world things that, like Mr. Tod's old dinner bones, "had much better have been buried"—that your parents, to whom you remained loyal, despised you (she felt they had), or that you went to books in lieu of a life and stole little pieces of them for kinship.

If this is so; if her true family *can* be found in literature, then her nearest adopted own were those sources she would be least likely to acknowledge — and, in fact, did not. They are the children's author Dinah Mulock Craik and, from a race apart, *Uncle Remus*.

I have seen no copy of a book by Craik that could be identified as Potter's; nonetheless, I think it is incontrovertible that she knew at least one of them, *The Adventures of a Brownie*, published in 1872 when she was six. Without this book *Jemima Puddle-duck* could not have become the tale it is, nor could Potter have spoken in prose quite the way she spoke. Potter had said that *Jemima* was *Little Red Riding Hood* retold; there is that to it, of course — the debonair wolf, now a fox, luring the innocent female — but *Little Red Riding Hood* is not really at all what *Jemima* is about. Potter's tale is the portrait of a woman "desperate" like herself, and a "simpleton" who is unable to fulfil her wanted destiny. The parent, here being the farmer's wife, "would not let her hatch her own eggs." Jemima's sister-in-law (brother Bertram's wife?) consoles her with the thought that she hasn't the patience for it anyway, but Jemima is determined to have her career. Like Potter she will do it "all by myself" if need be. And when at last it seems she will have ducklings to mother after all, what happens is what usually happened to Potter, an absurd turn of events that denies her everything, and she is "escorted home in tears." (A coda allowing Jemima the compromised later success of "only four" hatchlings does not alter the tenor of the story.) Of all Potter's books *Jemima Puddle-duck* bears the greatest burden of adult emotion and wisdom; the comic rue that permeates it is unlike anything else she achieved. This cannot have come from *Little Red Riding Hood* alone. It did, I think, come from the third of Craik's stories in *The Adventures of a Brownie*, the one titled "Brownie in the Farmyard."

In this tale within a tale (the Brownie remains in the background) Craik relates the parallel histories of two hens and their respective experiences at motherhood. One is raising her own chicks, the other is foster mother to an abandoned brood of ducklings. This latter conceit not only becomes the premise of Potter's tale, it becomes her opening line: "What a funny sight it is to see a brood of ducklings with a hen!" The "superfluous hen," as Jemima will call her, has in Craik no more luck at mothering than Jemima herself and, having lost the brood in her care, is "seen wandering forlornly about." The first hen, who will successfully hatch and raise her own chicks, takes that journey into the woods that Jemima will take when she is "determined to make a nest right away from the farm." Writes Craik, "She was a hen who hatched her brood on independent principles. Instead of sitting upon the nice nest that the Gardener made for her, she had twice gone into a little wood close by and made a nest for herself, which nobody could ever find." Jemima, then, is a composite of the two hens; her misadventure, essentially a sequel from the same fictional farmyard.

There is something more in Craik, however, than mere plotting, or even the recognition of a thwarted need, that puts me in mind of Potter here—it is that Potterish voice. In this and others of Craik's books what we hear is a woman of good sense and kindness, talking in a voice that is clear, wise, and inviting. She tells the truth about the way things are, and often with wit, but does no damage in the telling. Sometimes she will go on, looking for further kindnesses, where Potter would get right to the point, but otherwise it strikes me that Craik's is a voice Potter grew up remembering—the voice of a woman of "independent principles" who did go into the world and has both assurances and truth to report.

Here is a line from *Pigling Bland*:

> They led prosperous, uneventful lives and their end was bacon.

And here is the same thought from Craik, as she tells what became of those ducklings:

> They lived a lazy, peaceful, pleasant life for a long time, and were at last killed and eaten with green peas, one after the other, to the family's great satisfaction, if not to their own.

In the matter of kinship and family, it seems Potter had found, or had always had, an Aunt Dinah. In *Jemima Puddle-duck*, the most autobiographical of her tales, she brought the aunt together with an uncle known to her from her books, and sat down in the middle.

4

> "I lay yo' ma got company," said Uncle Remus, as the little boy entered the old man's door with a huge piece of mince-pie in his hand, "en ef she ain't got comp'ny, den she done gone en drap de cubberd key somers whar you done run up wid it."
>
> "Well, I saw the pie lying there, Uncle Remus, and I just thought I'd fetch it out to you."
>
> "Tooby sho, honey," replied the old man, regarding the child with admiration. "Tooby sho, honey; dat changes matters."

These are the opening lines to the first of six *Uncle Remus* tales that Potter illustrated[26] beginning in 1893 when she was giving serious thought to becoming a book illustrator. The tale appears in *Songs & Sayings* as "Mr. Wolf Makes a Failure" (sometimes titled "Wahoo!"). It is one of the funnier tales in the series, but it is only one of more than a hundred available to Potter in that year, and I am led to ask why she would have chosen to illustrate this one before any other. Most of the tales have introductions as congenial; she would have felt welcome in any one of them. The answer, I think, is this: "Mr. Wolf Makes a Failure" marks the first time in the series that the little boy appears at Uncle Remus's door because his parents are too busy for him. As we know too well, Potter's own parents shared virtually nothing with their daughter, not even their time. Never did they regard her with the admiration Uncle Remus bestows on this little boy. There was never a moment like this in her life.

Copies of *Songs & Sayings* and its first sequel, *Nights with Uncle Remus*, each of them bearing a Rupert Potter bookplate, were found in Beatrix's own library in Sawrey on her death in 1943 at the age of seventy-seven.[27] From the fact alone of their having been preserved over six decades like two slices of mince pie, one would have to conclude that they meant something, and, of course, they did. When in her later years she made the remark in a letter from Sawrey that Americans were always welcome there because they "love the same old tales that I do,"[28] these were most certainly the tales she meant. In 1893 *Songs & Sayings* and *Nights* will be the all-important volumes lying open at her desk as she first tries her hand at the business of Caldecott and Greenaway and then slowly finds her way to the sand-bank to become Beatrix Potter of the tales.

There will be other books open there as well. Over the next few years she will try to illustrate an *Aesop*, an alphabet, some *Mother Goose*, a fairy tale, and so on—anything, it seems, with a likely chance of success. All of these will be put aside. Her "Cinderella" is skilled work but too regressively whimsical, busy with characters coming and going, and all of them tiny, and all of them rabbits and moles and mice. The alphabet bores her, and she is tentative with *Aesop*. The technical display in a set of pictures for "Three little mice sat down to spin" is dazzling—photorealism applied to the world of make-believe—but the thing lacks real life. There have been enough tableaux already, enough creatures like herself frozen in place. What she needs to find now is a way of shaking herself loose from the picture's frame, of moving herself and her images through time and space—and to do that she must find a story to tell, and a line that talks.

Not surprisingly, as she thinks to invent a story of her own, she takes as her first models Edward Lear's happy runaways, the Owl and the Pussycat. It is a natural choice for someone in her straits. It is also the wrong choice. Lear wrote his songs nearer the end of his life than the beginning and, existing as he did in a state of melancholic grace, could take a more playful measure of the need to escape. Potter is too young, even at twenty-seven, to play this game, and too earnest. Also, she is translating from the wrong medium. A nonsense song, being once more removed from reality than a story, can bear more whimsy than a story can. Runcible spoons and Bong trees simply will not take root in Potter's world. What will take root, as *Little Pig Robinson* is retired to the drawer, is a bit of wisdom intuited from *Uncle Remus*, to keep her forays into the world more reasonable, more close to home. In Jeremy Fisher's outing at the local pond, or Peter's raid of McGregor's garden, there is story enough.

Looking over the evidence, I think it is clear that Potter was so taken with *Uncle Remus* that she followed the series faithfully through its first five volumes, to 1895, and possibly farther. She necessarily had the third volume of 1889, *Daddy Jake the Runaway* (the title alone would have appealed to her), because in 1897, in a picture-letter to a child friend, she quotes from it.[29] There is a great likelihood that she had the 1892 *Uncle Remus and His Friends*, the first volume to be illustrated by A. B. Frost. Three years later, when the famous Frost reissue of *Songs & Sayings* is published, she is ready with pencil and brush in hand: her illustration for "The Awful Fate of Mr. Wolf" in March of that year will be a copy of the Frost rendering. The March date attributed to this picture is so close to the book's publication date, in fact, as to suggest she was there at the bookshop waiting when the first copies arrived.

Over the next decade she will take from the tales as liberally as Peter from McGregor's vegetable patch. It seems to have been so much a family matter with her that we even find her slipping private jokes about *Uncle Remus* into her books. Who is this "little black rabbit" who pops up as a suitor "tapping at Cottontail's door" in *Appley Dapply's Nursery Rhymes*? Is it the same black rabbit mentioned in *Mr. Tod*? ("Cottontail had married a black rabbit, and gone to live on the hill.") Could they both be that same Brer Rabbit who courted one of the gals by singing nursery rhymes down her chimney, and made Miss Molly Cottontail his wife? Should there be any doubt about this, or about all of Potter's rabbits being black rabbits, there is her own testimony in the matter. Asked once to explain the success of *Peter Rabbit* and *Benjamin Bunny*, she did so by way of *Uncle Tom's Cabin*. "Like Topsy," she said, "they just 'grow'd'."[30]

How they grow'd — how rabbits born black in one neighborhood grew up English in another, and why, significantly, Potter chose to translate them from one tale in *Uncle Remus* and not the next — is exhibited in her books most clearly by her method in making *The Tale of Mr. Tod*.

The last of her major works to be published, this trickster epic about the neighborhood bullies was begun in May of 1895 with Potter's third attempt at a picture for *Uncle Remus*, this time for the tale "Brother Rabbit Rescues Brother Terrapin" (*Nights*). I say attempt only because her plump and hesitant hero is far from the rangy cut-up and bordello dandy found in the tales. She knows it is wrong, and I think even as she executes this picture she is imagining her way toward something else.

"The Bag in the Corner," as the tale is sometimes known, is the story of a kidnapping, a rescue, and a brawl, which at its most primitive level is the story of *Mr. Tod* as well. In the original, Brer Fox, having toted Brer Terrapin home in the bag of the title, has no sooner lit his pipe than "Brer Rabbit stick he head in de do' en holler":

> "Brer Fox! O Brer Fox! You better take yo' walkin-cane en run down yan . . . dar wuz a whole passel er folks in yo' water-million patch des a-tromplin' 'roun'. . . . "

In his absence a hornet nest is substituted for Brer Terrapin, and rescuer and victim hide outside to witness the ruckus that ensues when the returning villain unties the bag looking for his supper. Potter begins to build *Mr. Tod* from this scenario by a series of substitutions of her own. Flopsy's and Benjamin's babies replace Brer Terrapin in the bag; the hornet nest becomes the badger Tommy Brock, who in turn replaces Brer Fox as the kidnapper; and it is Peter and Benjamin who witness the climactic battle from hiding. Having no experience of a brawl herself, Potter paraphrases *Uncle Remus* directly:

Seem like, fum whar Brer Rabbit en Brer Tarrypin settin' dat dey wuz a whole passel er cows runnin' 'roun' in Brer Fox house. Dey year de cheers a-fallin', en de table turnin' over, en de crock'ry breakin', en den de do' flew'd open, en out come Brer Fox, a-squallin' lak de Ole Boy wuz atter 'im. En sech a sight ez dem t'er creeturs seed den en dar ain't never bin seed befo' ner sence.

. . . there was a terrific battle all over the kitchen. To the rabbits underneath it sounded as if the floor would give way at each crash of falling furniture.
. . . Everything was upset except the kitchen table.
. . . The crockery was smashed to atoms.
. . . The chairs were broken.
. . . Tommy Brock . . . rolled Mr. Tod over and over like a log, out at the door.
Then the snarling and worrying went on outside; and they rolled over the bank, and down hill, bumping over the rocks. There will never be any love lost between Tommy Brock and Mr. Tod.

For the elaborate trick that constitutes the heart of the book Potter returns to the first tale she illustrated for *Uncle Remus*, "Mr. Wolf Makes a Failure" (*Songs & Sayings*). Here she uses the dead-scene in which Brer Fox fools Brer Rabbit by lying abed feigning his own demise. By substituting Tommy Brock in the bed for Brer Fox, and giving Tod thereby an anxious twenty-two pages of contriving to get him out, Potter is able to set up a comic counterpoint to the air of dread that otherwise pervades the book. The badger's invasion of Tod's house in the first place, and his insolence there, may derive from a third tale, "Brother Rabbit Breaks Up a Party" (*Nights*), in which Brer Rabbit takes advantage of Brer Fox's absence to "make hisse'f at home wid puttin' his foots on de sofy en spittin' on de flo'." Tod's wary investigation of his invaded premises, his withdrawal to the yard and attempt at a trick on the intruder within all bear a strong resemblance to yet another tale, "Heyo, House!" (*Friends*).

Together, these four tales account for every element Potter needed to construct *The Tale of Mr. Tod*. In Brer Fox and in Brer Rabbit and family they gave her Tod, Peter, Benjamin, and Flopsy.[31] In the little rabs they gave her the abducted children; and in the hornet nest, Tommy Brock. They gave her the bag, the posse, Tod's walking stick, the dead-scene in the bed, the idea of playing a trick on the intruder (but not the mechanics, which she fumbles), the climactic battle, and the witnesses in hiding. What they did not give her, of course, was *The Tale of Mr. Tod* itself, the living character of the book: its physical personality as a countrywoman's chapbook with woodcuts; its intimately observed sense of neighborhood, the me-to-you tone of voice, the gothic dread. Nor did they give her Tommy Brock, really. There are no badgers in *Uncle Remus*; "The Bag in the Corner" could give her only the occasion for a Brock. Potter shaped the occasion into one of the great minor characters in children's story:

> Tommy Brock was a short bristly fat waddling person with a grin; he grinned all over his face. He was not nice in his habits. He ate wasp nests [a nod to Brock's origin?] and frogs and worms; and he waddled about by moonlight, digging things up.

Once satisfied that her translation from *Uncle Remus* has grow'd sufficiently English, Potter stamps it officially hers in the first-person singular:

> I have made many books about well-behaved people. Now, for a change, I am going to make a story about two disagreeable people, called Tommy Brock and Mr. Tod.

Only one other of her books begins on such a personal note. Potter had digressed into this lighter-hearted version of "The Bag in the Corner" at some point during her long hesitation over whether or not to publish *Mr. Tod*. Once again it is Benjamin's and Flopsy's children in the bag; and, as before, there is a row in the villain's kitchen and witnesses to it in hiding. *Mr. Tod* and *The Flopsy Bunnies* are different stories but they are the same tale. They differ structurally only in Potter's use in the latter of the original rescue by substitution, with rotten vegetables for hornets, and with Mrs. Tittlemouse standing in for Brer Rabbit as trickster. The book will precede its parent story into print by three years, and with an even more assertive opening in the first person:

> It is said that the effect of eating too much lettuce is "soporific." *I* have never felt sleepy after eating lettuces; but then *I* am not a rabbit.

What the two introductions imply is that fresh work is being undertaken extemporaneously here, and this is a deception. To us, Potter's borrowing habit can hardly matter; *Mr. Tod* and *The Flopsy Bunnies* are not imitation *Uncle Remus* but a new order of story altogether, and one for which she deserves sole credit. To Potter herself it may have seemed, however, more the poaching of an amateur than the modus operandi of a real artist. It can be no accident that of all her books only these two, of the three most heavily in debt to *Uncle Remus*, open with a pretence of absolute originality. It may be no accident either that she should be so knowing of Tommy Brock's appropriating ways. Had she not, with her six illustrations and subsequent borrowings, trespassed in *Uncle Remus* "without asking leave,"[32] exactly as Brock had helped himself to Tod's six houses? Hadn't she hopped the wall like Brock, carrying a full bag of tricks? Throughout her work Potter's real sympathies will lie not with "well-behaved people" but with trespassers and sneaks and thieves. For an aging child in her father's house it could hardly have been otherwise. An errand down to the kitchen from the third-floor nursery was as furtive a trip for Potter as it was for the rat-wife Anna Maria in *The Roly-Poly Pudding*.

Her stealthy habits put her in a quandary, though, when she came to publish. What do you say to the world about tales in which you strove to tell the truth, when you grubbed them up by moonlight? It is a problem she will never resolve. In 1911, a celebrated author with seventeen books to her credit, she backs into the submission of *Mr. Tod* with an almost plaintive apology:

> I think this story is amusing. . . . Its principal defect is imitation of "Uncle Remus." It is no drawback for children, because they cannot read the negro dialect—I hardly think the publishers could object to it? I wrote it some time ago.[33]

No one ever did notice how closely she had paraphrased *Uncle Remus*, but, as her letter implies, she thought *Mr. Tod* a dead giveaway. After the perjury of her opening paragraph she seems to feel compelled to leave self-incriminating traces behind, like Tommy Brock's footprints it the mud or the "ravellings of a sack . . . caught on a briar." When Tod is returning home along Bull Banks, for example, she slips in the phrase "a fox coming up the plantation." The only thing that is unclear about this hint is what her mood might have been in dropping it. Did she mean it as a playful tribute? A grudging nod to the truth? Or is it a guilty child's hedge against some feared charge of copying with intent? Was it a conscious gesture even, or the carelessness of a shoplifter who secretly hopes to be caught? It is as ambiguous in the end as the wasp nests she associates with Tommy Brock.

More problematical than the plantation clue is Potter's gossip regarding Cotton-tail's husband. When Peter and Benjamin stop to enlist him in their rescue party, the black rabbit—whom I think we can assume is meant to be Brer Rabbit—is made to show the white feather. Why Potter would introduce Brer Rabbit into the story only to brand him a coward is a mystery. As I suggested earlier, she may have meant it merely as a quip—a way of saying (if only to herself), Never mind the Yank, our boys can do the job. It smells naughtier than that to me, however, and slightly irrational, as if Potter, like Mr. McGregor in *The Flopsy Bunnies*, had "done it a purpose," perhaps to balance accounts for needing to drop the plantation clue in the first place.

What these little anomalies suggest to me, really, is that a more personal disturbance underlies *Mr. Tod* than just a fear of being caught out as a copyist. Potter had no such problem covering her tracks in her other work. *The Roly-Poly Pudding* and *Jemima* are as easily traceable to famous sources as *Mr. Tod*, yet there are no apparent ambiguities in the text of either book. That *Mr. Tod* was giving her some deeper kind of anxiety is accented, too, by her attempt to bypass it altogether in 1909 with *The Flopsy Bunnies*, which is even more obviously beholden to "The Bag in the Corner" than its parent story.

Whatever name we might put to this anxiety—and I am not sure that I have one myself—its source does lie, I think, in her encounter with *Uncle Remus* in 1895. It is here that the character of Potter's work begins its metamorphosis from mere whimsy to the darker vocabulary of behavior that we find throughout her tales. Here the laconic observer begins to emerge who can put Peter Rabbit's father in a pie, or insinuate that when Mr. Jackson next opens his mouth "most unnecessarily wide" his appetite might be for Mr. Tittlemouse herself. Potter's ability to caricature villainy will come, too, from Dickens, much of it; and from Craik I believe she has learned to say "Their end was bacon" and move calmly on. But access to the whole of her mind, and her ability to say the whole of her mind on paper began (insofar as we have a record) in May of 1895 with her illustration for "The Bag in the Corner."

It is a transitional picture for Potter, a hesitant step away from her earlier tableaux and the toward the kind of animated drawing we find in *Peter Rabbit*. The pencil work is conversational, but she has stopped short of actually letting the picture speak. Brer Rabbit stands alone in his enemy's house. Brer Terrapin is a prisoner still in the bag. A few cleavers and a chopper are visible in the gloom; also a mess of feathers and a skull. The scene feels stillborn, suspended in utter silence. And the cleavers, the chopper, and the skull do not belong. There are no such details to be found in *Uncle Remus*; nor could Potter have copied them from A. B. Frost—he never illustrated "The Bag in the Corner." These emblems she dreamed herself. When she submits *Mr. Tod* in 1911, a kitchen table will display the knife and chopper and Tod's yard will recall the rest:

> The sun had set; an owl began to hoot in the wood. There were many unpleasant things lying about, that had much better have been buried; rabbit bones and skulls, and chickens' legs and other horrors. It was a shocking place, and very dark.

Strong stuff for an illustrator of greeting cards, and lovingly preserved. What was there about "The Bag in the Corner" that could have provoked cleavers and a chopper and skulls from Potter's imagination? Earlier I said that whenever we find her borrowing from a text we almost always find in that text some speaking likeness to Potter herself. The rule holds especially true here, I think. The frame story to "The Bag in the Corner" dramatizes a conflict of loyalties very much like Beatrix's own. The young and "complacent" house-girl Tildy, for somewhat muddled reasons, has fixed on the notion that she has a duty to marry the Gullah Negro, Daddy Jack, a cantankerous old man who ordinarily sends her into fits of wanting to knock his brains out. "Somebody bleedzd to take keer er dat ole nigger," she tells Uncle Remus, "an I dunner gwine ter do it ef I don't." Potter is twenty-nine. Her history we know. She is a daughter duty bound to the stewardship of her aging parents, a keeper to her keepers. Her only marriage will likely be the pseudo-marriage of an indentured spinsterhood at home. Her parents and her own hateful shyness will see to it.

There is often a fine line dividing the artistic from the criminal act. We know the famous story of that other dutiful daughter of Potter's day, an American stifled and exemplary who, having no art to install her cutlery in one sweltering summer's morn, installed it in her parents instead. Perhaps for the space of one held breath as she bent over her drawing table in May of 1895 Beatrix Potter felt what Lizzie Borden felt. I don't know why we can't allow a children's author at least one hating moment in a lifetime of disappointment. Perhaps *Uncle Remus* gave Beatrix more than just characters and plots; perhaps it gave her a place to encode truer signs of her feelings than she could ever admit to her journal. For sixteen years she would hold onto a story whose source promised rescue and, when there was none, allowed her cleavers. It was not the fear of being branded a copyist that caused the long wait. Nearly all of her books were copies. Her fear of being thought derivative was real, but it was not specific to *Mr. Tod. The Flopsy Bunnies*, remember, was a copy of the very same tale. The real answer to why she waited can be found, I believe, in the book's publication date. When Potter finally released it to her publishers late in 1911, she had reached the moment in her life when escape to Sawrey and a husband seemed certain at last. Her long service to her parents was coming to an end, and so was her need for the unfinishable *Mr. Tod*.

"I feel younger at thirty than I did at twenty"[34] she had written in 1896, midway between discovering "The Bag in the Corner" and abandoning her journal forever; "firmer and stronger in both mind and body." Burying the hatchet in *Mr. Tod* may have helped.

5

In the end she was a trickster in her own right, a teller of tales more witty, more subversive, and more attentive to the truth than the children's field is accustomed to seeing. We tend to forget today what writers of the last century took as an article of faith, that however fanciful or benign a gesture children's story may be, its purpose is to tell us what the world is and what will happen to us when we go into it. This Potter did do—with irony, acid, and utter charm. At her best she never thought how the world might be if it were not as it is. Sending an apprentice everyman like Peter Rabbit to squeeze under the garden gate was not an occasion to warm our hearts; she thought only to get the thing right. We are all of us engaged in a comically lamentable business; our fate is to keep putting ourselves at risk and to come home again and again, like Brer Fox, "wid a spell er de dry grins." This is what she knew and what she told in tale after tale. Her stories are little dramatizations of her own thwarted longing to be joined with the world; the wonder of them is how much stoical sport she can eke out of each new abortive mission. The calamities she visits on Peter Rabbit, Tom Kitten, Jeremy Fisher, and Jemima Puddle-duck; the rage and disappointment of Tom Thumb and Hunca Munca, the distraction and weariness of the neurotic Mrs. Tittlemouse — when detailed to such perfection these do provide us with a kind of enchantment. The real pleasures of story, after all, are not the pleasures of escape but those of recognition, and what is recognized, however baleful, can be made, the stoic knows, into comedy.

Once she did go too far, even for her own rueful brand of humor. In *Johnny Town-mouse*, her meditation on Aesop, she succumbed to telling about the one thing children understand best, loneliness, and the one thing they prize most, friendship. Her country mouse is a plain and solitary cousin like herself, and naive. Patronized and left to his own devices by his more sophisticated kind in town, he still hopes that "his new friends" will pay him a return visit. Johnny Town-mouse, who "had half promised," does turn up after a year or so, looking for some diversion in a slow season. What Timmy Willie has to offer simply won't do. "I am sure you will never want to live in town again," said Timmy Willie hopefully; the crushing line at the book's conclusion reads, "But he did."

This is harsh. Potter has done some damage here, and she knows it. Her penultimate line, "One place suits one person, another place suits another person," is too little consolation. *Johnny Town-mouse* is not a simple fable about choices. The book must close on a more saving note. And in fact Potter's last line is the tale's most necessary gesture. She writes, "For my part I prefer to live in the country, like Timmy Willie." She has given him, in herself, a friend of sorts after all.

Published in 1918, *Johnny Town-mouse* had been written a decade earlier, at the time of *Jemima Puddle-duck*, which it resembles as an autobiographical testament. What Potter has succumbed to here finally, I think, is the weight of her own solitude. It was enough of a weight that she had no comedy in her here to save the story. It is this same, utter loneliness, of course, that will drive her to seek the true level of her mind and imagine a new kind of literature. Throughout the descent of story loneliness has been the improbable fountain of youth. Andersen, Carroll, Lear, and Collodi all lived by it; each encoded what he knew of it into fantasy; and each would tell a kind of story that had never been told before.

This is the one thing to consider when reading a *Johnny Town-mouse*, or a *Mr. Tod*, or an apparently self-evident book like *Peter Rabbit* — how much of her life Potter spent alone and how entirely her real life was a life lived in secret. By the time of her books, dealing in signs had become her accustomed way. The semicolons that foreclose on a thought; the evasively quick paragraphing; her characters' self-absorbed or guarded rejoinders; their small thefts and trespasses — remember, until she was thirty-one Potter had talked to herself in code. Now the books were a continuation of the journal, and her characters a new code. Their success, and through them her own, will lie, as she said, in how they "keep on their way; busily absorbed in their own doings."[35] It is how we might describe Potter's style as well. Pick a page from any of her books; you can see how involved she becomes in odd bits of business usually passed by in the pursuit of plot and meaning and how she achieves curious effects by pacing alone:

> First he ate some lettuces and some French beans; and then he ate some radishes;
> And then, feeling rather sick, he went to look for some parsley.

The Potter telling *Peter Rabbit* is not the detached observer we hear in more complex books like *Jemima* or *Mr. Tod* or *Ginger & Pickles*; nor is she the seasoned entertainer summoned for the occasion of a *Two Bad Mice*. All these books call for some distance between teller and tale. *Mr. Tod*, for example, is a tale that has taken on the character of a gothic novel. It is built up of several tales to contain a traditional apparatus of subplot and atmosphere more complex than any one tale could bear; and it was built up to contain something of Potter herself that, like Mr. Jackson's bumblebees or the knots in Samuel Whiskers's pudding, was "all over bristles" and "indigestible." The book that made Potter famous was never so heavily burdened. It was first set to paper as an entertainment for a five-year-old child, and it represents perhaps the simplest narrative gesture a storyteller can make. The voice in which it is told is a modulation of the tone in which she reported her pets' eccentricities to her journal. It has become a voice very much like Craik's or Uncle Remus's: easy with itself, straightforward, and intimate in its attentiveness to the small things of the moment. It is the voice of someone who is a friend of the hero and a friend of the reader and who is passing on information of interest:

> I think he might have got away altogether if he had not unfortunately run into a gooseberry net, and got caught by the large buttons on his jacket. It was a blue jacket with brass buttons, quite new.

Potter's friend here, the little boy listening to the tale, was Noel Moore, the son of her former German tutor. The story is well known, how in a moment of inspiration while on vacation in September of 1893 Potter dashed off the early draft of *Peter Rabbit* in a picture-letter to Noel, who was then ill. It is one of those little legends peculiar to the history of children's literature, and it is not wrong exactly, just misleading. She did writer the letter; and since she asked for it back several years later, it is likely that, if not the only copy to have survived her inspiration, it was the version she preferred. You have only to look at a facsimile of the letter, however, to see that it is too composed to be anything dashed off, and is almost certainly a second or third draft from notes and sketches. What it represents, I believe, is a telling, perhaps the first, of a tale then fresh in Potter's mind from a recent reading of *Uncle Remus*. In 1893, remember, *Songs & Sayings* lay open at her drawing table. *The Tale of Peter Rabbit and Mr. McGregor's Garden*, as she first titled it, comes from "A Story About the Little Rabbits" in that collection and from two tales in *Nights*, "Brother Rabbit and the Little Girl" and "In Some Lady's Garden." It possibly owes something also to "Why Brother Wolf Didn't Eat the Little Rabbits" from *Uncle Remus and His Friends*, published the year before the picture-letter and containing the first illustration of the little rabbits, by A. B. Frost.

In the passage below I have interwoven Potter's lines with several from *Uncle Remus* to demonstrate just how easily they can be made to describe one and the same event:

> Once upon a time there were four little Rabbits, and their names were Flopsy, Mopsy, Cotton-tail, and Peter. They lived with their Mother in a sand-bank, underneath the root of a very big fir-tree. Dey minded der mammy fum day's een' ter day's een'. Dey kep' der cloze clean, en dey ain't had no smut on der nose nudder. W'en old Miss Rabbit say 'scat', dey scatted. En w'en ole Miss Rabbit say, 'run along and don't get into mischief', dey did dat. Flopsy, Mopsy, and Cotton-tail were good little bunnies, en dey useter run down the lane to gather blackberries. Dey wuz all good chilluns; 'cept'n' der wuz one time . . .
>
> "What time was that, Uncle Remus?" the little boy asked.
>
> De time w'en Peter, who was very naughty, ran straight away to Mr. McGregor's garden and squeezed under the gate! Ole Brer Rabbit, he wuz off somers, en ole Miss Rabbit she wuz tendin' on a quiltin in de neighborhood. W'en Peter see Mr. McGregor, he squat behime a collud leaf, but 'twa'n't no use. Mr. McGregor done seed him . . .

As it would with *Mr. Tod, Uncle Remus* gave Potter every element she needed to construct her story. It gave her those most essential components, the little rabbits themselves and a garden to raid, complete with irate gardener. It gave her such lesser details as the name Cotton-tail, the idea of capitalizing "Rabbits," Mrs. Rabbit's errand, and the notion that Mr. Rabbit was the gardener's supper ("I want yo' meat fer ter put in de pot"). It gave her Peter's tears, his running "lippity lippity," and in the phrase that opens the first story, "good chilluns allers gits tuck keer on," it gave her the conceit of Flopsy, Mopsy, and Cotton-tail who are "good little bunnies" who get milk and blackberries for supper.

When fleshing out her tale from the original picture-letter she ensures that Peter gets took keer on as well by reaching back into "A Story About the Little Rabbits" for the figure of the helpful bird. Here the little rabs have been set an impossible task by Brer Fox, failing which they:

> sot down en 'gun ter cry. Den de little bird settin' up in de tree he begin fer ter sing, en dish yer's de song w'at he sing:
>
> > Sifter hol' water same ez a tray,
> > Ef you fill it wid moss en dob it wid clay;
> > De Fox git madder de longer you stay —
> > Fill it wid moss en dob it wid clay.

Up dey jump, de little Rabbits did, en dey fix de sifter so twon't leak . . .

In Potter this becomes

Peter gave himself up for lost, and shed big tears; but his sobs were overheard by some friendly sparrows, who flew to him in great excitement, and implored him to exert himself.

Mr. McGregor came up with a sieve, which he intended to pop upon the top of Peter; but Peter wriggled out just in time, leaving his jacket behind him.

The resemblance between the two scenes might seem accidental were it not for a small but telling change of one word from the picture-letter to the published draft. The text of the original version reads, "Mr. McGregor came up with a basket," not a sieve. Clearly, when she went back to *Uncle Remus* for the helpful bird, she brought out the little rabbits' sifter with it. The only question is, why? In dramatic and pictorial terms the change is all but pointless.

The answer, I think, leads us back to one of those anomalies found in *Mr. Tod*:

a fox was coming up the plantation

Mr. McGregor came up with a sieve

There is more here than just a tic in phrasing. The scenes in which these lines appear are similar enough, in fact, for use to conclude that at some point between 1895 and 1900 Potter had written them concurrently and was likely playing the same game in each. Both scenes tell us that something has been lost (Tod's anonymity, Peter's jacket), and the consequent revelation of identity (real fox, real rabbit) is attended in each instance by birds. In *Peter Rabbit* it is a trio of friendly sparrows; in *Mr. Tod*, a jaybird warning everyone in the neighborhood to pay attention to an intruder. Both jay and sparrow can be found paired, as it happens, in the next tale Potter will use in making *Peter Rabbit*, "Brother Rabbit and the Little Girl." Here Brer Rabbit is charming his way into the little girl's favor with a nonsense song:

> De jay-bird hunt de sparrer-nes',
> De bee-martin sail all 'roun';
> De squer'l, he holler from de top er de tree,
> Mr. Mole, he stay in de groun';
> He hide en he stay twel de dark drap down —
> Mr. Mole, he hide in de groun'.

Look back to the early pages of *Mr. Tod*. What is it that Tommy Brock is doing as he makes his rounds of the neighborhood? The person who "grinned all over his face" is setting mole traps. In her opening two scenes Potter thinks to mention the fact four times, most noticeably in the passage beginning "There was not much difficulty in tracking him" and ending with "the badger's heavy steps showed plainly in the mud."

Could Potter have meant her telltale sieve as yet another clue that here she had left a track of her own to follow? Her fear of being exposed as a copyist would lead to a lifelong silence about *Uncle Remus*, but when she first set *Peter Rabbit* to paper in 1893 her mood may have been different. "De Little Gal . . . she laugh, she did, and she up'n ax Brer Rabbit fer ter sing some mo," says the tale, and I suspect it was with brash self-amusement that Potter set about planting clues that here at this exact point, and there at that exact point, is where we should look to find her exiting *Uncle Remus* with her bag of tricks. What she had done, after all, was artfully done, and a real trickster would have itched to strut it a bit. Interestingly, she would later take some pride that the creator of Sherlock Holmes had a good opinion of her first book. Could she not make a modest claim in the arts of cunning and detection herself? The anomalies in *Mr. Tod* and *Peter Rabbit*, the tics and slips of phrase, the allusions to black rabbits, the trail of footprints and calls to pay attention are subliminal clues but too many and too tempting not to think them a deliberate effort to leave behind a modus operandi for us to uncover one day when she was past all embarrassment. Footwork this adroit wanted appreciating.

It is in the pair of garden tales in *Nights with Uncle Remus* that we can see how Potter might have come to cast herself as Sis Beatrix the trickster. In 1893 she is a twenty-seven-year-old spinster with a beloved pet rabbit and an unloving and unloved father. What she will find in each of these tales is a promising little drama of duty and deception, played out by an obdurate daddy, a daughter sent to mind the garden gate, and a rabbit determined to stuff greens. In the sentimental portrait illustrating the first of these tales, "Brother Rabbit and the Little Girl," she may well have recognized two of the players in the flesh. Harris's original illustrator, F. S. Church, has depicted not the black farm girl we should expect here but the sort of well-dressed white miss found in the pages of *St. Nicholas Magazine*. The rabbity character perched in her lap is wooing her with the instinctive savvy of an adoring pet. Potter will later use this same tale as a source for the autobiographical *Jemima Puddle-duck*. Elsewhere in *Nights* she will discover Jemima's rescue by the dogs (in "Mr. Fox and Miss Goose") and the name Miss Puddle-duck itself. But it is in "Brother Rabbit and the Little Girl" that she found ready-cut the debonair manner of that gentleman with the sandy whiskers whom Jemima thought "mighty civil and handsome." For a rustic seducer she needed to look no farther than this bowing Brer Rabbit come to court a girl's favor by talking "mighty nice en slick."

"In Some Lady's Garden," the second of the two tales, continues the flirtation several years later. Brer Rabbit's "I aint seed you sence you 'uz a little bit er baby, en now yer you is mighty nigh a grown 'oman" might well have said something to the lonely daughter who thought of her childhood as a paradise lost, yet could not grow up; certainly his joke about the girl's father would have: Brer Rabbit, "wunk he off eye . . . en 'low, 'You oughter be monstous glad, honey, dat you got sech a good daddy.'"

Did Sis Beatrix wink back? It is not hard to read *Peter Rabbit* as a natural sequel to "In Some Lady's Garden." This is the tale in which the little girl's daddy wants Brer Rabbit's meat for the pot. To invent her own tale Potter had only to imagine how life might have gone on for the widow and the little rabbits if he *had* become the gardener's supper. I think she did wink back. She did it by squeezing Brer Rabbit's son under that same gate a dutiful daughter was meant to guard and allowing him to have his way with the father's produce. *Peter Rabbit* began in the privacy of a smile, as a trick played on her own daddy by a Beatrix who had learned from *Uncle Remus* that hers were the habits of the trickster and could be turned to good and profitable account. The famous Mr. McGregor was modeled not on any of the real gardeners in Potter's life who have been promoted for the role but on Mr. Potter himself, and from a book in his own library. Beatrix is the thief's accomplice, the little girl who by stepping out of the frame to tell the tale found a place in story that was unavailable to her in real life, where she could "tuck'n' fling de gate wide open" and upset, for a moment, the daily round.

This is how she came to the now and forever by the sand-bank, not through greeting cards and affecting whimsy but by the coarser route of *Uncle Remus*, by the back door of small imaginary acts against orders and imposed routine, and by tricks of the trade that would become, through her silence, tricks played on the whole world. It was naughty, like Peter's trespass, and despite her fear of being caught out it was probably the only real fun she ever had. It wouldn't have mattered to her, perhaps, but she did entirely change the nature of storytelling while she was about it. The actual gesture that would translate folklore into a more personal and intimate kind of tale was no more than a glance away once she had reached the right place in the existing literature. If a picture could be called up to show it happening, I think we would see Beatrix in her third-floor room with a copy of *Uncle Remus* in her lap, staring intently at one of Frost's portraits of the little rabbits and calling out like Brer Fox, "You young Rab in der back dar, sail' 'roun' here."

The thought has just come to her to give one of the little rabbits a name and a book of his own. In two centuries of working up folklore into books for children, no one has ever thought of this before. It took someone forced to read for her very life to discover the simple thing.

8

THE GREEN PASTURES
The Descent of the Fable

In 1895 Joel Chandler Harris characterized *Uncle Remus* with a euphemism that misrepresented black lore by a country mile but did nicely describe the demeanor of the literature waiting in the wings. The blurb appeared in the introduction of the reissue of *Songs & Sayings*, in an open letter to its new illustrator, A. B. Frost. "The book was mine," Harris wrote in admiration, "but now you have made it yours. . . . You have breathed the breath of life into these amiable brethren of wood and field."

Neighbors as deeply in the employ of satire as Brer Rabbit and Brer Fox, who must daily make it their business to dupe and mug one another, could hardly be called amiable brethren, of course. Harris may only have been speechifying here. On the other hand, he may actually have believed his little caricature, as Charles Dodgson had done when pronouncing *Wonderland* a "friendly chat." In any case, he was prophetic. This third great class of make-believe, which for eighty years will dominate the literature as the natural best way of telling a children's story, is going to be amiable indeed.

We have seen Beatrix Potter at work. Hers was the patient faith of the stoic that page by page, year by year, things might be agreeably worked out. This was the most subtle sleight of hand in her bag of tricks, the subliminal lesson that history and fiction are the slow turning of pages and attention must be paid:

> Once upon a time there
> were four little Rabbits,

318

and their names were—
> Flopsy,
> Mopsy,
> Cotton-tail,
> and Peter.

They lived with their Mother in a sand-bank, underneath the root of a very big fir-tree.

[here we turn the page]

"Now, my dears," said old Mrs. Rabbit one morning. . . .

This opening to *Peter Rabbit* is cunning. The hares we have surprised at their burrow are not yet story characters but feral rabbits, crouching on all fours and ready to bolt at the least danger. Turn the page and they vanish. A mother in dress and apron is passing out baskets to three sisters in red cloaks while a brother stands by, looking itchy in his new, blue jacket. In getting us from page one to page two, Potter has worked a double trick, actually. She has taken us from the natural world into make-believe, and then from the once-upon-a-time of folklore into a new storytime called "*Now*, my dears." There is a feeling of privileged intimacy that comes with turning quietly crafted pages. What amiability Potter achieved she achieved not as a sentimentalist, using the fable as a literature of first convenience, but honestly, through the wry applications of art.

A good storyteller will ordinarily be working too economically to over-play the kindnesses implied by Harris's euphemism. At greater risk of turning these hard-scrabble biographies into a branch of the emotive arts is the novelist. This next advance in the descent of the fable was neither an inherently good nor a required step for entertaining children, but it was a necessary one if the talking beast was to be given every narrative advantage. Ideally, the conversion to the novel meant no loquacious uncle waiting to greet us, no once-upon-a-time to invoke the magic in store, but only the offstage trick of making a miracle story about critters in pants seem as normal to the reader as a new Trollope or Conan Doyle.

The most amiable such experiment appeared in the year of Potter's *Jemima Puddle-duck* and *Roly-Poly Pudding*. It opened in medias res with the casual notation that "The Mole had been working very hard all the morning, spring-cleaning his little home."

The Wind in the Willows (1908)

The beast fable's first novelization chronicles some eighteen months and a dozen or so episodes in the lives of four neighbors living along an English riverbank. The fifth member of the party, Kenneth Grahame (1859–1932), was an aging but gifted amateur of country ways when he set out to record the adventures of Mole, Rat, Toad, and Badger. He came to the project with two agendas and made a book that pulls in two directions. Toad's harebrained pursuit of that latest craze, the motorcar, was the original point of departure; four or more of the twelve chapters are gatherings from yarns Grahame had contrived for his son at bedtime and continued in a series of letters. The book took on its celebrated resonance when he retired to his desk to ponder the great and ancient question, How shall a man live his life? In the bucolic chapters devoted to Mole and Rat, Grahame would give his best-felt answer. Here, too, though, we find the country enthusiast running into difficulties. So long as he remains the novelist and one with the brethren, enjoying the idle pleasures of being "an animal with few wants and fond of a bijou riverside residence," the book is as alive and as amiable as any ever written for children. Let him stand erect to take a journalist's measure of the wildlife, however, and he is at once betrayed by a taste for fin-de-siècle embroidery and a weakness for the pathetic fallacy. Indeed, in the intrusive chapter "The Piper at the Gates of Dawn" and in innumerable other passages, *The Wind in the Willows* is revealed as something of a pantheistic tract. Grahame had published his first hymn to country life in 1893 in *Pagan Papers*. Here is the pagan reborn, evangelizing the reader with lauds to Nature divine:

> Purple loosestrife arrived early, shaking luxuriant tangled locks along the edge of the mirror whence its own face laughed back at it. Willow-herb, tender and wistful, like a pink sunset cloud, was not slow to follow. Comfrey, the purple hand-in-hand with the white, crept forth to take its place in the line; and at last one morning the diffident and delaying dog-rose stepped delicately onto the stage, and one knew, as if string-music had announced it in stately chords that strayed into a gavotte, that June at last was here. One member of the company was still awaited; the shepherd-boy for the nymphs to woo, the knight for whom the ladies waited at the window, the prince that was to kiss the sleeping summer back to life and love.

He did spare us nymphs. The god Pan will make an appearance, inspiring Mole and Rat to weepy prayer, but there are no Isadora Duncans tutoring the meadows with risings and pliés in these passages. A sense of audience kept Grahame grounded, generally, and he saved his best praises for humbler moments like "simply messing about in boats" or the comforts found one terrible night in the Wild Wood when refuge is taken at Badger's house. His greatest strength as a novelist lay in his talent for portraying friendship. For a book that becomes politically more reactionary as it goes along, *Willows* remains everywhere motivated by the most generous impulses. Recall Rat coming to inspect the long-neglected Mole End and how he and his shy chum respond to its "narrow, meagre dimensions, its worn and shabby contents." The would-be host collapses in mortification. What must be done next is managed just as we would want to see it done for ourselves:

> The Rat paid no heed to his doleful self-reproaches. He was running here and there, opening doors, inspecting rooms and cupboards, and lighting lamps and candles and sticking them up everywhere. "What a capital little house this

is!" he called out cheerily. "So compact! So well planned! Everything here and everything in its place! We'll make a jolly night of it. The first thing we want is a good fire; I'll see to that—I always know where to find things. So this is the parlour? Splendid! Your own idea, those little sleeping-bunks in the wall? Capital! Now, I'll fetch the wood and the coals, and you get a duster, Mole— you'll find one in the drawer of the kitchen table—and try and smarten things up a bit. Bustle about, old chap!"

Storytellers in this genre are almost all of them to remain grownups spinning yarns about animal folk for nursery folk. Grahame alone will get inside the skins of his characters. He speaks for them, and for Mole in particular, as naturally as a Dickens speaking for a David Copperfield. So perfectly has he wedded the human and the animal kingdoms that it is no effort at all to imagine the book retold on film in live action, with the roles being played by British character actors. A Michael Palin or the unassuming John Mills might be the Everyman Mole, for example, and Michael Redgrave, perhaps, the sophisticated Rat who initiates him into the pleasures of river-banking. A testy country squire is scrabbling about underground in the person of Alastair Sim, while into the busy outside world roars the collegiate aristocrat with parvenu impulses, gap-toothed Terry-Thomas. You could not make such a reverse translation with *Uncle Remus* or the works of Beatrix Potter. The novelist is able to say things about human needs and choices that would be difficult to express in their worlds. Grahame's exploration of what it means to be a friend remains the literature's best expression of childhood's greatest abiding concern.

A narrative commitment to sensibility over action exposes the children's author to certain hazards, of course. He can easily misspeak the parts, fabricate inanities, or, as often happens, turn hideously whimsical. The form virtually invites the author to hedgerow off a neighborhood as a haven from the cares of the world. Part of Grahame's expansive success in his way with the brethren can be attributed, I suspect, to his drawing from sources that complemented his vast shyness. We might expect this, given the story-hour needs that occasioned the book, but it seems to have been Grahame's mole-ish nature ever to be seeking out the gregarious Rat. As a young man in London he had cultivated bohemian friends, and so has he done here, I think. Humphrey Carpenter has noted a possible precedent for *Willows* in the comic river expedition of Jerome K. Jerome's *Three Men in a Boat* (1889), and in the network of tunnels beneath Badger's home, which are said to be the ruins of a lost city of men, we may be seeing an image from H. G. Wells's *The Time Machine* (1895). The travels and mishaps of Toad, from which the saga grew, were likely prompted by the popular Golliwogg stories of Bertha and Florence Upton (thirteen volumes from 1895 to 1909), and in particular by a bedtime session with *The Golliwogg's Auto-Go-Cart* (1901). Grahame's familiarity with the earliest of the Potter tales I think can be assumed. His acquaintance with *Uncle Remus* comes documented in a letter about Toad that Grahame sent his son in 1907. "I have sent you two picture-books," he wrote, "one about Brer Rabbit, from Daddy, and one about some other animals, from Mummy."[1] This would have been the seventh title in the Harris series, *Uncle Remus and Brer Rabbit* (1907), a larger-format book boasting one or two color illustrations each page, with the stories printed below as captions. It is the only *Uncle Remus* title that could be described as a picture book. Like Potter with her black rabbits, Grahame may even have footnoted *Willows* with a covert citation. Three of the four major British fantasists—Milne would later join this pair—seem to have felt some obligation to insert into their work a token acknowledgment of Brer Rabbit's influence. Grahame appears to be discharging the debt straightaway, as Mole sets out on his adventure. "'Hold up!' said an elderly rabbit at the gap. 'Sixpence for the privilege of passing by the private road!'" As had Potter before him with her little trespasses, he meant to travel this road of story; unlike her, however, he considered it to be a public wayfare and had no apologies to make. The rabbit is "bowled over in an instant by the impatient and contemptuous Mole, who trotted along the side of the hedge chaffing the other rabbits as they peeped hurriedly from their holes to see what the row was about. 'Onion-sauce! Onion-sauce!' he remarked jeeringly, and was gone before they could think of a thoroughly satisfactory reply." The "other rabbits" being trespassed upon here could be Potter's, of course.

What Grahame saw in *Uncle Remus* was not a model that might be imitated but a simple premise. A new kind of story was at hand: pick your ground, pick your most congenial players. The locale, a ramble Thames-side with its eddies and weir, he had chosen long since. The beast fable would give him a way of articulating his desires and a neighborhood to contain them, but the specific site had probably come recommended to him first by a poem in *A Child's Garden of Verses*. What we hear in Grahame and Stevenson is that same conflict between a man's need for the familiar hearthside and his longing for new horizons. In "Where Go the Boats" and "Travel" Stevenson dreamed of sailing to foreign lands, and these are the very dreams Grahame set Rat to dreaming in the chapter "Wayfarers All." For Toad, too, "the dusty roads go up and down." But it is Mole's impetuous maiden voyage up from his narrow confines one spring morning and down to the riverbank that most implicates a source in Stevenson. The spirit of the journey, and its destination and details, were all foretold in 1885 in the poem "Keepsake Mill," published when Grahame was a twenty-six-year-old gentlemen clerk in London and beginning his successful but less than fulfilling banking career:

> Over the border, a sin without pardon,
>   Breaking the branches and crawling below,
> Out through the breach in the wall of the garden,
>   Down by the banks of the river, we go.

> Here is the mill with the humming of thunder,
> Here is the weir with the wonder of foam,
> Here is the sluice with the race running under —
> Marvelous places, though handy to home!

The realized hereness of Grahame's marvelous places handy to home found its visual complement in the 1933 edition of *The Wind in the Willows*, illustrated by Ernest H. Shepard (1879–1976). This running commentary of ninety or so black-and-white spot drawings is the definitive reading of the book and, like its acknowledged ancestor, A. B. Frost's *Uncle Remus*, will likely never be improved upon.

Potter had gone one way with the tale after *Uncle Remus* by turning the heroic role over to one of the little rabbits. Grahame worked a similar feat by making his hero a childlike adult. Rudyard Kipling and A. A. Milne would take the perhaps more obvious next step of translating the listening child out of the frame stories and into the neighborhood to live with the beasts. This is who we find in *The Jungle Book* and *Winnie-the-Pooh*, the little boy of *Uncle Remus*, now wandering the woods as Mowgli and Christopher Robin. Kipling eliminated the artifice of the story hour and achieved a novelistic verisimilitude for his hero by beginning the action in medias res, as Grahame had done. In Milne's nursery saga, which wanted to remain a collection of trickster tales like its predecessor, the better to be, like *Alice*, a game of recognitions, we see the translation into the woods actually being performed and hear the boy's wonder as the trick is worked.

The first animal fantasy to follow *Uncle Remus*, Kipling's tale appeared while Harris was still at midstream in his own series and fourteen years before Grahame arrived with the fable's first novel. It is actually something of an anomaly in this company, bearing few of the form's true hallmarks.

The Jungle Book (1894), *The Second Jungle Book* (1895), *Just So Stories* (1902)

In 1893, while Potter puzzled out *Peter Rabbit* from the copies of *Uncle Remus* in her lap, Kipling (1865–1936) was in America. Newly famous as a teller of tales, the knockabout journalist had come with his American wife to Brattleboro, Vermont, there to raise his family and, if possible, to write in the American vein about American things. As it happened, the native stock was to surrender a *Captains Courageous* (1897) to his pen but only baffle him otherwise. It confounded even his children's stories, deflecting them back abroad to India and the world. "The failure of America finally to act on Kipling's mind," Angus Wilson has written, "is seen . . . in his failure to produce a fable from the wild life, although it fascinated him greatly."[2]

That the American experiment should founder in his imagination is perhaps not surprising. Kipling was by circumstance cosmopolitan and by habit peripatetic. His childhood in Bombay, with its "dimly-seen, friendly Gods,"[3] had been terminated abruptly at the age of six when he was sent to England with his sister to live in a place they would come to call the "House of Desolation." In good faith the British abroad commonly sent their children home to be raised; unbeknownst to his parents, however, Kipling had come to a bad place. For six years the woman who ran the establishment ill fed him, beat him, and lectured him with evangelical zeal on the refinements of hell. When his parents rescued him at last, he was half-blind and suffering a nervous breakdown. Although no one has ever adequately explained exactly why the center does not hold in much of his work, this dislocation that passed for his childhood would seem the likely cause. There is the sense of an unease always at Kipling's back, the closing tread of some specter that impelled him to rush his stories into print before they were fully realized. In his journalist's haste to say things once and quickly, of course, may lie the secret of his appeal. Lacking knowledge of a particular homeland and lingo, he had the whole world to call home and some marvel to report from every corner of it.

In *Just So Stories* he imagined, in comically heroic terms, how the creatures of the world got themselves made—how the camel got its hump, the leopard its spots, the elephant its trunk. Many such origin myths can be found in *Uncle Remus*—"Why Brother Bear Has No Tail," "Why the Negro Is Black," "The Origin of the Ocean," "Why Mr. Possum Loves Peace," and so on. Kipling's passion for things American had sprung partly from his boyhood reading of the early Harris collections. Years later, in a letter of tribute, he would tell his distant tutor,

> I wonder if you could realize how "Uncle Remus," his sayings, and the sayings of the noble beasties ran like wild fire through an English public school when I was about fifteen. . . . Six years ago in India, meeting an old schoolmate of those days, we found ourselves quoting whole pages of "Uncle Remus" that had got mixed in with the fabric of the old school life.[4]

Now in Vermont he began improvising his own collection of creation stories. He could not in good conscience place himself in competition with Harris, who was still at work explaining the lives of the local fauna, so he cast his net wide. He looked to the oceans for "How the Whale got His Throat" and "The Crab that Played with the Sea," to Arabia for "How the Camel got His Hump," and to an island in the Red Sea for "How the Rhinoceros got His Skin." The veldt and jungle of Africa gave him "How the Leopard got His Spots" and "The Elephant's Child." From Australia he took "The Sing-Song of Old Man Kangaroo" and from Brazil "The Beginning of the Armadillos." A neolithic cave yielded three more tales, including "The Cat that Walked by Himself," and, lastly, *The Arabian Nights* suggested the fairy tale "The Butterfly that Stamped." From Eastern storytelling tradition he also borrowed his manner of address, turning the "one time way back yander" of *Uncle Remus* into "Before the High and Far-Off Times, O my Best Beloved, came the Time of the Very Beginnings."

The invention in these tales is profligate, and the spirit is that of a magician who cannot contain his secrets. The two best stories, "The Elephant's Child" and "The Cat that Walked," are literary trickster tales embellished after the manner of Negro tradition. His summoning up of Africa with the book's most famous line, "the great grey-green, greasy Limpopo River, all set about with fever-trees," is so much the epitome of what make-believe means to evoke that it is a pity there are not more like it. Some images are nearly as numinous—the Parsee, for example, "from whose hat the rays of the sun were reflected in more-than-oriental splendour"—but, curiously, Kipling did not or could not or dared not tarry to find in himself an entire book all set about with fever-trees and settled instead for the self-conscious witticisms and the precious, lisping cadences then in fashion. These are not, most of them, good imitations of creation myths but darting flights of fancy, like Eugene Fields's imitations of Mother Goose. In Harris's "The Story of the Deluge" the animals "spoke speeches, en hollered, en cusst, en flung der langwidge 'roun'." Kipling flung the language too handsomely to serve the tales well. Like the elephant's child filling all Africa with his "satiable curtiosity," he filled his book to overflowing with the sound of black dialect babied into nursery dialect, and as a result the tales survive only as charming relics of their period.

No such problem obtains with *The Jungle Books*. The Seeonee Hills of India were one of those jewels shining out there in the world, like the locales of his creation myths. Kipling began extracting from them this other and greater myth, the story of Mowgli the wolf boy, at about the same time he began the *Just So Stories*. A fiction for older readers, it was to be more novel than tale, and a make-believe in want of some dignity, and so he sensibly put aside the exuberance of the storyteller for the occasion and stepped back into the voice of the narrator.

Mowgli's saga is clearly a fantasy of sorts, but in bringing the little boy of *Uncle Remus* inside the tale Kipling did not at the same time anthropomorphize his amiable brethren. *The Jungle Books* are a dramatized speculation, rather, of how it might go were a real child actually to be raised by wolves and trained in the ways of the wild by a bear, a panther, and a python. These being real, if reasoning, creatures inhabiting a real and not a make-believe jungle, their story is consequently not truly an animal fantasy but a hybrid of beast fable, coming-of-age novel, and the kind of wildlife biography soon to be practiced by the Canadian naturalist Ernest Seton-Thompson. It is a species of origin myth unique to Kipling. His most ingenious innovation, perhaps, was allowing the creatures to speak like Quakers. Mishandled, this could have betrayed the tales as surely as baby talk had spoiled the *Just So Stories*. Instead, it is pleasingly effective. A bear rolling his thoughts over "thees" and "thous" imbues the saga with a strange reality, even a kind of grandeur.

Alas, as with all his work, Kipling wrote the tales in haste and hurried them into print. It is difficult to settle in the mind whether one is reading a collection of tales or in fact a failed novel. Children taking the stories straight through may experience some confusion as to the time of any given tale in relation to the others. They were not written, and are not printed, in chronological sequence.

As Published		Chronological
Book 1	"Mowgli's Brothers"	Mowgli's Brothers," first half
	"Kaa's Hunting"	"Kaa's Hunting"
	"Tiger, Tiger"	"How Fear Came"/"The King's Ankus"
Book 2	"How Fear Came"	"Mowgli's Brothers," second half
	"Letting in the Jungle"	"Tiger, Tiger"
	"The King's Ankus"	"Letting in the Jungle"
	"Red Dog"	"Red Dog"
	"Spring Running"	"Spring Running"

Read in proper order, these eight tales tell the story of Mowgli's life from his infant orphanage to his becoming a man and a forest ranger at the age of seventeen. The first relates how, with the tiger Shere Khan stalking him, he is adopted by the wolf pack; midway through it Kipling writes, "Now you must be content to skip ten or eleven whole years, and only guess at all the wonderful life that Mowgli led." The second half of "Mowgli's Brothers" tells of his expulsion from the pack, and the final four stories relate the events that followed—how he defeated Shere Khan and what happened next. "Kaa's Hunting," "How Fear Came," and "The King's Ankus" fill that hiatus of ten or eleven years alluded to in the opening story.

The book's title was a publishing convenience and may mislead readers mindful of a famous story written in imitation of *The Jungle Books*, Edgar Rice Burroughs's *Tarzan of the Apes*. Of the fifteen tales in the two volumes, only the eight are set in the jungle (there is even a story here about Eskimos), and the lush appointments of a tropical rain forest are absent in any case. What Kipling meant by jungle was forested up-country. Angus Wilson finds it an "extraordinary evocation."[5] It seems to me to be hardly evoked at all. The one exception can be found in the superior trickster story "Red Dog," in which Mowgli uses bees to turn the day against the wild dogs of India:

> The split and weatherworn rocks of the gorge of the Waingunga had been used since the beginning of the Jungle by the Little People of the Rocks—the busy, furious, black, wild bees of India. . . . For centuries the Little People had hived and swarmed from cleft to cleft and swarmed again, staining the white marble with stale honey, and made their combs tall and deep and black in the dark of the inner caves, and neither man nor beast nor fire nor water had ever touched them.

For a long hour Mowgli lay back among the coils playing with his knife, while Kaa, his head motionless on the ground, thought of all that he had seen and known since the day he came from the egg. The light seemed to go out of his eyes and leave them like stale opals, and now and again he made little stiff passes with his head to right and left, as though he were hunting in his sleep. Mowgli dozed quietly, for he knew that there is nothing like sleep before hunting, and he was trained to take it at any hour of the day or night.

Then he felt Kaa grow bigger and broader below him as the huge python puffed himself out, hissing with the noise of a sword drawn from a steel scabbard.

"I have seen all the dead seasons," Kaa said at last, "and the great trees and the old elephants and the rocks that were bare and sharp-pointed ere the moss grew. Art *thou* still alive, Manling?"

These passages are quite fine, but even so, there is nothing of the jungle in either volume to equal Kipling's vision of the "great grey-green, greasy Limpopo River, all set about with fever-trees." What readers tend to remember about the books is neither the neighborhood nor the brethren but the to-do that Kipling has made of the "Law of the Jungle." This is the real engine driving the book, an agnostic's search for some principle that might ratify the myth. And it is here, I think, that the book fell apart before it had begun to cohere. If Kipling had known what the Law of the Jungle was, he would have said it, and he did not say it. He has many ways of phrasing it, and many ways of singing songs around it, but in the end the Law is only an abstraction, romanticized as the wisdom of a friendly bear.

His storybook solution to how things shall be regulated and made right in the world came from those dark days of his childhood in the House of Desolation. Granted the reprieve of a holiday at an uncle's house, he had there heard an impromptu recitation of what must be the bleakest document of the human condition ever recorded, the Icelandic saga *Burnt Njal*. This "tale full of fascinating horrors," as he later recalled it,[6] whose hero is given to lament, "More people become killers than I ever expected," what could it have impressed upon the eight-year-old but the squalid reality of the abuse he was suffering and the absolute need for some code of law as protection from the anarchy of the wicked? The Law Rock at the Al-thing, where the Icelanders learned to arbitrate their blood feuds, Kipling took for his Council Rock, where the wolves decide Mowgli's fate.

With laws shall our land be built up but with lawlessness laid waste.
Njal's Saga

Now this is the Law of the Jungle — as old and
    as true as the sky;
And the Wolf that shall keep it may prosper, but
    the Wolf that shall break it must die.
"The Law of the Jungle"

Over and above what else he valued in life—fellowship, honest labor, children—this is what he longed for, some healing certainty "as old and as true as the sky." But what it might be he could not say. The Christian God he kept confusing with godless Christians, and the friendly gods of Bombay were a make-believe from long ago. He dreamed he was a foundling, benignly tutored by the naturally savage Baloo rather than savagely tutored in England by a family of abusive fundamentalists. He would be Rousseau's Emile, raised in the forest as one of nature's nobility. It was a fine dream, but haunted perhaps by some spector of doubt that drove him to write it in haste and walk away from it too soon, praying that he had got it right.

Curiously, it is just now, in 1895, with *The Second Jungle Book* in print and the saga closed, that we find Kipling writing to Joel Chandler Harris with the urgent afterthought "One thing I want to know badly . . . from what nature myth or *what* come 'Miss Meadows and the girls?'"

To say that a thing is "as true as the sky" is only blowing hot air, after all. That elusive something to make things right in the world and ratify his dream, it may have been under his nose all the while, laying down the law in a good spirit at the down-to-earth center of a beloved book. He with the talent for more than oriental splendor had missed it.

His mother had always told him he was careless with his plots.

Winnie-the-Pooh (1926), The House at Pooh Corner (1928)

Like *Where the Wild Things Are*, the Pooh stories were a new kind of make-believe that bore the stamp of nearly everything that had gone before them. There are echoes of *Uncle Remus* in these pages, and Robert Louis Stevenson, *Peter Pan* and Kipling, and Kipling yet again. Cataloguing *Pooh* in the library of make-believe as a bedtime *Jungle Book* for younger children, in fact, would not be misrepresenting it by much. In both sagas the little boy of *Uncle Remus* is translated into the neighborhood to live among the beasts, and in both he must grow up and come out again. Playing tricks and playing school are games common to both. The felt experiences of being in the Seeonee Hills and at Pooh Corner could not be more different, of course. To see *Pooh* as a junior *Jungle Book*, we must cast an enchantment over those hills and picture Baloo as a bear with stuffing for brains and Mowgli with his thumb in his mouth. The author of this transmogrification, A. A. Milne (1882–1956), would have offered no apologies. It had been his express intent to make a popular success by translating the worlds of *Uncle Remus* and Kipling into the sentimental realm of the nursery toy. That he achieved as richly felt a little world as he did must be attributed as much to affection as to calculation, however. His redefinition of the brethren's amiability as unadulterated sweetness I do not doubt was sincere. "Could you very sweetly" is Christopher Robin's request for a story, and what we see in this pair of originally Piglet-small volumes with perfect

Piglet-small pictures by E. H. Shepard is a father very sweetly complying by relating twenty imaginary episodes from the lives of the stuffed animals in the nursery. The grounds of the Milne country estate in Sussex provided the neighborhood, with its "floody place" and "sandy pit" and "100 aker wood." The toys given voice there are Edward Bear, or Pooh, who lives in the forest under the name of Sanders; the pocket-sized Piglet, who inhabits a beech tree; and nearby Piglet, in a gloomy, wet place, the donkey, Eeyore. Filling out the cast are Owl and Rabbit, the latecomers Kanga and baby Roo, and the hyperactive tiger, Tigger. "Behind a green door in another part of the forest" we find our Edwardian Mowgli, the translated boy himself, Christopher Robin. The story-hour setting pictured in the frontispiece to Perrault's fairy tales and brought to life in *Uncle Remus* proves no impediment to his becoming a part of the fiction here. By a magic trick known only to grownups, into the tale he goes as his favorite stuffed companion

> began to think again. And the first person he thought of was Christopher Robin.
> (*"Was that me?" said Christopher Robin in an awed voice, hardly daring to believe it.*
> *"That was you."*
> *Christopher Robin said nothing, but his eyes got larger and larger, and his face got pinker and pinker.*)
> So Winnie-the-Pooh went round to his friend Christopher Robin, who lived behind a green door in another part of the forest.
> "Good morning, Christopher Robin," he said.

The sketches acted out by these principals are variations on the Brer Rabbit trickster tale, many of them, with the child-pleasing spin that it is the putative trickster — usually Pooh, the bear of little brain — who is fooled. No one gets hurt; no dust flies; no teeth are bared in these entertainments. At the close of each are only the hero's endearing befuddlement and our own amusement. If it all sounds the toney apotheosis of baby talk as a form of narrative, that is just what it was meant to be. The tee shirt was Pooh's great destiny; much of his history will one day be found outside the bookshop, racked for display in shopping-mall arcades. Cozy locutions like "Friendly with Bears," "Affectionate Disposition," "Don't Blame Me," and "Cunning Trap" do the tales little real harm, however. In Kipling's *Just So Stories* they were rather superfluous to the book, and a distraction. Here, they *are* the book. One either swallows them whole or one doesn't, and Milne does make them easy to stomach. He was not acknowledged in his day as the legitimate heir to J. M. Barrie without good reason. His voice was as graceful as any yet heard in children's books, and for this kind of tale he had the stand-up comic's perfect timing. The precision of delivery that in oral tradition takes generations to perfect was Milne's for a song. To say that because he was facile he was also superficial seems beside the point. He set out to entertain, and this he did supremely well. *Pooh* is one of the most beautifully crafted of all children's books, and, whimsical or not, the characters are as real as any in the literature.

The reason why those who do not like these stories really do not like them at all, I think, is the casual game Milne makes of the notion of the Inner Circle. His happy band is not a true freemasonry as in Kipling, nor can Christopher Robin be one of the brethren, as Mowgli had been for those ten or eleven years in the middle of his history. He is at the outset, and must always be, the Edwardian seignior, master of the playroom plantation, issuing invitations to parties, passing judgment, confirming who are the favorites and who the mascots. *Pooh* is a highly charged work emotionally. Children, note, do not identify with their counterpart in these adventures but with the fable's real children, the toy brethren. The immediacy Milne brings to their every pathetic hope and blunder can only compound the reader's sense of his own vulnerability. The story that concludes the first volume, "Christopher Robin Gives Pooh a Party," is really rather a weight to bear for a book that means to be buoyant. We have just seen Eeyore presented with a burst balloon at his own miserable dud of a birthday party, and now here he is making a fool of himself at Pooh's gala affair. And in the end he is still excluded from the inner circle of Christopher Robin, Pooh, and Piglet. Their remonstrances at the opening of the second volume notwithstanding, he will be left to sit alone in his stickhouse in the snow while the favored three, laughing and singing songs, walk off together in search of lunch. "So they left him in it" is not an innocent line. And, yes, children do notice these things.

Milne's almost obtuse indifference to those outside the circle and his imperviousness to the affective dangers in bringing such anxiety to bear in tales of birthday parties and picnic lunches can be traced directly to Robert Louis Stevenson, whose *Child's Garden* was the study for Milne's own collections of verse, *When We Were Very Young* (1924) and *Now We Are Six* (1927). What we see in *Pooh* is the last refinement of that growing sense of prerogative audience that Harvey Darton had identified among the Victorians. Great intimacy and textual richness would come of this sense, but also the narrowing satisfactions of class that we saw in Stevenson's "System":

> The child that is not clean and neat,
> With lots of toys and things to eat,
> He is a naughty child, I'm sure —
> Or else his dear papa is poor.

If the little boy of *Uncle Remus* was the grandfather of Christopher Robin's comings and goings, the grandfather of his sensibility was this sublimely egocentric and patronizing narrator of Stevenson's poems, whose innocence is never more than an inflection away from total fatuity.

For his plot mechanics Milne looked to a number of recent and famous children's stories. *The Wind in the Willows* was a particular favorite of his — in a few years he would be adapting the play *Toad of Toad Hall* from it — and there seems at least a touch of Grahame in *Winnie-the-Pooh*. "Tigger's getting so Bouncy nowadays that it's time we taught him a lesson," for example, may be an echo of Rat's "We'll convert him! He'll be the most converted Toad that ever was before we've done with him!" For the Tigger episodes Milne may have drawn from Helen Bannerman as well. The tiger's penchant for "hiding behind trees and jumping out on Pooh's shadow when it wasn't looking" certainly sounds like the habit of a jungle cat from *Little Black Sambo*. What we may be hearing between the lines of "Tigger Has Breakfast" is the thought process of a professional wordsmith testing the plausibility of introducing yet another hungry tiger into the nursery and wondering up a plot over the question of what it might want to eat if it weren't merely to be a paraphrase of Sambo's tigers. (Extract of Malt: when not being Bouncy, this is a Quiet and Refined tiger.)

Trickster tales to revamp for the patrician toddler were, of course, a legacy from *Uncle Remus*, and proof of ancestry is abundant in *Pooh*, in the dedicatory mode of Potter and Grahame. We are so used to thinking of these books as the adventures of Pooh, Piglet, Christopher Robin, and Eeyore, it comes as a surprise going back to them and seeing how often "There's Rabbit. He hasn't Learnt in Books, but he can always Think of a Clever Plan." Curiously, this new hand at the trickster tale would later feel compelled to raise the Milne flag of Total Originality over his variations:

> When, forty years later, I wrote a book called *Winnie-the-Pooh*, and saw Shepard's drawing of Pooh, the bear, standing on the branch of a tree outside Owl's house, I remembered all that *Reynard the Fox* and *Uncle Remus* and the animal stories in *Aunt Judy's Magazine* had meant to us. Even if none of their magic had descended on me, at least it had inspired my collaborator.[7]

Milne preferred the public to fancy him inventing his tales extempore, with a laughing Mrs. Milne taking them down as dictation. This happy family snapshot leaves much unsaid. Below for comparison are scenes from "Pooh Goes Visiting" and "Heyo, House!" (*Uncle Remus and His Friends*), with an initial line borrowed from the similar tale "Brother Rabbit Breaks Up a Party" (*Nights*). This latter pair the reader will recall as two of the tales used by Beatrix Potter to construct *The Tale of Mr. Tod*.

. . . *Rum-tum-tum-tiddle-um.*

So he bent down, put his head into the hole, and called out:

"Is anybody at home?"

There was a sudden scuffling noise from inside the hole, and then silence.

"What I said was, 'Is anybody at home?'" called out Pooh very loudly.

. . . yer come Brer Rabbit: *Diddy-bum, diddybum, diddybum-bum-bum.*

He 'low, "Heyo, house!"

De house ain't make no answer, en Brer Wolf, in dar behime de do', open his eyes wide. He ain't know what ter make er dat kinder doin's. . . .

Brer Rabbit holler hard ez he kin, but

"No!" said a voice; and then added, "You needn't shout so loud. I heard you quite well the first time."

"Bother!" said Pooh. "Isn't there anybody here at all?"

"Nobody."

Winnie-the-Pooh took his head out of the hole, and thought for a little, and he thought to himself, "There must be somebody there, because somebody must have said 'Nobody.'" So he put his head back in the hole and said:

"Hallo, Rabbit, isn't that you?"

"No," said Rabbit, in a different sort of voice this time.

"But isn't that Rabbit's voice?"

"I don't *think* so," said Rabbit. "It isn't *meant* to be."

still he ain't git no answer, en den he 'low, "Sholy sump'n nudder is de matter wid dat house, kaza all de times befo' dis, it been holler'n back at me, Heyo, you'se'f!"

Den Brer Rabbit wait little bit, en bime by he holler one mo' time, "Heyo, house!"

Ole Brer Wolf try ter talk like he speck a house 'ud talk, en he holler back, "Heyo, yo'se'f!"

Brer Rabbit wunk at hisse'f. He low, "Heyo, house! Whyn't you talk hoarse like you got a bad col'?"

Den Brer Wolf holler back, hoarse ez he kin, "Heyo, yo'se'f!"

Dis make Brer Rabbit laugh twel a little mo' en he'd a drapt off'n dat ar simmon stump en hurt hisse'f.

He 'low "Eh-eh, Brer Wolf! dat ain't nigh gwine ter do. You'll hatter stan' out in de rain a mighty long time 'fo' you kin talk hoarse ez dat house!"

The quirk of turning every thought into a slogan Milne probably took from Kipling's "How the Leopard got His Spots," with its "Big Tummy-ache" and "Quite the Wisest Animal." The mannered nursery inflections in use throughout the book also seem a legacy of the *Just So Stories*. "'Scuse me,' said the Elephant's Child most politely, 'but have you seen such a thing as a Crocodile in these promiscuous parts?'" is a question that could as easily have been asked by Pooh or Christopher Robin. Kipling may have learned his bad habits from Gilbert and Sullivan operettas, which in turn suggests an origin for the name Pooh-bear in its near-homonym, Pooh-Bah, "the Lord-High-Everything-Else" from W. S. Gilbert's *Mikado*.

Milne had followed Kipling's example in translating his hero into the forest to live with the brethren; he takes him out again much as Kipling had extracted Mowgli, but with less achieved. The curtain-closing last chapter to the saga, "In which Christopher Robin and Pooh Come to an Enchanted Place, and We Leave Them There," is a theatrical set-piece of little merit. Kipling did not sentimentalize the loss of childhood but granted the passage its proper dignity. An almost biblical covenant is being sealed between Mowgli and his wolf brothers when they tell him that, should he come to the foot of the hills when he is a man, "we will talk to thee; and we will come into the croplands to play with thee by night." In *Pooh* this becomes very fey: "Pooh . . . will you come up here sometimes? . . . Pooh, *promise* you won't forget about me, ever. Not even when I'm a hundred. . . . Pooh, *whatever* happens, you *will* understand, won't you?" This is effective stage-craft but as false to children and literature as the jerked tears of *The Velveteen Rabbit* or *The Little Prince*. Milne had enjoyed a happy child-hood and had departed it happily; there is no evidence he ever felt exiled from what might have been, like Kipling, or that he could be in the least sincere in closing his book with the words

> So they went off together. But wherever they go, and whatever happens to them on the way, in that enchanted place on the top of the Forest, a little boy and his Bear will always be playing.

These are lines composed according to a *Peter Pan* or "Little Boy Blue" code of aesthetics. They have nothing to do with real make-believe.

In America there was not the radical leap into new ways of saying a story that we find in Potter and Grahame, Kipling and Milne. On home ground, with good, gray Uncle Remus present to assume all responsibility for the genre, the new fables tended more or less faithfully to reproduce the old neighborhood of the South or else to scamper off into the future on little cartoon feet.

The first American to see that a children's genre was in the offing may have taken the enterprise too seriously to work any real magic with it. Albert Bigelow Paine (1861–1937) had recently founded the St. Nicholas League for Mary Mapes Dodge's famous magazine, hoping to foster good writing among subscribers. As overseer of the club, Paine would be the first to publish such tyros as Ring Lardner and Edmund Wilson. In 1898 the New York journalist published his earnest attempt at recasting the dialect of his Southern counterpart into standard English. Harris had noted in "Brer Rabbit and the Gingercakes" (*Daddy Jake*) that "Brer Mink en Brer Coon en Brer Polecat all live terge'er in de same settlement . . . a great holler log," and this humble gathering place Paine appropriated to himself for his own experiment, *The Hollow Tree*. Unfortunately, with his neigh-borhood and brethren all in place, he now found himself in the uncomfort-able position of having no stories to tell. Relieved of dialect, rudeness, and pranks, *The Hollow Tree* could at best be only a decorous and becalmed imitation of *Uncle Remus*. Paine's fellows sit around in this men's-club-cum-boarding-house, kibitzing and killing time in their shabby morning coats, and nothing ever happens. Miss Meadows is introduced, but Paine cannot think what to do with her, either. About the whole project hangs the torpor of a mens' marching-and-chowder society on a sweltry afternoon with too much cigar smoke in the air. A sequel, *In the Deep Woods*, followed in 1899. Being the only such tales then available in standard En-glish, they enjoyed a brief vogue but were quickly supplanted by two series that would soon number among the most popular children's books ever written.

Uncle Wiggily's Adventures (1912)

Popular culture's corrective to Paine was the unrestrained invention of an author who in one way or another has played stepfather to half of all the make-believe you have ever seen or read. "He had the sort of mind which traveled along the path of fiction, like a train on a downhill grade," his son wrote of him;[8] and it must have been so, for Howard Garis (1873–1962) is surely the most prolific author of all time. Ghost-writing for the syndicate of dime-novelist Edward Stratemeyer, Garis found his niche early in the mass market; while his wife, Lilian Garis, scripted the Bobbsey Twins books Howard wrote *The Motor Boys*, *Tom Swift*, and others, and he wrote some seven hundred of them. His most notable invention, however, was the work of his free time. Beginning in 1910 in the New Jersey *Newark News* and averaging six installments a week for fifty years in national syndication, Garis would tote up not seven hundred, or seven thousand, but the comically disproportionate number of fifteen thousand bedtime stories about a kindly old gentleman rabbit, Uncle Wiggily Longears, his muskrat housekeeper, Nurse Jane, and a circusy crew of villains known as the Bad Chaps. Over the decades the best of these were gathered into seventy-five books whose crippled charm, alas, did not spell ultimate survival:

> Once upon a time, not so very many years ago, there happened to meet, in the woods, the Pipsisewah, the Skeezicks, the Skuddlemagoon, the Boozap, the Blue Nosed Baboon and the Fuzzy Fox. "I don't know how you feel about it, friends," gargled the Pip, "but I am hungry for some of Uncle Wiggily's souse!"[9] They all said they were. "Then," went on the Pip, "let's go, one after another, to his hollow stump bungalow and try to get some. He may fool one of us but he can not fool us all! We'll take turns trying to catch him."
>
> Uncle Wiggily's Visit to the Farm *(1922)*

Garis helped himself to his contemporaries' stories in a way so blatant as to be almost innocent of guile. His Uncle Wiggily is Brer Rabbit playing Uncle Remus, or Uncle Remus playing his own Brer Rabbit, however Garis imagined this merger of the two characters. He is also Paine's Jack Rabbit, who lived "alone, an old bachelor, with nobody to share his home." The Hollow Stump Bungalow is Paine's Hollow Tree. The company provided the old bachelor in the person of Nurse Jane is Miss Meadows without her gals, and the little rabs have here become various nieces, nephews, and neighborhood children. The little girl rab named Bunty Garis transported verbatim from the *Hollow Tree* stories, along with tails and a top hat for his hero. Rheumatic Uncle Remus's walking stick became Uncle Wiggily's red-white-and-blue-striped rheumatism crutch; Paine's Mr. Billy-Goat became Uncle Butter; and the signature tag-lines Garis used to move the reader from tale to tale ("And if the potato salad doesn't jump off the table to have a race with the baked beans, I'll tell you next about Uncle Wiggily and—") are a dilation of similar conceits in Harris ("The wind was blowing and the keyhole was trying to learn how to whistle").

Brer Fox and Brer Wolf sometimes appear as themselves in *Uncle Wiggily*, but generally we find our new hero's archenemies recast as a motley of hoboes and mutants in clown suits, led by the rhinoceros-horned Pip and by Uncle Wiggily's great nemesis, the Skeezicks, a lanky, pipe-stemmed geek of a crow in red, white, and blue striped bathing togs. Thanks largely to Garis's primary illustrator, Lang Campbell, these pranksters are the screwiest interpretation of the stock villain to be found anywhere in children's literature. Poor chaps, it is their destiny never to prevail against the nimble old bunny; they exist only for the pratfall. Uncle Wiggily is as equal to the moment as Brer Rabbit ever was at confounding nursery outlaws, and twice as up to date. The old dear may live in a stump, but he can tune in to all the latest advisories on that new marvel, the radio, and like Grahame's Toad or his maker's other hero, Tom Swift, can more than handle himself behind the wheel of an automobile. Whatever the latest technological advance being announced to Mr. Garis in his newspaper, more than likely it will be turning up a week later in Uncle Wiggily's syndicated corner as the next expedient to save the day. The talking beast of folklore is breaking clear of the sticks in 1912 and motoring into the mass markets of the future at full throttle. Bugs Bunny and Big Bird await.

The fable's influence on popular entertainment lies outside the compass of this study, most of it. A chapter of appreciations ranging from George Herriman's Krazy Kat of 1913 to Carl Barks's Donald Duck comic books of the 1940s could be worked up easily and with pleasure. But in the end I think it would have to be conceded that the corporate effect of the mass market has been to turn a literature of substance and sometimes even vision into a traffic jam of assembly-line skits and gags. Real art is only occasionally even on the same road. Decades before *Uncle Wiggily* accelerated this trend, Beatrix Potter had considered the two ways you can take anthropomorphism in a story; in her sketchbook for 1876 we see her testing her line on some little rabbits dressed in scarves and boots and gone skating and sledding.[10] Nearby, two grown-up town rabbits stand with their backs to the wind. Their umbrella has blown out, and one rabbit, with a pipe clenched between his teeth, is holding down his hat. These renditions are terribly accomplished for a child of nine years and are unlike anything that would later appear in her books. The rabbits here are not really rabbits at all, but people with longer ears. They could pick up their lunch pails and newspapers and stroll into almost any picture book today, or almost any product endorsement, and not look dated in the least. And yet, following her encounter with *Uncle Remus* (and a few summers in the country), Potter abandoned this kind of translation in which rabbits can eventually be shown driving automobiles. As a rule, she preferred to keep her little people in their proper niches. And it was this allegiance to the first-told reality of the world that gave her books their authenticity and their authority. In taking a step back into nature, she took a step up in art. Nearly everyone to follow will go the way of *Uncle Wiggily* and, withdrawing from nature, take an artistic step backward into whimsy.[11] The make-believe of the talking beast will be absolving itself of its own reality in the twentieth century, gradually to become only a convenient trope for sentimental tales of Toyland or for the kind of cartoon shtick that puts Mickey Mouse on the beanstalk in place of Jack and usurps Mother Goose with Muppets.

As I read these pawky old Garis editions, on the other hand, I cannot deny that Uncle Wiggily leaves an oddly pleasing ghost of himself suspended in the mind. It is hard to fault the insouciance of a storyteller who can set us adrift in a washtub ship and save us from the piracy of the Bad Chaps by suddenly announcing the presence of a cannon on board and a handy cache of "old shoes that Uncle Wiggily didn't want anymore." Hokeyness does have its charm. Fooling around, at any artistic level, was never the best destiny of this literature of the countryside, however. When the fable descended into narrative fantasy, it brought with it the gift of real addresses in the world and that sense of neighborhood without which the creatures must be deprived of any semblance of their true nature—and so, too, we of ours. In fairy tales and stories like *Alice* or *Pinocchio*, our progress is ever forward, with little time allotted for hesitant steps or necessary retreats. The neighborhood, or place, fantasy gives us a place to contemplate who we are at the brink of life. In its serial format in particular, it stalls history indefinitely in our behalf and thus affords us a way of imagining ourselves going into the world in reasonable good time. Undeniably, any invitation to become naturalized as a member of a make-believe community carries with it the risk that, having found a good place, we may never want to leave it. The author is wise, I think, either to follow Grahame in making the neighborhood as open to the world as possible or, like Potter, simply to announce it with a few words or pictures and get on with the story.

Old Mother West Wind (1911)

We begin each day of these friendly annals with a comforting salute to the regularity of the universe. A jolly sun not unlike Stevenson's sun that goes wide and without repose begins his climb into a blue, blue sky and, right on schedule, Old Mother West Wind arrives to turn out her children, the Merry Little Breezes, onto the Green Meadows to play. We end each day with a similar, if now more melancholy, reassurance as "she gathers them into the great bag and, putting it over her shoulder, takes them to their home behind the Purple Hills." The neighborhood here blessed is Massachusetts farmland expressed as a pastoral lingua franca. The amiable brethren are generic country boys with names like Johnny Chuck, Reddy Fox, Peter Rabbit, and Jimmy Skunk. What grownups can be found trotting or flying about the premises are agreeably tutorial, when asked, unless you should ask at the breakfast or supper hour, when you would be better advised to seek your burrow or briar patch. Becoming someone else's supply of protein is a fate constantly alluded to in these pages. It is never actually allowed to happen, of course, or it won't be happening anytime soon, at least, for our presence is requested down by the Smiling Pool at the moment, where Grandfather Frog is always happy, after "a good breakfast of fat foolish green flies," to clear his throat, "Chug-a-rum," and spin yarns about why things are, and were, and ever shall be the way things are.

The creator of this world without end was an author now mostly forgotten, who could nonetheless lay just claim to having been for half a century the most beloved children's author in America. I know of only one study of children's literature that even mentions him, and that only in passing. His name was Thornton Waldo Burgess, and in a lifetime (1874–1964) of work in the shadow of *Uncle Remus* he managed to build a corpus in excess of one hundred and seventy volumes. Like Howard Garis he wrote for syndication, and over the same period of years. His narrative equivalent of the daily comic strip would equal that fabled total, achieved by Garis, of fifteen thousand tales.

Between 1911 and 1918, the opening chapters of the saga were gathered into the eight collections *Old Mother West Wind, Mother West Wind's Children,* . . . *Friends,* and . . . *Neighbors* and *Grandfather Frog's Why* . . . *Where* . . . *How* . . . and *When Stories.* In 1913, with the novelized adventures of Johnny Chuck, Reddy Fox, and Peter Cottontail, Burgess began his more naturalistic Bedtime Story Series. The twenty volumes of these in print by 1919 marked the beginning of a multiple-points-of-view biography of the neighborhood that, under various series titles, would proliferate over the decades until the life story of nearly every common animal, bird, amphibian, and reptile in eastern North America had been told in make-believe, along with scattered accounts of insects, spiders, and fish. Whatever creature a country boy might run through the kitchen door to show his mother has here found its history immortalized for the nursery.

The country boy had been Burgess himself, needless to say, whose upbringing on Cape Cod rather resembled that of the also fatherless Joel Chandler Harris. It was from the hardworking mother who raised him that Old Mother West Wind took her benign and practical soul. Burgess began telling these tales about her patch of the world to his own son, whose mother had died in childbirth in 1906, and once he started he never stopped.

The collections are not without variety—there are trickster tales here, and creation myths, nature lessons, and stuff about boys prowling about being boys (albeit muskrats and skunks and rabbits)—but it all goes down like the same glass of warm milk. Thinking back on any given episode, you would be hard pressed to say exactly what it was all about. Someone was curious, or lonely, or hungry and the tale proferred some small moment of relief from the problem. Burgess's English is transparently simple and utterly lacking the saturation of pleasures to be found in *Uncle Remus* or the Edwardians. He had none of Potter's or Milne's talent for making great events of small doings. The tales are more about belonging to a place and having friends there than about raids on gardens or honeybee trees. Burgess was no innovator in the pastoral form but a syndicated caretaker, intent on telling the ingenuous half of the world something about itself and nature that acknowledged the loneliness and ferocity of life while yet investing the world with a kind of grace.

Perhaps because they are a yeoman's vision, the Green Meadows remain, for all their perils, a child's paradise. This is the difference between Burgess and *Uncle Remus*. At no point in the Harris series does the little boy listening to the tales ever express a wish actually to live in that world. Burgess created a neighborhood that was equally full of risk but still eminently desirable. The librarian and critic Anne Carroll Moore once reported of a small patron that "if he could live always in the country as Danny Meadow Mouse, he would almost be willing to change his own being."[12] Burgess may put the lie to various arguments on what does or does not constitute good writing for children. His is not an artful prose, but it is not a bad prose, either. It always goes something like this:

> Right in the very middle of the pleasantest of pleasant dreams he was awakened. Instantly he was wide awake. He was just as wide awake as if he hadn't been asleep at all. Without stopping to think anything about it, he knew what had awakened him. Someone had just passed his hiding place.
>
> Billy Mink *(1924)*

You will never catch Potter lingering over a scene like this, much less lapsing into a "Yes, sir, he did that" parody of children's-book writing. What Burgess is doing here is extending a courtesy to his five- or seven-year-old listener. He is saying four times in succession that Billy Mink has woken up, thus giving the child a moment to absorb what is happening and the time to realize that something else is *about* to happen. His assumption is that prose may run along quicker than a child can follow — a truth that might profitably be attached as a rider to every law proscribing writing down to children. There is a simple power to these stories that may be inaccessible to adults and that rather confounds C. S. Lewis's dictum that the only good writing for the nursery is that which brings equal pleasure to the grownups. The easy conclusions about Burgess, that he was either a commercial drudge or an emotional recluse, simply do not hold up. The strain of the hack is never heard here; he speaks with the same serene ease from his first book to his last. Nor could this honest an adherence to the hard truths of nature be read as the mark of a damaged personality. These are warm stories but not whimsical ones. The creatures do not play at forest games, or attend birthday parties, or cozy up to cottage fires with hot cocoa as they do in so many works of this nature. Burgess seems to have been about some other business, honoring some unspoken contract, as it were, to care for this make-believe preserve. To tend each day to the upkeep of a prose lullaby for children, every day for forty-five years, is a strange calling, perhaps, but admirable in the achievement.

The animal fable came as second nature to the country boy, obviously—he was no visitor to the genre, like Kipling, to make Kipling's unwitting mistakes—but he did take reference to the literature in forming up his fictional domain. He knew Potter's books well, having read them to his son at bedtime. In *The Adventures of Peter Cottontail* (1914) we find him fretting his hero through a little debate over whether to use a name that was already a world trademark. Peter will briefly adopt the name Cottontail instead, with a popular song even coming of his identity crisis ("Here Comes Peter Cottontail"), but in the end Burgess deemed the whole business foolish and had Peter revert to calling himself a Rabbit, in better keeping with his image of himself as something of a trickster, like his parent down South in Georgia.

The translation of *Uncle Remus* into Burgess country is clear enough. He made no pretense about it. *Uncle Remus* became the neighborhood storyteller, Grandfather Frog; Miss Meadows, after lending her name to the tales' central theater, the Green Meadows (almost always called fields in Massachusetts), became Old Mother West Wind, with some reference, perhaps, to MacDonald's North Wind; and the gals were etherealized (alas) into the Merry Little Breezes. Brer Rabbit's famous briar patch Burgess accepted as an inalterable given and transplanted whole. For others of the brethren he drew from that same passage in *Uncle Remus* that had inspired Paine's *Hollow Tree* stories, "Brer Mink [Billy] en Brer Coon [Bobby] en Brer Polecat [Jimmy Skunk] all live terge'er in de same settlement . . . a great holler log." This residence he multiplied throughout his own settlement, the Green Forest, while at the same time leaving the topography somewhat vague, as Harris had done. There are signposts here—the Crooked Little Path, the Lone Little Path, the Laughing Brook—but there are no maps or show-me-the-way passages, and not a trace of Grahame's lush way with the greenery and the seasons. You accept that Peter knows the way to Johnny Chuck's house and follow along without thinking to look for way markers. What Burgess created is a generic storybook countryside serviceable anywhere in the world's temperate zone. A character like Mistah Buzzard can drop in from *Uncle Remus*, still speaking in dialect, as if he had only wandered over from next door. In the story "Peter Rabbit Fools Jimmy Skunk," for example, we read of our hero how "Unc' Billy Possum always calls him Brer Rabbit, but everybody else calls him Peter." This is the tale in which Potter's American cousin is given to reflect on his name and concludes, "I guess that Peter Rabbit is a good enough name, after all."

How we visualize this neighborhood and its denizens was wholly the doing of the *St. Nicholas Magazine* illustrator Harrison Cady (1877–1970). Cady had begun by translating A. B. Frost's pictures almost literally in duotone but quickly evolved the trademark cartoon style that would stay with the series to the end and which can be seen echoed in the work of Walt Kelly and Arnold Lobel, among others. His way with a line nicely complemented his author's unassuming prose, and its very whimsicality may have helped to discharge Burgess's second agenda here, to teach natural history. Tutorials that are indistinguishable from make-believe are simply that much easier to sit still for.

In making a world to explain the world, Burgess had looked to Charles Kingsley and Ernest Seton-Thompson (1860–1946). Seven years after *The Water Babies*, Kingsley had published the fictionalized tutorial *Madam How and Lady Why; or, First Lessons in Earth Lore for Children* (1870). This work suggested to Burgess his own *How* and *Why Stories* and the later idea of complementing Grandfather Frog and Old Mother West Wind with a series of lady tutors employed for more intricate lessons—those grandames of the spider world, for example, who will teach Peter his natural history in the 1940s. From Seton-Thompson he learned, or found ways of confirming in story, that among the hunters and the hunted in nature there are no villains, only points of view. The Canadian naturalist, working perhaps with Kipling's *Jungle Book* tale "The White Seal" as a model, had virtually invented this order of realistic animal biography. His harsh and moving *Biography of a Grizzly* (1900) may be the finest example we have of this kind of extrapolation from nature, which depends so much on an author's ability to find the balance between a knowledgeable empathy and the tendency to anthropomorphize his subject. Burgess admired Seton-Thompson's earlier experiment, *Wild Animals I Have Known* (1898); the realities documented in tales like "Raggylug, the Story of a Cottontail Rabbit," "Silverspot, the Story of a Crow," and "Redruff, the Story of the Don Valley Partridge" can be seen everywhere in the *Old Mother West Wind* books—in *Buster Bear's Twins* (1923), for example, where we learn the alarming truth of why it is that fathers are often cast out in nature, or *Old Granny Fox* (1920), in which Reddy and his grandmother can find nothing to eat one hard winter but a single, dead fish. The difference between Seton-Thompson's make-believe (for every animal biography must be make-believe in the end) and these later novelizations by Burgess is a difference only of degree. In the story "Raggylug" the Canadian writes, "No wild animal dies of old age. Its life has soon or late a tragic end. It is only a question of how long it can hold out against its foes." In Burgess's vision of the world, the end is always as imminent as the next fellow's hunger pangs, but for the sake of a younger audience the "how long" is forever.

Charlotte's Web (1952)

Prolonging the "how long" is the plot that drives this popular novel by the *New Yorker* essayist E. B. White (1899–1985). A desire to restore a sense of order and tranquility to the world can be seen reflected in a number of children's stories published after World War II. Between 1944 and 1949

Burgess would produce a matched set of five books that seem at least a token response to the disruptions of the decade. Here he has titled his work not for any of the brethren but, for the first time in the series, after features of the neighborhood itself — *On the Green Meadows, At Smiling Pool, The Crooked Little Path, The Dear Old Briar Patch, Along Laughing Brook* — a topography to come home to, perhaps, at war's end. White's neighborhood fantasy, the next major American narrative in the descent of the fable, will identify the good, safe place not with the terrain but with the architecture:

> The barn was very large. It was very old. It smelled of hay and it smelled of manure. It smelled of the perspiration of tired horses and the wonderful sweet breath of patient cows. It often had a sort of peaceful smell — as though nothing bad could happen ever again in the world.

Fantasy was a form for which White admitted he was not especially suited. In *Stuart Little* (1945) he had set his mouse hero loose in a real Manhattan, given him an invisible car, arranged a love affair for him with a bird, and introduced him to a young woman two inches tall — many kinds of make-believe bumping together, with only mixed success, in a tale that is otherwise very well told. For his second effort he appears to have done what Potter had done in crafting her tales, or the Reverend Dodgson when "desperate to strike out some new line of fairy-lore" — he referred to the literature. Or his wife may have done it for him. *New Yorker* editor Katharine White was then reviewing children's books for the magazine, and it seems only reasonable to assume her familiarity with current trends and with the existence of two titles published in 1944 in particular. In one, the hero, a pig, finds the message "Patriotic Mass Meeting" woven into a spider's web; in the other, spider whys and wherefores are explained to the hero by a pair of lady arachnids, one of whom is about to give birth. The first of the two books was the eleventh title in a series by Walter R. Brooks, *Freddy and Mr. Camphor*; the second was Burgess's novel-length natural history *On the Green Meadows*. As a possible source for *Charlotte's Web* the Brooks fantasy is intriguing, with its pig-to-pig and web-message-to-web-message correspondences; here, too, White may have found a precedent for using populist slang to speed the tale on its narrative way, and possibly even for the blush of coyness that closes the story: "It is not often that someone comes along who is a true friend and a good writer." Brooks cannot, however, account for the heart of *Charlotte's Web*. The presence of an in-house muse, her temperament and spiderly explanations, and at least the occasion for the quasi-spiritual scene of renewal at book's end — these all seem, rather, to have been informed by Burgess, with White telescoping into two dramatic episodes (Chapter V plus some of IX, and Chapters XIX and XXII) what Burgess had spun out over five chapters as a continuing nature lesson. [13] The similarities between their respective ways of setting up and saying a scene are striking; the differences are no less so. It is not the bedtimey Burgess we find playing the sentimentalist in his work for children, but the ordinarily discreet and witty essayist for grownups. White needed somehow to redeem the fact of death. But for a wholly secular make-believe, what article of faith, what liturgical rhetoric could even be implied? The muse he chose for his hybrid fable, though she operates like a Blue Fairy or a North Wind, can only be a muse for the meantime, a surrogate mimic for a disbelieving age—mortal, small, obedient to the laws of nature. The three gifts she grants Wilbur—her skill, her friendship, her children—would of course be hard for any of us to better. But in assigning the word "miracle" to Charlotte's promise, "I am not going to let you die, Wilbur," White engages us in what must ultimately be a lie.

Five years before *Charlotte's Web* he had written, in a way that Seton-Thompson would have endorsed, that in fact no one can save the pig:

> The scheme of buying a spring pig in blossom time, feeding it through summer and fall, and butchering it when the solid cold weather arrives, is a familiar scheme to me and follows an antique pattern. It is a tragedy enacted on most farms with perfect fidelity to the original script. The murder, being premeditated, is in the first degree but is quick and skillful, and the smoked bacon and ham provide a ceremonial ending whose fitness is seldom questioned.
>
> "Death of a Pig" (1947)

His closing image here recalls Craik's ducklings, who "were at last killed and eaten with green peas, one after the other, to the family's great satisfaction, if not to their own." Or, as Beatrix Potter put it of her pigs, "They led prosperous, uneventful lives and their end was bacon." Both Potter and White were city folk who had gone north and turned to farming. Neither was especially religious; both were matter-of-fact about how the bacon was got. But only White was susceptible to the pathos that can be worked up from the thought. Not killing the pig for the sake of a children's story betrayed him into exalting the little tricks of his trickster heroine as "the miracle of the web" and into shushing death with a pantheistic hymn to "the glory of everything." Where Potter's art is intent on the moment and precise, White's is inspirational and dubious. As beast fable, *Charlotte's Web* is a compromised specimen. It proves yet again, I think, that the open fantasy of serialization, and not the closure of the single novel, is the fable's best home. Charlotte's death scene is as alien to the form as Milne's melodramatically dropped curtain at the end of *Winnie-the-Pooh*. Death in animal stories is either a comic pratfall or else postponed forever. The contrived desolation of the spider's passing at the fairgrounds ("No one was with her when she died") completes the disqualification of her book as third-generation *Uncle Remus*—which through Burgess it might have been otherwise—and pushes it into the emotive camp of White's contemporaries, Walt Disney and Antoine de Saint-Exupéry, who in 1943 concluded *The Little Prince* by plucking the reader's sleeve with the moan "please comfort me."

If a partial failure as make-believe, *Charlotte's Web* does succeed nicely in animating the character and civic virtues White stood for as an essayist, however. The book could be read as the corporate voice of a generation that entered the twentieth century immersed in *St. Nicholas Magazine* and went on — some of it — to write for *The New Yorker*. It is emblematic of what the boys and girls of Paine's St. Nicholas League did and thought and wrote when they grew up. One of them invented a fable which, if faulty, nevertheless renews our sense of how, in a country barn, for example, "familiarity is the thing — the sense of belonging. It grants exemption from all evil, all shabbiness."[14]

The children's book possesses a virtue that obtains with no other medium, I think, and that is its capacity to convey White's saving familiarity through size, shape, look, and heft alone. Think of the pleasurable primer sensations generated by picking up a Potter first edition or Rojankovsky's *Tall Mother Goose*, for example. Among the select number of picture-book authors able to deliver this extra gift of the physical book, none has gone about it more felicitously than Jean de Brunhoff (1899–1937). Uninhibited by any native tradition, de Brunhoff, like the English, was able to explore the beast fable with a radical leap into a new art and to make as well, in the manufacture of the thing, a book as much to be desired in its physical presence as White's welcoming barn.

L'Histoire de Babar, Le Petit Eléphant (1931)

Potter had foreseen the coming of such a book as this. Dissatisfied with a French translation of her *Pierre Lapin*, she argued to her publisher in 1907, "[I]t is too English and rather *flat* for French. I should think a French person would tell the story in the present tense with many exclamation marks."[15]

Babar is the beast fable retold by Potter's French person. With it de Brunhoff brought to an end the long absence of fancy in France. The nineteenth century had not wanted for Gallic invention, but make-believe of this quality and purely for children had not been seen since Perrault. The manner of the telling is as Potter had predicted — the picture book as slide presentation: *Babar has grown bigger* (click). . . . *See him digging in the sand* (click). . . . *The hunter has killed Babar's mother!* (click). . . . *He comes to a town* (click). . . . *The automobiles and busses!* (click). . . . and so on. The text and the charm go much deeper than this, of course, but it is a device worth noting of a picture book that wants all the room of a novel. De Brunhoff made a success of the same narrative strategy that Dodgson had fumbled in *The Nursery Alice*, and with it was able, like Potter, to leap whole pages of reasons how and why things are happening. We turn a page and something has changed; already we are at play with the new information, without having to articulate that it *is* new, or why.

Through elisions, a new way of experiencing the world has been created, as it was in the nursery rhyme "The man in the moon." An orphaned elephant fleeing the forest arrives at once in a French city. What a wonderful world in which a Paris or a Marseilles lies just a dash around the corner from Africa and elephants! Lucky fellow, no sooner does he realize that in the city one must wear clothes than "a very rich Old Lady who has always been fond of little elephants understands right away that he is longing for a fine suit. As she likes to make people happy, she gives him her purse."[16] Six pages of shopping later, courtesy of this sidewalk fairy godmother, out of the store he comes, a certified grownup, who only a moment ago was playing in a sandbox. Nothing is remarked of this small miracle; it is a fait accompli by virtue of a new suit, a derby hat, and shoes with spats. Happiness, every child imagines, lies in being one of the privileged class, an adult. And the secret to that, the tale suggests, lies in merely having a good suit.

Thus, with a wink to his forebear Charles Perrault, whose Cinderella was similarly blessed, does de Brunhoff open his saga of innocence and esprit following the pain of the Great War. His world is as realistically hazardous as the world of *Pinocchio* — a mother is murdered, the king dies of mushroom poisoning, Babar and Celeste are abducted on their honeymoon, the rhinos wage war, a loose pram carries away the children — but in every line and expanse of color breathes the author's benign best hope for the innocents who must live in it.

On the surface, with its onward rush of exclamation marks, the adventure is that slipperiest of enterprises for make-believe, a burlesque. Everywhere, de Brunhoff is risking all by having fun with the conventions and taboos of children's literature. Like Perrault with "Little Red Riding Hood," he is getting away with it very nicely:

> "My dear children, I am indeed pleased with you. Go to the pastry shop and select whatever cakes you like."

> "I must explain to you that, while we were traveling in the car, Celeste and I became engaged."

> "Let's work hard and cheerfully and we'll continue to be happy."

The seven books in the *Babar* series amount to a lexicon of the kinds of stories you can develop from a traditional premise once you have decided to kick out all the stops. The opening chapter in the saga, *The Story of Babar*, is the one true tale here. It is not a beast fable exactly, but something new, a beast fable told as a fairy tale, or perhaps a fairy tale told with beasts. The Jacques we see setting out on his adventures and returning home the hero who will be king is now — an elephant. The remaining six books, which appeared almost annually following the first, are the tale's "and they lived happily ever after." *The Travels of Babar* is the picture book as picaresque novel, *Babar the King* is a mock Utopia, and *Babar and His Children* a domestic comedy detailing the life of our hero now the hard work of building a civilization is done. The first three and the sixth volumes thus trace the history of Babar, his childhood, marriage, travels, kingship, and patriarchy. The remaining three—the *A,B,C of Babar*, *Babar and Father Christmas*, and *Babar and Zephyr*—are extensions within the chronicle. *Babar and Zephyr*, a school-holiday adventure charged with the wonders of ancient travelers' tales, is a discrete work in its own right and the most satisfying of the three.

The exact secret to all this apparently unpremeditated charm is likely to remain a mystery. If de Brunhoff had been in the least solemn about his evocative powers, or whimsical, or coy with his burlesques, the whole enterprise would have collapsed. He has gotten away with whatever it is that he has done here by doing things in a spirit of play that would have spelled ruination in less capable hands. He has gone over the top with everything— size, immediacy, speed, caricature—and then, his best sleight of hand, he has made it all quiet again with a soothing palette of colors. He clearly loved the whole business, and if his tongue was in his cheek he was yet participating in the play with a full, not a guarded heart. *Babar* wants to be a big book physically. Originally, it was. First published in a folio edition, it had the appeal of a full spread of the Sunday funnies. With its hand-lettered text, soft paper, and fresh fields of color, it enveloped the small reader, conveying the sensual news that here with the book itself was a neighborhood—an architecture like White's barn, bearing in its physical presence alone the familiarity that grants exception from all evil.

Put the talking beast into the picture book, give him the advantage of working the middle ground between literature and popular entertainment, and two things will happen. First, the possibilities for saying the fable in new ways will multiply. An artist might choose to work within the tradition, only in smaller focus, as did Arnold Lobel in *Frog and Toad Are Friends* (1970), whose eponymous heroes pay each other visits much like Peter Rabbit and Johnny Chuck, and along paths from the same generic countryside. He might, on the other hand, follow de Brunhoff into the big book, as did William Steig, and, crossing the fable and the fairy tale, make a *Sylvester and the Magic Pebble* (1969). Or he might look to locate the next logical step in the descent of animal make-believe as James Stevenson had done when taking his characters onto the open road. In this variation on the form the direction taken will matter less than the author's success in making his crew real and not whimsical wayfarers. In *Wilfred the Rat* (1977) and *Howard* (1980), we find our heroes sniffing out a living in a boarded-up carnival and the odd, unpeopled corners of Manhattan. In *The Bear Who Had No Place to Go* (1972), Stevenson has reversed the trend begun by *Uncle Wiggily* and sent his circus-bear hero bicycling back to the woods. In each of these books the talking beast goes credibly about his business as a creature with anthropomorphic limitations, seeking his own true niche in the world.

The second consequence of putting the beast into the picture book is the negative one of domain lost and authority forfeited. The fable's power to stand as an analog for the world is necessarily diminished to whatever of the world can be fit into thirty-two pages. A thoughtful artist like Potter can pace out a satisfying measure, but most authors as they clip along from picture to picture achieve only a caricature. A gathering sense of place and time cannot be experienced in so brief a span. There are rhythms of make-believe that are deeper than a picture book can say. When the talking beast quit its native home for the short shelf and the cartoon, much was lost.

The two sagas concluding this chapter in the history of story debuted some fifty years ago. Tove Jansson's Moomin tales and Walt Kelly's *Pogo* are half a world apart in space and sensibility but are endowed equally with personalities, neighborhood, and language. Appearing serially over the years, these two domains have each attained that same weight of authority that had accrued to the worlds of *Uncle Remus*, Beatrix Potter, and Thornton Burgess.

Finn Family Moomintroll (1946–71)

Notwithstanding a family resemblance to *Winnie-the-Pooh* and *Babar*, it would hardly do to call these inventions animal fantasies. The old neighborhood is here—now relocated to a fictional Moomin Valley on the Finnish coast—but the fauna inhabiting the place are an indescribable, hybrid population of human, beast, and troll, bearing names like Hattifattener, Mymble, Groke, Fillyjonk, Snork Maiden, woodie, and Hemulen. They and a host of other likably odd folk frequent the periphery of the lives of a family of generally contented middle-class hippopotomoids called Moomins. Or the Moomins frequent the periphery of their lives, perhaps. No one in Moomin Valley is inclined to think of him or herself as a bit player in someone else's script. Like the Ancestor who lives behind the stove, or Snufkin, "a calm person who knew an immense lot of things but never talked about them unnecessarily," each comes and goes on his own mysterious recognizance. This is a tribe to whom privacy and hospitality, civility and crankiness are equal and indispensable virtues. Someone will courteously hear you out before recommending you "shut up, please." They are most of them either bracingly sane or else a little nuts, reader to choose. The hero, Moomintroll, like Charlie Brown, is not always quite sure himself. Life in Moomin Valley can be as serene and down-to-earth as Moominmamma or as unlatched as Moominpapa, with his idle itch for some new adventure to justify his memoirs-in-progress. A visit to Jansson's shores is often eerie, always busy, and rarely what you expected. Character is destiny in this land, and some are ahead of the game, while others are forever trying to catch up:

> Strangely enough it was the most timid of them all, Salome the Little Creep, who really liked the Hemulen. She longed to hear him play the horn. But alas! the Hemulen was so big and always in such a hurry that he never noticed her.

No matter how fast she ran he always left her far behind, on his skis, and when she at last overtook the music, it ceased, and the Hemulen began doing something else.

A couple of times Salome the Little Creep tried to explain how much she admired him. But she was far too shy and ceremonious, and the Hemulen had never been a good listener.

So nothing of any consequence was said. [17]

Tove Jansson (1914–) began her serial fable in 1946 with *Comet in Moominland* (*Kometjakten*). *Finn Family Moomintroll* followed in 1948, and then *The Exploits of Moominpapa* (1952), *Moomin, Mymble, and Little My* (1953), *Moominsummer Madness* (1955), *Moominland Midwinter* (1958, and arguably the best of the series), the picture book *Who Will Comfort Toffle?* (1961), *Tales from Moomin Valley* (1963), *Moominpapa at Sea* (1966), and *Moomin Valley in November* (1971). To my knowledge she is the first author of note to introduce into the bachelor's paradise of the place fantasy a cast fully balanced between male and female characters. From her Everyman Moomintroll to scowling Little My, the circle is rounded in Jansson's world; strong personalities of both genders come and go through magical landscapes talked to life and drawn to life by the best, and the canniest, author-illustrator since Potter. The reader will find here, too, a portrait of middle-class life as a potentially high and eccentric calling that is unequaled in children's literature. Everything and everyone in these tales has an eccentric calling, it seems, including the weather and the times of day. The reader may even find such a calling in himself, should he spend enough time in Jansson's domain. There seems to be some uncharacterized presence about the place, some thing inhabiting the quiet of the in-between times, as if the Ancestor behind the stove had been sublimated into the air as a pure quality. What to call this presence I am not really sure—a palpable sensation of time, of contemplation, of the author's own presence, perhaps, as she warily gathers this odd community of neighboring solitudes into the family of her fiction. Its exact nature, I confess, eludes me. But then, the best things about make-believe seldom rush to announce their names to over-inquisitive critics.

As Jansson was beginning her tour with the genre in Finland in 1946, a cartoonist in New York, ironically, was laying out the route for the fable's return home to Georgia.

Pogo (1951)

The translation of the beast fable back to its place of origin in the South was effected by a Connecticut Yankee, and the modes of transport were the comic book and the comic strip. I have given the year of *Pogo's* first book publication as an official date here, but the populist hero had been appearing in print in various guises for more than six years at that point. Walt

Kelly (1913–73) had arrived in New York in 1941, following six years in Hollywood as a Disney animator. To the 4-Color Comics line at Dell Publishing he brought a tale of his own invention, about a black boy living in Georgia's Okefenokee Swamp with his pet alligator. While the Disney Studio prepared its film version of the *Uncle Remus* stories, *Song of the South* (1946), Kelly experimented with his strip narrative, *Bumbazine and Albert the Alligator*, and supported the effort by writing and illustrating all or part of more than one hundred and seventy other comic books. Many of these were mass-market versions of the *Uncle Wiggily* stories. Kelly had long been a student as well of the illustrator Harrison Cady, whose independent strip and comic-book versions of Thornton Burgess's *Peter Rabbit* were then quite popular in their own right. Both Garis and Cady were to prove instructive when he made the decision to drop the boy, Bumbazine, from his Okefenokee adventure. Reversing the translation made by Kipling and Milne now left him in need of some replacement companion for his alligator; Garis and Cady, as it happened, had earlier introduced possums into their work in minor roles, Joel Chandler Harris's Brer Possum becoming a Dr. Possum in *Uncle Wiggily* and a Professor Possum in Cady's cartoons. The evolution of Pogo as a character can be seen played out on some of the scores of covers Kelly drew for Dell's Animal Comics series during his tour with the house. In one issue for 1945, for example, we find Albert paddling about the swamp with Uncle Wiggily perched on his back with a fishing pole. Five months later, Uncle Wiggily has disappeared and the alligator is being rowed along like a boat by an opposum now fully recognizable as the future star of books like *I Go Pogo* and *The Pogo Papers*. The following year, as Disney released *Song of the South*, Kelly put out the inaugural issue of his comic book, *Albert the Alligator & Pogo Possum*. It would not be until 1948, however, when the pair appeared in their first newspaper strip, that the fable would evolve from a kiddie-comics aesthetics into the more sophisticated vehicle for which Kelly is known.

Once installed in syndication, with a potential audience of some twenty-five million readers, the brethren and their antics grew apace. To his two principals, the amiable Pogo and his loose-cannon sidekick, Albert, Kelly added a pair of meddlesome foils, Dr. Howland Owl and the turtle Churchy-la-Femme. The little rabs of *Uncle Remus* proliferated as a swarm of "tads," and Pogo and Porky, the porcupine Eeyore of Okefenokee, acquired a Miz Meadows of their own to court in the Creole skunk Miz Mamzelle Hepzibah. Brer Fox and Brer Wolf, by way of Garis's Bad Chaps, became the bully boys and swindlers Wiley Catt, Sarcophagus Mac-Abre, Deacon Mushrat, and Seminole Sam. A vast crowd of neighbors, dupes, blowhards, and poltroons was to issue from Kelly's pen over the years. Each new episode would become an occasion for some new character to take up residence in the neighborhood—a Tammany Tiger, a war veteran bloodhound named Beauregard, an Hon. Mole MacCaroney. P. T. Bridgeport, a pontificating bear named after Kelly's Connecticut hometown, is, more or less, the historical P. T. Barnum as interpreted by W. C. Fields. Some of the best sequences in the series involve bit players like the trio of hobo bats, Bewitched, Bothered, and Bewildered, or the pair of self-serving cowbirds given to threats of "[a] proletarian pox on absentee landlordism." Folks commonly stand on political or personal soapboxes to take umbrage in these pages. Children parade through the panels bearing placards cautioning "Warn the gentry" or "Arise!" Neighbors stalk off from one another sniffing, "Stuffy is as stuffy do!" But on the whole the brethren are too amiable and the living too easy in Okefenokee for anyone to stay exercised for very long. The place is a swampy paradise of water lanes and forest corners, with baseball afoot and the tads gathering for a story while catfish-fries smoke up the twilight. Kelly has blown away the cigar fumes that dulled the air in A. B. Paine's *Hollow Tree* stories (notwithstanding the stogie permanently clenched in Albert's jaw). The marching and chowder society here brought to life, if sometimes sentimentally drawn, is always raucously bad-mannered. The language itself is in an uproar. Characters speak and shout a democratic patois of folk and regional accents, contemporary slang, obsolete slang, and the bombast of the stage melodrama and the political caucus. The most benighted citizen is replete with literary allusions. Panels run over with puns good, bad, and outrageous and with nonsense songs like "Deck us all with Boston Charlie." One speech balloon might be reproduced in a biblical, black-letter font, and the next resemble a circus poster. Highbrow slapstick for a lowbrow medium or low brow antics with highbrow aspirations? Better to call it, perhaps, the noise of a democracy at play.

Kelly's comic inventions gained in domain and authority throughout the 1950s as the daily and Sunday strips were collected into a series of brightly colored, pliable volumes that were perfectly designed to convey the spirit of the enterprise while at the same time giving it a certain needed heft as literature. *Pogo* was succeeded in 1952 by *I Go Pogo*, and then annually by *The Pogo Papers*, *The Incompleat Pogo*, *Pot Luck Pogo*, *The Pogo Party*, *The Pogo Sunday Book*, *Positively Pogo*, *Pogo's Sunday Punch*, *G.O. Fizzickle Pogo*, and *The Pogo Sunday Parade*. Three special annuals published between 1953 and 1955, *Uncle Pogo's So-So Stories* (an obvious marriage of *Uncle Remus* and Kipling), *The Pogo Stepmother Goose*, and *The Pogo Peek-a-Book* would seem the fallout from Kelly's days at Dell, doing kiddie comics. All the tales and songs in these three are spoofs, mostly of children's classics; Kelly lampoons *Robin Hood*, *A Child's Garden of Verses*, *Mother Goose*. A prissy Chicken Little directs a stage production of "A Frog He Would a-Wooing Go." The Army-McCarthy hearings are recast as the trial scene from *Alice in Wonderland*. Of all the postmodern uses to which children's story has been subjected, Kelly's burlesques go down the easiest. In making them, he did not undermine the literature for young children before they could know it, as is the fashion today in commercial make-believe and some picture books; the audience for *Pogo* is the older child crossing over into puberty—those boys to whom Proverbs was once addressed, or the older brothers and sisters of the ancien régime who enjoyed Perrault's racy tales. And even with an audience eager to shed its childhood, Kelly is solicitous of his targets. There is no feeling here that the pleasures of childhood are being scorned in order that some adolescent level of sophistication might be established. Rather, Kelly set himself to playing with the forms because they were enjoyable in themselves. As it had been with de Brunhoff, it was a way of sharing in something he really did love.

A passage from Isaiah that Kelly was fond of quoting says more in conclusion about this modern Uncle Remus than anything I could contrive:

> The wolf also shall dwell with the lamb, and the leopard shall lie down with the kid; and the calf and the young lion and the fatling together; and a little child shall lead them.

AFTERWORD
Wisdom Justified of All Her Children

Make-believe can be an education in the fullness of reality or a schooling in intellectual fraud. The course of instruction will in either case proceed from the fabrication of a lie. Some precipitous scribbler has thought to surprise and amuse us by effecting a breach in natural law which, were it to be reported in the morning papers, would have to be reckoned miraculous. Rabbits in trousers, tigers into butter, excursions through Wonderland or Oz — we have seen the range of miracles the liars' bench can produce. Their higher purpose was announced by George MacDonald when he offered of his own tales that they were meant to awaken a meaning. What this meaning might be for make-believe as a whole I have tried to suggest with the term allsense and the thought that the reader lost in the right story at the right moment may be visited by a transcendent awareness that the world itself is in a condition we could only call a state of grace. This visitation is a phenomenon I trust no one has been confusing with the generic suppositions known as pantheism. Superficially, the two do resemble one another, but pantheism is really little more than primitive animism smartened up for an audience too skeptical for dogma yet still in want of the religious aura. As a warrant for a literature of miracles it must necessarily be a counterfeit. Like the prayer lately issued from Hollywood, "May the Force be with you," it presumes a kind of grace in the world but without the bother of having to name its author. Pantheism today has degenerated from the Romantics' expression of it into the popular New Age whimsy that there are, all around and within us, latent powers that can be — how to put this? — mentally siphoned out of the material world — if, of course, one can only

351

locate that elusive guru with a working siphon. The allsense implies no such power. It is, rather, a gift of understanding, a confirmation to the meek and the powerless that they are alive in a world that is indeed invested with the imminence of wonder, which we call mystery, and the imminence of joy, which we call gladness. If these two imminences do not intimate the one immanence of a creative and self-revealing God, furthermore, they must by definition be specious and the miracle stories conveying them vain and sentimental entertainments.

I will not strain the argument by suggesting that lesser forms of make-believe like the cartoon might themselves be instruments for bestowing the grace of knowing there is a grace to be bestowed, but trace a cartoon or other entertainment back to its parent story and you will find the tale that is. By direct descent or by adoption into children's literature, each of these parent stories belongs to that one tradition announced by Charles Perrault when he summoned fairy godmothers to Beauty's christening and Cinderella's kitchen. Its place in world literature is exactly that of any godparent electing to instruct a child in his spiritual upbringing. If an author can discharge his role with a sympathetic wink and a push of the swings like his French ancestor, so much the better. Never, however, should he deceive himself that because his tale is only a make-believe for children there is nothing more involved than a jolly hour or two at the playground. You cannot write in this tradition and with impunity claim a secular exemption for yourself. Every work of make-believe bears the same implicit message. Its miracles may be mysterious like MacDonald's, they may be tricks for fun like Helen Bannerman's, but they all announce to a credulous audience that the world is possessed of a quality that is beyond empirical knowing. We like to congratulate ourselves that we know better today than to belabor the reader with messages, but we are living in a fool's paradise if we are so blithe as to think that our make-believes are not all of them introductions to one or another brand of metaphysics. Every choice to work within this godparent branch of literature is a tutorial presumption and a potential danger to the audience. Children are natural theists. They are also superstitious and animistic and therefore naturally pantheistic and pagan. These are the raw understandings out of which any knowledge will evolve and the understandings to which the mind will always revert when unguided by reason or faith. The hedonistic pursuit of superstitious fictions is a threat to the commonweal that has been recognized by Puritans and atheists alike. To awaken a meaning, make-believe must of course speak to children according to their understanding. That it be nondenominational is only sound aesthetics; that it be to some degree animistic is pretty much a given of let's-pretend storytelling. But beyond these accommodations make-believe becomes a very problematical enterprise. For if all of it is religious indoctrination, with what subtle waters might an author, even unconsciously, be baptizing children's imaginations? Could he today even say what they are? The vocabulary of make-believe has survived ages of condemnation to become a matter of habit in our own time, universally accepted as a good in itself. How many of those authors, illustrators, filmmakers, and advertisers now employing it as a language of convenience ever give a thought to its implications and effects or even recognize that the happy little miracles of our secular entertainments might be a paradox and a fraud? For if I do not believe in God, why would I be writing make-believe at all? I cannot believe in miracles and so presumably I would see no merit in a literature of miracles. After all, of what other reality could my disruptions of natural law be the expression? There can be none, and I must be the fatuous tutor indicted by John Newbery when he warned how "People stuff Children's Heads with Stories of Ghosts, Fairies, Witches, and such Nonsense when they are young, and so they continue Fools all their Days."

My one warrant for dabbling in gnostic wonders is itself a make-believe, the ancient custom of literary paganism, reclaimed by the Renaissance and perpetuated by the Romantics and the Moderns. Man's itch to worship his talent for making things up has been proscribed by a spoilsport God since the beginning of history—certainly since Moses brought the First and Second Commandments down from Sinai—but it is the original sin that will not be denied. The golden calf of self-expression is an idol with ten thousand faces—John Keats, Lewis Carroll, James Joyce; every communicant will find talents to revere according to his own affinities and aspirations. The dogma proselytized by the priesthood of Poetic Genius is a generous one—Blake's Proverb of Hell, "Every thing possible to be believ'd is an image of truth." In children's books we have seen this sophism sanctioned as the Land of Make-Believe, where "there's never a dream but must come true." Through the tender mercies of the entertainment industry it has become a global creed in the twentieth century. Ironically, the first place everyone now thinks to look for make-believe is one of the last places it will ever be found. The movies and television have expropriated the entire corpus of classical children's story on the conceit that it must all naturally aspire to a state of show business. A movie, however, can never itself be a make-believe but only an entertainment based on a make-believe. The pulse of the literature simply cannot be conveyed by the soundtrack and the moving image. The Second Commandment, so blithely dismissed as the fussy Blue Law of a jealous God, is in fact an aesthetic principle. The quickening of the allsense is a gift pledged to the printed page, a property encoded into language and into language alone. The still, small voice of God belongs to those moments of utter quiet when one is bent over a book and working in collaboration with its deepest possibilities. Musical cues and special effects are third parties intruding upon a private conversation.

This understanding of make-believe as a silent tutorial brings us back, finally, to a text the reader may recall from the Introduction. Though not itself a fanciful work, it has been, more than any other book, the one true warrant for our library of miracles. Tolkien called this moment of unveiling a *Eucatastrophe*, "the Consolation of a Happy Ending." The concept applies to a chronicle of books begetting books quite as much as it would to any story within the chronicle; the terms do need to be reversed, however. A true *Eucatastrophe* prefigures the narrative and inhabits it throughout. The Happy Ending must have a Happy Beginning. Think of a child proceeding through a *Peter Rabbit* or a *Pinocchio*. Imagining himself to be at risk with the hero, he cannot help but feel some trepidation as he reads along. But the heart of the story is not itself anxious. Foreknowledge of the end has lightened the author's voice, his choice of elements, and whatever else might work to summon the sense of a free grace in the world. Since we first saw this happening in Perrault, it would be tempting to call his little collection the happy beginning that prefigures modern make-believe and to leave it at that. Perrault alone, however, cannot account for the fullness of all that we have seen here. In the figure of the fairy godmother Kingsley, MacDonald, Collodi, and Craik realized a personage only hinted at in the earlier tales. They expressly associated their tutorial muses with the Holy Ghost and in so doing identified God's Immanence in the world as feminine in character. If our historical *Eucatastrophe* is to be valid, it must reveal their authority for such a dilation. What book, then, what first cause other than Perrault, could have given four Christian writers of considerable discernment and piety the warrant to advance so unorthodox a thought? By the same token, what same book was it that could have sent their equally pious contemporary, Charles Dodgson, reeling scornfully off in the opposite direction to win the world over to a make-believe that was anxiously secular and marginally pagan?

The sacred godmother, who to some scribes has been a blessing and to some others a reproach, is not the invention of a few modern storytellers but a rediscovery. Long before Collodi's Blue Fairy or Kingsley's Irish Woman; long before MacDonald's North Wind and grandmother Irene; long before Craik's fairy godmother or her speaking heirs, Helen Bannerman and Beatrix Potter—some two thousand years, in fact, before their nearest common ancestor, Perrault—the true teacher and universal friend of our need was fully in place in literature and already hard at work calling home the errant Pinocchios, Toms, and Peters of the day:

> She crieth in the chief place of concourse, in the openings of the gates; in the city she uttereth her words, saying,
>
> How long, ye simple ones, will ye love simplicity? and the scorners delight in their scorning, and fools hate knowledge?
>
> Turn you at my reproof: behold, I will pour out my spirit unto you, I will make known my words unto you.

The Happy Beginning that will justify the Happy Ending of our *Eucatastrophe* is to be found precisely where we should expect to find it—in the world's oldest surviving text for children, the book of Proverbs. The meaning awakened when Perrault conceived the fairy godmother was a meaning being reawakened. The words being made known to us had been called by the ancients, Wisdom. She who first brought it into the world—in one of the most numinous and troublesome accounts in all of Scripture — they had known as Lady Wisdom.

Over the centuries, an uneasy consensus has declared this biblical anomaly to be a personification, not unlike our own Lady Liberty or Mother Nature. As She is introduced in the first and subsequent chapters of Proverbs, She might indeed seem to be so, and little more in the end than a pedagogical conceit. In the eighth chapter, however, and beginning especially with the testimony "I am understanding," something happens for which I think no ordinary explanation will suffice. Here it does seem that a revelation is being made that no scribe or teacher of the time would have dared make, or priestly redactor let stand, solely on his own recognizance. A curtain parts, if you will, and onto the stage of Scripture, fully visible at last, steps the Spirit of God. Her words are not those of a teacher struggling with a class of sluggards, nor are they the accident of some scribe turned whimsical:

I was set up from everlasting, from the beginning, or ever the earth was.

When there were no depths, I was brought forth; when there were no fountains abounding with water.

Before the mountains were settled, before the hills was I brought forth:

While as yet he had not made the earth, nor the fields, nor the highest part of the dust of the world.

When he prepared the heavens, I was there: when he set a compass upon the face of the depth:

When he established the clouds above: when he strengthened the fountains of the deep:

When he gave to the sea his decree, that the waters should not pass his commandment: when he appointed the fountains of the earth:

Then I was by him, as one brought up with him: and I was daily his delight, rejoicing always before him:

Rejoicing in the habitable part of his earth; and my delights were with the sons of men.

Now therefore hearken unto me, O ye children: for blessed are they that keep my ways.

In theology, such a revelation is called (by some) an hypostasis. What this means, crudely put, is that the passage just quoted is not to be thought symbolic or make-believe. Lady Wisdom's existence is to be accepted as actual and as stated. Her words to the sons, and latterly to the daughters, of men are the voice of reality. Her reappearance in the seventeenth and nineteenth centuries may therefore be read, literally, as the Spirit of God bridging two millennia of literature to step into the pages of some of our most famous children's books.

Charles Kingsley knew whom he was serving in *The Water Babies*. His profession of faith in "woman as the teacher, the natural and therefore divine guide, purifier, inspirer of the man" is his homage to this universal muse. His fantasy is rather closely modeled after Proverbs, actually. It is the story of that same boy, "my son," who without wisdom must live the life of the fool and die, as does his master, fulfilling the fool's prophecy, "The man that wandereth out of the way of understanding shall remain in the congregation of the dead." In the Irish Woman we again see Lady Wisdom being introduced into a work as the personage whose guidance will effect a boy's salvation. Since She waits for young sluggards "in the places of the paths," that is where we find Tom's muse appearing as he trudges along to work, and, not surprisingly, when she leaves him she leaves him with a proverb to ponder: "Those that wish to be clean, clean they will be; and those that wish to be foul, foul they will be." Fittingly, the Irish Woman takes on the guise of Mrs. Bedonebyasyoudid, the Spirit of the Old Testament, to carry out Wisdom's teachings. She who in Proverbs "was set up from everlasting" comes to rid Tom of his prickles as one who "shall go for ever and ever; for I am as old as Eternity, and yet as young as Time."

Alas, together with the fool and his muse, Kingsley resurrected from Proverbs that annoying refrain "My son, hear the instruction of thy father" and, playing the clerical Polonius, filled *The Water Babies* with reams of his own homiletic counsel. It is this last translation forward, so uncongenial to the modern fairy tale, that kept his ground-breaking work from being the unqualified success it might otherwise have been. In retrospect, his failure to see that Charles Kingsley must step aside for the muse seems a bit odd, for he understood full well the larger implication of what he had wrought for a Christian audience. He could not have spelled it out more clearly than he did at book's end with his revelation that the Spirit of the Old Testament, Mrs. Bedonebyasyoudid, and the Spirit of the New Testament, Mrs. Doasyouwouldbedoneby, were one and the same person. This would shortly be MacDonald's understanding of the name-that-is-not-yet, and Collodi's also. These writers, and after them Mrs. Craik, accepted and built upon what Scripture patently suggests, that the Immanence of God — these fairy godmothers — is the Spirit of God, and the Spirit of God is the Wisdom of God, and the Wisdom of God *is* God, and is feminine. Lady Wisdom is the Holy Ghost; the Holy Ghost is Lady Wisdom. Mac-Donald was supple enough in his use of the fictional theophany to find justification as well for his North Wind, who might otherwise be thought pantheistic and pagan and who, being a servant of heaven rather than the actual Immanence of God, could not, like his grandmotherly Princess Irene, be Lady Wisdom Herself. In Proverbs it is written that for those times when Wisdom is not Herself on the roads or in the marketplace, bestowing grace and understanding, "She hath sent forth her maidens." And thus can a North Wind be justified in Christian make-believe as a divine emissary to a dying boy's bedside.

The pronoun here attaching to God will undoubtedly strike some readers as unorthodox, but in its defense it should be recalled that wisdom is frequently identified with the Holy Ghost in the New Testament and that the identification of Lady Wisdom with the Spirit has not entirely lacked church acceptance, even in those perilous times when having to contend with the efforts of gnostics to excerpt Her from revealed tradition for the most fanciful of purposes. The argument to be made for the consubstantiality of Lady Wisdom and the Holy Ghost is, I think, a sound one. For the sake of brevity I note here only that we have Jesus's own witness to the feminine character of the Spirit. His remark "But wisdom is justified of all her children" appears in Luke (7:31–35). There he is comparing "the men of this generation" to "children sitting in the marketplace" and observing how they will play the fool with those who, like himself, have come to teach understanding. The setting, though badly transmitted by some redactor, seems clearly the mise-en-scène from Proverbs. To say, then, that Wisdom and the Holy Ghost cannot be one and the same Person of God is to raise certain difficulties. Foremost among these would be having to accept the possibility of a God in not three but four Persons—Father, Son, Holy Ghost, and Wisdom. Surely Jesus was not inviting us to imagine such a thing. He did not come to baptize us with one Person of God only then to refer our understanding to a make-believe. The argument that his allusion to Lady Wisdom can be set aside as a harmless personification is footless for it must presume that Jesus would give us something to imagine that did not reflect the truth. Not only would such an argument create a discontinuity between the two Testaments; it would be tantamount to accusing Christ of frivolity or carelessness or error.

The consubstantiality of the spirit of the literature and the Spirit of the literature leads me to interpose one last thought here before we finish. On page 2 of this book you will find half a proverb. It is from Lady Wisdom, and it reads in full "The fear of the Lord is the beginning of wisdom: and the knowledge of the holy is understanding." I deleted the antecedent clause not to devalue it but because in practice it has meant not respect or awe but actual fear, and this is an inappropriate precept for a children's literature. The Puritans and early tutors drummed home the trepidation and scarcely knew where to find the understanding. When a Christian speaks of seeing the light he does not mean—at least he ought not to mean—while quaking in his boots. Knowledge of the holy is born in gladness. "The fear of the Lord" is a call to humility—a call, really, to adults, not children. Through the successes of those who have listened and the failures of all who have preferred to play the high priest or the literary pagan instead, the proverb has been borne out again and again: those who have not honored the Spirit of the literature, but only their own genius, have done poorly in relaying its spirit. The many misappropriations we have seen from the past century— some for pagan, some for gnostic, some for whimsical or commercial purposes—have amused the world, and a few have even brought to children's story a certain intellectual cachet; but unfortunately their net effect has been to divorce make-believe from its traditional patronage and to deprive it of its true potency. There is a gravity of purpose that holds the fanciful to the world, and only those stories that are grounded in the lived life of the world can summon a gladness that is not itself merely a make-believe. Literary paganism and that great failure of the imagination before reality, sentimentalism, tell us nothing valid about life and so can convey nothing real to us nor ever awaken a meaning worth living with. The only lasting justification for the literature is the redemptive grace of agape, through which the world, with all its perils and squalor, may be revealed to children as a comic arena socially and a terra incognita invested with true mystery and true light.

That said, let me close with a word about one of the great *Eucatastrophes* now available to the makers of make-believe, that most perfect of all the children of Proverbs, *The Adventures of Pinocchio*. This tale of a puppet dancing by the strings of his appetites is what Tom's adventures wanted to be in *The Water Babies* but never really became. *Pinocchio* is the dry matter of Proverbs brought fully alive through the persuasions of story. *Pinocchio is* the book of Proverbs. If someone were to commission a writer to make a Second Proverbs, a *Lady Wisdom and the Fool*, they could not hope for better than this epical comedy told by a repentant grasshopper. Here is the young sluggard, "my son," who will not study the ways of the ant but wishes only "to eat, drink, sleep, and amuse myself, and to lead a vagabond life from morning to night." Here is the ant, now a Cricket, offering the proverbial wisdom, "Woe to those boys who rebel against their parents." Here is the bad company a fool is promised to keep, and here is the prodigal forever dragging his sorry tail home again. Spliced together, the self-recriminations of our puppet and the good-for-nothing son of Proverbs are virtually indistinguishable:

> "Oh, how much better it would have been, a thousand times better, if I had only gone to school! I wanted to be obedient. I wished to study and earn a good character. But I am obstinate . . . a willful fool. How have I hated instruction, and my heart despised reproof; and have not obeyed the voice of my teachers. I let them talk and then I always take my own way!"

The Blue Fairy, Collodi's benefactress "come from the other world," is Lady Wisdom's finest theophany outside the Bible. A few critics have found her punishments a bit unpleasant and others unnecessary, but then, I suppose, so would they find the book that inspired them. Each of her lessons is modeled after some antecedent proverb. When Pinocchio nails his foot to the door, for example, and must wail through the night untended while the Fairy lies asleep upstairs, we are hearing Wisdom's caution to those who would mock Her, "Then shall they call upon me, but I will not answer." In every instance, however, the lesson is carried out in the benevolent spirit of the proverb "Whom the Lord loveth he correcteth," and always there is the invitation "Come, eat of my bread, and drink of the wine." In *Pinocchio*, recall how "[a]ll his schoolfellows were to be invited for the following day to a grand breakfast at the Fairy's house." It is not as judge and jury that Wisdom abides in make-believe but as an affectionately scolding older sister with long patience and a ready "Well done." In Proverbs fools are told, "Say unto wisdom, Thou art my sister." In *Pinocchio* this has become, "'I love you also,' answered the Fairy, 'and if you will remain with me, you shall be my little brother and I will be your good little sister.'"

It would be a stretch to suppose Collodi anything but resentful of his initial encounter with biblical wisdom — indeed, what more likely to have provoked him over the seminary wall than an assignment to commit a list of proverbs to memory? — but the make-believe and the hypostasis at the heart of the book did apparently stay with him all his life, and the voice saying, "I am understanding. . . . I love them that love me." In his middle age, Wisdom reimposed Herself on his imagination — possibly in a dream; possibly, too, through his translations of Perrault — and he surrendered his pen. *La bella bambina dai capelli turchini*, though she grew into a woman as the pages turned, remained ever the good sister watching over him and his puppet, much as an older sister Ann had tutored the age's other poet of gladness, Edward Lear.

The one thing she did not do was stuff his head with Nonsense and tempt him with vain imaginings. We live at a time when the expected thing in fantasy is a flight to some pleasant, or, increasingly, some unpleasant Land of Make-Believe. The Blue Fairy takes Pinocchio nowhere. This is the aesthetics I have called open fantasy — the make-believe of the world. It is the way of Mother Goose and *Little Black Sambo* and all fairy tales and animal fables properly conveyed. The promise borne through the allsense in these tales, "Come, eat of my bread," is the offering of communion with a presence who wishes only to be justified of all her children, that She may bestow Her "Well done" and reveal to us the grandness of all Her Sambos in a world that was, and is, and ever shall be a world abounding in grace.

NOTES

Introduction

1. Gore Vidal, *Homage to Daniel Shays* (Vintage, 1973), p. 85
2. Older individual tales for children can be found in the Bible, of course. The story of David and Goliath is probably the best known of these.
3. Prov. 30:24–28. All scriptural quotations in this study are taken from the Authorized King James Version.

Chapter 1

1. For a plausible definition of the term, see "Do You Admire the View? The Critics Go Looking for Nonsense," *Signal* 67 (Jan. 1992), pp. 41–65.
2. Sir Edward Strachey, "Nonsense as a Fine Art" [1888], reprinted in Lance Salway's *A Peculiar Gift: Nineteenth Century Writings on Books for Children* (Kestrel, 1976), p. 206.
3. Ibid.
4. Cornelia Meigs, *A Critical History of Children's Literature*, rev. ed. (Macmillan, 1969), p. 57.
5. Oliver Goldsmith, *The Vicar of Wakefield* (Dutton, Everyman's Library, 1965), p. 101.
6. John Rowe Townsend, *Written for Children: An Outline of English-Language Children's Literature*, rev. ed. (Lippincott, 1975), p. 47.
7. Iona Opie and Peter Opie, *The Oxford Dictionary of Nursery Rhymes* (Oxford, 1951), p. v.
8. Anne Anderson, *The Old Mother Goose Nursery Rhyme Book*, (Thomas Nelson, n.d., but probably within five years either side of World War I).

9. Townsend, *Written for Children*, p. 336.

10. F. J. Harvey Darton, *Children's Books in England: Five Centuries of Social Life*, 2nd ed. (Cambridge, 1958), p. 249.

11. Vivien Noakes, *Edward Lear: The Life of a Wanderer* (Houghton Mifflin, 1969), pp. 115-16.

12. Ibid., p. 201.

13. Ibid., p. 58.

14. Ibid., p. 160.

15. Selma Lanes, *Down the Rabbit Hole: Adventures and Misadventures in the Realm of Children's Literature* (Atheneum, 1971), p. 83.

16. Ibid.

Chapter 2

1. Wanda Gág, "Hansel and Gretel," *Tales from Grimm* (Coward-McCann, 1936), p. 20.

2. All Perrault quotations are from the A. E. Johnson translation of *Perrault's Fairy Tales*, ill. Gustave Doré (reprint, Dover, 1969).

3. Meigs, *Critical History*, p. 103.

4. Katherine Pyle, *Mother's Nursery Tales* (Dutton, 1918), p. 331.

5. Iona Opie and Peter Opie, *The Classic Fairy Tales* (Oxford, 1974), p. 81.

6. Ibid., p. 162.

7. Samuel Goodrich, *Recollections of a Lifetime*, vol. 2 (Miller, Orton, 1857), p. 320.

8. "The Twelve Apostles," *The Complete Grimm's Fairy Tales*, trans. Margaret Hunt, rev. James Stern (Pantheon, 1944), 1974.

9. All quotations are from Hans Christian Andersen, *The Complete Fairy Tales and Stories*, trans. Erik Christian Haugaard (Doubleday, 1974).

10. Elias Bredsdorff, *Hans Christian Andersen: The Story of His Life and Work* (Scribner's, 1975), p. 126.

11. Ibid., p. 297.

12. Ibid., p. 13.

13. Salway, *A Peculiar Gift*, p. 137.

14. Ibid., p. 163.

15. *Charles Kingsley: His Letters and Memories of His Life*, vol. 2, edited by his wife [Fanny Grenfell Kingsley] (Henry S. King, 1877), p. 330.

16. Darton, *Children's Books in England*, p. 259.

Chapter 3

1. Darton, *Children's Books in England*, p. 262.

2. Derek Hudson, *Lewis Carroll* (Potter, 1960), p. 128; Roger Lancelyn Green, "The Golden Age of Children's Books," *Only Connect: Readings on Children's Literature*, ed. Sheila Egoff et al. (Oxford, 1969), p. 7; Townsend, *Written for Children*, p. 100; Meigs, *Critical History*, p. 194; Morton N. Cohen, "Curiouser and Curiouser! The Endurance of Little Alice," *The New York Times Book Review*, November 1990, p. 54; Jacqueline Flescher, "The Language of Nonsense in *Alice*," in *The Child's Part*, ed. Peter Brooks (Beacon, 1972), p. 144.

3. Alexander Woollcott, "'Lewis Carroll's Gay Tapestry," in *Aspects of Alice*, ed. Robert Phillips (orig. pub. 1971, reprint Vintage Books, 1977, pp. 50–56).

4. Cohen, "Curiouser and Curiouser" (see note 2).

5. Woollcott, "Lewis Carroll's Gay Tapestry," p. 53.

6. Ibid., p. 52.

7. Hudson, *Lewis Carroll*, p. 106 (see note 2).

8. Shane Leslie, "Lewis Carroll and the Oxford Movement," in Phillips, ed., *Aspects of Alice*, pp. 211–19.

9. Hudson, *Lewis Carroll*, p. 114.

10. Ibid., p. 102. The fact that Carroll was called "Uncle Dodgson" by the children of his friend, George MacDonald, leads me to take this liberty with some confidence.

11. Roger Lancelyn Green, "Alice," in Phillips, ed., *Aspects of Alice*, p. 28.

12. Roger Sale, *Fairy Tales and After* (Harvard, 1978), p. 103.

13. Hudson, *Lewis Carroll*, p. 126.

14. Green, "Alice," p. 28.

15. Ibid., p. 29.

16. Ibid., p. 30.

17. Ibid., p. 31.

18. Herbert Read, *English Prose Style*, rev. ed. (Beacon, 1952), p. 132.

19. *The Complete Works of Lewis Carroll* (Random House, Modern Library, 1937), p. 279.

20. Ibid., p. 277.

21. Roger Lancelyn Green, ed., *The Diaries of Lewis Carroll*, 2 vols. (Oxford, 1953), as cited by date of entry.

22. *Yesterday's Authors of Books for Children*, vol. 2, ed. Anne Commire (Gale Research, 1978), p. 182.

23. Ibid., p. 183.

24. Hudson, *Lewis Carroll*, p. 52.

25. Green, ed., *Diaries*, see Editor's Note for July 26, 1879.

26. Hudson, *Lewis Carroll*, p. 75.

27. Commire, ed., *Yesterday's Authors*, p. 191.

28. Hudson, *Lewis Carroll*, p. 101.

29. Ibid., p. 128.

30. Green, "Golden Age," p. 7.

31. Hudson, *Lewis Carroll*, p. 115.

32. Martin Gardner, *Alice's Adventures Under Ground: A Facsimile of the 1864 Manuscript* (McGraw-Hill, 1966).

33. Hudson, *Lewis Carroll*, p. 118.

34. Ibid., pp. 45–46.

35. See chapter 1, note 1.

36. Hudson, *Lewis Carroll*, p. 143.

37. Martin Gardner, *The Annotated Alice* (World, 1960), p.195, note 21.

38. Ibid., note 28.

39. Martin Gardner, *The Annotated Snark* (Bramhall House, 1962), p. 75, note 48.

40. Humphrey Carpenter, *Secret Gardens* (Houghton Mifflin, 1985), p. 66. I have argued elsewhere against Carpenter's thesis that the *Alice* books are gospels of nihilism. (See Chapter 1, note 1 in this study.) Carpenter is the first critic, I

believe, to recognize the conflict informing *Alice* as being—somehow—a religious one, but, while I agree that Dodgson begrudged God the use of his life, I cannot concur that he actually lost his faith or designed *Wonderland* "specifically as a mockery of Christian belief." A predeliction for some "much needed rejection of the old secure system of beliefs" (pp. 68–69) seems also to have guided Carpenter's misreadings of Kingsley and MacDonald as closet gnostics seeking to replace their faith with "alternative religions."

41. Hudson, *Lewis Carroll*, p. 102.
42. I am unable to identify Gardner's source for this.
43. Green, "Alice," in Phillips, ed., *Aspects*, p. 37.
44. Green, *Diaries*, entry for Dec. 5, 1863.
45. Hudson, *Lewis Carroll*, p. 97. All subsequent quotes relating to Tennyson are from this source.
46. Dodgson denied being an insomniac, but we may only be splitting hairs here. The man stayed up very late nights.
47. Gardner, *Alice's Adventures*, p. 37.
48. Green, *Diaries*, entry for Oct. 18, 1881.
49. Ibid., entry for Jan. 7, 1856.
50. J. R. R. Tolkien, *Tree and Leaf* (Houghton Mifflin, 1965), p. 68.

Chapter 4

1. *Grimm's Fairy Tales*, p. 812.
2. MacDonald, "The Fantastic Imagination," in Salway, *A Peculiar Gift*, pp. 167, 165.
3. Ibid., p. 164.
4. Ibid., p. 166.
5. William Carlos Williams, *In the American Grain* (orig. pub. 1925, reprint, New Directions, 1956), p. 234.
6. Too ancient and too potent to be mistaken for a saint, MacDonald's grandmother at the top of the stairs does however suggest a likely patronage for this literature of make-believe, in the person of St. Anne, who grandmothered the words "Whosoever shall not receive the kingdom of God as a little child, he shall not enter therein."
7. *The Adventures of Pinocchio*, translated by M[ary] A. Murray. This first English translation appeared in 1892 under the title *The Story of a Puppet*. It is one of the very few I have seen that takes no liberties with the text and is still, I think, the best available.
8. Martha Bacon, "Puppet's Progress; Pinocchio," *Atlantic Monthly*, no. 225 (April 1970), pp. 88–90, 92.
9. *The Adventures of Pinocchio*, translated with an Introductory Essay and Notes by Nicolas J. Perella (University of California Press, 1986), p. 6.
10. Margery Fisher, *Who's Who in Children's Books* (Holt, Rinehart and Winston, 1975), p. 283.
11. From a fairy tale of MacDonald's not otherwise treated here, *The Princess and Curdie* (1883).
12. W. H. Auden, "Lewis Carroll," *Forewords & Afterwords* (Vintage, 1974), p. 291.

Chapter 5

1. Selma Lanes and Margery Fisher have both noted a likely secondary source for *Sambo* in Heinrich Hoffman's famous collection of cautionary tales, *Der Struwwelpeter* (1846). In "The Story of the Inky Boys" some local bullies are given their comeuppance for abusing a "black-a-moor." Bannerman's illustration of an innocent out walking with his green umbrella is almost identical to Hoffman's.
2. Edmund Wilson, "Oo, Those Awful Orcs!" *The Bit Between My Teeth* (Farrar, Straus and Giroux, 1965), p. 327.
3. Tolkien, *Tree and Leaf*, p. 13.
4. Ibid., p. 9.
5. Ibid., pp. 70–71.
6. Ibid., pp. 64–65.
7. Roger Lancelyn Green and Walter Hooper, *C. S. Lewis: A Biography* (Harcourt Brace Jovanovich, Harvest, 1976), p. 252.
8. Ibid., p. 238.
9. Pyle, *Mother's Nursery Tales*.
10. William Blake, "Proverbs of Hell," *The Marriage of Heaven and Hell*, in *The Portable Blake* (Viking, 1946), p. 254.
11. C. S. Lewis, *Of Other Worlds* (Harcourt, Brace & World, 1967), p. 37.
12. Green and Hooper, *C. S. Lewis*, p. 213.
13. A. N. Wilson, *C. S. Lewis* (Norton, 1990), p. 213.
14. Ibid., p. 220.
15. Green and Hopper, *C. S. Lewis*, p. 252.
16. Ibid., p. 253.
17. Townsend, *Written for Children*, p. 239, and M. Fisher, *Who's Who*, p. 29.
18. W. H. Auden, "The Protestant Mystics," *Forewords & Afterwords*, p. 57.
19. Ibid., p. 62.
20. See, for example, Selma G. Lanes, *The Art of Maurice Sendak* (Harry N. Abrams, 1980), pp. 85–96.
21. My thanks to Jane Conger for bringing this to my attention.
22. Virginia Haviland, *Questions to an Artist Who Is Also an Author* (Library of Congress, 1972), p. 273.

Chapter 6

1. The title page reads 1881 and I have referred to *Songs & Sayings* throughout this study as an 1881 book.
2. Angus Wilson, *The Strange Ride of Rudyard Kipling* (Viking, 1978), p. 44.
3. Leslie Linder, ed., *The Journal of Beatrix Potter, from 1881–1897* (Warne, 1966), p. 103.
4. This is pure speculation, of course, and has been disputed.
5. The editions of *Uncle Remus*, in order of publication:

   Uncle Remus: His Songs and His Sayings, ill. Frederick S. Church and J. H. Moser (D. Appleton, 1881). New and revised edition with illustrations by Arthur Burdette Frost (D. Appleton-Century, 1895).
   Nights with Uncle Remus: Myths and Legends of the Old Plantation, ill. F. S. Church and William Holbrook Beard (James R. Osgood, 1883).

Daddy Jake the Runaway: And Short Stories Told After Dark, ill. Edward
Windsor Kemble (Century Co., 1889).

*Uncle Remus and His Friends: Old Plantation Stories, Songs, and Ballads with
Sketches of Negro Character*, ill. A. B. Frost (Houghton Mifflin, 1892).

The Tar-Baby and Other Rhymes of Uncle Remus (D. Appleton, 1904).

Told By Uncle Remus: New Stories of the Old Plantation, ill. A. B. Frost, J.
M. Condé, and Frank Verbeck (McClure, Phillips, 1905).

Uncle Remus and Brer Rabbit, ill. J. M. Condé (Frederick A. Stokes, 1907).

Uncle Remus and the Little Boy, ill. J. M. Condé (Small, Maynard, 1910).

Uncle Remus Returns, ill. A. B. Frost and J. M. Condé (Houghton Mifflin, 1918).

Seven Tales of Uncle Remus, ed. Thomas H. English (Emory University, 1948).

The Favorite Uncle Remus, comp. and ed. George Van Santvoord and Archi-
bald C. Coolidge (Houghton Mifflin, 1948).

The Complete Tales of Uncle Remus, comp. and ed. Richard Chase (Houghton
Mifflin, 1955). See also note 6.

6. Two years after these remarks appeared in *Signal*, the scholar and children's
author Julius Lester nicely obviated them with *The Tales of Uncle Remus* (Dial,
1987), a four-volume series that concludes with *The Last Tales of Uncle Remus*.
Lester's solution to the problems in any retelling of the tales — how to reclaim
the appropriated lore of a slave culture for the modern, and especially for the
modern African-American, reader — is a supple blend of dialect and standard
English that would be hard to improve upon.

7. Mark Twain, *Life on the Mississippi* (Harper, 1917), p. 380. Harris was the
only white master of it, certainly. His rendering of black dialect, while unques-
tionably displaying literary touches, does compare well, I think, with that of,
say, Zora Neale Hurston in *Mules and Men*.

8. Julia Collier Harris, *The Life and Letters of Joel Chandler Harris* (Houghton
Mifflin, 1918), p. 403. Unless otherwise attributed, subsequent excerpts from
the Harris correspondence are taken from this volume. Harris's general remarks
regarding the tales will be found in the Introductions to *Songs & Sayings* and
Nights.

9. For each quotation I have cited the story's original title, the volume in which it
first appeared, and, when substantially different, the title given it in *The Favorite Uncle Remus*.

10. "Views on the African Exodus," *Uncle Remus and His Friends*, p. 317.

11. Inexplicably, this unique sequence has been deleted from *The Favorite Uncle
Remus*, where the tale appears under the title "Brer Rabbit Loses his Luck."

12. In the lines, for example, "Sat'dy night, w'en de sun goes down" (*Songs &
Sayings*, p. 197) and "De shadders, dey er creepin' todes de top er de hill"
(*Friends*, p. 194) can be heard the opening chords for much of the music of the
1950s and 1960s. Chuck Berry's "Maybellene" comes specifically to mind. And
Berry's performances: you have only to see it once to recognize in his mocking
strut across the stage a parody of running away — as the slave from his "pater-
rollers," so the teenager from overseers of school and squad car — and only once
to see in his rolling eye and sly grin the countenance of Brer Rabbit himself.

13. Needless to say, many of my remarks on the origins of the *Uncle Remus* tales
are also speculative.

14. There is no textual evidence in *Uncle Remus* to indicate if Man is black, white,
or either, depending on the tale. Illustrators invariably portray him as black,

but to the little boy's query "Was he a white man or a black man?" Uncle Remus responds, "I'm des tellin' you de tale, en you kin take en take de man en w'ite wash 'im, er you kin black 'im up des ez yu please."

15. Not to work the rhetoric of this too hard in Freud's, Jung's, or Frazer's behalf (take your pick), but the sun here is a she, Brer Wolf assumes the fetal position, and when Brer Rabbit cons Brer Wolf into believing that the sun, now down low in the woods, is a fire at which he might warm himself, the creature that sold his mother runs and runs but "de nigher you come ter dat fier de furder hit's off." *Are* there residual mythic elements here? Or should we call this particular scene more Joel Chandler Harris than folklore and leave it at that?

16. See the story "Brer Coon and the Frogs" (*Daddy Jake*; listed in Chase as "Crazy Sue's Story"). It is one of the three or four best-told and funniest tales in the *Uncle Remus* corpus, finely balanced between the comic and the horrific (note especially the economy of the last paragraph), and is interesting also as a rare example of altruism in these tales. When Brer Rabbit tells Brer Coon, "[B]ein' ez you bin so sociable 'long wid me . . . I'll des whirl in en he'p you out," we are just around the corner from Kipling and within imagining range of the intimate alliances found in Burgess, Grahame, and Milne.

17. The helper seldom works for us without asking us to work for ourselves somehow. Cinderella's white bird, the soul of her dead mother, helps her to recognize her true self in the Grimms' version of the tale, without which knowledge she must remain catatonic. The bird of "A Story About the Little Rabbits" serves the same function in the terms of the trickster tale. The solutions it gives the rabs are only those they already know if only they could quell their fear and self-doubt long enough to realize it. Quite simply, it is the thought in their minds, how would daddy do it?

18. In *The Favorite Uncle Remus*, where she is seen to best advantage, Miss Meadows turns up in fifteen tales and brings, through the continuity given them by Uncle Remus, some twenty-two within her sphere of influence. Fourteen of these, twelve of them from *Songs & Sayings*, have been reshuffled by the editors into a sort of narrative sequence. (See 10, "The Wonderful Tar-baby"—23, "Brer Rabbit Raises a Dust.")

19. See Chapter 8, note 4.

20. Compare Zora Neale Hurston, *Mules and Men* (Lippincott, 1935; Perennial Library edition, Harper & Row, 1990). Miss Meadows's establishment would be the "jook" (whence our modern juke box) reported by Hurston as a "fun house. Where they sing, dance, gamble, love, and compose 'blues' songs" (p. 57), or "a mere bawdy house" (p. 248).

21. In *Joel Chandler Harris, Folklorist* (University of Georgia Press, 1950), Stella Brookes remarks of Miss Motts that "she remains as shadowy a character as Miss Meadows."

22. Compare Hurston, *Mules and Men*, p. 35, in which a character boasts of being too smart for the "plow lines" of marriage and recommends instead a life without "de trace chains. Never no shack up. Ah want dis tip-in love and tip yo' hat and walk out."

23. Reproduced in full in Brookes, *Joel Chandler Harris*, pp. 153–165. Harris found the piece deficient in understanding, and I would add that it is also obscenely racist. That Harris first saw Negro lore paired in print with such attitudes as these could have contributed to any decision of his to play down

hard evidence of Miss Meadows's calling. Blacks—now free, political, and dangerous to the status quo—were being rendered harmless again by being cast as the object of every crude joke and cartoon imaginable about "Coon Town," and to allow a muse of their literature to remain a whore would only have exacerbated this image of them in the public eye.

24. R. B. Dobson and J. Taylor, *Rymes of Robyn Hood* (University of Pittsburgh Press, 1976), p. 42.

Chapter 7

1. Lanes, *Down the Rabbit Hole*, p. 180.
2. Marcus Crouch, *Beatrix Potter* (Bodley Head Monograph Series, 1961), p. 67.
3. Graham Greene, "Beatrix Potter," reprinted in Egoff et al., eds., *Only Connect*, p. 291.
4. Margaret Lane, *The Tale of Beatrix Potter*, rev. ed. (Warne, 1968), Chapter 6.
5. Eleanor Cameron, *The Green and Burning Tree* (Atlantic, Little Brown, 1969), p. 27.
6. Humphrey Carpenter, *Secret Gardens*, p. 144.
7. Townsend, *Written for Children*, p. 156.
8. Hereafter referred to by its original title, *The Roly-Poly Pudding*.
9. In a letter to *The Horn Book*, 1940. Reprinted in *Beatrix Potter's Americans: Selected Letters*, ed. Jane Crowell Morse (Horn Book, 1982), p. 147.
10. Since Potter is known to have kept a darkroom, it seems likely she photographed before drawing the scene and that the cat's confusion was short-lived.
11. Jane Gardam, "On Writing for Children: Some Wasps in the Marmalade, Part II," *The Horn Book* (Dec. 1978), pp. 676–7.
12. Linder, *Journal*, p. 81.
13. Lane, *Tale*, p. 17.
14. Linder, *Journal*, p. 116.
15. Ibid., p. 117.
16. Ibid., p. 161.
17. Ibid., p. 143.
18. Ibid., p. 55.
19. Ibid., p. 161.
20. My thanks to W. D. Emrys Evans for pointing out to me that the names Hunca Munca and Tom Thumb were taken from Henry Fielding's tragedy, *Tom Thumb the Great* (1731).
21. Leslie Linder, ed. *A History of the Writings of Beatrix Potter*, (Warne, 1971), p. 97.
22. Sale, p. 129.
23. Linder, *Journal*, p. 55.
24. Margaret Lane, *The Magic Years of Beatrix Potter*, (Warne, 1978), p. 200.
25. Linder, *History*, p. 225.
26. All six illustrations can be found reproduced in *The Art of Beatrix Potter*, ed. Leslie Linder, rev. ed. (Warne, 1972), under "Early Ideas for Illustrated Books." Captions penciled in by Potter are quotations from the respective source tales.
27. I am indebted for this information to Mrs. Joan Duke, widow of the late Capt.

K. W. G. Duke, who had earlier made available many of the pictures reproduced in *The Art of Beatrix Potter*.

28. Morse, ed., *Beatrix Potter's Americans*, p. 35. (See note 9 in this study.)
29. Letter to Freda Moore, November 1897. Reproduced in Linder, *History*, p. 135. Note the interlinear remark "They say Pot Rack! Pot Rack!" which she added as an afterthought. The guineas' cry can be found variously in *Uncle Remus*; I am assuming that the resemblance between her own anecdote here and the tale "Why the Guineas Stay Awake" in *Daddy Jake* prompted her to look it up in that volume.
30. Letter to *The Horn Book*, 1940. Reproduced in Morse, ed., *Beatrix Potter's Americans*, p. 146.
31. Determining what parts of the story might have appeared in which draft between the book's inception in 1895 and its submission in 1911 is probably impossible. By the latter year Potter will have published seventeen other books. Benjamin, for example, will apparently be cross-referenced into *Mr. Tod* from his own tale of 1904 and consequently in 1909, out of the *Tod* draft and into *The Flopsy Bunnies*.
32. Technically, Potter had been raiding the copyrighted work of a living author and not folklore in the public domain.
33. Linder, *History*, p. 210.
34. Linder, *Journal*, p. 210.
35. See note 30 in this study.

Chapter 8

1. Patrick Chalmers, *Kenneth Grahame: Life, Letters and Unpublished Work*, in Commire, ed., *Yesterday's Authors*, vol. 1, p. 146. The letter is dated May 10, 1907.
2. Angus Wilson, *Strange Ride*, p. 185.
3. Rudyard Kipling, *Something of Myself* (Penguin, 1977), p. 7.
4. Harris, *Life and Letters*, pp. 333–4. Kipling had written to thank Harris for his favorable review of *The Second Jungle Book*. The letter is dated Dec. 6, 1895.
5. Wilson, op. cit., p. 125.
6. Kipling, *Something of Myself*, p. 16.
7. A. A. Milne, *It's Too Late Now* (1939); see Commire, ed. *Yesterday's Authors*, p. 176.
8. Roger Garis, *My Father Was Uncle Wiggily* (McGraw-Hill, 1966), p. 8.
9. Souse is pickled rabbit ears, or rabbit ears in want of pickling. Pipsissewa is the Cree word for wintergreen; as used here, a nonsense word. The name Skeezicks was probably suggested by Eugene Fields's "The Two Little Skeezucks . . . who lived in the isle / Of Boo in a southern sea."
10. These drawings can be found reproduced in Lane *The Magic Years*, p. 23.
11. In England this trend had its own antecedents, of course. One of its best early products was Mary Tourtel's popular *Rupert* series, which debuted in 1920.
12. Anne Carroll Moore, *My Roads to Childhood* (Horn Book), 1961.
13. White testified early on that the character of Charlotte was based upon a real spider at his farm in Maine. "I had been watching a large spider in the backhouse," he wrote a correspondent in 1953 (*Letters of E. B. White*, ed. Dorothy Lobrano Guth, [Harper & Row, 1976], p. 375), "and what with one thing and

another, the idea came to me." That one thing and another — all those details of authorship too intricate for the simple myths that children's-book lore and correspondents require — he expanded upon twenty years later for some school-children: "Before attempting the book, however, I studied spiders and boned up on them. I watched Charlotte at work, here on my place, and I also read books about the life of spiders. . . . It took me two years to write the story. Having finished it, I found I was dissatisfied with it, so instead of submitting it to my publisher, I laid it aside for a while, then rewrote it, introducing Fern and other characters" (p. 644). Could his dissatisfaction with the early draft have followed from some recognition that a *Charlotte's Web* without a Fern too much resembled *On the Green Meadows* to be publishable? His quandary recalls Beatrix Potters's hesitation, perhaps, over submitting *The Tale of Mr. Tod*.

N.B.: The textual evidence linking White to Burgess (some four pages of match-ing quotations) has been removed from this book at the last moment — literally, from the hands of the typesetter — following HarperCollins's eleventh-hour deci-sion to deny me permission to quote from *Charlotte's Web*. Those words of White's that I have left in place I construe to constitute a bare minimum of the fair use allowance.

14. "Home Coming," *The Essays of E. B. White* (Harper & Row, 1977).
15. Leslie Linder, *The History of The Tale of Peter Rabbit* (Warne, 1976), p. 34.
16. Merle Haas, translator.
17. Tove Jansson, *Moominland Midwinter*, trans. Thomas Warburton (Walck, 1962), pp. 110–11.

INDEX

KING ALFRED'S COLLEGE
WINCHESTER

Library: 01962 827306

To be returned on or before the day
marked below, subject to recall

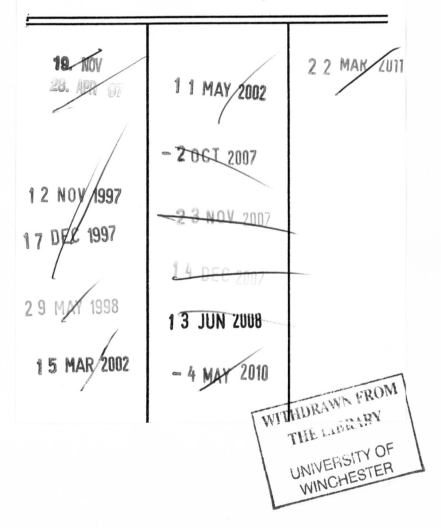